720.47MCC

The Built Environment

The Built Environment

A Collaborative Inquiry into Design and Planning

Second Edition

EDITED BY

Wendy R. McClure and Tom J. Bartuska

John Wiley & Sons, Inc.

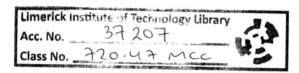
This book is printed on acid-free paper. ∞

Library of Congress Cataloging-in-Publication Data:

The built environment : a collaborative inquiry into design and planning /
Wendy McClure & Tom Bartuska, editors.-- 2nd ed.
      p.   cm.
   Rev. ed. of: The built environment / Tom J. Bartuska, Gerald L. Young. c1994.
   Icludes bibliographical references and index.
   ISBN 978-0-470-00752-5 (cloth)
1. Architectural design.   2. Design.   I. McClure, Wendy.   II. Bartuska, Tom J.
Built environment.
   NA2750.B35   2007
   720'.47--dc22
                                                        2006103532

Printed in the United States of America

10 9 8 7 6 5 4 3 2 1

Contents

Editors' Notes and Acknowledgments

The built environment is a challenging subject. It is pervasive and relevant to all who live in the human-made or arranged world—to all who live on this planet. A healthy built environment makes significant contributions to human life. It fulfills human needs and values; it extends and increases comfort, productivity, and enjoyment. A quality environment can foster a greater sense of belonging, involvement, and pride. An environment created without supportive qualities can have unfortunate influences on people, decreasing the ability to learn, perform, and enjoy life's activities. An unhealthy built environment breeds high levels of apathy, crime, vandalism, and disease.

The built and natural environments are shaped by many human, environmental, and technological factors. The character and quality of the built environment is dependent on everyone, and effective design and planning are critical to an inclusive, proactive process. It is important for everyone to be aware, involved, and responsible. Each of us is an influential part of the ongoing story of the built environment.

"Built environment" is a relatively new term and an inclusive concept. It emerged in the 1980s, and its importance awaits fuller appreciation and comprehension. In reality, the built environment is as old as the beginning of time, dating back to when humans first fashioned stone tools, created clothes and discovered (utilized) fire for warmth, modified caves for shelter, and formed cooperative communities. The term embodies all human creation—past, present, and future plans.

The primary purpose of this book is to explore and clarify the many interrelated aspects of the built environment and to demonstrate that design and planning for human, environmental, and technical needs overlap many fields of interest and study. Interdisciplinary, collaborative design and planning are critical to understanding and resolving the many societal human-environmental problems, locally and globally. This need to integrate across traditional specialized boundaries is expressed not only in students'/readers' and authors' interests, but also in professional and societal concerns found in contemporary literature and mandated by state and federal policies. This book is dedicated to the elimination of apathy and, conversely, to the encouragement of people to become aware of and involved in the life-supportive qualities of the built environment. Awareness and involvement are important prerequisites for all responsible citizens. The book attempts to develop an interdisciplinary forum for collaborative study of the built environment. It encourages people from all disciplines to enter into an inclusive study of the built world in which we all share and live, work and play. It demonstrates the importance of collaborative effort in dealing with complex subjects in a unified and holistic framework, fostering constructive ideas and positive developments.

The genesis of this particular collaborative investigation began at Washington State University. A graduate-level, collaborative, special topics seminar in Environmental Science was first offered in 1974 to explore the related interdisciplinary aspects of the built environment. The seminar met with considerable enthusiasm from a diverse group of students and faculty. They concluded that this subject was critically important to everyone and should be offered earlier to beginning university students from all disciplines. This evolved into the development of another experimental course for undergraduate students in 1975. The same positive results occurred, and in 1979 the course achieved permanent status as an interdisciplinary, team-taught course in Architecture/Interior Design/Landscape Architecture. In 1984, it was approved as a class, which fulfills one of the General University Requirements in Humanities.

Early on, our collaborative group carried out an exhaustive search for appropriate books for this new study. We determined that libraries were full of definitive references on each component of the built environment, but few addressed the important overlapping aspects of the humanly created world. None existed that were appropriate in scope and integrative enough in concept to be useful to our work. Consequently, we developed the first collaborative book on the subject—*The Built Environment: A Creative Inquiry into Design and Planning*, published by Crisp in 1994. The book has been used by a number of colleges and universities throughout the country.

In 1997, the University of Idaho's Architecture Program redesigned their introductory course offerings. They carried out a nationwide investigation of introductory courses, their syllabi and textbooks. This study concluded that the course and book at Washington State University best matched their needs. In 1999, they implemented a similar interdisciplinary, team-taught course using the above textbook for beginning students in all the design fields.

In 2002, the coordinators of the University of Idaho and Washington State University investigated the feasibility of updating the original book. We carried out a series of discussions on the future of the courses and the textbook. We concluded that the fundamentals of the first book were sound but that it could be updated with more state-of-the-art advances in environmental design/planning. The editors carried out a four-year development process for this new, updated book.

We, the editors, would like to express our sincere appreciation to the many past and present participants who have collaborated to evolve this book into its present form. All the authors, individually and collectively, have made critically important contributions to this work. The authors have been able to convey their important part in context with the whole, their chapter within the framework of the book. Their willingness to collaborate effectively in this integrative process was fundamental to this interdisciplinary process and was very much appreciated. The following Contributors List identifies the authors and their affiliations. The reader is encouraged to do a Web search of their distinguished resumés and the continuing contributions they have made to the design and planning of the built environment. All the authors and editors have personally absorbed the costs of developing this manuscript and have agreed to donate all royalties to a university development fund.

The collaboration between environmental science and environmental design has been an important interdisciplinary thread and a unifying influence on this work. There exists a challenging but compatible relationship between environmental science, which deals primarily with the natural but humanly impacted environment, and this study, which focuses on environmental design and planning and the built or humanly created world. We are particularly appreciative of the scholarship and wisdom of Gerald L. Young, a human ecologist and coeditor of the first edition of this book. His interdisciplinary understanding of environmental science, ecology, and design/planning has made a major integrative contribution to this work.

Special thanks are also extended to the students who, over the years, have provided constant feedback through their interest and encouragement, and their concerns and complaints—challenging us to do a better job. The hidden but extensive work of Sandra Tyacke needs recognition. She, and others, have been most helpful in typing and retyping a seemingly endless array of written drafts, outlines, references, letters, and memos. Sandra's remarkable patience, professionalism, and word processing skills have made this whole process run smoothly. We express our sincere appreciation to our families, who have patiently seen this volume through many drafts—and many hours, days and nights "away." We thank them for years of caring and support.

The graphics and illustrations are the responsibility of the authors of each chapter, unless otherwise noted. The graphic design of the circular logo and linear formats are by Sarah Recken and Jon Singleton of Washington State University. We express our appreciation to David Lim, Peter Wolfe, Karl Heitman, Janet Archer, and Zulqaisar Hamidin, students at Washington State University, for developing many of the graphic diagrams and sketches and Jarod Hall of the University of Idaho for his development of the cover design. Finally, we express our gratitude to Pamela Overholtzer, graduate student at the University of Idaho, for her technical editing, graphic and photographic skills, which she generously shared during our final push to the finish line.

To all of the above contributors and collaborators, we are deeply thankful.

WENDY R. MCCLURE AND TOM J. BARTUSKA, COEDITORS

Contributing Authors and Their Affiliations

Diane Armpriest, Associate Professor of Architecture, University of Idaho

Robert M. Baron, Professor and Associate Dean, University of Texas, San Antonio

Tom J. Bartuska, Professor Emeritus of Architecture and Construction Management, Washington State University

Catherine M. Bicknell, Professor Emeritus of Interior Design, Washington State University

Nancy H. Blossom, Professor and Director of Interior Design, Washington State University

Kenneth R. Brooks, Professor and Associate Dean, College of Design, Arizona State University

William W. Budd, Professor and Chair of Environmental Science/Regional Planning Program, Washington State University

Kenneth L. Carper, Professor of Architecture and Construction Management, Washington State University

Eldon H. Franz, Professor Emeritus of Environmental Science/Regional Planning Program, Washington State University

Bruce T. Haglund, Professor of Architecture and former chair, University of Idaho

Carl W. Hall, Deputy Assistant Director for Engineering (retired), National Science Foundation, Washington, DC

Tina H. Johansen, Assistant Professor of Interior Design, Washington State University

Bashir A. Kazimee, Professor of Architecture and Construction Management, Washington State University

Katherine M. Keane, Associate Professor and Assistant Director of Architecture and Construction Management, Washington State University

Gregory A. Kessler, Associate Professor and Director of Architecture and Construction Management, Washington State University

W. Max Kirk, Associate Professor and Program Director of Construction Management, Washington State University

Henry C. Matthews, Professor Emeritus of Architecture and Construction Management, Washington State University

Wendy R. McClure, Professor and Chair of Architecture, University of Idaho

Ian L. McHarg, Professor Emeritus and former Chair of Landscape Architecture (deceased), University of Pennsylvania

Michael S. Owen, Associate Professor of Architecture and Construction Management, Washington State University

Barbara M. Parmenter, Lecturer, Urban and Environmental Policy and Planning, Tufts University

Robert J. Patton, Professor Emeritus and former Chair of Architecture and Construction Management, Washington State University

Frederick R. Steiner, Professor and Dean of Architecture and Planning, University of Texas

Matthew A. Taylor, Assistant Professor of Architecture and Construction Management, Washington State University

Jo Ann A. Thompson, Professor of Interior Design and Associate Dean, Interdisciplinary Design Institute, Washington State University

John C. Turpin, Associate Professor and Program Coordinator of Interior Design, Washington State University

Phillip S. Waite, Associate Professor of Landscape Architecture, Washington State University

Paul G. Windley, Professor Emeritus and former Dean of Art and Architecture, University of Idaho

Preface to the First Edition

Ian L. McHarg

Educator, author, landscape architect/planner and ecologist Ian McHarg. Author of *Design with Nature*, a most important and very influential work (courtesy of Ian L. McHarg).

Environments that bear no visible human marks are rare—possibly some realms of ocean, the poles, deserts, mountain summits. There, human works may seem absent, but nonetheless, these environments have all relinquished the magic qualities of the term "primeval." That most pervasive sphere, the envelope of gases that protects and sustains us, is now disturbed, tainted, and has corrupted the innocence of the last natural refuge.

The world is now the human-created environment—a built environment.

As long as humans played a minor role in relationship to an irreplaceable, all-powerful nature, their works mattered little. They were only another predator limited by their prey, their works trivial—ephemeral incidents in the biosphere. Today, human works have global effect, often accomplished without thought or knowledge. It would be reasonable to assume them to be random—some harmful, some neutral, others beneficial—but not so: they seem to be capriciously destructive. Who would have imagined global effects from aerosol cans, abandoned refrigerators? Who would have assumed that human acts could cause serious transformations to world climate, induced warming, violent weather, sea level rise, and disruption of the protective ozone layer? Can the mind adjust to the transformation of benign rain into a toxin threatening forests in North America and Europe?

Humans have, knowingly or not, accumulated powers to control and modify the environment, and at last have come to the realization that our impact is destructive to ourselves and to the systems upon which we depend. We have no recourse but to come to understand the way the world works and initiate behavior that will maintain the biosphere and enhance human health and well-being.

The built environment must reflect the intelligence of humans, not their ignorance—a belated conclusion, not widely understood, it awaits application and realization.

The view of the Earth from the moon was a profound transformation. After centuries of observing the lunar procession from Earth, the subject and object were reversed and we looked from moon to Earth to perceive the lonely orb, the Earth our home, blue-green from oceans, maritime algae, and terrestrial vegetation. The astronauts view this green layer, this celestial fruit, and observe blemishes and lesions pocking the tissue. They and we must ask, are humans but a planetary disease? The answer is blunt: there is disease upon the Earth, and the lesions are the works of human beings. There are humans and institutions whose fulfillment involves the continuous infliction of disease and death on the world's life body. It is intolerable.

Yet, can we possibly contemplate the role of world steward, "designing with nature," understanding the operation of this vast system, planning human affairs in such a way as to perpetuate and enrich the biosphere, including the human-created built environment?

We can take heart from the realization of the past accomplishments and the current operations of simpler organisms. It is now widely accepted that the atmosphere, oceans, and lands are the creation of life. The transformation of the lethal primeval atmosphere into the benign envelope that encompasses us was the work of simple microorganisms. Its regulation is largely their work today. It is believed that the evolution of the oceans, their salinity, temperature, pH, are a product of life. Without doubt, microorganisms, plants, later animals, colonized the Earth, producing soils, modifying climate, the hydrologic cycle, creating habitats, successively making environments more fit for life.

There is one further analogy to give heart. One simple animal has accomplished greater environmental transformations, uniformly benign, than the sum of all human works in all of human time. The coral polyp with its photosynthetic associates has transformed vast oceanic deserts, incorporating calcium carbonate and silicate into their beings to create one of the richest environments of the world, habitat for incredibly diverse and stable ecosystems.

So, modifying environments is not unnatural. Indeed, it seems to be critical to evolution. Nor were these transformations trivial. So, we can accept that modifying environments and creating a built environment to accommodate human life is perfectly natural and appropriate. But there is a caveat. There were and will be costs and benefits.

So, we can assume that people have reason to undertake the role of consciously manipulating the environment to make it more fitting for all life, including humans. We have already demonstrated that we can dispose great powers of destruction, so why not reverse this power to create a sustainable world?

Charles Darwin stated that the surviving organism is fit for the environment. Lawrence Henderson augmented this proposition. The world includes a multiplicity of organisms and environments. It is necessary for all organisms to find the fittest available environment, and adapt it and oneself to achieve better fitness. Implied, but not explicit, was the definition of a fit environment as one in which the user found the maximum benefits on any given site, where the least work of adaptation need be undertaken.

At the beginning of the twentieth century, Lawrence Henderson observed that the oceans exhibited self-regulation and thus "responsiveness," a term usually reserved for life. In 1969, moved by Henderson's arguments on "The Fitness of the Environment," I wrote that if Henderson's description of organic life fit the oceans, why not then the atmosphere and the biosphere?

This inquiry was developed brilliantly by the English chemist James Lovelock, who advanced the Gaia Hypothesis, which, simply stated, suggested that we best consider the Earth, its inert and living systems, as a single superorganism. As humans are comprised of many organs, tissues, and billions of cells, and include water, sundry gases, and calcium, acting as a single integrated organism, so too the earth, rocks, oceans, soils, microorganisms, plants, and animals seem to interact coherently as a unitary system.

James Lovelock then investigated the matter of the regulating system—did this require a god-like creator? His conclusions were to the contrary; thermostatic devices widely used by living systems would be perfectly adequate. To establish this point, Lovelock invented Daisyworld, with light and dark flowers, higher and lower reflectance. Preponderance of lighter flowers reduced temperature, darker flowers increased it. If each has a selective temperature range, increasing or decreasing in numbers would create a natural thermostatic device that would regulate temperatures.

Evidence to support the hypothesis is only preliminary, but quite positive and certainly provocative. I can imagine no greater challenge to science than to investigate the Gaia Hypothesis. Should it be proven conclusively, the results could be dramatic. The most immediate result would be the necessity for a holistic view and the relegation of reductionism to contributor rather than final product. All parts must be seen as agents in the whole. I suspect that economics would be the next arena of change. If the Gaia Hypothesis is true and the bulk of the world's work in regulating atmosphere, oceans, temperatures, and terrestrial ecosystems is performed by microorganisms, it becomes necessary to identify them, and their roles, and give them value. Perversely, natural areas should assume inordinate value; highly urbanized areas may well incur significant global costs.

Philosophy and theology would also be subject to revision. How many prayers have issued from people asking for interventions—prevention of flood, drought, earthquakes, volcanoes, hurricanes, pestilence, pleas for good harvests of livestock, game, grains, and fish? What effect they have had we will never know. What change will occur when it becomes clear that many of these matters have been and are regulated by Gaia? So, the agents who could respond to prayers will be creatures and processes among us. How do we view these powerful god-like creatures? How do we negotiate, collaborate? We may remain ignorant of the cosmic but encounter a more modest planetary benefactor and control agent—ourselves, individually and collectively, as human inhabitants of the Earth. This requires a new stewardship—a new theology and philosophy advancing sustainability. Clearly, biology will be affected. No longer will plants and animals be categorized into taxonomic lists; even ecosystems or biosphere are too limiting. The Gaia Hypothesis integrates inert and living systems into a biological whole. The challenge to us all is to understand the living processes that comprise Gaia, the Earth.

In my own realm of planning and design—that which leads directly to a human-created built environment—a transformation is necessary. Given a world system with elaborate self-regulating processes, the human role is first to understand these and thereafter to engage in conscious modifications for human use that are not destructive of the critical processes. We must evaluate our creations in terms of their contribution to global processes that must be maintained. These environments can then be evaluated to ascertain their tolerance or intolerance to prospective modification. Planning and design must then include responses to global and regional contributions to Gaia, be responsive and expressive to world, region, place, and people.

This brings us back to the astronauts' view of the Earth, a blue-green celestial fruit on which lesions are visible. The fundamental role for humanity is to contribute to the health of the planet, the Earth, our home, to heal disease, to engage in modifications to enhance the global environment, among which none may be more important than the built environment.

Until the advent of the Industrial Revolution, the built environment worldwide injected small-scale, local interventions into the natural environment of little damage to world ecology. Since then, the scale has changed dramatically. Megacities—Calcutta, San Paõlo, Mexico City—exceed all world urbanism prior to the nineteenth century. Apparently, the rapid increase in carbon dioxide caused by humans may not only induce world warming, but also exacerbate violent climatic, hydrological, and terrestrial events. We are bringing violence upon ourselves. Can we reduce it? The human capability of environmental transformations has moved from little consequence to global threat.

While the prospect is frightening, history is reassuring. For most of human history, modifying the environment, including city building, has been appropriate to natural systems, responsive in materials and forms, of limited scale, and generally humane. One should not overlook epidemics, floods, earthquakes, or oppression, slavery, feudalism, war, but these events are not necessarily a direct consequence of built form. It appears that there are human, environmental, and technological factors that are identified with successful societal accomplishments. There have been vernacular adaptations in the built environment that are exemplary. In addition, there has developed an extensive body of knowledge on the environment that is fundamental to human health and understanding, and that permits planning and design based upon objective principles. It is challenges such as these that are addressed in this book on the built environment.

PART I

Introduction: Definition, Design, and Development of the Built Environment

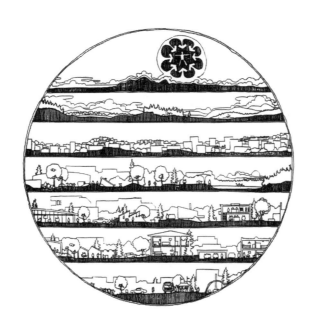

CHAPTER 1

The Built Environment: Definition and Scope

Tom J. Bartuska

We all build and therefore make important contributions to the built environment. We design and build our lives from one experience to another. Based on those experiences, components of the built environment emerge from human needs, thoughts, and actions. Sometimes the substances of human actions are grand, and we design and plan quality life experiences for ourselves and others. At other times, human actions are shortsighted, creating uncomfortable situations that are less fit for healthy human activities and negatively impact the environments that surround us and with which we are in constant interaction.

There are many reasons to design, plan, and build. Each aspect of the built environment is created to fulfill human purpose. As those purposes and actions are manifold, so too are the reasons to design and build. Where you are sitting while reading this page, you are surrounded by hundreds of human-created objects, all contributing components of your built environment. The words on this page, this book, your chair and desk, the nearby stereo, the cell phone and Internet that connect you to many others throughout the world, even the walls, floor, and ceiling of the space are humanly made or arranged and therefore part of the built environment. These components are constructed by dozens, hundreds, even thousands of material products and production sys-

tems. Look further afield and observe the variety of objects and environments out of the window. Buildings, automobiles, roads, bridges, the landscaped areas, parks, and the surrounding city are also part of a human-made or -arranged built environment. Imagine the range and complexity of environmental components, the magnitude of environments beyond your home: cities, highways, and other transport systems, parcels of agricultural land, even domesticated plants and animals—all are to some degree the products of human artifice and should be included.

All people everywhere are surrounded by an abundance of components of the human-created world. It may actually be harder to find environments that are completely outside the built environment, *not* made or arranged, maintained or controlled by people or society, if such still exist on this planet. The sky, weather, free-flowing rivers, and wilderness areas may seem untouched, but none are totally free from human intervention and impacts.

The cumulative results of the changes people have made in their surrounding environment are extensive expressions of past and present cultures. A large percentage of humanity lives in urban metropolitan areas. These massive urban and suburban developments are the largest, most complex human systems ever created. Perhaps less evident but equally extensive are human modi-

Figures 1-1 and 1-2 Reflections of the built environment—outside and within. *The Cloud Gate*/2006/Anish Kapoor, Millennium Park, Chicago, Illinois. Courtesy of the artist and Gladstone Gallery, New York. (Photograph by Jon Bartuska)

fications of the rural regions of the world: farmlands; domestication and genetic alterations of animals and plants; manipulation and management of forests and wildlife; dams built on a multitude of rivers for power, navigation, and flood control. The count is endless. The built environment fills every nook and cranny of the everyday world; it strongly influences human lives concurrent with their creation and modification of it.

To meet their most basic needs, people first created tools, harnessed fire, and developed shelter to survive in the wilderness. Once human survival needs became less uncertain (though that uncertainty still afflicts many even now), people turned their attention beyond survival and continued to modify the environment at an accelerating rate to make their lives safer and more comfortable, productive, and enjoyable. Times have changed, change has accelerated, and populations have exploded, but the basic reasons for creating a built environment remain essentially the same as people design and construct tools and products, modify and manipulate space, build structures, plan and shape landscapes and cities, and manage regions and the Earth.

Certain questions, though, can never be asked too many times, if only to remind us of the power we have to change environmental conditions. Why do humans make such extensive changes to their surroundings? Do we take equally extensive responsibility for the actions or changes involved? How often do we consider the long-term consequences of these actions? Are we concerned enough about the overall effects these actions have upon neighbors or upon the Earth, its finite resources, and its complex ecological systems? What are the limits to human intrusions on natural systems? How can meaning

and significance be created and maintained in the built environment?[1]

Movements to protect or restore the environment have focused somewhat narrowly on natural systems, neglecting the idea that the environments with which people interact most directly are often products of human initiated processes. Collectively, these products and processes of human creation are called the **built environment**. This term is comparatively new, but it describes in one holistic and integrated concept the creative (and not so creative) results of human activities throughout history. The term emerged in the 1980s and came into widespread use in the 1990s.[2] To illustrate, the term built environment is an integral part of a new definition of landscape architecture approved in 2003 by the International Federation of Landscape Architects. Tasks considered to be central to their work include the "planning, design, management, maintenance and monitoring of functional and aesthetic layouts of built environments" and "identifying and developing appropriate solutions regarding the quality and use of the built environment in urban, suburban and rural areas."[3] These are broad goals for a profession long considered to be focused on yards and gardens, yet typical of the recognition by the design disciplines today of the need to be more collaborative and inclusive.[4]

Most of society's knowledge of past civilizations is derived from remnants of the built environment. Similarly, present cultures will be judged in the future by what they have created. Will the results, and the remainders, be profound and expressive of the very best of society or condemned as careless of healthy human-environmental relationships?

The primary purpose of this book is to develop an appreciation and understanding of the objects and places (even the organisms) built and modified by humans, how they are created, and how they affect life on the planet. Increased involvement in and awareness of the design of the built environment should lead to human actions that influence our lives today, and those of our descendants, in a positive, contributing way. Quality tends to encourage more quality, more personal enjoyment, enrichment, productivity, and greater involvement, which in turn should improve quality. Poor quality creates apathy and has negative impacts on human health and well-being.

Every person is immersed in environments, including the built environment. Since the built environment is manifested in physical objects and places, it is relatively easy to observe and study (if not so easy to understand). It is critical for the reader to participate in, to visualize, and to experience real environments. This involvement can more easily be achieved by paying attention, by being aware, by directly experiencing and analyzing the many examples that exist in your local environment, home, and community, as well as throughout the surrounding region, country, and world. This book encourages your active participation and tries to increase your interest in and sensitivity to the wide range of variables in the built environment. The best way to create better environments is to actively engage with those environments, perhaps especially those we shape so intimately and so extensively. Get involved! Your active participation in this exploration will increase your appreciation, enjoyment, and success. And ours!

A working knowledge of the built environment, and of the design and planning professions that help shape it, is vital for all responsible citizens. Such knowledge allows a citizen, the reader of this book, to be aware of, search out, and help create more positive aspects of the built environment. Better understanding enables citizens to be more effective in taking corrective measures to eliminate or change the negative aspects. In general, better environments are created when people work together in cooperative ways. Any puzzle is easier to understand when the pieces are designed to fit together, and when people understand how and where they fit. It is urgent to realize that we are all interdependent participants in the collective building process; we can all effect positive change. Citizens and politicians, bankers and lawyers, engineers and planners, designers and scientists are all indispensable and influential parts in the design, planning, and management of a quality environment for all.

Definition and Scope of the Built Environment

The built environment is certainly pervasive (look again out that window), but both the term and its reach and implications are evasive, more comprehensive, and far-reaching than most of us realize, even though we live in it every day. It may be helpful, then, to start simply and define the built environment by four interrelated characteristics. First, it is extensive; it is *everywhere*; it provides the context for all human endeavors. More specifically, it is *everything* humanly created, modified, or constructed, humanly made, arranged, or maintained. Second, it is the creation of human minds and the result of human purposes; it is intended to serve human needs, wants, and values. Third, much of it is created to help us deal with, and to protect us from, the overall environment, to mediate or change this environment for our comfort and well-being. Last, an obvious but often forgotten characteristic is that every component of the built environment is defined and shaped by context; each and all of the individual elements contribute either positively or negatively to the overall quality of environments both built and natural and to human-environment relationships. These impacts are almost always local, and more and more are experienced at every scale, including global and even planetary.[5]

The simple but inclusive diagram in Figure 1-3 is intended to help visualize and define the built environment by these four interrelated characteristics.

The triangle (Δ) is intentionally used to symbolize the designed/built aspects of this definition. The triangle looks like a structure. It is the most stable geometric form

The Built Environment

 The built environment is everything humanly made, arranged, or maintained;

 to fulfill human purposes (needs, wants, and values);

 to mediate the overall environment;

 with results that affect the environmental context.

Figure 1-3 Definition of the built environment and its four related characteristics.

Figure 1-4 Exploring the interesting qualities of the triangle.

and unites three distinct sides and three points. It is used later in this chapter and others to integrate three sides of an issue and/or three points of view.

Components of the Built Environment

Understanding of any subject is advanced when it is organized into sets and subsets illustrating interrelated parts and wholes.[6] The variety and scope of the built environment, its diverse content, and its subtle contexts are organized in this book into seven interrelated components: products, interiors, structures, landscapes, cities, regions, and Earth. The sum of the seven defines the scope of the total built environment.

1. PRODUCTS

Products include materials and commodities generally created to extend the human capacity to perform specific tasks: graphic symbols such as the Western alphabet (letters form words, sentences combine into paragraphs and chapters, such as in this book); tools (pen and pencil, hammer and saw, peace pipe or weapon); materials (bricks and mortar, wood, concrete and steel, polymers and plastics); machines (radios and stereos, televisions and telecommunication systems, calculators and computers, roller skates and automobiles, aircraft and spaceships).

2. INTERIORS

Interior spaces are defined by an arranged grouping of products and generally enclosed within a structure. They are generally created to enhance activities and mediate external factors (living room, workrooms, private rooms, public assembly halls, stadiums, etc.).

3. STRUCTURES

Structures are planned groupings of spaces defined by and constructed of products; generally, related activities are combined into composite structures (housing, schools, office buildings, churches, factories, highways, tunnels, bridges, dams, etc.). Generally, structures have both an internal space and an external form.

4. LANDSCAPES

Landscapes are exterior areas and/or settings for planned groupings of spaces and structures (courtyards, malls, parks; gardens, sites for homes or other structures; farms, countryside, national forests and parks). Landscapes generally combine both natural and built environments.

5. CITIES

Cities are groupings of structures and landscapes of varying sizes and complexities, generally clustered together to define a community for economic, social, cultural, and/or environmental reasons (subdivisions, neighborhoods, districts, villages, towns, and cities of varying sizes).

6. REGIONS

Regions are groupings of cities and landscapes of various sizes and complexities; they are generally defined by common political, social, economic, and/or environmental characteristics (the surrounding region of cities, counties, or multicounty areas, a state or multistate regions, countries, continents).

7. EARTH

The Earth includes all of the above, the groupings of regions consisting of cities and landscapes—the entire planet, the spectacular, complex, beautiful, still mysterious Earth, which, as human power expands, may be considered the ultimate artifact.

These components can be better understood as connected layers or levels of varying scales interwoven together to form the built environment. These seven layers, this nested set of components, provide the organizing categories for this book, conceptualized in Figure 1-5.

The listing and descriptions of the seven components illustrate a significant overall theme: the interrelationships of each component with each of the others. The content of each component consists of a combination of smaller components. In turn, each component is a part of a larger context and contributes to the next larger component. For example, products can be considered the content for interiors and, for those products, interiors are the context. The **content-component-context** hierarchy is a useful tool in this book for organizing and presenting component parts and the myriad ways seemingly individual elements interrelate to form the whole of the built environment.[7]

In an age of specialization, many have lost sight of the interrelationships among the components of the built environment, including those who actively participate in the creative processes. Complex webs of elemental interrelationships are critical in creating a quality built

environment and require considerable understanding, forethought, and collaborative planning. Too often, designs have been project specific and bounded by disciplines. There is an understandable tendency for product designers to talk primarily to their own colleagues, for engineers to discuss common issues with other engineers, for architects to seek solutions from other architects. But the designs, and the built environment, that emerge from a limited or channeled discourse tend to be fragmented and isolated from the context. Designers need to establish common ties that bind them, and their ideas, together and help integrate content-component-context linkages within the built environment. A lack of integration often results in a fragmented and chaotic environment. We all suffer the consequences.

Reminding the design and planning disciplines and professions of their common base and shared goals is an important objective of this book.[8] The term built environment is presented as a holistic concept formed from the integration of separately designed components. Understanding this is necessary to acknowledge the interdependencies not only among the many components, but also between people, their professions, and areas of study.

Fortunately, increased numbers of designers, both educators and practitioners in various fields, are combining their talents in interdisciplinary teams to strengthen

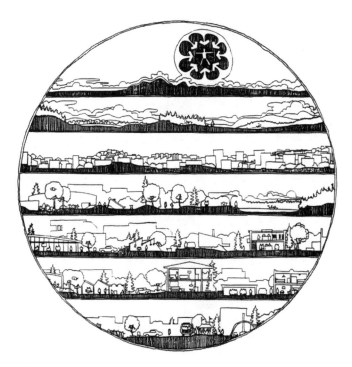

Figure 1-5 The layers of the built environment (the integrative or composite symbol design by S. Recken; the linear graphic formats by J. Singleton).

interrelationships. Societal and governmental pressures are encouraging more integration. National, state, and many local environmental policy acts mandate interdisciplinary analysis and citizen participation in addressing complex problems. Environmental reviews and approval processes mandate more collaboration. There is, however, significant room for continued improvement in education and practice.[9]

The arts and sciences, traditionally organized in a taxonomy of separate disciplines, are sharing their understanding of the environment through renewed awareness of ecology, study of the interactions of organisms (including humans) and their environments. Concurrently, the applied design and planning fields, which have also traditionally been organized into separate disciplines, are combining their talents into a general field of environmental design, often specifically expressed as a focus on the built environment. Robert Reekie, an English planner, architect, and educator, and author of one of the first books on

the built environment, emphasizes this need for integration, participation, and interdisciplinary collaboration:

[We all should] intelligently participate in the urgent task of abolishing ugliness, dreariness, squalor and also offensiveness from towns, villages and countryside, and in restoring and producing [human] pleasure in the environment, so that life can be lived therein more healthily and happily. . . . One of the points made in this book is that environmental design, now and in the future, is and will be a matter of expert teamwork supported by public appreciation and participation. . . . Integration may well be the key word in good design. Not only does it mean the correct combining of parts into a whole, but also it implies . . . integrity, soundness and honesty.[10]

Why Humans Build

An encompassing definition of the built environment can also provide some understanding of why humans build. There is a clear cause-and-effect relationship between human purpose and the things we create. An eloquent historian and English Prime Minister, Sir Winston Churchill, forcefully expressed this: "We shape our buildings; thereafter they shape us." Another noted historian, Arthur Cortell, conveys this same interdependency by claiming: "Tell me the landscape you grew up in and I will tell you about yourself." To aid in understanding this relationship, it is useful to explore more specifically the nature of human needs, wants, and values.

Human Needs as Manifested in the Built Environment

To survive, all organisms must satisfy certain basic needs. Humans are no exception. Abraham Maslow,[11] a psychologist, outlined a well-known hierarchy of human needs.

The most basic set of needs are physiological—those required for proper functioning of the body and mind. Maslow's idea is that we humans concentrate on the most basic needs (at least to a significant degree) until those needs are met with some degree of certainty and satisfaction. Then we turn our attention to those needs not strictly essential to body function and survival. The same transition occurs at each level of the hierarchy; humans become concerned with psychological needs, such as the need to belong to a group or to achieve self-realization, when they reach some level of provision of physiological

Figures 1-6 and 1-7 "Continuum," 5,000 images expressing the human, environmental, and technological history of the city (B. Brother, 2003, Seattle, Washington).

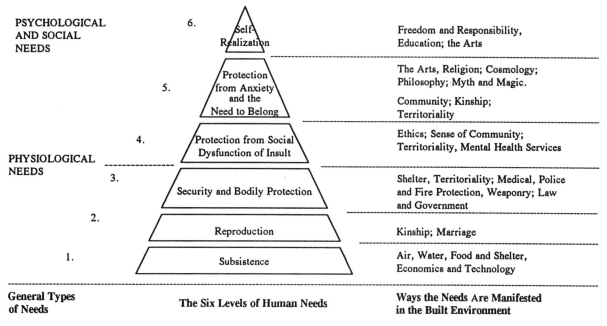

Figure 1-8 Human needs and various ways they are manifested in the built environment.

needs. Maslow's ideas, of course, are only a model of reality, a deliberately simple sketch full of overlaps and uncertainties; humans in all but the worst situations are concerned with several (if not all) of the levels all of the time; concern is a matter of degree and emphasis. But the hierarchy is useful and does underline the fact that elements of the built environment do correspond, often directly, to expressions of human needs and wants. Figure 1-8 identifies the general types of physical and psychological needs (on the left), the hierarchy of six levels of human needs (in the center), and the way these needs are expressed in the built environment (on the right).

Beyond the realm of needs is that of wants, those material goods that are not really needed at any level but that emerge from the desire for self-gratification. For example, we biologically need food and water, but instead of beans and rice we may want gourmet foods. We need clothing but many want expensive designer brands. We need efficient transportation systems, but we may want a car; we may even need a car in the context of where we live, but we want a newer, bigger, or faster car. Market forces, especially energy prices, are pushing people again toward more energy-efficient cars, and designers and producers are responding with gas/electric hybrids.

Comparisons in the needs hierarchy can also help us better understand many of the social differences in the world. It is naive and hypocritical to think that the millions of people in the world suffering from malnutrition and starvation are very concerned with the ego gratifica-

tion gained from a louder stereo, designer clothes, or a bigger car.

For every need and want, there must be an adaptive response, an **adaptive design strategy**. The need is satisfied (by every human) through exploitation of the environment, processes that form complex varieties of human-environmental relationships. These relationships are established through the use of various technologies (see Chapters 6 and 16). The design response also requires the use of material and energy resources and the combining of various components into some portion of the built environment. Recognizing that needs are generally more basic than wants helps to establish priorities in order to minimize costs, to reduce the use of finite resources, and to mediate human impacts on the environment.

Since needs are similar and reoccur, many of them based in the biology of the organism, they are quite predictable throughout every life span and in each succeeding generation. The adaptive design responses then become organized, institutionalized, and slow to change. It seems obvious, but is often forgotten, that the most fundamental needs are air, water, and food. One can only live a few minutes without air, a few days without water, and a few weeks without food. These are the fundamental building blocks of life, and they must be protected from harmful substances throughout the world. Part of the food for humans comes from agriculture, a human endeavor. Though still rooted in natural systems, a field of grain is an artifact of the built environment, as is the grain itself, usually a highly developed hybrid far removed from its origins in a wild plant. All of the other adaptive responses necessary to modern agriculture (equipment, fertilizers, pesticides, etc.) are also modified or created and operated by humans.

To satisfy reproductive needs, every culture develops kinship systems, including the institution of marriage. For bodily protection, we have developed various systems of microenvironmental control: clothing and shelter, the medical professions, even weaponry. To protect ourselves from social dysfunction, we have developed law and politics, and for protection against anxiety, we have developed the varied institutions that deal with art, science, technology, religion, philosophy, etc. Every culture has such institutions in some form; it is the way societies have elaborated these institutions that makes them different. Much of that elaboration is expressed in the various created forms in the built environment.

Human Values as Manifested in the Built Environment

The built environment is an expression not only of human attempts to fulfill personal and societal needs and wants, but also of personal and collective values and aspirations. Human values may be more abstract than needs, but a general understanding of them can enhance our sensitivity to the attitudes people have about the built environment. Value-formed attitudes manifest themselves in the way we relate to our surroundings, the way we solve problems, and consequently are expressed in the intrinsic characteristics of culture. Human values are subjective—they deal with beliefs, opinions, and attitudes. They influence the setting of priorities and are analogous to the value or the price we are willing to pay for something. In objective terms, money can serve as a measure of value, but some objects, concepts, or places may be difficult or impossible to measure in economic terms. How can the value of beauty, quality, freedom, equality, a mountain range, the ocean, or even an ecosystem be assessed objectively? Many attempts have been made to assign prices in such areas, but their value remains subjective and elusive.

Values affect subjective attitudes, and many of these find expression in the built environment. For example, many Americans place a high value on individual rights and freedoms. On the face of it, that should be as good, but it has a range of ramifications for the built environment. The individual house on its own site is an important value to many, but detached structures can create energy inefficiency and sprawl. The same is true of transportation: The United States has developed a very exten-

sive auto-oriented lifestyle and a complex of systems to support it. So far, North Americans have been willing to pay the high costs in taxes and energy for these sprawling, auto-driven land use patterns. Such attitudes or values can blind people to consideration of other alternatives; many other countries judge such patterns as wasteful, even as antisocial. Also, in U.S. and Canadian cities, private corporations and commercial interests dominate the cityscape; the tallest buildings dominating contemporary skylines are those owned by banks, insurance companies, and large investment firms. In some cities in other countries, the most prominent features are public spaces, civic structures, or cathedrals.

Values fundamentally affect people's perceptions of the built environment. Values and the ethics emerge from every decision in shaping and reshaping the built environment: decisions on selection of sites and materials, environmental impacts, energy use, and sustainability.[12] Despite this, there is too little conscious effort to deal with human values openly and directly, yet they are at the heart of the design professions' contribution to society.

Lawrence Kohlberg, extending the work of Jean Piaget, gives clarity and utility to the understanding of various human values.[13] Kohlberg constructed a useful scale of six levels of moral development, illustrated in Figure 1-9. Each level is referenced to what are considered conventional norms (on the left). The hierarchy of human values (in the middle) is similar to the human needs scale. The implied attitudes formed are also included (on the right).

In very general terms, human values affect personal philosophy and how we set priorities or solve problems, be they individualistic or based upon popular style, on functionalism, on humanistic ideals, or on a total integration of all concerns. Kohlberg's conventional values represent the general operational level of people in market-based urban/industrial nations. These people live and work in an arena of laws, codes, and economics. Success derives from reality of individual and market conventions. But societal values emerge at the postconventional level and give greater weight to equality and public participation. Though conventional values may lead to individual success, they aren't necessarily as successful in the public realm. Conventional and postconventional values don't need to be in conflict if people can incorporate both into their perspectives and actions. Kohlberg's scale has been criticized as too Western, too male-oriented, and even anticaring and anticommunity. We are not recommending using the scale to measure people, but we present it as a visual

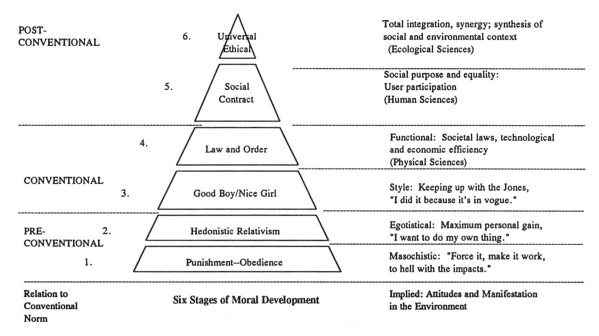

Figure 1-9 Human values (levels of moral development) and various ways they are manifested in the built environment.

tool for people to achieve what they can and should transcend conventional values to help realize a better environment for all. Looking at the visual depiction of this value scale, we may get a better grasp of where people are coming from when ideas are in conflict over issues of design or of life.

Thematic Ideas and Ideals

Social, Environmental, and Technological Issues

The built environment involves a fascinating and challenging set of issues. Human/social and cultural issues deal with why people build. Environmental issues deal with the natural and built context, locally and globally. And finally, technological issues deal with the materials, energy and financial resources, methods, and systems required to establish interrelationships and construct the built environment. All the authors of this book will expand on these triad relationships in various ways in order to create unifying themes throughout this study.

Integrative Design: Issues, Art, and Science

The best design and planning decisions respond to a comprehensive set of issues. Design and planning can be defined as the art and science of creatively resolving issues, of solving inherent conflicts in human–environmental relationships. Creative design and planning allow us to be agents of change rather than victims of it. Interrelationships between issues, science, and art are expressed in the triangle in Figure 1-10. Design and planning occur at all levels and extremes; they can be expressive as pure art or pure science but are usually expressions of both.

Any of the three extremes can lead to designs that are expressive and to objects that at times are favored by the public and the press. But, ideally, integrated design and planning embrace an inclusive design process—the middle of the triangle. Designers and planners of the future need to accept the challenge of attempting to understand and integrate the full range of this complex triad of relationships as they work to create new integrated layers of the built environment.

Design and Planning

Throughout this exploration into the built environment, the terms **design** and **planning** play important and reiterated roles. They are action-oriented words that express human intentions to engage in the creative process. Design is a process to plan and implement an idea in a creative, intentional, and skillful way; planning is the design or formulation of a scheme for making, doing or arranging something [in a skillful way].

Although there are subtle differences between the two terms (design tends to be more specific, planning more general), for the purpose of this work they are equally important and at times are used interchangeably. Design requires careful planning; planning requires careful design. More specifically, design tends to deal with three-dimensional development of smaller-scale components (products and interiors, structures, and landscapes), whereas planning tends to deal with two-dimensional schemes for larger components (landscapes, cities, and regions). The medium-scaled components tend to use both terms (landscape design and city planning, urban design and planning).

Inclusive, Interdisciplinary, Integrative and Involvement

This collaborative effort sets a model for modern design and planning; it attempts to be inclusive, interdisciplinary, and integrative while encouraging user involvement. The term and definition of the built environment are inclusive: all things designed, planned, and managed by humans. The book is interdisciplinary, written by a variety of authors from all the design and planning disciplines. Throughout the book, integrative concepts weave the content and components of the built environment together. The goal throughout is involvement; greater involvement increases each person's potential to realize his or her objectives; public participation can greatly enhance understanding and thus the quality of the resultant built environment.

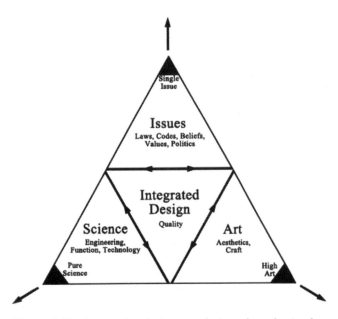

Figure 1-10 Integrative design—analysis and synthesis of issues through science and art (W. McClure).

As emphasized before, aspects of the built environment are everywhere. They are readily accessible through the Internet and discussed daily in various local and national newspapers and radio and television programs. Take advantage of the model provided here; take advantage of all the resources available. People learn more if they are engaged and involved. The more venues the better, because we all retain information in different ways and in different percentages, though some generalizations can be made. Some studies estimate that people retain approximately 10% of what they read, 20% of what they hear, 30% of what they see, 50% of what they see *and* hear, 70% of what they say, and 90% of what they do. So, get involved! Personal participation may be the most critical action the readers of this book can take to improve the quality of the built environment for themselves and for others.

Organization of the Book

To reveal and clarify the complexities and challenges of design of the built environment, the book is organized into four parts.

I. Introduction: Definition, Design, and Development of the Built Environment

The first chapter discusses the purpose, definition, and scope of the built environment. The second chapter establishes four general traditions expressed in the evolution of the built environment and explores the meanings of each development.

II. Central Human-Environmental-Technical Dimensions of a Quality Environment

The first chapter in Part II explores the concept of the word environment, its meaning and its complexity and hierarchical relationships. It also addresses quantitative and qualitative dimensions of the built environment. The next three chapters introduce the importance of designing with human, environmental, and technical aspects of the built environment in mind. Designing with the human aspects of this triad relationship is explored in the second chapter of Part II. How to design with the natural environment is introduced in the third chapter. The importance of technology is explored in the fourth chapter, and how people attempt to compose, order, and give meaning to the diverse characteristics of their environments is addressed in the final chapter.

III. Design and Planning Components (Levels of Integration) in the Built Environment

The third and main part of the book organizes the built environment into seven components and explores in greater detail the human, environmental, and technical aspects of each. Each component is defined and then explained in terms of the past, present, and future: past precedents (historic developments), present developments including discussion of contemporary design issues, and future design challenges. In particular, Part III examines the important contributions the design and planning professions make in helping to shape the built environment. Although the seven components must be considered as integrated together, individual readers may elect to concentrate on one or more of the following seven components, which include the following:

1. **Products:** Industrial and Product Design
2. **Interiors:** Interiors and Interior Design
3. **Structures:** Architecture, Engineering, and Construction
4. **Landscapes:** Landscape Architecture and Planning
5. **Cities:** Urban Design and Planning
6. **Regions:** Regional Planning and Management
7. **Earth:** Global Policies, Planning, and Management

IV. Challenges: Designing/Planning a Quality and Sustainable Environment for All

Part IV offers a brief concluding perspective, one that hopefully will foster further insight and increase involvement in meeting the challenges raised throughout the book, challenges for a quality and sustainable built environment for all. The overall purpose of this book is to foster interest and involvement in the built environment. It seeks to open a series of doors that invite a more thorough understanding of the fascinating complexity, intricacy, and multilayered structure of the built world. Most chapters conclude with a list of references to encourage further investigation and study. Readers are encouraged to further investigate the concepts and components of the built environment in that literature and within their local communities.

Acknowledgment

This chapter is a revised and updated version of T. Bartuska and G. Young, "The Built Environment Definition and Scope" in *The Built Environment: A Creative Inquiry into Design and Planning*, Crisp Publications, Inc., 1994.

References

Bartuska, T. "Values, Architecture and Context: The Emergence of an Ecological Approach to Architecture and the Built Environment." *ACSA Annual Conference Proceedings*, March 1981.

Boyer, E., and L. Mitgang. *Building Community: A New Future for Architecture Education and Practice*. Carnegie Foundation, 1996.

Charles, J., and J. Kibert. *Reshaping the Built Environment: Ecology, Ethics, and Economics*. Island Press, 1999.

Crowe, N. *Nature and the Idea of a Man-made World: An Investigation into the Evolutionary Roots of Form and Order in the Built Environment*. MIT Press, 1997.

Habraken, N.J., and J. Teicher, editors. *The Structure of the Ordinary: Form and Control in the Built Environment*. MIT Press, 2000.

International Federation of Landscape Architects. "Definition of the Profession of Landscape Architecture." *IFLA News*, No. 48, 2003.

Knox, P., and P. Ozolins (eds.). *The Design Professions and the Built Environment*. Wiley, 2000.

Maslow, A. *The Farther Reaches of Human Nature*. Viking, 1971.

Muir, T., and B. Rance. *Collaborative Practice in the Built Environment*. Routledge, 1995.

Rapoport, A. *Meaning of the Built Environment: A Nonverbal Communication Approach*. University of Arizona Press, 1990.

Reekie, R. *Design in the Built Environment*. Edward Arnold, 1972.

Young, G.L. "A Piece of the Main: Parts and Wholes in Human Ecology." *Advances in Human Ecology*, No. 8, 1–32, 1999.

Endnotes

1. A. Rapoport, *Meaning of the Built Environment: A Nonverbal Communication Approach* (University of Arizona Press, 1990).
2. N. Crowe, *Nature and the Idea of a Man-made World: An Investigation into the Evolutionary Roots of Form and Order in the Built Environment* (MIT Press, 1997).
3. International Federation of Landscape Architects, "Definition of the Profession of Landscape Architecture" (*IFLA News*, No. 48, 2003).
4. T. Muir and B. Rance, *Collaborative Practice in the Built Environment* (Routledge, 1995).
5. N.J. Habraken and J. Teicher, editors, *The Structure of the Ordinary: Form and Control in the Built Environment* (MIT Press, 2000).

6. G.L. Young, "A Piece of the Main: Parts and Wholes in Human Ecology." *Advances in Human Ecology*, No. 8, 1–32, 1999.

7. See Note 5.

8. P. Knox and P. Ozolins (eds.), *The Design Professions and the Built Environment* (Wiley, 2000).

9. E. Boyer and L. Mitgang, *Building Community: A New Future for Architecture Education and Practice* (Carnegie Foundation, 1996).

10. R. Reekie, *Design in the Built Environment* (Edward Arnold, 1972): pp. v and 5.

11. See footnote 3.

12. J. Charles and J. Kibert, *Reshaping the Built Environment: Ecology, Ethics, and Economics* (Island Press, 1999).

13. T. Bartuska, "Values, Architecture and Context: The Emergence of an Ecological Approach to Architecture and the Built Environment" (Annual *ACSA Proceedings*, 1981), San Francisco.

CHAPTER 2

Four Traditions in the Built Environment

Henry C. Matthews

Few places on the surface of planet Earth have escaped radical change by human intervention. In densely populated or intensively farmed regions, the landscape is essentially a human creation. City dwellers may go out into the countryside and feel that they are experiencing nature; but what they see is a natural world under human control, very different from the landscape that would have survived if humans had never taken charge. We have harnessed natural processes for our own advantage and suppressed others that do not suit us. We have used backbreaking labor for countless generations to reshape the land for our use, and, more recently, have employed vast machines to speed up such tasks. When we talk about the built environment, we are referring to something far broader than the places defined by products and buildings, for we have constructed around us a world controlled by our own powerful systems. We have transformed it with systems of human settlement and of defense, land management and agriculture, power generation, irrigation and flood control, as well as networks of communication and transportation. Unfortunately, we have rendered large areas dangerous or uninhabitable by contaminating them with chemicals, nuclear waste, land mines, or depleted uranium from weapons. Even high mountain ranges and the snowy wastes of polar regions that once seemed immune

to human intervention are changing as a result of global warming. The decisions we make locally about the built environment often have global repercussions.

Although many animals create efficient, complex, and beautiful shelters, the human race has distinguished itself by building far more than is necessary for survival. The beaver may dam streams and build lodges on artificial islands; ants may engineer fantastic vertical structures, teeming with organized life. However, these creatures always follow predetermined patterns. In contrast, *Homo sapiens* has created products, structures, and settlements that adapt to widely different circumstances, with original and unique design ideas. Centuries after they were made, we can study human artifacts and buildings and see in them evidence of the beliefs, fears, and obsessions of their makers. They not only provide shelter and tools for survival but also act as symbols of ideals and aspirations.

Human endeavors in the built environment have been governed by two distinct traditions that have existed side by side since the beginnings of civilization. Each tradition can be identified by its own priorities and design principles. The first, known as the **vernacular** or folk tradition, has served ordinary people in their daily lives; the second, the **high-style** tradition, has belonged to the elite, to governments, religious cults, and institu-

Figure 2-1 Systems of water supply and defense, a Roman aqueduct and a medieval castle, dominate a landscape. Arghyrokastro, Albania (E. Lear, 1848).

tions. Its purpose is often ceremonial rather than practical. In more recent times, two other traditions have developed—the **speculative** tradition, which is concerned with building for profit, and the democratic tradition of public participation in the process of design, also known as the **participatory** tradition.

The Vernacular Tradition

The first artifacts and human shelters were made of materials found close at hand. Through a long process of trial and experimentation, designs evolved to serve the users as efficiently as possible. They were shaped according to their purpose, and their form changed only if a refinement in design or a new approach made a significant improvement in their performance. They followed old traditions, linking the present with a distant past. Early forms of tools and shelter provide excellent examples of human ingenuity. They show how locally available materials could be exploited to make sound dwellings, well adapted to their site and climate and appealing to the eye.

For example, in the fertile river valleys of the Tigris and Euphrates in Mesopotamia, revered as the cradle of Western civilization, two materials proved outstandingly successful and are still used today much as they were 6,000 years ago. In vernacular traditions, mud was molded into blocks, dried in the sun, and used as a strong, stable walling material. Reeds were bound together into bundles to make columns and woven into mats to serve as wall panels or roofs. Where light was needed, the reeds were formed into decorative openwork screens. With the use of local mud or reeds, there was no need to bring materials from far away or to deplete non-renewable resources. We might feel that dwellings of

mud or reeds are bound to be inferior to our own homes, produced in an industrialized society. Yet, we would be astonished by the quality of the spaces, the expertise of construction, and the appealing simplicity of form of the houses proudly built by their own inhabitants. We might also be impressed by their natural methods of adaptation to the climate. Mud bricks are ideal for a desert climate. The heavy walls with a high thermal capacity absorb heat during the day and transfer it to the interior at night. The lighter reed dwellings allow the necessary ventilation in humid marsh areas and provide comfortable living conditions.

Vernacular traditions respond to the lives of the people. Obviously, fisherfolk, animal herders, and farmers who raise crops build different kinds of settlements. Nomadic peoples have developed highly specialized portable buildings. An example is the yurt of the nomads living in the area between eastern Turkey and Mongolia, which collapse for transportation on horseback. It is interesting to note that some of the finest carpets are made by nomadic people who cannot carry much furniture. Easily laid out on the ground, they bring immeasurable richness to otherwise simple homes. In a desert environment, a woven rug can even symbolize a garden of flowers.

Similarly, throughout the world, building types have emerged that solve the housing problems of different cultures in a wide range of climatic zones. The longhouses of the Northwest Coast, the tipis of the Central Plains, log houses of forested regions, and adobe houses in the Southwest of the United States all belong to strong vernacular traditions in domestic building, which lasted into the twentieth century.

The availability of materials has also governed the making of common artifacts. A container fashioned by its owner for daily use may be made in the Arctic of whalebone and sealskin; in Europe of hardwood; in Southeast Asia of woven palm leaves. In Africa, a calabash will serve the same purpose, and elsewhere it may be made of pottery or wrought iron. In each place, a traditional

Figure 2-2 Ancient Egyptians making bricks. The same method is used in many places today.

Figure 2-5 The yurt is ideally adapted to the life of nomads in Afghanistan. It collapses for transportation, yet provides protection in a harsh climate (T. Bartuska).

Figures 2-3 and 2-4 A dwelling of the Marsh Arabs of Iraq. Such buildings consume no nonrenewable resources, yet serve their purpose well (W. Thesinger).

method of manufacture is passed down from generation to generation.

Throughout the world, the exploitation and conservation of the land have been controlled by conventional wisdom and tradition. Holland was formed out of unin-

habitable salt marshes by building dikes and pumping the water away by windmills. Ancient Egypt was made fertile by irrigation canals distributing the waters of the Nile at its annual flooding. Vast areas of Asia retain the waters of monsoon rains in their rice paddies, while in more arid places, whole hillsides are terraced to contain precious soil behind stone walls. Within the vernacular tradition, farmers have generally worked in harmony with nature and paid attention to the conservation of vital resources. They have known only too well that quick ways of obtaining higher yields make little sense in the long run.

Often agriculture and buildings go hand and hand. In southern Italy near the town of Alberobello, dwellings known as *trulli* are built of stones cleared from previously infertile fields. In this region, the upper layers of

Figure 2-6 Cliff dwellings of the Anasazi Indians at Mesa Verde, Colorado. Heavy masonry walls absorb the heat of the low winter sun, while the overhanging cliff provides protection from the high summer sun.

Figure 2-7   African women carrying calabashes, the dried skins of gourd-like plants (D. Hill).

Figure 2-8   Terraced fields of Winaywwayna, Peru (developed in the 16th century by the Inca civilization). Throughout the world, generations of hard labor have made rocky mountainsides productive, prevent soil erosion and water runoff (T. Bartuska).

limestone have been broken up by centuries of changing weather. The farmers have used the largest blocks of stone to build their houses and the thin, naturally split stones to form their roofs. Rougher stones have sufficed for boundary walls. The remaining rubble has been put back over the solid beds of impervious limestone and topsoil then replaced over the gravel beds. This system traps and stores winter rains among the small stones, and the reservoir below the sparse topsoil nourishes crops during the dry seasons. Remarkable clusters of *trulli* stand among the fields, conical structures unique to the area, a testament to human creativity of the vernacular tradition.

Although vernacular traditions can be explained as a response to material needs and practical opportunities, these factors alone cannot explain the rich variety of form. Many types of artifacts and dwellings can only be understood as cultural symbols. Ritual and ceremony have been important in determining the organization and design of buildings. The value systems and social hierar-

chies of the owners are often clearly expressed. For example, in many African villages, the design of a family compound will show how many wives the head of the family has, the status of children, and whether cattle are more important than grain.

Sometimes the forms of dwellings can be traced to an earlier phase in the history of the group that built them. House types can survive even though prevailing conditions change. An outstanding example of such survival is the kiva, the ceremonial space of the Anasazi Indians of Colorado and New Mexico. This subterranean space originated in ancient dwellings of Siberia. People there responded to the harsh climate by living in sunken pits with a central hearth, covered with a thick, insulated layer of turf over a wooden roof. The original inhabitants of the North American continent migrated from that

Figure 2-9   Trulli near Alberobello in southern Italy—a harmony of fields and buildings in the vernacular tradition.

Figure 2-10 The kiva, the ceremonial space of the Anasazi Indians, Mesa Verde, Colorado. Originally covered and provided with a central fire pit, it closely resembled the Siberian pit dwelling.

region over the Bering Straits, bringing building traditions with them. As they moved south and adapted to milder climates, they still retained their former type of dwelling. At such places as Mesa Verde and Chaco Canyon in the Southwest of the United States, where they built villages with stone walls above ground, the subterranean pit dwelling survived as a ceremonial space centered around a fire. The fire is provided with an elaborate air intake and draft deflector, a reminder of the time when fire was the key to survival.

Vernacular traditions tend to conform to certain general rules that distinguish them from the high-style tradition:

- Vernacular building and crafts belong to ordinary people. They are built or made by the owners or by specialists within their community.
- Materials are found close at hand, and designs have strong local or regional character.
- Designs are utilitarian. They are made for their purpose, fitting proven functional patterns.
- Building and village design is well adapted to climate, solving problems by the use of natural systems.
- Changes in design develop slowly. Craftspeople are conservative, preferring to use the experience of previous generations. The quality of work is sound and capable but often rough and unrefined.
- Cultural symbolism, ceremony, and ritual also play a part as influences in design. Sometimes practical needs are overruled by the desire for symbolic elements.

High-Style Tradition

From the beginnings of civilization, certain individuals emerged as leaders with power over others. Whether they excelled in hunting and battle or gained power through wisdom or magic and ritual, they sought to distinguish themselves from ordinary people. They wore rich and unique clothing and created luxurious palaces, forbidding citadels, and awe-inspiring temples furnished with precious objects. They summoned the best artisans and imported fine materials to create high-style designs.

At least five thousand years ago, tribal leaders in many places demanded unique structures that rose above local vernacular dwellings in scale, in strength, and in artistic quality. Their expert builders experimented with new materials and engineering skills to produce unique structures that inspired awe in those who saw them and gave protection and pleasure to their patrons. The human desire for high-style design has continued ever since. While vernacular traditions provided buildings suitable for villages and the edges of towns, the growth of cities promoted the development of grander architecture and urban landscapes. Both despotic rulers and democratic governments have employed skilled designers to create urban spaces that express civic pride and a sense of order.

As in vernacular design, change in high-style design was often slow. Successful forms often survived for many generations. However, radical changes sometimes took place in response to new religious beliefs or aesthetic impulses. Vernacular traditions reflect the conservatism of rural people, and it is rare for foreign ideas to

Figure 2-11 Worship of the Babylonian Sun God in a richly designed temple (from a stone tablet of 900 B.C.).

be accepted. But in the high style, foreign influence is admired and originality is often a sign of prestige.

The Egyptian Pharaoh Zoser, who ruled in the third millennium B.C.E., built a great temple tomb for himself to preserve his body and soul for eternity. It was first constructed in the conventional way as a low structure in which material goods were stored over the grave. However, the architect, Imhotep, breaking with tradition, conceived a new design of unprecedented splendor. He enlarged it into a stepped pyramid 200 feet high, perhaps symbolizing a stairway to the heavens. Around this, in a 35-acre enclosure, he built a necropolis, or city of the dead, made up of stone replicas of palaces, shrines, government buildings, and storehouses to serve the dead king to eternity. Such buildings for the living had nor-mally been made of mud bricks and reeds; so, to create familiarity, Imhotep imitated the texture of reeds in stone. The columns of the entrance hall symbolized bundles of reeds; he adorned other columns with capitals based on the flower heads of lotus and papyrus that once decorated reed houses. Deep underground by the tomb chamber, stone panels faced with lapis lazuli, a rich blue stone, were carved with the texture of reed matting. Such ornament, carved with the utmost confidence and precision, celebrated traditional building techniques in a to-tally original way.

Stonehenge, in southwest England, follows none of the normal rules for vernacular building. Far from being useful for shelter or agriculture, the monument appears to have possessed symbolic meaning as a great astronomical computer. The materials were imported at the cost of enormous human labor. Eighty-two stone blocks, weighing about 4 tons each, were brought 240 miles from Wales. Similar feats of art and engineering have been achieved in many places around the world.

The Greek temple exemplifies the search for excel-

Figure 2-13   Stonehenge, Salisbury Plain, England. This structure demonstrates the human will to overcome obstacles to build religious or symbolic structures (T. Bartuska).

lence. This building type evolved gradually from a simple hut constructed of wooden posts and beams to such impressive monuments of the fifth century B.C.E. as the Parthenon of Athens. For permanence, the material was changed from wood to stone; but just as Zoser's tomb contained details of reed buildings, the Parthenon retains symbols of wood construction in solid stone. Each part of the temple expresses its purpose through refinement of form. Columns clearly carry loads, beams span between them, the triangular pediment proclaims the function of the roof. Decoration subtly emphasizes form, as in the fluting of the columns, or appears in nonstructural elements, such as the panels of the frieze, carved with scenes from mythology. Greek temples were often built in dominant positions above cities. Their beauty and permanence demonstrated reverence for the gods.

The Romans adopted the Greek temple as the model for their own temples and spread this classical design

Figure 2-12   The temple tomb of the Pharaoh Zoser, 2750 B.C. A symbolic structure designed for the eternal afterlife of the powerful ruler (model reconstruction made and photographed by Jean-Phillipe Lauer from his book *Saqqara*, published by Thames and Hudson, Ltd., London).

Figure 2-14   The Parthenon, Athens (mid-fifth century B.C.) The Doric temple perfected.

Figure 2-15   The Virginia State Capitol designed by Thomas Jefferson in 1748, based on the Maison Carrée, a Roman temple in France.

throughout their empire. So potent was this form as a symbol of beauty, order, and permanence that its use has been revived many times. For example, in the late eighteenth century, Thomas Jefferson, the third president of the United States, built the Virginia State Capitol as a close replica of a Roman temple he had seen and admired in France. Although his building was to be a democratic place of assembly, he adopted the Roman temple form to show the people of the United States what architecture should be. Many later generations have endorsed Jefferson's ideas by building residences, banks, churches, and several other building types to similar designs.

The Romans exploited the potential of vaulting and dome construction, creating vast interior spaces. To ensure that the importance of their imperial buildings was perceived, they decorated their surfaces with columns like those of the temple. Thus, the column became something other than a means of support. It was now a symbol expressing power and beauty. In the Islamic world, where science was greatly valued, significant advances were made in dome construction. Space, light, and structure were united as the essence of sixteenth-century Ottoman mosques.

Roman vaulted spaces were the direct ancestors of the Gothic cathedral. The medieval masons refined the principles of vaulting practiced by the Romans to use a minimum amount of stone. In the late twelfth century, master masons strove to create an image of heaven on earth made of stone and glass. Amiens Cathedral represents the high point of French Gothic. Looking up into the vaults, one cannot believe that thousands of tons of stone can be made to appear so weightless. This astonishing achievement was only made possible by the daring ingenuity of the masons. The combination of flying buttress, pointed arch, and ribbed vault allowed them to open up huge areas of wall to stained glass windows. This design through which a dream was realized became a celebration of structure and space.

Historians describe the Middle Ages, which produced the Gothic cathedral, as an age of faith. In the fifteenth and sixteenth centuries, a more secular age, known as the Renaissance, followed in which artists, architects, and their patrons tried to revive the architecture of ancient Rome. Of course, they adapted their borrowed forms to suit their own society, but their theorists developed rules governing the correct use of the "orders" of Roman architecture. Since artists rarely accept rules for long, the Renaissance style was challenged in the seventeenth century by the Baroque, with its more expressive and dynamic approach to painting, architecture, interior design, and landscape. Other styles followed: the sober Georgian of the eighteenth century, the Greek and Gothic revivals in the nineteenth, and a variety of experimental movements at the turn of the twentieth century. Styles, like fashions, followed so fast, one upon the other, that it seemed as if style was more important than purpose.

In the early twentieth century, a modern movement developed in which designers of all disciplines rebelled against the continued revival of historic styles and the excessive use of imitated decoration. They sincerely believed that, by using new technology, they could rise above the concept of style to solve human problems in a universal way with truly functional buildings and products. As autocratic rule was replaced by democracy, social housing became a priority in many countries. Architects, working in an idealistic manner for govern-

Figure 2-16   The Pantheon, Rome, 120 C.E. A vast interior space relying on sheer mass for stability. The only opening is the oculus at the top.

Figure 2-17 Selimiye Mosque, Edirne, Turkey, 1570 C.E.
The architect Sinan used amazing engineering skill to lighten
the structure and open up many windows.

ment agencies, developed innovative approaches to
housing. Unfortunately, the designers often paid insufficient attention to the realities of family life. Their projects
lacked human scale and ignored local traditions. Those
who lived in them missed familiar patterns of settlement
and social life and often found them alienating.

The most prestigious examples of modern architecture can be appreciated as works of art, or as brilliant
essays in the use of new technology, designed to enclose
space with clearly articulated structural systems. Corporate headquarters of shining glass have brought excitement to city skylines, but the plazas at their feet are often
unappealing empty spaces or parking lots. It has been
found that the modernist environment was not particularly functional. Glass walls, for example, proved wasteful of energy, gaining excessive heat from the sun in
summer and losing valuable heat in the winter. Modernist planners believed that it was important to separate
urban functions such as living, working, and shopping.

Rigid zoning for such separation denied the complexity
of real life and reduced urban vitality.

During the 1970s and 1980s, designers began to react
against the principles of the modernists and returned to a
richer design vocabulary. Many have tried to evoke the
character of historic styles or regional types. They have
attempted to be more responsive to the users, and some
have ascribed symbolic value to their work. At best, Post
Modern buildings are sensitive to human needs, appropriate to their context, and environmentally efficient.
However, too many are simply modern structures

Figure 2-18 Amiens Cathedral, France, 1220 C.E. The
dynamic structure of pointed arches, ribbed vaults, and flying buttresses makes it possible to open up the walls to huge
stained glass windows (Viollet-le-Duc).

Figure 2-19   Amiens Cathedral. The vault, consisting of thousands of tons of stone, appears almost weightless. The interior is flooded with light.

Figure 2-20   Crown Hall, Illinois Institute of Technology of Chicago, 1956, by Mies van der Rohe, architect. The architect's preoccupation with structure, space, and proportion links it to a Greek temple or Gothic cathedral.

Figure 2-21   High-rise housing at Roehampton, near London, built in the 1950s. An award-winning project that was later criticized for being unsuited to family life.

Figure 2-22   Kimbell Art Musum, Fort Worth, Texas, by Louis Kahn, architect, 1972. The architect invokes classical principles in a truly human way (T. Bartuska).

dressed up in a decorative exterior with details borrowed arbitrarily from historic sources.

One aspect of high style design in the twentieth century was the quest for originality. The same phenomenon occurred in clothing, vehicles, advertising signs, and consumer products designed to fulfill a seemingly insatiable desire for novelty. Unfortunately, the premium placed on originality often produced confusion and ugliness.

The high-style tradition applies equally to small objects and to treatment of the landscape. The objects found in Egyptian tombs demonstrate the superb quality achieved by ancient craftspeople. Modern industry has also given scope to furniture and product designers who have made use of new manufacturing processes to produce goods in original ways. For example, chairs, instead of being made of jointed and glued wood, have been manufactured of tubular steel.

In ancient Egypt, the landscape around temples was carefully ordered for ritual purposes. Long causeways lined by sphinxes linked one temple with another. This was a sacred landscape separate from the surrounding fields. Centuries later, Louis XIV, the absolute monarch who ruled France in the seventeenth century, laid out the pleasure gardens of his palace at Versailles with ruthless formal, axial symmetry. His design has been interpreted as a symbol of the divine right of kings. In contrast, English gardens in the eighteenth century responded to informal natural features of the landscape and exploited picturesque qualities.

Designers have also controlled the landscape around important buildings. The Washington Mall linking the Capitol with the White House is an example of formal axial planning in the classical tradition. In contrast, the suburban community of Riverside, Illinois, belongs to a romantic movement in landscape design. Its designer, Frederick Law Olmstead, avoided symmetry and gave the neighborhoods a picturesque character. He made use of surprise, gradually revealing the landscape to people

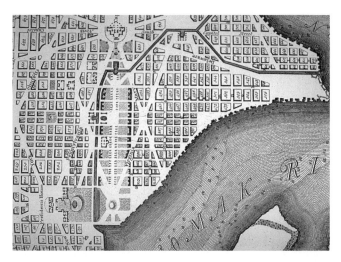

Figure 2-24 The Ellicott Plan of 1792 for Washington, DC, 1792. Formal axial landscape design.

as they move along curving roads. Riverside is intended to simulate certain qualities of a natural rural landscape, but it is, of course, humanly designed.

High-style tradition differs from those of the vernacular tradition in the following ways:

- It is the property of the elite.
- Designs are conceived and executed by specialists, who are often brought a long way to carry out the work. The designer is usually not the maker or builder,

Figure 2-23 Office building, Boston, by Philip Johnson, architect, 1989. The Palladian windows, based crudely on the designs of the Italian architect Andrea Palladio, have little relationship to twentieth-century Boston.

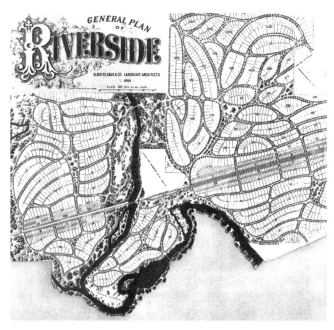

Figure 2-25 Riverside, Illinois. Plan by Olmsted, Vaux, and Co., 1869. Planning in the picturesque manner was intended to simulate certain informal qualities of a natural rural landscape, but it is, of course, humanly designed.

but rather the overseer of the work. The makers or builders are skilled artisans.

- The quality of work is of the highest standard. Materials are of high quality; if necessary, they are imported from far away. Rare and precious materials are frequently used.
- Symbolism, decoration, and refinement are often more important than usefulness.
- Designs do not evolve primarily as a response to climate and site, but they may be adapted to suit local conditions.
- National and regional character is developed, but designs from other cultures are often adopted to satisfy the desire for change or prestige.
- Changes in design style occur regularly. Great importance is attached to originality.

The Speculative Tradition

In the past 300 years, vast numbers of rural people have migrated to the cities. The old-fashioned ways of housing people were no longer feasible, and speculative builders motivated by financial profit filled the gap. Such developers built many fine residential districts, but throughout the industrializing world, housing units of minimum standard were built on street after street. In the country the poor had suffered in appalling hovels, but in the city they were concentrated in horrifying slums. Even in the wealthier nations, the conditions created during the Industrial Revolution have never been fully alleviated, and in some developing countries, industrialization has only just begun. Since the mid-nineteenth century, many affluent people have fled from the cities to the suburbs, giving further scope to developers.

While the profit motive has often encouraged speculative builders to adopt high standards of design, they have generally put up what was easiest to build and have concentrated more on marketing than on creating viable communities. Speculators have drawn something from vernacular and high-style traditions. There is often a simple logic and appropriateness in the houses they have built, but they have also sought the superfluous trappings of elite and high-style characteristics. In many cities, there are hundreds of small houses attempting to imitate the mansions of the wealthy without any regard to regional identity.

As long as life was not too complex, vernacular traditions guided the building endeavors of the human race. The high-style tradition has endowed cities and countryside with splendid monuments to wealth, power, and creativity. But the speculative tradition has not very suc-

cessfully fulfilled the remaining requirements. Uncontrolled private enterprise has not demonstrated sufficient thought for the needs of society or care of environmental resources. Housing has sprawled over the countryside, often without proper provision of community services. Commercial strip developments have spread along highways, providing easy access and parking for those with automobiles and cheap land for the developers, but at considerable cost in terms of social amenities. The result has been the sacrifice of agricultural land and the decline of city centers, as well as the loss of regional identity and unique character in individual cities. Auto-driven suburban sprawl has made excessive demands on air, water, and land resources and has dramatically increased the consumption of nonrenewable energy sources.

Similarly, products of all kinds have proliferated in today's enterprising economy. In earlier times, a family had few household objects, but those they possessed were useful and solidly made by hand to last a lifetime. Today factories around the world turn out countless products, many of them unnecessary, few of them very durable, and millions of dollars are spent on advertising to persuade people to buy them. While industrialization has given us possessions our ancestors never had, it has also turned us into a wasteful society. We are also discovering that the manufacture of many goods produces dangerous by-products that poison the environment.

Modern agriculture is transforming the world in many ways. Where traditional farming techniques tended to maintain the productivity of the land by rotation of crops and the use of organic fertilizers, today's intensive "agribusiness" has chased short-term profits

Figure 2-26 Houses built in London during the Industrial Revolution (G. Doré).

Figure 2-27 Speculatively built houses, Daly City, California, 1960s. The backs of another row of houses, behind them, are absolutely plain and uniform.

while ignoring long-term effects. In the Amazon Basin, vast rain forests, essential to the production of oxygen for human survival, are being cut to make way for beef production even though the land will be viable for pasture for only a few years. In England, where hedges separated fields for centuries, their removal to make way for larger machinery has caused unprecedented soil erosion.

Speculative tradition's general characteristics are as follows:

- The profit motive is the guiding force, and marketability is the key. Instant appeal to the buyer is more important than durability or environmental issues.
- Designs are rationalized to be cost effective and mass produced.
- There is a loss of local and regional character.

Figure 2-28 Suburban sprawl extending onto some of the richest farmland in the nation, the Palouse Region of eastern Washington and northwestern Idaho. While land lies vacant within or near cities, new sprawling land-use patterns destroy farmland, increase traffic, and demand expensive infrastructure (T. Bartuska).

- Social amenities and environmental effects are often ignored.

Participatory Tradition: The Future of the Built Environment

The building of sound communities has always needed the participation of their members. In the vernacular tradition, the simplest tribes made group decisions and built together for mutual benefit. Idealistic early settlers in ancient Greece, South and North America, and other regions of the world planned their towns democratically and worked together to develop them. But as populations have grown and societies have become more complex, people have lost touch with the planning process. Democracy can provide mechanisms for public participation in planning and design, but most of us play no part in the massive building schemes that do so much to change our lives and the built environment, often abruptly and drastically. Elected representatives and public officials have often failed to make the best decisions. In the past four decades, many cities in the United States have been subjected to more construction than ever before. Whole downtown areas have been demolished and rebuilt as a result of urban renewal programs. New suburbs have proliferated; thousands of acres of agricultural land have been buried under asphalt and concrete. The largest single building program ever undertaken was the construction of roadways in the United States as the result of the 1956 Federal Highway Act. Broad ribbons of concrete, sometimes meeting at complex intersections, forced their way across the countryside and through every major city in the nation. To make way for these roadways, thousands of buildings and their neighborhoods were destroyed. Much of the finest building of the past is gone forever. Individuals, corporations, and city, state, and federal governments contrived to make decisions without fully understanding their implications.

The boom years between the 1950s and the 1980s were a period of unshakable belief in the future and in the need to sweep away familiar surroundings to make a more modern world. Through this process, we have discovered just how important our familiar environment is to us. Communities are made of human beings, and they thrive on ordinary social activity. The disruption of human groups and their activities, even to make way for dazzling new developments, has often been disastrous.

Today, at the beginning of a new century, we seem to appreciate once more the value of old traditions. Urban renewal is now often a much gentler process. Strategies such as the preservation of historic buildings and land-

Figure 2-29 Freeway, Dallas, Texas. A broad ribbon of concrete dominates valuable land (T. Bartuska).

Figure 2-31 The reanimated historic Pioneer Square District, Seattle, Washington.

scapes, the careful insertion of appropriate new structures, the revitalization of entire neighborhoods, and the conservation of regional open space are being implemented in many cities where only decades ago the bulldozer and the wrecking ball rampaged. The preservation movement has sprung from the grass roots of society to become a potent force reviving lost qualities in the built environment. While it began with the preservation of mansions and places associated with important figures from history, preservationists today are equally concerned with vernacular buildings, ordinary neighborhoods, landscapes, the main streets of small towns, greenways, farmland, and open space. The Pioneer Square district of Seattle offers an example of urban revitalization. It was successful because public demand, financial incentives for preservation, and design worked

Figure 2-30 The Pioneer Square District of Seattle in 1970. Today, this once run-down area has been reanimated into a delightful historic district with an enjoyable mix of urban activities (R. Anderson).

creatively together. This mixed-use neighborhood possesses a human scale and offers a variety of activities. The topic of preservation will be discussed in more detail in Chapter 14.

A truly **participatory tradition** in the built environment can only be attained when the following conditions are met:

- The public is well educated in environmental design and ready to take a part in the decision-making process.
- Designers are trained to respond to human needs and desires.
- Designers give a higher priority to concern for the environment and the long-term effects of our design decisions.

Today we can still admire the grand and beautiful high-style designs commissioned throughout history by great leaders. We can also appreciate the simplicity and appropriateness of vernacular builders. We are capable of rivaling their works with what we build ourselves, but often we accept mediocrity, leaving it to others to build for their own profit. If we are to attain a sustainable built environment that fulfills the needs and ideals of a democratic society, we need to play a greater role in its creation.

In the twenty-first century, the vital concern for **sustainability** has changed the way responsible designers, planners, developers, and building officials think. We have the scientific data to warn us that the very future of life on our planet is threatened by our overconsumption of resources and by our pollution of earth, air, and water. While modernists were infatuated with new technology for its own sake, they rarely showed sufficient concern for ecological issues. Today's leading designers are putting sustainability at the top of their agenda. They aim, as much as possible, to use renewable and recycled materials; they design for conservation of water and energy, and attempt to create healthy interior and exterior environments. Some U.S. cities are ahead of state and federal authorities in demanding sustainable practices. The city of Seattle, for example, has won a Leadership in Energy and Environmental Design (LEED) award from the U.S. Green Building Council for the design of its new City Hall. The building, designed by Bassetti Architects and Bohlin Cywinski Jackson, fulfills the city's desire for transparency so that government does not seem to be hidden behind monumental walls; it appears open and welcoming. Issues of water and energy conservation were treated with utmost care; concrete from the old city hall was recycled on site, and to avoid long-distance transportation many materials were procured locally.

There is also a growing interest in regionalism. In the modern era, designers promoted the idea of universal values and an **International Style**, but to avoid global homogenization of the built environment, many designers today want to express the unique qualities of the places for which they design. David E. Miller, in his book *Toward a New Regionalism: Environmental Architecture in the Pacific Northwest,* suggests that there is indeed a connection between the creation of regional character and sustainability. Climate, terrain, available materials, and cultural concerns are all significant determinants of architectural form in the buildings designed by his firm.

Each era of history has demonstrated its major preoccupations in built works. In ancient Egypt, an obsession with the afterlife drove the building of great pyramids; in medieval Europe, the desire to create an image of heaven on earth inspired the building of the lofty cathedrals illuminated by stained glass windows; in the twentieth century, designers felt compelled to express the desires and opportunities of modern life. Today, our transcending goal must be to design and construct in a sustainable manner, and to satisfy real human and environmental needs through the use of renewable resources and appropriate technologies. The sustainability movement may be demonstrating the emergence of a fifth tradition. As examples later in this book clearly demonstrate, there need be no conflict between human and environmental quality, design principles, and sustainability.

References

Alanen, A.R., and R. Melnick. *Preserving Cultural Landscapes in America.* Johns Hopkins University Press, 2000.

Beatley, T., and K. Manning. *The Ecology of Place: Planning for Environment, Economy, and Community.* Island Press, 1997.

Bruegmann, R. *Sprawl: A Compact History.* University of Chicago Press, 2005.

Lauer, J. *Saqqara: The Royal Cemetery of Memphis.* Thames and Hudson, 1976.

Loeb, C.S. *Entrepreneurial Vernacular: Developers' Subdivisions in the 1920's.* Johns Hopkins University Press, 2001.

McMurry, S.A. *Families and Farmhouses in Nineteenth Century America: Vernacular Design and Social Change.* University of Tennessee Press, 1997.

Miller, D. *Toward a New Regionalism: Environmental Architecture in the Pacific Northwest.* University of Washington Press, 2005.

Moffett, M., et al. *Buildings across Time: An Introduction to World Architecture.* McGraw-Hill, 2004.

Rapoport, A. *House, Form and Culture.* Prentice Hall, 1969.

Rudofsky, B. *Architecture without Architects.* University of New Mexico Press, 1987.

Scobey, D. M., R. Rosenzweig, and S. P. Benson (eds.). *Empire City: The Making and Meaning of the New York Landscape.* Temple University Press, 2002.

Thesiger, W. *The Marsh Arabs.* Longmans, 1964.

Figure 2-32 Seattle City Hall by Bassetti and Bohlin Cywinski Jackson, architects, 2005. Although its walls are of glass in the Modernist manner, it was designed to conserve energy and resources.

PART II

Central Issues: Human-Environmental-Technical Dimensions of a Quality Environment

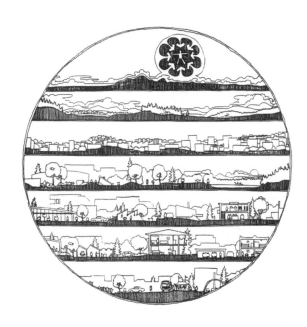

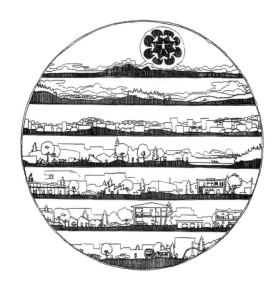

II. Central Issues: Human-Environmental-Technological Dimensions of a Quality Built Environment

An Introduction

First and foremost, the study of the built environment involves a closer analysis of three essential variables that are critical to any human-environmental investigation—**people**, the **built environment** we create, and the **environmental context**, both built and natural, within which we live, work, socialize, celebrate, and recreate. It is important not only to understand these variables individually, but also to comprehend how they interrelate and interact with each other. These three variables were introduced in the definition of the built environment (reference Chapter 1), and they will recur throughout the text.

The graphic depicts these variables individually and collectively within the overall environmental context.

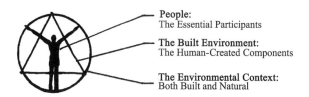

People:
The Essential Participants

The Built Environment:
The Human-Created Components

The Environmental Context:
Both Built and Natural

Studying these central concerns will help develop a more complete understanding of people, society, and cultures; the components of the built environments (created to satisfy human needs and values); and the resultant built and natural environments.

It is useful to realize that a more general concept is formed by the interaction of the three factors. This general concept is central to the study of almost all subjects; it is particularly important to the study of the design and planning disciplines that participate in the process of shaping the built world. This general concept is commonly referred to as **human-environmental relationships** (in this case *environment* includes both the descriptive adjectives *natural* and *built*) and relationships that are formed by design/planning and the use of **technology**. The following built environment diagram emphasizes the dynamic interaction or interrelationship between people, environment, and technology).

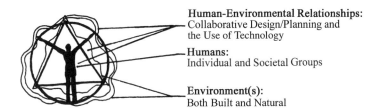

Human-Environmental Relationships:
Collaborative Design/Planning and
the Use of Technology
Humans:
Individual and Societal Groups

Environment(s):
Both Built and Natural

This human-environmental relationship theme is, in reality, a four-part concept: (1) people, (2) the natural environment, (3) the built environment, and (4) the dynamic interrelationship between parts developed through **collaborative design/planning** and **technology**. This interplay between the terms is emphasized by the hyphen "-" between the two terms "human-environment" and is reemphasized by the word *relationships* (sometimes stated as interrelationships).

This interplay is an important **adaptive strategy**. Design and planning are like a two-way street: humans adapt environments to fit their needs and values, and humans have to adapt their needs to fit various environments. Ideally, a mutual harmony and balance or symbiotic condition emerges—one adapting to the other, and vice versa. Serious consequences can occur when people overbuild and cause environmental deterioration (polluted air and water, urban sprawl destroying prime farmland, traffic congestion, etc.). Serious consequences also occur when the natural environment destroys human habitat (floods, earthquakes, volcanic eruptions, tornadoes, etc.). By understanding these central variables as a two-way adaptive design strategy, people are able to do a better job in celebrating life and its creative processes, while living in harmony with the best qualities of relationships within both built and natural environments.

Adaptive strategies are then created through the use of technology. Designing/planning with a deeper understanding of the variables of the human-environment-technology triad helps to evaluate the purpose and function of the built environment and helps determine its supportive and disruptive characteristics. Knowledge of this triad of issues can direct our time and talents toward corrective measures to improve the design quality of the things that humans create and the things that they build.

The following chapters investigate the three main domains of this human-environment-technology triad concept.

Understanding Environment(s): Built and Natural by Tom J. Bartuska

This first chapter explores the meaning of the word *environment*. It is commonly used, and yet its precise meanings can be elusive. What is included? What is excluded? Words are an important artifact of human creation and thus an important part of the built environment. The purpose of this chapter is to explore the meaning of key words and to encourage reading between the lines— to understand critical implications and interconnections between words. This chapter also outlines a number of conceptual tools that give us better access and a deeper understanding of our built world. Words and their interrelationships are fundamental to understanding the deeper meanings of life, design, and environment(s).

Designing with People: Human Behavior, Culture, and User Participation by Paul G. Windley and Wendy R. McClure

Designers and planners who understand ways to design with people are more likely to help improve the quality of the built and natural environment. This chapter introduces the field of environment behavior studies that apply insights generated by scholars, researchers, and practitioners to better interpret and respond to human needs, cultural values, and traditions. The discussion also introduces participatory strategies to engage people in decision making—those who are most impacted by a particular designed environment in which they must live, work, recreate, or socialize.

Designing with the Environment by Michael S. Owen and Bruce T. Haglund

This chapter introduces the need for "designing with nature"—with land ecology and climate. It is just common sense to design with nature instead of against it. Recognizing the inherent vulnerability of relying solely on fossil fuels and mechanical control systems, people seek new methods to reduce this dependency by designing with nature. Ironically, the "new methods" being sought are not new methods at all. They have been employed for centuries before the advent of the Industrial Revolution; they are the vernacular methods of traditional, indigenous societies which, by necessity and adaptive ingenuity, shaped built environment in harmony with nature.

Designing with Technological and Creative Processes by Matt A. Taylor and Kenneth L. Carper

Technology has a profound influence on the design of the built environment. The word *technology* is often misunderstood or misapplied. Technology may be associated with positive or negative connotations because of the limited experiences of people with appropriate or inappropriate applications of technology. Examination of a few definitions, however, show that "technology" is, in fact, a neutral term. It is demonstrated that an understanding of technological processes is essential to the development of quality design in the built environment. As applied at any scale, technology is the means whereby conflicts between the natural environment and human needs are resolved.

Designing with a Visual Language: Elements and Ordering Systems by Greg Kessler

In the final chapter of this section, the built environment is explored through investigation of the meanings that various elements and ordering systems have on design. Designers and planners communicate and articulate ideas, beliefs, and social/cutural values in the built environment by effectively using a visual language—composing elements into ordering systems to create a quality and meaningful built environment.

CHAPTER 3

Understanding Environment(s): Built and Natural

Tom J. Bartuska

What do we mean when we use the word *environment*? Everyone seems to know. It is in common usage in English, and yet its precise meanings can be elusive. What is included? What is excluded? *Environment* is a fascinating and challenging word. Words are an important artifact of human creation and thus an important part of the built environment. The purpose of this chapter is to explore the meaning of key words and to encourage reading between the lines—to understand the critical implications and interconnections between words. This chapter will also outline a number of conceptual tools that give us better access and a deeper understanding of our built world. Words and their interrelationships are fundamental to our understanding of life, design, and environment(s).

Exploring the Meaning of the Word

Humans evolved in multiple environments, and by necessity, they adapted and at times prospered. Aboriginal groups did alter their environments, sometimes extensively but mostly in moderate ways. With the beginning of agriculture and fixed settlements, humans began to create built environments of real significance.

Now humans dominate, and most contemporary societies adapt natural environments to their own wishes rather than adapting their needs to environments. Humans are transforming earth environments so radically that we increasingly live in a world largely of our own making.

Natural/Built Environment(s)

Today, human imprints are essentially everywhere on the globe. Seemingly, we are transforming almost every acre of its immensity, leaving not even the farthest reaches free of human impact. The result is a challenging and, at times, confusing overlap between the natural world and that created by humans.

The human-modified world has been tagged with assorted labels, including "artificial," "synthetic," "physical," "fabricated," and/or "constructed" environment(s). But the phrase **built environment** used in this book does seem to be emerging as the dominant form in the literature for a number of reasons. Built environment avoids the negative connotations of other terms such as artificial and synthetic. "Built" as a modifier avoids the implication that this kind of human creation is unnatural, somehow counterfeit, even unreal. The built environment is not

Figures 3-1 and 3-2 The wonders of the natural and built environment(s). Mount Rainier National Park, Washington, USA, and the City of Vancouver, British Columbia, Canada.

unnatural or false. It is conceived by the human mind and built by the human hand, and humans are natural organisms. Indeed, all artifacts are fabricated from the resources of nature. Also, the adjective built is inclusive of the actions of both men and women and avoids the unfortunate and very dated terms "man" (or "woman)-made."

Carefully selected modifiers (adjectives) can help clarify the term environment in very useful ways. At a minimum, the built environment must be understood to intertwine with the natural environment—either in a state of harmony or discord. Also, as the above discussion suggests, the descriptive adjective "natural" could include those changes humans naturally create to live on this planet. These two descriptive adjectives are highly interrelated.

Perceptual/Functional/Conceptual Environment(s)

Perhaps the main reason to distinguish between the natural and built is that many people (perhaps most) see themselves carrying on their daily activities within the built environment. Humans now live with the realities of smog much more than sky, in concrete instead of stone, in contemplation of a flower box more than wild flowers.

Every organism lives in a different perceptual world. A dog, for example, sniffing the air, lives in a perceptual world all its own, one that we humans can only vaguely appreciate. The **perceptual** environment is that part of the environment intercepted by the senses. We often confuse this with total reality. We cannot hope to under-

stand behavior without knowing the stimuli to which humans react, both favorable and unfavorable.

Most humans are primarily interested in that part of the environment that most directly affects them. This is commonly referred to as the "functional," "near," or "operational environment." The **functional** environment is defined as that portion of the environment that physically impinges on an organism (even though we might not directly perceive these influential factors). This designation focuses on the environment in which we operate or function—places where we carry out our day-to-day personal and community interactions. This functional emphasis is that of our personal world that we physically occupy as opposed to that larger world of which we must be increasingly aware. But that larger world is real also. As Thoreau suggested in *Walden*, "the imagination, give it the least license, dives deeper and soars higher than [even] Nature goes." Education provides that license, expanding our awareness and appreciation of the world's levels of complexity.

Beyond the perceptual and functional environment is what many call the **conceptual** environment—society's cultural world, including the built environment, a world shaped by human ideas and the meanings they convey. Human experience and the built environment are enriched by human thought, concepts, and ideas. But even in this conceptual environment, the subject-object or human-environmental relationship remains the fundamental structure of experience. We name our concepts and abstractions, attaching symbols to express reality, and can then interact with them as a seemingly real part of our environment. So, even abstractions, such as spirits of human myth or legend, are part of the built environment.

The term built environment can be used in a **reductionist** or in a **holistic** way. To some, the built environment may be furniture or a room. To others it can mean everything humanly made or arranged—products, interiors, structures, cities, regions, even the heavily modified Earth. This study of the built environment strives to be **inclusive**, not exclusive. An important objective of this book is to foster holistic thinking about the built and natural worlds.

Defining Environment by Levels

Levels of Organization

Because of the wide range and complexity of the environment(s) in which humans exist, it is necessary to think of human–environmental relationships in holistic terms. Modifiers such as "natural" or "built" help develop subcategories of the whole topic. They also help to further organize the complexities of any subject into its component **parts and wholes**. Environments can be more completely understood by using concepts and methods that allow shifts from analysis of individual parts to how those parts are organized into wholes. Such shifts provide access to **content** for each **component** part, and the way parts connect together provides a fuller understanding of **context**. Shifts between parts and wholes, and wholes and parts, contributes to the ongoing effort to understand linkages individually and holistically.

Contemporary critics of the reductionist methods of science and specialization in engineering and design have become increasingly vocal in recent years. They claim that reductionist methods, necessary (and successful) as they certainly are, tend to isolate entities and deemphasize connections. They worry that, in the process of analysis, a great deal of information about relationships between people and environments, if not lost, is often disregarded or

misplaced, resulting in a fragmentation of our environment(s). We organize reality in categories of knowledge and related disciplines and then miss the richness and excitement of interdisciplinary dialogue and collaboration. Many have responded with attempts to ensure that connections are restored, linking parts to their functional wholes. Hierarchy, a device suitable for such integration, is time tested and readily available as an organizing framework for accessing the intrinsic organization of nature and the diversity of the built environment.

What archaeologists call the "Persian Carpet Effect" illustrates the importance of studying not only the parts of the environment but also the wonderment of the overall context. "Imagine you're a mouse running across an elaborately decorated rug. The ground would merely be a blur of shapes and colors. You could spend your life going back and forth, studying every inch . . . and never see the patterns."[1] Like the mouse, many scientists, designers, and citizens may concentrate solely on studying the parts without appreciating and comprehending the whole.

Hierarchy or Levels of Integration: A Useful Systems Framework for Design

Two concepts have been commonly used for centuries to illustrate part-whole relationships and clarify linkages and connections: "hierarchy" and "levels of integration." The two have slightly different meanings but form a single general concept, and both are useful in studying the built environment. They are used interchangeably in this book to emphasize important integrated linkages.

The book's organization is based upon levels of integration, which effectively link subjects, design levels, and design disciplines/professions together. At different times and in various ways, the authors in this book introduce various aspects of this integrative concept from their individual perspectives. Each approach is a reaffirmation of its importance and utility in design analysis and in the ultimate synthesis of components of the built environment.

The term **hierarchy** can create negative connotations. It may, for example, raise images of a social order in which human relationships are determined by the degree of authority exercised by one group of people over another. However, hierarchy has been widely and commonly used as a simple organizational tool to order and relate the parts of numerous structures and topics, linking small to large, simple to complex, and innumerable others. It should be used in a neutral sense where all components at every level are unique and significant.

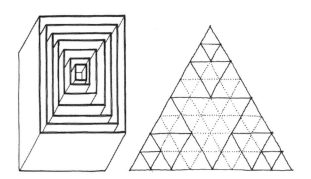

Figure 3-3   Nested hierarchy in Chinese boxes and subdivided sets of triangles.

Fundamental to one's comprehension of the built environment is the fact that hierarchies make complex subjects more understandable, meaningful, and, hopefully, enjoyable. A reductionist view of the world confines and limits design/planning processes and too often isolates the various components of our built world. Hierarchy frees scientists, scholars, and designers from the shackles of the analytical mode without requiring them to reject it and provides, as well, an appreciation of a wider, more diverse and interesting world.[2]

Alternative terms are perhaps less negatively perceived than hierarchy but are also not as widely shared across disciplines. The concept of levels of organization is sometimes used but does not emphasize integration, whereas **levels-of-integration** suggests integrated linkages among various levels. Some people prefer "levels of complexity," "levels of analysis," or simply the words *levels, layers,* and/or *scales.* But hierarchy remains the term in widest use in most disciplines.

Several additional terms and concepts—"holism," "holon," "functionalism"—are derivatives of hierarchy and come into play in discussing linkages across levels. Holism emphasizes the existence of an ever-widening totality, a comprehensiveness in dealing with human environments. **Holism**, a very general term, is refined by introducing a new term—**holon**—which was defined by its originator as any (and every) entity that is in one sense a whole and in another sense a part.[3] Holon reminds us that every object or entity we work with has a double identity, and that when placed in such a series of levels, each is both a whole by itself and part of a larger system. Think of any entity—the human eye, for example. We can speak of the eye as a specific entity with fascinating subparts, but to understand how it works or functions, we must place it back in the whole human body. To illustrate further, each of us considers ourselves whole individuals, but to understand how we relate as human beings, it is necessary to look beyond the individual to the family, the neighborhood, the community, and so on. Working with one level to the exclusion of others is simplistic and incomplete.

Functionalism is another common term in the design/planning disciplines, especially as embodied in the dialectic that interrelates form and function. Functionalism has other meanings: first, it addresses how the parts of an object function internally, and second, how objects interrelate with each other to make up a larger functional whole or system. Functionalism is a reminder to creators of the built environment that systems work because the parts fit together; each is a holon, and each fits into its context.

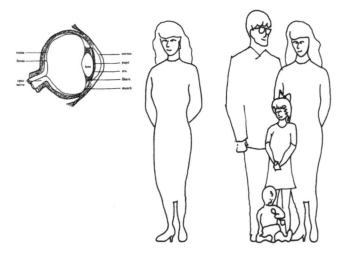

Figure 3-4 The human, its parts (the eye and its subparts), and a person's larger context, the family.

What all this really means is a shift in mindset, in perspective, from focusing on the isolated object or subject to focusing on objects "as content" "in context," both defined by hierarchy or levels-of-integration. Placement in a series of integrated levels clarifies the parts from which an object or entity is made and reveals more clearly the setting of which the object is itself a part. The creation of a healthy, functioning individual in a healthy, functioning environment demands both perspectives.

Hierarchical structures and linkages are pervasive, fascinating, and useful. Examples abound: this text book integrates just 26 letters of the alphabet to form words; a word

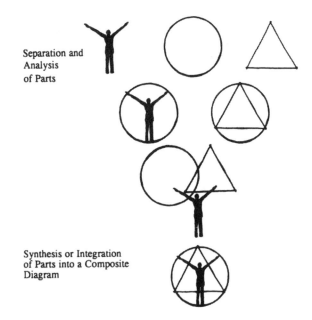

Separation and Analysis of Parts

Synthesis or Integration of Parts into a Composite Diagram

Figure 3-5 Analysis and synthesis within the definition of the built environment.

by itself conveys a minimum of information, but a word integrated into a phrase, then a sentence, has more meaning, meaning created by context and linkages. Sentences set in a paragraph, then in parts of a chapter, and finally in a book can convey all the richness of human thought. The organization of a book is like a comprehensive plan of construction. It is, in effect, a process of integrating levels, of creating and building by putting pieces together into larger wholes. Books are then organized in libraries to be shared—conveying the depth of human knowledge.

The hierarchical word "stratify" comes from the Latin *strata*, which means literally a system of roads—the hierarchical system one uses from driveway to residential street to community-shared arterial roads and eventually to a major thoroughfare or freeway. While doing so, one is negotiating an amazing landscape of human design constructed with hierarchical levels and integrated linkages.

Across much of the central United States, the road and street pattern corresponds to grids imposed by the land survey system. The township-and-range survey system is a hierarchical system, ranging from a subdivision of an acre of land to the quarter-section (160 acres) through the section (640 acres) to the township (36 square miles). This integrated system of townships ties into the latitudinal and longitudinal lines that circle the Earth. In the midwestern region of the United States and Canada, aerial photographs frequently reveal a precise correspondence between township lines and transportation patterns (Fig. 3-6). Other human systems are tied even more subtly into this same regular grid pattern, notably patterns of land ownership and settlement.

Other countries use the metric system of measurement, a similar integrated, hierarchical system. Humans have also invented a system of units to measure time that interlinks with natural systems of sun-Earth relationships and cycles: seconds, minutes, hours, days, weeks, months, seasons, years, centuries, and so on. Like so many of the hierarchical systems discussed in these pages, time scales provide the context for human affairs, organizing and giving order to human activities and life cycles.

Figure 3-6 The Jeffersonian land survey system—organizing land from subdivisions of an acre to the prime latitude and longitude lines that encircle the Earth.

Design and Planning: Analysis and Synthesis within the Built Environment

Hierarchical structures foster interplay between the two basic modes of thinking—analysis and synthesis. In general, the design process deals with the analysis of the **content** *and* **context** of a problem and then with the synthesis of the various issues in order to create effective alternative solutions. These two important modes of thought are more specially defined below and in Figure 3-5.

- **Analysis**: The separation of the whole into its parts; the examination and study of the content of each part
- **Synthesis**: The integration of the parts into a unified whole; the integration of the parts into a new context

Content-Component-Context Strategies

In the built environment, as in all of nature, each level or part becomes integrated to form the **content** of the next larger component. Then this **component** is integrated to form the next more complex levels; higher levels form the **context** for each component level. This relationship between content and context may seem simplistic, but optimum design, especially in correspondence to natural systems, requires a grasp of the concept. The concern for

wholeness requires that "every building increment (large or small) must help form at least one larger whole" within a continuum of design levels.[4]

Products (furniture, walls, floor and ceiling, etc.) form interiors. Interior spaces are collectively arranged to form structures. Structures, along with exterior spaces (both natural and built), form landscapes. Extended further, this content-component relationship forms cities, regions, and, finally, the content of the Earth. The fundamental quest is not in the simple connection, one forming the other, but the quality of the interrelationship—how well the parts integrate, contribute to, and create the whole. The same relationship can be expressed in a different way to emphasize context. Products are composed to fit their context—interiors. Generally, structures serve as the context for interiors; the context for a structure is its landscape and urban setting, and so on throughout the hierarchy. Again, the quest emphasizes integration: how well each component of the built environment fits its context.

Any hierarchical structure has this important three part level-of-integration relationship: each **component** is formed by its **content** and must fit into its **context**.

Integrative Design and Planning with the Hidden Grain

The basic reason for this exploration of the pervasive and evasive nature of the term environment is to gain appreciation and understanding of the underlying order or organization of the environments in which humans must live, work, and play. "Everything in our world reveals a structure below the surface, a hidden grain which, when it is laid bare, makes it possible to take natural formations apart and assemble them in new arrangements."[5] Assembling new arrangements is a fundamental aspect of the **art** *and* **science** of design and planning. And the best way to design is with the grain, not against it.

The conceptual layering of human built and natural systems provides the basis for first understanding and then developing creative arrangements that fit together and make healthy contributions to the built environment. The hidden grains of human built and natural systems are briefly listed in Figure 3-7 (please observe their similarities and differences).

Designing with Understanding and Quality

Quality is a most challenging word. It is best understood as a multiple, variable concept. It deals with analysis and synthesis, art and science, mind and matter, and designing with the hidden grain. Integration is the essence of quality (reading between the lines). A quality marriage requires quality components (people) and a loving relationship.

The qualitative dimensions in the built and natural environments are further explored in the following related triad sets of terms. Do you know what they have in common?—a deeper appreciation of some of the critical aspects of quality. As introduced in Chapter 1, the triangle (△) was first used to symbolize the built environment. Here it is used to express the important triadic relationships between terms, which are embedded in the design of our built world. The points of the triangle represent the **analysis** of singular issues, whereas moving toward the center requires design **synthesis** and integration.

Ecological Design: Human-Environmental Relationships

As emphasized throughout this chapter and book, "human-environment relationships" (HE/HER) is an important ecological concept. This interactive triad of terms is central to our understanding of reality and quality. Design must address and creatively integrate the following three terms:

- **Human** (and societal purpose: needs and values)
- **Environment(s)** (built and natural)
- **Relationships** (adaptive design strategies, creative and appropriate use of technologies)

Life on Earth is a constant interchange between organisms (including humans) and their environment.

People and Society	Natural Environment	Built Environment
Individual	Subatomic Particles	Products
Families	Atoms/Molecules	Interiors
Neighbors/Neighborhoods	Cells	Structures
Communities/Cities	Organisms	Landscapes
Counties/Regions	Communities	Cities
States/Nations	Ecosystems	Regions
Earth	Ecosphere/Earth	Earth

Solar System Universe

Figure 3-7 The intrinsic levels of human-environmental relationships within the definition of the built environment.

Design/planning is, in its most basic sense, an integrative strategy—creatively developing healthy relationships between human/social needs and values with environmental conditions. The better we understand this most important triad relationship, the better we can effectively design/plan the built environment with the natural context, creating effective relationships with appropriate technologies.

Comprehensive Design: Social-Environmental-Technological

Parallel to the above HE/HER triad are three similar terms more commonly used in the design disciplines; these form the second but very similar SET (social-environmental-technological) of relationships. Our understanding of the built environment is enhanced by recognizing that these three issues are also interactive relationships. In general, technologies establish relationships and are an integrative, adaptive design strategy. This three-part interactive concept forms three important threads, which are carried throughout this study of our built world. They are first explored individually in the next three chapters and then emphasized throughout the book.

Sustainable Design: Social-Environmental-Economic

Sustainability is generally defined as a process of satisfying human/societal needs without compromising the needs of future generations. Searching for sustainable design requires a more holistic, long-term perspective and challenges us to get our HE/HER or SET relationships right not only for now but also for the future. Sustainability requires the optimization of three similar variables—social, environmental, and economic (SEE). Human concerns shift to social issues, and technological relationships are integrated with costs into the broader concept of economics (a prominent topic of interchange in society). It is critical to the concept of sustainability to consider all three together. Emphasizing one over the other is neither an effective thought process nor a creative approach to design and planning of quality parts and relationships.

In society's constant (and at times confusing) play with terms and acronyms, the triad relationships are used to define a healthy, sustainable society as one that creatively addresses the three E's—(social) equity, (environmental) ecology, and economy.[6] The reader is encouraged to explore the many dimensions of a sustainable society at Ecotone's Web site, www.conserva-

Relating Triad Interrelationships	Acronyms
Human - Environmental - Relationships	HE/HER
Social - Environmental - Technological	SET
Social - Environmental - Economics	SEE

Figure 3-8   Two related sets of qualitative terms and related acronyms.

tioneconomy.net (then go to "view the pattern map" and its interactive "spheres" of information). The application of these terms and concepts by the design/planning professions will be examined in greater depth in later chapters of this book.

Integrated Design

The above three triads convey the same theme and use similar words. They link ecology (HE/HER) with important relationships within the built environment (SETs) with the very critical global concern for sustainability (SEE). These terms are integrated in the table and triad (Figs. 3-8 and 3-9).

Quality: A Search for Health, Fitness, and Creativity in the Built Environment

Integrated relationships of the triad dimensions lead to greater effectiveness in planning and design decisions. **Health, fitness, and creativity** are action-oriented terms

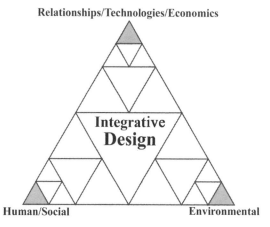

Figure 3-9   Integrating the important triads for quality design.

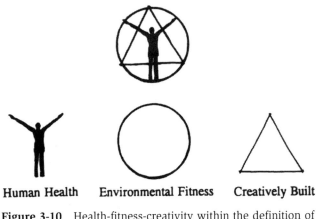

Human Health   Environmental Fitness   Creatively Built

Figure 3-10 Health-fitness-creativity within the definition of the built environment.

included in this discussion of these triad relationships to provide more descriptive dimensions to **quality**. These terms should be attached to the definition of the built environment (Fig. 3-10) as well as the other triad relationships in the following ways:

- **Health** of human, societal, and natural systems
- **Fitness** within the built and natural environments
- **Creativity** in the integration of all components to their context through the effective use of appropriate technology

These three terms have been in use for centuries and parallel those left to us by the Roman architect Vitruvius: successful built environments must exhibit "commodity, firmness and delight." Two thousand years later, the landscape architect and planner Ian McHarg[7] rephrased

Vitruvius' triad of qualities as "health, fitness, and creativity" to describe desirable qualities of successful, life-sustaining environments. These ideas interlock as another dynamic triad: fitness requires **health** and creativity, health emerges from creative fitness, and creativity is measured by an optimum degree of health and fitness (Fig. 3-14).

McHarg emphasized the importance of health in the development of ecological design and planning. He built on the work of Patrick Geddes, an early-twentieth-century Scottish planner and scholar, who stated that a healthy life is completeness of the relationships between organism, function, and environment, and all at their best (healthy human-environment relationships). McHarg also

Figures 3-12 and 3-13 Bringing the human-environmental-technical relationships together is like fitting the pieces of a puzzle together.

Human Health

Environmental Fitness

Creatively Built

Figure 3-11 The interaction of health-fitness-creativity within the definition of the built environment.

Figure 3-14 The importance of health and fitness. A student's creative design of a poster (WSU student—unknown).

used a definition of health from the World Health Organization: "the ability to seek and solve problems," implying that the most important demonstration of health is finding creative fitness. Health is also emphasized in U.S. state and federal laws and professional license requirements enacted to protect the health, safety, and welfare of society.

Fitness can be understood as a measure of how well an entity is integrated into its context in the search for optimum creativity and health. The interrelationship of fitness with health is commonly conceived as proper, in fine physical condition, in good health, right in respect to the nature of circumstance and/or use, etc. The creative act of finding fitness, then, becomes a fundamental challenge for designers and for all people. "The quest of the surviving organism is to find the fittest possible environment and adapt that environment and itself."[8] "The fittest survive, the fitting-est thrive."[9] These statements emphasize the importance of appropriate adaptive strategies: designing quality components that are integrated into their environment(s). This process, if undertaken in a sustainable way, results in a mutual adaptation or balancing of human needs and environmental conditions.

The elements of design are part of the process. As with any puzzle, designers must also make sure that the elements, the parts or pieces, fit together. A concept of fitness deals with adaptive human-environmental design strategies—how a design adapts and fits its context.

Quality in the built environment can then be more closely approximated by defining optimum as "fitness in context," fitting into larger social/cultural-environmental-

economic patterns. Health and fitness are often used in creating a nurturing environment for the human body (see Fig. 3-14). In a similar way, these challenging terms are critical directives for quality and creativity in the built environment.

Creativity is the process of finding fitness and health. *Webster's Unabridged 1996 Edition Dictionary* defines creativity as the act of bringing into being, to cause to happen, to arrange as by intent or design. McHarg defined creativity in more challenging ecological terms as "the employment of energy and matter to reach higher levels of order," and stated that successful evolution is a **maximum success/minimum work** solution (working with the hidden grain). In measuring creativity, some will unfortunately emphasize merely newness and uniqueness. But it is more important to emphasize appropriateness and sustainability within the context. In practical design and planning decisions, the terms quality and creativity need to be clearly defined. Some design decisions are considered to be higher in quality and more creative than others, though the distinctions are often subjective. Understanding the value of each component provides a means to compare the relative creativity of one design to that of another by estimating, in a holistic way, the benefits and costs. The **benefit/cost ratio** is widely used throughout governmental, engineering, and planning segments of society. This general benefit/cost ratio is:

$$\textbf{Quality} \text{ and/or } \textbf{Creativity} :: \frac{\text{Benefits}}{\text{Costs}}$$

$$= \frac{\text{Human Health and Environmental Fitness}}{\text{Costs, Energy, and/or Impacts}}$$

Quality should be our most important measure of creativity. Quality is a comparative term and includes a variety of factors. Because of all the costs and potential benefits, quality is difficult to measure. But health, fitness, and related costs can be measured in descriptive terms (listing and describing in verbal and written form the positive and negative characteristics of each alternative). It can also be evaluated in quantifiable terms (number of issues, years of service, quantity of energy, and costs in dollars) or in relative terms (probably the measure most often used because of the variety of factors and information). Regardless of the method, the exploration of an integrated benefit/cost ratio approach to decision making helps individuals and society make more effective and knowledgeable decisions.

Figures 3-15 and 3-16 Comparing quality in the built environment. Two adjacent streets in San Francisco, one void and the other expressive of human creativity—health (appreciative people) and environmental fitness (pride in place and the landscape).

Environment: A Challenging Framework for Life

Understanding environment(s) as a series of integrated levels provides an initial point of access to understanding. William Wurster, former Dean of Environmental Design at the University of California at Berkeley, has repeatedly described buildings as resembling frames rather than pictures. Pictures represent human life; buildings provide a framework through which to view and interpret life.

To make sense of the world in which we live, we use hierarchical systems to organize our various environments, including the natural and the built. This book is organized into a hierarchical set of seven levels or components of the built environment: products, interiors,

Figures 3-17, 18, and 19 Creative integration of a building (inside and out) with built and natural environments. Provincial Law Court building in Vancouver, British Columbia, Canada.

structures, landscapes, settlements and cities, regions, and, finally, the Earth. Each level and related design/ planning discipline are then linked to all the others through connections that are subtle and complex. The listing is not perfect, exhibiting overlaps and discontinuities, but it does illustrate general categories and relationships. It can serve as a useful approximation, a series of frames that help to expand understanding and awareness of this complex and fascinating subject—the built environment.

Acknowledgment

This chapter is a condensed, updated combination of G. Young, "Environment: Definition and Organization" and the author's "Designing with the Intrinsic Organization of the Built Environment" in *The Built Environment: A Creative Inquiry into Design and Planning* (Crisp Publications, 1994).

References

Alexander, C. *The Nature of Order: An Essay on the Art of Building and the Nature of the Universe. Book One: The Phenomenon of Life*. Center for Environmental Structure, 2002.

Barabasi, A. *Linked: The New Science of Networks*. Perseus, 2002.

Bronowski, J. *The Ascent of Man*. Little, Brown, 1973.

Capra, F. *The Hidden Connection: Integrating the Biological, Cognitive and Social Dimensions of Life into a Science of Sustainability*. Doubleday, 2002.

Curry, A. "Airborne Archaeology." *Smithsonian*, December 2005.

Ecotone (view the pattern map). 2006. www.conservation-economy.net.

Henderson, L. *The Fitness of the Environment: An Inquiry into the Biological Significance of the Properties of Matter*. Beacon Press, 1913.

Koestler, A. "The Hierarchy and the Game." In Lila L. Gatlin (ed.), *Information Theory and the Living System*. Columbia University Press, 1972.

McDonough, W. 2006. www.mcdonough.com.

McDonough, W., and M. Braungart. *Cradle to Cradle: Remaking the Way We Make Things*. North Point Press, 2002.

McHarg, I., and Frederick R. Steiner (eds.). *To Heal the Earth: The Selected Writings of Ian McHarg*. Island Press, 1998.

Molnar, F. "The Unit and the Whole: Fundamental Problem of the Plastic Arts." In G. Kepes (ed.), *Module, Proportion, Symmetry, Rhythm*. George Braziller, 1966.

Patten, B., and S. Jørgensen (eds.). *Complex Ecology: The Part-Whole Relation in Ecosystems*. Prentice Hall, 1995.

Young, G. "Between the Atom and the Void: Hierarchy Theory in Human Ecology," *Advances in Human Ecology*, Vol. 1, 119–147, 1992.

Endnotes

1. A. Curry, "Airborne Archaeology," *Smithsonian* (December 2005): p. 71.

2. G. Young, "Between the Atom and the Void: Hierarchy Theory in Human Ecology," *Advances in Human Ecology*, 1992. p. 119–147.

3. A. Koestler, "The Hierarchy and the Game," in Lila L. Gatlin (ed.), *Information Theory and the Living System* (Columbia University Press, 1972).

4. C. Alexander, *The Nature of Order: An Essay on the Art of Building and the Nature of the Universe. Book One: The Phenomenon of Life* (Center for Environmental Structure, 2002).

5. J. Bronowski, *The Ascent of Man* (Little, Brown, 1973).

6. McDonough, W. 2006: www.mcdonough.com; and Ecotone (view the pattern map), 2006, www.conservationeconomy.net.

7. I. McHarg, and Frederick R. Steiner (eds.), *To Heal the Earth: The Selected Writings of Ian McHarg* (Island Press, 1998).

8. L. Henderson, *The Fitness of the Environment: An Inquiry into the Biological Significance of the Properties of Matter* (Beacon Press, 1913): p. 5.

9. W. McDonough and M. Braungart, *Cradle to Cradle: Remaking the Way We Make Things* (North Point Press, 2002): p. 120.

CHAPTER 4

Designing with People: Human Behavior, Culture, and User Participation

Paul G. Windley and Wendy R. McClure

Designers and planners who understand ways to design with people are more likely to help improve the quality of the built and natural environments. This chapter will introduce the field of environment and behavior studies (EBS) by applying insights generated by scholars, researchers, and practitioners to better interpret and respond to human needs, cultural values, and traditions. The discussion will also introduce strategies to engage in design decision making people who are most impacted by a particular designed environment or plan for a community context in which they must live, work, recreate, or socialize. The chapter will explore in greater detail how one designs with human, social, and cultural influences. It is the first in the triad of linked chapters expanding upon the **human-environmental-technological** themes.

What Are Environment and Behavior Studies?

A Definition

EBS explores the reciprocal relationship between people and their built environments—a further exploration of human-environmental relationships. That is, the built environment influences our behavior and, in turn, our behavior influences the built environment. EBS includes fields such as human ecology, environmental psychology, behavioral architecture, environmental sociology, behavioral geography, and environmental anthropology—each with a slightly different focus. In this chapter, we will use the collective term "environment and behavior studies" to refer to all disciplines that study the relationship between behavior and the environment, both built and natural. The term "behavior" refers to human behavior that is observable.

This chapter will briefly note the historical and interdisciplinary roots of EBS, discuss why this field is important to people who design, plan, and manage the built environment, and introduce a vocabulary of EBS attributes that leads to quality place making and place experience. It will conclude with a discussion of how EBS contributes to design methods, including the role of participatory planning, environmental evaluation, ecology, technology, and cultural issues.

Interdisciplinary Roots

The exact time EBS emerged as a discipline is still in debate. Some scholars believe it began with studies in the 1920s of how heat and noise affected work performance.[1]

Figure 4-1 The Louvre (former palace of Louis XIV) and Museum Additon by I. M. Pei provide a dynamic built environment for people to sightsee; experience art, history and culture; and socialize in Paris.

In subsequent years, EBS was represented in a variety of publications, academic programs offering graduate degrees in EBS, associations that focus on EBS, and many architectural and planning firms that based their design philosophies on the EBS perspective. The developmental history of EBS documents an exciting period when scholars from the social sciences and design fields, practicing architects and designers, and regional and community planners were trying to be more socially responsible in their understanding and design of the built environment.[2]

EBS and Place Making

Place Making

From the 1960s to the present, EBS has responded to criticism directed toward designers and planners for not creating environments that respond to human needs and values. Representative of this criticism is the comment by Gans,[3] a sociologist and planner, who stated that many designers have been peer-oriented and have pursued originality, so that too often designers were more concerned about how a project would look in the design publications than about how it would actually work. Collectively, these critics have identified serious flaws in current design practice. Multiple studies demonstrate that population groups such as the elderly, the disabled, and those with low incomes are frequently marginalized because they must cope with designed environments that do not enable them to function independently or successfully. Designers place undue emphasis on aesthetics and appearance at the expense of function. They

are more preoccupied with making a "personal visual statement" with their designs than with making places that meet the needs of their clients and users. As evidence of this whimsical preoccupation, critics cite the common practice of designers giving other designers awards for projects not yet constructed. Some design projects, even when constructed, have served as icons of failure to address human needs, including the Pruitt-Igo public housing project in St. Louis, where in 1960 rampant crime and other social dysfunctions were attributed to building design, and the University of Cincinnati's College of Design, Art, Architecture and Planning, where wayfinding is difficult for building users.

However, some designs demonstrate successful consideration of human needs, including the Federal Aviation Administration's Northwest Regional Headquarters in Seattle, Washington, where employees were very satisfied with their work settings and appreciated a design process that included them in the planning. The design of the Contra Costa County Detention Center in Martinez, California, was highly praised for its ability to suppress violence and promote safety for professional staff through innovative design. William Whyte's Exxon Minipark Redesign Project in New York City and Oscar Newman's redesign of Clason Point Gardens in New York City were successful in creating defensible space by promoting surveillance and control over public spaces.[4] Other success stories are revealed in the works of architect Michael Pyatok, who regularly involves low-income residents in the process of designing their own (multifamily) co-housing communities.

Processes in Making Places

EBS offers designers and planners a different paradigm for the making of places. Rather than focusing on aesthetics and appearance as priority criteria for design, EBS emphasizes meeting the needs of people through correct application of behavioral design criteria. Aesthetic principles are integrated into behavioral criteria but never allowed to dominate the final design. An important principle in this paradigm is the reciprocal effects of behavior and environment, in which environment shapes behavior and then behavior shapes environment. A second principle is that the correct application of EBS to place making requires a theoretical context for the behavioral goals of a place. Human activities are then identified that meet these goals, followed by environmental attributes that support these activities. Thus, the EBS perspective helps the designer to be accountable for meeting behavioral goals by using a more systematic design process.

Design outcomes are later evaluated against their original goals, and the results are used to improve the theoretical concepts from which they originally emerged. So then, what are the environmental attributes of places that support human needs and values?[5]

Human Attributes of Place Making:

Physical Attributes of Places

Many beginning design students are taught what is often called the "vocabulary of design," including concepts such as mass and void, scale, proportion, and rhythm. These concepts are based on the aesthetic perspective. The EBS perspective offers a different vocabulary comprised of environmental attributes that are linked to human behavior. Several of these attributes will be described below.[6] Each of them is defined somewhat differently, depending on the client, the facility users, and the scale of the environment in question.

Accessibility promotes access to neighborhoods, buildings, and objects for all potential users. This is a component of **universal design** discussed in other chapters. It includes accessible or barrier-free buildings and neighborhoods that allow a person to move from one place to another unencumbered, and the degree to which objects, such as furniture, can be manipulated to successfully accomplish a specific task. Wheelchair-bound individuals and elderly people are particularly vulnerable to environmental barriers such as stairs, steep slopes and ramps, and uneven surfaces. Their ability to function autonomously within an environment is compromised by such barriers as narrow doorways, high countertops, or ramps or supported by environments designed to be barrier free. Sensitive designers create accessible environments and objects for all users, being careful not to make those who are physically disadvantaged feel conspicuous in a given space. Adaptability is an attribute that enables environments to be modified to fit changing human activities. Adaptable environments include movable partitions and furnishings, flexible lighting and heating systems, and spatial configurations that allow for multiple and alternative uses. Because of the increasing complexity of human activity, the rapid change in such activities, the expanding use of technology, and the high cost of building construction, many building types must serve a variety of functions. Settings where adaptability is important include educational classrooms, most work environments, hospital patient rooms, student dormitories, and homes.

Social interaction, privacy, and territoriality are often referred to as **proxemics**.[7] Some settings facilitate **social interaction**, while others hinder it. The way buildings or landscapes are arranged on a site may encourage informal contact with neighbors. The configuration of rooms in a building or the arrangement of tables and chairs in a space can encourage or discourage social interaction among users. Most airport seating is known to hinder social contact among inhabitants, while seating in a restaurant is often more conducive to social interaction.

Privacy is the degree to which the built environment controls inputs from others and outputs to others.[8] The way rooms are arranged in a building, the way doors are arranged in a corridor, the placement of windows, and the use of sound-attenuating materials in walls, floors, and ceilings can either promote or prevent the experience of privacy. Similar elements also define the exterior environment in parks, plazas, and other public spaces. Privacy is important in many settings, especially correc-

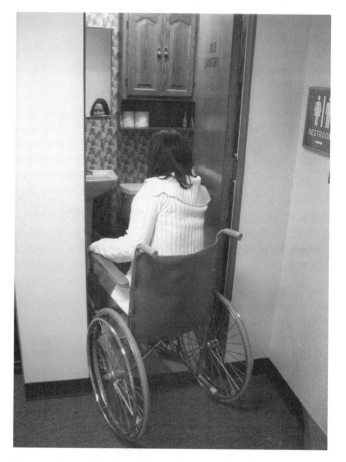

Figure 4-2 Accessibility. The built environment must accommodate individuals with disabilities. The photo illustrates the restriction to free access that a wheelchair-bound woman encounters as she tries to use the restroom because the doorway is too narrow (Pamela Overholtzer).

Figure 4-3 Accessibility. This workstation enables wheelchair users to work comfortably at daily office tasks by affording adequate clearance under the desk and an appropriate desk height (Pamela Overholtzer).

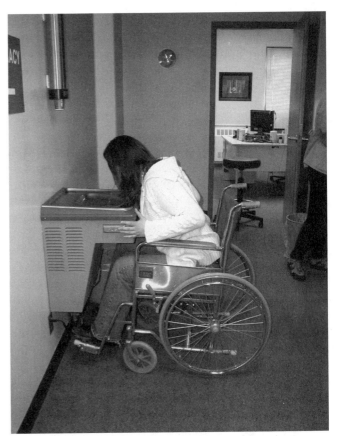

Figure 4-4 Accessible drinking fountain (Pamela Overholtzer).

tional facilities, hospitals, counseling centers, most work settings, and residential and urban environments. **Territoriality** is the degree to which the built environment promotes identity by allowing a person or group to defend **personal space**. How an environment is designed can either facilitate or hinder territorial expression. Such factors as room configuration, building height, building shape, and the placement of windows and doors can either hinder or facilitate surveillance and territorial expression.[9]

Legibility is the degree to which a setting possesses spatial organization, incorporates the components of identity and structure, and is perceptually understandable.[10] The degree to which a person can identify and structure environmental components to form a functional internal representation or mental image of a place is influenced by the way that environment is configured. Legible environments promote orientation, predictability, and wayfinding, all of which are important in cities, landscapes, and public buildings such as courthouses, elder care facilities, and health care facilities.

Density is the number of people per unit area. Density can have both negative and positive effects on individuals. For example, highly dense cities can create ample opportunities for social interaction but may restrict privacy. High density in hospital settings creates efficiency but may cause health problems, multiple-occupancy cells in a correctional facility can foster violence, and crowded classrooms can inhibit learning. On the other hand, low-density settings are often unable to create a sufficient critical mass of individuals to carry out the functions of the setting, such as in a suburban neighborhood area or a small rural community.[11] The designer and planner must anticipate the effects of density on behavior for specific users and environmental conditions.[12]

Comfort and **sensory** stimulation are attributes that promote human comfort include thermal, acoustical, luminous, and anthropometric properties of settings. These attributes can work in combination with other dimensions of the environment, such as temperature and humidity. In other cases, they can have their own indi-

Figure 4-5   Privacy. This chair in the Seattle Public Library is designed to allow library users who are strangers to face away from one another and to establish adequate privacy.

Figure 4-7   Personal space. Seagulls and other members of the animal world naturally create a comfortable distance between one another.

vidual impacts on perceived comfort, such as when a properly designed chair accommodates body dimensions and movement. The experience of comfort is somewhat subjective but is usually based on a specific task that is being carried out under specific environmental conditions. Individuals who have visual and auditory difficulties and body limitations may need special environmental attributes to be able to complete a task comfortably. Attributes such as color, spatial variety, visual pattern, and contrast can create a visually stimulating setting. Other environmental features such as the odor,

Figure 4-8   Personal space. Similar to the animal world, humans maintain an invisible bubble around themselves to preserve their identity (Pamela Overholtzer).

Figure 4-6   Territoriality. Individuals have a natural tendency to claim space, as evidenced by this person, whose purse, coat, bag, and umbrella serve as personal markers (Pamela Overholtzer).

Figure 4-9   Personal space. Library users have a natural tendency to space themselves out evenly at a common table.

sound, and texture of materials can also contribute to a setting's stimulation potential. Physical settings can be over- or understimulating, resulting in overload or deprivation for users.[13] Designers must determine the appropriate level of stimulation for individual users within specific environmental settings.

It is useful to view the attributes described above as an interdependent network or fabric. In combination these attributes always yield a holistic condition greater than the sum of its parts. These attributes, although not exhaustive, comprise the operational vocabulary of EBS and the raw material needed for place making in community and urban planning, landscape architecture, architecture, and interior design. When appropriately applied, these attributes lead to specific place experiences that contribute to a healthy quality of life. The following section will describe some of these experiences.

Domains of Place Experience

Wayfinding is one outcome of the processes of perception and cognition. It is related to spatial orientation, which is a function of a building or landscape's legibility. Other environmental attributes such as sensory stimulation and accessibility are also related to wayfinding. Wayfinding is the ability to know where one is in the built environment and how to reach a destination without getting lost. Lynch[14] identified five environmental components of cities that contributed to city legibility and wayfinding: nodes, paths, edges, districts, and landmarks. Wayfinding is important because it enables people to predict the consequences of their actions, reduces anxiety associated with getting lost, results in better adjustment to a new environment, increases the use of environmental amenities, and leads to greater satisfaction with and preference for a setting.[15]

Autonomy is defined as situation-specific freedom of choice, action, and self-regulation of one's space. EBS also asserts that autonomy is important to affirm one's competence and develop a sense of self-mastery in interacting with the built environment.[16] EBS attributes that relate to this dimension of experience include accessibility, adaptability, privacy, density, legibility, and territoriality.

Place attachment is the "bonding of people to places."[17] Low and Altman state that the term "place" refers to all scales of the environment, ranging from nations to cities and neighborhoods to residences and specific objects, and note that individuals form attachments to places in their past that may be used to assess present and future places. It also has a social dimension where individual and group associations become inte-

grated with a place and are as important as the place itself. These scholars conclude that individuals who have strong attachments to a place are usually highly satisfied with it as well. Place attachment promotes a sense of security; provides continuity to our lives; encourages exploration; enables one to predict the consequences of one's actions; enhances control; and creates individual, group, and cultural identity. Nearly all EBS attributes are associated with place attachment.[18]

Cultural Influences on Place Making and Design

Culture also plays a significant role in shaping the built environment. Cultural traditions are rich and complex, with each society viewing the built environment in different ways. Through his book, *House Form and Culture*, Amos Rapoport revolutionized thinking about the influence of culture on the built environment by explaining that variety in the built environment, particularly vernacular traditions, is the direct manifestation of cultural differences. People shape built environments to express and support their cultural values, beliefs, and traditions.[19] People around the world respond to similar climatic conditions differently. Cultures differ in the way they organize space, orient buildings, and respond to natural surroundings. For example, Native Americans traditionally locate the entry to their structures facing east, whereas Western cultures in urban settings typically orient entryways to primary streets, regardless of compass direction. Traditional Japanese dwellings are organized so that those entering the dwelling are immediately introduced into family common spaces, where they are expected to interact before retiring to private areas. By contrast, houses constructed by Western cultures in similar climatic conditions allow people a choice upon entering the home—whether to enter common living areas or retreat to private areas. Western cultures tend to configure the spatial organization of their homes according to similar traditions and sequences irrespective of climatic conditions; the floor plan for a house in Florida may not differ radically from one in Minnesota.

In order to design effectively, designers must develop an understanding of cultural norms and meanings and how to interpret them appropriately. Through work with the Lemhi Shoshone tribe for the design of a new facility celebrating the life of Lewis and Clark's Indian guide Sacajawea, a design team of faculty and students learned about significant tribal traditions and the need to interpret their meaning accurately in the articulation of space.

Figure 4-10 In Mexico, the town square is an important gathering place, reflecting cultural values and traditions. Many plazas have raised planted areas or fountains that serve as focal points.

During planning meetings, tribal members encouraged the design team to respect their most precious tribal traditions and to incorporate them into the design of the facility. Tribal members explained the importance and associated meaning of particular colors, as well as the significance of relationships between those colors and specific cardinal directions of the compass.

Human Behavior, Culture, and Design Method

Quality environments are responsive to human needs, values, and aspirations (see Chapters 1 and 3). Successful designs and healthy environments are inclusive and embrace multidimensional goals; they support the particular needs of a user; they respect and reflect the values and traditions of user populations; and they include **stakeholders** (people most impacted) in design decision-making processes. Designers can achieve a better understanding of their user populations by engaging them in the design process and by relying on established bodies of research to help guide design decision making.

Participatory design is a process that emerged during the 1960s, initially as a reaction to modernist design, which was very directive about how people should work and live. Modernist theory promoted an International Style that failed to acknowledge important differences in cultural traditions, regional climates, and design contexts. Modernist designers were touted as professional experts who made autonomous design decisions for their clients that were often based on artistic intent and theoretical values concerning how people should live rather than on appropriate information about actual users. The result in many cases was to alienate people as they tried to cope with dysfunctional environments.

Participatory design is rooted in the conviction that, in a democratic society, people should be able to participate in decisions that most impact them. Design is not and should not be the exclusive realm of the designer. Research demonstrates that user satisfaction is higher for designs people believe they have influenced.[20]

There are several types of participatory design processes, ranging from passive to proactive involvement. On one end of the spectrum, users' interests, much as in an elected government, are represented to the designer, who acts on their behalf. More interactive engagement encourages participants to become involved as co-decision makers in partnership with design professionals. Participants help to generate design alternatives, evaluate them, and reach a consensus concerning preferred alternatives.[21]

Strategies for participatory design vary according to the stage in the design process. Participants can become involved in initial stages or throughout the design and construction process.

Work completed with northwestern U.S. communities has successfully adapted and refined established participatory processes to involve citizens and civic leaders in community design and planning projects.[22] One strategy, known as "dot sticker voting," has been used by the planning profession since the 1970s. Participants vote for preferred ideas by placing dot stickers on a public display of work to determine common goals and objectives or preferred conceptual design ideas. Dot sticker voting can readily engage a broad cross section of a community. Other strategies involve helping participants to visualize opportunities. For downtown revitalization projects in Colfax and Colville, Washington, a consulting team had citizen participants create poster boards from photographs they had taken of their community indicating features that they liked and did not like. In other design workshop settings, citizens were asked to create land-use plans using color markers or to construct models of an entire neighborhood or a downtown area using a kit of parts or wooden blocks.[23] Each strategy is tailored to support the types of decisions that citizens must make.

Use of participatory processes offers several advantages for communities and design professionals:

- Research shows that user satisfaction is higher in participatory design projects because stakeholders own the outcome.

Figure 4-11 Citizens from Star, Idaho, partner with university design students and faculty to create alternative comprehensive plans for a new mixed-use commercial district using a "kit of parts" consisting of wooden blocks and plant materials.

- Participatory design helps to build support for a project within the community.
- Design professionals may actually save time in the long run on a project because their clients have wrestled firsthand with the design issues involved and therefore have a clearer understanding of what is possible.

Implementation of participatory design techniques and strategies by design professionals helps to create win-win situations for clients, community groups,

designers, and users. Several states have passed legislation mandating public participation in publicly funded projects, no longer allowing design consultants to practice in isolation. Design professionals who adopt an inclusive model for design will be better prepared to deal with the significant and diverse challenges of each design context, address cultural diversity, and better support human needs, values, and aspirations.

Built Environment as Hypothesis, Research Translation, and the Design Process

Environment-behavior studies and participatory design promote a more inclusive and systematic design process by identifying and solving design problems within a holistic human/societal framework—one of the three domains in the human-environmental-technology concept. Human behavioral objectives emerge from these frameworks and can be defended by documented research. However, one of the problems with the application of research in design is that research findings are often difficult to translate into design criteria because many findings are generated by nondesigners, often with other objectives in mind. The gap between research and design is resolved in a four-stage design process proposed to guide design decision making to achieve behavioral objectives. This process is illustrated in Figure 4-12.[24]

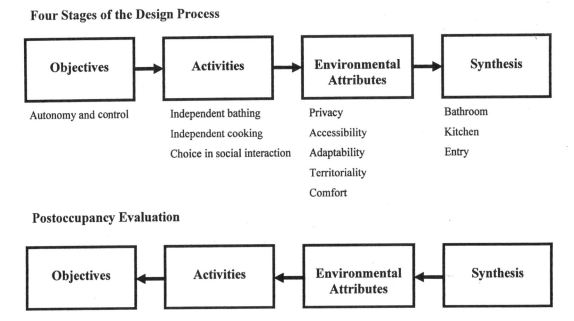

Figure 4-12 Four stages of the research translation and design process.

Design objectives are described in behavioral and cultural terms; activities are identified that meet these objectives; environmental characteristics that support these activities are then identified and include the EBS attributes described earlier; and finally, these characteristics are synthesized into larger spatial configurations that eventually evolve into schematic proposals. For example, assume that a designer's objective in a housing project for older people is to increase autonomy and control among residents. Through the research literature, the designer identifies three essential activities necessary for autonomy to occur: bathing without help, meal preparation in the unit, and control over when to engage in social interaction with other residents. Research demonstrates that environmental attributes such as accessibility, adaptability, privacy, and territoriality in various combinations are likely to support these activities. Finally, a synthesis of these attributes will lead to appropriate design of the bathroom, kitchen, and apartment entry. Movement from one stage in the process to the next is based on a design **hypothesis**—that is, an anticipated cause-and-effect relationship supported by research as one moves through the four stages. The generation of these design hypotheses is central to the research translation process and enables entire projects to be viewed as a system of hypotheses. The process is then reversed when buildings are completed to determine if environmental attributes accommodated needed activities and met overall behavioral objectives as hypothesized. This reverse process is called **postoccupancy evaluation**. Design hypotheses are then modified if needed and added to the experience and theoretical knowledge base for other designers and planners to employ in future designs.

Designing with Human/Social, Environmental, and Technology Domains

There are several dimensions to the ecological movement that span the natural, biological, and social sciences, economics, and environmental design and planning. As discussed in other chapters, **ecology** is the study of life in all of its forms within a specific environmental context and is based on the **ecosystem** as the basic unit of study. Human activities are a part of this unit. In the last few decades, many have argued that the world is experiencing an ecological crisis resulting from the misuse of Earth's resources, uncontrolled growth, unbridled use of technology, and misplaced priorities.[25] Because the built environment is part of the ecosystem, this translates into a design and planning crisis as well. The ecological movement has brought back into focus the finite and interactive nature of Earth's resources and the role human behavior plays in designing a more ecologically responsible environment. In the current use of terms, ecological design is synonymous with sustainable design.

The role sustainable design and technology play in EBS is centered in the place experience domain of autonomy discussed earlier. Our need to exercise design control in interacting with the built environment must be tempered by our knowledge of the interdependence of the ecosystem. Many argue that interdependence and individual behaviors that support sustainability are governed by awareness of needs, consequences, and responsibilities.[26] These different levels of awareness are most effective when developed in concert with all decision makers, including the designer. The concept of human-environmental relationships then suggests that design decisions emerging from this collective awareness maximize everyone's long-term autonomy and control within the ecosystem. Van Der Ryn and Cowan[27] recommend that designers follow five principles in order to increase awareness, promote interdependent sustainable design, and use technology appropriately:

- Design solutions grow from place—meaning that we learn from the human, cultural, and environmental opportunities and limitations of a place and the values of users.
- Ecological accounting informs design—suggesting that all ecological benefits and costs must be assessed and used to define and solve design problems.
- Design with nature—arguing that human-environmental impacts of good design are reduced when the processes in nature are integrated into design solutions.
- Everyone is a designer—meaning that often the best designs are created when distinctions between designer, owner, and user vanish in an inclusive participatory process and no one takes sole credit for the design.
- Make nature visible—asserting that designers creatively express the regional and often invisible qualities of a place.

As **ecological design** principles confront current design practice, trade-offs will always be required between the interests of individuals, the broader interests of society, and the environmental context (both built and natural). However, "In a social dilemma situation, each individual always receives a higher payoff for defecting than for cooperating, but all are better off if all co-operate than if all defect."[28]

Conclusion

This chapter introduced the role of EBS, culture, and user participation in understanding the relationship between people and their physical environment. It presented a vocabulary of environmental attributes that support place experience, discussed how human and cultural qualities enhance more inclusive and systematic design processes and methods of evaluation, and considered how design professionals can engage project stakeholders in design decision making. The chapter has expanded our understanding of how ecology, technology, and culture impact the built environment. Later chapters will further explore the environmental and technological domains of an inclusive understanding of the humanly created world. In addition, the concepts of human behavior and universal design (built environments that are accessible to all users) and proxemics will be explored in more detail in the product and interior components described in Part II.

References

Altman, I. *Environment and Social Behavior*, Brooks/Cole, 1975.

Bechtel, R. A. "A Behavioral Comparison of Urban and Small Town Environments." In J. Archea and C. Eastman (eds.), *EDRA 2: Proceedings of the Second Annual Environmental Design Research Association Conference*, 1970, 347–353.

Berkeley, E. "More Than You Wanted to Know About the Boston City Hall." *Architecture Plus*, January 1973.

Bonnes, M., and M. Bonaiuto. "Environmental Psychology: From Spatial-Physical Environment to Sustainable Development." In R. Bechtel and A. Churchman (eds.), *Handbook of Environmental Psychology*. Wiley, 2002.

Brill, M. "Evaluating Buildings on a Performance Basis." In J. Lang (ed.), *Designing for Human Behavior*. Dowden, Hutchinson and Ross, 1974.

Cherulnik, P. *Applications of Environment-Behavior Research: Case Studies and Analysis*. Cambridge University Press, 1993.

Dawes, R. "Human Cooperation: The Critical Role of Group Identity and Commitment." Paper presented at the Diplomacy and Psychology Dag Hammarskjold Memorial Seminar, Twenty-Seventh International Congress of Psychology, Stockholm, 2000.

Gans, H. "Toward a Human Architecture: A Sociologist's View of the Profession." In J. R. Blau (ed.), *Professionals and Urban Form*. State University of New York Press, 1983.

Gifford, R. *Environmental Psychology: Principles and Practice*. Optimal Books, 2002.

Hall, E. *The Hidden Dimension*. Anchor Books, 1969.

Kent, S. "The Cultural Revolution in Architecture." In K. Diaz-Moore (ed.), *Culture, Meaning, Architecture: Critical Reflections on the Work of Amos Rapoport*. Ashgate Publishing, 2000.

Korobkin, B. "Images for Design: Communicating Social Science Research to Architects." Architecture Research Office, Harvard Graduate School of Design, 1976.

Low, S., and I. Altman. "Place Attachment: A Conceptual Inquiry." In I. Altman and S. Low (eds.), *Place Attachment: Human Behavior and Environment: Advances in Theory and Research*. Plenum Press, 1992.

Lynch, K. *The Image of the City*. MIT Press, 1960.

McClure, W., A. Byrne, and Hurand, F. "Visualization Techniques for Citizen Participation." In W. McClure (ed.), *The Rural Town: Designing for Growth and Sustainability*. University of Idaho, Center for Business Development and Research, 1997.

Parmelee, P., and M. Lawton. "The Design of Special Environments for the Aged." In J. Birren and W. Schaie (eds.), *Handbook of the Psychology of Aging*. Academic Press, 1990.

Rainwater, L. "Fear and the House-as-Haven in the Lower Class." *Journal of the American Institute of Planners*, January 1966.

Rapaport, Amos. *House Form and Culture*. Prentice-Hall, 1969.

Regnier, V. *Assisted Living: Housing for the Elderly*. Van Nostrand Reinhold, 1994.

Sanoff, H. *Participatory Design: Theory and Techniques*. North Carolina State University Press, 1990.

Stokols, D. "On the Distinction Between Density and Crowding: Some Implications for Further Research." *Psychological Review*, 1972.

Van Der Ryn, S., and S. Cowan. *Ecological Design*. Island Press, 1996.

Weisman, J. "Evaluating Architectural Legibility: Wayfinding in the Built Environment." *Environment and Behavior*. February 1982.

Windley, P., and R. Scheidt. "Person-Environment Dialectics: Implications for Competent Functioning in Old Age." In L. Poon (ed.), *Aging in the 1980s: Psychological Issues*. American Psychological Association, 1980.

Windley, P., and J. Weisman, "Social Science and Environmental Design: The Translation Process." *Journal of Architectural Education*, 31, 1, January 1974.

Endnotes

1. R. Gifford, *Environmental Psychology: Principles and Practice* (Optimal Books, 2002).
2. See Note 1.

3. H. Gans, "Toward a Human Architecture: A Sociologist's View of the Profession," in J. R. Blau (ed.), *Professionals and Urban Form* (State University of New York Press, 1983).

4. P. Cherulnik, *Applications of Environment-Behavior Research: Case Studies and Analysis* (Cambridge University Press, 1993).

5. B. Korobkin, "Images for Design: Communicating Social Science Research to Architects" (Architecture Research Office, Harvard Graduate School of Design, 1976).

6. P. Windley and R. Scheidt, "Person-Environment Dialectics: Implications for Competent Functioning in Old Age," in L. Poon (ed.), *Aging in the 1980s: Psychological Issues* (American Psychological Association, 1980; adapted from Windley and Scheidt, 1980).

7. E. Hall, *The Hidden Dimension* (Anchor Books, 1969).

8. I. Altman, *Environment and Social Behavior* (Brooks/Cole, 1975).

9. See Note 7.

10. K. Lynch, *The Image of the City* (MIT Press, 1960).

11. R. A. Bechtel, "A Behavioral Comparison of Urban and Small Town Environments," in J. Archea and C. Eastman (eds.), *EDRA 2: Proceedings of the Second Annual Environmental Design Research Association Conference* (1970), 347–353.

12. D. Stokols, "On the Distinction Between Density and Crowding: Some Implications for Further Research," *Psychological Review*, 79, February 1972.

13. V. Regnier, *Assisted Living: Housing for the Elderly* (Van Nostrand Reinhold, 1994).

14. See Note 10.

15. J. Weisman, "Evaluating Architectural Legibility: Wayfinding in the Built Environment," *Environment and Behavior*, 13:2, February 1982.

16. P. Parmelee and M. Lawton, "The Design of Special Environments for the Aged," in J. Birren and W. Schaie (eds.), *Handbook of the Psychology of Aging* (Academic Press, 1990).

17. S. Low and I. Altman, "Place Attachment: A Conceptual Inquiry," in I. Altman and S. Low (eds.), *Place Attachment: Human Behavior and Environment: Advances in Theory and Research* (Plenum Press, 1992).

18. See Note 17.

19. S. Kent, "The Cultural Revolution in Architecture," in K. Diaz-Moore (ed.), *Culture, Meaning, Architecture: Critical Reflections on the Work of Amos Rapoport* (Ashgate Publishing, 2000).

20. H. Sanoff, *Participatory Design: Theory and Techniques* (North Carolina State University Press, 1990).

21. See Note 20.

22. W. McClure, A. Byrne, and F. Hurand, "Visualization Techniques for Citizen Participation," in W. McClure (ed.), *The Rural Town: Designing for Growth and Sustainability* (University of Idaho, Center for Business Development and Research, 1997).

23. See Note 22.

24. M. Brill, "Evaluating Buildings on a Performance Basis," in J. Lang (ed.), *Designing for Human Behavior* (Dowden, Hutchinson and Ross, 1974). This process is based on the work of Brill (1974), Korobkin (1976), and Windley and Weisman (1974).

25. M. Bonnes and M. Bonaiuto, "Environmental Psychology: From Spatial-Physical Environment to Sustainable Development," in R. Bechtel and A. Churchman (eds.), *Handbook of Environmental Psychology* (Wiley, 2002). These ideas are discussed in more detail in Van Der Ryn and Cowan (1996).

26. See Note 25.

27. S. Van Der Ryn and S. Cowan, *Ecological Design* (Island Press, 1996).

28. R. Dawes, "Human Cooperation: The Critical Role of Group Identity and Commitment," Paper presented at the Diplomacy and Psychology Dag Hammarskjold Memorial Seminar (Stockholm: Twenty-Seventh International Congress of Psychology, 2000).

CHAPTER 5

Designing with the Environment: Land and Climate

Michael S. Owen and Bruce T. Haglund

Life, in sickness and in health, is bound up with the forces of nature, and that nature, so far from being opposed and conquered, must rather be treated as an ally and friend, whose ways must be understood, and whose counsel must be respected.

—Lewis Mumford, on Hippocrates' ancient Greek treatise titled *Airs, Waters and Places*[1]

I t is common sense to design with nature instead of against it. Designing against the grain of nature is inherently problematic, can cause extensive difficultly from natural disasters, and requires more reliance on fossil fuels and mechanical control systems. People are seeking new ecological understanding and methods to reduce this dependency on nonrenewable resources and artificial systems. Ironically, the "new methods" being sought are not new methods at all! They are methods that were employed for centuries before the advent of the Industrial Revolution. They are the vernacular methods of traditional, indigenous societies that, by necessity and adaptive ingenuity, shaped the built environment in harmony with nature. This chapter will explore designing with nature's influential land and climatic context. It is the second in the triad of linked chapters expanding upon human-**environmental**-technological themes.

Land and Its Natural Context

Preindustrial societies relied on an inherent understanding of the natural cycles—related to air, land, and water—to locate and design human settlements. At the beginning of the twenty-first century, regional and urban planners are applying scientific methods, such as computer-based geographic information systems (GIS), to accomplish the same thing. GIS is used to analyze potential development sites by overlaying aerial photos, satellite images, and maps pertaining to topography, geology, soils, hydrology, and other natural features. These influential factors and methods are explored in detail in Chapters 19, 25, and 26. The purpose of such careful analysis is to determine where to locate structures, roads, and landscapes to ensure human and environmental sustainability for the future.

This so-called **layer-cake method** of site analysis originated with the internationally recognized landscape architect and ecological planner Ian McHarg, author of *Design with Nature*, first published in 1969, considered one of the most important books of the twentieth century. McHarg argued that before a site is developed, it should be evaluated from the point of view of natural factors (namely, climate, topography, geology, soils, hydrology, vegetation, and wildlife) to ascertain the "best places to build." Once the analysis is complete, new development is recommended according to the following ecological principles:

- Avoid building on steep slopes and away from natural hazards—flooding, earthquakes, slides, fire.
- Avoid building on farmlands and fertile organic soils.
- Build on land that is dry, with sufficient drainage, and avoid wetlands.
- Build where there is insolation (sunshine) and protection from hostile winds.
- Build near sources of potable water.

Although a major contributor to modern methods of ecological planning, McHarg recognized the innate ability of early humans to make intelligent decisions about locating and shaping their settlements:

> . . . [so-called primitive people] frequently acquired an astonishing empirical knowledge of their environment, its creatures and their processes. . . . Societies that sustained themselves for these many millennia are testimony to this understanding. . . .[2]

Early civilizations, based on agricultural economies, located their settlements in fertile valleys with abundant water nearby. As societies became more specialized and complex, settlements spread into ever more diverse geographic areas. Today, human settlements can be found in the climatic extremes of the Arctic Circle and great inland deserts. Much of the global diversity and variety in human habitat may be traced to specialized means of adaptation to widely divergent ecosystems determined by climate and geography.

Climate and Geographic Context

Simply stated, climate is a function or consequence of geography. The general climate of a region is determined by its level of **insolation** (the amount of sunlight that reaches the Earth). Insolation is most constant at the equator, where days and nights are nearly equal in length all year long. Temperatures at the equator are typically warm and constant.

Moving north or south of the equator, insolation periods begin to vary (e.g., longer summer days, shorter winter days). The closer to the poles, the greater the variations; hence, the solstices in arctic climates are characterized by 24 hours of darkness (winter) or 24 hours of

Figure 5-1 A city created by an indigenous society designing with the environment—Machu Picchu, Peru (T. Bartuska).

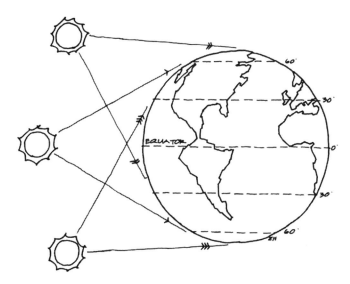

Figure 5-3 The elevation or altitude of an area also modifies temperature. Typically, temperatures lower by 3° for every 1,000-foot rise in altitude.

Figure 5-2 Latitude/insolation of the Earth influences weather patterns by the amount of sun reaching the surface. The highest, most consistent insolation occurs at the equator and becomes less and less as one moves north or south. Distances from the equator are measured in degrees of latitude.

light (summer—the "midnight sun"). Movement away from the equator is measured by degrees of latitude: the equator is 0° latitude, Mexico City is 19°, Seattle is 49°, and the Arctic Circle is 67°. Latitude therefore is the primary determinant of general climatic conditions. Longitude, which measures distances east-west around the globe, is not a determinant of climate; it functions as an indicator of location and time.

In addition to latitude, other primary geographic features determining general climatic conditions are large areas of water and land. Large water bodies tend to mediate temperature extremes of adjacent lands because of their capacity to absorb and store heat for maintaining a constant temperature and their property of evaporation, which produces cloud cover that reduces daytime solar gain and reduces nighttime heat loss. Large land areas tend to suffer the greatest temperature extremes (both seasonally and daily)—the greater the distance from water, the greater the variation. For example, the Great Plains area of the United States and Canada typically experiences extremely cold winters and hot summers, as well as large variations in day versus nighttime temperature.

Latitude and the relationships of land and water masses are geographic features, which establish the general or larger **macro-climate** patterns of a region. Geographic features, particularly elevation (above or below sea level), landforms (valleys, ridges, buttes, etc.), and vegetation, also influence the local or **micro-climate** conditions of a specific area. Typically, higher elevations

yield relatively lower temperatures and greater quantities of precipitation (rain and snow). In mountainous areas, solar orientation plays a major role because exposures facing the sun (southern exposure in the Northern Hemisphere) can be far warmer than shaded exposures. Landforms act to channel prevailing winds and to create thermal winds caused by temperature differences from variations in solar exposure.

Trees and other forms of vegetation are very important as potential windbreaks, heat absorbers, and air cleaners. Like water bodies, forests tend to mediate temperature extremes. The lack of significant vegetation in arctic and desert climates testifies to this fact. The properties of snow and sand tend to amplify temperature extremes in these climates; snow tends to reflect the heat and sand to absorb it.

What are the design consequences of this range of geographic and climatic zones? What are the weather conditions humans must contend with when developing their settlements? What are the critical geographic and climatic factors that must be taken into account when creating a living environment?

Although the subject of climate and geography appears complex in its diversity and variety, the number of factors that must be taken into account for design of

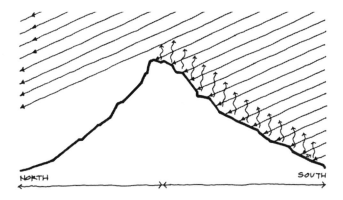

Figure 5-4 Solar exposure is important in building. Especially when building on slopes, it is wise to locate major developments on exposure facing the southern sun.

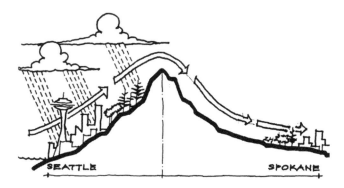

Figure 5-5 Water, mountains, and other land masses also determine weather patterns. Areas near or surrounded by water tend to be more temperate, with only minor fluctuations in temperature. Inland areas, on the other hand, exhibit severe temperature ranges from icy cold to desert hot. Mountains also modify the weather by creating barriers to the movement of warm air and precipitation.

the built environment is small: insolation, temperature, wind, humidity, and precipitation—rain and snow.

The design objectives of adapting the built environment to these factors are twofold. The first is to reduce the extremes of each condition that might cause discomfort and dysfunction in the daily lives of humans; hence, the built environment should be structured to:

• Shade occupants from the summer sun and allow them to bask in winter sun
• Protect occupants from freezing winter winds but allow cooling breezes in the summer
• Provide protection from rain and snow

The second factor is to celebrate the special qualities of each climatic zone and seasons—making nature visible.[3] The built environment should be created to enhance such opportunities as:

• The warm feeling of the sun indoors and out
• The beauty of the sound and movement of rain
• The quiet beauty of snow blanketing the outdoors
• The movement of trees and banners in the wind

Designing with Climate and Geography

How can the dual objectives of mediation and celebration be achieved in human settlements? Again, the principles are simple, but the diversity of climatic conditions must be taken into account. The categorization of climates derives from two principal factors of latitude and

proximity to large bodies of water. Latitudes closest to the equator are called "equatorial" and may have either arid or tropical climates. Mid-latitudes exhibit temperate climates of four distinct seasons—mild springs and autumns, hot summers, and cold winters. Arctic latitudes are uniformly cold. In addition to latitude, proximity to large bodies of water will create climates that are either dry or humid. Each of these climates requires a different set of design strategies regarding the built environment.

Hot-Dry Climates (Equatorial Arid)

In hot-dry climates, human habitats must be structured to minimize insolation on buildings and streets, encourage air movement for ventilation and cooling, and capture and retain precipitation. In these climates, during certain seasons, nights can be quite cool because the sky acts as a heat sink. Often it is necessary to retain the heat of the day to mediate nighttime coolness. Conversely, the cool air of night can be stored in thermal masses to mediate the daytime heat.

Inhabitants of human settlements sited in desert regions have a long history of fine-tuning their built environment to respond to hot-dry conditions. The street systems are structured to minimize building exposure to the rays of the sun. Streets are narrow so that they can be shaded by surrounding buildings during most parts of the day. Settlements are built compactly to minimize exposed surface areas and to enhance the effects of thick

Figure 5-6 In desert towns, designing with nature means constructing compact settlements with narrow streets, which can be shaded by adjacent buildings. Buildings are often constructed with thick mud walls to insulate the inhabitants from the hot sun during the day and to release radiant warmth during the cool of the evening.

Figure 5-7 Water and greenery are celebrated in desert settlements through the creation of oases, or lush verdant gardens.

mud and masonry walls shared by neighbors. Thick walls absorb the heat and "insulate" inhabitants from the heat of the day but release the day's heat in the cool of the night. Courtyards are used to trap pools of cool night air for use in their surrounding buildings.

The compact design of settlements also shields desert people from severe winds while allowing cooling breezes to ventilate living areas and streets during the day through careful siting of buildings and through the use of

Figure 5-8 Shaded streets are useful in desert and jungle settlements. Awnings and cloth screens provide color and shade while allowing breezes to cool the city on hot days.

such devices as "wind scoops," which direct breezes into cool subterranean spaces, forcing cool air into rooms above. Such settlements are also designed to capture and retain precious rains through the careful crafting of drainage systems to feed into underground cisterns. Water, and the green growth it creates, are celebrated in desert communities through specially sited and protected plazas designed to serve as spectacular oases for public use. When water is available, it is used to moisten and cool the built environment.

Hot-Humid Climates (Equatorial Tropical)

People living in hot-humid climates (e.g., jungle habitats) approach design of the built environment in a way just the opposite to that of desert cultures. In hot-humid climates, shade and air movement are the most critical factors in ensuring human comfort; hence, buildings are separated from one another and often set on stilts above the ground. This allows maximum air movement around and through streets and structures. Shade is achieved by large roof overhangs and arcades (covered sidewalks along building and street fronts), which provide protection from rain but are open to breezes.

Typically, temperatures in hot-humid climates do not drop significantly during evening hours. Structures are therefore made of light materials such as wood, bamboo, and palm leaves—which do not appreciably retain heat. Light, elevated structures minimize the effects of heavy, humid air. Consequently, tropical settlements are not

Figure 5-9 Jungle towns in hot-wet climates are constructed less compactly than those in desert climates to avoid blocking cooling breezes. Construction materials such as bamboo and palm leaves are employed to minimize heat retention in buildings (T. Bartuska).

designed compactly; instead, buildings are separated to maximize airflow. Public landscapes and plazas are designed to be used in the hours of early evening and are surrounded by arcades, where people can sit protected while watching and listening to the cooling afternoon rains.

Temperate Climates (Mid-Latitude)

Temperate climates are typified by four-season weather patterns. Summer conditions can be similar to those in hot-arid or tropical climates, and winter conditions can approach arctic conditions. Near large bodies of water, temperate climates tend to have less pronounced seasonal differences than those located well inland.

In temperate climates, settlements must be designed to achieve the greatest exposure of streets and buildings to the warming rays of the winter sun. In mountainous areas, settlements should be located on the sunny side of slopes (on the south side in the Northern Hemisphere).

Temperate zones tend to mediate climatic extremes; consequently, most of the world's largest cities are located there. Designers of such cities need to pay special attention to seasonal variations. They should attempt to locate streets and buildings to protect inhabitants from cold winter winds but allow cooling summer breezes. This can be accomplished because prevailing winds in the winter and summer generally blow from different directions. Also, designers must pay attention to protec-

Figure 5-11 An arcade of plants provides shade and evaporative cooling from the hot sun. Expo 92 in Seville, Spain. (T. Bartuska).

tion from sun and rain. As in hot-humid regions, arcades and canopies are employed to shelter people from hard-driving rains and hot summer sun. In mid-latitude temperate climates snow may occasionally fall, but it does not typically remain for long periods of time and therefore is not a primary determinant of settlement design. In northern temperate climates, however, winters can be

Figure 5-10 Arcades are excellent for protecting people from the sun and rain.

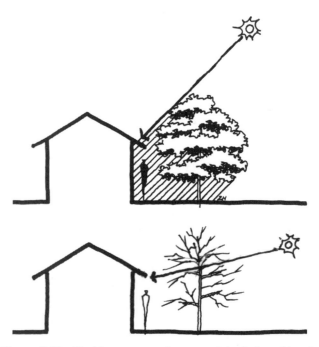

Figure 5-12 Deciduous trees play a special role in cold and temperate climates. During the summer, when their leaves are full, they provide needed shade and evaporative cooling. During the winter, when their leaves have fallen, the sun's rays are able to penetrate to warm buildings and open spaces.

more severe and solar insolation is more important. Snow should be one of the design/planning considerations (cold climates are explored in the next section).

Appropriately designed settlements in temperate regions allow people to celebrate the special climatic qualities of each season—summer, fall, winter, and spring. Summers are spent outdoors; the arcades and canopies, which protect against the rain, also provide shaded areas for especially hot days. In fall, people celebrate the brightly colored leaves of deciduous trees and the special delight of feeling the warmth of sunshine in combination with cool, brisk temperatures. Winter is a time for quiet contemplation; the pace slows, dense fog can occur and turn people's thoughts inward, and frequent rains keep people indoors to be warmed by fires. Spring unleashes the rebirth of greenery and flowers; rain and sunshine alternate and heighten people's feeling of being alive.

Landscaping is an important dimension in the design of settlements to mediate seasonal climatic extremes and to celebrate climatic variations. Deciduous trees and shrubs planted on the west side of buildings and streets offer shade from the intense afternoon summer sun; the loss of foliage in the fall allows the sun's rays to penetrate and warm the cool surfaces in winter. Dense groves of evergreen trees and shrubs can be strategically planted to reduce the freezing effects of cold winter winds. Trees and ground cover also contribute to visual beauty in human settlements by providing color and texture while absorbing excess heat, dampening excess noise, and filtering airborne dust and particles.

Cold Climates (Arctic)

Cold climates typically are found in inland regions, such as the Great Plains of North America and the Siberian Plains of Russia, in alpine regions, and in high-latitude areas. These climates also exhibit variations in season, but the transitional periods (spring and fall) are less pronounced, and winters are longer and more severe. The extreme cold means that precipitation generally falls in the form of snow and may remain for several months.

In response to these conditions, people living in these areas attempt to expose as much building and street area as possible to the warming rays of the sun. As in any cold climate, habitable structures should be located on the sunny side of slopes to conserve heat, and settlements should be compact. Living areas should ideally have as much insulation as possible to retain the maximum degree of warmth. Whenever possible, the sun should be allowed to penetrate into buildings, especially during the short days of the winter months. The sun's warmth

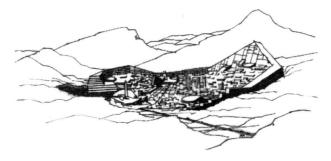

Figure 5-13 Ralph Erskine, an English architect practicing in Sweden, designed an ideal arctic town, developed on the sun-facing slope. Compact buildings share many common walls; large, continuous buildings on the perimeter block the arctic wind; and streets, paths, and green spaces are organized for maximum sun exposure and wind protection.

should be retained by heat-absorbing materials and released during the long, cold evenings.

Since people will spend 60% to 70% of the wintertime indoors, buildings and streets should be connected, enclosed, and shaped to protect them from freezing winds. As in cool-wet climates, outdoor landscaping should be used to shield against cold winds, to provide shade in the summertime, and to contribute to the visual quality of the environment. In addition, trees and shrubs should be employed inside buildings to absorb heat, release moisture, and soften the inevitable effects of "cabin fever."

Snow is the special feature of winter. It is a natural insulation material; as such, it can aid in retaining heat in buildings and in softening sounds. Snow-covered ground reflects light, helping to brighten interior spaces and lessening the effects of daylight deprivation during winter months. It provides unusual opportunities for transport such as sleigh rides, snowmobiling, and cross-country skiing, as well as recreational uses such as sledding, skating, and downhill skiing. Aesthetically, snow provides a white background against which rich building and landscape colors may be contrasted.

Designing with Appropriate Technologies

The preceding descriptions emphasized **appropriate technologies** and **adaptive design** responses to various climatic conditions. Appropriate technologies are those that work with nature instead of against it (the next chapter will further discuss the importance of this concept). They focus on approaches or methods that address climatic factors through the manipulation of spaces, structures, materials, and vegetation. Note that no mention has been made of mechanical environmental controls such as furnaces, air conditioners, ventilating fans, and the like. In fact, advanced technology and the widespread use of mechanical devices have had a major impact on the way planners and designers have responded to climatic and regional factors. The overall impact of mechanical environmental controls has been to reduce the use of more traditional or **vernacular** design responses in shaping the built environment. In other words, ever since humans have been capable of heating, cooling, dehumidifying, and ventilating buildings by mechanical means, the need and, to some extent, the knowledge to make the built environment more responsive to the natural environment have declined or been lost. These mechanical methods consume fossil fuels and higher amounts of energy throughout the world and contribute significantly to global warming.

When humans shaped the built environment in accordance with the forces of nature, buildings and cities in cold climates looked very different from those of hot climates. The use of mechanical air conditioning, heat-

ing, and ventilating has resulted in a reduction of the rich variation of regional expression that existed in the past.

Most contemporary cities, especially suburbs, are not compact: streets frequently sprawl over the land without attention to solar orientation or wind protection; tall buildings shade streets and other buildings from solar access; snow is plowed, not used; the built and natural ecology of the site are ignored. Cities have in fact created their own miserable micro-climates: wind-swept streets and plazas; places that are too hot in the summer and too cold in the winter; places that cannot sustain pedestrian activity and social contact, but instead rely on people going about their business separated from each other in disconnected buildings and isolated vehicles.

Heavy reliance on mechanical control of the environment has not only reduced human ability to appreciate the benefits of nature, the ecological qualities of our finite land resources and climate, but has also contributed in no small way to contemporary manifestations of social dysfunction and alienation. A significant challenge designers face today and in the future is to reduce reliance on mechanical controls and non-renewable energy sources and continue to discover (and rediscover) appropriate ways to design with the environment at all levels—the products we use, our interior spaces, buildings, and landscapes, our cities and regions, and, ultimately the Earth itself.

References

Fitch, J. M., and W. Bobenhausen. *American Building: The Environmental Forces That Shape It*. Oxford University Press, 1999.

Hanna, K., and R. Culpepper. *GIS and Site Design: New Tools for Design Professionals*. Wiley, 1998.

Hyde, R., and P. Woods. *Climate Responsive Design: A Study of Buildings in Moderate and Hot Humid Climates*. Spon Press, 2000.

McHarg, I. *Design with Nature*. Natural History Press, 1969.

Miller, D. *Toward a New Regionalism: Environmental Architecture in the Pacific Northwest*. University of Washington Press, 2005.

Pressman, N. *Northern Cityscape: Linking Design to Climate*. Winter Cities Press, 1995.

Van Der Ryn, S., and S. Cowan. *Ecological Design*. Island Press, 1996.

Endnotes

1. I. McHarg, *Design with Nature* (Natural History Press, 1969): p. vi.
2. McHarg, *Design with Nature*: p. 68.
3. S. Van Der Ryn and S. Cowan, *Ecological Design* (Island Press, 1996).

Figure 5-14 Banners "celebrate" the wind and add color to community streets (T. Bartuska).

CHAPTER 6

Designing with Technology: A Collaborative and Creative Process

Matthew A. Taylor and Kenneth L. Carper

Technology has a profound influence on the design of the components of the built environment. The word "technology" is often misunderstood or misapplied. Technology may have positive or negative connotations for people because of their limited experience with appropriate or inappropriate applications of technology. Examination of a few definitions, however, will show that technology is, in fact, a neutral term. It will be seen that an understanding of technological processes is essential to the development of quality design in the built environment. At the "structures" scale and at the "systems" level, **technology** is the means whereby conflicts between the natural environment and human needs are resolved. This chapter will explore in greater detail how one designs with technology. It is the third in the triad of linked chapters expanding upon the human-environmental-**technological** concept.

Definitions: Creativity, Technology, and Design

Creativity

There is much to be learned about creativity and the creative process from direct observation of the natural and built environments in their various forms. In this chapter, we will emphasize Ian McHarg's definition: Creativity is the "process of seeking fitness and health."[1] Other aspects of this concept are given in the following definitions:

- The employment of energy and matter to reach higher levels of order . . . evolution is a least work maximum success solution . . . the surviving organism is an energy-conserver and is successful by finding creative fitness and health. . . .[2]
- To create is "to cause to come into being as something unique that would not naturally evolve or that is not made by ordinary processes. To cause to happen; to bring about; to arrange as by intent or design."[3]
- Creativity is "The ability to transcend traditional ideas, rules, patterns, relationships or the like and to create meaningful new ideas, forms, methods, interpretations, etc.[4]

Technology

The origin of the word technology is found in two Greek words, *techne* and *logos*. *Techne* means "art or craft," and *logos* means "creating or making." Thus, the word **technology** implies "the making of something." Interestingly, this word serves to bridge the arts, the humanities, and the sciences. Art, craft, or science has no tangible expression apart from systems or technology. While ideas may certainly exist separately from technology, the making of an idea through the creative process implies application of technology.

Three additional definitions of technology are given here: one short and two more comprehensive:

- Technology is applied science[5]
- The totality of the means employed to provide objects necessary for human sustenance and comfort[6]
- The branch of knowledge that deals with the creation and use of technical means and their interrelation with life, society, and the environment[7]

The third definition indicates the essential character of technology as related to design processes. It is evident that to achieve quality design in the built environment, designers must have an understanding of how to apply and integrate art, science, and appropriate technologies.

Both aesthetic and scientific judgments are important factors in the application of technology, perhaps even more important than mathematical formulas. Whether or not the built environment can coexist in harmony with the natural environment depends to a great extent on the designer's ability to understand and creatively integrate the various

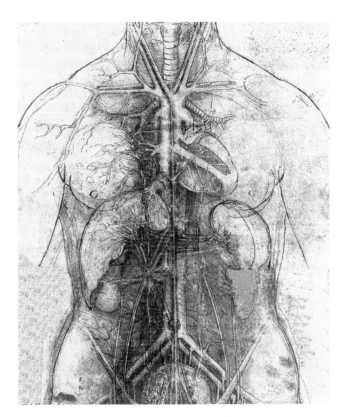

Figure 6-1 The body, like many of the components of the built environment, is supported by a series of systems (drawing of the human body by Leonardo da Vinci).

technologies in an appropriate manner. Concepts of art and science will be discussed further in the section "Technology and the Natural Environment: What Is Appropriate?"

As noted above and in previous chapters, the natural environment is a valuable and accessible resource from which to gain an understanding of technology. Natural forms and systems have often served to inspire designer's as they pursued efficient, functional, and aesthetically pleasing solutions to built environment problems. Today we seek to resolve current problems in the face of energy and material resource limitations. We will continue to find partial solutions to contemporary problems by adapting technological examples from nature (natural analogies) to the built environment.

Natural systems applied to design are sometimes obvious. Designers speak of "circulation spines" and "arms" or "wings" of built forms. The same can be said for technology. The structural system forms the "skeletal system" of a project, and the environmental systems become the "organs." This anthropomorphic model is a useful way to explain design, but more importantly, a "natural" model can be the design concept.

Design

Many definitions of design (and/or planning) have been attempted, some narrow in scope and others more comprehensive. Design is an activity that integrates the arts and sciences and encompasses many scales and many objectives. Perhaps this is why it is so difficult to define it. However, for the purpose of this discussion, the following definition is useful: **Design** at most scales requires the creative integration of technology. If the above definitions of creativity and technology are accepted, this definition is sufficiently comprehensive to include most activities in the design of the components within the built environment.

The Need for Technology: Resolution of Conflicts

Technology is the means whereby conflicts between the natural environment and human needs are resolved. Clearly, conflicts exist at the most basic levels. Indeed, the very reason for the existence of the built environment is the conflict between the unmodified natural environment and human environmental needs.

For example, consider structural engineering, one of the principal built environment technologies. A structure is a three-dimensional design, which differs from a sculpture only in the fact that a structure exists for some utilitarian purpose. A structure may exist to connect two points (a bridge), to withstand natural forces (a dam or a retaining wall), or to span and enclose space so that the environment can be made suitable for habitation (a building).

For example, in buildings, the structural system spans and encloses space. Enclosure of space is often an essential first step toward humanization of the natural environment. In one sense, the technology of structural design can be seen as a resolution of a conflict.

The conflict resolved by structural design is the conflict between natural forces (called "loads") and space requirements. Most building loads that need to be resolved are directed vertically because most load forces are the result of gravitational attraction. In structures, the vertically directed forces must be resisted in such a way that human activity spaces remain unobstructed. Human activity spaces tend to exist on horizontal planes, because we move horizontally more easily than vertically. Thus, a fundamental conflict exists between the vertical direction of most load forces and the human need for unobstructed, horizontally oriented spaces.

Structural design resolves this basic conflict by providing a spanning system that causes the load forces to change direction so that the human activity spaces can be unobstructed. Therefore, a general definition of structural design is "the art and science of causing forces to change direction."[8]

Environmental control systems (the systems used for heating, ventilating, cooling, and lighting) also attempt to

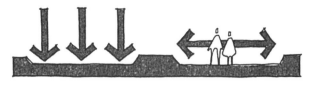
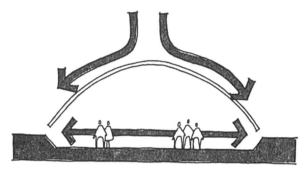

Figure 6-3 A structural system causes vertical load forces to change direction so that human activity spaces are unobstructed.

solve the conflict between the natural environment and the comfort needs of people in buildings. In a cold winter, a solar and/or mechanical heating system is employed to make occupants feel comfortable; the same is true for a cooling system in summer. Because buildings are well-enclosed systems, a means for bringing fresh air to occupants is usually needed. Thus, operable windows and the ventilation system become the "lungs" of the building.

Similarly, lighting technology is required because the natural environment provides light only part of the time and only a very specific type of light. Even when daylight is available, it must be modified using appropriate technologies. Heating, ventilating, and air-conditioning technology

Figure 6-2 A structure that connects two points using "legs" (steel members) and "tendons" (cables) for support: the San Francisco–Oakland Bay Bridge, San Francisco, California (T. Bartuska).

Figure 6-4 Enclosing space: the Palm House by Decimus Burton, 1844, Kew Gardens, London, England (T. Bartuska).

is needed because the natural environment does not always provide constant thermal conditions that are consistent with human needs or tasks. The other built environment technologies can be described as well in terms of the resolution of conflicts between human needs and what the natural environment provides.

The need for technology is evident. Conflicts exist that must be resolved if human needs are to be satisfied. The purpose of technology is to creatively resolve these conflicts.

Technology and the Natural Environment: What Is Appropriate?

The natural environment demonstrates processes that serve as examples of built environment technologies. Structural forms found in nature often exhibit efficiencies in material utilization beyond the achievements of human technology. Energy is conserved and converted efficiently from one form to another in living organisms and ecosystems. These processes deserve study. Much can be learned from natural analogies as we seek to develop an appropriate response in the built environment.

The natural environment is complex, and is constantly changing and adapting, involving a multitude of interrelated variables. One of the beauties of natural environment technologies is that they have evolved in a way that produces a dynamic compatibility within the overall system, generally with renewal or a minimal use of materials and energy.

The natural environment is not static or stagnant. It is a dynamic system, one in which changes are constantly occurring. These changes can be dramatic or even cataclysmic. Natural disasters such as earthquakes, floods, tornados, and hurricanes are examples of the destructive dynamics of the natural environment. But present within the system is the capacity to restore equilibrium—to replace temporary chaos with order and direction.

The more we develop our understanding of the equilibrium-seeking processes at work in the natural environment, the closer we will come to providing fitness and health in the built environment. The concept of appropriate technology deals with the issue of fitness. **Appropriate technology** can be defined as that which fits with or is compatible with the natural environment while also fulfilling human needs. The achievement of successful solutions based on appropriate technology implies an understanding of natural processes and an appreciation

for natural systems. An important criterion for fitness and health is compatibility with the natural environment.

Technology applied to the built environment can be inherently incompatible or compatible with natural processes and living systems. The act of building, regardless of its sensitivity to natural systems, uses resources in some way in the form of materials, processes, or operating energy. Building, in general, is incompatible with nature unless the act of building uses resources in a sustainable way (i.e., uses renewable resources). This is how the natural world works. In a forest, for example, there is no such thing as garbage or waste. A healthy tree uses the by-products of fallen trees to grow more vigorously; it uses leaves, soil, and rainwater to sustain growth. When it dies, it falls to the forest floor and a new growth process starts again. There is no concept of waste in nature; the by-products of one system are food for another.[9]

Common construction practices produce the human product called waste. Leftover materials, energy needed during construction, fuel used in transportation, and energy used for operation and maintenance use natural resources and do not "give back" to the environment. In a sense, most buildings and other design projects accomplish the goal of providing for human needs, but they do not address the "zero waste" model demonstrated by the natural world.

> The earth is a bank account, except [that] we only take out. You have to replenish; you have to put it back in. Western civilization in the 20th century has done virtually nothing but take out. When are we going to start putting it all back in?[10]

There has been a recent trend in all aspects of design called "sustainability." The proponents of sustainable practices ask that the built environment use resources at the same rate at which they are replenished. Sustainable design is a practice that provides for human needs while helping to ensure that the natural environment is not compromised and, hopefully, is enhanced by human actions. Until technology can ensure that the "bank account" is balanced, it is suggested that another term be used: **ecological design**. "Ecological" (rather than "sustainable") is preferred in discussing technology since humans are not yet sustaining the natural world. Ecological design acknowledges the inherent unsustainable nature of development and tries its best to "design with nature."

It should also be understood that technology always responds to requirements placed on it by society. What is

Figure 6-5 A spiderweb network of tension structures by Frei Otto, 1972, Munich, Germany (T. Bartuska).

deemed appropriate at one point in history, or in one particular culture, may not be considered at all appropriate in another context. This is discussed later in this chapter.

Static Objects in a Dynamic Universe

Objects built by humans and placed in the environment are temporary. This is because they are static objects with a limited capacity to adapt to changes in the surrounding natural environment.

The entire physical world is most properly regarded as a great energy system: an enormous marketplace in which one form of energy is forever being traded for another form according to set rules and values. That which is energetically advantageous is that which will sooner or later happen. In one sense, a structure is a device that exists in order to delay some event, which is energetically favored. It is energetically advantageous, for instance, for a weight to fall to the ground, for strain energy to be released, and so on. Sooner or later, the weight will fall to the ground and the strain energy will be released; but it is the business of a structure to delay such events for a season, for a lifetime, or for thousands of years. All structures will be broken or destroyed in the end, just as all people will die in the end. It is the purpose of medicine and engineering to postpone these occurrences for a decent interval.[11]

In the natural environment, some locations are more susceptible to violent dynamic changes than others. One useful application of technology is the ability to identify those locations that are most likely to experience the hostile effects of change. Those sites that are most sensitive to the effects of strong winds, flooding, or earthquakes (seismic events) can be identified using the tools provided by modern technology. Public policy, **land-use planning**, and **design guidelines** can be implemented so that these sites are avoided and conflicts between static objects and the dynamic environment are minimized.

Unfortunately, political concerns and economic considerations often take precedence over ecological sustainable design and land-use planning. Coastal regions, susceptible to hurricanes and tsunamis, may be the most dynamic environments of all. Yet, these regions have been developed, even recently, to a dangerous degree. For example, the coastal regions of Florida and the Gulf Coast states have experienced dramatic increases in population and property development, with very little regard for potential hurricane activity. Many schools, hospitals, and other essential facilities in California have been located close to clearly defined seismic faults. The prediction capability provided by modern technology has been largely ignored in these decisions. When natural disastrous events occur, society pays dearly (in loss of life and the economic, social, and ecological costs of rebuilding or of relocating the residents of devastated areas).

As a result of inappropriate land-use planning and settlement patterns, many problems and conflicts have arisen. These add unnecessarily to those already inherent in the design process. Those responsible for unwise land-use development have sometimes belatedly turned to technology, requiring solutions to these conflicts. This, of course, is not appropriate technology. At best, technology can provide only temporary relief from these problems, often with devastating effects on the natural environment.

Judgment is an important component in the application of technology. The natural environment cannot be controlled, or even successfully modified, at the whim of shortsighted politicians or real estate developers. When technology is asked to address problems that should have been avoided by foresight, appropriate planning, and enlightened leadership, the results are generally unsuccessful.

Overview of Built Environment Technologies

There are many specialized technologies involved in the creation of the built environment. Designers identified with each of the technologies devote their skills and creative energies to the resolution of specific conflicts in their areas of expertise. Some of these specialized technologies that are making significant contributions to the design of the built environment are listed below.

- **Structural Engineering**: the design of systems that span and enclose space for human activities. Structural engineers rely on a number of other disciplines, such as geotechnical engineering, foundation engineering, and fracture mechanics.
- **Heating, Ventilating, and Air Conditioning (HVAC)**: the technology that modifies interior thermal and humidity conditions to support human activities. This discipline has become more prominent in the past few decades because of concerns about energy conservation, combined with increased expectations for environmental comfort. HVAC system design includes both passive (working with nature) and active (mechanical equipment) technologies.
- **Electrical Engineering**: the development of electrical energy resources and the design of systems that supply and distribute energy in the built environment.
- **Sanitation Engineering and Plumbing Design**: distribution systems for supply and waste products in buildings and communities. Conservation and/or recycling of water resources have become important issues.
- **Lighting or Illumination Engineering**: the design of systems and products that provide general and task illumination, including artificial systems and daylighting.
- **Acoustical Engineering**: the control of unwanted noise, and the enhancement of desirable sound in buildings and the environment.
- **Communications Engineering**: the design of systems that contribute to efficiencies or safety through communication, including computer technologies.
- **Data Processing**: emerging technologies that help to control response to changing environmental conditions. This specialty is finding applications in each of the specialized technologies.
- **Conveying Systems Design**: the design of systems that move people or products either horizontally or vertically, such as escalators, elevators, and industrial conveying systems.
- **Materials Science**: research in the development or application of new materials for the built environment.
- **Detailing Specialists**: construction techniques for combining materials, such as in building curtain wall systems.
- **Fire Safety Engineering**: a new and rapidly developing profession that specializes in the mitigation of the effects of fire in the built environment.

Figure 6-6 An excellent example of systems integration: Stansted Airport by Norman Foster & Associates, north of London, England (T. Bartuska).

- **Construction Management, Equipment, and Process Technology**: the construction of quality components of the built environment safely and economically.
- **Security Engineering**: planning and design of systems that increase the level of security for buildings and their occupants, including enhancement of resistance to terrorism.
- **Forensic Engineering**: investigating and reporting on failures and performance deficiencies in buildings for the purpose of improving design and construction practices.

Each of these technologies is evolving rapidly as contemporary design becomes more complicated. The process of designing the built environment has become more technically challenging, requiring specialists in each of these disciplines. Successful design of constructed facilities must be the result of a team approach, with each specialist serving as a consultant to the team. It has become impossible for a single individual to maintain the necessary knowledge or skills in all the specialized technologies required for design of any work of significant scale. Chapters 16 and 17 will expand upon the important role engineering and construction management play in the development of the built environment.

The Role of Collaboration and Coordination

The complexity of most design and construction projects usually creates the need for a team-oriented and integrated approach to design. A **collaborative** approach, while necessary, may result in design solutions that lack coordination or unity. There is a definite need for a single creative individual or a small group to act as design **coordinator**. Such a coordinator must assemble information from each of the specialized consultants and synthesize that information into a cohesive solution.

Quality design, whether it involves a single project or planning the development of an entire region, has always exhibited the need for integration, harmony, and overall coordination. The spaces, buildings, landscapes, and communities to which we respond most favorably are those where conscious effort has gone into the selection and integration of systems that enhance one another. The solutions that are not satisfactory tend to contain contradictory or incompatible elements.

The professional orientation of the coordinator will vary, depending upon the scale of the project. Often, on large-scale projects, the coordinator is a landscape architect, urban planner, and/or regional planner. Sometimes the coordinator is an interior designer, architect, engineer, or construction manager. To be successful, the coordinator must be a generalist, having the ability to understand and appreciate the role of others, communicate effectively with each of the specialists, and blend diverse issues and areas of expertise. The coordinator must be able to recognize the implications of individual decisions for the overall project design.

As knowledge in each of the technologies expands, the design team will include an ever-increasing number of specialized consultants. The role of the coordinator will become ever more important to achieve quality design in the future built environment.

Emerging Demands on Built Environment Technologies

Societal trends, demands, and expectations influence the evolution of technology. Changing settlement patterns and functional requirements have given rise to new technologies and revisions to traditional technologies throughout history. During the past century, societal changes have occurred at an unprecedented rate, placing extraordinary demands on technology.

Urbanization and Population Density

The trend toward centralization of the population that accompanied the Industrial Revolution forced the development of new technologies at increasing scales and densities. Building systems and community life-support systems that worked well for small population clusters simply did not work in the urban context with its greater density. Most of the technological developments that occurred as a result of urbanization have focused on the health and safety of large groups of people living in close proximity.

Technology has responded to the demands of urbanization in many successful ways. The technology is available to develop dense urban environments. Many of the problems associated with urban density, however, are social or political problems, beyond the scope of technological solutions. Consider the skyscraper, for example, made possible by the development of technologies responding to urban density requirements. While even taller buildings are now technologically possible, there is need for further research on their social and ecological implications.

Figure 6-7 One of the world's tallest buildings: The 109-story Sears Tower by Skidmore, Owings & Merrill, 1974, Chicago, Illinois (T. Bartuska).

The consequences to the urban environment of close grouping of tall buildings are of utmost importance. The impact of the scale of some of the superskyscrapers on the city, such as the 109-story Sears Tower in Chicago, more than a quarter-mile high, is apparent. The building's electrical system can serve a city of 147,000 people, and its air conditioning complex can cool 6,000 one-family houses. A total of 102 elevators are needed to distribute about 16,500 daily users to different parts of the building. Visualize the many elevators as equivalent to a dead-end street system and the sky lobbies as plazas where people pass from one part of the building to another either by nonstop, double-deck, express elevators to the next sky lobby or by local low-speed shuttle elevators. Since the building contains all necessary services and amenities, theoretically the people never have to leave it. The support facilities, such as transportation, parking, utilities, water and sewage services, and waste collection, are equivalent to the services needed for a small city. A building of this scale forms a city within a city. The design of such an intricate interacting system requires systematic programming of the social, ecological, economic, and political effects exerted not just on the surrounding urban context, but also on its own environment.[12]

Historic versus Contemporary Buildings

As technologies have developed, it has become possible to design things that were never before imagined. For this reason, society has placed greater and greater demands on technologies. Larger, more complicated designs have been made possible, and society has come to expect this complexity, often with little regard to the cost in energy and material resources. Society has come to expect a greater degree of comfort and the ability to modify environments instantly, again with little concern for the cost in energy utilization.

Prior to the development of modern "artificial" technologies, a building had to respond to contextual environmental conditions; otherwise, it could not function as a habitable environment. For example, dimensions and configurations of spaces and buildings were limited so that daylighting and natural ventilation potential could be maximized. Many historic buildings rely on the mass of masonry bearing walls to provide constant thermal conditions throughout the daily thermal cycle. Environmental criteria influenced the selection of materials, plan configuration, and site orientation.

One of the benefits of adaptive reuse or conservation of historic structures is the minimal external energy required for these buildings compared to contemporary buildings. Many of these historic buildings are excellent examples of a creative response to natural environmental conditions. Compatibility with the natural environment was essential—the only way in which comfort could be achieved. Equipment was simply not available to provide comfort to the occupants. Such buildings provide lessons in the application of appropriate technologies (those that are integral with natural systems).

With the tools and equipment of modern technology, it has become possible to ignore the natural context in the design of structures. Large groups of people are housed in spaces deep within buildings, far from exterior walls and windows. Equipment is available to provide comfort to the occupants—an unprecedented degree of comfort—with little concern for the natural environment. Building forms have evolved that have no relationship to natural systems. In the societal context and at the time these buildings were developed, they were considered an appropriate response.

However, we now understand that there has been a cost associated with this movement away from compatibility with the natural environment. When energy costs were less, the high-technology building, with its limitless complexity and planning freedom, was considered a bargain. Only recently has society begun to realize the substantial human and environmental costs of solving problems without concern for natural systems.

As society has awakened to the fact that energy and material resources are finite in quantity, the current definition of appropriate technology has emerged. Traditional forms based on rational natural principles are again appearing in all the components of the built world. Fresh air and daylight are now seen as desirable, perhaps even preferable to conditioned air and artificial light.

Natural versus Artificial Systems

New appropriate technologies are rapidly emerging and evolving. Research is under way in many disciplines to identify solutions that are more compatible with the natural environment. These solutions promise a greater level of sustainability.

It is important to note that this activity is not a turning away from technology, but instead represents an evolution in technology. The "natural" technologies require at least as much artistic and scientific creativity as do the artificial ones. In many ways, a higher level of intellectual and intuitive skill is required to successfully design functional daylighting or nonmechanical ventilation systems than is required to address the same problems with typical energy-consuming systems and equipment.

But the rewards of such efforts are already evident. Carefully designed building projects are now collecting a high percentage of the energy they require from the sun, demonstrating that a reasonable degree of comfort is possible. Larger buildings illustrate that compatibility with nature can be aesthetically and economically desirable. New materials and systems are designed to enhance natural processes rather than conflict with them. Along with these developments, society will need to reevaluate comfort requirements and other demands placed upon the built environment technologies if significant efficiencies are truly valued.

Designs that incorporate naturally driven technologies save energy, money, and resources, but a more important result is clear—people like them. Buildings that use passive heating and cooling systems, natural lighting systems, and other new trends in design are simply healthier, more effective, and desirable. For businesses, this means fewer worker absences and higher profits for the company. Good design is proving to be a good investment, and the natural environment is reaping the benefits as well.

Conclusion

Technology is the means employed to resolve conflicts between what the natural environment provides and what humans need. Technology is necessary for human sustenance and comfort. Society is a dynamic community, constantly redefining its needs and comfort requirements. Technology, throughout the history of the built environment, has responded to society's changing demands.

Appropriate technology has been defined as technology that is compatible with the natural environment while simultaneously providing for human needs. Within the context of this definition, technology can be inappropriately applied or applied to inappropriate problems. All objects in the built environment are temporary, but those based on appropriate technologies have the greatest opportunity for survival.

The application of technology is a creative activity involving both art and science. Design in the built environment has become a complicated activity, relying on many technical specialists, each employing both artistic and scientific judgment. A collaborative team approach to design and planning has become essential, along with the need for a coordinator to provide integration and unity in the final solution. Quality design, planning, and engineering, now and in the future, will always require creative integration of appropriate technologies.

References

Benyus, J. *Biomimicry: Innovation Inspired by Nature*. William Morrow, 1997.

Carper, K. *Forensic Engineering*, 2nd ed. CRC Press, 2001.

Carper, K. *Why Buildings Fail*. National Council of Architectural Registration Boards, 2001.

Engel, H. *Structure Systems*. Praeger, 1978.

Gordon, J. *Structures, or Why Things Don't Fall Down*. Penguin Books, 1978.

McDonough, W., and M. Braungart. *Cradle to Cradle: Remaking the Way We Make Things*. North Point Press, 2002.

McHarg, I. "Energy and the Built Environment: A Conceptual Framework." Lecture given to the ACSA Summer Institute on Energy Conscious Design, Harvard University, 1978.

Salvadori, M. *Why Buildings Stand Up: The Strength of Architecture*. W. W. Norton, 1980.

Schueller, W. *High-Rise Building Structures*. Wiley, 1997.

Wines, J. Video interview on "Ecological Design: Reinventing the Future." Knossus Publishing, 1994.

Wines, J. *Green Architecture: The Art of Architecture in the Age of Ecology*. Taschen, 2000.

Zollner, F. *Leonardo da Vinci 1452 to 1519: Sketches and Drawings*. Taschen, 2000.

Endnotes

1. I. McHarg, "Energy and the Built Environment: A Conceptual Framework," lecture given to the ACSA Summer Institute on Energy Conscious Design (Harvard University, 1978).
2. See Note 1.
3. *Webster's Seventh New Collegiate Dictionary*, 1977. G.C. Merriam, 1977.
4. *Webster's Encyclopedic Unabridged Dictionary of the English Language* (Gramercy Books, 1996).
5. See Note 3.
6. See Note 3.
7. See Note 3.
8. H. Engel, *Structure Systems* (Praeger, 1978).
9. W. McDonough and M. Braungart, *Cradle to Cradle: Remaking the Way We Make Things* (North Point Press, 2002).
10. J. Wines, Video interview on "Ecological Design: Reinventing the Future" (Knossus Publishing, 1994).
11. J. Gordon, *Structures, or Why Things Don't Fall Down* (Penguin Books, 1978).
12. W. Schueller, *High-Rise Building Structures* (Wiley, 1997).

CHAPTER 7

Designing with a Visual Language: Elements and Ordering Systems

Gregory A. Kessler

In this chapter, the built environment is explored through investigation of selected elements and ordering systems of design. Design elements and ordering systems are employed by designers to integrate, articulate, and communicate ideas, beliefs, and social values in the built environment.

The built environment is composed of many elements and components. A building, landscape, or interior space utilizes a common series of elements in order to create a comprehensive functional, experiential, and symbolic environment. The built environment communicates ideas, values, and beliefs that reflect the material culture of our civilization. In this way, our spaces and places can be understood as a language of communication in the same way that our written and verbal language allows us to communicate with each other.

A designer can utilize the language of design to communicate—to individuals, groups, and society at large—ideas, emotions, values, and beliefs. Design can project somber and serious emotions or can be humorous, ironic, and sensual. The types of experiences and values that can be expressed in the built environment evolve from many sources. Examples include the function or use of a place; the history, culture, or social value; and the surrounding context. Designers can utilize a series of sources that help to determine the nature of what will be

expressed through the built environment. Ultimately, in designing a place, designers need to be mindful that all the built and natural elements (content, components, and context) express and communicate some type of meaning. The act of design and construction goes beyond the boundaries of simply providing shelter when it creates places that communicate ideas, feelings, and emotions and provokes thought.

This chapter discusses three important aspects of a design language. The first aspect identifies five elements of the built environment that serve as building blocks, a developing alphabet if you will, for the language of design. The second identifies means of assembling the elements into comprehensive ordering systems that are placed in the landscape, and the third identifies rationales that designers may use for selecting certain ordering systems and their means of expression through specific elements.

The Elements of a Visual Language

In order for our written and spoken language to have meaning, there are rules and elements for organizing it. Nouns, verbs, adjectives, pronouns, etc. form the basis for organizing words into sentences, which in turn are used to construct paragraphs that convey coherent ideas. In the same way, elements of the built environment can be composed to create and convey ideas or values that the designer wishes to communicate. In this part of the chapter, five elements of design are presented. It is important to remember that these elements can be utilized to form a foundation of design for application to multiple contexts and at multiple scales of resolution, including interiors, structures, landscapes, spaces, and urban designs. Most projects will generally utilize all of the elements, but whatever the intent, elements are organized into more integrated designs.

1. Vertical Elements: Columns, Poles, Trees

In the language of design, vertical elements are most often displayed by the use of columns. Columnar elements can be made from many different materials, such as stone, concrete, and wood, as well as water and vegetation (Fig. 7-1).

The essential purpose of columns is to establish vertical relationships. Columns can be used to establish relationships with the earth and sky, as well as with horizontal elements such as floors. As an example, the French architect Corbusier utilized columns in a structural manner that he called "piloti." This system established a series of relationships with other building elements such as floors, walls, and windows that allowed Corbusier to establish what he called the "domino system." In the Villa Savoye, the domino system allows the façade and windows to be free of structure so that they can provide opportunities for humans to experience the landscape through ribbon windows and the sky through roof gardens. At the same time, this system allows the building to engage the earth softly, creating a sense of openness and transparency at ground level. Corbusier was well aware of the effect that the columns would have on his building. His ideas were

linked with concepts concerning how humans should live in the modern technological world.

Columns can also be created using landscape materials and vegetation. For example, the architect Luis Barragan often uses columns of water in his gardens. Such columns used as focal points within gardens unite the ground plane with the sky. Landscape architects may also use trees to create vertical connections between earth and sky. Certain types of trees (such as cypress and lombardy poplar) have a columnar structure and can be used to create vertical experiences. Many of the Moorish gardens in Spain, northern Italy, and southern France incorporate the cypress tree and columns of water to help engage the Mediterranean sky with the garden.

2. Vertical Planes: Walls, Fences, Hedges

Vertical planar elements such as walls, fences, berms, and hedgerows are other elements of design that can be used in creating the built environment (Fig. 7-2). The architect Tadao Ando often uses walls as the primary element in organizing his buildings. In his Church of the Light and his St. Louis Art Museum, walls are the principal means by which space is enclosed. Vertical planes are used to define a specific enclosure or activity and also provide a sense of refuge from the outside world.

Walls are often used in Islamic gardens in the same way. The creation of a lush, beautiful garden full of water and aromatic flowers symbolizes the earthly representation of paradise. In these gardens, walls provide a secure and protected enclosure from the harsh desert climate.

Like columns, walls can be made from landscape elements. Shrubs can be situated to create a hedge or wall of vegetation. In the same way, trees can be planted closely together to create large walls that form a natural enclosure or separation between activities. Buildings in cities positioned close to one another form walls and define the streetscape. An excellent example of this is Central Park in New York, where buildings align the outside perimeter of the boundary streets to form a wall that defines the park.

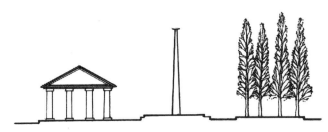

Figure 7-1 Vertical elements such as buildings, columns, symbols, and vegetation.

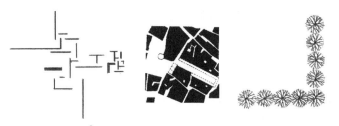

Figure 7-2 Vertical planes of cities, streetscapes, landscapes, and buildings.

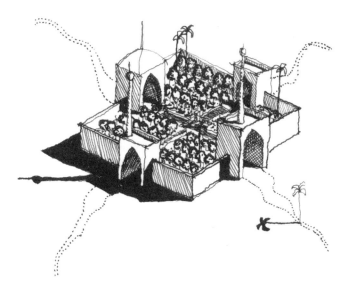

Figure 7-3 Paradise as a garden contained within walls.

3. Horizontal Planes: Floors, Terraces

A third element of the language of design is horizontal elements such as floor planes and horizontal roofs (Fig. 7-4). Horizontal planes comprise the surfaces that we walk upon, as well as surfaces above.

Horizontal planes can be used to create unique experiences within buildings and the landscape. These "floors" can include horizontal or inclined planes used to extend or reach into the natural landscape or urban terrace. They can be elevated off the ground, placed on the ground, or embedded in the ground. Each condition will establish a unique set of circumstances and experiences relative to the relationship between the natural and built environments.

In Mies Van Der Rohe's Farnsworth House (Fig. 7-5), floor planes elevated off the ground and horizontal roof planes are used as the dominant elements to provide a sense of lightness. The elevated floors create the feeling that the floors float above the ground plane, which seems to continue indefinitely into the surrounding landscape.

Like the two previous elements, landscape elements can be utilized as floors. For example, expanses of lawn, fields, and meadows may be seen as floors that provide soft surfaces for walking and sitting.

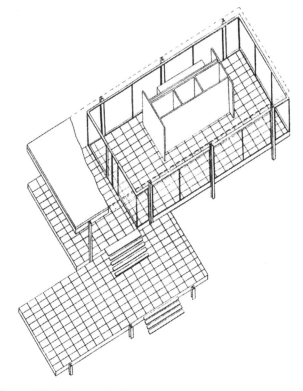

Figure 7-5 Horizontal planes of the Farnsworth House by Mies Van der Rohe (Washington State University student).

Floors can also be made and experienced through the use of water. In front of the palace of the Chehel Sutun in Isfahan, Iran, also called the Palace of Forty Columns, (Fig. 7-6), is a large pool of water that serves as a floor, providing a mirror to reflect the building. Although there are 20 columns that actually support the building,

Figure 7-4 Horizontal elements such as floors, water, terraces, and land.

Figure 7-6 Horizontal planes and vertical elements (real and reflected columns), Sutun Palace in Isfahan, Iran.

the floor of water provides the illusion of an additional 20, resulting in the image of a building possessing 40 columns.

4. Diagonal Elements: Stairs, Ramps

Diagonal elements, such as stairs and ramps, provide a utilitarian component in design allowing humans to move between floors and traverse topography in the landscape (Fig. 7-7). At the same time, these elements can be used to provide unique experiences. By simply varying the rise-to-tread ratio or the width, stairs can be integrated into a building or place to create sensations of uncertainty, mystery, grandeur, or formalism. Luis Barragan often utilized width, structure, and materials to create stairs that evoke a feeling of the unknown as well as to provide privacy.

Designs for diagonal elements that move between different levels in the built environment can include water to create a variety of expectations. The garden of Nishat Bagh in the province of Kashmir utilizes water to mirror the stair configuration leading from the upper levels of the garden. Water can also be incorporated into other stair-stepped elements. For example, in the garden of the Generalife in Granada, Spain, one of the stairs leading from or to the upper garden utilizes water in the handrail, creating a dynamic and audible element in the stair.

5. Openings: Gateways, Doors, Windows

Openings, as expressed through elements such as gateways, doors, and windows, etc. also contribute to the language of the built environment. Windows and doors serve as portals to rooms and to the landscape and/or cityscape beyond. They mediate between inside and outside environments. We normally take gateways, doors, and windows for granted, but they can be some of the most important and experiential qualities in the built environment. Windows can be focused on the horizon, sky, or earth. When placed correctly, they help to intensify the interaction between humans and their surroundings. Opening placement, height, depth, and orientation

Figure 7-7 Diagonal elements such as stairs, waterfalls, sloped landscapes, and hills.

help people integrate buildings and places. Local conditions such as sun location, precipitation, or wind influence the placement and size of windows and doors. As mentioned earlier, in the Villa Savoye, Corbusier used horizontal ribbon windows distributed across the façade to provide a sense of connection to the horizon. Likewise, Tadao Ando in his Church of the Light utilized windows symbolically. The window at the front of the church creates a cross in the concrete wall and serves as a focal point.

The architect Peter Zumthor also uses windows to create unique experiences. Many of his windows filter light to create a soft glow, and in some instances provide light of a certain color. This is also true of Steven Holl's chapel at Seattle University, where soft lights of various colors in different parts of the chapel evoke a meditative mood. The entrance to the building is exaggerated by the use of a large, heavy, textured door, which helps to symbolize the entrance to a sacred place.

Like other elements, plant materials and vegetation can be used to create windows or portals to other places or spaces. Deliberate voids in planting materials can create openings that serve as windows. In the same way, trees planted in certain configurations can provide openings to view particular events.

Summary

The five elements discussed here help to create a language of the built environment. Understanding their role and limitations is most important for creating exceptional places. Part II of this chapter considers how different elements are assembled to form a comprehensive ordering system of design.

Ordering Systems in the Language of Design

How do designers organize the five basic design elements into meaningful compositions? Various ordering systems are used. For example, walls may be used to form a linear ordering system, as in the city of Isfahan, or a radial system, as in the city of Palma Nova. Ordering systems are applicable to many different scales of design, ranging from the large urban scale to buildings, landscapes, and interiors, and even products and graphic design. In each of the examples considered here, a predominant element is utilized to express a particular ordering system. Although a design may feature a combination of several ordering systems, one system will generally serve to organize it. The ordering systems can be designed as **formal** or **informal** compositions. Formal designs are those that are highly controlled and often symmetrical, whereas informal compositions can be more casual, asymmetrical, organic, and/or dynamic.

Five ordering systems are presented here: linear, radial, grid, courtyard, and repetitive. Each system, when used appropriately, responds to a unique set of circumstances such as use, cultural forces, landscape, and topography. These forces, and others, are utilized by insightful designers to determine the best system for establishing a particular language of design.

1. Linear Systems

Linear systems are often utilized if the designer wants to develop a sequence of experiences or a hierarchy leading to an important space, icon, or event. They can be utilized at the urban scale, as well as at the individual building and garden scale. Linear systems can be created by the use of columns, walls, stairs, or other elements. The city of Isfahan in Iran (Fig. 7-8) is an excellent example of a linear ordering system: the Chahar Bagh forms an informal central linear axis that stretches for several miles. Perpendicular to the main axis is a series of formal gardens and religious schools. In the original city plan, a single water trough lined with trees on either side ran the entire length of the street, which reinforced its linearity. It is said that the inhabitants of the city filled the trough with fresh flower petals each day in order to fill the city with a sweet aroma. The bazaar in the city of Isfahan is an informal example of a linear system that undulates in what seems to be a flowing or organic manner. The segmented pattern, which was developed over time, creates a unique series of spaces and experiences.

Another example of an informal linear system is the Baker Dormitory at the Massachusetts Institute of Technology. In this building, designed by the Finnish architect Alvar Aalto, the linear system is undulating in response to the adjacent Charles River. Rooms and dining spaces are organized to take full advantage of the river view. The dormitory illustrates how ordering systems evolve as a result of contextual forces.

2. Radial Systems

Radial systems are most often used when designers wish to create a central space or building as a focal point.

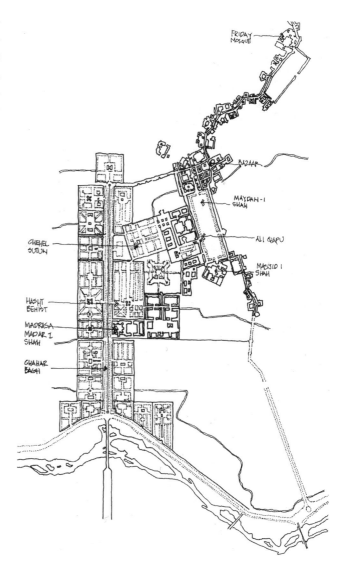

Figure 7-8 Informal (bazaar and river) and formal (gardens) linear systems in Isfahan, Iran.

Streets, rooms, and circulation paths generally radiate from the focal point. The radial spines are then often linked together by secondary streets or circulation. The city of Palma Nova in Italy serves as a classic example of a formal radial system. The radial pattern is clearly evident emanating from the central open space through a series of streets terminating in a wall that rings the entire city. The city of Detroit (Fig. 7-9) was originally organized as a radial plan. The symmetry and defined hierarchy are harmonious and fit the Platonic ideal of perfect geometry and order.

Another example of a radial system is the Piazza de Popolo in Rome. Three radial streets intersect the piazza and move from there to engage the city. The enclosed open space of the piazza becomes the focal point.

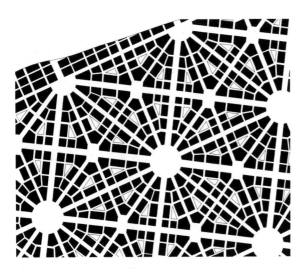

Figure 7-9 Proposed radial plan for the city of Detroit (Washington State University student).

3. Grid Systems

Grid systems are utilized in many different forms and types. In the United States the grid has been the dominant system for organizing cities, particularly in the West. Thomas Jefferson believed that the grid was the best expression for a democratic country in which egalitarianism and the rights of all were to be protected. For Jefferson, the grid was the perfect manifestation for a new and optimistic country. The Jeffersonian grid was seen as a way of ordering the western landscape and taming a wilderness. Jefferson's grid was superimposed on the land as a survey system still in use today, utilizing a hierarchy of ranges, townships and sections (as discussed in Chapter 3).

Historically, the grid was used in the earliest cities of Mesopotamia and Greece and was continued in Roman

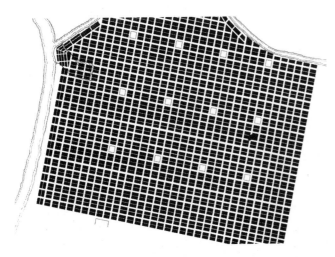

Figure 7-10 Typical Jeffersonian grid (Washington State University student).

cities. Roman grid cities evolved from military camps that were organized for efficiency and order. Grid cities are often perceived as unimaginative and uninspired. However, some of the most beautiful cites today utilize grid systems. One example is Savannah, Georgia, founded by the Englishman George Oglethorpe as a debtor's colony. His city featured a series of open spaces or squares set in the midst of each grid integrating landscape with the city. Facing each open space were civic buildings such as churches used to unite the inhabitants of the city. Savannah demonstrates how grids can be designed to create a very beautiful and exceptional place.

There are many other examples of the grid system in both buildings and landscape. Architects such as Corbusier, Kahn, and van der Rohe used the grid to organize the plans of many of their buildings, as well as structural and circulation systems. The Yale Center for British Art, designed by Kahn, is an excellent example of the grid system. Though often criticized as mundane and banal, in the hands of thoughtful designers the grid can be an excellent means of integrating human settlements with their surroundings. The landscape architect Frederick Law Olmsted designed Riverside, Illinois, with a formal grid pattern in the village center and then used an informal grid pattern to relate to the flowing river and organic landscape for the parks and residential area (see Chapter 2).

4. Courtyard Systems

Courtyard systems have a long tradition in many cultures throughout the world. Courtyards can be used to provide a sense of privacy and protection from both the outside world and climatic conditions. Courtyards also allow a focus on a central space—a garden or an enclosed space. One of the principal differences between a courtyard and a radial system is that courtyards are often surrounded by main circulation paths rather than radiating from the central space.

As mentioned earlier, Islamic architecture is generally organized through courtyard systems, with gardens being the principal use of the court. The garden of the Generalife in Granada, Spain, is composed of a series of courtyards that provide beautiful, lush vegetation within a very condensed space (Fig. 7-11). Courtyard systems are also traditions in Spanish, Mexican, and Latin American cultures. In the United States, courtyard systems often appear in the Southwest, where Hispanic influences and warm climates are predominant. Courtyard systems work well in warm, dry climates, where the courtyard helps to cool the building through the circulation of air. Since the courtyard essentially doubles the

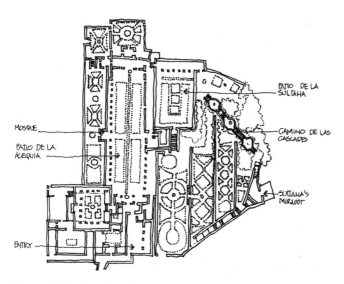

Figure 7-11 Courtyard gardens of the Generalife in Granada, Spain.

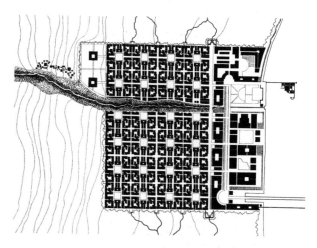

Figure 7-12 Repetitive system illustrated in an urban block structure.

surface perimeter of the building compared to traditional buildings, there is more opportunity for ventilation through doors and windows. Due to the increased perimeter of the building, courtyard systems are generally less effective in the cooler northern climates.

The architect Rick Joy, who practices in Tucson, Arizona, has utilized the courtyard system in many of his buildings. These unique structures, in response to climate, materials, and culture, incorporate many traditional methods of building in the desert environment. At the same time, their construction represents contemporary architecture. Joy has developed a unique ability to utilize the past while integrating it with current technologies and lifestyles.

5. Repetitive Systems

Design programs often call for repetition of a particular building element. Urban housing or high-density housing often utilizes a repetitive organization system (Fig. 7-12). In this design, the urban blocks and buildings are established through a repetition of open space and structures. Repetitive systems can provide a great variety of experiences at both the urban and building scales. Buildings or other places that require a modular system of design can also use the repetitive system. For example, in the Unité housing complex, in Marseille, France, Corbusier generated a modular system of housing types that were repeated both in plan and in section. Modules, when joined together, create a series of repetitive forms that can be seen and experienced through the building. The Unité project incorporates a repetitive (egg crate–like)

system in the elevation, reflecting the repetitive system used in the plan and section. Repetitive systems provide the opportunity to connect or group together similar parts that may be related to issues of use, experience, or expression.

Summary

The selected five systems present methods of organizing elements. It is important to note that many designed environments may utilize more than one of the systems mentioned, though one system generally predominates. A linear system, for example, may also have repetitive elements as part of the design. What is critical is that the designer be aware of the predominant system and use that system as a reference for design decisions.

Determining Rationales for a Language of Design

So far, the elements of design, along with specific ordering systems for expressing the language of design, have been discussed. One method for thinking about the elements of design and the ordering systems is to compare them to elements of written and spoken language. As noted earlier, elements of design can be equated to nouns, verbs, and adjectives, or to the parts or segments of sentences in language. The ordering systems of the built environment become the sentences, which unite the elements to provide a comprehensive experience and meaning. A city, landscape, building, and/or interior can be thought of as a story that describes the values, ideas, beliefs, and principles of individuals and cultures. This is one of the reasons that the built environment is so important and must be studied and designed with great conviction. How we build and what we build are a direct reflection of what humans and society value.

Determining which ordering system to use and the dominant element used to express the system is dependent upon many factors. Identified here are some of the rationales for selecting a system. The most important concept to remember however, is that each project is unique and engages a specific set of circumstances. Use of ordering systems and elements arises from the uniqueness of each project. Each of the projects discussed in this chapter has been conceived through the designer's understanding of a specific set of human/social/cultural, technological, or environmental forces.

The following rationales may be seen as forces that may determine ordering systems and define the use of predominant elements of design. It is important to remember that an ordering system and its predominant element are critically important choices that must be made with care. Selection should never be done arbitrarily or capriciously.

Physical Environment: Climate, Topography, Landscape

These three factors are often critical in determining which element will be dominant and which ordering system will be utilized. Islamic gardens are often organized in a courtyard system enclosed by walls to define a specific place. The harsh desert climate and the desire to create a garden of lush vegetation require that gardens be very compact, enclosed, and protected. Another environmental factor contributing to this system is the scarcity of water. The ability to utilize water and all other natural resources in the most efficient ways is critical to the success of the garden. Topography is also an important issue that may determine ordering systems and elements. A steeply sloped site, for example, may suggest that the building or garden traverse the hillside through a series of stairs or terraces or be composed in an informal linear pattern following a contour (level).

Culture, Typology, and Precedent

These three forces also play important roles in determining the language of a particular environment. As an example, many places have distinct linkages to the past through heritage and tradition. Buildings and landscapes are often tied to the history of a place, which in turn can

influence the language of that place. As an example, new buildings placed within a historic context need to be responsive to existing patterns of movement, materials, and structure. While the new building need not mimic older buildings, its ordering system and elements may be derived from existing conditions. In addition, cultural values and the building's position within that culture influence the particular system chosen. Designers must understand the role of culture and precedent in their projects. This is not to say that the best designs mimic history or try to establish a nostalgic link with the past. Rather, as humans we are inexorably linked with our past, and only through understanding our past can we move into the future.

Community, Client, and Utility

These three factors are also influential in the language of design. Unique community and client needs and desires will often determine the ordering mechanism of a place. Clients often have a direct impact on design through a particular type of environment or idea that they want to express. For example, in 1947 Le Corbusier began design of the city of Chandigarh in India (Fig. 7-13). Prime Minister Jawaharlal Nehru was very influential in the design, insisting that the new city reflect a new technological and modern image to advance India into a new age of democracy. Nehru's influence and direction were instrumental in developing the language of design for the new city. Le Corbusier's plan integrated a formal transit/vehicular grid with a more informal pedestrian walkways/park grid.

Utility plays an important role in establishing the ordering system. For example, some building types, such as jails and prisons, require linear or radial systems in

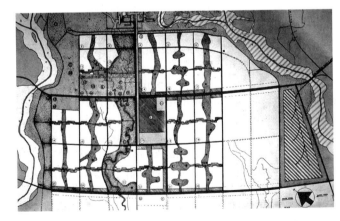

Figure 7-13 Formal (roads) and informal (rivers, pedestrian ways, and parks) linear systems, Chandigarh, India. © 2006 Artists Rights Society (ARS), New York/ADAGP, Paris/FLC.

order to maintain visual contact with inmates. Typically, buildings with complex programs and functional requirements, such as hospitals and some government buildings, have dramatic forms of organization. The designer's ability to understand these conditions and integrate them into an appropriate ordering system to create a supportive, meaningful place is critical.

Other forces impact the way a place may be organized, including view or orientation, as well as specific regulations such as zoning, local codes, and covenants. Ultimately, each designer must understand the total scope of the project and understand and assess the most important issues informing his or her decisions about ordering systems and elements.

Summary

This chapter identified selected elements and ordering systems of the built environment. Creation of the built environment is a reflection of cultural, technological, and environmental forces. Designers must be cognizant of these forces. The design professions are very complex,

and designers must be capable of managing many different forces simultaneously. Understanding the languages of the built environment allows designers to control their decisions. In many ways, the design professions require general as well as specific knowledge. Design professions unite the arts, sciences, and technology to make a comprehensive environment that serves human and societal needs and values and fits its context. The ability to understand the languages of design is important to all the design disciplines, as the built environment is the ultimate representation of our civilization.

References

Brookes, J. *Gardens of Paradise.* Meredith Press, 1987.

Ching, D. *Architecture: Form, Space and Order.* Van Nostrand Reinhold, 1979.

Clark, R., and M. Pause. *Precedents in Architecture.* Van Nostrand Reinhold, 1985.

Mann, W. *Space and Time in Landscape Architectural History.* Landscape Architecture Foundation, 1981.

Moore, C., W. Mitchell, and W. Turnbull, Jr. *Poetics of Gardens.* MIT Press, 1988.

Thiis-Evensen, T. *Archetypes in Architecture.* Norwegian University Press, 1987.

Introduction: The Design and Planning Components (Levels of Integration) in the Built Environment

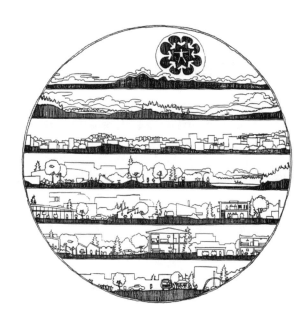

This part marks a transitional point in this study of the built environment.

Parts I and II explored various definitions and concepts intended to clarify the vast scope, purpose, and interrelated complexity of the built environment. Emphasis was placed on the importance of being inclusive, not exclusive, and of designing with an understanding of the complex human/social, environmental, and technological dimensions of our world. It is necessary to comprehend these issues and integrative concepts to fully appreciate the contributions each component can make to the humanly created world. Important terms and concepts from Parts I and II are summarized below:

- Definition of the built environment and its four characteristics
- The seven selected components of the built environment
- Why humans build: human needs and values
- Integrative design: holistic understanding of issues, art, science, and technology
- Five traditions: vernacular, high style, speculative, participatory, and conservation/sustainability
- Understanding the meanings of the term environment(s) and related descriptive adjectives
- Levels of integration, analysis, and synthesis
- Quality: integration of the triad of relationships, maximizing health and fitness while minimizing costs/impacts
- Triad of issues: human-environmental relationships (HE/HER) and adaptive design strategies, human/social, environmental, and technology (SET) and sustainability: social equity, environmental ecology and economic parity (SEE).
- Designing with people: culture, participatory design, and applications for human-environmental behavioral studies, particularly for marginalized populations such as the disabled or elderly

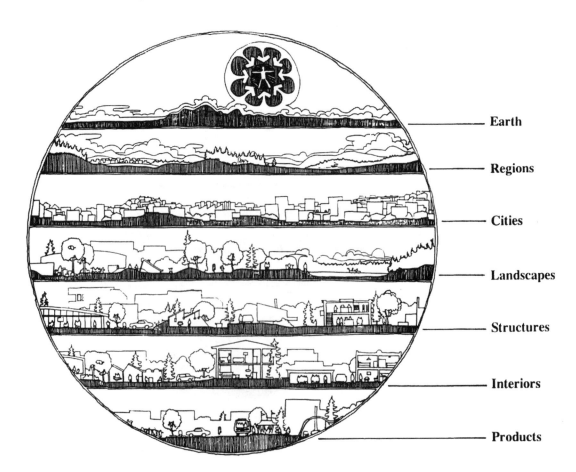

Figure III-1
Graphic logo illustrating levels of integration in the built environment (S. Recken and J. Singleton).

Earth

Regions

Cities

Landscapes

Structures

Interiors

Products

- Designing with environment(s): nature of the site, land, context, and climate
- Designing with technology: creativity, appropriate technologies, and coordination
- Designing with visual language: elements, ordering systems, and rationales

Part III explores in greater detail the characteristics and qualities of the selected **components** or **layers** within the built environment: **products-interiors-structures-landscapes-cities-regions-Earth**.

Each of the seven components also addresses in greater depth the human creative contribution, the people and professions that, individually and collaboratively, participate in the design and planning of the various components or layers, each adding to the others to form the overall built environment (Fig. III-1). The design and planning professionals are better understood as cooperative rather than competitive agents in the creative process. Through participation or collaborative teamwork, a more fitting and appropriate design can be developed, thereby integrating quality components into the total environment. These disciplines (as areas of study) and professions (as areas of practice) are commonly and collectively referred to as the **environmental design disciplines and professions**. The following list shows the seven selected components (on the left) and the related environmental design disciplines/professions (on the right) that collaborate in design, maintenance, and construction of the built environment.

Products: Industrial Designers, Graphic Designers, Artists, and Craftspeople
Interiors: Interior Designers and Architects
Structures: Architects, Engineers, and Construction Managers
Landscapes: Landscape Architects and Planners
Cities: Urban Designers, Planners, and Managers
Regions: Regional Planners, Managers, and Environmental Scientists
Earth: Environmental Scientists and Global Planners

Fundamental to the study of this pervasive and, at times, evasive subject is to integrate and apply the overall definitions and concepts to the study of each component. The reader will be continually challenged to put all the pieces of the puzzle together, to ask whether issues and design/planning ideas and ideals are isolated or integrated, and to fully address each component in context with the others. The sections in this part of the book, each with several chapters, peel back and examine the layers that reveal the primary components that need to be interwoven into the intricate and beautiful tapestry of the built world. Each set of chapters explores **past** (the historic development), **present** (contemporary issues and development), and **future** challenges.

The seven selected components are **layers** that are organized and tabulated into sections, as illustrated in Figure III-2.

Products: Component 1 Introduction and Chapters 8 and 9
Interior: Component 2 Introduction and Chapters 10, 11, and 12
Structures: Component 3 Introduction and Chapters 13, 14, and 15; 16 (Engineering); and 17 (Construction Management).
Landscapes: Component 4 Introduction and Chapters 18, 19, and 20
Cities: Component 5 Introduction and Chapters 21, 22, 23, and 24
Regions: Component 6 Introduction and Chapters 25, 26, and 27
Earth: Component 7 Introduction and Chapters 28 and 29

The reader will find some overlap between the components and between the various design and/or planning professionals' roles. In general, each set of professionals specializes in one level but extends to the margins of others.

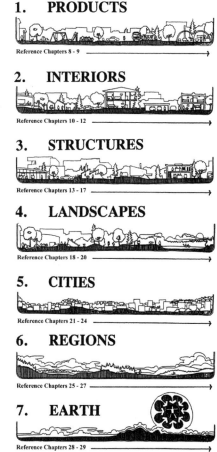

1. **PRODUCTS**
Reference Chapters 8 - 9

2. **INTERIORS**
Reference Chapters 10 - 12

3. **STRUCTURES**
Reference Chapters 13 - 17

4. **LANDSCAPES**
Reference Chapters 18 - 20

5. **CITIES**
Reference Chapters 21 - 24

6. **REGIONS**
Reference Chapters 25 - 27

7. **EARTH**
Reference Chapters 28 - 29

Figure III-2 The seven selected levels of the built environment (J. Singleton).

Quality emerges if each professional is aware of overlapping responsibilities, conveys respect for others, and encourages cooperation, collaboration, and teamwork. **Integration** is key to quality design. Environmental designers/planners, to be successful in a larger or holistic sense, must comprehend interrelationships while fully identifying with the specific characteristics and requirements of each area of specialization. In other words, designers/planners need to be generalists with an area of specialization or, as the great inventor, architect, and futurist R. Buckminster Fuller stated, they should provide for "macro comprehension and micro incisive solutions."[1]

The special aspects of each component or professional role can be defined by differing **space/time perspectives** (Fig. III-3). For example, a product or interior designer deals with a smaller scale than a landscape architect or urban planner. The **human-environmental-technological** variables are similar in kind but are applied at different scales. Also, the time required to design and/or plan at each scale or level of resolution is different. For example, interior designers may take a few weeks or months to design a space, whereas the urban planner may need years, even decades, to change the design of a city or region. These temporal differences should be understood and appreciated. They should also be matched with each individual's personal traits, talents, and interests. If a person's space/time perspective is compatible with the demands of the task at hand, the potential for successful engagement will be greater. A compatible, integrated space/time fit is necessary for each professional role, but just as important is that the public appreciates the differences in the space/time dimensions of each component and its associated design professional to arrive at a collective, integrated understanding of the built environment. Table III-1 below summarizes these space/time characteristics.

In addition to space/time perspectives, the type of client each design discipline works with is very different. Even though all environmental design disciplines are confronted with somewhat similar human/environmental/technical relationships, interior designers and architects may work with an individual or a family in the design of a home, while urban or regional planners are required to deal with the collective hopes and aspirations of people in large political or geographical regions. Landscape architects can deal with clients directly around a conference table, whereas urban/regional planners may have to deal with political representatives, take public surveys, and use public media to approach projects, programs, and policies at larger scales. Actually, it should be remembered that there are always **five clients** in most environmental design projects: the actual owner/client, the users, the site, members of the surrounding community or the general public, and the Earth.

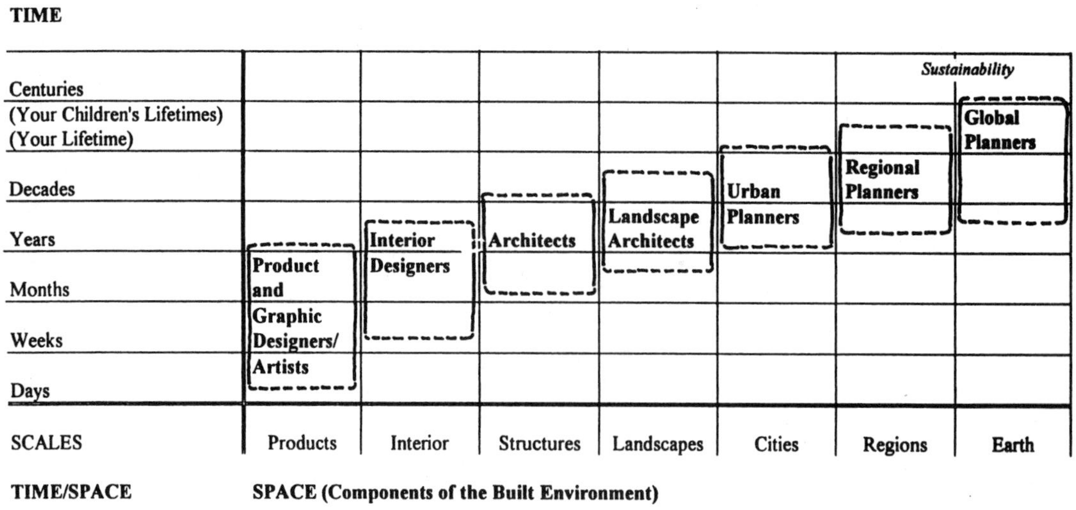

TIME

	Products	Interior	Structures	Landscapes	Cities	Regions	Earth
Centuries (Your Children's Lifetimes) (Your Lifetime)							*Sustainability* Global Planners
Decades					Urban Planners	Regional Planners	
Years		Interior Designers	Architects	Landscape Architects			
Months	Product and						
Weeks	Graphic Designers/						
Days	Artists						
SCALES	Products	Interior	Structures	Landscapes	Cities	Regions	Earth

TIME/SPACE   **SPACE (Components of the Built Environment)**

Figure III-3 Space/time perspective(s) of the environmental design disciplines/professions.

All the environmental design fields have a common professional mission—to develop a quality built environment for their clients. There are, of course, many differences in scale (from products to the Earth) and great variety in the variables each design discipline deals with. Commonalities enable all those engaged in design/planning to understand one another and collaborate more effectively on complex problems/opportunities in the built environment.

Also emerging from the following sections are working definitions of each design profession. By comparing the evolution of these definitions, one discovers additional similarities. In general, all the design professions deal with the **art** *and* **science** of creating their particular component of the built environment. This dual charge evolves from the arts (and crafts) and scientific, technological, and engineering discoveries of an advancing global society. Therefore, the design **professions** deal with the highest aspirations of the **art, craft,** *and* **science(s)** of the built environment. The following four terms also imply **quality** by the inclusion of the following definitions and related characteristics:

- **Art:** Skill in performance acquired by experience, study or observation, and ingenuity
- **Craft:** An art trade or occupation (referencing profession) requiring special skills; to make or manufacture (objects, products, etc.) with skill and careful attention to detail
- **Science:** Knowledge obtained by studying and experiments; accumulated knowledge, discovery of general truths or operation of general laws (technologies and engineering, including physical, biological, human/social/psychological, and environmental sciences)
- **Profession:** A public declaration of an occupation to which one devotes oneself (licensing is required by most professions in order to protect human and societal health, safety, and welfare)

Robert Pirsig,[2] a popular yet probing author, argues that quality combines the arts and sciences: it is "a kind of harmony . . . to produce a complete structure of thought [and design] capable of uniting the separate languages of science and art into one."[3]

As noted, this part of the book is divided into seven sections, which explore multiple dimensions of the seven selected components of the built environment. Each level provides a context for smaller-scale components; and conversely, larger components act as an umbrella by providing a context for smaller components. Thus, products are the components of interiors, interiors are the components of structures, as each level nests within the next larger one in scale and scope. Conversely, cities provide a context for landscapes and structures, structures for interiors, and interiors for products. These seven components interlock and form the **content-components-context** of this study of the built environment. Each section contains several chapters and starts with an introduction to help remind the reader of the unifying definitions and concepts.

Table III-1 summarizes the environmental design disciplines, professionals, and consultants who participate and collaborate in the design and planning of the built environment. It is a useful guide relating employment and business opportunities in these environmental design, planning, and management fields. For further investigation, the table contains some national and international Web sites for further investigation (please note: the addresses of Web sites do change). It also provides numerous keywords for readers to pursue their own Internet explorations and discoveries.

Table III-1 The Environmental Design Disciplines/Professions

BUILT ENVIRONMENT COMPONENTS	DESIGN PROFESSIONS	DISCIPLINES WORKING AT THIS SCALE	SOME SUPPORT SPECIALISTS
Products	Industrial Designer	**Industrial Designer** **Product Designer** Designer Interior Designer Architect Furniture Designer Engineer	Graphic Artists and Illustrators CAD: Computer-Aided Design Textile Designers Costume Designers Manufacturer Representatives • Materials • Furniture • Appliances/Equipment • Lighting • Computers • Etc. Engineers Production Specialists Materials Scientists Context: See below ↓
Interiors	Interior Designer	**Interior Designer** Architect (Interiors) Interior Decorator Exhibit Designer Stage Designer Space Programmer	Content: See above ↑ Space Programmer CAD: Computer-Aided Design Architects and Engineers Functional Specialist • Hospital • Airport, Airplanes • Factory, etc. • Ships, Trains, Cars Manufacturer Representatives • Furniture • Carpets, Textiles, Paints, Stains • Kitchen, Bathroom, etc. • Lighting Engineer or Designer • Maintenance Specialists • Industrial Scientists, etc. Context: See below ↓
Structures	Architect	**Architects** Environmental Designer Building Designer Engineer Draftsperson Interior Designer Designer Developer Builder/Contractor	Content: See above ↑ Programmer Space Planner CAD: Computer-Aided Design/Drafting Computer Modeling (Building Performance) • Energy • Structures • Lighting • Mechanical, etc. Engineers • Soils • Structural • Mechanical • Electrical • Acoustical/Life Cycle Cost Consultants • Landscape Architect • Interior Designer • Construction Manager

Table III-1 The Environmental Design Disciplines/Professions (Continued)

BUILT ENVIRONMENT COMPONENTS	DESIGN PROFESSIONS	DISCIPLINES WORKING AT THIS SCALE	SOME SUPPORT SPECIALISTS
Structures	**Architect**		Engineers • Developer • Urban Designer & Planners • City Planner & Engineers
	Construction Manager	**Construction Manager** General Contractor Design-Build Firms Developers	Subcontractors • Excavation • Foundations • Framing: Wood, Steel, Concrete, Masonry, etc. • Walls, Roofing • Material Specialists • Mechanical, Electrical, Plumbing, Communications, etc.
	Engineer	**Engineers** Aerospace Agricultural Bio/Medical Chemical Civil Electrical Environmental Material Mechanical, etc. Technician Scientists	Numerous Specialists Relating to Materials, Processes and Production Context: See below ↓
Landscapes	**Landscape Architect**	**Landscape Architect** Gardener Horticulturalist Ecologists Urban Designer Urban Planner Regional Planner	Content: See above ↑ CAD: Computer-Aided Design and Planning GIS Specialist (Geographic Information Systems) Developer Builder Contractor Horticulturalist Botanist Nursery Keeper Attorney Real Estate Broker Economist Marketing Analyst Sociologist Psychologist Geographer Soil Scientist Geologist Forester Context: See below ↓

Table III-1 The Environmental Design Disciplines/Professions (Continued)

BUILT ENVIRONMENT COMPONENTS	DESIGN PROFESSIONS	DISCIPLINES WORKING AT THIS SCALE	SOME SUPPORT SPECIALISTS

Cities	Urban Designer
	City Planner
		Urban Designer
		Architect
		
		Landscape Architect
		Urban Planner
		Urban Historian
		City Planners
		City Manager
		Urban Designer
		Architect
		Landscape Architect
		Civil Engineers
			Content: See above ↑
			All Human-Environmental Disciplines/
			   Professions
			Governance
			Public Safety (Police, Fire, etc.)
			Code Enforcement
			Economic
			Transportation and Urban Infrastructure
			   Engineering
			Social, Cultural, Recreational
			Educational, etc. Disciplines
			Context: See below ↓

Regions	Regional Planner	**Regional Planner** Environmental Scientist Economists and Geographers (In Regional Science) Ecologists Systems Analyst	Content: See above ↑ All Human-Environmental Disciplines/ Professions GIS: Geographic Information Systems CAD: Computer-Aided Design/Planning Geologists Meteorologists Botanists Hydrologists Soils Scientists Behavioral & Social Scientists Biologists, etc. Context: See below ↓
Earth	Global Planner	**Global Planner** Environmental Scientists Ecologist Systems Analyst Politicians and Diplomat International Organization (UN, AID, World Bank, etc.) Futurist	Content: See above ↑ All Human-Environmental Disciplines

REFERENCES

Fuller, R. Buckminster. *Operating Manual for Spaceship Earth*. Pocket Books, 1970.
Pirsig, R. *Zen and the Art of Motorcycle Maintenance*. Bantam, 1974.

ENDNOTES

1. R. Buckminster Fuller. *Operating Manual for Spaceship Earth* (Pocket Books, 1970).
2. R. Pirsig, *Zen and the Art of Motorcycle Maintenance* (Bantam, 1974).
3. See Note 2.

PRODUCTS
Industrial and Product Design

Introduction

Products are the first and most basic building blocks of the built environment. Products are so numerous that they are often overlooked and taken for granted, yet they are of fundamental importance to everyone. In the most basic sense, the ability to create products distinguishes humans from other species of the animal kingdom. Products enable us to pursue many diverse activities and support human endeavors, both noble and ignoble.

Products extend not only human capacities, but also responsibilities. With a stone, axe, or spear, one may have dominance over a few, but a red button connected to a nuclear arsenal provides the capacity to control or destroy the world. This creates huge responsibilities. Consequently, when dealing with products, it is important to connect human intellectual capacities to create with human and environmental responsibilities. The simplest products (e.g., a soda pop can) can be produced many, many times and collectively consume large amounts of resources, causing considerable human-environmental impacts if they are not reused or recycled.

Products are effectively defined by adapting the definition of the built environment presented in Chapter 1:

- Products are objects that are humanly made or arranged;
- to fulfill human needs, wants, and values;
- to extend human capacities; and
- to mediate the overall environment; with results that affect the overall environmental context. (The context for products ranges from interiors to the Earth. As noted previously, products such as nuclear weapons systems can affect the ultimate context; that is, they can destroy all life on Earth.)

Products begin the layering of the components that form the built environment. In general, these layers are as follows:

- **Products** build interiors.
- Interiors combine into structures.
- Structures and external spaces combine into landscapes.
- Landscapes combine with structures and form cities.
- Cities grow within regions.
- Regions are subunits of the Earth.
- Earth, the ultimate context for all the above, is referred to by some as a type of product: "spaceship" Earth.

This layering, one component building upon another, can be placed into a levels-of-integration continuum. A series of component-context interrelationships are nested within the holistic concept and unifying sphere of the built environment.

Products—Interiors—Structures—Landscapes— Cities—Regions—Earth

Readers may find it enjoyable and challenging to observe and analyze the products that surround them and help them perform the activities of life. Many products are made from multiple materials that are products themselves. Products may require elaborate manufacturing processes. The following list defines various products and their implied purpose and meanings:

- Books convey the authors' ideas and concerns through humanly created letters arranged in words, sentences, paragraphs, and chapters—the created languages of civilizations.
- Eyeglasses extend the human capacity to see, while microscopes and telescopes allow us to study the worlds smaller and larger in scale than normal vision can perceive.
- Clothing keeps us comfortable and warm, helps convey moods, and expresses informal or formal values.
- Machines and appliances help people cook, wash clothes, create, and envelop human life with music and electronic communication from distant places.
- Walls are made of a variety of products that help mediate the external climate. They are designed to define quality spaces for almost all life activities.
- Phones connect us to friends and family, fire, police, and health care professionals, associates, companies—almost anyone around the world.
- Computers, once room size, now are pocket size and allow us to explore the World Wide Web, communicate with others, save huge amounts of information, carry out extension work, and enjoy electronic games.

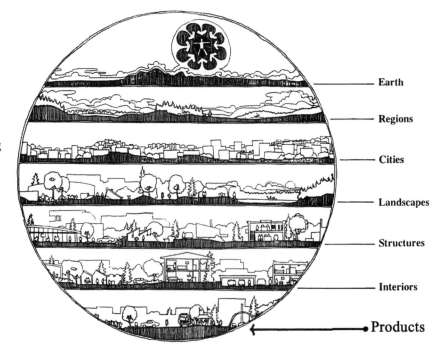

Graphic logo illustrating levels of integration in the built environment (S. Recken and J. Singleton).

Earth

Regions

Cities

Landscapes

Structures

Interiors

Products

The products that surround us are extensive. They are important extensions of human capacity. The following two chapters will explore various aspects of products and their design.

The Humanly Made Object
by Catherine M. Bicknell

This chapter explores the human impulse to create objects or products and discusses their functional and cognitive impact on human life. The chapter analyzes various traditions in product development. The author concludes with a discussion of how products have caused a shift in society from natural to human dominance and how products are now part of and dependent on extensive human, environmental, and technological systems in the built environment.

From Craft Tradition to Industrial Design
by Catherine M. Bicknell

This chapter examines product development from hand-crafted items to industrial designs today. The author concludes with a discussion of the impact of products on contemporary society and the important responsibilities created for the users and designers of products today.

References

Each chapter concludes with a list of relevant references.

Association of Women Industrial Designers (AWID): www.awidweb.com
Industrial Design Schools (IDS): www.ArtSchools.com
Industrial Designers Society of America (IDSA): www.idsa.org
International Council of Societies of industrial Design (ICSID): www.icsid.org

CHAPTER 8

The Humanly Made Object

Catherine M. Bicknell

Human beings cannot survive in isolation. In order to live, they need air, water, food, and light and are, therefore, dependent on their surroundings. They are just part of a much larger whole. Beyond the bare necessities, the human race impulsively modifies the environment to create objects and to provide shelter and protection.

The Primary Impulse to Create Objects

People from prehistoric times to the present have deliberately shaped utensils, tools, clothes, weapons, and ritual or decorative artifacts as extensions of themselves. For example, clothes are created to improve thermal protection, and tools and weapons are developed to extend the use of hands to perform tasks beyond their original capabilities. These objects are found in a variety of forms in different parts of the world. Objects made for the same use may vary considerably in different places according to local materials and traditions and to different levels of ingenuity and skill.

The First Artifacts

Archaeological evidence indicates that from earliest times, humans have exhibited the skill to fashion artifacts. The skill to sharpen flint, for example, has appeared in the form of arrowheads, knives, and axe heads found all over the world. The original axe, as an object and a tool, was conceived through selection of an appropriate material and discovery of a functional form.

The first stages in development of the axe were obviously practical. The toolmaker had to select the right material for the axe head and then concentrate on perfecting its cutting power. This involved the gradual smoothing, polishing, and refining of the blade until it reached its optimum point of efficiency. The shaping and attachment of the handle posed a difficult problem, for it needed to be comfortable in the hand, easy to grip, and well balanced. By a long process of trial and experimentation, the flint axe developed the characteristic form not very different from the one we use today. But though its general appearance may have remained the same, the cutting material has been changed and refined beyond its original concept in stone. The search for the best materials and the most effective functional form emerges even today as an important aspect of contemporary product design.

The Cognitive Aspects of Objects Form and Function

Form and Function

An axe is a familiar object with a known purpose, like a fork, cup, or bowl. This familiarity is visible in the external shape of the object. It communicates its purpose

Figure 8-1 Primitive axe—shaping and refining the functional form and searching for the most effective materials.

without words—creating a **visual language**. Certain objects communicate what they are by the familiarity of what they do: their function. We observe them performing their **function** and, therefore, we know what they are. Others communicate through their appearance: their **form**. We recognize their form and know their function. Some objects do not possess a practical function but have qualities that are purely aesthetic or symbolic. They were made to be looked at and enjoyed or to convey ideas or meanings. Their significance or even beauty may not be immediately understood by the uninitiated observer; the growth of an aesthetic sense or the comprehension of complex symbolism may require a process of learning.

Figure 8-2 Products—their form expressing the functional purpose, sense of place, and symbolic meaning.

For this learning process, we need the help of our perceptive abilities. Perception of an object is the way we tell whether things are close to us or far away, whether they are large or small, flat or curved. This overall knowledge and meaning of objects developed over time from human experience with nature and with the built environment. Perception is the action of a person's mind to identify objects from external sensations.

Recognition of an object through perception is a communication that transcends the spoken language. For example, most people will recognize the distinct image of a San Francisco cable car or a double-decker London bus; the image alone will communicate a sense of place much faster than the spoken word.

Sense of Place: Universal, National, and Regional Objects

Today, as never before, certain common objects can be seen anywhere. For instance, the transistor radio can be seen all over the world and is universally recognized. The bicycle has become an object of universal human culture.

Other articles are universally used but have distinct differences from country to country. For instance, brooms in Britain and the United States are made of different materials and are of contrasting shape even though the availability of materials and the job they have to do are the same in both countries. Although the broom may be universally known, such differences in materials and use emerge from and contribute to a national identity.

Some unique cultural or symbolic objects can also be identified with a particular region. Like the cable car or the London bus, the totem pole is recognizable and representative of the Pacific Northwest coastal region of Canada and the United States.

The Object as Symbol

The axe as an object is at times endowed with unique qualities not connected with its function. In such cases, the axe has reached a satisfactory shape as a working tool, and the toolmakers have taken their craft a step further. The handle may have a carved or painted pattern or the head may be decorated in some way, perhaps by an engraved design. Then it is no longer a mere tool; it is also an example of the maker's attempt to create a unique symbol that may endow its owner with special symbolic qualities. After such alterations, a simple tool can become a ceremonial axe, an object for purely ritual purposes. For instance, the ancient Chinese had such a ritual axe,

Figure 8-3 A totem pole—a unique regional artifact from the Pacific Northwest.

a highly elaborate cult object for ceremonial use. To enhance its special non-utilitarian qualities, it was beautifully carved out of the rare and precious jadeite.

The Shift from Natural to Human Dominance

Until very recently, most human life was dominated by the larger environmental context. Natural environments were used and understood by hunters, sailors, and fisherfolk with little significant modification. These people needed what such environments could offer and used what they could obtain from them to create their artifacts—their shelters, huts and tents, their implements and their boats. Aboriginal peoples sometimes effected considerable change in their surroundings, but their impacts were specific as to organisms and locales. Nature remained dominant, and only in the past 4,000 to 5,000 years, with the coming of agriculture, towns, and cities, has nature's domination seemed to have gradually diminished. Only in the past two hundred years has this

relationship altered to such a degree that human experience now seems primarily one of humanly made places and things—the built environment. How much power or dominion humans have over nature is debatable. We are consistently reminded of nature's power and devastating impact on the built environment through cataclysmic events such as hurricanes, earthquakes, tsunamis, and tornados, and more recently and subtly, by changes to natural system that occur as the result of humanly made products such as automobiles, air conditioners, fertilizers, and soaps.

Products and their designs are manifested in the various traditions introduced in Chapter 2 and further examined and applied the product development. They represent the social-environment-technology (SET) relationships introduced in Chapter 3.

The Vernacular Tradition

In the biological process of **natural selection**, the least fit members of the species die and the strongest members survive. A parallel can be seen in the development of certain objects, a survival of the fittest in which the appropriate object survives over inappropriate ones.

The survivor could be a domestic utensil that has been made over and over again; tiny improvements have accrued to the objects, and faults and problems have been gradually eliminated or at least minimized. A modern example familiar to us is the copper, tin, and brass saucepan used for cooking. The combination of copper for good heat conduction, tin to protect the food, and brass as a stronger metal for the handle make a functionally superior article respected by all who enjoy traditional quality.

Experiments in nonstick and easy-to-clean surfaces for saucepans have produced many new approaches and finishes, but it is interesting to note that for quality cooking, many modern users are going back to the older, tried-and-true materials and are using traditional pots again, not for convenience but for performance.

Selection by gradual elimination and refinement is common to objects for everyday use. These objects are

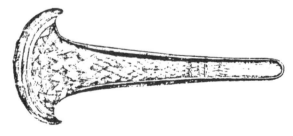

Figure 8-4 A ceremonial axe and its symbolic meaning.

unself-consciously developed by a cultural group rather than a single individual. This gradual and anonymous process is known as the **vernacular tradition**. Drastic innovation or radical improvements are not typical of vernacular products. Consistency and continuity are intrinsic to their development.

The vernacular tradition is exemplified by the hand implements commonly found even on today's farms and by the common tools that many of us still use, such as the hammer and saw. The household dishes, glassware, and flatware of today reflect strong vernacular traditions, customs that have long provided for the needs of ordinary people in the form of functional everyday wares.

High Style and the Ceremonial Object

On the other hand, the richness and elaboration of household artifacts serve the sophisticated desires of wealthy people who endeavor to emphasize ceremonial occasions rather than ordinary everyday needs. Such elaborations constitute the parts of another tradition, commonly referred to as **high style**. The adornments and embellishments of this tradition often show an enjoyment of form for its own sake and a pleasure in decoration. Many cult and ceremonial objects are beautifully made and hand decorated from elegant materials that have particular meaning for selective groups of people.

For many, the high-style object is exemplified by the luxuries that some people choose to possess because they admire their decorative designs. Compare an elaborate candelabra to a simple candleholder; both have the same function, but contrasting decorative qualities mark one as vernacular, the other as high style.

The difference between the vernacular and the high style can easily be seen in common household objects such as the chair or the candleholder. The differences also reveal a wide variety of values among the elite. An ordinary chair in the vernacular tradition is solid, well made, and comfortable but unpretentious. Its upper-class counterpart may be richly decorated with carving and upholstered with tapestry or satin, and embellishments may be more important than comfort. Some expensive chairs may conform to the latest style but may not be comfortable to sit on. A high-style chair may be based on a vernacular design but developed with a more precious material, perhaps rosewood instead of traditional oak or beech. Rarity has always had value in high-style tradition. However, the beauty of simplicity is also enjoyed by high-style makers and consumers. Eighteenth-century furniture makers often produced chairs of utmost simplicity but with perfect proportions,

Figure 8-5 Candleholders—expressing the vernacular and high-style traditions.

so that their beauty came from inherent qualities of form, not from applied decoration. Many modern furniture designers have used vernacular products for inspiration, achieving a high quality of design through simplicity.

The Growth of Materialism

We have gone a long way beyond people's first necessities—the word "materialistic" is often used when describing the modern world. We work to produce things and then work to earn what we can to acquire more things. For example, houses, cars, televisions, washers, freezers,

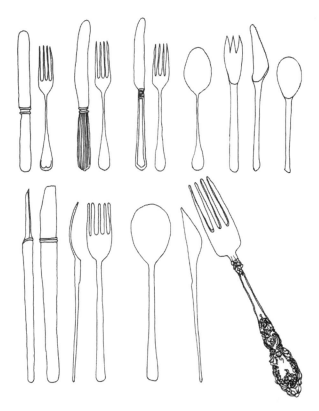

Figure 8-6 The variety of personalities expressed in many forms of tableware.

books, furniture, ornaments, and souvenirs are produced in abundance and are very much a part of the everyday built environment. We are now a population not only dependent on our natural surroundings, but also interdependent with humanly made objects and the complex systems that produce them. To our detriment, we have tended to lose sight of our original interdependency with the natural environment.

We do not typically live close to places where we can hunt and fish. In order to enjoy naturally fresh food, we rely on complex energy and supply systems, even fast, motorized transport. We have moved an immense distance from the directness and immediacy of early, uncomplicated ways of living to interdependent, complex industrial and societal support systems. Most of us probably cannot think of examples of people who still live with a minimum of means and material goods. A lack of modern conveniences may seem empty and inconvenient to many, perhaps most of us.

The Development of Mass Production: A Speculative Tradition

Production in recent times has allowed the cheapest industrially made household utensils to imitate the wares of previous ages. Easily obtained dishes, silverware, and glasses are often imitations of high-style objects, reproduced in great numbers in cheap materials, too often of poor quality. Quick and easy reproduction, created by the Industrial Age, has led to a widespread **speculative tradition**, developed for profit through mass production.

To the uninformed person, a new version of an object that deviates from high-style or vernacular forms might be attractive and preferable to buy. A plastic bucket can look bright and colorful and be more enticing than the solid and more expensive traditional product. But vernacular products are often still surprisingly successful, both in practical and visual ways, with an excellence built to last. For instance, when a traditional metal spoon and certain new kinds of plastic spoons are both put in a mug of hot coffee, each shows a totally different performance: the metal spoon remains rigid, but some plastic spoons can weaken and bend. These plastic products are intentionally designed to be used once and discarded—manifestations of a "throwaway society." Likewise, plastic knives simply do not approach the cutting performance of metal ones. The cutting edge of stainless steel knives is not as sharp as that of the earlier carbon steel. Many cooks are still prepared to sacrifice the convenience of stainless steel for the keen edge of carbon steel blades.

The Artificial Need for More Objects

Today, manufacturers are also producing objects that never existed before and have no traditional uses; through advertising and exposure, a public demand is created. No longer content with having mere necessities, consumers and manufacturers have created artificial needs. We can all think of examples of objects for the person who has everything. Our acquisitive society falls for such odd articles as electric fingernail polish dryers or mink-covered toilet seats. Victor Papanek, an international design expert, found a distributor who was selling 20,000 diapers a month—for parakeets.[1]

You may not own any of the above, but if you shut your eyes for a moment and imagine all of your possessions, from your toothbrush to the pictures on your wall, you will probably find that the list is very long. If you left the room in a panic, could you possibly carry it all? Yet, a household possessing only necessities need not be thought of as impoverished. The ordinary sixteenth-century household, for instance, enjoyed good food and fine living. The following inventory from one such household has nothing in it that is superfluous or unnecessary: one brass pot, a frying pan, a kettle, a gridiron, a skillet and spit, 5 pieces of pewter and a candlestick, 3 pairs of sheets, a cover, 12 pieces of linen, 2 coffers, 2 pillows, a cupboard, a table, and some chairs.

This list is in striking contrast to the modem equivalent. Can you imagine listing all the contents of your home in part of one short paragraph? Two aspects of this medieval list should be remembered: all these objects were expertly and carefully handmade, and all the articles were cherished and valued. Most of these items could be presented proudly today as quality historical exhibits in any museum. Can we predict the same admiration for the quality of our possessions?

The Object as Part of a System

Many of the objects in the medieval house can be thought of as independent, self-sufficient and long-lasting, without the need for external sources of energy or for external connections to support their continued existence.

Our homes today still contain such objects, like tables and chairs, but in addition televisions, telephones, lights, washers, dryers, sinks, and toilets. Many of these other products must be connected beyond the limits of the house to a complex of roads, sewers, electric lines, and other external systems (commonly referred to as

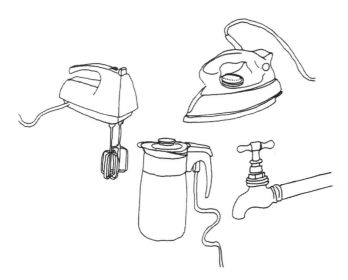

Figure 8-7 Many products today are dependent upon various support systems.

"infrastructure"). The home, as we know it, has become divorced from its natural surroundings and turned into a small part of a much larger network of support systems, all of which can fail on short notice or without notice.

In its simplest form, shelter itself can exist without artificial connections to an external support system. The simple shelter was originally for people's protection, but it has changed and become a place to display our many possessions and ourselves. As early as 1851, the English designer **William Morris**, founder of the Arts and Crafts Movement, spoke of our houses being filled with "tons and tons of unutterable rubbish." Since Morris's time, our houses have grown to contain more, more, and still more. The house itself has become a very complex modern appliance; it has become a machine for living with all the problems inherent in keeping a machine running smoothly. Earlier houses may have had inconveniences, but their simplicity also had advantages.

How many of us are ready to look at the social responsibility that we owe to one another and to ourselves, the responsibility to reduce this excessive demand for more products, for more and more complex objects?

As noted, the natural world has its own process of survival of the fittest, and people first created objects that did not interfere with the natural dominance. The long line of humanly made objects (especially those in the vernacular tradition) can gradually show us which objects are of real value, which are most appropriate—if we care to carefully study their qualities. Meanwhile, the built environment supports our ability to inundate our surroundings with products. Do we have to wait until we are buried under our own possessions before we can see the need to slow down? Again, if we had to abandon our households in a hurry, perhaps to escape a fire or flood caused by a hurricane, would we know what few things to take with us?

Products are also connected to natural resources and to the natural systems of the Earth. Often, in highly industrialized societies, especially in the United States, a single design is manufactured into many thousands, sometimes millions, even billions of individual products, an explosion that can cause significant loss of resources and corresponding environmental impacts. For example, the design of an aluminum soda pop can may appear quite simple. It is a relatively small product, but it is reproduced billions of times and consumes huge amounts of resources. The smallest incremental change in efficiency can make a significant saving in total resources. In 2004, 100 billion aluminum cans were used in the United States—45 billion were recycled but, unfortunately, 55 billion were wasted.[2] "If you throw away two aluminum cans, you waste more energy than is used daily by each of a billion individual human beings in less developed nations."[3] Today, it is critical for designers to practice the **three (or four) R's**—to **reuse, reduce,** and **recycle** (and use **renewable** resources). This creative and more comprehensive "Cradle-to-Cradle" approach to design is critically important to a sustainable society and will be addressed in a number of future chapters.[4] "In 1988 alone, aluminum can recycling saved more than 11 billion kilowatt hours of electricity, enough to supply the residential electrical needs of New York City for six months. Recycling aluminum cuts air pollution by 95% . . . [and] uses 90% less energy than making aluminum from scratch."[5] Reduction of consumption, reuse, and recycling of the simplest products can often save huge amounts of energy and resources, as well as minimize the air and water pollution associated with manufacturing and distribution systems. Unfortunately, the United States is slipping; it recycled 65% of its cans in 1992 but now only recycles 45%. Sweden currently recycles 85%.[6]

Designers especially, but all humans (and particularly those in industrialized consumer societies), must continue to think about such connections between human needs and wants, must consider seriously the level of satisfaction obtained through creation of products and objects in the built environment, and must increasingly understand the implications of such creations and consumption, not only in the household but multiplied throughout the world.

References

CRI (Container Recycling Institute). 2006: www.container-recycling.org.

EarthWorks Group. *50 Simple Things You Can Do to Save the Earth*. EarthWorks Press, 1989.

McDonough, W., and M. Braungart. *Cradle to Cradle: Remaking the Way We Make Things*. North Point Press, 2002.

Papanek, V. *The Green Imperative: Design for the Real World*. Thames and Hudson, 1995.

Papanek, V. *Design for the Real World: Human Ecology and Social Change*. Academy Chicago, 1985.

Endnotes

1. V. Papanek, *Design for the Real World: Human Ecology and Social Change* (Academy Chicago, 1985).

2. CRI (Container Recycling Institute), 2006: www.container-recycling.org.

3. EarthWorks Group, *50 Simple Things You Can Do to Save the Earth* (EarthWorks Press, 1989): p. 64.

4. W. McDonough and M. Braungart, *Cradle to Cradle: Remaking the Way We Make Things* (North Point Press, 2002).

5. EarthWorks Group, *50 Simple Things You Can Do to Save the Earth*: p. 64.

6. See Note 2.

CHAPTER 9

From Craft Tradition to Industrial Design

Catherine M. Bicknell

The design of ordinary products affects everyone. Objects that we use every day can give us pleasure or cause serious problems with human, environmental, and technical systems. A tea kettle that does not pour or a door handle with a rough surface that hurts your hand are in direct contrast to the kettle that pours beautifully or the handle whose silky smooth finish caresses your hand. This chapter is concerned with ordinary everyday objects and with the design processes and professions that make their realization possible. The transition from the traditional craftsperson to the contemporary industrial designer is explored in its historical context.

Historical Developments

Medieval Design

In the Middle Ages, most people had few possessions. In the great medieval halls of the time, the king, the queen, or the lord was provided with an elevated platform and throne or chair to sit in state and survey the fine silver or gold plates on the table, the stained glass in the windows,

the tapestries on the walls, and the costly table linens. So important were all these objects, that when royalty moved from house to house, everything was taken by horse and wagon to furnish the next house. Even the glass in the windows was moved, and everything was designed, from the glass to the chair, to withstand these rough journeys.

We have inherited the term "chair" as a Western title to designate success as a leader in a position of authority. It is not only the lord who has the chair; it can now be the "chair of the board," a term that comes to us directly from the elevated status of that important chair at a medieval table. The table at which royalty was seated was known as the "board," and that is exactly what it was, a board on trestles. Such historic roots are still symbols of contemporary society—we still refer to the chair as one who sits above the board of directors.

The making of the important chair and table in medieval times required an expert craftsperson whose skill had been passed down from generation to generation but who might add individual artistry. The table was even an object of pride, for in those early days, cutting a thin board by hand from a great tree was no easy task.

For most of human time on earth, the availability of materials and technology was severely limited. Obtain-

Figure 9-1   The medieval board and chair (M. Girouard).

ing materials was restricted to those close at hand, like wood, clay, or bone, and artisans had to learn to make the most of them. But limitations have often inspired human creativity; many objects of beauty and utility have been made from the simplest of materials. Certainly, there were fewer colors to choose from, and all were made from natural substances, but the pigments and dyes made from local plants and minerals were in many ways superior to those we make today through complex, and often toxic, chemical processes.

The Traditional Craftsperson

Throughout the world and throughout most of history, craftspeople or artisans working at skilled trades (pottery, cabinet making, weaving, or metal work) learned their skills from their parents, who in turn had been taught by their own parents. Or they were apprenticed to experienced artisans at a young age, first paying for the privilege of learning, later receiving modest pay, and finally themselves becoming masters, perhaps with apprentices of their own. This system ensured proper training and an understanding of the work—from selecting raw materials to manufacturing, finishing, and selling whatever was produced. Originality was rarely important to such workers. Their role was to make what was needed according to traditional standards, and perhaps to refine or modify standard designs to suit particular needs. Occasionally, outstanding artisans produced new designs that were greatly admired, and thus they initiated new traditions or styles. Most of these people worked anonymously, but some were so skilled at their craft that they have been regarded as artists. For example, Thomas Chippendale, the eighteenth-century English cabinetmaker, gave name to a style still well known today. Although educated through an apprenticeship, the artist/craftsperson came to represent the design spirit of an age.

The Industrial Revolution

Age-old traditions of handwork by skilled artisans were challenged and, in some cases, brought to an end by the Industrial Revolution. The improved design of the steam engine by James Watt in 1769 was a catalyst in the development of factory production. The use of coke in iron production made possible the casting of large sections of iron required for the machines of industrial production. By the nineteenth century, many articles previously made by craftspeople at home were made in factories. With the coming of the machine, standards in both visual and functional design rapidly changed. In the Victorian age, machines could instantly stamp out elaborate effects that would have taken a craftsperson days or weeks to create.

This resulted in an increase in ornamentation on all consumer goods—furnishings, household objects, and artifacts; manufacturers strove constantly to outdo each other in lavish decoration. Craftspeople might help set up the model for running the machines, but they themselves were no longer making individual, beautiful objects.

In the nineteenth century, the number of products increased rapidly. Between 1790 and 1900, 600,000 patents for new devices were granted in the United States alone. Many of those patents covered designs for machines that would transform the size and character of the farm, the office, and the home. Locomotives, steamships, and bicycles led to mechanized transportation just as the typewriter, the adding machine, the cash register, the Dictaphone, and the telephone, all introduced between 1875

Figure 9-2   English carved oak armchair, c. 1250.

and 1900, brought about the mechanization of office work and eventually led to development of the computer.

Factory canning and baking and home appliances such as washing machines, vacuum cleaners, and sewing machines simplified housework, even if they did not mechanize it. The nineteenth-century poet Ralph Waldo Emerson's claim that "things are in the saddle and are riding us" was true at the time and seems even more so today. The big question of the day was, "What should everything look like?" Should designers clothe their products in historic costume or should they forge new styles for machine-made products?

On the whole, most product designers of the eighteenth and nineteenth centuries turned to past styles or to nature as a source of inspiration for their designs. Instead of finding new designs appropriate for the machine age, factory owners preferred to imitate designs from earlier historical periods. Today we tend to look back to this period as a time when the means of production was progressive but designs were regressive.

Despite the regressive historicism of the majority of designers, a few responded to the conversion from hand to machine production by adapting to the new technology and by evolving appropriate styles for it. Engineers

Figure 9-3 Wooden handcrafted Windsor chair.

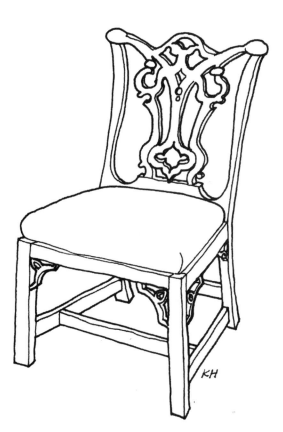

Figure 9-4 Chippendale chair.

Figure 9-5 Victorian chair.

Figure 9-6 A patented swimming device (L. De Vries).

and inventors were the first to develop "styleless" products and structures, and to introduce the modern look, well before product designers did.

This was particularly well illustrated in the Great Exhibition at the Crystal Palace in London in 1851. Products were exhibited from all over the world. The general impression was that ornament, embellishment, and historicism were at their height. Inside the palace, with its eclectic pleasures, all the glories of Victorian times were apparent. In direct contrast to the exhibits, the building

Figure 9-8 The Crystal Palace of the Great Exhibition 1851, showing the simple structure and the overly elaborate exhibits.

housing the exhibition itself was an incredibly modern iron and glass structure designed by Joseph Paxton, a particularly creative landscape architect. Stripped to its structural basics, it heralded a whole new era in which simplicity and a functional approach to design were admired. Its clean lines and lack of ornamentation were quite shocking to some of its viewers.

Also shocking were two contributions to the exhibition from the United States. Cyrus McCormick's Virginia Reaper and Samuel Colt's revolver were seen as so stark and apparently unstyled that they were a public joke. The *London Times* reported that the reaper was "a cross between an Astley chariot, a wheelbarrow and a flying machine." But when it cut 20 acres a day, the machine was reported to be "the most valuable contribution from abroad to the stock of previous knowledge yet discovered."

The 'Remington' typewriter [1891]

Figure 9-7 Remington typewriter.

Figure 9-9 Victorian taste: products in the Crystal Palace (The Crystal Palace Catalogue).

Figure 9-10 McCormick's Virginia Reaper (S. Giedion).

The simplicity of the Colt revolver contrasted dramatically with the decoratively engraved, handcrafted weapons of France and England. It was the British who were most amazed by its advancement in technology—its performance and capability of shooting five or six rounds in succession without reloading and the fact that it was mass produced, not handcrafted, and in production each part was duplicated by die-cutting machines. The British Institute of Civil Engineers was so impressed that it invited Colt to set up a factory in England similar to the one that he had established in the United States.

Not only could Colt's machines stamp out a part many times faster than the human hand could fashion it, but each part was reproduced with sufficient precision to make it interchangeable with the same part from any other unit. This was one of the key elements in the mass

Figure 9-11 The invention of the telephone (L. De Vries).

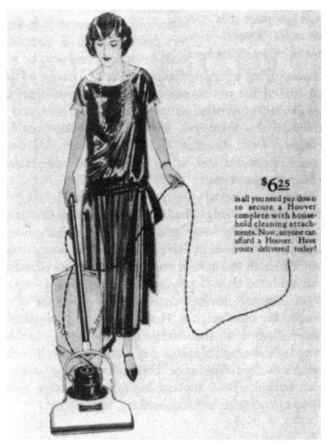

Figure 9-12 Household inventions (S. Strasser).

production process and an inherent strength of this new system developed in the United States.

A lack of concern for good design in mass production is evidenced by the fact that most manufacturers during the Victorian period failed to record the names of the designers of their products. The names of Thomas Edison, Alexander Graham Bell, and others who patented new products are recorded, but the names of the designers who decoratively styled the phonograph, telephone, and typewriter are not. Neither the Bell Company nor Western Electric has records of any designers in 1877, when Bell introduced the first commercial model of the telephone. But by 1936, times had changed; in that year, Western Electric, the actual manufacturer of later telephones, retained Henry Dreyfus as a consultant designer.

The Arts and Crafts Movement and the Bauhaus

At the time of the Great Exhibition in London, most designers produced overly elaborate, highly decorated work. A few were so dismayed by the results of machine production that they attempted to turn back the clock and return to the methods of the Middle Ages. They became part of the **Arts and Crafts Movement** under the leadership of **William Morris**. Compared to medieval artisans, who took pride in their work and were directly involved in its final form and finish, Morris saw the factory worker as degraded. Arts and Crafts designers saw machinists as slaves without any influence on what they were making. The movement also protested against the devaluation of beautiful handmade objects, and its members designed objects of great simplicity.

Their aim was to restore the dignity of the craftsperson. Unfortunately, the fine handcrafted furniture, fabrics, tapestries, and other products they produced were too expensive for the mass market and could only be purchased by wealthy people. They were also based too firmly on medieval traditions and, therefore, did not meet the challenge of the new age. The influence of the Arts and Crafts Movement, however, was tremendous. The origins of modern design are found in its honest, simplified forms.

Not until 1919, when **Walter Gropius** founded the **Bauhaus School of Design** in Germany, was an attempt made in design education to work with technology. The

Figure 9-14 Barcelona chair, steel construction, cantilevered, designed by Mies van der Rohe, 1929.

Bauhaus accepted mechanization and attempted to work with it. Bauhaus designers worked alongside skilled engineers so that both could make contributions to the finished product. Students were taught three kinds of skills—those of an artist, those of a craftsperson, and those of a scientist or technologist.

Shortly before World War II, the Bauhaus School was closed by the Nazis and many of the faculty left Germany. They migrated to England, spread across the United States, and took their ideals with them. Design

Figure 9-13 Morris ladderback chair.

Figure 9-15 The "Swan" chair, glass-fiber shell, leather- or fabric-covered, designed by Arne Jacobsen, 1958.

and design education in the Western world became heavily influenced by the Bauhaus. Unlike members of the Arts and Crafts Movement, Bauhaus teachers knew they had to work with the realities of their own age and design for machine production, but they also placed great stress on the development of creativity. In the words of Walter Gropius, only the artist "can breathe life into the dead hand of the machine."

Contemporary Industrial Design

The Artist/Craftsperson Today

In the spirit of the Arts and Crafts Movement, which stressed the satisfaction that individuals can derive from working creatively with their hands, many artistic people chose to work in one of the crafts. Artists/craftspeople today have mostly been educated at a university or art school, but they work like the medieval artisans—from selecting the raw material to finishing and even selling the product. Artists/craftspeople design things through direct contact with the consumer. Their working methods, however, may not be the same as those in the days of medieval craft apprenticeships. And they have emerged from the anonymity of the artisan to become artists known by name, of whom patrons expect some originality. Exhibitions in contemporary galleries show an abundance of examples of the high standards and refinements that a contemporary artist/craftsperson can attain, from original conception to final completion of the object.

The Industrial Designer of Today

Industrial designers today stand as a bridge between the old world of the craftsperson and the incredibly sophisticated world of mass production. The best of them integrate the highest aspects of human, environmental, and technological systems.

Industrial designers have seldom been trained in a particular trade or to work with a specific material. They are very often educated professionals, such as engineers who, through special studies, become qualified to supervise and coordinate the complicated process on which industrial production is based. They stand between the customer and the manufacturer, with the moral duty to protect the customer's interest. They act as coordinators of many different specialists: technicians, artisans, manufacturers, and salespeople. Collaboration is the key to success in the design process today.

Design has many influences, but a clear thread of development is discernible. Design has become progressively integrated, embodying the highest aspirations of the arts and sciences with the making or manufacturing of an artifact. The designer's professional status has become increasingly sophisticated, but the basic role is that of a problem solver.

Industrial designers today must still possess the analytical and creative abilities of the artist/craftsperson, but also the manager's will to organize and cooperate. They stand in the midst of an explosive development of new materials and new techniques of manufacturing.

Contemporary designers have an infinite choice of synthetic, humanly made substances, as well as natural materials from all over the world. Any color can be selected. New types of malleable materials, such as plastics, can be formed to meet demanding performance criteria.

New materials and technology go hand in hand; today a chair can be molded out of a single flexible material, dispensing with the traditional wood joints of the medieval craftsperson. That chair can be made so strong that it can survive a journey not just from house to house, but from Earth to moon and back; or we can make a similar molded chair that is attractive enough to sell well and make a profit but is not at all durable. Such a chair will soon end up on the junk heap with all the other billions of abandoned consumer goods of the speculative tradition.

Designers of molded plastic chairs are necessarily members of a team of specialists, from chemists to manufacturers and marketing experts. They have studied

Figure 9-16 Gallery of fine art and craft products, the Stonington Gallery, Seattle, Washington (T. Bartuska).

ergonomics, **anthropometric**s, structural principles, visual design, and many other complex subjects. Modern industrial designers will not—perhaps cannot—make the chair by hand, but delegate the task of manufacturing to others.

Design at whatever scale, whether it be a small pot or a high-speed train, is not only a matter of aesthetic judgment. The designer is expected to make the creative leap, to synthesize, and to bring all the conflicting human/social, environmental, and technical factors to an optimum visual and functional solution.

Challenges of the Twenty-First Century

The potential benefits to society of advanced technology and improved materials are obvious. For example, the development of North American bathrooms, kitchens, and laundry rooms, with their numerous appliances, has given us improved health, comfort, and convenience. We might expect that the entire built environment and all the objects that constitute it would show a similar improvement. Unfortunately, this hope has not been fulfilled. We have the means, but it seems that collectively, we lack the wisdom and resolution.

People today seem to expect that the quality of life should be completely satisfactory, with adequate food, clothing, housing, work, leisure, and means of transportation. Satisfaction of all of these is taken for granted by the majority of people in developed countries. Paradoxically, we have not succeeded collectively in designing a coherent and meaningful environment complete with all its constituent parts. The human ability to identify and solve material problems seems inexhaustible, but the ability to anticipate the impact of unlimited production remains comparatively weak. We are only just beginning to realize the collective result of the accelerating multitude of individual decisions and consumer habits. It is hard for us to absorb the fact that each of us individually contributes actively to massive large-scale problems caused by our desire for more and more products.

The common way of thinking about objects is to view them as separate, isolated units unconnected with anything else. The process of making an object, with its need for materials, tools, and power, too often seems remote from the finished product and our immediate convenience.

The automobile is a product that was invented and designed in the light of a certain ideal vision, a vision of

Figures 9-17 and 9-18 An abundance of industrial products, IKEA, Chicago, Illinois, and Seattle, Washington (T. Bartuska).

easy, hopefully efficient, independent mobility and/or of an attractive, seductive, powerful object that each of us can own. Only in recent years have the full consequences of its use begun to catch up with and overtake its advantages. The automobile creates a need for costly and irreplaceable construction materials, a seemingly insatiable demand for increasingly scarce operating fuel, and an extensive landscape of roads and parking lots. It creates extreme problems of safe operation, a distressing output of wastes, and a complicated, multi-ton carcass after it becomes inoperative. Autos need and create a diffuse landscape of sprawling developments that fosters more and more auto-dependent lifestyles, more and more traffic and congestion, air pollution, and related health problems, even global warming. Tragically, as this product multiplies, it takes huge amounts from individual, family, and city budgets, and in the United States alone, cars cause 40,000 to 50,000 deaths per year (a total that exceeds all those killed in all U.S. wars). Many are searching for answers to the problems caused by this product. Effective strategies include smaller, more efficient designs; more clustered communities where people can walk or bike to stores and schools and take public transit to work; and growth management strategies to control sprawl, protect regional resources, and reduce global warming. It is inescapable that most of us work at a small scale but feed large-scale human, environmental, and technical problems. The need to regain a sense of scale is not helped by the massive transformation achieved through mechanized industry, advertising media, and the speculative tradition.

We no longer go to the tailor or cabinetmaker in order to have things "made to measure," to choose the materials, the size, and style. We have lost direct contact with the things we enjoyed when handicraft traditions formed a firm basis of design. When clothes and utility wares were made at home, everyone knew about materials and how they should be employed.

In the handcraft tradition, the whole process of design and manufacture could be accomplished by one person. Handicraft skills represent a conscious effort to impose meaningful order and can be applied by a person at any scale, from landscapes and cities down to a tiny bit of jewelry. Designers continue to make decisions about finding and producing an appropriate form, but the handicraft tradition allowed the design process and its realization to be experienced by both the designer and the observer as a comprehensible unity. In this way, the product could be followed from raw material to finished form.

Now, more often than not, we buy things that are ready-made, out of unknown materials, things in which contacts between practitioner, observer, and user have been eliminated.

A Designer's Responsibility

Industrial designers obviously must have a sense of responsibility for human/social, environmental, and technical sets of issues—from the manufacturer who commissions a design to global users/consumers. As professionals, they also have a responsibility to society now and in the future. Everyone involved today in creating the complex built environment and its individual components must be willing to confront many issues and concerns that are all too easy to neglect. A comprehensive, sustainable approach to product design must con-

sider not only the effective design of the product, but also the context in which it is to be placed. More specifically, the designer today needs to consider such human, environmental, and technical issues such as those described in the following subsections.

What Are the Environmental Impacts of the Object?

"Everything is connected to everything else" is a widely quoted statement about the world in which we live. Many designers are beginning to grasp the essence of this statement and are considering the total implications and full production cycle of what they create—where the raw materials come from, the efficiency of their production, the energy and resources used (and pollution expended), the longevity of product usefulness, if it can be reused or recycled, and so on. This complete cycle analysis is not a cradle-to-grave (beginning to end of life) design but is commonly referred to as **cradle-to-cradle** design (birth, life, and beginning a new life through reuse and recycling).[1] These issues are more fully addressed in other chapters of this book. But when keeping a hamburger warm in a Styrofoam container or recharging the air conditioner in a personal automobile can erode the ozone layer, we still have massive problems to resolve. When choosing exotic woods to enhance a design can contribute to the destruction of tropical forests and ultimately to deterioration in the quality of the atmosphere, neither the design nor the resulting object seems so personal or so isolated from the immensity of the Earth.

How Does It Affect the Availability and Sustainability of Scarce Materials?

If designing a more powerful, fuel-inefficient car means a faster drawdown of petroleum supplies, leaving less for future generations, or if invasion of wilderness areas by loggers and mechanized tourists means less appreciation of nature by future generations or degradation of ecosystem health, then the decision to design, to manufacture, or to buy that car transcends the personal, the pocketbook, or even the gross national product. We must consider renewable resources within cradle-to-cradle design.

Does It Produce Wastes?

Designers (and consumers) need to be concerned not only with products, but also with by-products. Is an object designed so that all of it is consumed or used up? Is it designed to be recycled—or deliberately designed to be disposable? Is packaging necessary? Is the packaging excessive and, if needed, biodegradable or will it be found in landfills or littering roadways, even harming wildlife, decades after the time of purchase and use? We must consider the three Rs (reduce, reuse, and recycle) and cradle-to-cradle design.[2]

Is It Safe?

Do designers think about whether they would want their own children to wear the flammable dress they just created, or is caring lessened by the faceless, nameless people who will eventually buy the product? Is protection or profit the bottom line? The U.S. Constitution states that society and the design professions must protect the "health, safety and welfare" of the citizens.

What Is Its Impact on Human Health?

Who designs a cigarette, the seductive packaging, and the colorful, attractive advertising? Considering what we know now about tobacco's impacts on human health, what are the ethical considerations for the designers of such things? How far does their responsibility extend? Do we consider the total impact of each product design? Pollution not only occurs during manufacturing but also is caused by all the transportation needed to bring the product to life and during the use of many products. Currently, there is considerable concern over the many chemicals that are used in products. Many of them compromise human health and are known to off-gas (release their chemicals) into the air after they are manufactured and while being used. Artificial fragrances in perfumes, deodorants, shampoos, dryer sheets, and so on are known to cause health problems in some people with multiple chemical sensitivity. The off-gassing chemicals accumulate in the interior environment and can cause indoor air quality (IAQ) problems in homes, commercial spaces, and office interiors. These human-environmental concerns will be discussed in the set of chapters in Section 2.

Products are a most important building block of the built environment. Many exist in great numbers, multiplying far faster than world's population. Some have enduring usefulness and beauty; others may be initially attractive but are wasteful and destructive. Society and industrial design, now and in the future, must creatively respond to the many advances in human/social, environmental, and technological factors as we all work toward a more sustainable society.

References

Attfield, J. *Wild Things: The Material Culture of Everyday Life.* Berg, 2000.

The Crystal Palace Exhibition Illustrated Catalogue. Dover, 1970.

De Vries, L. *Victorian Inventions.* John Murray, 1971.

Gibbs-Smith, C. H. *The Great Exhibition of 1851.* Her Majesty's Stationery Office, 1851.

Giedion, S. *Mechanization Takes Command.* Oxford University Press, 1947.

Girouard, M. *Life in the English Country House.* Yale University Press, 1978.

Hesket. J. *Toothpicks and Logos: Designing Everyday Life.* Oxford University Press, 2002.

McDonough, W. 2004: www.mcdonough.com.

McDonough, W., and M. Braungart. *Cradle to Cradle: Remaking the Way We Make Things.* North Point Press, 2002.

Naylor, G. *The Bauhaus Studio.* Vista, 1968.

Naylor, G. *The Bauhaus Reassessed.* E. P. Dutton, 1985.

Norman, D. *The Design of Everyday Things.* Basic Books, 2002.

Oates, P. B. *The Story of Western Furniture.* Bennett Press, 1981.

Papanek, V. *Design for the Real World.* Academy Chicago, 1985.

Papanek, V. *The Green Imperative.* Thames and Hudson, 1995.

Reed, H. *Art and Industry.* Faber and Faber, 1953.

Sexton, R. *American Style: Classic Product Design from Airstream to Zippo.* Chronicle Books, 1987.

Strasser, S. *Never Done: A History of American Housework.* Pantheon Books, 1982.

Endnotes

1. W. McDonough and M. Braungart, *Cradle to Cradle: Remaking the Way We Make Things* (North Point Press, 2002).
2. See Note 2.

INTERIORS
Interior Design

Introduction

Interiors are formed largely from products and constitute the second building block of the built environment. Interiors are commonly referred to as "three-dimensional enclosed space" and as the "near environment."

Interiors are an environment created using a combination of products to satisfy human needs and embody human values. The ability to design effective interiors has increased human comfort, efficiency, and enjoyment. Some spaces fulfill individual and family needs for privacy; others are more public and reinforce social interaction, culture, and commerce. Interiors protect people from external factors and disturbances such as climate, noise, and intruding public eyes. Some specialized spaces, such as ships, aircraft, or space exploration vehicles, are designed to maximize efficiency within limited spatial dimensions. Like the other seven components of the built environment, interiors can be understood as an essential part of the **content-component-context** continuum. Products are designed together to form interiors, and interiors are integrated into a structural enclosure. The resultant artifact is an interior space.

Interiors can be further defined by adapting the following four-part definition of the built environment. The defining four characteristics also clarify the following content-component-context interrelationships:

- **Interiors** are created spaces that are humanly made or arranged;
- to fulfill human purposes, to satisfy human needs and embody human values; and
- to mediate the overall environment;
- with results that affect the overall environmental context (contexts for interiors include structures, landscapes, cities, regions and the Earth).

This connected content-component-context relationship can be simply understood by the following levels of integration continuum:

Products—**Interiors**—Structures—Landscapes—Cities—Regions—Earth

The three chapters in this section encourage the reader to explore more fully the human-environmental-technological aspects of interiors and interior design:

Interiors: Cultural Blueprint of Human Existence
by John C. Turpin

This chapter explores the historical relationships between humans and interior space. In an attempt to create quality interiors through the orchestration of aesthetic and functional requirements, designers are often challenged by the continued advances in societies' understanding of human/social, environmental, and technical issues. The integration of their responses to these external forces with the intention/function of interiors is the focus of this chapter.

Human Nature and the Near Environment
by Nancy H. Blossom

The idea of the near environment is based on the concepts of shelter and enclosure. Speaking of the near environment involves a focus on the interior spaces of a building. These are the spaces where we live and work. Interior designers strive to understand people by exploring the relationship between human nature and the near environment. Their goal is to design spaces that are supportive functionally as well as aesthetically. The designer plans not only for the physical comfort but also for the psychological comfort of people in these spaces.

Interior Design: Contemporary Issues and Challenges
by Jo Ann A. Thompson and Tina H. Johansen

This chapter addresses the issues and challenges manifested by the interaction between people and the interior spaces in which they experience life and interior design as a professional career. The goal of interior designers is to create interior environments that successfully address the functional, psychological, aesthetic, and cultural needs of

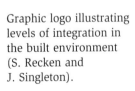

Graphic logo illustrating levels of integration in the built environment (S. Recken and J. Singleton).

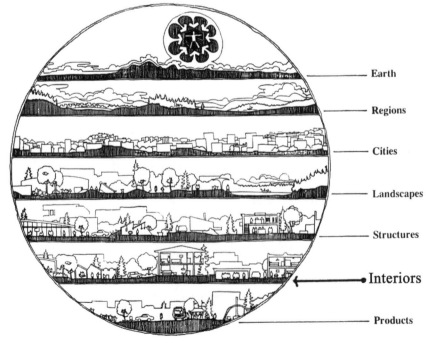

— Earth

— Regions

— Cities

— Landscapes

— Structures

— Interiors

— Products

people. Today's interior designer is a skilled professional who, through collaboration with other allied professionals, creates interior spaces that optimize the art and science of design by maximizing relationships among humans, the environment, and technological advances.

References

Each chapter concludes with a list of relevant references.

American Society of Interior Design (ASID): www.asid.org

Council for Interior Design Accreditation (CIDA): www.accredit-id.org

Foundation for Interior Design Education and Research (FIDER): www.fider.org

Interior Design Schools: www.InteriorDesignSchools.com or www.allartschools.com

International Interior Design Associations (IIDA): www.iida.org

National Council of Interior Design Qualification (NCIDQ): www.ncidq.org

CHAPTER 10

Cultural Blueprints of Human Existence

John C. Turpin

This chapter takes a historical look at the relationship between humans and interior space. In an attempt to create quality interiors through the orchestration of aesthetics and functional requirements, designers are often challenged by social, technological, and environmental issues. This investigation of interior spaces will reveal how corresponding responses to external issues have shaped select historic and contemporary developments and increase one's awareness of how interiors are cultural blueprints of human existence.

Recent studies have shown that humans spend approximately 80% of their life indoors. As children, the home embraces us, acting as a surrogate parent keeping us safe and secure. Our bedrooms become private shrines of identification as we search for self throughout our formative adolescent years. Educational institutions absorb close to one-third of our day from the ages of 5 to 21, with the majority of us selecting careers that are housed in an interior space. We have even begun to focus our entertainment inside movie theaters, shopping malls, sports arenas—and our own homes, initially with the advent of TV and increasingly with the development of computer technology. Consequently, it is very important to understand the forces that help mold these spaces and their impact on the human experience. When we speak of the human experience, we are, in fact, dis-

cussing "quality." The search for quality is, therefore, a major focus of this discussion.

Generally, quality depends on whether or not the interior sustains human life (physically, psychologically, and physiologically) by being aesthetically pleasing and supporting certain functions. In interior design, both of these criteria should be met to maximize the quality and usefulness of the space by employing methods from both art (aesthetics) and science (function, ergonomics, accessibility, technological advances).

History of Interiors

History provides a full-scale living laboratory for designers to analyze and understand the impacts of certain design decisions and the role of external forces. These forces can be divided into three categories: social issues, technological issues, and environmental issues. There is a continuum between time periods relative to each of these categories.

Social Issues

The mere fact that we have so many different types of interior space is an acknowledgment that human/social needs are driving the production of the built environment. Interiors are a crucial part of the infrastructure by which we define ourselves and interact with others. Social institutions are manifested clearly in the built environment and carry a great deal of meaning for the people they represent. The most common social institutions are domestic, commercial, political, and religious. Each of these provides various levels of interaction. Religious and political structures are public, while the home is private and intimate. In the home, social customs, etiquette, and life's basic necessities specifically drive interiors.

Fire is a major component of life for all human cultures. In early dwellings, a hearth, brazier, or fire pit was centrally located in the home for heat, cooking, and light. This necessity impacted space planning, as well as furniture design and arrangement. In ancient Egypt, the space containing the fire was centrally located, with all other rooms radially disposed. As cultures harnessed fire, space plans were freed from this composition as heat and light were provided for each room. Eventually, as the fireplace was introduced and moved to the wall, the center of the room was freed for other functions. An interesting response to this change was reflected in furniture.

With the central location of the brazier in Egypt and early Greece, furniture was created to be movable in order to support the various social functions that occurred around the fire (eating, conversation). This need for mobility required furniture to be lightweight and easy to transport from room to room. Consider an Egyptian and a Greek stool. Both were made of wood and were lightweight. One obvious difference was the number of legs. Why did an Egyptian stool have only three legs? In ancient Egypt, the floors were made of stone or earth and were often uneven. A three-legged stool was always stable on an uneven floor. Greek culture was able to create floors that were much more even and chose to design stools with four legs.

With the use of mobile furniture, what is now called a **classical arrangement** of furniture developed. Often used in more formal or aristocratic interiors, this particular arrangement keeps all pieces of furniture lined against the wall until needed. Depending on the required function, only certain pieces are utilized at any given time. The implication is that rooms, for the most part, remain multifunctional. One such example is the English great hall found in most medieval manor houses. The manor house was the center of the community. The great hall acted as dining hall, court, and festivities space. During a dining function, large trestle tables and benches were moved to the center of the room. But when court was in

session, these tables were moved back to the walls to provide more space for the masses.

One example of a radically changed social issue is privacy. This is quite a concern, considering that the hallway or corridor as a clearly defined and separate entity does not really appear until the nineteenth century in Victorian England. Previously, people moved directly from space to space and personal privacy was a considerable challenge. Medieval England and France used tester beds that could be enclosed completely in heavy textiles, providing protection from cold drafts and separation from the flow of traffic.

In seventeenth-century France, interiors aided in stratifying society. Both the monsieur and madam of the house had their own apartments, a series of rooms including an antechamber, chamber (bedroom), and cabinet (closet). A single salon connected the two. During social gatherings, guests' status relative to the host or hostess was clearly indicated by which rooms they were permitted to enter. Some guests had to stay in the salon, while the host/hostess permitted others to enter the antechamber or bedchamber. Only the most intimate friends entered the cabinet. It is interesting to note that the term "cabinet" is still used today to signify one's close associates, such as the President's cabinet.

Technological Issues

Interiors prior to the twentieth century had quite a few similarities. The most significant is the fact that the shape of interior space was a by-product of architectural design. The design of the exterior superseded the design of the interior. Not until the nineteenth century did a tradition emerge whereby interior spaces began to define the structure. Consequently, construction methods played a considerable role in defining the character of the spaces enclosed.

There are two basic methods of construction: trabeated and arcuated. **Trabeated construction**, also known as "post and lintel," is composed of a series of vertical elements (posts or columns) that support horizontal beams (lintels). The distance between the two vertical elements defines the width of the space. This can sometimes be rather limiting. For example, the temple complexes of Egypt are grand in scale, but the interiors were somewhat limited due to the use of stone in the construction system. Because of stone's poor tensile strength, the beams could not span large distances. As a result, some of the largest "rooms" in the complex are filled with columns. One space in particular, known as the "hypostyle hall," was roughly 50% structure and

50% space. Imagine being in a space like this; because of the massive size of the columns, the entire interior could not be viewed at once. The interior's uncomfortable, maze-like effect can cause visitors to wander rather aimlessly through the space. Only the clearly articulated central circulation path provides orientation.

As new materials and technologies were introduced, the spatial limitations of the post-and-lintel system were overcome. Consider a contemporary home; it is likely a wood-frame construction composed of studs placed in vertical and horizontal framing members. Some interiors can be quite large and yet are not interrupted by structural columns. The vast majority of office buildings also feature column-free interior spaces, employing steel or concrete to span longer distances between columns and allowing construction of taller structures. While columns do appear on every floor, they are considerably smaller, easily disguised in partition walls, or treated as design elements to help define spatial zones.

The second major system is known as **arcuated construction**, based on the Roman invention of the arch. The arch's success lies in its use of stone in compression. Unlike the trabeated system, the arch redirects the weight of the stone into the legs of the arch. The result is an ability to span much larger distances uninterrupted by structure. The earliest and perhaps most famous example is the Pantheon in Rome. Constructed in 79 C.E., the interior of the Pantheon is a dome (an arch spun on a vertical axis) 148 feet in diameter and 148 feet in height. Unlike orthogonal spaces, domed spaces have a unique effect on humans. What do people do when they enter a domed space? First, they look up. Then they walk toward the center of the room. They may think they are responding to the height, but in reality they are responding to the nature of a sphere. People are innately aware that a circle has a clearly defined center, whether it is articulated by some form of ornamentation or not. As a result, a domed space draws people to the center, directs their attention upward, and causes them to pause. On the other hand, a rectangular vaulted space, which is composed of a series of arches aligned on a horizontal axis, makes people move quickly through the space because the length of the space is typically greater than the height. Other famous arcuated spaces include Gothic cathedrals (see Fig. 10-1) and most state and national capitol buildings.

Environmental Issues

Humans' relationship with nature is clearly visible in the design of interiors. As discussed in Chapters 2 and 5, throughout history vernacular traditions have been a

Figure 10-1 Ste. Chappelle is an excellent example of Gothic construction. Notice the emphasis on height and the large number of windows relative to the structure (Patrick Snadon).

source of inspiration for design with indigenous environments—their culture, materials, and climate. The most common and easily recognizable tribute to nature in interiors of the high-style tradition can be found in their use of daylighting, views, ornamentation, or decoration. Countless cultures have re-created their surrounding environment in moldings, paintings, frescoes, and numerous other media. Examples include the Egyptian lotus capital, the Greek deer hoof, French vine work, and the U.S. eagle. But the connection between humans and nature is often obstructed by the limits of technology and construction, creating a conflict between interiors, buildings, and exterior spaces.

For the wealthy, a garden was incorporated into the design of the home and acted as an oasis or courtyard in an otherwise masonry jungle. Courtyard dwellings are also an effective design response to hot climates (see

Figure 10-3 Hall of Mirrors of the Palace of Versailles, seventeenth-century France (Patrick Snadon).

Figure 10-2 A Roman fresco from Pompeii depicting a garden scene, c. 79 B.C. (Dwight D. Rose © 2005).

Chapter 5). In response to the minimal opportunities for windows, Romans took advantage of their knowledge of frescoes (applying paint to wet plaster), covering their walls with images that attempted to dematerialize the wall and extend the perception of the interior by recreating garden scenes or fanciful city vistas (Fig. 10-2).

Virtually everyone appreciates a well-placed opening that leads to an extraordinary view, especially of nature. However, such views are often not available. In ancient Pompei, town homes were densely packed together. All houses had common walls with their neighbors and no external areas.

There is an inherent conflict between the human need for shelter and the need to be connected to the surrounding natural context. As a result, examples of solutions that demonstrate a capacity to accommodate both needs are rare. However, during the French Baroque period, a group of designers tackled the problem head-on and created one of the most successful relationships between the built and natural environments.

Built around an existing chateau at Versailles, the Hall of Mirrors connected two wings with an impressive expanse along a garden front. With spectacular gardens

Figure 10-4 The Salon Ovale in the Hotel de Soubise (1750) is the quintessential example of French Rococo style: nature, synthesis of the arts, and the impact of women (Patrick Snadon).

as far as the eye could see, the designers Charles LeBrun and Louis LeVau wanted to incorporate and André Le Notre's geometric gardens. Le Notre was a famous French landscape gardener. With the clear repetition of arched windows on the exterior wall of the hall, LeBrun copied the wall elevation on the other side, replacing glass with mirrors. The effect is stunning, as visitors are led to believe that the hall actually has two exterior walls, both looking out onto extravagant gardens. In addition, the geometry of the gardens is repeated on the wall elevations through contrasting marble accented by ormolu (gilded bronze).

For a brief descriptive summary of historic periods and related social-environmental-technological developments, see Table 10-1 at the end of this chapter.

The Twentieth Century: Transitions to Contemporary Design

Interior developments of the twentieth century can be illustrated by a look at the work of **Frank Lloyd Wright**, the development of the **Modern Movement** and the **International Style**, and the individualism that influenced the second half of the twentieth century.

As mentioned earlier, designers in the twentieth century approached space differently in that they designed both the inside and outside congruently. Frank Lloyd Wright was one of the earliest designers to implement this process. As a designer, Wright is difficult to categorize. Some historians consider him a participant of the **Arts and Crafts Movement** because he used natural materials and a natural color palette. Others regard his use of organic motifs as characteristic of the **Art Nouveau** period. Many settle the debate by crediting him for initiating a new type of **regionalism** through his residential works known as the **Prairie Style**. The term comes from an emphasis on the horizontal line, which Wright attributes to the prairies of the midwestern United States. If anything, Wright can be given credit for masterfully integrating the ideals of the Arts and Crafts Movement, the Art Nouveau period, and his own vision of regional design.

Social Issues

Socially, the Robie House design was guided by the implicit requirements of a wealthy client, as well as by Wright's own view of the importance of family and how it should be symbolically represented in the home. As the

quintessential example of the Prairie Style, the Robie House (1909) in Chicago was considered extremely progressive. Wright's clients took a significant risk in departing from the accepted options of the time, which included Victorian and neoclassical mansions. But the Robies were not typical aristocrats. They shied away from the social scene and desired greater privacy. With this in mind, Wright created an exquisite architectural shell that hid the front door and balconies that accented the horizontal line of the exterior and shielded views of the inside.

Wright designed the house around the fireplace because he believed it was a critical element in the development of the family. The double-sided fireplace is massive and separates the living room and dining room. The absence of walls allowed the spaces to flow together in an **open plan**, one of the unique traits of the Prairie Style. The open floor plan supported the more casual gatherings that many enjoyed; guests were expected to mingle between the rooms.

Socially, the rich were expected to have servants maintain the home. This is clearly evident by the **zoning** of public, private, and service areas. The kitchen, laundry, and maids' quarters were located in the back of the house. This grouping kept guests and the help from coming into contact with one another. The mechanics of the house were intentionally hidden.

Technological Issues

While the fireplace is the major focal point for the two main rooms, it is not the major heat source. The Robie House was equipped with central heating, with small floor vents throughout the living/dining room. Without

Figure 10-5 The living room of the Robie House by Frank Lloyd Wright (1909) demonstrates the use of horizontal line and windows with abstracted natural motifs.

this system of heating, the open plan would have been inefficient.

The most significant technological advance impacting the aesthetic of the interior was Wright's use of horizontal steel beams hidden in the ceiling. The steel spans the length of the living room uninterrupted. But the beams do not stop there; they continue as cantilevered elements far beyond the exterior wall, creating connections to an outdoor room. This arrangement achieved two goals. First, the cantilevered elements enhanced the horizontal lines of the exterior. Second, the "exterior" rooms connected the interior to nature.

Environmental Issues

The integration of indoor/outdoor spaces is not coincidental. Wright had a very clear desire to create **organic architecture**. This was not meant to involve copying nature, but instead a reinterpretation of nature's principles. Wright's designs responded to the climate and landscape of the prairie region (i.e., his Prairie Style). His designs expressed sensitivity to site qualities, daylighting, and orientation to the sun. Other important trademarks included his focus on a central symbolic fireplace and solar access in winter, and shade and cross-ventilation in summer. He also emphasized designing with and expressing the inherent nature of materials, much like the Arts and Crafts Movement. The living room was extended visually out to nature through the exterior rooms and by opening up or dematerializing walls with casement windows. The windows might seem to provide an "easy" connection to nature, but Wright creatively maintained a sense of privacy. To provide an additional "layer" of nature, each window was designed with an abstracted floral motif of the sumac, a local plant. Tempered geometry was another concept employed by Wright: to see the real thing, first look through an abstracted version of the actual view.

Human Experience

The Robie House has been preserved as a museum enabling visitors to experience Wright's design ideas and ideals firsthand. The experience of moving to and through the house is one of compression. As visitors look for the entrance to the home, they find that the architecture slowly closes in around them, leading to a recessed front door framed by a 7-foot clearance overhead. The foyer beyond is quite small, with equally low ceilings. The feeling is very intimate and warm, quite unusual for the house of a wealthy family during that period.

The space continues to constrict as the guest ascends the stairway; it is only at the top of the stairs and through one more turn that Wright releases the space and the living room breathes like a clearing in a forest. The warm colors and generally low ceilings are typical of the Arts and Crafts Movement and enhance the sense of warmth and intimacy. Clearly, Wright was successful in addressing both aesthetic and functional issues, creating a quality interior.

The Bauhaus and the International Style

The International Style originated in Germany. Designers sought to exploit recent developments in mechanization to deliver well-designed products to a much larger audience. With the machine as a crucial component in the design process, **functionalism** became a key feature of modern design. Walter Gropius[1] employed this philosophy in the curriculum of the **Bauhaus School** in Germany by implementing a design process that required handcrafted prototypes intended for mass production. It was perhaps the ultimate integration between the arts, crafts, and sciences, the human, and machine, as designers were intimately involved in the design and production processes, while the machine made the product available to a wider audience.

With the final phase requiring machine production, all the designs focused on an efficient and effective use of materials and industrial processes. There was to be no excess. As a matter of fact, decoration was seen as superfluous and did not represent German societal values of the early twentieth century.

The teachings of the Bauhaus School were disseminated throughout the United States and Europe through a show at the Museum of Modern Art in New York City and a book called *The International Style*.[2] Gropius and Mies van der Rohe migrated to the United States after the Nazis closed the Bauhaus School in 1933. Their designs for dwellings eventually impacted the design of commercial skyscrapers, which exploited their concepts of **functionalism**, **universality**, and **standardization**. The office environment was a major benefactor.

Social Issues

At the beginning of the twentieth century, businesses were burgeoning as a result of the growing application of mass production processes. More products reached a larger consumer base at a lower per unit cost. The workforce exploded to keep pace. During this time, the office environment took form and massive numbers of individuals began "desk jobs." By the mid-twentieth century, the modern office building was in full bloom and was greatly influenced by the new International Style.

The appearance of the new skyscraper differed considerably from that of earlier historic periods because of its lack of ornamentation. The Modern Movement style removed any sense of regionalism. Buildings were not tailored to their cultural and environmental surroundings. Structures in the United States looked the same as those in Europe and Asia, hence the designation International Style.

Technological Issues

The typical office environment is a large open space divided by columns or furnishings. The open grid system has a history linked to the Chicago Fire of 1871. With a large portion of downtown Chicago destroyed, a huge rebuilding campaign ensued. William Jenney employed the fastest method of constructing a building by utilizing a skeletal steel frame system of posts and beams creating a three-dimensional grid. With all of the weight and structure of the building localized in these elements, walls were freed from any load-bearing responsibilities. This included the exterior façade, which eventually became almost entirely glass, thanks to Mies van der Rohe, permitting light to flood the interior.

The interior columns created spaces that could accommodate an endless arrangement of partitions. Since most companies began creating corporate headquarters in the middle of the twentieth century, the skyscraper's ability to provide open, flexible space was crucial.

Environmental Issues

As the skyscraper reached a climax in the 1950s, the aesthetics of postwar modernism presented a more **biomorphic** approach to interior furnishings. As discussed in the previous chapter on product design, earlier examples of Modern Movement furniture were characterized by exposed structures of tubular steel demonstrating the most efficient and effective use of materials. However, post–World War II attitudes were dramatically different. Feelings of hope and faith in the democratic ideal prevailed, and consumers yearned for warmer, more inviting environments. Alvar Aalto, a Finnish designer, began working in bentwood, a material more acceptable to the

public. In the United States, Charles Eames and Eero Saarinen created more casual contemporary furniture. Humanism and technological innovation were combined in Eames' new chair through "his use of molded plywood bonded to rubber and metal, creating a chair that was elegantly light, functional, strong, with the flexibility and comfort of heavier furniture."[3]

While the seating clearly responded to the human form through sculptural planes, desks and cabinets remained rectilinear and focused on function and flexibility. Seating and work surfaces shared a feeling of levity, with a noticeable separation between the floor and the furniture through thin tubular legs. The contrast of the two types of furniture created an interior environment of interest and comfort. Many modernists worked caringly with the "nature" of new materials, climate, sun orientation and views, and natural light and ventilation, while others relied upon the new developments in mechanical technologies.

Human Experience

The human experience was a central issue in the development of the office environment. Frank Lloyd Wright's Larkin Building, constructed in 1906 in Buffalo, New York, responded to employees' need for comfort. He created a central atrium topped by a skylight that delivered natural light to the workers and incorporated a rooftop restaurant, library, infirmary, and pipe organ at the top of the atrium to provide lunchtime concerts.

Wright also developed one of the first open office systems, which was further developed by the Quickborner team, a German management consultancy, during the 1950s. The new optimism generated by the end of the war created a feeling of egalitarianism and dynamism. Interiors were opened up as small offices and corridors gave way to rows of desks and small dividing screens and the use of plant life. The term **office landscape** came into use as designers attempted to create a visually interesting environment by selecting furnishings and decorative elements that would produce multiple layers. Even though many private offices continued to ring the perimeter, inner glass walls brought natural light and distant views to the employees.

A prevailing impetus for design decisions that supported quality work environments was the desire to boost employee productivity. With the science of **ergonomics** (human engineering) at the forefront, seating focused on conforming to the human body. Back support, padded armrests, and casters allowed time at the desk to be less physically straining. Researchers studied posture, human reach, and external conditions that would enhance human comfort and productivity. This is an excellent example of how interior design incorporates science (human science in this case) in the design process.

The Late Twentieth Century: Individualism?

"Stylistic heterogeneity" continued to be a prevalent trend in the late twentieth century, with an inexhaustible range of styles available to reflect individual identities.[4] Three movements beginning in the 1960s seem to offer a logical foundation for this trend. Pop, Post Modern, and Memphis styles share the common goal of individual expression. With designers' liberation from clearly defined rules of "good taste," environments of whimsy and playfulness ensued.

Figure 10-6 The central atrium of the DAAP by Peter Eisenman (1996). The Grand Staircase is not revealed. It starts on the second floor on the right-hand side.

The Pop culture of the 1960s severely criticized the functionalism characteristic of the Modern Movement. Pop culture embodied the values of an affluent teenage population and its growing dissatisfaction with the social and cultural values of its parents. As a strong consumer force, teens created a unique identity in their selection of music, clothes, furnishings, and behavior. A vibrant energy spread across the United States through use of the expressive power of form and color.

By the early 1970s, the achievements of the Modern Movement had largely been discredited and a mannerist phase had begun. Designers had grown weary of the rigidity of the International Style's dogma and had begun experimenting with a new interpretation of classicism. By the end of the decade, designers were exaggerating the classical orders in a very playful manner. Post Modernists argued that historic styles and the visual immediacy of mass culture had something to teach designers. In conjunction with this movement, a group of Italian designers flouted the notions of good taste, which in Italy had become closely bound up with Modernism. Known as the Memphis Style, their designs soon became part of the mass-consumer experience. Interiors were adorned with brightly patterned plastic laminates creating a witty, bold style intended to be fun.

On the heels of the prevailing individualism of the past three decades, designers like Peter Eisenman were primed to continue to reinvent space, but at what cost? Some answers may be found in a building for the College of Design, Art, Architecture, and Planning (DAAP) at the University of Cincinnati, completed in 1996.

Social Issues

Much like the Pop era, the late 1990s were empowering for youth. The students who would be the main users of the DAAP environment grew up with MTV and a wide array of computer games. As a result, these young consumers processed and fed off of rapid-fire visual information like no generation before. Numerous discussions in the design community have focused on how this upbringing might alter demands for designed objects. Was Eisenman aware of this issue when he designed an unconventional interior for DAAP that seems to be in constant motion? Most interesting is the manner in which Eisenman relates the interior to the user. The interior does not reveal itself to the user. Instead, the user is treated much like a player in a video game in which there is little knowledge of what is around the next corner. One example is the juxtaposition of the central atrium (Fig. 10-6) with the grand stair (Fig. 10-7). Neither of the two elements gives a clue of its presence to

Figure 10-7 The grand staircase of the DAAP. The atrium is immediately behind the columns on the right.

the other. Another example is the use of solid 5-foot walls to surround atrium spaces, which, unlike conventional open railings of a typical 3-foot height, prevent the average building user from making visual connections between floors or watching activities in common spaces. Situations like this are difficult and can cause considerable frustration to users trying to navigate the space or connect with other building users.

Another interesting social issue is the prevailing relationship of humans with their own bodies. In a society riddled with violent images from cartoons like "Itchy and Scratchy" on *The Simpsons* to unending sequels of slasher movies like *Friday the 13th*, the human form has been under attack. Unlike the Renaissance period, when the body was revered as the key to the universe, today's society is much more irreverent toward the body. This perspective shows up in the DAAP. There is a spot in the atrium where people can sit and view a bridge that connects two separate areas of the building. As people walk across the bridge, the structure seems to decapitate them and viewers in the atrium witness a torso floating above them.

Technological Issues

The strongest driving force in the creation of the DAAP is the impact of the computer. Eisenman used complex computer-generated formulas to assist in the design of the structure. The geometry of the interior creates movement and interest (Fig. 10-8). However, because of a lack of light, paint played a major role in articulating the numerous shapes and forms and providing a sense of order.

The complex planes and connections stressed the construction budget for DAAP. One sacrifice was the use of dryvet, a new material, for the interior. Much like gyp-

sum board, dryvet was adhered to a metal frame. Unfortunately, holes can easily be punched into this material. Once students discovered this, there was a backlash of vandalism—perhaps a criticism by the students of the "cheap" material used for "their" school.

Environmental Issues

The site for DAAP presented design challenges. Eisenman responded to the site by embedding a profile of a one-story building on its north façade. Thanks to the landscape architect George Hargraves, the building graciously follows the contours of the hill; the relationship between structure and site is quite sensitive. In addition, the south side of the building has been integrated with existing buildings. Unfortunately, this limits the fenestration, leaving many spaces without exterior views or natural light. DAAP does not address a strong response to environmental issues or advance the many design qualities and benefits of "designing with nature" (the nature

Figure 10-8 The atrium of the DAAP reveals some of the complexity of the computer-generated geometry.

Table 10-1 An Overview of the Prevailing Periods and Their Characteristics Prior to the Twentieth Century. (Dates Are Approximate)

HISTORICAL PERIODS	SOCIAL	TECHNOLOGICAL	ENVIRONMENTAL	HUMAN EXPERIENCE
Ancient Egyptian 2800–1000 B.C.E.	• Fire is center of home. • Furniture is mobile to provide flexibility. • Religion is a dominant force.	• Use of post and lintel. • Mastery of wood joinery evident in furniture.	• Natural imagery: lotus, reeds, alligators. • Natural color palette. • Hypostyle hall is abstraction of forest. • Design with sun, climate.	• Domestic spaces have minimal windows/light. • Extreme division of material possessions.
Classical Greece 400–0 B.C.E.	• Democratic ideals prevent excessive display of individual wealth. • Drive toward perfection.	• Refinement of post and lintel. • Use of lathe to create turnings.	• Uses human form to define proportion of columns. • Response to site.	• An appreciation of perfection in beauty. • Minimal ornamentation on furniture.
Classical Roman 0–400 C.E.	• Interiors/furnishings are massive and ornate to display the wealth and power of the empire.	• Invention of arch and concrete provides more spatial options. • Perfection of frescoes.	• Expanse of empire allows wide range of marbles. • Natural motifs: lion's paw, eagle, festoons. • Use of formal geometry with spaces and gardens.	• Scale of interiors evokes awe. • Emphasis on pleasures, both physical and visual.
Gothic 1100–1500	• Christianity is the major authority. • Immense civil pride in the construction of cathedrals.	• Flying buttress and pointed arch allow spaces to soar upward and walls to be mainly of windows (Fig. 10-1).	• Light is a major element as it is filtered through stained glass windows. • Human forms stretch to respond to interior.	• Interiors evoke awe, wonder, and humility in order to visually enhance relationship between God and worshipper.
Renaissance 1410–1525	• New wealth from banking class creates a patron class for the arts. • Belief that the human was center of the universe.	• Craft traditions are revived, in part, by the return of artisans to Rome from the fallen capital of Byzantium.	• Nature is manifested through formal geometry because the human form can make a perfect square and circle. This is reflected in room proportions and ornamentation.	• Interiors display art or become works of art themselves. • Classical arrangement of furniture.
Baroque 1640–1700	• Catholic Church becomes a major influence by using interiors as propaganda to bring people back to the Church.	• Growing mastery of construction methods provide complex, dynamic interior spaces.	• Strong movement to connect interiors visually with gardens in domestic commissions.	• Baroque churches intend to engage the viewer emotionally with dramatic, energetic religious scenes.
Rococo 1700–1760	• Women ascend socially. • Etiquette is loosened slightly (Fig. 10-4).	• French and Italians create large sheets of plate glass.	• Nature becomes a major force, and motifs of vines, shells, cherubs are prolific.	• Interiors become more intimate and casual as women become patrons.
English Neoclassical 1760–1800	• Discovery of Pompeii allows a more accurate interpretation of interiors.	• Invention of mechanical loom provides more textiles for interiors.	• Classical swags and festoons are smaller to fit the scale of an interior.	• Interior ornamentation is more appropriately scaled. • Formality returns.

Table 10-1 An Overview of the Prevailing Periods and Their Characteristics Prior to the Twentieth Century. (Dates Are Approximate) (Continued)

HISTORICAL PERIODS	SOCIAL	TECHNOLOGICAL	ENVIRONMENTAL	HUMAN EXPERIENCE
Victorian 1840–1920	• The emphasis on etiquette by Queen Victoria causes introduction of hallways and rooms with only one function.	• Machine production creates high-style products at lower prices.	• Materials are considered dishonest because they are represented as something other than what they are in reality.	• Interiors become dense with furnishings, accessories, and pattern.
Arts and Crafts 1860–1900	• Reaction against the evils of machine production that created unhappy workers.	• Methods of production return to hand craftsmanship.	• Use of materials "honestly" according to physical and performance properties.	• Interiors are very simple, with low ceilings and a large amount of wood.
Art Nouveau 1890–1910	• A growing tendency for cultures to adopt a new style that represents their entrance to the twentieth century.	• Experimentation with all manner of production as long as it is faithful to the material.	• Organicism is fully embraced, especially in decorative arts.	• Interiors have molded appearance and relate to the biological form of the inhabitant.

of human and environmental systems)—using terms such as "green," "ecological," or "sustainable design." Many of these advances will be further developed in the next two chapters and in other related components of the built environment discussed throughout this book.

Human Experience

While the interior of the DAAP is a fascinating experiment in computer-generated aesthetics, designers and many users have not given it high marks for function. The building does not provide a supportive environment for human needs such as wayfinding and legibility, discussed in Chapter 4. The lack of views and natural light in numerous classrooms and faculty offices is uncomfortable, undermining the ability to concentrate. The lack of signage and architectural cues for orientation is another problem many have identified. Directions are impossible to give, and people often need to be escorted to ensure their arrival.

Conclusion

This chapter has looked at a variety of spaces, their response to social, technological, and environmental issues, and their integration in final design solutions during major historic periods. The ultimate goal for designers of interior spaces should be to ensure a supportive environment for human activity. Research has found

unequivocally that interior environments impact human health and productivity. Since interiors are so powerful in their manipulation of human experiences, everyone should be more aware and appreciative of the supportive qualities (aesthetics and function) of interior space.

References

Blakemore, R. *History of Interior Design and Furniture: From Ancient Egypt to Nineteenth-Century Europe.* Wiley, 1997.

Giedion, S. *Space, Time and Architecture.* Cambridge University Press, 1982.

Harwood, B., B. May, and C. Sherman. *Architecture and Interior Design Through the 18th Century: An Integrated History.* Prentice Hall, 2001.

Hitchcock, H., and P. Johnson. *The International Style.* W. W. Norton, 1966.

Massey, A. *Interior Design of the 20th Century.* Thames and Hudson, 2001.

Pelegrin-Genel, E. *The Office.* Flammarian, 1996.

Sparke, P. *Design in Context.* Bloomsbury, 1987.

Whiton, S. *Interior Design and Decoration.* Lippincott, Williams & Wilkins, 1991.

Endnotes

1. H. Hitchcock and P. Johnson, *The International Style* (W. W. Norton, 1966).
2. See Note 1.
3. P. Sparke, *Design in Context* (Bloomsbury, 1987): page 191.
4. A. Massey, *Interior Design of the 20th Century* (Thames and Hudson, 2001).

CHAPTER 11

Human Nature and the Near Environment

Nancy H. Blossom

The idea of the near environment is based on the concepts of shelter and enclosure—focusing on the interior spaces of a building. These are the spaces where we live and work. Designers strive to understand people by exploring the relationships between human nature and the near environment. Their goal is to design spaces that are supportive functionally as well as aesthetically. The designer plans not only for the physical comfort but also for the psychological comfort of people in these spaces.

Human nature and the near environment are core concerns for interior designers and other design disciplines that focus on **human scale** and **human performance** in the built environment. All designers strive to understand clients and users by exploring in depth the relationship between human nature, interior spaces, and the near environment. Key to this understanding is the recognition that the interior environment has a strong impact on the personal nature of the built environment, whether urban or rural. This discussion will be a more applied exploration of many of the issues discussed in Chapter 4.

Human nature describes characteristics that all humans have in common. When this term is used in the context of interior design, its meaning is expanded to include not only the character but also the characteristics that all or most humans share in the built environment. These characteristics can be divided into two basic categories: functional and behavioral.

Functional characteristics relate to the size, shape, and form of the human body, as well as to movement and activity. These characteristics can be as simple as height and weight or as complex as the measurements of specific bones. These characteristics shape the ability of people to work and play in various environments. Physical measurements of functional characteristics assess whether a person can sit comfortably in a chair or reach the top shelf in the closet.

Behavioral characteristics relate to the way humans act in a group or individually. It is very difficult to make generalizations about people, as they come in all sizes and shapes and act in very different ways. However, some characteristics are shared by many people. It is important for all designers to recognize both the traits that people share and those that make them different. Social scientists study behavior and recognize that individuals often behave differently from people in groups. The study or science of individual behavior is psychology, relating to the mind or mental processes. Sociology is the study of group behavior in social settings. Designers of both interior and exterior spaces need to understand how the built environment affects individual

Figure 11-1 Humans come in all shapes and sizes. As the marketplace becomes more global, interior designers need to be aware of both the similarities and differences among a wide variety of people.

mental processes and how it affects the way groups of people behave. Designers depend on the work of psychologists and sociologists to help them understand how people will react to the spaces they design.

Figure 11-2 A well-designed reception desk serves many purposes. First, it welcomes strangers to an office suite and signals the character or identity of a company. It also serves as a multipurpose workstation with multiple surfaces at different heights. The transaction surface is designed to support a person who is standing to sign a paper or read a document. The work surface is designed to support a person who is sitting to work at the computer or speak on the phone.

What does the near environment mean? While landscape architects view the natural environment as their palette and architects tend to look at the structure, exterior, and interior of a building as their domain, interior designers focus on designing spaces within a building. The near environment is the space that surrounds the human body and is separated from the natural environment by the walls of buildings. These are the spaces where people live and work.

Functional Issues in the Near Environment

Designers take a close look at functional issues in the near environment, particularly as they relate to the health, safety, and welfare of the people who use the spaces. The way people fit the spaces they occupy can impact their safety. The way furniture and equipment fit the bodies of the people who use them can impact their health. The study of human body measurements on a comparative basis is known as **anthropometrics**. It is a useful science for interior design, providing the tools to understand the physical fit or interface between the human body and various components of interior space.

In the twentieth century, concern for human dimensions and body size became critical factors in the design process. In turn, this focus on human dimensions in interior spaces such as homes, offices, health facilities, and schools, became a significant field of research.

Any interface between people and the near environment must ensure comfortable, safe, and efficient use of space. For instance, the heights of countertops in a kitchen or work surface heights in an office must reflect

Figure 11-3 People can spend a great deal of their time in the workspace.

Figure 11-4 The size and shape of individuals impact their safety and comfort in interior spaces. A mixed user population includes people of all sizes and shapes.

Figure 11-5 Designers must consider the special needs of specific populations—for example, a toddler in a playschool environment. Providing tables, cubbies, and easels that a child can access gives an opportunity to learn independence.

dimensions are measurements taken in working positions or during the movement associated with certain tasks.

All designers must keep in mind the huge number of variables involved in assessing human dimensions. Many researchers believe that there is no such thing as an "average" human size when dealing with **ergonomic** fit. Designing for a standard or average human size often prevents many people from using equipment, furniture, or space. What are a designer's options then? One approach is to deal with human dimensions in ranges. Another

Figure 11-6 Ergonomics is the study of how a workplace and its equipment are designed for comfort, safety, efficiency, and productivity. This traditional design studio does not demonstrate consideration for a good ergonomic fit between student and furniture and would not allow access for all people.

the human factor of body size. Human dimensions also impact such considerations as the number of seats around a kitchen table or the size of a restaurant booth. In public areas like restaurants, designers must take into account not only the comfortable fit of the seats in a booth, but also the distances between tables that allow customers to walk safely and waiters to work efficiently.

In some situations, designers create spaces for a large **mixed user population**, which includes people of all sizes and shapes. At other times, designers work out spaces for just a single user. In still other situations, the focus may be on a specific demographic group such as young children or the elderly. In order to do their jobs well, designers must be aware of their intended audience, as well as the metrology of body size—that is, the system of measurement.

Human body dimensions that impact the design of interior spaces are of two basic types—**static and dynamic**. Static dimensions are measurements of body parts such as the head, torso, and limbs in standard positions. Dynamic

Figure 11-7 The use of ergonomics to create flex and flexibility within the various aspects of the traditional studio/work environment.

approach is to design with the capacity to adjust to varying users. The selection of appropriate anthropometric data is based on the nature of the particular design problem under consideration and who will be using the spaces. Another approach is to design for all users. Data that should be considered in this case are the statistical extremes of the user population. In other words, consider the tallest and the shortest, the widest and most narrow humans. This is called **universal design**, a philosophical approach to design that advocates designing for all people rather than an average. It is based on the belief that all people deserve equal access to all environments and should be able to use and navigate them without challenges.

Of equal concern to all designers are the sensory

characteristics of humans, those related to the **five human senses**: hearing, sight, smell, taste, and touch. While most people have good use of all five senses, some do not. A diminished sense of sight, for instance, can pose significant safety and welfare challenges to a person in any environment. Routine decisions about the placement of furniture or the use of hard materials that create sharp edges may need to be modified. Similarly, people who cannot hear may need special accommodations in the design of their living spaces. For instance, routine elements such as light fixtures can become means for communication as well as a way to illuminate space. A light fixture in each room of the apartment of a hearing-impaired adult can be wired to the doorbell. When a visitor presses the button, the lights will blink, signaling that someone is at the door. The same light fixtures can be programmed to blink very fast, like a strobe light, if there is a fire alarm in the building.

While bad odors are often a sign of danger—for example, leaking natural gas or spoiling food—even harmless odors have been known to disrupt a workplace. Careful consideration of the impact of odors is important in the design of specialty interiors, from the highly technical, such as laboratories, to the recreational, such as snack bars and fast food restaurants. Finally, humans depend on their sense of touch to understand and appreciate the environments around them.

It is difficult to consider a single sense as a key human

Figure 11-8 Universal design advocates designing for all people, regardless of age, size, or gender. This approach acknowledges and values the wide variety of people who use interior spaces. This sculpture shows how easily an elderly woman and two children share a public bench.

Figure 11-9 Color, texture, and light all impact the way people feel in the near environment. The open office landscape also allows the distribution of daylight in the work environment and provides for a semiprivate work zone as well as an open community for teamwork and collaboration. IslandWood, Bainbridge Island, Washington (T. Bartuska).

characteristic because people use their senses in concert when navigating space. It is often not until a sense is challenged that people realize how they use it and how important it is to a feeling of security within a space.

Behavioral Issues in the Near Environment

The built environment profoundly affects attitudes and behavior. The designer has to plan not only for the physical comfort of the user but also for the psychological comfort. Many components in the near environment impact human behavior. Of particular significance are the products that give character and definition to interior spaces. Variables like the color and texture of fabrics and materials or the scale and proportion of furniture all play a big role in the communication exchange between the built environment and the people who inhabit it.

Something as simple as the way chairs are placed in a room can communicate to people how they should behave in the space. Chairs set up in rows facing in one direction suggest a more formal or controlled setting and signal the need for similar behavior. A circle of chairs or groups of two and three chairs scattered throughout the room suggest a more informal setting and help to trigger more communication between people as well as more relaxed behavior.

Supportive spaces make people of all ages feel more comfortable. Designers cultivate an awareness of the key issues and objectives upon which support design should be based. One of these is the concept of **personal space**. Edward Hall,[1] an anthropologist, conducted one of the earliest studies of how people relate socially and psychologically to the physical space around them. Hall developed the concept of **proxemics**—the study of the distance individuals maintain between each other in group or social interaction. Hall's concept is based on the idea that every individual is surrounded by a perceptual bubble of what he called personal space—that is, the space that separates an individual from the rest of the world. When a stranger infringes upon that space, a sense of discomfort follows. Hall noticed that people tolerate different levels of closeness, depending upon the activity in which they are engaged. He imagined that personal space is like a bubble around a person that changes shape as the activities and circumstances change. Think about a packed elevator. People crowd together without much concern, usually facing toward the door. But if someone enters the elevator and does not turn around,

squeezing closer face to face, it's likely that a high level of discomfort will follow. Once people leave the elevator, the bubble of personal space normally expands, particularly in front.

Hall determined that when people interact socially, they typically function within **four zones of space**: the intimate zone, the personal zone, the social zone, and the public zone. Various cultures may have the same zone but different sizes. Each of these zones has a near phase and a far phase. Hall maintains that people will select a particular zone for social interaction, depending upon relationships, status, and the nature of the activity involved. This is an important concept for all designers to understand as they consider the sizes of rooms and the placement of furniture for different activities. Hall's studies predicted that people would not interact with one another beyond a certain distance. If the goal is for a group of people to get to know one another, it would be self-defeating to place chairs in such a large circle that interactions become prohibitive. Based on proxemics,

Figure 11-10 The study of proxemics explores the distance that individuals maintain between each other in social interaction. This closeness demonstrates that friends can infringe on personal space without creating stress (courtesy Washington State University/Spokane).

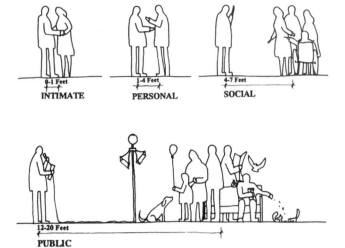

Figure 11-11 The four zones of proxemics developed by Hall—used to develop private-to-public spaces of appropriate sizes.

chairs placed in twos and threes support better interaction between people.

Do students behave differently in a large lecture hall than in a seminar room? It is very easy to opt out of the discussion in a large lecture. The distance between student and teacher is great, and it is easy to feel removed from the conversation. The dynamic changes in more intimate settings such as a seminar room, where everyone is seated around a table. Designers can make good decisions about the furniture to use in a room and how to arrange it if they know how the room will be used, who the users will be, and what their goals and objectives are for each anticipated function.

Consider the impact of proxemics in an elder care facility. Someone noticed that older men and women liv-

ing together did not talk during social hours, when they were brought from private rooms to be together in public spaces. A close look at the situation revealed that for the most part, the chairs in these public rooms were lined up along the walls, all facing the center. The social distance was too far for people to interact across the room, and it was easy to ignore people on either side. Many of the residents had diminished eyesight or hearing. Even though the goal was to promote social life, the placement of the chairs around the room promoted isolation rather than interaction. A simple experiment with chair placement changed the social activity: chairs were arranged in smaller groups so that people could interact face to face, giving them an opportunity to become acquainted and make friends—to, in fact, be social.

Another factor important to all people is the concept of **privacy**, the state of being apart from other people and not being seen, heard, or disturbed by them. All people have a need for privacy, although this need is as diverse as the many different types of humans.

While privacy is something that we can expect in the places we call our own, especially our homes, it is harder to achieve, but no less important, in places we share

Figure 11-13 Workspaces in a computer lab are designed to provide minimum privacy while students work. A sense of privacy is as important to individuals as real privacy, even though it is an illusion (Pamela Overholtzer).

Figure 11-12 Students are far more likely to engage in classroom discussion in a seminar or small-group setting.

with relative strangers—for example, offices, schools, and hospitals.

What is the relationship between privacy and the design of the near environment? Consider the placement of hallways in homes. In early homes in the United States, rooms were all connected by simple doorways. In order to move through the house, people passed from room to room. What happens to privacy in circumstances such as these? After hallways became commonplace in most homes, privacy could be taken for granted. Simply closing a door gives most people the opportunity to be apart from others and relatively undisturbed. Designers make decisions about where doors are placed, how rooms and hallways relate to one another, and how homes and workplaces are divided into public and private spaces.

It is important to note that no matter what type of space people find themselves in, they have a huge capacity to **adapt** to it. This is why, if there are no other options, we are able to live in the most unpleasant circumstances. We can live in rooms that are too dark or too smelly. Eventually, we adapt and no longer notice the annoyance. But more typically, we attempt to change the environment to meet our needs. Usually people try to improve their surroundings by making changes, plugging holes in the wall or covering cold floors. But people also change their environments just because they want to. People tend to rearrange furniture freely in public spaces—for example, to create privacy or to enhance a group dynamic.

Dorm rooms are excellent examples of adaptation. To some extent, students change their behavior to adapt to

Figure 11-15   This office allows a close relationship to the outside and the bustling activity of the city. For an extroverted individual, this is an excellent work environment. For an introverted person, it might be very difficult.

dorm room circumstances, such as lack of privacy and cramped quarters. But they also move furniture, hang barriers, and divide spaces. A well-designed dorm room allows for some flexibility in arrangement, recognizing that college students are very diverse and have many different needs. For example, beds that can be raised to create extra storage space beneath, or made into lofts to create study alcoves, help students personalize and feel comfortable in their dorm environment.

Cultural Reference

Cultural reference affects the way people respond to the details of the near environment and the products that give character and definition to the interior space. **Cultural reference** can be defined as the belief patterns that surround all people as they pass through life. Typically, these belief patterns are shared by a number of people who come together as a group. For example, race, religion, social connections, or status tie people within a group together and can influence their belief patterns. Most humans claim allegiance to multiple groups at one time and are influenced by all of them.

A more complex definition of culture is that of an integrated pattern of human behavior that includes thought, speech, action, and artifacts. Culture is dependent upon humans' capacity for learning and for passing knowledge on to succeeding generations. Designers know that thought, speech, and actions are all connected

Figure 11-14   Fixed seating in a lecture hall makes it hard for students to participate in small-group discussions. Flexible seating allows students to adapt the classroom in order to interact with a speaker or to work individually or in small groups.

Figure 11-16 Posters, photographs, and the red flyer wagon are all artifacts that make a statement about the person who works in the space.

to artifacts. **Artifacts** are human-made objects and materials such as tools or ornaments. If thought, speech, and actions are tied to artifacts, then artifacts have the potential to represent meanings or ideas. Designers must understand how these things convey meanings to their clients and other users.

People desire (and expect) their material worlds to express or reinforce their personal identities. They use materials or artifacts to symbolize their sense of self, that is, what they want the world to know about them. The way a house is furnished, the type of car chosen, or the clothes worn are all factors in the expression of self. The idea, however, is not limited to homes and personal

belongings. In public or shared spaces, people will often strive to claim or identify their ownership of space. Men and women spend so much time in the workplace that their sense of self is closely tied to their desks, offices, studios, and so on. Most make some effort to personalize, modify, or mark these spaces as their own.

Built Components of the Near Environment

The messages conveyed by the near environment are closely related to the built components that surround it. As introduced in Chapter 7, **planes** define the space of the near environment: two horizontal planes and a series of vertical planes. The ceiling plane, the floor plane, and four wall planes, for instance, define a typical room. In its simplest form, an interior space is like the inside of an empty box. But these spaces can be manipulated; the walls can be curved or angled, and the ceilings and floor planes can be raised or lowered to varying heights. Texture and color can be added to create interest. As planes are manipulated or changed in appearance, the character of the space also

Figure 11-17 What does this office say about the person who uses it? Note the saddle in the far right corner.

Figure 11-18 This room communicates something about the people who live in it through the combination of Chinese and North American furniture and artifacts.

the reality of the building did not consist in the walls and the roof, but in the space within to be lived in.[2]

Wright's use of concrete in the Unity Temple was key to this discovery of the interior. The structural qualities of concrete allowed him to manipulate the volumes of space and to experiment with the ideas he had been contemplating. Wright's genius was in recognizing that all components of interior spaces affect users. He not only manipulated the volumes of space but also recognized that the articulation of planes, the application of color and texture and decorative motif, all impacted the quality of spaces. He saw the design as a whole and often insisted on designing all the components of the interiors, structure, walls, furniture, rugs, lights, and even objects of daily living such as china and utensils.

From Wright's era on, designers have continued to experiment with structure and new technologies to manipulate and exploit interior space. The growing concern with interior space as a design element led to the

Figure 11-19 The planes of the interior can be manipulated to create a strong sense of volume. In this case, the overhead planes of the ceiling slant and the heights of vertical planes are varied, creating a very dramatic interior space.

changes. Openings in the wall planes let light into the interior environment. If daylight is not available, artificial light can be used to illuminate the space, to change the atmosphere, and to make the space more appealing.

Let us look a little more closely at the idea of space. For the most part, **space** is something that is taken for granted in contemporary times, but it was only in the early twentieth century that designers recognized the importance of interior space as a design element and a vital environment. In the sanctuary of the Unity Temple in Oak Park, Illinois, Frank Lloyd Wright discovered the importance of the interior space:

I think that was about the first time when the interior space began to come through as the reality of the building. . . . You will notice that features were arranged against that interior space allowing a sense of it to come to the beholder . . . wherever he happened to be. And I have been working on that thesis for a long time because it was dawning on me that when I built that building that

Figure 11-20 Integration of the exterior and interior, along with manipulation of light, texture, and color, create positive environments (Courtesy of Washington State University/Spokane).

Figure 11-21 People of all sizes, shapes, and abilities are the focus in the design of the near environment. As people change, so do their demands on the space that surrounds them (Spokane, Washington).

specialty of interior design. As the field grew, designers recognized that manipulation of volumes of space, as well as the application of decorative elements, has an impact on the quality of interior spaces. As research demonstrated that elements such as light, texture, and color have a profound effect on the way people work and play in these spaces, more emphasis was placed on the integration of elements in the design of the near environment. Design teams now recognize that good design demonstrates strong relationships between the interior and exterior of a building.

Contemporary designers continue to recognize all these components as key to a viable near environment. New products and technology play a big role in the development of contemporary near environments. Instead of a basic white wall, designers might imagine a wall of multilayered ribbons of fabric that cascade from a ceiling and unfold into pieces of furniture as they approach the floor. As a basic component of the interior, a wall becomes a sculptural unit that defines a space and is beautiful to

look at as well as comfortable to sit on or within. The possible combinations of color are endless, limited only by the imagination. Walls of acrylic that can change color from the vivid reds and yellows of a sunset to a calm blue to suit the whims or moods of the people inside are being tested. Computers program spaces to recognize when a person enters and adjust the light level or change the temperature. In all instances, the key is the effect on people within the space, and the palette that the designer works with to achieve that effect constitutes the near environment.

Today's interior designer is an educated and experienced individual in a complex profession. Designers impact, discreetly or indiscreetly, all phases of people's lives. Interior design professionals work with spaces that have great potential to affect the safety, health, and well-being of diverse groups of people. Interiors of nearly every description are professionally designed: schools, health care facilities, restaurants, offices, institutions, and more.

Design should be a continuous collaborative effort. There is an expanding need for well-trained interior designers who can create a space that is responsive to all users' needs and who take responsibility for the impact of design on the psychosocial well-being of all users. The temptation to guess at answers to complex design problems must be resisted. In today's world, mistakes last a long time and the penalties for wrong guesses can be punishing.

Out of this need to understand the complexity of contemporary design, interior designers and researchers cooperate to solve more broadly defined problems that cannot be solved alone. Research and design cooperation grows out of the variability of social reality. Boundaries of problems change; situations differ; viewpoints are flexible; people grow. An interior designer's main objective is to change the physical settings of the near environment. A good designer wants his or her design decisions to support desired behavioral effects and to create environments that meet the social and psychological needs of those who use them.

Interior design is a dynamic, complex field that challenges skilled practitioners to think creatively and critically to solve problems that affect human nature in the near environment.

References

Bremer, J. *Proxemics, How We Use Space*. 2002: www.bremer-communications.com.

Dreyfus, Henry. *The Measure of Man and Woman: Human Factors in Design.* Wiley, 2002.

Hall, E. *The Silent Language.* Anchor, 1973.

Hall, E. *The Hidden Dimension.* Doubleday, 1996.

Harmon, S., and K. Kennon. *The Codes Guidebook for Interiors.* Wiley, 2001.

HVM. *Human Variance Model.* 2003: www.hf.faa.gov.

InformeDesign. *Where Research Informs Design.* University of Minnesota, 2004. www.informedesign.umn.edu.

Malnar, J., and F. Vodvarka. *The Interior Dimension: A Theoretical Approach to Enclosed Space.* Van Nostrand Reinhold, 1992.

Protrowski, C. *Professional Interior Designers.* Wiley, 2001.

Steinfield, E., and S. Danford. *Enabling Environments.* Plenum, 1999.

Stumpf, B., D. Chadwick, and B. Dowell. *The Anthropometrics of Fit.* 2004: www.hermanmiller.com/us/pdf/workplace/wp_Anthropometrics.pdf.

Endnotes

1. E. Hall, *The Hidden Dimension* (Doubleday, 1996).
2. J. Malnar and F. Vodvarka, *The Interior Dimension: A Theoretical Approach to Enclosed Space* (Van Nostrand Reinhold, 1992): 41.

CHAPTER 12

Interior Design: Contemporary Issues and Challenges

Jo Ann A. Thompson and Tina H. Johansen

Interior design is a professional career that addresses the issues and challenges created by interactions between people and the interior spaces in which they experience life. The goal of interior designers is to create interior environments that successfully address the functional, psychological, aesthetic, and cultural needs of people. As an emerging discipline, interior design has faced many challenges. Today's interior designer is a skilled professional who, through collaboration with practitioners in other allied disciplines, creates interior spaces that optimize the art and science of design by maximizing relationships among humans, environments, and technological advances.

Throughout their lifetime, people spend a majority of time in some form of interior environment. These environments vary in size, scale, and function and range from small private living spaces to large public spaces—with a multitude of variations in between. Interior spaces, therefore, are a dominant component of each individual's lifetime of experiences and are three-dimensional reflections of the needs, values, and social norms of individuals, families, and cultures. Designing interior environments that address the behavioral, social, and cultural needs of the human beings who will inhabit and interact with them is a central concern of interior design professionals.

An interior space, whether it is an office, a restaurant, a home, or a large auditorium, is by its very nature a "personal" space in the sense that each space is interpreted differently, depending upon the individual's experiences, memories, and capabilities. Thus, designers are challenged to create interior environments that are sensitive to the dynamic relationship between people, experience, and space.

Hierarchy of Needs

Several social and cultural concepts have been developed to help explain how and why people behave the way they do. One of the most frequently cited and comprehensive models used to explain human behavior is known as the **hierarchy of needs** postulated by the psychologist Abraham Maslow.[1] As discussed in Chapter 1, Maslow believed that human needs are dynamic and can be arrayed in an ascending hierarchy—from simple and most basic to most complex. In other words, when one set of needs is satisfied, another set emerges to replace it.

Maslow's hierarchy of needs begins with the basic physiological requirements that sustain life—air, water, food, clothing, and shelter. Once these needs are met, Maslow contends that security and safety become

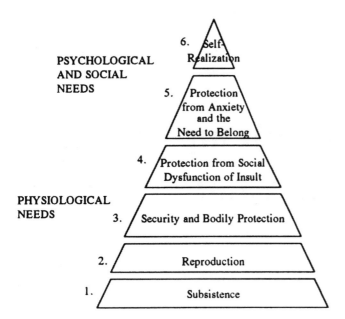

Figure 12-1 The six levels of human needs developed by Maslow.

important needs—that is, a concern with avoiding harm and protecting what has been gained, particularly in hostile environments.

According to Maslow, these basic needs have to be met before people become concerned about the psychological set of needs in the hierarchy—protection from insult and the need to belong. After these needs are achieved, the individual then strives to achieve social status within the group or organization. The final step in Maslow's hierarchy of needs is fulfillment of an individual's own highest need, or self-realization. Maslow contends that people continually strive to reach this highest level in the hierarchy, and may cycle up and down many times in the course of a lifetime.

Applying this basic needs hierarchy of human behavior can help designers understand why people react the way they do and predict the way people will behave in relation to interior adaptations and components. For example, the president or CEO of an organization may achieve self-realization through being assigned to the largest office in the building with a panoramic view of the city. Self-realization for a computer specialist in the same company may be quite different and may be achieved instead by recognition in a technical journal or having state-of-the-art computer equipment in his or her office environment.

The importance of Maslow's hierarchy to interior design provides the designer with insights into the nature of human beings and how that knowledge translates into user satisfaction. Issues such as territoriality, comfort (both physical and psychological), privacy, and function are easier to understand if Maslow's hierarchy is applied

during the design process. This allows for better designer/client relationships.

Professional Issues and Challenges

Recognition of the importance of interior spaces in fulfilling human needs has led to the emergence of interior design as a professional endeavor. What exactly does this mean? What's the difference between a profession and a vocation?

In order to have a clearer understanding of this difference and the importance of interior design's professional evolution, it is necessary to examine the characteristics common to all professions. There is general agreement among scholars that all professions have the following common indicators:

- Certification or licensing preceded by an extensive period of formal training in a systematic field of knowledge that allows those who possess this knowledge to claim authority over its application. This knowledge must go beyond a simple understanding of complex skills.
- The existence of distinct cultures and identities for members of the profession that enforce ethical practices both formally and informally.
- A commitment to provide service to society. In return, society is expected to give deference to those who create and apply the profession's specialized knowledge.
- A "monopoly of judgment" in the field. Peer review of individual treatments and research is encouraged, while review by nonmembers is resisted.[2]

These indicators suggest that all professions depend upon the existence of specialized knowledge. This specialized knowledge is the true signpost of a profession, and professions define their jurisdictional boundaries through control of this knowledge and skill set. In most cases, this specialized knowledge is derived from academic research, which provides the focus for what builds and defines a profession's body of knowledge.[3]

An examination of interior design's evolution as a profession reveals that it closely adheres to the indicators cited above. In particular, interior design's evolution as a profession can be seen through (1) the development of formal programs of study in interior design at recognized institutions of higher education, (2) the identification of a distinct body of knowledge that underpins and provides the foundation for interior design as a professional endeavor and an academic discipline, (3) the establishment of accreditation standards for educational programs in interior design, and (4) legislation mandating certification and/or licensing requirements to practice as a professional interior designer.

Interior Design Education

As pointed out, one of the most fundamental aspects of a mature profession is the educational foundation upon which it is built. When examined from this perspective, interior design represents a relatively new and emerging discipline—particularly in the United States. This is in contrast to European countries, where the educational roots of interior design have been embedded for centuries.

In the United States, formal programs of study in interior design at recognized institutions of higher education began to emerge only around 1950. Initially, many of these educational programs focused on residential design and decoration. As these programs matured, the scope of interior space design increased. Most programs of study available at educational institutions today do not limit interior design to home environments, but instead offer opportunities for students to explore the design of any interior space in which people live, work, or play.

By nature, interior design is interdisciplinary. For this reason, interior design educational programs historically developed under a variety of academic umbrellas, including art, architecture, and home economics. Most programs in the United States still function under one of these academic umbrellas. Each promotes a different philosophical perspective, but all recognize that dependence upon subject matter from other disciplines is critical to the education of a professional interior designer.

A significant benchmark in the evolution of educational standards for interior design was the establishment of the Foundation for Interior Design Education and Research (FIDER). FIDER, founded in 1970, is an international nonprofit organization that accredits postsecondary interior design education programs in the United States and Canada. Its primary purpose is to ensure a high level of quality in interior design education that meets the needs of students, the interior design profession, and society. The primary accreditation organization for interior design is the Council of Interior Design Accreditation or CIDA. Today, CIDA is recognized internationally by design professionals as a force for determining the hallmarks of a quality education in interior design.

Definition of a Professional Interior Designer

Interior designers are well-educated professionals who create environments that meet the physical, psychological, and aesthetic needs of the people who interact within these environments. Other professions that deal with the design and creation of built and natural environments that are closely allied with interior design include architecture, landscape architecture, and industrial design. Although these professions have attributes similar to those of interior design, there are important differences. These distinguishing characteristics are best articulated through the qualifications and services provided.

According to CIDA's (formerly FIDER) definition, a professional interior designer is a person qualified by education, experience, and examination to enhance the function and quality of interior spaces for the purpose of improving the quality of life, increasing productivity, and protecting the health, safety, and welfare of the public. This definition goes on to specify that a professional interior designer:

- analyzes the client's needs, goals, and life safety requirements;
- integrates findings with knowledge of interior design;
- formulates preliminary design concepts that are aesthetic, appropriate, and functional, and in accordance with codes and standards;
- develops and presents final design recommendations through appropriate presentation media;
- prepares working drawings and specifications for non-load-bearing interior construction, reflected ceiling plans, lighting, interior detailing, materials, finishes, space planning, furnishings, fixtures, and equipment in compliance with universal accessibility guidelines and all applicable codes;
- collaborates with professional services of other licensed practitioners in the technical areas of mechanical, electrical and load-bearing design as required for regulatory approval;
- prepares and administers bids and contract documents as the client's agent; and
- reviews and evaluates design solutions during implementation and upon completion.[4]

Professional Certification and Registration

In addition to strong educational underpinnings, a key component of any profession is certification of individuals who possess specialized knowledge in a field or discipline. For interior design, this requirement is fulfilled through the National Council of Interior Design Qualification (NCIDQ) exam. This exam was developed in the late 1960s to serve as a basis for issuing credentials to professional interior design practitioners and has been in effect since 1972.

The purpose of the NCIDQ is to identify to the public those designers who have met the minimum standards for professional practice by passing the NCIDQ exam. The exam is continually updated to reflect expanding professional knowledge and design development techniques with the intent of setting a universal standard by which to measure the competency of interior designers to practice as professionals.

Successful completion of the NCIDQ exam is a prerequisite for professional registration in the United States and in Canadian provinces that have enacted licensing or certification statutes to protect the health, safety, and welfare of the public. In addition, the NCIDQ exam must be passed by everyone applying for professional membership in a recognized interior design organization.[5]

The process of certification through legal recognition of interior designers varies among U.S. states and Canadian provinces. To date, 23 jurisdictions in the United States (including the District of Columbia and Puerto Rico) have a registration, certification, or licensing requirement for interior designers. Eight Canadian provinces have a similar requirement.

State or provincial legislation to regulate and limit practice can be described in two categories: practice acts and title acts. A practice act prohibits the actual practice or provision of professional services by anyone not licensed by the state. In most states, architects, engineers, and doctors have practice acts. At this time, only a few states have passed practice acts for interior designers.

A title act prohibits anyone not certified or registered by the state from representing or identifying himself or herself as a certified or registered interior designer or registered architect, professional engineer, or landscape

Title State
Title/Practice State
Permitting State
Self-Certification State

Figure 12-2 This U.S. map gives an overview of the growing number of states that require interior designers to obtain licensing.

architect. It does not prohibit professional practice or provision of services by nonregistered individuals, but it does prohibit persons from calling themselves an interior designer unless they have met specific requirements. Figure 12-2 shows the current status of licensing for interior designers in the United States.

Sustainability and Universal Design

Interior design is a distinct professional endeavor that addresses a wide array of issues that impact the human condition. Paramount among these issues and challenges are those of sustainability and universal design.

Sustainable Interior Design

An interior design that is considered sustainable must meet the needs of the present occupants without compromising the ability of future generations to meet their needs. To provide successful sustainable interiors, designers must first be environmentally aware. Environmentally sensitive interior designers can positively influence the sustainability of the built environment. Through effective space planning, heating and lighting design, product specification, and the education of clients, interior designers can create spaces that conserve energy and improve indoor air quality.

Things as simple as environmentally sensitive arrangements of furniture and the strategic use of color, texture, and materials can encourage a client to turn down the thermostat by creating the perception of warmth in an interior space. For example, most browns, yellows, oranges, and reds are perceived as warm, while violets, blues, and greens are perceived as cool. By selecting a warm color scheme, together with inviting textures and intimate furniture arrangements, a perceived feeling of warmth can be achieved.

Other means of addressing sustainability issues require collaboration with architects and landscape architects to maximize the natural amenities that may be present. For example, correctly orienting a building can maximize natural light in an interior environment without overheating the space. Important considerations include locating areas primarily used in the early morning, such as kitchens, dining rooms, and bedrooms, toward the east to take advantage of the rising sun and locating high-activity areas such as living rooms and family rooms toward the south and southwest. Interior spaces such as home offices, storage spaces, and other areas that require uniform light levels should be oriented toward the north. By organizing the interior spaces within a home, the interior designer can take advantage of the natural attributes of a site, providing the client with functional, psychological, and aesthetic benefits.

An environmentally sensitive lighting design is another critical component of sustainable interiors. By strategically placing natural and artificial light sources and varying the quality and intensity of light to suit the specific space and task at hand, the amount of energy consumed is lowered without lessening the quality of the interior environment.

In addition to a carefully designed lighting plan that includes sensitivity to both natural and artificial lighting sources, the interior designer must consider the placement of heating, ventilation, and air conditioning components. Decisions such as centrally locating the hot water

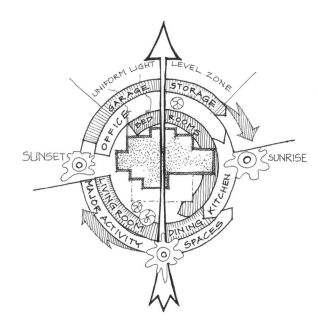

Figure 12-4 Orienting a building to maximize the use of natural light in the interior saves energy and creates healthy interior spaces.

Figure 12-3 The warm incandescent lighting and the colorful banners dropped into this space, together with the large amount of wood being used, bring a sense of warmth and human scale to this grand interior at Hearst Castle, California.

heater and other major heat sources will make it possible to minimize the length of water pipes and ductwork, thereby saving both energy and water. Selecting energy-efficient lighting systems, heating or cooling units, and water-conserving appliances and fixtures can further reduce global impact on natural resources.

One important task of an interior designer is the selection and assemblage of materials and finishes. The products selected influence the way people think, feel, and function, thereby helping to shape the patterns of their behavior. Thus, it is imperative that interior designers understand the consequences of the material and finish choices that they specify. Keeping up with new sustainable products and current research on sustainability is essential in order to make informed decisions about materials and finishes for interior environments.

A material's or product's life cycle is described as either "cradle to grave" or **cradle to cradle**.[6] A material with a life cycle categorized as cradle to grave cannot be recycled at the end of its useful life. By contrast, a material with a cradle-to-cradle life cycle can be reclaimed for another use. The goal of the interior designer is to specify as many materials, finishes, and products as possible that are cradle to cradle. Another consideration when specifying interior materials and finishes is to determine if the material is classified as "green," that is, environmentally friendly. The following factors help to determine the green quality of a product: (1) extraction and manufacturing processes, (2) transportation and

Figure 12-5 An environmentally sensitive lighting design utilizes natural light to its fullest. Punch Bowl Cemetery, Hawaii.

Figure 12-6 Good kitchen lighting designs require numerous light sources to best support the various tasks, providing the client with options and thus the potential to reduce energy consumption.

packaging, (3) installation, (4) performance, and (5) maintenance.

Extraction and Manufacturing Processes. Once a designer has decided on the type of material or product that meets the needs of the project, a search should be done for the most sustainable options among manufacturers. Most manufacturers that strive for environmentally friendly products have published environmental policies that can be researched. A valid environmental policy will dictate resource extraction or harvesting processes that have minimal environmental impact and a manufacturing process that is least taxing on the environment. For example, a good representative policy for wood products is one that requires harvesting from sustainably managed forests that do not harm natural ecosystems.

Many products require lengthy and complicated manufacturing making it difficult to determine whether or not the manufacturing processes are environmentally

sound. In such instances, the designer can usually determine if the manufacturer uses energy from renewable sources or, at a minimum, whether the manufacturer tries to make the processes as energy efficient as possible. Additional indicators of the green quality of a product can be found in an examination of the following: (1) whether or not waste materials from the manufacturing process are recycled into other products, materials, or finishes; (2) whether or not waste materials are biodegradable; and (3) whether or not hazardous chemical treatments are part of the production process.

Certain material or product manufacturing processes produce gaseous or solid hazardous waste. In these situations, it is the responsibility of the designer to choose alternative materials and products, such as a natural material over a manufactured one.

Transportation and Packaging. Whenever possible, specifying regionally produced materials is a good prac-

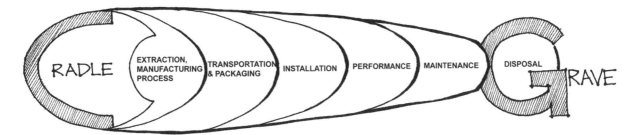

Figure 12-7   A material with a cradle-to-grave life cycle cannot be recycled at the end of its useful life.

tice. By doing this, the designer supports the regional economy, while at the same time drastically reducing the energy and resources required to transport and handle the product from its extraction through its end use. Packaging may also be reduced by specifying regional materials and products. Products that are packaged in recyclable materials are also important in creating environmentally sensitive interiors.

Installation. The installation of a product may require the use of several additional materials—such as subsurfaces, various glues and adhesives, or added final fin-

ishes. This may mean that an otherwise harmless product is no longer the best environmental choice. An environmentally sensitive designer will examine the products required for final installation to determine if these products are toxic and if they produce an environmentally hazardous end product. In addition, a designer should determine whether or not the installation products might contribute to a reduction in worker safety or a high level of energy consumption during installation.

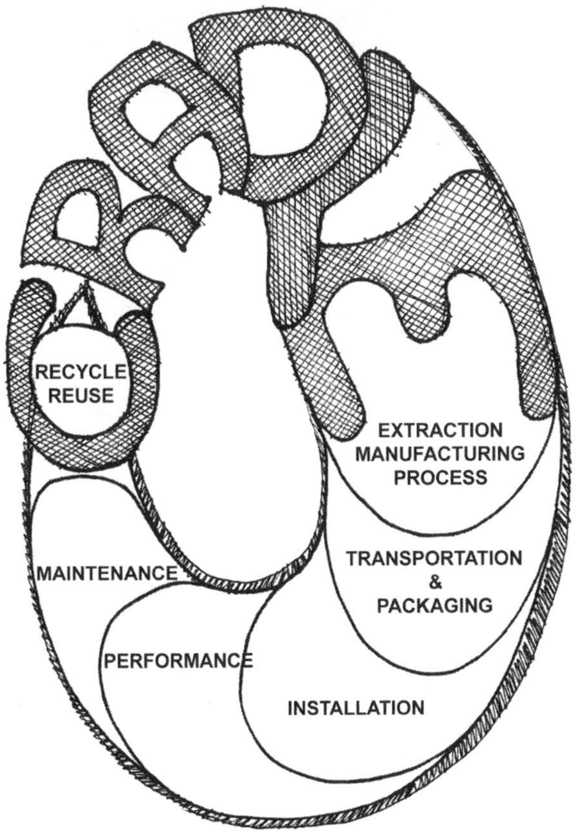

Performance. All clients have their own expectations of how long interior materials and products should last. The client's budget, the company's philosophy, and the type of interior that is being created mainly determine the expected material life span. The designer should, therefore, use these guidelines for all product specifications. The client should be able to expect, at a minimum, that a professional designer will specify environmentally sound products that will absorb and/or release no, or only minimal amounts, of **volatile organic compounds** (VOCs)

Figure 12-8   A material with a cradle-to-cradle life cycle can be reclaimed for another use.

Figure 12-9   By specifying regional wood species from sustainably managed forests, designers can make environmentally conscious material selections.

while at the same time offering durability and adaptability for reuse and recycling purposes.

Maintenance. Performance is often greatly affected by maintenance; thus, it is critical that the designer understand the client's maintenance schedule. This will help to ensure that the materials and products selected will last and reduce the need for harsh, environmentally dangerous chemicals to revive their original appearance. It is also important to check to see if the material specified requires extensive energy and resource-consuming maintenance procedures to maintain its appearance and usefulness.

Indoor Air Quality. In an effort to create energy-efficient interiors, an unexpected negative consequence has occurred in certain situations—poor indoor air quality (IAQ). A lack of adequate air exchange between interior and exterior spaces results from a tighter building envelope, and inadequate ventilation traps air pollutants inside. Indoor air pollution is defined as the concentration of compounds for certain periods of time in the air, causing negative health effects in humans.[7]

The World Health Organization has diagnosed public, nonindustrial buildings suffering from poor IAQ as having **sick building syndrome**, a condition that has become one of the most serious chemical or environmental health threats in the world, commonly referred to as **multiple chemical sensitivity** (MCS).[8] Interestingly enough, however, research shows that people experience the most exposure to poor IAQ in their own homes because these dwellings are not covered by public regulations.[8] Most likely this is because people do not often associate or appreciate the importance of healthy indoor air in their personal environments. Thus, educating the public and clients to the potential dangers of toxic IAQ is an important responsibility of all designers.

The source of poor IAQ is matter in the air that causes indoor air pollution. This may be viable, organic matter or inorganic particulate matter, gases, or vapors. Dust, mildew, and VOCs are classified as viable organic matter. Even artificial fragrances from most perfumes, colognes, soaps, and dryer sheets are very toxic to some people. Formaldehyde, radon, sulfur, carbon monoxide, ozone, and tobacco smoke fall into the category of inorganic particulate matters. Frequently, it is not the various toxic matters themselves, but rather the interactions between them or multicomponent exposure, that cause adverse health effects—MCS.

Formaldehyde was first recognized to cause indoor air problems in 1975, and VOCs were first noted as a cause in 1982. Designers must be aware of the most sig-

Figure 12-10 The introduction of live vegetation and humidity control can help alleviate the buildup of VOCs within a space, creating healthier IAQ.

nificant **off-gassing** offenders releasing VOCs found in synthetic materials, finishes, furnishings, and composite building materials.

Depending on the level of VOCs present, an inhabitant may experience one or more of the following symptoms: nonspecific hypersensitivity, chronic tissue irritation, respiratory problems such as asthma or allergies, headaches, difficulty concentrating, or a feeling of sleepiness. In extreme cases, diseases such as cancer and cardiovascular effects have been attributed to poor IAQ.[9]

A designer can help alleviate the problem by suggesting a design that includes the specification of natural materials, improved mechanical or natural ventilation, humidity control, and the introduction of live vegetation. Potted plants such as philodendrons, spider plants, and golden pothos act as air filters, extracting harmful air pollutants from the indoor air. The simple concept of an operable window that allows the inhabitants to manually ventilate their home is often overlooked. Well-located windows can capture not only valuable natural daylight, but also refreshing breezes.

Universal Design

As noted earlier, people spend a significant amount of time in a built environment. Unfortunately, barriers often limit the safety, security, and comfort of inhabitants within these environments. When one considers the fact that approximately 43 million people in the United States are disabled, making up the largest minority group in the country, the continued existence of barriers in our built environment is unsettling.

Basic access to the built environment should be an inherent right of all people. Policies that help to ensure this right for everyone, including individuals with disabilities, have taken decades to implement and enforce. With the passage of the **Americans with Disabilities Act** (ADA) in 1990, every disabled individual was provided with legal entitlement to a barrier-free, public built environment. Another act, the **Fair Housing Amendments Act** (FHAA), passed in 1988, provided for the existence of accessible multifamily dwellings.

Although the ADA and FHAA are significant benchmarks ensuring access to buildings for everyone, they establish only minimum access requirements. In recent years a broader concept, known as **universal design**, has become the focus of accessibility advocates. A universally designed interior space strives to provide equal access for all users, including able-bodied adults, children, the elderly, and individuals with disabilities. The goal of universal design is to decrease the stigma of spe-

Figure 12-12 Many multifamily dwellings are inaccessible. Passage of the Fair Housing Amendments Act provided the legal base for a continuing increase in accessible units.

cial populations and increase social participation and functional independence for all—a fundamental shift in thinking.[10]

The difference between universal design and accessibility is that accessibility is a function of compliance with regulations or criteria that establish a minimum level of design necessary to accommodate people with disabilities. In contrast, universal design is the art, science, and practice of design to accommodate the widest variety of people throughout their life span.[11]

The **principles of universal design** provide for (1) equitable use, (2) flexibility in use, (3) simple, intuitive use, (4) perceptible information, (5) tolerance for error, (6) low physical effort, and (7) size and space for approach/use. By applying these simple principles to the design of both public and personal interior spaces, interior designers can make a significant contribution to the creation of a comprehensive built environment in which all people can interact freely.

Figure 12-11 The Americans with Disabilities Act helps ensure a barrier-free public built environment. This picture shows the level entry of the Mount Saint Helens Visitors Center in Washington.

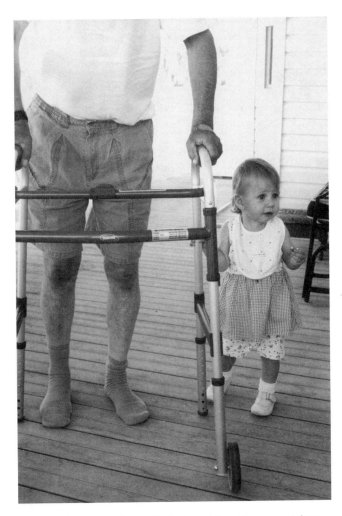

Figure 12-13 A universally designed interior space strives to provide equal access for all users, regardless of age and mobility.

Summary

The issues and challenges facing interior design professionals are varied and complex—ranging from macro-level challenges faced by the profession at large (such as certification and licensing issues) to micro-level challenges that each designer must deal with on a daily basis (such as creating sustainable interior environments that are friendly to all users). As a young and maturing profession, interior design will continue to change and evolve as each challenge is addressed.

Interior design is interdisciplinary; thus, collaboration with other disciplines is essential in the creation of interior spaces that optimize the art and science of design. By maximizing relationships among humans, the environment, and technological advances, interior design positively influences the way people live, play, work, and experience the world around them.

References

Abbot, A. *The System of Professions: An Essay on the Division of Expert Labor.* University of Chicago Press, 1988.

Ballast, D. *Interior Design Reference Manual: A Guide to the NCIDQ Exam.* Professional Publications, 2002.

Harmon, S., and K. Kennon. *The Code Guidebook for Interiors.* Wiley, 2001.

Klay, W. E., R. Brower, and B. Williams. "A Community-Oriented Model of Academic Professionalism." *Metropolitan Universities: An International Forum,* March 2001.

Martin, C. "Professionalization: Architecture, Interior Decoration, and Interior Design as Defined by Abbott." Master's thesis, Department of Design, Housing, and Apparel, University of Minnesota, 1998.

Maslow, A. *The Further Reaches of Human Nature.* Viking, 1971.

McDonough, W., and M. Braungart. *Cradle to Cradle: Remaking the Way We Make Things.* North Point Press, 2002.

Molhave, L. "Organic Compounds as Indicators of Air Pollution." *Indoor Air,* 13, 6, 2003.

Molhave, L., and M. Krzyzanowski. "The Right to Healthy Indoor Air: Status by 2002." *Indoor Air,* 13, 6, 2003.

Piotrowski, C. *Professional Practice for Interior Designers.* Wiley, 2001.

Salmen, J. "U.S. Accessibility Codes and Standards: Challenges for Universal Design." In W. Presier and E. Ostroff (eds.), *Universal Design Handbook.* McGraw-Hill, 2002.

Steinfeld, E., and S. Danford. *Enabling Environments.* Kluwer Academic/Plenum, 1999.

Endnotes

1. A. Maslow, *The Further Reaches of Human Nature* (Viking, 1971).
2. W. E. Klay, R. Brower, and B. Williams, "A Community-Oriented Model of Academic Professionalism," *Metropolitan Universities: An International Forum,* March 2001.
3. A. Abbot, *The System of Professions: An Essay on the Division of Expert Labor* (University of Chicago Press, 1988).
4. See the FIDER Web site: www.fider.org.
5. See the NCIDQ Web site: www.ncidq.org.
6. W. McDonough, and M. Braungart, *Cradle to Cradle: Remaking the Way We Make Things* (North Point Press, 2002).
7. L. Molhave, "Organic Compounds as Indicators of Air Pollution," *Indoor Air,* 13, 6 2003.
8. L. Molhave and M. Krzyzanowski, "The Right to Healthy Indoor Air: Status by 2002," *Indoor Air,* 13, 6 2003.
9. See Note 8.
10. E. Steinfeld and S. Danford, *Enabling Environments* (Kluwer Academic/Plenum, 1999).
11. J. Salmen, "U.S. Accessibility Codes and Standards: Challenges for Universal Design," *Universal Design Handbook,* edited by W. Presier and E. Ostroff (McGraw-Hill, 2002).

STRUCTURES
Architecture, Engineering, and Construction

Introduction

Structures represent the third component of the seven layers of the built environment to be examined. The building of structures establishes human/social, environmental, and technical relationships and constitutes a basic creative act, one that has occurred throughout human history. Building is a primary adaptive design strategy for humans and, for that matter, for many other animals and insects—an **adaptive strategy** developed in order to live more comfortably and more effectively within the natural and built environments. The act of building symbolically expresses shelter, permanence, and cultural values.

It is difficult to generalize about structures; they exist in many different types and sizes. Structures, old and new, crude and refined, express many reasons to build. Only human insights, interests, and imagination limit the types of structures possible.

Simply observing the built environment should enable anyone to list a variety of structures that serve individual and collective needs, wants, and values. Shelters, the most basic structures, have been created in an enormous variety of shapes and sizes. Community structures accommodate cultural, commercial, governmental, educational, and recreational interests. Even bridges, circulation systems, dams, power plants, and energy networks are structures created to interconnect society in various ways.

The cumulative effect of building on or with the land creates larger components of the built environment. For example, a farmstead, a campus, a neighborhood, village, or city, even large metropolitan and rural regions, are influenced by the way we collectively build and arrange structures.

Structures, especially buildings, have a unique and dual role in the built environment—they have both an inside and an outside. Structures help to mediate between people, and between both the natural environment and the surrounding built environment, creating a unique and dynamic relationship within the total built environment. This dual role of designing both an interior and an exterior is not shared by the other design fields. Exploring interior and exterior characteristics can expand the appreciation and understanding of structures and their human-environmental interrelationships within the natural and built environments.

Internally, structures satisfy and symbolize human spatial needs, wants, and values. They creatively configure products and interior spaces in a variety of ways to support human needs and aspirations. Spaces for human activities are essential ingredients of a structure. This internal characteristic is commonly referred to as the "spatial" or **functional** aspect of structures.

Externally, structures also provide and symbolize a protective envelope, an interrelationship with the outside environment. This external expression is commonly referred to as the **form** of structures. The form becomes, in a sense, an enclosure that mediates the conflict between internal functional needs and the external environment. This enclosure forms the interior environment, which protects humans from the unwanted aspects of the exterior environment, such as uncomfortable temperatures, strong winds, or disruptive noises. The enclosure can also open up to beneficial aspects of the outside environment, such as a beautiful garden or landscape, daylight, fresh air and ventilation, even pleasant fragrances and the sounds of water, birds, and music. The external enclosure can be considered closely analogous to the "skin" of the human body, which also welcomes the sun's warmth (clothing provides insulation from the winter cold); its pores open to provide evaporative cooling in very hot temperatures. Hair screens unwanted contacts while accepting the appreciative touch of a friend or loved one.

Human comfort (light, fresh air, optimum temperatures, etc.) is based upon human senses and is provided either by natural means (windows for light and ventilation, solar energy for heat, shade for cooling, etc.) or by artificial means (electric lights, heating, air conditioning, etc.). Designing without a full understanding of the advantages and disadvantages of natural and built technologies generally causes high operating costs and high rates of energy consumption.

The external expression, the characteristics of form, also has a direct effect, even at times a major impact, on the overall built environment. Structures can be created to enhance or disrupt the landscapes, cities, and regions in which they are built. How structures "fit" into their context, or adjacent environment, is an important topic in studying the external form of structures.

Structures, both inside and out, can be summarized by the basic definition of the built environment introduced in Chapter 1 and by the levels-of-integration concept (content-component-context) discussed in Chapter 3. In general, structures can be defined as follows:

- **Structures** (the contents of which are products and interiors) are humanly made or arranged;
- to fulfill human purposes; to satisfy human needs, wants, and values;
- to mediate the overall external environment;
- with results that affect the overall environmental context (the context for structures includes landscapes, cities, regions, and, ultimately, the Earth upon which they are built).

Structures are in the middle of this interlocking continuum of content-component-context relationships. The concept of levels of integration emphasizes that the structures component must integrate content and must fit within its context, as represented by the following parts-to-whole continuum:

Products—Interiors—**Structures**—Landscapes—Cities—Regions—Earth

Important quantitative and qualitative differences are apparent in the definitions of related terms: "structure," "building," and "architecture":

- **Structure:** Something constructed, such as a building, a dam, or a bridge; and/or to arrange, compose, or interrelate all parts to a whole.
- **Building:** A structure that is built, generally implying human occupancy; and/or to construct, the art or work of assembling materials into a structure.
- **Architecture:** The art and science of designing and building quality open areas, structures, communities, and other artificial constructions or environments, with attention to their aesthetic effect. Furthermore, insights can be gained from the word "architecture" itself:

Arch-i-tecture: Art + technology (art + craft + science + engineering)

Arch + tecture: Tecture refers to "texture," the characteristic of the interwoven or intertwined fabric; the integration of a structure with its internal content and external context.

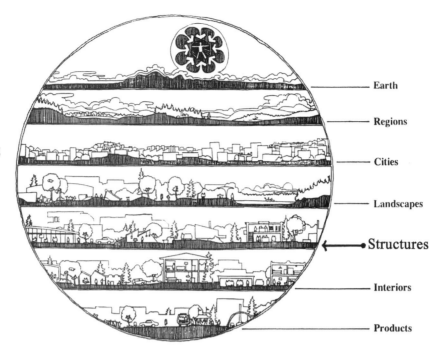

Earth

Regions

Cities

Landscapes

◄ •Structures

Interiors

Products

Graphic logo illustrating levels of integration in the built environment (S. Recken and J. Singleton).

The quantitative and qualitative dimensions of structure, building, and architecture are implied in the above words. Structure is the most general, all-encompassing word used to represent this level of the built environment. Architecture represents a special subset of structures that are for the most part designed by licensed professionals. Architecture places emphasis on quality—the art, craft, and science of building. The definition of building and architecture combines the noun and the verb. The verb emphasizes the design process, while the noun emphasizes the product or component of the built world.

To practice architecture, a person is required to become knowledgeable, skilled, and licensed before being legally entitled to use the term **architect**. National and state laws, which attempt to ensure public health, safety, and welfare, generally require an individual to undertake five to seven years of university studies leading to a nationally accredited professional degree in architecture, complete the three-year Internship Development Program (IDP) by working under the guidance of an architect, and pass the architecture registration examination before becoming a licensed professional.

The chapters in this section explore past, present, and future aspects and qualitative dimensions of the art and science of building. Also explored are the many aspects of function and form in the creative building of healthy human spaces that fit environmental contexts and emphasize the importance of carefully using technology. The chapters are organized as follows:

Historic and Contemporary Trends in Architecture
by Katherine M. Keane

This chapter presents a brief conceptual survey of major architectural trends from historic periods to contemporary practice. It describes the principal characteristics of each trend, emphasizing concepts that recur and recycle throughout history. The main goals are to present a concise overview of how trends manifest and mature throughout history and to propose that this understanding may facilitate the prediction of future trends.

Architecture as a Cultural Layer
by Wendy R. McClure

Historic structures, contexts, and neighborhoods create cultural layers in the built environment that offer temporal dimension and enrich the texture of our cities, towns, campuses, and neighborhoods. This chapter provides an overview of the historic preservation movement in the United States, including why preservation is important and how it is accomplished. Processes sanctioned by the U.S. Secretary of the Interior and the professional preservation and design communities are discussed, including preservation, restoration, and rehabilitation (or adaptive use).

The Fitness Test: Building with Human and Environmental Factors
by Bruce T. Haglund and Tom J. Bartuska

Buildings and architecture have a unique dual character embodied in their external forms and internal spatial/functional developments. This chapter explores the dual human-environmental dimensions of design. Ideally, this duality is integrated to fit the environment and support human activities. These internal-external relationships must be creatively addressed and resolved for each building in order to pass the fitness test.

Engineering Contributions
by Carl W. Hall

This chapter analyzes the history and mission of engineering contributions to the built environment. It emphasizes the important interface between science, engineering, and the environmental design disciplines and suggests that design synthesis is the common thread that directs their work to meet the challenges of the future.

Constructing the Built Environment
by W. Max Kirk

Construction produces tangible structures from the dreams and designs of owners, developers, designers, and builders. Whether the structure is a house, apartment, school, or library, a multitude of people contribute to the construction of the built environment. All of the products and systems found in rooms, buildings, landscapes, and cities involve a vast amount of design, technology, and construction in their composition. Through the knowledge and efforts of those in the construction industry, these products and systems are assembled to meet design specifications and the needs of inhabitants, society, and the environment.

References

Each chapter concludes with a list of useful references

Accredition Board for Engineering and Technology (ABET): www.abet.org

American Council for Construction Education (ACCE): www.acce-hg.org

American Institute of Architects (AIA): www.aia.org

American Institute of Architecture Students (AIAS): www.aias.org

American Society of Engineering Education (ASEE): www.asee.org

Architectural Research Centers Consortium (ARCC): www.arccnet.org

Association of Collegiate Schools of Architecture (ACSA): www.acsa.org

Construction Management Association of America (CMAA): www.cmaa.net

National Certification of Architectural Registration Boards (NCARB): www.ncarb.org

Society of Building Science Educators (SBSE): www.sbse.org

CHAPTER 13

Historic and Contemporary Trends in Architecture

Katherine M. Keane

This chapter presents a brief survey of major architectural trends from historic periods to the contemporary era. It attempts to describe the principal high-style characteristics of each trend, emphasizing concepts that recur and recycle throughout history. The main goals are to present a concise overview of how trends manifest and mature throughout history and to propose that this understanding may help to both predict and inform more effective and sustainable trends in the future.

Is it possible to predict the future by looking at the past and, in particular, by identifying patterns that have the tendency to repeat over time? It is certainly important to understand history and the nuances that influenced the development of society and, in turn, the development periods or high-style traditions (see Chapter 2) in order to fully comprehend contemporary environmental design. In order to provide concise information on critical periods of development, this chapter is divided into conceptual segments and attempts to discuss their salient qualities and characteristics. While this chapter focuses primarily on developments in Western civilization, achievements of non-Western civilization are equally impressive.

Distant Past: 7000 B.C.–1770 A.D.

Egyptian Period
Greek Period

Roman Period
Medieval and Gothic periods
Renaissance and Baroque periods

Recent Past: 1770–1960

Industrial Revolution
Arts and Crafts Movement
Art Nouveau
Modern Movement
International Style

Contemporary: 1960–present

Post Modernism
Environmentalism
High-Tech
Deconstruction
Participation

All dates in this chapter are rounded off for simplicity and, therefore, are not precise. Historic periods very rarely occurred at the same time in different countries or ended abruptly, as they tended to transition into succeeding periods.

The following outline of different periods and trends in architecture highlights how ideas developed and/or recycled through action and reaction.

Figure 13-1 National Space Science Center, Leicester, England (architect, Grimshaw).

Distant Past: 7000 B.C.–1770 A.D.

Evidence and fragments of human construction dating back to 7000 B.C.E. have been found around the globe in the form of a concrete-like material made by combining ingredients from the earth into a paste with water and then left to sun dry and harden in the open air. Examples include a lime concrete floor in Galilee, Israel, dating to 7000 B.C.E., and a red lime cement with gravel hut floor along the Danube River in Eastern Europe dating to 5600 B.C.E. In Mesopotamia in 4000 B.C.E., palaces and temples were constructed using stone and bricks formed by mixing clay from the earth with water and dried in the sun to create a hard unit of construction.

Egyptian Period

In Egypt along the Nile River from about 3000 B.C.E., stone was used for the construction of magnificent temples, pyramids, and ziggurats. These all represent massive load-bearing structures, although columns were also used to punctuate processional spatial sequences. Illus-

trations dating from 1950 B.C.E. in Thebes, Egypt, describe construction with a concrete material.

Greek Period

From about 500 B.C.E., Greek civilization used limestone and marble to construct temples, home to statues of the gods embodied in human form. These solid-walled spaces surrounded by colonnades of columns were witness to the glorification of the human body. The massiveness of the wall began to be replaced by the use of columns. Their close spacing reflected the limited spanning capacity of the material used in the trabeated (post and beam) method of construction. Spatial planning extended to deliberate placing of clusters of buildings in a complex such as an acropolis.

Greek sensibility permitted the natural character of place to dictate a less formal plan of organization characterized by integration with nature.

Roman Period

Roman civilization at its height developed many architectural innovations. The Romans carried their conquering spirit into the layout and placement of their cities. Nature was conquered, controlled, and made subservient to their will. Formal designed environments evolved that, in turn, provided an influential atmosphere controlling the inhabitants. The advance of Roman civilization is typically attributed to the use of innovative technology. Development of the arch for spanning permitted larger openings in walls and much larger spaces. Elements used by the Romans that could span spaces included the arch, the vault, and the dome. All of them

Figure 13-2 Greek Ephesus library complex, modern Turkey.

Figure 13-3 Greek Priene Theater integrated with the hillside, modern Turkey.

Figure 13-4 Medieval Norwich Cathedral, England—earlier Romanesque round arches (lower level) and later Gothic pointed arches and vaulting (upper level and ceiling).

provided a whole range of new experiences and possibilities, emphasized in the dome of the Pantheon constructed in Rome 127 C.E. and spanning 43.3 meters (approx. 145 feet). For almost 2,000 years the Pantheon was the largest spanning structure in the Western world. The arch was also utilized in the construction of aqueducts or channels that carried fresh water into inhabited areas. Aqueducts were often elevated to provide a natural slope over great distances. Other developments included systems of construction that utilized a concrete-like material as inner fill to walls constructed from stones, rubble, or brick and lightweight construction techniques. Support technology included hot-water heating and wastewater removal. In these early civilizations, spatial development was influenced and limited by aqueduct technology and construction.

Medieval and Gothic Periods

As the Roman Empire declined, a period often identified as the Dark Ages emerged. During this time, also known as the "medieval period," Romanesque and Gothic architecture evolved from round arch masonry construction technology developed by the ancient Romans. In medieval Europe and Islam, masonry vaulting was the technique that defined spatial development. In the Islamic world, the principal building typologies were palaces, markets, and mosques constructed from brick with glazed tile facing. In Europe, stone and brick were the primary materials for constructing fortresses and cathedrals supported by construction techniques such as pointed vaults and buttresses. The Dark Ages gave way to a new spirit of religious fervor in Europe. Crusaders, motivated to travel by this spirit, returned from Middle

Eastern countries with new ideas about building and spatial development. This energy was expressed in architecture, and the Gothic period emerged.

The Gothic period had a theocentric focus (a concern with God), which was translated into architecture by

Figure 13-5 Medieval Salisbury Cathedral, England.

reaching up toward heaven—an opening up or a dematerialization of cathedral walls to allow "heavenly light" to penetrate dark interiors and human minds. These desires required vast innovation in construction technology. The techniques that made the architecture possible included vaulted interiors, arched windows, buttresses to support the loads transferred from the dematerialized walls, and, later, flying buttresses as walls further dematerialized. The Gothic period in Europe began at different times in different countries. All periods of development have many subcategories and distinctive characteristics. For example, the three recognizable periods of Gothic architecture in England were Early, Decorated, and Perpendicular, distinguished by the differing characteristics described in Table 13-1 at the end of this chapter.

Renaissance and Baroque Periods (1420–1750)

Renaissance (1420–1600). The transition from the Middle Ages of the Gothic period took place during the Renaissance and Baroque periods, which created critical turning points in the development of Western civilization. The Renaissance represented a rebirth and return to the round arch and more formal Roman ideas. This resurgence was fueled by looking to the past in an attempt to capture the spirit of antiquity and synthesize the culture of classical forms of architecture. In contrast to the theocentric nature of the Gothic period, the Renaissance emerged as an anthropocentric or human-centered movement. This fundamental focus and value were translated into architecture by emphasizing the human body and its place in space. Measurements were inspired by human proportions, by interrelationships between the whole human body and its parts. The proportions used related directly to the human body and harmonized with it. The Renaissance idealized nature and represented this

Figure 13-7 High Renaissance addition to Hampton Court, England (architect, Wren).

idealization visually in the form of decoration. The main scientific development that influenced the built environment in this period was mathematical perspective. In the use of constructed perspectives and theories of proportion, designers sought to understand how appearances conformed to formal geometric rules.

By the time the High Renaissance culminated in 1500, the characteristics of this period were clearly identifiable. Buildings had unified, harmonious compositions. They were typically represented by formal organization and monumental form. The unified whole related harmoniously to its parts. Buildings and gardens were centrally planned and organized symmetrically around a central focus. Important High Renaissance practitioners in Rome include Bramante, Michelangelo, Raphael, and da Vinci and Jones and Wren in England.

Baroque (1600–1750). The Baroque style originated in Rome with Michelangelo. It was based on the Renaissance order, but its principal quality was a painterly approach to representation. What something looked like was more important than its actual essence. Baroque

Figure 13-6 Renaissance Queen's House, Greenwich, England (architect, Jones).

Figure 13-8 High Renaissance/Baroque St. Paul's Cathedral, London, by Sir Christopher Wren (T. Bartuska).

style was concerned with movement in the sense that the active notion of becoming was emphasized over the static role of being. As in the Renaissance, the individual parts and units of a design related to the human scale, as did every aspect and detail of decoration. Critical players during this period include Rubens, Rembrandt, Bernini, Borromini, Fisher von Erlach, Wren, and Nash. The Baroque has often been summarized as a wild and bizarre interpretation of the formal Renaissance style.

Recent Past: 1770–1960

Industrial Revolution

The Industrial Revolution started in England in 1770 and spread throughout Europe and North America. It is characterized by a shift from hand-created to machine-manufactured products, from dispersed to concentrated centers of production, and from rural to urban living. The new centers of industry utilizing mechanized manufacture began to draw the displaced rural populations into densely overcrowded urban areas. The Industrial Revolution led to difficult social conditions, including extensive

factory production (and pollution), densely populated new urban areas, and brutal factory labor practices. These conditions provided the impetus for many significant social changes, including development of the first environmental laws, building codes, and labor laws. The Industrial Revolution was also a major turning point in architecture. New construction materials were developed. Methods for mechanized manufacture led to systems of assembly rather than individual custom designs.

The production of iron in the late eighteenth century provided a new construction material that, in turn, produced innovations in methods and systems of construction. Large spans using minimal material became possible, and spatial possibilities expanded. The use of iron for construction was originally relegated to industrial building because of aesthetic concerns. In the mid-1800s, most designers were fascinated with copying historic styles. As in product design, cast iron in classical motifs appeared on façades. As its benefits became more widely appreciated, it was utilized for construction of bridges, the Crystal Palace (see Chapter 9), and train stations and was slowly incorporated into major innovations in architecture. The use of iron for the frames of buildings was a major departure from the load-bearing wall construction of the past. As the relatively small iron members took the major loads in a building, the enclosing wall or façade no longer had to bear this weight. The façade became free, hung as a skin supported on the iron frame, which was lighter and less expensive than previous load-bearing construction systems. Much larger openings became possible, as the skin supported only its own weight. With a lighter structural frame and the invention of the elevator, increased building heights became possible and the first

Figure 13-9 The world's first iron-manufactured bridge, Ironbridge, Telford, England.

skyscrapers emerged. Steel production evolved by refining the properties of iron through the removal of impurities in a blast furnace. The result was a material far superior to iron. Construction practices became less restrictive, and new advances resulting from the use of iron were surpassed by steel. In architecture, this period is marked by light frames and the repetitive rhythm of construction elements that evolved from the economics of mechanized production and assembly.

During the Industrial Revolution, the science of concrete technology, which had lain dormant since the fall of the Roman Empire, was reactivated. Although the ingredients changed from those used by the Romans, the principles were the same. A critical ingredient, portland cement, was developed in 1824. As concrete and its plastic nature gained acceptance, structures combining concrete with steel to form reinforced concrete emerged, a marriage that used the qualities of each material to advantage: steel for tension and concrete for compression. Other construction systems developed in the early twentieth century, including hollow concrete block and reinforced masonry wall construction.

Arts and Crafts Movement (1850–1920)

In the mid-nineteenth century, designers began to rebel against industrialization and its commercialism. This reaction, which became known as the Arts and Crafts Movement, spread throughout the British Isles, Northern and Central European industrial cities, and North America. Prominent in the Arts and Crafts Movement in the British Isles was William Morris, who focused on pattern design and attempted to reenergize abandoned craft techniques. Charles Rennie Mackintosh founded the Glasgow School of Art and worked with a small group of associates in architecture, furniture design, and graphic arts. A second-generation member of the Arts and Crafts Movement was M. H. Ballie Scott, who promoted simple abstract designs and open planning in domestic architecture.

This movement was not an isolated phenomenon. Contemporary philosophies of the period reflected similar dissatisfaction with the industrialization of human nature. The Garden City Movement promoted a return to a quality living environment lost in the rush to overcrowded, polluted industrialized centers of population. A romantic notion of the rural country garden was utilized in the planning and design of new Garden Cities, intended to provide both proximity to sources of employment and a lifestyle centered on nature. There was also a developing interest in vegetarianism and in reviving the folk song. Factory work was viewed as soulless and

Figure 13-10 Arts and Crafts Movement, Hill House, Hellensburgh, Scotland (architect, Mackintosh).

degrading to humanity. These philosophies rejected the artificiality of postindustrialized life and favored the Romantic values of nature and folk culture.

The Arts and Craft Movement looked to diverse sources for influence, including India, Japan, the Middle East,

Figure 13-11 Arts and Crafts Movement, Glasgow School of Art, Glasgow, Scotland (architect, Mackintosh).

Scandinavia, Celtic Ireland, Byzantium, medieval Europe, Renaissance Italy, and sixteenth- and seventeenth-century England.

The essence of the Arts and Crafts Movement is a unity of arts and crafts rather than a mechanical division of parts, the value and experience of individual craftspeople, and expressions of the qualities of materials and construction. The spirit of this movement materialized in small workshops—located away from the centers of industry—in which old craft techniques were revived. Objects of the preindustrialized period, including humble household items, became valued for expressing the essence of the human spirit. The pleasure of working with traditional craft methods defined the essence of a product's aesthetic. Machine-made objects were considered to be disconnected from the human condition and, therefore, without meaning. Design was to be simple and unpretentious, executed with honest construction, material, and appropriate decoration. High value was placed on the craftsperson who revived traditional methods and worked for the sake of achieving creative satisfaction. This purity of aesthetic echoed a romantic view of rural life and the past.

Art Nouveau Movement

The Gallerie L'Art Nouveau opened in Paris in 1884; its name was adopted by a movement emergent from the Arts and Crafts Movement. The Art Nouveau Movement rejected the academic tradition and all forms of ornament based on classical or Renaissance precedent. It promoted the abolishment of hierarchy in favor of the unification of all the arts and crafts. The roots of Art Nouveau philoso-

Figure 13-12   Garden Cities Movement, Letchworth Garden City, England.

phy were in utility and the alliance of form with need. The observation and imitation of nature was a central focus. Sinuous, asymmetrical lines of organic forms, simple outlines, and the influence of exotic flowers and plants characterized Art Nouveau designs.

Modern Movement

Nikolaus Pevsner is credited with originating the term "Modern Movement" in his book *Pioneers of Modern Design*. This movement had its origins in the philosophy of the Arts and Crafts Movement in Britain, where the handcrafted ideal was favored over industrialization of the building process. The early Modern Movement had the following characteristics:

- Surfaces were uninterrupted and plainly extended, with unadorned walls.
- Volume and form were simple and bold, with abstracted rectilinear geometry.
- Organization followed a structural rationale that produced elegant, uncomplicated interior spaces and exterior forms.
- Detailing included extensive glazed areas, horizontal windows, unadorned masses, and undecorated surfaces.

The German Bauhaus (*bau* = building, *haus* = house) was a school of art, architecture, and industrial design founded by the architect Walter Gropius in 1919. It was, unfortunately, closed by the Nazi government in 1933. Initially the school shunned the academic studio in favor of historical training methods in workshop environments that created a closer connection between fine and applied art and attempted to reestablish the connection between arts, crafts, and sciences (manufacturing and technology). In 1923, the Bauhaus began to dissociate itself from the handcrafted ideal and to embrace the machine age, recognizing that the new technology could play an integral role in quality design. The Bauhaus investigated the role of technology in determining form while admiring the beauty and purity of the machine aesthetic and began to produce a rational, modern architecture using new building techniques.

International Style

The Museum of Modern Art in New York held an exhibition in 1932 that included the work of many European avant-garde architects. The catalog of the exhibition was titled *The International Style: Architecture since 1922*. The term "International Style" came to denote a style of architecture that evolved through the late Modern Movement. The International Style was distinguished by the following practices:

- Geometric forms were used that were frequently rectilinear grids, asymmetrical, or simple cubes.
- Structures were organized in grid patterns and divided into different volumes by non-load-bearing planes.
- Space was emphasized rather than mass.
- Surfaces were plain and free of historical styles or references.
- Façades were arranged according to a regularly placed structure and the use of standardized parts.
- Decoration was eliminated or minimized.

Because the structure was disconnected from the articulation of enclosed interior space, it became functionally adaptable. Its most memorable characteristic, however, was an anonymous and banal appearance. This aesthetic developed further through technology and structural techniques that used steel and concrete frames with prefabricated infill panels. This standardized appearance is synonymous with the curtain wall and grid pattern of the corporate "glass box." In many cases, internal comfort was achieved by extensive use of energy-consuming mechanical systems. Because it was void of culture and regional influences and was used throughout the world, it has been labeled the International Style.

Contemporary Trends (1960s to Present)

Post Modernism

The Post Modern Movement evolved in the 1960s as a challenge to ideas associated with the Modern Movement; Post Modernism appeared as a reaction to the rationalism of modernism and the uniformity of the International Style. The Post Modern palette made eclectic selections from classical and neo-classical vocabularies. The Post Modern architect Robert Venturi coined the phrase "**less is a bore**" in response and reference to the famous quote "**less is more**" by the Modernist architect Mies van der Rohe. The Post Modernists abstracted historical elements into hybrid compositions that emanated a lively richness. A new formalism began to emerge that echoed Renaissance values materialized with modern technological expression. Post Modernism attempted to respond to the site by using historical and contextual references. The anthropocentric nature of the Renaissance was visible in efforts made to re-create a relationship between people and their architectural environment. Key players in the Post Modern era were Robert Stern, Mario

Figure 13-13 Post Modern, Number One, Poultry, London (architect, Stirling).

Botta, Oswald Ungers, Charles Moore, Robert Venturi, and Michael Graves.

Environmentalism

Buildings act as modifiers of the natural environment to provide interior environments appropriate for human habitation and production. A building can do this in a passive manner without utilizing mechanical devices, relying solely on design, orientation, organization, form, material and construction to filter unwanted elements, reduce the ingress of undesirable qualities, and encourage the admission of all desirable elements of climate. When a building uses active mechanical systems, it depends on technology and energy to create human comfort. Active design is frequently combined with passive control systems.

Traditional **vernacular** buildings often utilized passive methods of control. In hot climates, passive controls include thick walls to insulate; courtyards to provide cool, shaded space; small, deep wall openings to prevent solar ingress; and wind catchers—tall chimney-like elements that stimulate the venting of hot interior air by rotating to catch external air movement and sucking up interior air currents. In hot, humid climates, passive-planning techniques include open-sided buildings with shaded verandahs often elevated to encourage air movement and subsequent cooling.

In the twentieth century, mechanical technological methods for heating, cooling, and ventilating buildings developed. There was a growth in the use of active systems of environmental control, especially in urban areas of the United States. This growth was encouraged by

Figure 13-14 A solar-responsive design in which air stacks, chimneys, and operable windows passively ventilate the building. Building Research Establishment (BRE), Watford, England.

Figure 13-16 Effective window shading, daylight strategies, air stacks, chimneys, and operable windows that passively ventilate the building. Inland Revenue Complex, Nottingham, England (architect, Hopkins).

plentiful sources of energy at relatively low cost. The International Style, which promoted the use of steel and glass structures for all climate types, also demanded active mechanical systems. The glass façade, if used indiscriminately, overheated, resulting in the need for cooling, and since it did not provide insulation against the cold, the need for heating also increased. These extreme needs were somewhat modified by the development of tinted and reflective glass designed to minimize solar heat gain and double-glazed window systems designed to modify heat loss.

The reliance on mechanical systems to satisfy heating and cooling demands came under review when an energy crisis began in 1973. A shortage of fuel, and the compounding effects of an oil embargo, resulted in a move to conserve energy. Early experiments in energy-

Figure 13-15 Air stack-chimneys, and operable windows that passively ventilate the building. New Parliament Building, London, England (architect, Hopkins).

conserving buildings included highly engineered environments that were tightly sealed against climatic elements. These "artificially controlled buildings," managed by computers, created unhealthy interior environments. Efforts to seal buildings not only prevented the ingress of fresh air, but the buildings, burdened by inadequate air-handling and purifying systems, developed polluted interior environments, a condition that came to be known as "sick building syndrome." Interest in more **sustainable** solutions led to renewed use of passive systems of control coupled with investigations into alternative renewable energy sources. Research and experimentation focused on cost- and energy-efficient active systems and direct and indirect solar-powered systems. Like the vernacular concepts, the passive design response began to change the appearance of the buildings utilizing these strategies.

High-Tech

In the 1960s and 1970s, there was a growing concern in the West about profuse use of technology to solve all problems, regardless of cost. The environmental awareness motivated by the energy crisis of the 1970s was accompanied by concern for the less developed areas of the world. For some, the answer was for the West to develop a more modest, less energy-intensive culture. At the same time, the first high-tech buildings appeared. High-tech architects sought to find an expressive use of modern technology and industrial components, and many found it by blatantly utilizing brightly colored elements of industry. High-tech was not always greeted favorably. It represented the opposite of low-tech, which,

Figure 13-17   High-tech Sainsbury Art Center, Norwich, England (architect, Foster).

in the light of environmental and energy issues, was considered the more appropriate choice.

This debate was further energized when two prominent projects were executed in the high-tech motif. Sir Norman Foster's design for the Hong-Kong and Shanghai Bank Building of 1985 and Richard Rogers' Lloyds of London building aligned with the high-tech aesthetic. Another prominent high-tech building was the Pompidou Center in Paris, completed in 1976 and designed by Renzo Piano and Rogers. The main characteristics of high-tech aesthetics include compact rectangular forms that are transparent and lightweight, emphasis on precision engineering and machine detailing, and exposure of structure and mechanical systems, often exhibited in bright colors with high finishes.

Deconstruction

In 1988, the Museum of Modern Art in New York presented an exhibition of work by seven avant-garde architects from Europe and the United States under the label of "deconstructivist" architecture. The group was composed of Peter Eisenman, Frank Gehry, Zaha Hadid, Coop Himmelblau, Rem Koolhaus, Daniel Libeskind, and Bernard Tschumi. The deconstructivist philosophy was a strong

Figure 13-18   High-tech expression of Lloyds of London (architect, Rogers).

Figure 13-19   High-tech, environmentally responsive Greater London Council Building, London, by architects Foster and Partners (T. Bartuska).

Figure 13-20 Deconstructivist design of the School of Art and Architecture, University of Cincinnati, Ohio (architect, Eiseman).

departure from or reaction to what had preceded it, especially the historical eclecticism of the Post Modern period.

Deconstruction as a philosophical movement emerged from the writings of the French philosopher Jacques Derrida in the 1970s. Typically, philosophers focused on deconstructing or analyzing texts to search for conflicts and possibilities. With so many differences and possibilities, meaning was open to interpretation, though connections could be recognized. A deconstructivist approach includes an attempt to deconstruct the elements of architecture, treating buildings as the philosophers did texts. Often elements from other traditions are incorporated in the composition, altering their function and meaning to provide an innovative three-dimensional spatial experience.

Participation

An exhibition titled "Architecture without Architects" opened at the Museum of Modern Art in New York in

1964; it was later incorporated into a publication of the same title by the exhibition's designer, Bernard Rudolfsky. The exhibition and publication explore nonformal, nonclassical architecture, emphasizing the immutable nature of vernacular architecture and its ability to satisfy its function. In exploring the content of the exhibition, which spans millennia, the role of the designer emerges in a participatory process involving diverse components including the site and the user. In contrast to the solo, isolated architect depicted in Ayn Rand's novel *The Fountainhead*, Rudolfsky presents a participant in a collaborative process.

In the twenty-first century, the collaborative participatory process can be divided into three principal areas, one or more of which can be included in a project. First, participation may take place in the project conception phase, where individual, group, or community stakeholders are involved in initiating and conceiving a design project. Village Homes in Davis, California, is an example; future inhabitants initiated the project in consultation with an architect. This group wished the development to embody a philosophy of living not readily available at that time in commercially developed residential communities. This philosophy included concepts to promote community-oriented design and harmonious living with one another and the site. Second, participation may take place during the design process. This is most evident in the design methodology of architect Ralph Erskine, who plays the role of facilitator and mobilizes community creativity. As well as facilitating community involvement in the design process, Erskine is very sensitive to the use of materials and methods of construction that represent a humanistic approach to living. Third, participation may take place in

Figure 13-21 Participatory and environmentally responsive design, University Allhouse, Stockholm, Sweden (architect, Erskine).

Table 13-1 Medieval/Gothic Characteristics

	ROMANESQUE (NORMAN) 1060–1200	EARLY GOTHIC 1200–1300	DECORATED GOTHIC 1300–1400	PERPENDICULAR GOTHIC 1400–1575
Form	• Cruciform • Apsidal ends • Nave arcades	• Simple design	• Flowing geometric shapes	• Rectangular module • Slenderness + delicacy in design • Vertical lines
Walls	• Thick walls • Massive pillars • Triforium • Clerestory	• Reduced thickness • More slender pillars • Detached pillars • Lancet windows • Early tracery	• Increased window area • Reduced height • Triforium • Enlarged clerestory windows	• Increased window area • Increased number of mullions and transoms • Triforium almost gone
Span	• Rounded arches • Barrel vaulting	• Pointed arches	• Abutments + flying buttresses • Intricate rib vaulting	• Abutments advanced • Vaulting advanced • Four-centered flattened arch
Decoration	• Decorated carving	• Simple decoration	• Greater ornament of surface	• Slenderness + delicacy in design

the construction phase, where the project is created physically. This concept is illustrated by volunteer organizations such as Habitat for Humanity. Strategies for keeping costs down include involvement of a volunteer, semi-skilled workforce from the community.

Participation in making contemporary design shatters the image of the designer as the elite, all-knowing individual who creates in isolation from future users. This image has been replaced by one of the designer as a member of a team where collaborative efforts materialize in collective visions with humanistic sensibility.

Conclusion

This brief overview of trends in Western architecture has presented the idea that trends overlap and run concurrently. Many approaches are recycled and mature in later periods; in other cases, designers combine or fuse together multiple ideas in a more effective way to address human/social, environmental, and technological issues. Thus, the study of past trends may allow us to predict trends in the future and understand the maturation of the various approaches to architecture. The human/social, cultural, and environmental issues will be expanded upon in the next two chapters.

References

Allen, E. *Fundamentals of Building Construction*. Wiley, 1990.

Jordan, J. *A Concise History of Western Architecture*. Thames and Hudson, 1969.

Moffett, M., et al. *A World History of Architecture*. McGraw-Hill, 2004.

Papadakes, A. *New Architecture*, St. Martin's Press, 2000.

Pevsner, N. *Pioneers of Modern Design*. Penguin, 1960.

Rudolfsky, B. *Architecture without Architects*. Doubleday, 1965.

CHAPTER 14

Architecture as a Cultural Layer

Wendy R. McClure

Historic places create cultural layers in the built environment that offer temporal dimension and enrich the texture of our cities, towns, campuses, neighborhoods, and buildings. This chapter will provide an overview of the historic preservation movement in the United States, including why preservation is important and how it is accomplished. Processes sanctioned by the U.S. Secretary of the Interior and the professional preservation and design communities will also be discussed, including preservation, restoration, and rehabilitation (or adaptive use). This chapter will emphasize buildings and neighborhoods; Chapter 22 will apply similar principles and process to cities.

What Is Historic Preservation?

A substantial portion of the built environment includes structures, landscapes, infrastructure, and cities constructed by previous generations. These inherited artifacts provide a tangible record of the aspirations, technologies, and cultural values of human civilization. Current and future generations must make choices concerning how to treat historic buildings and neighborhoods. A small percentage of structures, revered for their association with famous persons or architectural achievements, should be protected from alterations. However, a vast majority of historic buildings are capable of being reshaped and adapted to suit the needs and aspirations of contemporary culture. Some buildings and neighborhoods will be recycled for new uses, while others will be replaced by new development.

Although historic buildings, landscapes and districts in the United States are relatively young compared to those in Europe, Asia, or the Middle East, they constitute our history. Some western towns have only recently celebrated their centennials, but their historic buildings are important to sustain cultural and regional identity. The Department of the Interior, a federal organization known best for its role in protecting national parks, is also responsible for identifying and protecting historic structures. Buildings and neighborhoods over 50 years old are considered to be historic and are potentially eligible for the National Register of Historic Places.

Early preservation efforts in the United States were initiated primarily to protect buildings associated with famous persons or important works of architecture. In 1853 the first preservation organization in the United States, the Mount Vernon Ladies Association, was formed by Anne Pamela Cunningham to rescue President George Washington's home and grounds, Mount Vernon, from conversion to a luxury hotel. A primary motivation was to restore the decaying plantation to a state that would accurately interpret Washington's life. During the early twentieth century, preservationists expanded their focus from single buildings to entire historic contexts. The city of Williamsburg, Virginia, was meticulously restored to its original colonial state. All buildings constructed after 1776 were demolished, and buildings that had been lost were accurately reconstructed. The city became frozen in time; it serves as a museum to interpret colonial life and no longer functions as a living city.

The Battery District of Charleston, South Carolina, was the nation's first living historic district. In the 1920s, neighborhood residents organized to prevent pillaging of fine antebellum homes. Homeowners, architects, interior designers, and construction companies from the Northeast were purchasing Charleston homes and removing exterior features and interior materials for use in new homes. The American Institute of Architects (AIA) responded to a plea from Battery District residents by declaring such practices professionally unethical.

Charleston served as a paradigm for other urban historic districts that followed, including the French Quarter in New Orleans and the Pioneer Square District in Seattle. During the later twentieth century, the historic preservation movement expanded to include less extraordinary buildings and districts. While not considered national icons, these cultural resources provide historic continuity and contribute to regional character.

Preservation Terminology and Strategies

Historic Preservation

Historic preservation is an umbrella term used to describe the advocacy, research, planning, design, and construction activities associated with protecting historic structures and contexts. Most planners, architects, and interior designers will work with historic structures and contexts during their professional careers. Their specialized knowledge is required to make appropriate design decisions concerning historic structures.

In the United States, the Secretary of the Interior sets standards for historic preservation. The Secretary sanctions three basic design strategies for design professionals, contractors, and building owners to use on historic structures: preservation, restoration, and rehabilitation/adaptive use. Selection of a strategy depends upon the goals of a particular project.

Preservation

Preservation as a design strategy involves taking actions to "sustain the existing form, integrity and material of an historic property" (Secretary of the Interior's Standards).

In a sense, preservation can be considered an ongoing maintenance program. Change happens gradually and incrementally. Historic materials, which may be quite worn, are maintained rather than replaced, so that the wear and the aging process are visible and continue to convey a sense of time—for example, the original, unpainted siding on a barn or old glass in a storefront window.

Examples of places where preservation strategies are used to maintain structures for their intended purposes include barns, private homes, university classroom buildings, and theatres. Mixed-use buildings in Salzburg, Austria (Fig. 14-1), have been in continuous use since the Middle Ages. Changes made during the Renaissance and in the modern era are reflected in the medieval structures.

Figure 14-1 Preservation in Salzburg, Austria. A mixed-use commercial building with housing above that has been in continuous use since the sixteenth century through a process of ongoing preservation. Note the cornice line, which proudly displays the date of original construction (1558) and most recent improvements in 1986.

Figure 14-2 Preservation. The Jefferson County Courthouse in Port Towsend, Washington, has been in continuous use as a courthouse since it was constructed in 1892. Repairs continue to be made to keep the building in use without changing its purpose or compromising its historic or architectural integrity. The building serves as an example of ongoing preservation.

Cultural layer is laid on cultural layer. Dates at the cornice line, showing when the buildings were originally constructed and most recently improved, are indicative of community pride in their continued use and preservation.

During the life of most historic structures, modifications are made to accommodate changes in functional needs or stylistic trends. These changes may assume historic significance in their own right. For example, a theater in Moscow, Idaho, constructed in 1890 as a vaudeville theater, was remodeled in the late 1930s as a movie house and updated to reflect the Art Deco style of the time. In 2002, the building in its current condition was listed on the National Register of Historic Places, because the architectural changes made during the 1930s and 1940s were considered to be historic in their own right.

Restoration

The process of **restoration** is used to bring a building back to a specific and significant point in time, usually its original state, by "accurately depicting the form, features, and character of a property as it appeared at a particular period of time by means of removal of features from other periods . . . and reconstruction of missing features from the restoration period" (Secretary of the Interior's Standards). Restoration processes involve

removing materials and layers of changes that may have been added in order to clarify the original design intent, or architectural style, or association with a significant historic event or famous person. In some cases, materials and changes that may have become significant in their own right are removed to more accurately reflect an earlier period. As a result, restoration processes can be the most invasive of the three primary preservation strategies (Fig 14-3).

Candidates for restoration include buildings associated with famous persons or works of high-style architecture. The restoration of Mount Vernon in 1853 by the Mount Vernon Ladies Association was one of the first restoration projects in the United States. Many buildings by Frank Lloyd Wright have been meticulously restored to their original state to accurately reflect the renowned architect's original design intent.

Ironically, the restoration process can freeze a building in time, making it more difficult to accommodate its original purposes, especially if technologies or practices have changed. The restoration of building façades is generally more easily accomplished than that of interior spaces, which are more vulnerable to changes in function. Some notable exceptions include grand spaces such as hotel lobbies, train stations, and capitol rotundas, which can be restored to their original purpose and style. Buildings that have been restored on the inside frequently become museums. This is the case with Frank Lloyd Wright's Oak Park home and studio, which serve as a museum to help interpret his life and earliest professional work. Restoration of these structures required the removal of alterations that

Figure 14-3 Restoration. Constructed in 1865 by French missionary Father Ravalli and members of the Coeur d'Alene (Schitsu'umsh) tribe, Cataldo Mission is the oldest surviving building in Idaho. The mission represents the use of restoration as a preservation strategy.

Figure 14-4   Restoration. The Wallowa County Museum in Joseph, Oregon, was originally built as a bank. The structure has been carefully restored on the exterior and interior. It is used as a museum because it can no longer support the functions of a contemporary bank.

Wright himself had made when he converted those spaces into an apartment building.

There is a tendency among architects and others involved in restoration projects to envision an historic structure as more grand than it actually was and subsequently to be overly zealous about the restoration process. During the late nineteenth century, the French architect Violet Le Duc was renowned for his embellishments of historic structures to make them appear, according to him, "more grand than they ever were." Sanctioned restoration projects in the United States today, however, require scholarly detective work to reveal the original materials and conditions, as well as archival research of photographs and/or drawings.

Rehabilitation and Adaptive Use

Rehabilitation and **adaptive use** are the most commonly used historic preservation strategies. Rehabilitation is defined as "the act or process of making possible a compatible use for a property through repair, alteration and addition while preserving those portions or features which convey its historical, cultural or architectural

Figure 14-5   Rehabilitation. Visionaries at Washington State University rescued the campus's historic dairy barn from demolition by demonstrating its potential for adaptive use as an alumni center. The former stalls are arranged as small-group gathering areas for alumni.

value."[1] Rehabilitation involves preserving the original design and materials of an historic structure while making the alterations necessary to accommodate changes in function and/or use. When buildings can no longer accommodate their original uses, they are often recycled for other purposes. Examples include conversion of warehouses to condominiums and school buildings to community centers. Access the U.S. Department of the Interior Web site for complete definitions of, and guidelines for, each preservation strategy.

Figure 14-6   Rehabilitation. The former hayloft of the Washington State University Alumni Center retains the integrity of its barn gambrel roof structure as a dramatic setting for large-group alumni events.

Figure 14-7 Combining strategies. Daniel Burnham's Union Station in Washington, DC, represents one of the most significant historic preservation projects of the twentieth century in the United States. The main head house (above) and the President's Room were meticulously restored, the areas used for train travel were preserved, and the concourse, basement, and train shed areas were adaptively reused for retail purposes to reactivate the station.

Washington, DC's, Union Station, designed by Daniel Burnham in 1907, was one of the most significant preservation projects in the United States during the twentieth century, involving all three design strategies—preservation, restoration, and adaptive use (Fig. 14-7). During the peak period of train travel, the Beaux Arts–style station was a virtual city serving travelers, temporarily housing immigrants in its basement area, and acting as a site for presidential banquets and inaugural balls. The once celebrated train station fell into disrepair when train travel declined during the 1950s and 1960s. An act of Congress in 1981 rescued the building from demolition and set the stage for a public-private partnership to complete its restoration and rehabilitation in 1988.

The renowned preservation architect Harold Weese was engaged to restore the grandest spaces of the station. Celebrated retail architect Benjamin Thompson was hired to infuse life and economic vitality into the station once again by adapting secondary spaces for new retail and entertainment uses. The partnership forged a highly successful preservation plan and gave the remarkable station new life. First and foremost, Union Station continues to function as a train station. The most elaborate and ceremonial spaces in the station have been carefully restored to their original grandeur, including the head house and President's Room. Contemporary design interventions injected new vitality by drawing crowds of people to participate in a wide range of activities. Former

concourses, train sheds, and basement areas now feature retail stores, food courts, and cinema complexes, contributing to the project's overwhelming success as a hub of human activity. Design integrity has been maintained and economic viability and social vitality restored.

Integrity is critical. Most buildings undergo varying degrees of change over time, either through natural wear on materials or modifications to accommodate changes in human needs. An historic building that has been neglected or poorly maintained can still retain its historic and/or architectural **integrity—clarity of design intent**— even if its physical condition is allowed to decline. By contrast, buildings that have been dramatically altered or overly restored may lose that integrity.

Why Is Historic Preservation Important?

The benefits of historic preservation are multifaceted. Historic preservation processes help to preserve cultural continuity, protect neighborhoods, conserve energy, interpret history, and enable people to experience the vitality and complexity of a multilayered built environment.

Energy and Resource Efficiency

Every structure features materials that contain **embodied energy**, or energy that has already been expended and can continue to be harnessed. The sources of embodied energy include energy used to manufacture original materials and transport them to job sites, as well as labor and energy used during construction. Embodied energy is lost through demolition. Instead, additional energy must be used for new construction to extract, manufacture, and transport new materials to job sites, build structures, and dispose of old materials in landfills. Preservation, by capturing embodied energy onsite, can be considered the ultimate recycling program.

Because mechanical support systems did not exist, historic buildings were frequently designed to use passive technologies, optimize access to daylight, and conserve energy. For example, school buildings generally had rectangular footprints, with their long axis running east-west, affording generous access to high-angle or indirect daylight and ventilation through operable windows on the north- and south-facing sides of the building. The advent of mechanical systems and electricity enabled designers to substitute natural/renewable energy sources for daylight and ventilation, with energy-intensive artificial life support systems to regulate comfort for occupants. Their intentions often backfired. The impact of artificial substitutes on health, productivity, and energy consumption are being reconsidered in the design of contemporary workplaces. Historic buildings can provide a paradigm for more effective design responses to climate.

Cultural Identity

Historic components of the built environment embody the hopes and aspirations of previous generations. They are living artifacts, affording opportunities for firsthand, tangible contact with history. For example, as students ascend the well-worn marble steps of their campus buildings, they can feel a connection to the students who climbed those same steps one hundred years before them and to the traditions that help to forge institutional identity. Historic contexts provide cultural layers and experiential complexity that cannot be replicated in new developments. Historic buildings convey a sense of permanence and contribute to the unique cultural heritage and regional identity of a community. They provide a tangible connection to a community's history. For example, the eloquent half-timbered railroad depot constructed by the Great Northern Railroad in 1927 in Whitefish, Montana, adds character and interest to the downtown area. The depot serves as a tangible connection to the community's origin as a railroad town and its continuing role as a regional hub for rail transport (Fig. 14-8).

The preservation of Pike Place Market in Seattle is important not because it represents a significant work of

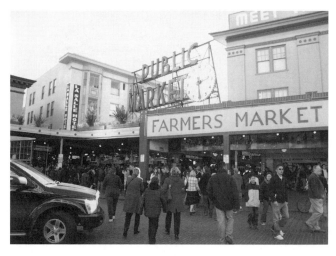

Figure 14-9 The Pike Place Market in Seattle is an example of ongoing preservation of structures, as well as use of policies to preserve the economic viability of the area for fish and fruit vendors and the cultural character of the district by preventing infiltration of chain stores and gentrification.

architecture, but because the urban market sustains cultural and economic traditions. Market structures are vernacular, makeshift, and reflective of incremental expansion of spaces for independent entrepreneurs to sell fish, produce, and crafts (Figs. 14-9, 14-10).

The once expansive farmer's market was threatened with demolition when it fell into decline in the 1960s. Seattle architect Victor Steinbrook championed the cause to rescue the market by convincing the city government to invest in revitalization.

Today, the Pike Place Market Corporation manages the market and institutes policies to ensure that its unique character and heritage are protected. Rents are

Figure 14-8 This Great Northern Railroad depot, constructed in 1927, provides both a visual icon and an important connection to the town of Whitefish, Montana's railroad history.

Figure 14-10 The preservation strategy used for the Pike Place Market has been to retain its simple, vernacular character.

Figure 14-11 Restrictive zoning limiting the height of surrounding development is implemented in the Pike Place Market Historic District to help preserve its intimate street scale.

structured to ensure viability of traditional, independent businesses such as meat, fish, and produce vendors and to prevent intrusion of national chain stores. One notable exception is Starbucks Coffee Company, because its original store was located at Pike Place. During the 1970s, architecture students at the University of Washington engaged the once tiny retail company in its first commercial contract to supply coffee beans for the college's campus coffee shops.

Zoning laws created to protect the market from encroachment of high-rise development are reflected directly in the surrounding urban form. Luxury high-rise condominiums literally step down in height toward the market district. Upper-level spaces in the market provide subsidized, affordable housing for single-room occupants, preventing displacement of lower-income residents (Fig. 14-11).

Urban, Neighborhood, and Small-Town Revitalization

Urban Revitalization

During the 1960s, blighted neighborhoods in cities throughout the United States were being destroyed to achieve planning goals established by urban renewal

programs designed to improve conditions in the inner city. One of Seattle's earliest settlements, Pioneer Square, was targeted for urban renewal. Fortunately, the neighborhood was revitalized instead and provides a successful paradigm for reanimation of blighted neighborhoods using historic preservation as the primary design strategy.

Pioneer Square was rebuilt from the ashes of a devastating fire in 1889. Following World War II, the neighborhood gradually fell into economic decline as the center of commercial activity shifted north and masses of inner-city residents moved to the suburbs. During the 1960s the neighborhood was declared blighted. Urban renewal plans called for razing the district's many abandoned and dilapidated late-nineteenth-century buildings and replacing them with a new waterfront highway system. The plans were successfully averted, largely due to the visionary architect Ralph Anderson, who helped to launch a revitalization campaign. Anderson demonstrated the area's potential and instilled confidence in investors by acquiring several buildings and rehabilitating them. The Seattle-based landscape architecture firm Jones and Jones developed two of the abandoned plazas, Occidental Square and Pioneer Square, helping to restore areas for public gatherings, public art, and outdoor entertainment. The revitalization process took nearly 25 years. Throughout the 1970s and early 1980s, building owners "land banked" their buildings by inflating prices and refusing to rehabilitate them. Eventually, the expanding Seattle economy attracted adequate investment capital to revitalize the vast majority of the remaining structures. Today the neighborhood is a vital center for the arts, tourism, and entertainment (Figs. 14-12 to 14-14).

Figure 14-12 Pioneer Square in the heart of Seattle's oldest historic district continues to serve as the heart of the neighborhood.

Figure 14-13   Before—photo taken by visionary architect Ralph Anderson of the Pioneer Building in Seattle on Pioneer Square demonstrates the condition of buildings in the district before they were rehabilitated.

Neighborhood Revitalization

Enlightened investors and the firm of Peter Trapolin and Associates, Architects, partnered to transform two blocks of abandoned housing in a blighted New Orleans neighborhood into a luxury hotel. The site, which included

Figure 14-14   After—the revitalized Pioneer Building in 2006.

Figure 14-15   Before—a decaying neighborhood surrounding the site of a unique inner-city hotel in New Orleans, Louisiana.

houses constructed before the Civil War, had become a staging area for drug trafficking and other criminal activities. The investment was very risky. The houses, each featuring balconies with iron railings, elaborate millwork, and slave quarters, were adapted as unique hotel suites. Vacant lots between the houses were infilled with similarly scaled new hotel units to ensure the economic viability of the project. The city street network through the site was preserved, but vehicular access was limited to provide security for guests while retaining pedestrian access for neighborhood residents. Parking was located offsite, affording opportunities to create a garden sanctuary at the core of the development. Backyards were aggregated into a landscaped courtyard (Figs. 14-15 to 14-17). Long-term goals of the project sought to turn the neighborhood around and provide needed employment for neighborhood residents.

Figure 14-16   After—eight abandoned houses in New Orleans were adapted to serve as a campus-style hotel (Peter Trapolin and Associates Architects).

Figure 14-17 After—revitalized streetscape resulting from rehabilitation of abandoned shotgun houses as hotel units.

The hotel has been successful in a neighborhood that most investors wouldn't have touched. It is still uncertain whether or not the project will serve as a catalyst to help revitalize the surrounding neighborhood, especially after the city suffered the devastating effects of Hurricane Katrina in 2005. The hotel fronts along St. Charles Avenue, at the edge of the historic Garden District, one of the higher areas of the city that fared relatively well during the floods. It reopened for business early in the recovery efforts.

Small-Town Revitalization

Main Street, the commercial spine of small towns, was historically and continues to be the center of public life in most small towns, providing a stage set for community parades and other important events. In the early years of commercial districts' lives, fires wreaked havoc, destroying entire blocks of buildings, particularly wood, false-front structures. Merchants frequently rebuilt them in brick or stone to increase fire resistance. They adopted fashionable architectural styles and more durable materials as a marketing strategy to convey a heightened sense of permanence and sophistication in the commercial district.

During the 1960s, the combined effects of federal highway expansion and increased automobile use disrupted the integrity of downtown areas in small towns. Highways were routed through the heart of downtowns, increasing the volume and pace of traffic along Main Street. Merchants initially responded to the emerging automobile-oriented culture by shrouding their historic building façades in modern materials such as corrugated metal and scaling signage to capture the attention of passing motorists. Gas stations and parking lots replaced prominent corner buildings such as banks and drugstores.

By the 1970s, many downtowns in small communities had declined. Businesses relocated to the highway strip at the edge of town, where provision of parking and access were perceived to be easier. Shopping malls sucked the life out of downtown. The new highway strips and shopping malls in every small town began to look like the next one, a landscape of large signs and stand-alone businesses surrounded by massive parking lots and accessed by arterial roadways with minimal sidewalks.

By the late 1970s, forward-thinking civic leaders, business owners, and citizens, inspired by successful recovery efforts in urban centers such as Pioneer Square, began to revitalize their downtowns. Misguided community projects sought quick fixes by adopting a theme town approach or by constructing a downtown mall.

In 1980, the **National Trust for Historic Preservation**, a quasi-public and privately funded organization, responded by launching the **Main Street Program**. Using a four-point approach, this program provides a process for small communities to bring life back to their downtowns by rehabilitating and restoring the assets they already have in their historic buildings. Design serves as a tool to organize long-term planning for rehabilitation (adaptive use) and restoration of historic buildings, appropriate new infill construction on vacant lots, and add streetscape improvements such as wider sidewalks, trees, lighting, and public art. The program provides a forum for downtown stakeholders to organize and promote the district to customers and investors and to strengthen the economic base of downtown (see the Main Street Program's Web site for more detailed information)[2] (Fig. 14-18).

According to Dick Ryan, architect with the Texas Main Street program, "there has been a long history of miracle approach failures—urban renewal, modernizing

Figure 14-18 A revitalized Main Street in Baker City, Oregon.

whole towns with slipcovers, streetscape improvements—any concept that meant all we had to do was one thing."[3] Ryan explains that successful revitalization requires a long-term commitment from the community and willingness to complete hundreds of projects, not just one. Ryan describes the transformation of one such community, Hillsboro, Texas:

> Hillsboro Texas, 1981—You can't buy a pair of Nike shoes or an IZOD shirt. There is a mannequin that has had the same dress on for three years. The sales people are talking on the telephone. There is a dog asleep in the middle of the street yet the merchants in town say that people go to shop in Dallas because there is not enough parking. . . . Hillsboro Texas 1996—the finishing touches are being put on a 6 million dollar restoration of the 3-story limestone courthouse. What happened in those 15 years to change the attitude of the people in Hillsboro from defeatist to can-do? Much of it is linked to historic preservation and the Main Street program.[4]

Through work with dozens of communities in the intermountain West to revitalize their downtowns and restore community pride, historic preservation has consistently been a key ingredient in the process.[5] In the western United States, political beliefs span the entire spectrum. Despite the potentially fragmented conditions in which community initiatives are launched, citizens unite behind efforts to preserve what is meaningful in their built environment. For example, in New Meadows, Idaho, citizens agreed that restoring their decaying railroad depot should play a pivotal role in their economic recovery plan. The depot serves as an architectural showpiece and living testimony to the community's railroad heritage.

Figure 14-20 Downtown Priest River, Idaho, after revitalization.

Citizens and civic leaders in Priest River, Idaho, a depressed logging town, have been able to capture a share of the regional tourist market and attract outside investment by chipping away, project by project, at a 30-year downtown revitalization plan that the author's architecture firm developed with them in 1989 (Figs. 14-19, 14-20).

In Moscow, Idaho, the Post Office and Federal Building, constructed in 1911, was rescued from demolition and converted to the City Hall, serving to strengthen community identity and pride (Fig. 14-21). After a 10-year battle, local preservationists succeeded in preventing the demolition of a high school constructed in 1912 for use as a school district parking lot. The first phases of a long-range plan to adapt the historic school as a community center are complete.

Conclusion

Since its inception in the early nineteenth century, the preservation movement in the United States has expanded beyond the realm of the exclusive, focusing on only grand buildings or those associated with famous persons, to include buildings and districts that play important roles in the lives of ordinary citizens. Extraordinary structures remain important candidates for restoration or ongoing preservation, but the vast majority of historic preservation efforts now target buildings constructed by ordinary people for everyday purposes. Many of these structures are candidates for rehabilitation/adaptive use to extend their life and usefulness to ordinary people for everyday uses. Their continued

Figure 14-19 Downtown Priest River, Idaho, before revitalization.

Figure 14-21   Following a twenty-year effort by local citizens and the city, a former 1911 post office in Moscow, Idaho, was adapted to serve as City Hall.

preservation or adaptive use enables communities to integrate past and present, ensure historic continuity, harness embodied energy, conserve resources, and develop a more sustainable vision for the future— socially/culturally, economically, and environmentally.

Today, the process of preservation is as important as the products, for it is through the process that we can learn, as individuals and as a society, who we are and where we came from. In this world of increasing uncertainty and divisiveness, preservation can be a rallying point for positive investment in future generations. As we preserve and reuse historic structures, our built environment reflects the forces of previous generations that helped to shape it. A multigenerational built environment is inherently more complex and diverse, visually richer, and reflects a more responsible attitude to the expenditure of precious energy and materials. Through our preservation efforts, we transfer a more complex and spatially rich palette of built resources to future generations. In the words of Winston Churchill, "We shape our buildings and afterwards they shape us."

References

Burayidi, M. *Downtowns: Revitalizing the Centers of Small Urban Communities*. Garland, 2001.

Fitch, J. *Historic Preservation: Curatorial Management of the Built Environment*. University Press of Virginia, 1992.

Jacobs, J. *The Death and Life of Great American Cities*. Random House, 1961.

McClure, W., and F. Hurand. "Re-engaging the Public Art of Community Place-Making." In M. Burayidi (ed.), *Downtowns: Revitalizing the Centers of Small Urban Communities*, Burayidi. Garland, 2001.

Murtagh, W. *The History and Theory of Preservation in America*. Main Street Press, 1988.

Ryan, D. "Rural Communities in Transition." In McClure (ed.), *The Rural Town: Designing for Growth and Sustainability*. University of Idaho Center for Business Development and Research, 1997.

Tyler, N. *Historic Preservation: An Introduction to Its History, Principles and Practice*. W. W. Norton, 2000.

U.S. National Park Service. *Secretary of Interior's Standards for Preservation, Rehabilitation and Restoration*. www.cr.nps.gov/hps/tps/standards_guidelines.htm.

Endnotes

1. See Secretary of Interior's Standards for Preservation, Rehabilitation and Restoration by U.S. National Park Service web site: www.cr.nps.gov/hps/tps/standards_guidelines.htm
2. See the Main Street Program Web site: www.mainstreet.org.
3. W. McClure (ed.), *The Rural Town: Designing for Growth and Sustainability* (University of Idaho Center for Business Development and Research, 1997).
4. See Note 3.
5. See Note 3.

CHAPTER 15

The Fitness Test: Building with Human and Environmental Factors

Bruce T. Haglund and Tom J. Bartuska

Buildings and architecture have a unique dual character embodied in their **external** form and **internal** spatial/functional development. This chapter explores the dual human-environmental dimensions of design. Ideally, this duality is integrated to fit the environment and to support human activities. Internal-external relationships must be creatively addressed and resolved for each building in order to pass the fitness test.

A deep understanding of the internal needs and external aspects of a building is a fundamental prerequisite to design. Internally, fine architecture provides delightful and supportive spaces to accommodate human needs, values, and activities in a way that shelters people from extreme environmental forces, inspires their performance, and satisfies their aesthetic sensibilities. Externally, the form of architecture is prominent, conveying expressive and symbolic qualities, be it an office building, a civic center, a cultural facility, or a house. This symbolic meaning is culturally based and may provide orientation and enjoyment for users and the public. The external form also interacts in a positive or negative way with its neighbors and surroundings. Levels of integration—levels that fit together—are required for a success-

ful design concept: products form interiors, interiors combine into buildings, and buildings and the spaces between them combine to form landscapes, cities, regions, and finally the Earth. This internal-external or form-function dualism creates the basis for a vital dialectic. Understanding this dialectic and designing with people and the environment, both built and natural, is the only way buildings can pass the fitness test.

Human Factors: The Spatial/Functional Aspects of Architecture

First, a building's internal spaces directly express the human aspects of human-environmental relationships. Buildings fulfill human needs and values through physical dimensions (anthropometrics, ergonomics, and proxemics), their spaces, organizational relationships, and systems (rooms, special sequences, circulation, and related support technologies for structure, natural and mechanical systems for communication, lighting, heating and cooling, etc.). These functional/spatial require-

ARCHITECTURE

Figure 15-1 What is architecture? A student's response—sitting at a drawing board and designing human-environment (built and natural) relationships (author unknown).

ments must be carefully studied and organized to effectively meet the needs of clients and users and are the primary experiential qualities of buildings. Louis Kahn, a world-renowned U.S. architect and educator, stated that a building "plan is a society of rooms in agreement."[1] This agreement requires fitness among spatial relationships and is achieved by carefully grouping needs and spaces to maximize positive interactions (combining compatible activities to foster a society) and minimize discord (separating conflicting activities). This concept of **zoning** is often used in design to organize a society or grouping of rooms to create agreement—maximize relationships and benefits of the external environment (view, sun, ventilation, etc.) and protect the user from unfavorable external and internal influences. Like clothing, the skin of a successful, environmentally responsive building provides a protective layer of walls, windows, and roofs. These elements mediate the external environ-

ment to help people carry out their activities effectively in a comfortable, convenient, and enjoyable internal environment bathed in daylight, shaded from the sun, insulated against extreme heat or cold, and flushed with fresh air.

Human functional requirements are the responsibilities of the interior designer and the architect. This overlapping responsibility can be fulfilled by a single individual on small projects and/or a team of professionals working closely together on larger developments. These human functional factors are discussed more fully in Section 2 and are not repeated here. It must be emphasized that designers should not only provide a successful environment for their clients (building owners), but should also consider the users of the building. Users' needs should never be compromised. Many techniques are available to assess users' needs. Users include occupants as well as the general public. The public may need to use the facilities and/or pass by them. They need to accept and enjoy each building as it adds to their envi-

Figure 15-2 and 15-3 Exterior and interior, new and old redevelopment of Liverpool Street Station, London, England.

ronmental context. Each building also affects the Earth through the resources used in construction, the energy used and embodied in its construction, and the energy consumed to provide for users' needs and comfort. The use of resources impacts the quality of the Earth's environment through air and water pollution, carbon dioxide generation, and solid wastes.

Environmental Factors: The Natural and Built Contexts for Architecture

The **external** character of a building's **form** is shaped not only by internal requirements, but also to fit its environment. The two extreme environmental contexts in which buildings are placed are completely natural (a wilderness) and totally built (a city). Both settings offer considerable challenges to the creative designer in integrating the built and natural environments.

Before the characteristics and qualities of each environment are investigated, it is necessary to discuss the reasons architecture should (or should not) relate to, contribute to, and/or be integrated with its environment. Any designer can think of many practical and philosophical reasons to design buildings harmonious with or contrasting to their surroundings. Should we place a building **on** its site or should we integrate a building **with** its context?

The easiest path for a designer is to place a building on its site without regard to context. This approach, commonly called "parachute architecture," gives a designer the personal freedom to be expressive and not limit design possibilities by the conditions of the context. It is an attractive strategy for chain corporations that seek to maintain the same image nationally or worldwide. On the other hand, there are many reasons to design with the context. Buildings can be more economical, requiring minimal excavation and foundation work. Creatively responding to similar construction methods and materials within a city can be more cost efficient and allow local builders to participate in the construction process. Also, designing in a neighbor-friendly manner produces long-term benefits by helping to create a sense of community. Taking advantage of the local climate and sun orientation can also increase human comfort and reduce energy consumption. This respect for others can nurture a fuller, even regional appreciation of design.

Regionalism in architecture has evolved within many vernacular traditions. Like vernacular design, regional-ism is responsive to local climates and culture(s), as well as to local materials and construction methods, and is very energy and resource efficient. Using the site's solar energy, natural lighting and ventilation, sun shading, earth sheltering, and indigenous landscaping are all possible regional-environmental strategies that substantially reduce costs and energy use and bond a building to the special qualities of a place.

Architecture and the Built Environmental Context

Architects designing for built-up areas have to consider the natural environment and the built environmental context. Many built-up areas have specific requirements (e.g., building codes, zoning ordinances, and regulations). Other issues are less tangible and are implied (local historic, social/cultural, and visual characteristics, etc.). All these influences combine into a challenging mix of issues and require a careful analysis of the built environmental context. Some communities attempt to define such contextual issues by establishing **design guidelines**—a set of recommendations that guide the design of the general characteristics of a building to fit sensitively into its urban or suburban setting. Some communities require design proposals to be reviewed by a **design commission**. These review procedures require a building's design character to pass a fitness test established by the community. Most communities, however, do not have such guidelines and, consequently, designs are not required to fit their surroundings. In these communities or even regions, contextual issues are responded to or ignored, depending upon the individual values of designers and/or developers.

In a legal sense, designers are obligated to consider contextual issues when a community has established design guidelines, has identified unique historic conservation areas, or has a design review commission. These communities have established contextual issues as law in order to protect the general societal welfare.

Regardless of what is legal, moral, or related to individual creative freedom or rights, designing within the built environmental context is a critical issue in the study of architecture. Modern architecture has been strongly criticized by the public and by many within the design profession because it is too abstract; it either ignores or deliberately contrasts with the environment; it is egocentric and shouts in isolation.

Portland, Oregon, has established an effective set of design guidelines. They were developed through student research, public participation, and governmental action.

The guidelines help direct the design of new buildings to fit the general urban and historic qualities of the city. They suggest that new projects reinforce urban organization, emphasize pedestrian spaces and street life (human scale and activities along the walkways of the city), and encourage harmonious architectural relationships (be friendly to their neighbors). The principles do not insist on a rigid formula for design, but instead promote a flexible way for the city to grow and change—allowing change while still respecting the existing contextual qualities of a place. The adaptive reuse of historic buildings is another significant way to build within the existing context (explored in Chapter 14). Portland's planning department and design committee reviews all building projects for conformance to the spirit of the guidelines. Portland also has advanced policies on sustainable development and urban growth management to control suburban sprawl.

Such guidelines can make a substantial contribution to the design of buildings and to the design of cities. Contextual designs can be achieved through levels of integration, which suggest that one component must be integrated into the next in order to create appropriate designs at the next larger scale—designs that pass the fitness test. Ignoring contextual issues at the building scale disrupts, diminishes, or even eliminates overall integration of larger environments such as landscapes, cities, and regions. Buildings designed to contrast with their neighbors generally create discord and can disrupt the overall quality of the built environment.

Architecture and the Natural Environmental Context

Besides the built environment, the fitness test also requires consideration of the natural environment. Considering both is important for the design disciplines and for society. Current advances in sustainable architecture are directing our attention, understanding, and renewed commitment to deal more effectively with natural resources and ecological systems. Three basic ways can be identified for achieving fitness with the natural environment.

Inspirational Achievements. Throughout most of human history, indigenous people have had deep understanding of and respect for nature. Native American and Asian cultures exhibit many ways of living in harmony with nature. A similar harmony with nature was also achieved in the Western world by the English Landscape Garden Movement and Ian McHarg's profound work, *Design with Nature*.

Figure 15-4 and 15-5 The new in harmony with the historic character of the city. Pioneer Center, downtown Portland, Oregon.

Vernacular architecture, a product of indigenous cultures, has evolved with its surrounding environment and is a source of inspiration for many designers. Conversely, some pioneers of the Modern Movement, such as Frank Lloyd Wright, Alvar Aalto, Walter Gropius, and Le Corbusier, can be considered ecological designers who paid close attention to context. Their seminal work provides insight and inspiration for contemporary design with nature. Many designers practicing today respond to these regional traditions of designing with the natural environment.

As for vernacular architecture, nature is an inspirational source of design ideas. Nature demonstrates effective adaptation of form to environmental factors such as climate, local materials, and site conditions. Evolution is based upon optimum adaptation to the environment. In nature, form and function are highly integrated, unified by ecological processes. **Natural analogies** can help designers understand ecological processes and achieve at least three of the following desirable characteristics:

- **Regionalism**: learning to design effectively with the regional climate, local materials, and site conditions
- **Creative integration of form and function**: discovering how form and function are united by ecological processes

Figure 15-7 The optics of the human eye (and shading cap).

- **Energy and resource conservation**: adapting appropriate technologies with minimal energy and resource requirements

Humans still see the world with natural equipment—their eyes. The eye illustrates how nature works. Our eyes adapt naturally to changing conditions. We have effective eyebrows and eyelids (overhangs) (Fig. 15-7). Filtering hair softens the contrast, overhangs can even be extended by squinting (or by hats), and light intensity is controlled by aperture changes; even dust and dirt are cleansed by automatic washing devices. Can designers translate such traits into effective window design? Can appropriate overhangs be provided that shield and soften light and aperture devices to control the desired quantity of light? The window in Figure 15-8 ignores these environmental factors and allows harsh contrast and glare to dominate the indoor environment. The window in Figure 15-9 develops optical quality by overhangs, filtering by landscape, and curtains to control the light admitted through the opening.

Appropriate design for the thermal environment can be more clearly understood by observing how plants and animals (and some humans) effectively adapt to regional climatic characteristics. Such natural analogies can enhance understanding of how to adapt effectively to desert or alpine conditions, to wet river basins or dry plateaus. Adaptive strategies for use of the sun, both summer and winter, the evaporative cooling of skin, the efficient wind forms of sand dunes, the structure of a spiderweb or seashells all form inspirational lessons for designing with nature and for developing more appropriate built form.

Figure 15-6 An inspirational example of designing with nature—Fallingwater by Frank Lloyd Wright.

Figure 15-9 A window with optical control.

protected from the west's hot evening sun and winter winds by berming and protective landscaping.

Natural analogies, or biomimicry,[2] offer numerous inspirational lessons. They provide examples not only of a conceptual basis for ecological design, but also of how designing with nature can produce more effective, regionally sensitive, and energy-efficient buildings.

Comprehensive Ecological Approach. The workaday world of contemporary society is too often directed to an objective, cost/benefit analysis of design. More and

Figure 15-8 Windows with glare.

Something as basic as rocks on a seashore may convey usable lessons for the design of a built environment. Rocks (Fig. 15-10) illustrate changing characteristics, which can occur from different orientations of any object—a rock, a building, or a landform. The sun side (the south side in the Northern Hemisphere) is warm, dry, and generally better for heating with solar energy. Orientation of a building is a critical first step in designing with the climate and the sun. A southern exposure can also cause overheating if not carefully shaded in summer months. The opposite side, generally the north side, has the reverse conditions—cool, shaded, and moist. These thermal characteristics are clearly understood in the design of the solar-responsive building in Portland, Oregon, illustrated in Figures 15-11 and 15-12. The south side allows a controlled amount of solar energy to be directed to collectors, windows, and the greenhouse. Low windows on the north side allow the cool air to be admitted in the summer (not the warm southern air) to cool the building. The building is also

Figure 15-10 Rocks on the seashore: warm south side; cool, even frosty, north side.

Figures 15-11 and 15-12   Solar demonstration home, Portland, Oregon. Warm south side, cool north side.

more, designers are meeting this challenge by comprehensively addressing natural environmental issues. Malcolm Wells, the late Ian McHarg, and National (and State) Environmental Policy Acts (NEPA and SEPA) have provided leadership in designing with nature. Examination of their work provides a basis for a comprehensive approach to design.

Malcolm B. Wells, an author and a practicing architect, outlined a comprehensive, environmentally sensitive approach to architecture in an article titled "The Absolutely Constant Incontestably Stable Architectural Values Scale."[3] Wells suggests a way to test designs by using an array of criteria developed from an analogy with a natural system. His checklist consists of fifteen issues that measure various criteria, such as "destroys pure air" versus "creates pure air." Each issue can be rated on a scale from "poor" (-100, "always destroys pure air") to "good" (+100, "always creates pure air"), with four levels in between. In Wells' opinion, wilderness scores a

perfect 1500, while a typical building scores a dismal -750. Wells' reasoning is passionately expressed below:

Architecture is the outward expression of a way of life and, as such, it must begin to express real reverence for life . . . actually helps support life. . . . We disagree about degree, about priorities, about directions and goals. . . . Our value criteria are so unstable that nothing can be objectively compared with anything.

But there is a way to evaluate what designers do. There's a cold, scientific, stable, constant, absolute and very simple scale on which one work can be rated versus another. That scale can measure, not only architecture, landscape architecture, engineering and planning, but also zoning laws and everything else that is likely to affect the environments of which humans are so visibly a part.

So far as we know, the only fully appropriate structures and the only truly successful communities ever to be established . . . were those myriad miracles that we now lump together under the word "wilderness" . . . [They] can be used as an unchanging standard against which we can measure our own solutions. . . .

The . . . forest [for example] must really have been something to see. It actually created pure air. It created pure water. It stored extra water for use during droughts. It created all the food needed for its inhabitants. It created fossil fuels. It created silence. It consumed all its own wastes. It required no detergents, no fertilizers and no insecticides. The forest was supremely in tune with the pace of all creation. And it was host to uncountable species of plants and animals, including more than a few of our own kind. . . . Wind was something to be heard only far above in the tops of the trees. And the moderating effect of the huge forest kept summers cooler and winters warmer than the ones we have today. . . .

Measuring the city of today against such a standard is so humiliating [that] we usually refuse to do it. We call the comparisons irrelevant or unfair or even silly. But they aren't; the wilderness and city have exactly the same goal: sustenance of a successful living community on the land. . . .

The shameful cities we've created have only one treasure (to human eyes, anyway), and that treasure is people—human beings and human resources; our culture; the arts, the sciences and the whole fund of knowledge and wealth that goes with them. The rest of the city is pure failure, for it does what the wilderness long since learned not to do. . . . The city destroys pure air. It destroys pure water. . . . It feeds, waters and powers itself by depleting the vast areas beyond its own borders. It destroys rich soil. It destroys silence. It consumes none of its own wastes. . . . It requires extensive maintenance and megatons of detergents and poisons. It is utterly out of step with all natural rhythms. It destroys beauty. It makes winters and summers more severe. . . .

That's why it's so important that we recognize the value of the lessons the wilderness offers and the need to apply them right now. We can't get well until we first find out just how sick we are. Which brings me back to the Absolutely Constant Incontestably Stable Architectural Value Scale.

[Figures 15-13 and 15-14] show how the long-lost . . . forest would have scored and, if you don't mind being depressed, how [most contemporary architecture compares] with the miracle of wilderness. . . . Wilderness know-how could teach us how to use solar energy to re-use all our wastes . . . start thinking of wilderness as a . . . guide for cities [and buildings] rather than as an antithesis of them. . . . And our architecture, as it begins to express the new values, will become really beautiful again, naturally an earth art.[4]

Wells' designs have achieved very positive ratings from his Absolutely Constant Incontestably Stable Architectural Value Scale, and he has received numerous design awards. His philosophy and work are more fully developed in his landmark book, *Gentle Architecture.*

Considerable progress has been made since Wells first presented his simple scale. His comprehensive approach has motivated many designers. At an annual Curriculum Development Retreat in 1999, a group of Society of Building Science Educators (SBSE) members reviewed Wells' checklist with the intention of updating it to incorporate advances in thinking about sustainable architecture made in the past 30 years. These three decades saw the revival of passive solar design techniques for both heating and cooling buildings, the rise of technologies for daylighting, the birth of green, sustainable, ecological architecture, and John Lyle's advocacy for **regenerative design**.[5]

Clearly, Wells' important scale, developed some 20 years ago, required an update. Although the SBSE educators confirmed its overall importance, they did make the

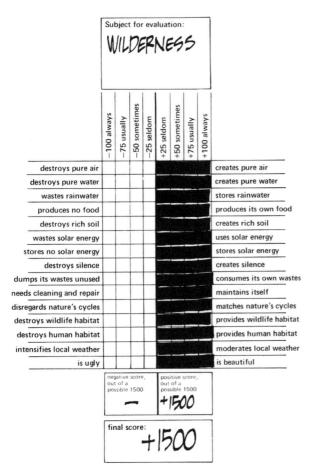

Figure 15-13 Wells' evaluation of wilderness (courtesy of M. Wells).

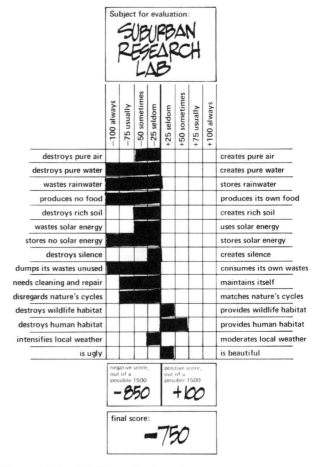

Figure 15-14 Wells' evaluation of a contemporary building (courtesy of M. Wells).

following recommendations, principally in scoring, organization, and inclusiveness.

- **Scoring**. Following John Lyle's logic, sustainability is a critical concept but it is just good enough to guarantee survival of the planet. A greater goal is to improve the planet through regenerative design, planning, and building. In order to acknowledge this distinction in Wells' scale, a column for balance (0 points) labeled "Sustainability" was added. Extremes are labeled "Degeneration" for the worst rating and "Regeneration" for the best. A total score of zero indicates that a building is sustainable; it does no further damage to the planet.
- **Organization**. Issues were sorted into two divisions, "the site" and "the building," to help scale users visualize the results of their efforts. Issues of site and building design are roughly equal in weight, which emphasizes that a building extends beyond its walls and beyond its site.
- **Inclusiveness**. Several issues were revised and the number increased from 15 to 22 to reflect changes

in technology and to address regenerative development more comprehensively. Prominent among the changes are addition of the issues of wastes, circulation, transportation, neighborliness, recyclability, and use of materials. More subtly, the solar energy issue was divided into heating, cooling, and lighting. The issue of beauty was retained and supplemented by the new issue of symbolism: "Is the building an icon for regeneration or degenerative design?"

The Regeneration-Based Checklist for Design and Construction and detailed instructions for its use are maintained on the SBSE Web site.[6] To extend its importance globally, the checklist is also developed in other languages.

Wells' work dovetails with the equally significant efforts of Ian McHarg, discussed in Chapter 3. McHarg, an ecologist, educator, and landscape architect/planner, developed a comprehensive ecological process for assessing the natural environment in order to make effective design decisions—maximizing fitness and

Regeneration-Based Checklist for Design and Construction

Project:

	degeneration				sustainability		regeneration		
the site	-100 always	-75 usually	-50 sometimes	-25 a bit	0 balances	25 a bit	50 sometimes	75 usually	100 always
pollutes air										cleans air
pollutes water										cleans water
wastes rainwater										stores rainwater
consumes food										produces food
destroys rich soil										creates rich soil
dumps wastes unused										consumes wastes
destroys wildlife habitat										provides wildlife habitat
imports energy										exports energy
requires fuel-powered transportation										requires human-powered transportation
intensifies local weather										moderates local weather
excludes daylight										uses daylight
uses mechanical heating										uses passive heating
uses mechanical cooling										uses passive cooling
needs cleaning and repair										maintains itself
produces human discomfort										provides human comfort
uses fuel-powered circulation										uses human-powered circulation
pollutes indoor air										creates pure indoor air
is built of virgin materials										is built of recycled materials
cannot be recycled										can be recycled
serves as an icon for the apocalypse										serves as an icon for regeneration
is a bad neighbor										is a good neighbor
is ugly										is beautiful

negative score 2200 possible   positive score 2200 possible

final score:

Figure 15-15 Regeneration-Based Checklist for Design and Construction (SBSE, 2003).

human-environmental health and well-being.[7] His work has made a profound change in the environmental design and planning professions by increasing use of his ecologically based process.

A comprehensive approach was also embodied in NEPA and SEPA legislation. The goal in each case was to create balance and harmony between people, the things they build, and the natural environment. This landmark legislation has, unfortunately, been compromised by erratic governmental leadership. Short-term profits have remained the controlling yardstick instead of a comprehensive approach to design with nature.

Sustainable Systems and Regenerative Design.

McHarg, Wells, and the SBSE group explored the variables of an integrated, sustainable systems approach to design—an approach that emphasizes the dynamic, symbiotic interactions of human-environmental, ecological processes of the Earth. This approach has come to be known as "sustainable systems and regenerative design (SS/RD)," which emphasizes that the comprehensive set of factors discussed are not stand-alone, static variables but rather interactive parts of a dynamic biological/ecological system. Throughout the world, many designers are directing their creativity toward making truly intelligent "green" projects based upon sustainable systems within the built and natural environments.

A truly Green architecture is much more than one that is bedecked with plants, conserves energy and minimizes pollution. It recognizes and gently engages all of the extraordinarily rich web of forces and relationships that can, and do, exist between architecture, its occupants, and its surroundings—both immediate and planet wide. . . . Because it is holistic, Green architecture is concerned with [a synthesis . . . that seeks] a delicate judged equilibrium rather than simplistic statement.[8]

The underlying concept of SS/RD is found in a symbiotic systems diagram. Projects without this diagram are probably not based upon the dynamic interaction of biological systems.

John Lyle's profound contribution to SS/RD is based upon both a book[9] and a live/learn project. Lyle is a landscape architect and educator. With his students, he developed the Center for Regenerative Studies (CRS) at the California State Polytechnic University. CRS began as an interdisciplinary studio project with landscape and architecture students. Their ideas were so profound that the university formed a public-private

partnership, solicited funding, and built the center. CRS is now a reality, available to students where they live and learn (gain credit) the best way by participating in its management and care. The underlying concept of this recent project is an ecological **systems diagram** illustrated in Figure 15-16.

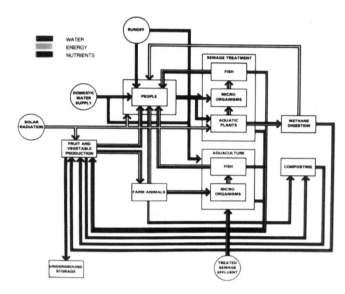

Figure 15-16 Human-environmental-technical systems of CRS.

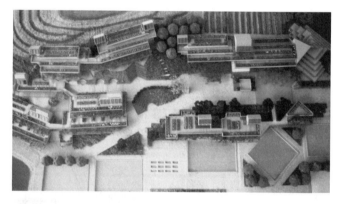

Figures 15-17 and 15-18 Student conceptual model of CRS and as it exists today. Pomona, California.

Internationally, there are many projects based upon advanced SS/RD strategies. Two "breakthrough" buildings that demonstrate the quality and effectiveness of sustainable design are the United Kingdom Pavilion, by Nicholas Grimshaw, and the Commerzbank, by Norman Foster. Both of these pioneering projects and many others were collaborative designs with Ove Arup and Partners, a very innovative engineering firm. The United Kingdom Pavilion was built for the 1992 Expo in Seville, Spain. It expresses a beautiful integration of passive technologies and renewable energies. Natural ventilation, a water wall, and shading sails with a photovoltaic system help cool the building in Spain's warm climate.

The Commerzbank, built in Frankfort, Germany, is a 53-story high-rise building designed with cascading greenhouses to clean the air and provide natural lighting, passive ventilation, and heating/cooling. Both the Commerzbank and the United Kingdom Pavilion afford excellent opportunities for further study of SS/RD projects.

Figure 15-20   The Commerzbank in Frankfort, Germany, by Norman Foster & Partners, et al.

Figure 15-19   The United Kingdom Pavilion at Expo 92 in Seville, Spain, by Nicholas Grimshaw & Partners, et al.

IslandWood, an educational center for youth based on a very advanced set of SS/RD principles, is another significant project located on Bainbridge Island, Washington.[10] Designed by Mithun (architects) and Berger Partnership (landscape architects), its goals are to foster community and environmental stewardship through the exploration and integration of science, technology, and the arts in a beautiful environment designed with people and nature in mind. The project brings city youngsters to its sustainable campus in the woods to demonstrate lessons in SS/RD, helping to educate them about a sustainable future. The education of the young is critical to a sustainable future.

Probably one of the most dramatic SS/RD developments occurred in England—the Eden Project. A center to study and celebrate the dynamic systems of the Earth, the Eden Project, collaboratively designed by Nicholas Grimshaw in partnership with Ove Arup and

Figures 15-21, 15-22, and 15-23   IslandWood, dedicated to science, technology, and the arts, sustainably designed with people and nature in mind. Bainbridge Island, Washington, by Mithun, et al.

Figures 15-24 and 15-25   The Eden Project, dedicated to the study and celebration of the important union of place, plants, and people, by Nicholas Grimshaw & Partners, et al.

others, unites place, plants, and people (human-environmental systems). An abandoned industrial clay pit has been regenerated into one of the most beautiful and intellectually provocative sites in the world. The project is so popular that the original design cannot accommodate the number of visitors who flock to experience and study its qualities and SS/RD mission. The Eden Project is truly a Garden of Eden and points the way to the future—a synthesis of place, plants, and people (and wonderful lessons in human-environmental relationships).

Creating a Sustainable Future: Designing with Human-Environment Systems

What is our vision of the future? What should be emphasized and studied? How can we formulate and design to meet the challenges of the future? In 1993, the American Institute of Architects (AIA) assembled hundreds of professionals from all the design disciplines throughout the country in a series of far-reaching probes into the future—Vision 2000. A major section of this national study dealt with mega "Trends Shaping the Future." One trend states, "a philosophy [of] ecological design will eventually have a profound impact on architecture and technology . . . biological metaphors [natural analogies and symbiotic relationships between natural and built systems] will increasingly supplant mechanical metaphors as the dominant paradigm or pattern of thought. Architecture will aspire to 'go with' natural systems [human and environmental] rather than overriding them, and . . . diversity will increase as buildings are better adapted to the climates and resources of different regions."[11]

Students of the American Institute of Architecture Students (AIAS) have expressed a profound concern for their education. Echoing the challenges set forth in the 1992 Rio Summit, the AIAS national membership passed a resolution stating, "It is vital that AIAS be active and at the forefront of environmental and ecological issues . . . that environmental issues be addressed in all phases of their architectural education."[12]

An increasing number of cities and countries, citizens

and clients, designers and planners are embracing sustainable development. One who is prominent and successful is William McDonough, an educator, practicing architect, and popular spokesperson for SS/RD. McDonough's firm is doing significant work throughout the world. His approach, principles, and extensive work can be reviewed on his Web site.

BREEAM is a dream comes true. **BREEAM** (the Building Research Establishment Environmental Assessment Method) was developed in England to comprehensively assess building performance and sustainability. Other countries followed and developed similar methods. **LEED** (Leadership in Energy and Environmental Design) was developed to lead the United States in sustainable, regenerative design. Currently, many states and cities have programs on sustainability and require LEED-certified development for all publicly funded projects.

Collectively, we must understand life's basic ecological premises and respond fully by creating truly integrated, symbiotic, human-environmental systems. The fitness test challenges all of the design professions, as well as leaders around the world, to continue the important work of pioneers and contemporary designers of SS/RD. We must pass this test, and design and manage with people and with the nurturing qualities of the built and natural environments. If we succeed, we will be able to celebrate sustainable life throughout the biosphere; if we don't, we will fail this fundamental fitness test.

Avoiding that failure and ensuring real success requires attention to how the parts fit together and how they are integrated into contextualized, sustainable wholes. Understanding of, and compliance with, such an approach allows us to understand how to design the internal functional aspects of structures, and also how the external form of structures should fit the natural and/or built environmental context and contribute to the creative design of landscapes, cities, regions, and ultimately the Earth.

References

AIA. *Vision 2000: Trends Shaping Architecture's Future and Architects for a New Century.* American Institute of Architects Press, 1988.

AIA. *A Nation at the Crossroads.* American Institute of Architects Press, 1993.

Benyus, J. *Biomimicry.* Morrow, 1997.

BREEAM. *Building Research Establishment Environmental Assessment Method.* 2005: www.breeam.com.

Buchanan, P. "Green Architecture." *Architectural Review*, September 1990.

IslandWood. *IslandWood: A School in the Woods.* 2005: www.islandwood.org.

Lobell, J. *Between Silence and Light: Spirit in the Architecture of Louis L. Kahn.* Shambhala, 1979.

Lyle, J. *Regenerative Design for Sustainable Development.* Wiley, 1994.

McDonough, W. *Resources, Publications, and Firms Projects.* 2003: www.mcdonough.com.

McHarg, I. *Design with Nature.* Doubleday Natural History Press, 1969.

McLennan, J. *The Philosophy of Sustainable Design.* Ecotone, 2006.

SBSE. *Regeneration-Based Checklist for Design and Construction. Society of Building Science Educators.* 2003: www.sbse.org/resources.

USGBC. *LEED—Leadership in Energy and Environmental Design.* United States Green Building Council. 2005: www.usgbc.org/leed/index.asp.

Van der Ryn, S., and S. Cowan. *Ecological Design.* Island Press, 1996.

Wann, D. *Deep Design: Pathways to a Livable Future.* Island Press, 1996.

Wells, M. *Gentle Architecture.* McGraw-Hill, 1981.

Endnotes

1. J. Lobell, *Between Silence and Light: Spirit in the Architecture of Louis L. Kahn* (Shambhala, 1979).
2. J. Benyus, *Biomimicry* (Morrow, 1997).
3. M. Wells, "The Absolutely Constant, Incontestably Stable Architectural Values Scale," *Progressive Architecture* (March, 1971): 93–95.
4. See Note 3.
5. J. Lyle, *Regenerative Design for Sustainable Development* (Wiley, 1994).
6. SBSE, *Regeneration-Based Checklist for Design and Construction* (Society of Building Science Educators, 2003): www.sbse.org/resources.
7. I. McHarg, *Design with Nature* (Doubleday Natural History Press, 1969).
8. P. Buchanan, "Green Architecture," *Architectural Review* (September 1990): 36–38.
9. See Note 5.
10. IslandWood, *IslandWood: A School in the Woods*: 2005, www.islandwood.org.
11. AIA, *A Nation at the Crossroads* (American Institute of Architects Press, 1993): and AIA, *Vision 2000: Trends Shaping Architecture's Future and Architects for a New Century* (American Institute of Architects Press, 1988), 33–34.
12. See the AIAS Web site: www.aias.org.

CHAPTER 16

Engineering Contributions

Carl W. Hall

Engineers work with many other professionals in developing the built environment. Engineers must be aware of the challenges confronting all persons designing, constructing, operating, and maintaining the components, contexts, and processes within the built environment. The particular responsibilities of engineers deal with energy, materials, and information. These must be used safely and economically to provide appropriate environments and infrastructure systems for society. This chapter is a further expansion of many of the issues discussed in Chapter 6.

Engineers are characterized by their training and ability to creatively apply scientific principles of design and planning to develop structures, machines, devices, and processes. Included in this characterization is the possibility that, in searching for the most appropriate design, several plausible designs are discarded. Designs not used generally have not adequately considered external influences during the design process.

The mission of engineering covers a wide spectrum—from research, designing, and building to operating and maintaining systems and processes. In this chapter, attention is focused on the built environment: creating appropriate products, structures, and technological systems within all the components of the environment that humans create and in which they live. The spectrum of requirements for providing humans with a built environment may range from fundamental research on the materials to the work of the craftsperson who builds and assembles components.

The design, planning, and construction of the built environment are based on using natural resources to meet the needs, wants, and expectations of people in a variety of roles. Government, education, business, and industry, along with individuals and families, make very different demands on the built environment. Environmental designers, engineers, and planners are often commissioned first to design the built environment for a particular client, whereas manufactured products are designed, built, and then sold to a speculative market.

The contributions of engineering to the built environment are largely dependent on external factors such as the following:

- **State of the Economy**: A vigorous economy not only enhances construction, but also encourages more innovation and new research developments.
- **Development of Science**: New materials, such as polymers, provide the basis of laminated construction or shapes not otherwise attempted.
- **Development of Technology**: Using conventional materials, such as fiberboard and particleboard, in new ways, provides the basis for the use of wood-based products; substitute products for piping, tubing and tile have come from new developments in science and technology.
- **Education of the Population**: The potential for use of new products and ideas is largely dependent on the results of research, codes, craftspeople, and the public response.

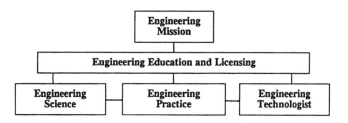

Figure 16-1 The mission of engineering in society.

Engineering Contributions: Antiquity and Change

Architecture and engineering began as a combined design field. Numerous engineering and architectural works were constructed before the 1500s by famous engineers (or architects), such as Archimedes and Vitruvius, as described and illustrated by de Camp (1963) in *The Ancient Engineers.* The early work of the Greeks laid the theoretical base for mathematics, measuring, and mechanics, as represented by *Mechanics*, the oldest known engineering book, attributed to Aristotle. The developments of the Greeks were followed by the more practical works of the Romans in highways and bridges, irrigation and drainage, canals and locks, mining, and building construction.

The Renaissance marked the beginning of more organized thinking, writing, and engineering design activities. The creativity of the Renaissance formed the foundations strengthening the professions of architecture and engineering, and this was the period in which the two professions assumed different identities.

Engineering and architecture, as well as other scholarly fields, claim Leonardo da Vinci. This is an indication not only of Leonardo's contribution, but also of the interrelated activities of many fields at the beginning of the two professions.

The early works of engineers primarily involved "engines" of war; thus, the term "engineer" or "military engineer" was created. From the 1700s to the 1800s, foreseeing the potential for contributing to nonwar endeavors, the profession of civil engineering began. Civil engineers and other professionals were primarily responsible for the components of that portion of the built environment used by "civilians," or nonmilitary people. The works of engineers followed the development of various economies throughout world history. Originally, agriculture, then mineral extraction, followed by manufacturing and industrial production, were paramount. Now, in the United States, service industries predominate.

Later, other branches of engineering (electrical and mechanical engineering and their subspecialties) devel-

oped and assisted in the design and environmental control mechanisms and systems. Both architecture and engineering have spawned many subsets and specialty areas. Interestingly, in some institutions, architectural engineering, a recognized field until the mid-1960s, is being reestablished.

Developments in materials have an important relationship to advances in engineering and the built environment. At first, stone was used, then wood and timber, brick and masonry, followed by portland cement and concrete, all of which are still used today. Cast and wrought iron followed, with the first iron bridge constructed in Ironbridge, England, in 1774–1779. Iron was followed by steel (the Bessemer process in 1856) and its alloys, some of which withstand high temperatures and high radiation levels.

Portland cement was developed in England in 1824, followed by reinforced concrete in the 1880s. The use of steel tension bars in concrete construction occurred in 1925 and prestressed concrete in 1945. These cement-concrete developments greatly changed the parameters of the design of structures (dams, highways, buildings, etc.). Structures previously considered impractical could now be built, a development that dramatically changed the built environment.

Aluminum and light metals were initially developed for movable structures but are now widely used in stationary structures. Sheet glass gave way to plate glass. Polymers and plastics are now available for many structural components. Using various combinations of these materials permits a wide variety of structures to serve the built environment. Variations in size, shape, geographical location, weather conditions, and uses can be accommodated with composite materials previously not available.

The development of materials was followed naturally by major advances in holding these materials together with fasteners, glue, adhesives, and welding. Traditional

Figure 16-2 The first iron bridge, 1774–1779, Ironbridge, England (T. Bartuska).

methods using rivets, bolts, nails, and screws are still used today but have been greatly improved.

New scientific discoveries have been the basis of many innovative technological developments. Likewise, many technological developments have been based on innovative ideas that themselves became the basis of scientific investigation. Technological developments have often been improved by the results of scientific developments and analysis, resulting in more efficient use of energy, materials, and human labor and creating the potential for better achievement of human endeavors.

The main branches of engineering are:

- Aerospace
- Agricultural
- Architectural
- Bioscience/medical
- Chemical
- Civil
- Computer
- Electrical
- Environmental
- Industrial
- Materials
- Mechanical
- Mining
- Nuclear
- Transportation

Engineering: Present and Future

The development and use of new materials made possible longer spans for buildings and bridges. In the United States, the longest span for a continuous steel truss bridge built is 376 meters (1,232 feet), crossing the Columbia River at Astoria, Oregon. The longest suspension bridge in the United States is 2,737 meters (8,981 feet), the Golden Gate Bridge in San Francisco. The longest bridge in the world is the Alashi Kaikyo in Japan, at 3,911 meters (12,828 feet).[1] Materials with high tensile strength, low corrosion, and light weight were developed to meet design needs. High-pressure devices, such as boilers and nuclear reactors, would have been impossible without the development of the materials that preceded them. Tall structures that withstand wind and earthquakes would not have occurred without the development of the elevator (1900–1910). From 1973 to 1997, the world's tallest building was the Sears Tower in

Chicago, Illinois, at 443 meters (1,454 feet). Today it is the Petronas Twin Towers in Kuala Lumpur, Malaysia, just 10 meters taller at 453 meters (1,483 feet). Even more towers are being proposed in the race up into the sky.[2] Improved materials for use in pavements, foundations, and drainage are continually being developed to serve the building and transportation industries.

One of the great engineering contributions of the world is the electrical power network. This network is used for construction and for controlling interior environments. Foremost in importance is artificial lighting used inside and outside structures. Air control and flow, as well as temperature and humidity control, are major domains that engineers contribute to the built environment. The industrial development of the southern United States is the result not only of resources there, but also the availability of air conditioning and energy to provide a desirable physical environment.

As in the recent past, science and technology reinforce each other and will continue to do so in the future. Science is the basis of much of the new technology, and technology assists science in its development and use. In many cases, technology leads science: a creative or innovative idea, such as the transmission of messages by wireless technology, can lead to many scientific studies and findings. Such new findings, whether in science or technology, increase design opportunities. Innovative and creative minds are continually at work at the scientific frontiers and in technological areas.

Recent developments, such as artificial intelligence, photonics, lasers, fiberoptics, and silicon chips, are having a tremendous impact on design. Growth in the use of computers—for manipulating numbers, for memory and recall, and for communication—is greatly influencing engineering and design. Communications networks, both within a structure and connecting to others throughout the world, are adding new dimensions to the built environment. The concept of the electronic cottage, as described by Toffler,[3] provides additional insights into future possibilities. The electronic cottage is a home equipped with electronic devices to communicate externally for business and to handle transactions. Only occasionally do employees need to go to the office. But telecommuting from home can also alienate individuals from the larger society.

New microprocessor controls can drastically reduce energy requirements for the built environment through sensory control of climatic conditions such as heating, ventilation, and cooling, as related to external environmental conditions. The capacity of microprocessors and computers has increased phenomenally. Computer capacity, which cost $1 million in 1955, $100,000 in

1965, and $1.00 in 1982, was $0.01 by the year 2000. Also, computers have gone from room-sized energy hogs to some that are very energy efficient and can fit in the palm of one's hand.

A major trend in recent times is the rapid transfer of scientific information and technological innovations to the marketplace. Photography, which was invented in 1727, did not become a reality until 1839 and did not become a common procedure until just prior to the American Civil War. The telephone was an idea in 1820 but required over 50 years to become a reality in 1876. In contrast, the transistor, solar cell, and artificial diamonds were in the marketplace within 5 years of conception. Table 16-1 presents the time required for various ideas or discoveries to be developed for societal use. Today's world is characterized by rapid, even accelerated, flows of knowledge and information to users.

The printing press and communication systems, which are technological rather than scientific developments, have helped to disseminate information. The Internet has made this information instantly available worldwide. This transfer now takes place throughout an educated society, whereas previously it occurred only among peers. The rapid spread of information in some ways makes designing more difficult, though also more effective. Designers must be knowledgeable about an incredible array of new developments to avoid the criticism of being out-of-date. However, they must also be wary. The parties considering a design may have unreasonable expectations for a new but untried or untested material.

The increasing number of people in the world (exceeding 6 billion), longer life expectancy (approaching an average of 80 years), and shifts in age distribution (e.g., more older people) challenge designers of the built environment. Besides being aware of these population changes, designers must recognize that a society's knowledge and economic levels, along with its needs, wants, and expectations, are also continually changing. "It is change, continuing change, inevitable change, that is the dominant factor in society today. No sensible decision can be made any longer without taking into account not only the world as it is, but the world as it will be," says Isaac Asimov.[4]

The exploration and utilization of outer space holds special fascination for many. The possibility of constructing a built environment in outer space, for whatever reason, challenges the imagination. Almost science fictional in concept, outer space could provide sites for low-gravity processing and manufacturing, as well as ports for space travel, locations for vacations, and space laboratories. Space colonization is predicted by some to occur within the twenty-first century. A space station close to the Earth is a reality, and a space settlement of 10,000 people is predicted within the next 50 years. In a space settlement, environmental conditions needed for life would be tightly controlled, and food would be produced within a wholly contained environment.

New materials have provided increased flexibility and variety in form and function for design applications. Polymers are available that can be shaped into forms; mastics exist to seal exterior surfaces; and numerous materials are available to provide vapor barriers and insulation. Water and waste-handling systems, formerly made of metal, now include a variety of polymers. Each new material must meet rigid standards for safety, strength, and economy. Economic considerations include the cost of the fabricated material, as well as the cost of installation, and should incorporate external environmental impacts and recycling at the end of its first life. Engineered wood materials such as particleboard, panelboard, and composites are now widely used, not only for building itself but also for forms and supports during construction. Safety has become even more important as structures become larger, involve more people, and must perform against earthquakes, floods, fire, wind, and water. The strength and durability of materials are important factors in designing for safety.

Experience has shown that some materials first considered safe are later found to be undesirable as a result of long-time experience or changed standards of requirements. Asbestos fibers have been found to harm the human respiratory system. Formaldehyde fumes given off by some manufactured materials pollute the atmosphere. Chlorofluorocarbons (CFCs), chemicals traditionally used for refrigerants, are destroying the ozone layer

Table 16-1 Time for an Idea or Discovery to Be Converted to Reality

ITEM	DATES OF IDEA TO REALITY		TIME LAG, YEARS
Photography	1727	1839	112
Electric Motor	1829	1894	65
Telephone	1820	1876	56
Radio	1867	1902	35
Radar	1925	1940	15
Television	1922	1934	12
Atomic Bomb	1939	1945	6
Transistors	1948	1953	5
Artificial Diamonds	1954	1957	3

and thus degrading the global environment. New materials have been developed to replace them. The seriousness of these undesirable effects becomes more evident as structures become tighter to conserve energy and as instruments become available to measure smaller concentrations of harmful chemicals.

Recent developments include "smart" or "intelligent" materials and structures. Sensors in these structures measure changes that warn of possible failure. The most obvious use is for bridges, but smart technology is also applicable for other structures and their attachments—such as balconies, canopies, chandeliers, stairways, and internal bridges. Structures can now be designed with internal optical fibers embedded in materials to warn when failure thresholds are being approached. Not only can these sensors warn of impending failure (by a sound, light, or recorded signal), but they can also be connected to other devices to correct for or compensate for destructive factors such as overloading of circuits or other systems. Other sensors detect changes in environmental conditions such as air quality, or smoke.

Manufacturing has taken on a new role in construction. Traditionally, most construction (manufacturing) took place at the site, particularly for large buildings. For small buildings, virtually the entire structure can now be built in a factory (manufactured) and transported to the site. For larger buildings, subsystems or parts, such as trusses, walls, floors, and arches, can be manufactured, shipped to the site, and put in place. Construction at the site itself has also changed drastically. Not only do derricks, cranes, and towers move components into place, at ever-increasing heights (telescoping towers), but computer-assisted planning and execution are now commonplace. All of these activities depend on engineering contributions, sometimes developed specifically for construction, often adapted from other fields.

Trends in technological development can be represented as an S-curve, sometimes called a "sigma curve" and originally used to represent growth. The S-curve starts out with a flat slope when basic information and technology are developed. A steeper slope follows in which rapid development takes place. As competitive or new technology is created, further development continues but increases more slowly. This concept is useful in projecting trends in technological development, diffusion of technology, and possible sales patterns for new products.

Predictions of technological developments based on projections usually give a conservative view of trends. One reason is that predictions based on possible new scientific developments are fraught with uncertainties. For example, predicting the date at which fusion nuclear power will be available is impossible because basic, complex scientific research and extensive development of technology are both needed, and a clear picture of the design is not yet available.

Interface of Engineering with Other Disciplines

Before World War II, the technology spectrum consisted of crafts-engineering-sciences. In the immediate postwar period, engineers and engineering education were criticized for not staying abreast of advances in the sciences, thereby causing a perceived gap between engineers and scientists. Various studies by members of the profession, assisted by many external to the profession, recommended that engineers should have a stronger base in the sciences to be better prepared to meet future needs. As a result of adoption of these recommendations, the education of the engineer moved closer to that of the scientist. For some education programs, the curriculum for engineers has been difficult to distinguish from that of scientists. These adjustments left another perceived gap between the craftsperson and the engineer, so an associate technician degree was developed.

While the scientific base of engineering was increasing, the involvement of engineers with a wide variety of nontechnical people was also increasing, and people with broad interests were attracted to the profession. Many engineers were becoming interpreters of science for society. Social sciences and humanities courses took on new roles and importance. One-eighth of all undergraduate courses now taken by engineering students are in the social sciences and humanities.

The mid-1960s witnessed a concern for what appeared to be a lack of commonality of engineering

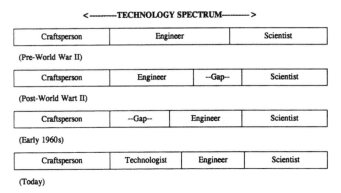

Figure 16-3 Technology spectrum: crafts-technology-engineering-sciences.

degree programs and a weakness in preparing highly skilled people to carry out expected problem-solving functions. The various engineering organizations joined efforts through the Accreditation Board for Engineering and Technology (ABET) to ensure that all programs of study incorporated adequate design instruction.

Engineering education has changed considerably in recent years—by moving from skill- to science-based courses, by increasing the humanities and social science content, and by strengthening communication skills. Design instruction has also changed in emphasis to a new synthesis or integrative approach dynamically supported by computer technologies.

Design: The Common Thread

Engineering design is defined as the "art [and/]or science of applying scientific knowledge to practice problems"[5] or "the application of science to the needs of humanity . . . through the application of knowledge, mathematics, and practical experience to design useful objects and process."[6] Professional (licensed) practitioners of engineering are called engineers. Engineering is a decision-making process (often interactive) in which the basic sciences, mathematics, and engineering sciences are applied to convert resources optimally to meet a stated objective. Central to the process are the essential and complementary roles of synthesis and analysis. Design is the common thread in engineering and the other design/problem-solving professions. Design involves not only analysis but also synthesis, not only of internal factors but also of external conditions. The design question has become more incorporative: no longer just "Will the design work?" but "Will it work socially, economically, and environmentally (SEE) with minimal unfavorable impacts?" SEE factors are the three variables of sustainability introduced in Chapter 3. Not only nature or natural conditions are involved; also, and primarily, the emphasis is on how built environments affect human-environmental relationships both locally and globally.

Obviously, science now has a much more important role in the engineering profession. Graduate programs in engineering often focus more on science and scientific research than in the past. The results of scientific research, however, as far as engineering is concerned, should be considered as information for design parameters. Simon[7] describes the study of "**what is**" as the task of science disciplines (to research the nature of things, what they are, and how they work). Scientific research focuses on **analysis**—answering questions about the nature of things. The scientific method is used to develop information.

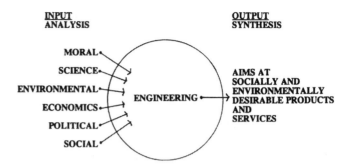

Figure 16-4 Engineering input-output model.

The task of design and engineering is to understand artificial things, or "**what can be**." This includes how to make artifacts that are a **synthesis** of design requirements and how to design to meet private and public wants or needs, often exemplified in the built environment. The challenge to the engineer is to solve problems, which often have many answers, posed by people outside the profession. In contrast, scientists are challenged to a greater extent to answer questions raised by peers. The design method (called by some, with slight variation, the "engineering method") is parallel to the scientific method. The similarities and differences are clarified in Table 16-2.

Scientific and Engineering Method

Design consists of translating the knowledge of art, science, and technology into artifacts such as a part, a component, an assembly, a product, a process, or a structure. Design **synthesis** is emphasized. Design can produce a very simple or a very complicated product. Design can result from a very creative, innovative, often unpredictable process or from a highly predictive process. Criteria for design can be established by people within the profession, in government or industry, and by the public. Consideration of these criteria is an important part of the design process. As designs are developed, they are tested against the criteria and evaluated for feasibility. Many designs are considered that are never built. Designers, like sculptors and painters, must be prepared for criticism when their designs are placed before the public. When evaluating the impacts of a design through a cost/benefit analysis, the designer should consider not only internal aspects of the problem, but also external factors such as energy, the environment, economics, and impacts upon society. The designer must also consider who pays the costs and who gets the benefits. These analyses should not stop with the primary impacts of the design, but should be extended to secondary and tertiary impacts—positive, neutral, or negative.

Table 16-2 Scientific and Engineering Method

SCIENTIFIC METHOD (SCIENTIFIC CURIOSITY: WHAT IS . . . ?)	ENGINEERING METHOD (CREATIVE APPROACH: WHAT CAN BE . . . ?)
Question identification	Problem identification
Research and analysis	Research and analysis
Hypothesis	Conceptualization
Analysis	**Synthesis**
Proof	Evaluation of alternatives
Publication	Decision/implementation/construction

Engineers, with a basic education in quantification, who are involved in designs and discussions of issues of political and social significance, are often at a loss to understand, let alone resolve, the conflict among these ideas. This conflict might be more easily ascertained and understood if we consider two general kinds of truth—**scientific truth** and **adversary truth**. Scientific truth involves scientific uncertainties. Adversary truth, as presented in public debate or in a court of law, usually includes only a selected part of the truth. The presentation of adversary truth includes the uncertainties, which are left to the audience or court. The decisions based on adversary truth are made by those not involved in the subject. People with expertise in the subject under consideration are often rejected from juries considering an issue.

The engineer or scientist questions and delves into uncertainties, attempting to clarify facts, data, procedures, or processes. The acceptance of scientific truth requires an overwhelming consensus of the engineering and scientific communities. If a consensus is not reached, considerable uncertainty remains about the subject being considered. In a scientific controversy, scientific truth is reached when all the parties involved accept the solution. However, in a legal process, adversary truth can be determined by an open and voluntary disclosure of issues. There may even be a willful withholding of certain information. For adversary truth, only a set of findings is presented and there is no effort to have the two sides agree to what is the truth. The jury or audience decides on the "truth," which may actually be counter to the facts. The quality of the truth depends considerably on the ability of the audience to fill in the uncertainties (known by the participants but not by the audience). Understanding of these relationships is helpful to those who place their designs before the public or adversary groups. An educated public, which can be critical of a design, can also be helpful in understanding the many variables in a complicated situation.

Many examples can illustrate the effect of new scientific and engineering discoveries on the design of the built environment. For example, Henry Bessemer and George A. Fuller studied engineering and contributed to the idea that engineering is an agent of change. In the process of improving guns, Henry Bessemer noted that some barrels burst because the cast iron from which they were made contained an excess of carbon. He reasoned that blowing air through the iron ore during smelting would help burn up and remove the carbon. This process to improve one product actually greatly improved many. After several experiments, his method provided a new way of making better steel at nearly half of its previous cost, and the process was quickly adopted by almost all industries. The availability of steel at a reasonable price made possible tall buildings. George Fuller was a leader in designing and building tall buildings, calculating weight and strength, and using steel as a construction material. The Flatiron Building in New York City was built in 1902 of steel instead of cast iron. The building was 20 stories, 87 meters (286 feet) high, three times as high as the usual buildings at the time. A new material was developed to serve a rather specific need but was soon used for many applications in construction of the built environment.

Conclusion: Moving to an Age of Synthesis

In the future, synthesis will become a major thrust in advanced technological societies. The twentieth century is widely recognized as the **Age of Analysis**, both philosophically and technologically. Evidence is now accumulating to demonstrate that the twenty-first century will be the **Age of Synthesis** (Hall, 1995). Synthesis involves a holistic understanding of all the human, economic, and environmental issues and creative integration of them into a new change in the built environment. Synthesis also helps give direction to analysis by identifying gaps in information. So, the trend will be to synthesis in contrast to the previous century's approach based on analysis. Synthesis is a valuable concept for the artificial domain, which includes built, constructed, or manufactured devices, systems, and processes. The design professions emphasize the synthetic approach; the sciences, the analytic approach, with the notable exception of physics, which uses a predominance of the synthetic approach.

Scholars are involved in a search for truth (science) and/or beauty (art and science). The approaches and processes used to search for truth have served society in the past but need to be considered in a new synthesis to meet the needs of the future more effectively. The emphasis has traditionally been primarily on analysis, with secondary consideration of synthesis. But in the recent past the use of synthesis has increased rapidly, particularly in the engineering, design, and planning of the built world. The stage is now set for major efforts to emerge, efforts based on synthesis.

Thinking synthetically encourages a more global view, considering larger systems that often involve human, environmental, and technological systems simultaneously. Often synthetic thinking directs one's thought to larger issues, whereas analysis is more narrowly focused on precision. The analysis approach does not provide a larger matrix for thinking but is an important part of the design process. Educators need to accept an enlarged role for synthesis and learn how to guide and teach synthetic thinking. A starting point is provided by some of the theorems developed for systems and hierarchical theory. Systems are characterized by connectivity, interfacing, interactions, complexity, interdependence, integration, and synergy—all of which relate to synthesis.

Synthesis is expressed in the patterns of nature. As more is learned about natural systems, that knowledge will be used not only to change those systems, but also to use this knowledge while developing artificial systems (bioengineering). People in the professions, people who design, in the broad sense—architects, engineers, veterinarians, and medical doctors—need a stronger understanding of the role of synthesis in their work.

In the past, most disciplines (scholarly, scientific, and applied) were built on analysis and reductionism rather than synthesis and integration. The growth of interdisciplinary or multidisciplinary fields, collaboration, and teamwork may be the result of established fields failing to change or to incorporate new integrative fields.

Recent history has witnessed tremendous advances in the science and engineering fields. Designers, indeed all people, now need to integrate these advance within a harmonious system with nature through continued collaboration between the environmental design/planning, engineering, and scientific fields.

References

Abel, C. *Sky High: Vertical Architecture.* Royal Academy Books, 2003.

ABET. Accreditation Board for Engineering and Technology. 2006: www.abet.org.

Amato, I. "Animating the Material World," *Science*, January 1992.

ASEE. *Engineering, Go for It.* American Society of Engineering Education, 2003.

de Camp, L. *The Ancient Engineers.* Ballantine Books, 1963.

Eide, A. (ed.). *Introduction to Engineering.* Wiley, 2002.

Garner, G. *Careers in Engineering.* McGraw-Hill, 2002.

Hall, C. *The Age of Synthesis: A Treatise and Sourcebook.* Worcester Polytechnic Institute for Science, Technology and Culture, 1995.

Koberg, D., and J. Bagnall. *The All New Universal Traveler: A Soft-Systems Guide to Creativity, Problem-Solving and the Process of Reaching Goals,* rev. ed. W. Kaufmann, 1981.

Papanek, V. *Design for the Real World,* 2nd ed. Academy Chicago, 1985.

PBS. 2006: www.pbs.org/wgbh/buildingbig/bridges.

Pool, R. *Beyond Engineering: How Society Shapes Technology.* Oxford University Press, 1999.

Pratt, F. *All About Famous Inventors and Their Inventions.* Random House, 1955.

Rubin, E., and C. Davidson. *Introduction to Engineering and the Environment.* McGraw-Hill, 2000.

Simon, H. *The Sciences of the Artificial,* 2nd ed. MIT Press, 1981.

Toffler, A. *The Third Wave.* Bantam Books, 1981.

Toffler, A. *Powershift.* Bantam Books, 1990.

WIKI. 2006: en.wikipedia.org.

Endnotes

1. PBS, 2006: www.pbs.org/wgbh/buildingbig/bridges.
2. C. Abel, *Sky High: Vertical Architecture* (Royal Academy Books, 2003).
3. A. Toffler, *The Third Wave* (Bantam Books, 1981).
4. ABET (Accreditation Board for Engineering and Technology, 2006): www.abet.org.
5. Wordnet, 2006: wordnet.princeton.edu
6. WIKI, 2006: en.wikipedia.org.
7. H. Simon, *The Sciences of the Artificial,* 2nd ed. (MIT Press, 1981).

CHAPTER 17

Constructing the Built Environment

W. Max Kirk

Construction produces tangible components of the built environment from the dreams and designs of owners, designers, developers, and builders. As you read this chapter, take a minute to look around you; whether you are in a home, dorm, apartment, classroom, or library, a variety of people contributed to your built environment. As you survey your surroundings, take note of all the materials that make up the place. If you are in a room, note that the ceiling, walls, doors, windows, and floor, as well as the lighting, heating, cooling, and plumbing systems, all contribute to your security and comfort. All of the products and systems found in this room involve a vast amount of design and technology in their composition and construction. Through knowledge and careful selection and assembly, these products are installed to meet design specifications and the needs of the inhabitants. So, the products, interior, and buildings where you live, attend school, work, shop, and so on, as well as the landscapes, roads, and bridges you traverse, are all the result of design and construction. However, as essential as construction is to our daily lives, many people have misconceptions about the construction industry.

Areas of Construction in the Building Industry

Within the broad industry of construction, there are three main areas: **Residential Building, Nonresidential Building,** and **Heavy/Highway Construction.** These areas can be further categorized into numerous subdivisions with their own specializations as determined by usage, products and materials, and construction methods for that particular division. For example, Residential Building includes single-family and multifamily residences (such as duplexes, apartment buildings, and condominiums). Nonresidential Building includes Commercial (such as office buildings, single- and multistory/high-rise, retail stores, hospitals, schools, and universities) and Industrial (such as factories, petroleum refineries, electrical substations, and nuclear reactors). Heavy/Highway construction includes dams, water distribution, roads, and bridges. To further illustrate, within the subdivision of retail stores there can be additional distinctions based on design and usage, such as a multistory department store compared to a single-story grocery store.

Figure 17-1 The constructed city—a collaborative process involving the design/planning professions, government, and the construction industries (T. Bartuska).

Figures 17-2 and 17-3 Residential townhouse and cottage housing during and after construction (T. Bartuska).

Because each area and subdivision within construction is very different, the knowledge base and expertise needed to manage them are so varied that they make the evolution of specialization within construction an accepted occurrence. To reflect this specialization, there are **general contractors**, also referred to as **prime contractors**, who typically provide construction services as well as oversee a particular development, and subcontractors, also referred to as **specialty contractors**, who specialize in a particular aspect of the project, such as plumbing or electrical.

In the above main areas of construction, general contractors specialize according to their areas of expertise. For example, you probably would not find a residential contractor building a bridge. A residential contractor specializing in single-family residences would not as a rule build apartment buildings or condominiums. The reason goes back to specialization found in the expertise of the personnel managing the building process, as well as those carrying out the daily field construction. That expertise is often honed by years of experience in that particular area of construction and by specialized knowledge of building codes, material usage, equipment, applications, and methods of installation, to name just a few. For example, building codes for single residential construction can be very different than codes required for multistory, multiunit housing such as condominiums. Also, some materials can be very different in application, such as finishes for single-family residences, which can be profoundly different from finishes used in commercial buildings for fire resistance and durability.

Specialty contracting has expanded not because of differing management methods, but rather due to new

materials and methods created by conditions such as technology, code requirements, installation procedures, and costs, etc. Every day, new materials are invented and introduced to the building process, or codes are added or

Figure 17-4 Commercial high-rise building under construction, showing a tower crane and the arm of a concrete pump truck.

Figure 17-5 Industrial construction of a steam plant showing the lifting of a large steel vessel.

altered that affect the construction process. Therefore, to keep abreast of these various changes, specialty contractors are used by the general contractor to bring the necessary expertise to the building process to enable the project to be built according to the owner's requirements. For example, there are contractors who specialize in excavation, concrete, mechanical (heating/air conditioning), plumbing, electrical, ceilings, floor coverings, windows and doors, carpentry, and many other areas.

Because of the vastness and complexity of specialization just within the subdivision of Commercial construction within the area of Nonresidential Building, the various specialty areas have been categorized by the Construction Specification Institute (CSI). The original 16 divisions, known by broad scope numbers, were developed over 40 years ago; they are:

01) General Requirements
02) Site Work
03) Concrete
04) Masonry
05) Metals
06) Wood and Plastics
07) Thermal and Moisture Protection
08) Doors and Windows
09) Finishes
10) Specialties
11) Equipment
12) Furnishings
13) Special Construction
14) Conveying Systems
15) Mechanical
16) Electrical

The above categories, or "broad scope numbers," were further subdivided into more detailed subsets or "narrow scope numbers." For example, broad scope number 09, Finishes, was divided into 15 additional narrow scope numbers, including such classifications as 09250, Gypsum wall board; 09300, Ceramic tile; 09500, Acoustical treatment; 09680, Carpeting; and 09900, Painting. Each of the CSI broad scope and narrow scope numbers represents literally hundreds of areas of construction specialties.

CSI recently released the 2004 edition of MasterFormat, which expands the original 16 divisions to up to 50 divisions. Some of the division numbers have been reserved to accommodate future areas as needed. According to *The Construction Specifier*:

With its expanded number of divisions, the new edition addresses project information's dramatic growth, driven by spectacular advances in construction technol-

Figure 17-6 Bridge construction with two cranes lifting and then setting a large steel girder.

ogy. For example, there are new divisions for fast-advancing areas such as computer and telecommunications networks, integrated building automation systems, and electronic safety and security.

While building technologies have grown in number and complexity, new construction priorities also have developed. Security and life safety, especially post-

September 11, impact project design as never before. Green building and sustainability, rarely mentioned 40 years ago, are growing concerns.[1]

As you can see, the construction industry is comprised of a multitude of specialized areas, each with its own types of contractors, management methods, organization, methods of construction, processes and procedures, and project delivery. In other words, the term "construction" is not very descriptive of the magnitude, depth, and breadth of the industry it tries to define. The construction industry is too broad to be characterized by a single word.

Contractual Relationships

Many people choose the profession of construction because they have a basic desire to be involved and see things built. Much like designers visualizing a design within their mind's eye, contractors visualize how the parts come together—the people, materials, equipment, and labor—and the project comes to fruition. As the opening sentence of this chapter stated, a contractor builds the dreams of the owner, the designer, the developer, and the builder. Of course, besides the satisfaction of seeing a project completed, contractors are in business to make a profit. Therefore, the **contract** and the contractual relationships between the owner, designer, and contractor are as critical to any project as the bricks and mortar. Outlined below are the four major types of contracts used in the construction industry: lump-sum or stipulated-sum contracts, unit price contracts, negotiated contracts, and design-build contracts.

Lump-Sum or Stipulated-Sum Contracts

In lump-sum contracts, the contractor quotes one price for every item in the plans (working drawings) and specifications. Lump-sum contracts are widely used in contracts for both residential and nonresidential (commercial) construction. In commercial contracting, the architect or another licensed professional creates the plans and specifications based on the owner's requirements. The plans and specifications are further broken down into seven major categories: working drawings, general conditions, supplementary general conditions, specifications, contract, addendum, and changes. Within the specifications, the various components of the project are further categorized into the CSI broad scope divisions and scores of narrow scope numbers. Then the project is

Figures 17-7 and 17-8   A university building during and after construction (T. Bartuska).

placed out to bid. Contractors will review the plans and submit bids for their work in specific areas of the proposed project. Award of the contract is usually given to the lowest responsive bidder. For public projects, the bids are publicly opened and read aloud, while many times on private projects the bids can be opened and read privately.

This bidding process has both positive and negative aspects, depending on the sector being bid, namely, public or private. Within the public sector and because of the competitive nature of lump-sum contracts, all contractors are generally treated equally, which can be seen as an advantage. In essence, the competitive bidding practice drives the pricing to its lowest competitive level. However, to ensure that the contractor can deliver a fair competitive price, the licensed designer (interior designer, architect, landscape architect, professional engineer, etc.) must deliver complete and accurate working drawings and specifications. When discrepancies occur, they can adversely affect the bid. Bidding within the private sector, especially where the bids are opened privately, can cause negative consequences because a contractor's bid can be altered through the intervention of the owner and the contractor behind the scenes. The process can also favor certain contractors over others.

In both private and public bids, contractors live or die by their bid price. For example, if they bid too low but are awarded the project, they will likely have to use change orders to alter their scope of work and their price. In essence, a contractor's profitability is largely based on the accuracy of his or her original estimate in addition to completing the contracted work in a timely manner.

Unit Price Contracts

In unit price contracts, a contractor quotes a price based on a certain unit of a construction line item. One example is concrete footings; a concrete footing is the line item and the measured unit is in cubic yards (CY). If the cost to install a concrete footing is $150.00 CY, this price would include all the items needed to install the concrete footing, including labor, job site overhead, profit, and company overhead cost. There is a major advantage of using unit pricing on a project where the actual concrete needed for footings could be substantially different than what was designed or indicated on the plans. When using unit pricing, the field measurements must be accurate or the contractor's profit could be in jeopardy. Unit pricing is often used in earthwork and is the predominant method of contracting in heavy and highway construction.

Negotiated Contracts

Negotiated contracts can take a variety of forms. In addition to the price, a contractor could negotiate the use of materials and/or the schedule. Selection of the contractor is based on the method of negotiation. In other words, the contractor is chosen based not only on price, but also on the projected schedule of completion, the materials and/or method(s) used to construct the project, and the contractor's experience.

Negotiated contracts can be an advantage for a contractor when the plans and specifications are not complete or the project has a high risk. There are four basic fee structures used in negotiated contracts: cost plus a percent fee; cost plus a fixed fee; cost plus a fixed fee and profit sharing; and cost plus a sliding fee. The cost plus a percent fee is probably the most common form and may be the most profitable for the contractor. In any negotiated contract, a savvy owner will insist that all units used to construct the project be subject to scrutiny and review. This can cause additional paperwork for the contractor and the need to defend proposed construction methods (also referred to as "methods of project delivery"). Whatever type of contract is used, the method of project delivery is vital to the success and profitability of the contractor.

Design-Build Contracts

As the term suggests, a design-build contract allows a project to be designed and built almost simultaneously. Design-build contracts have been used for many years. The building of the Brooklyn Bridge in the late 1880s basically used this approach. This bridge was an astonishing engineering feat considered a major accomplishment not only in the 1880s but today as well. However, design-build projects at the turn of the twentieth century lacked the internal integrity that we find in today's projects. Years ago, design-build projects usually were designed, engineered, and built by the same person or company. The difficulty was that there were few checks and balances. In other words, if there was a design flaw, there was no independent entity to check for it. In one project, this proved to be not only costly in terms of dollars but also deadly. In 1925–1926, the City of Los Angeles used the design-build approach to build the St. Francis Dam in the San Francisquito Canyon. A design error occurred when the height of the dam was increased without increasing the base and without understanding the nature of the soil beneath the dam. When the reservoir was filled to capacity in 1928 the dam failed, destroying property and claiming over 450 lives.[2]

Figure 17-9 Students engaged in a design-build project with straw bale construction (T. Bartuska).

Today this type of failure is extremely rare with the design-build approach because designers, architects, engineers (civil, structural, mechanical, and electrical), and contractors all work in a collaborative team to avoid disputes and errors. Each member of the team is at risk, and it is essential that they work to minimize delays and disputes.[3] Since the contractor works with the designers, a complete set of drawings is not needed and the project can proceed as the drawings are being completed.

A major advantage of a design-build contract is that the project can begin sooner than a project whose plans and specifications must be complete before the building process begins. Thus, a contractor can develop an estimate during the initial design period, eliminating costly change orders and aiding the designers to develop a design that hopefully can be built within the owners' budget. Design-build projects also have an advantage where the actual construction and/or the type of project has inherent difficulties. Industrial projects have been built using design-build contracts for many years. There is one disadvantage of design-build over design-bid build (see the discussion of lump-sum contracts) from the owner's point of view. With design-bid build the owner knows what the price will be at the bid opening, but with design-build, the total price of the construction may not be known until the completion of the project.

The Economy and Construction

Construction is one of the largest industries in the U.S. economy and, consequently, one of the nation's largest employers. Depending on the strength of the economy in any given year, the construction industry comprises nearly 9% of the gross national product;[4] only the military commands a larger sector. The following brief overview of the economics of the construction industry will explore how construction influences the national economy.

Residential construction comprises the largest portion of the construction industry, making **housing starts** (the number of new homes being built) a major economic indicator. The media often report current statistics on housing starts because new home construction sets a wide economic ripple effect in motion. In simple terms, the federal government, through the Federal Reserve, sets the rate at which banks can borrow money and therefore lend to their customers. The lending rate either stimulates the economy—by lowering or raising the rates at local banks and lending institutions—or slows it down during inflationary times. Because a home is the largest purchase the majority of U.S. citizens will make, an increase in home buying will significantly stimulate the economy. When lending rates are low, more customers are likely to borrow money for a home as well as other goods and services.

Where new houses are being built, communities are created that will likely need additional infrastructure, such as transit, new roads and bike/walkways, utilities, schools, stores, restaurants, parks, churches, and hospitals. In addition, these new homes will need furniture and other household goods. Thus, with housing construction being the largest sector of the industry that comprises a major portion of our economy, one of the fastest ways to stimulate the economy is to build homes.

Another way in which the federal and state governments stimulate the economy is through releasing funds to build federal and state projects: buildings, transit, highways, bikeways, and funding state agencies to improve their respective infrastructures. For example, many public university buildings have been built during poor economic times. Many of these government-funded projects are specifically developed and designed to utilize more labor during periods of high unemployment in order to get people back into the workforce. If more people are working, they will be able to buy more products and pay taxes, thus stimulating the economy.

The use of construction to stimulate the economy goes back to the Great Depression of the 1930s, when the federal government established programs under the **New Deal** such as the Works Progress Administration (WPA) and the Civilian Conservation Corps (CCC), creating thousands of construction jobs. Many roads, bridges, parks, lodges, and hiking trails were built across the nation under these programs. This type of economic stimulation has even reached beyond our country's borders, as in the Marshall Plan.

Under the Marshall Plan, the United States aided European countries from 1948 to 1952 in rebuilding their cities and infrastructures, which had been heavily damaged by bombing during World War II. Sending billions of dollars in machinery, food, and various products, this effort provided a great stimulus to the U.S. construction industry and contributed to development of many new building methods, products, and technology that we see today. The effects of the Marshall Plan are still being felt today, with new technology being created and applied in foreign countries and then finding its way to the United States.

The U.S. Census Bureau divides the economy into 20 major categories or sectors within the North American Industry Classification System (NAICS): Agriculture, forestry, fishing and hunting; Mining; Utilities; Construction; Manufacturing; Wholesale trade; Retail trade; Transportation and warehousing; Information; Finance and insurance; Real estate and rental and leasing; Professional, scientific, and technical services; Management of companies and enterprises; Administrative, support, waste management, and remediation services; Educational services; Health care and social assistance; Arts, entertainment, and recreation; Accommodation and food services; Other services (except public administration); and Public administration.[5]

Because construction is considered one of the major economic indicators, it also commands a complete NAICS category by itself. The category Construction is subdivided into three areas: Building, development and general contracting; Heavy construction; and Special trade contractors. These subcategories are similar to the three main areas of construction mentioned earlier.

So, just how large an industry is construction? According to the U.S. Census Bureau in 2004,[6] the category of Construction had sales or receipts worth $1.1 trillion, making it the sixth largest economic sector. By March 29, 2004, Construction trailed only Wholesale trade at $4.4 trillion, Manufacturing at $3.8 trillion, Retail trade at $3.2 trillion, Finance and insurance at $2.6 trillion, and Health care and social assistance at $1.2 trillion. More significantly, however, Construction had a much larger annual payroll per sales and receipts. For example, Wholesale trade (the largest sector) had an annual payroll of $255 million, compared to Construction with $235 million, even though its sales and receipts were only one-fourth those of Wholesale trade. Therefore, when the economy needs to be stimulated, economists look to the construction industry.

Figure 17-10   Mixed-use housing project: commercial and parking base with townhouses and apartments above (T. Bartuska).

Despite the enormous economic strength of the construction industry, there is deep concern about the current trend of the industry. Not enough young people are choosing careers in the business of construction and the multitude of construction trades, creating a severe skilled and unskilled labor shortage. One reason for this drop-off is the negative image of the construction industry.

Construction Image Concerns

Important as the construction industry is to our economy, it suffers from an inescapable negative image. Although they may admire a finished project such as an urban plaza, building, or road, many people become annoyed during the construction process due to inconvenient delays and detours, as well as dusty and noisy conditions. In an age when people want instant results, construction never seems to happen fast enough. In addition, construction workers are often viewed and depicted as uneducated, foul-mouthed people with big guts hanging over their belts, sweating and laboring away while the rest of society attains loftier goals. Construction is a labor-intensive, aggressive, get-your-hands-dirty type of job that many people do not see as a desirable career.

When high school students are asked about possible career choices, they usually rank construction, specifically construction trades, very low.[7] Why would anyone want to work in construction, out in the heat, cold, rain, and snow, when they could enjoy the comforts of working indoors in more professional attire? Many young people see working in construction as failure to achieve a higher-status career.

Yet, at one time, those who worked in manual trades were regarded as highly skilled and well respected in our society. In fact, for thousands of years, there has been the tradition of the apprentice learning under the master. Working through apprentice school to becoming a journeyman or craftsperson was a proud accomplishment. Bricklaying, cabinetry, carpentry, plumbing, and ironwork, to name a few, had many skilled workers.

Because fewer young people are choosing construction careers, many talented individuals are not entering the industry, leaving the backbone of the U.S. economy short of highly skilled workers. Over the past ten years some 200,000 construction workers have left the industry; between 30,000 and 40,000 exited in 1997 and 1998, respectively.[8] Additionally, as the workforce has become more diverse, the industry has been striving to reduce language and trade barriers, increase product knowledge and work production, and improve the industry's overall image.

There are still many talented men and women in the construction trades who are gifted at their crafts and take pride in what they build. They can visualize an idea on a two-dimensional set of drawings (often without the aid of a computer) and use their minds and hands to transform that idea into reality. They are truly builders of dreams and rival even Michelangelo and the great masters of old.

So, here we have an industry with a rich history, which comprises a major part of our economy and is producing the important built components and systems in our everyday lives with fewer and fewer highly skilled workers. At the same time, increasing technology, production costs, and time constraints are making construction a very demanding occupation. Successfully completing a construction project requires more than understanding the products, technology, and equipment involved in building the physical project; it also includes organizing and managing the various people involved in design and construction. In response to this need, a relatively new field has emerged in the education arena—**construction management**.

Construction Management

Construction management, like the vast and complex construction industry, is difficult to define. As in the tale of the three blind men describing an elephant, it depends on what part of the animal you are describing. Each sector of the industry—whether residential, commercial, heavy, or specialty—has its own unique perspective in the management of its projects. However, the common thread among them is the premise that all construction projects are kaleidoscopic in nature and that the management of these projects requires strong leadership and management skills. Thus, construction management encompasses the areas of contractual documents and relationships, project management, scheduling and estimating, and, perhaps most importantly, an ability to work in collaboration with a variety of people and professions.

For the construction project manager, change occurs daily—perhaps caused by the availability of labor and materials, weather conditions, or financial constraints—and each project has its own unique combination of situations. A construction project manager must not only be an effective administrator within the framework of his or her company, but must also be an effective leader and manager of people from the different companies and occupations that come together to construct a given project. Depending on the project, the construction project manager may be overseeing millions of dollars, estimating the various components of the project, scheduling these items, and managing people ranging from bankers to newly hired migrant workers. The construction project manager must deal with the physical development of the project as well as with the variety of people involved, foresee potential problems and analyze them as they occur, and devise methods to solve these problems. To become an effective leader and manager in the construction industry, one must "see the big picture"—that is, one must possess intuitive and visionary reasoning that can be applied to linear and sequential situations. One must "lead others to lead themselves."[9]

In response to the industry's need for persons educated in business management in conjunction with a solid background in design and engineering concepts, construction management programs began to develop in earnest within U.S. colleges and universities during the 1960s. These programs were generally housed in a college of architecture or engineering as an offshoot of civil engineering. Civil engineering graduates were often employed to manage heavy engineering projects such as roads, bridges, and dams. However, since architecture curricula focused more on design and civil engineering began a move toward more environmental design concerns, construction management programs began to flourish during the 1980s.

Presently, there are about 170 programs at the B.A. level from fully accredited schools in the United States. Of these, over 40 are members of the accrediting body

Figure 17-11 Renovation and additions to a historic university building, School of Architecture and Construction Management, Washington State University (T. Bartuska).

the American Council for Construction Education (ACCE) and have curriculums specifically designed for the management of construction projects. Over the past 10 years, graduate programs in construction management have been established and Ph.D. programs are being developed.

The curriculums for construction management generally consist of courses in business management, engineering and architectural principles, communication (both oral and written), and a variety of subjects specifically tailored for the industry, such as estimating, planning and scheduling, and the process, procedures, and materials found in all aspects of the industry. Though there is still the misconception that these programs are about learning how to use hammers and nails, graduates of construction management programs are now highly sought after for their specialized skills. As a result of the educational evolution in this field, a new professional title of "constructor" has been accepted in the industry, and this term has been added to the latest editions of *Webster's* dictionaries. As with all licensed design professionals and engineers, the new title distinguishes construction management as a professional.

Because the construction industry is a major player in the U.S. economy, there is an increasing demand for college-educated construction managers. Between 2001 and 2005 there was a projected 38% increase in the demand for construction graduates.[10] The *U.S. Occupational Outlook Quarterly* spring 2000 issue projected an increase of 38,000 construction manager's positions, or a 14% increase, from 1998 to 2008. Because of this demand and the nature of the construction industry, many students graduating from four-year accredited construction programs are earning high-paying starting salaries.

Conclusion

Construction has evolved into an enormous industry and a major influence in our nation's economy. Despite image concerns and a shrinking workforce, construction offers a wide variety of challenging and rewarding occupations, including a relatively recent field referred to as construction management.

As we examine all of the aspects of our built environment, one of the key components is constructing its various components and systems. For every person who designs a dream, and for every owner who desires to build a specific project, there must be a builder to construct it. The construction process brings these dreams to reality. As long as we continue to utilize and shape our world, how effectively we construct our built environment will determine our future as a society.

References

ACCE. American Council for Construction Education. 2005: www.acce-hg.org.

Bergman, M. *United States Department of Commerce News*. U.S. Census Bureau Public Information Office, 2004: www.census.gov/Press-Release.

Bilbo, D., T. Fetters, T. Burt, and J. Avant. "A Study and Demand for Construction Education Graduates." *Journal of Construction Education*, Spring 2000.

Bowditch, J. L., and A. F. Buono. *A Primer on Organizational Behavior*, 4th ed. Wiley, 1997.

Halpin, D. W. *Construction Management*. Wiley, 2006.

Kibert, C. *Sustainable Construction: Green Building Design and Delivery*. Wiley, 2005.

Kirk, W. M. "A Proposal for Obtaining Funding for Construction Research and Development at the State Level." Unpublished master's thesis, Arizona State University, 1990.

Krantz, L., and T. Lee. *National Business Employment Weekly: Jobs Rated Almanac*, 3rd ed. Wiley, 1995.

Liebing, R. W. *The Construction Industry: Processes, Players, and Practices*. Prentice Hall, 2001.

Nunis, D. B. "The St. Francis Dam Disaster Revisited," Historical Society of Southern California, Los Angeles and Ventura County Museum of History and Art, 1995.

U.S. Census Bureau. "Advance Comparative Statistics for the United States 1997," Table 2. NNAICS Basis, 2002: www.census.gov/econ/census02/advance/table2.htm.

U.S. Occupational Outlook Quarterly, Spring 2000.

Washington, E. S., and K. F. Borgstrom. "Why MasterFormat 2004?" *The Construction Specifier*, July 2004.

Endnotes

1. E. S. Washington and K. F. Borgstrom. "Why Master-Format 2004?" *The Construction Specifier* (July 2004): 80–82.
2. D. B. Nunis, "The St. Francis Dam Disaster Revisited" (Historical Society of Southern California, Los Angeles and Ventura County Museum of History and Art, 1995).
3. D. W. Halpin, *Construction Management* (Wiley, 2006).
4. W. M. Kirk, "A Proposal for Obtaining Funding for Construction Research and Development at the State Level" (unpublished Master's Thesis, Arizona State University, 1990).
5. U.S. Census Bureau, 2002: www.census.gov/econ/census.
6. M. Bergman, *United States Department of Commerce News* (U.S. Census Bureau Public Information Office, 2004): www.census.gov/Press-Release.
7. L. Krantz and T. Lee, *National Business Employment Weekly: Jobs Rated Almanac*, 3rd ed. (Wiley, 1995).
8. R. W. Liebing, *The Construction Industry: Processes, Players, and Practices* (Prentice Hall, 2001).
9. J. L. Bowditch and A. F. Buono, *A Primer on Organizational Behavior*, 4th ed. (Wiley, 1997).
10. D. Bilbo, T. Fetters, T. Burt, and J. Avant, "A Study and Demand for Construction Education Graduates," *Journal of Construction Education* (Spring 2000).

LANDSCAPES

Landscape Architecture and Planning

Introduction

Landscapes are the fourth selected component or layer in this study of the built environment. It may be more difficult for some to perceive landscapes as a component of the built environment because much of the landscape apparently seems to consist largely or entirely of natural features, including land, water, vegetation, insects, and living creatures (both wild and domesticated). However, many landscapes feature a combination of humanly created processes of design and products with or within the natural environment. This component integrates the human/social, environmental, and technical aspects of the built and natural "land" and creates a setting or "scape." And even the most natural-appearing landscape has undoubtedly been shaped, altered, or manipulated to some degree by humans. Plants may be arranged, placed, or manipulated by human hands and even partly created (genetically) by humans. Although land is the ultimate natural resource of ancient earthly origin, it can be formed and shaped by human hands or machines.

Landscapes incorporate a variety of shapes, sizes, and scales, including small, intimate or residential gardens, urban courtyards, plazas, parks, planned unit developments, large recreational developments, and regional watershed management/ecological plans. They can be rural, suburban, or urban places. Landscapes feature creative combinations of natural features such as plant materials, trees, water, and open space, and humanly made components such as structures, outdoor furnishings, walks/bikeways, and roads/parking. And most importantly, landscapes are alive; they grow and change over time, celebrating the wonderful delights of oxygen-producing plants and the changing beauty of the seasons.

Consequently, the people who work with the landscape component interrelate with almost all levels within the built and natural environments, as described by the following content-component-context continuum:

Products—Interiors—Structures—
Landscapes—Cities—Regions—Earth

Landscapes, their nature and characteristics, can be further defined by the use of the following four-part definition used for the built environment and adapted for all of its components:

- **Landscapes** (the contents of which are elements of the natural environment and components of the built environment, including products, interiors, and structures) are humanly made, arranged, or maintained;
- in order to fulfill human purposes, to satisfy human needs, wants and values; and
- to mediate the overall environment;
- the results affect the context (cities, regions, and Earth) in which they are placed.

Members of the design disciplines/professions that work at the level(s) of landscapes are usually called **landscape architects** but, depending on the scale, might be called "landscape or regional planners" or (in Europe and recently in the United States) "landscape ecologists." Landscape design professionals are intimately involved

at the interface between nature and the built environment, where the balance can be largely natural or largely humanly made. These designers/planners do not fit the stereotype of "backyard gardeners." Instead, they have always designed within a variety of contexts at scales ranging from small, intimate gardens to large regional state or national parks. For example, Central Park in New York City is no single person's backyard—it is everyone's. It is also New York City's front yard and a profound contribution to the quality of urban living.

A clearer understanding of the various dimensions of this component can be gained by thinking about the similarities and differences among three terms: landscape, landscaping, and landscape architecture.

Landscape is a portion of land, which the eye can comprehend in a single view, especially its pictorial aspects; a picture representing natural scenery; to improve by landscape architecture or gardening. Other similar words can be formed by changing the first syllable, such as "seascape," "townscape," and "riverscape." They mean, of course, a portion of the environment, either natural or built, that can be perceived in a single view.

As noted, this single view has a variety of scales, ranging from an enclosed yard to the panoramic view from an airplane or mountaintop. If we accept the above definition, which links scale to the human view, we can begin to understand the general and specific characteristics of a term that some would argue covers any landscape at any scale, just over the fence or far distant hills.

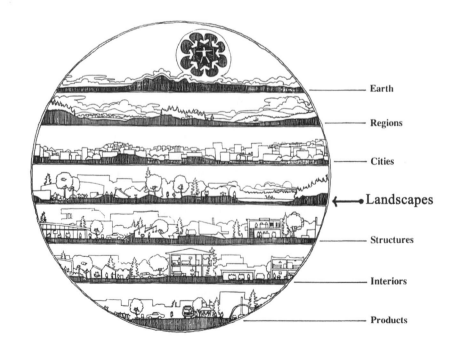

This may be true in a general sense. In a more specific sense, the landscapes beyond our view may have their own unique qualities, so we can conclude that there are interlinked landscapes perceived by sequential experiences of a mobile observer.

Landscaping means to improve the landscape, to make the land more beautiful, especially by adding trees and plants, water features, land and rock formations, and so on. It is synonymous with landscape gardening.

Landscape architecture is a profession focused on the art and science of designing/planning the natural and built characteristics and the stewardship of land to produce the best aesthetic, scientific, and ecological conditions, considering the uses to which the land is to be put.

Landscape profession implies public declaration, knowledge of the art, craft, and science of the design, management, and planning of landscapes. This includes education, apprenticeship, and professional licensing.

The American Society of Landscape Architecture (ASLA) incorporates various dimensions and responsibilities within the art and science of design, planning, or management of the land. ASLA is concerned with resource **conservation, stewardship,** and **sustainability.**

The chapters in this section investigate various characteristics and scales of landscapes:

Landscape Architecture through Time
by Frederick R. Steiner

This chapter discusses the art and science of landscape architecture as it has evolved through four transitional periods. European landscape gardening marks the first transition. Frederick Law Olmsted, Sr., advanced the field significantly through the late nineteenth century during the second period. Third, modernism became the defining force of mid-twentieth-century landscape architecture. In the most recent period, since the 1960s, landscape architects have developed ecologically based approaches to design that have influenced many of the allied environmental design, and planning disciplines.

Landscape Architecture Today: Purpose, Process, and Palette
by Kenneth R. Brooks

This chapter further examines landscape architecture today and how careful planning and design provides a more useful and pleasant context for human activities. It improves the natural and built environments and enhances human safety, health, and enjoyment of landscapes and larger environments. Landscape planning and design is an intentional, conscientious process, performed by landscape architects and other environmental designers/planners, to apply and integrate a wide range of science, art, and technology to improve the built environment.

Comparative Campus Design and Planning
by Phillip S. Waite

This chapter explores the campus environment, whether a college, corporate, or civic campus, as a distinctive form within the built environment. Campus planning and design are interdisciplinary efforts that combine all the design disciplines in such a way that the whole is greater than the sum of its parts. Although a campus deals with many of the same issues that affect cities, it often has many of the positive attributes of an urban environment without the negative aspects. This chapter also looks for lessons in campus planning that can be applied by designers/planners to improve the overall built environment, especially in cities.

References

Each chapter concludes with a list of useful references.

American Society of Landscape Architects (ASLA): www.asla.org

American Society of Landscape Students (ASLS): www.asla.org/nonmembers/students2.html

Council of Educators in Landscape Architecture (CELA): www.thecela.org

Landscape Architecture Foundation (LAF): www.laprofession.org

CHAPTER 18

Landscape Architecture Through Time

Frederick R. Steiner

The art and science of landscape architecture evolved through four transitional periods. European landscape gardening is the first. Frederick Law Olmsted, Sr., advanced the field significantly through the late nineteenth century during the second period. Third, Modernism became the defining force of mid-twentieth-century landscape architecture. In the most recent period, since the 1960s, landscape architects have developed ecologically based approaches to design that have influenced the allied environmental science, design, and planning disciplines.

Landscapes present a synthesis of all the natural and cultural features, such as fields, buildings, hills, forests, farms, deserts, water, or plants, that distinguish one part of the surface of the Earth from another part (Fig. 18-1). Landscape architecture is the art and science of designing and planning with land, plants, and all built components so as to adapt it ecologically most conveniently, economically, functionally, and aesthetically to any of the varied needs and wants of people.

Frederick Law Olmsted, Sr. (1822–1903) was largely responsible for creating the discipline of landscape architecture. He adapted European landscape gardening ideas to places in the United States. The driving force for Olmsted was how to make increasingly industrial and crowded cities more livable. Olmsted's work, as well as his goals for the discipline, defined the field. Beginning in the mid-nineteenth century, he and his colleagues designed urban parks, new suburban communities, parkways, campuses, state, national, and international parks, city and regional plans, cemeteries, and estates. In the process, a new design profession was born, which has international origins and worldwide influence.

Landscape architecture has developed in four periods. First, varied European styles emerged in landscape gardening, including the Moorish in Spain, the Italian Renaissance, the French Baroque, and the highly original English picturesque, as well as distinct, yet synthetic, styles in the Netherlands, Germany, and Poland. Second, the contributions of Olmsted and his collaborators established a broader social agenda. Third, a modern movement emerged just before World War II that reached fruition in the following decades. Finally, landscape architecture has played an influential role in the environmental movement from the 1960s to the present. In each of these four periods an Asian influence has been present. For example, the English landscape picturesque style especially exhibited an awareness of Chinese and Japanese gardens.

The Agricultural Transition and the Rise of Civilization

For most of its existence, the species *Homo sapiens* lived without government. In small groups, people lived off the land. Humans depended on hunting, fishing, gathering food, subsistence cultivation, and/or pastoralism for survival. The development of governments came with

Figure 18-1 Sardinian landscape.

the rise of agriculture. Advancing techniques of irrigation and cultivation transformed the fertile river valleys of the Nile, Tigris, Euphrates, Indus, and Hwang Ho into nation-states. These nation-states included urban areas with bureaucracies responsible for distributing agricultural surpluses. These new urban areas were dependent, as cities and towns are today, on the capability of land and people to produce food and fiber.

Greek and Roman Landscapes

Civilization spread to the rocky islands of the Aegean Sea and the plains of the Balkan Peninsula. In Greece, the hot, dry climate, the folded mountain ranges and rocky coastlines—the whole ecological matrix—was a major influence on the health of the people, as well as their economic activities and general view of life. Dark green orchards of olives and figs contrasted with sparse, dusty plains and white limestone crags juxtaposed against cerulean blue seas. Greek cities (the *poleis*) were the birthplace of ideas about democracy.

Just as the Greek landscape influenced the settlement patterns and political organization of the *polis*, the relatively open plains and uplands of the Italian Peninsula provided the base for the vast Roman Empire. The empire was connected by an elaborate network of roads and aqueducts, and as the empire expanded, new towns, known as *castra*, were built. The powerful Romans expressed their imperial dominance by designing new towns using formal, rigid geometries. By contrast, the city of Rome, heart of the Roman Empire, featured an intriguingly complex web of interlocking streets and spaces free of any dominating geometry or urban form.

Rome's proximity to the sea influenced the city's climate, resulting in high summer temperatures and low humidity. As the empire grew, the city became a large population center. Because of overcrowding in the city of Rome and the stench of hot summers, many of the wealthy patrician families built villas outside of the town: *villa rustica* were working farms, while *villa urbana* were used primarily for residents.

Islamic Landscapes

In Islam, the Mediterranean building, garden, and city design tradition of the Greeks and Romans was maintained as the Dark Ages descended on Europe. Like the Romans, the Islamic tradition emphasized the organization of space based on an application of principles of geometry and other branches of mathematics, with interior courtyards favored for housing. Water was used judiciously but played an important role, not only for drinking and irrigation, but also for cooling. The arrangement of space, the manipulation of water flows, and the careful application of building materials, such as masonry and ceramic tiles, contributed to a pleasant living environment.

The Islamic garden derives from the "paradise garden" of the Koran. These places were to be manifestations on

Figure 18-2 The Alhambra's Court of Myrtles, Granada, Spain (T. Bartuska).

earth of a heavenly condition. Their rigorous ordering according to geometric principles is a logical corollary and makes it equivalent to a mandala. The Islamic approach had a significant impact in the Iberian Peninsula. As Spain was conquered by the Christians, Islamic ideas about design and planning filtered into European thinking. Among the structures built by the Moors in Spain, their dramatic fortress palace at Granada, called the Alhambra (built between the thirteenth and fourteenth centuries), made an especially important impression. In particular, its inner courtyards (the Court of Myrtles and the Court of the Lions) provide models for how water and shade can be manipulated for human comfort and delight (Fig. 18-2).

Landscapes of the Renaissance

The Islamic world was one of the influences on the Italian Renaissance. The early phase of this learning revival was especially strong in Tuscany, where the influence of Moorish design on the hillside villas around Florence is still evident. For example, the powerful Medici family built hillside gardens at Fiesole (1458) overlooking Florence. They were also responsible for the extensive Boboli Gardens behind the Pitti Palace in Florence (Fig. 18-3). The outdoor spaces of these villas were remarkable both in Tuscany and later around Rome as the Medici introduced the style there and eventually elsewhere in Italy.

In addition to adapting Islamic ideas and uses of materials, the Italian designers drew on ideas from ancient Rome, especially those of Marcus Vitruvius Pollio, and forged a new style. In works such as the gardens of Villa Lante (1518) and Villa D'Este (begun c. 1550), Italian architects sculpted earth, water, and plants in new ways. Formal geometric patterns were carved into hillsides, with water flows directed to erupt strategically at dramatic fountains, framed by rows of trees and shrubs that guided the eye to

Figure 18-4 Villa Lante, Bagnaia, Italy.

various focal points. Water is an essential feature of Italian garden design and, along with stone and living plants, delights the polarities of human senses (Figs. 18-4 to 18-7).

The great French garden designer André Le Nôtre (1613–1700) took these Italian forms and enlarged them with Baroque proportions. The natural expanses of the French countryside were not as constrained as the hillsides of Italy, and the power of the Sun King eclipsed that of even the Medici. Begun in 1661, Louis XIV's palace at Versailles transformed a vast 5-square-mile portion of the French countryside into an elaborate, formally composed system of grand vistas (Fig. 18-8). The main east-west axis and several crossing axes of various sizes divide the space into a series of parterres with connecting allées bordered with massive, carefully manicured trees. As with the Italian gardens, Le Nôtre created fountains and other focal locations at strategic points along the sight lines, but where trickles of waters collected into gushing fountains in Italy, a grand canal and an elaborate mechanical pumping system were created at Versailles.

Figure 18-3 Boboli Gardens, Florence, Italy.

Figure 18-5 Water feature at Villa Lante, Bagnaia, Italy.

Figure 18-6   Water table at Villa Lante, Bagnaia, Italy.

Figure 18-7   Fountains at Villa D'Este, Tivoli, Italy.

Figure 18-8   Main vista of the Garden of Versailles. The palace (in the distance) was designed by André Le Nôtre and built by King Louis XIV in the seventeenth century.

From the apex at the chateau, the landscape underscored who controlled and ruled this place.

English Garden Design Tradition

A contrasting landscape style emerged in England, as it became a sea power connected to the Americas and the Orient and influenced by growing ideas about democracy. While John Locke (1632–1704) wrote about the inalienable rights of people to pursue life, liberty, and property, poets like Alexander Pope (1688–1744) celebrated learning from the genius of the place.

The innovative Lancelot "Capability" Brown (1716–1783) sought to improve the English landscape. He arranged estates with asymmetrically placed clumps of trees, broad undulating greenswards, serpentine lakes, and surrounding belts of woodlands. Capability Brown's romantic designs used small classical and Asian-influenced structures as focal points. The English landscape garden became known as an "animation of nature." Where straight lines dominated the Moorish, Italian, and French designs, curves predominated in the British Isles from the eighteenth century on (Fig. 18-9).

The English landscape tradition drew inspiration for its nongeometric "picturesque" qualities from the Chinese garden.[1] The English and other Europeans were exposed to the Chinese approach by returning French Jesuit priests. The Chinese garden contains complex symbolic meanings in its cultural and physical contexts. These gardens, as well as subsequent adaptations and transformations in Korea and Japan, are richly symbolic microcosms of nature (Fig. 18-10).

Ancient Roman gardens, as well as rising English nationalism, also influenced the picturesque approach.

Figure 18-9   A picturesque English landscape garden, Stourhead, England (T. Bartuska).

Figure 18-10   Changduk Palace in Seoul, an example of Korean traditional architecture and garden (Jusuch Koh).

Figure 18-12   Wilanow Palace Garden, Warsaw, Poland (E. Kaliszuk).

Watkin notes that the third Earl of Shaftesbury "called for the creation of a national style and national taste based on the spirit of national freedom, which he believed was enshrined in the Whig oligarchy," and to achieve this style the model was the "free commonwealth of republican Rome as well as the culture of China."[2]

This growing philosophy, affected largely by the teachings of Locke, coincided with the English colonization of the New World and would have a lasting imprint on North America.

Meanwhile, the English landscape style and the contrasting geometric forms from the continent impacted approaches in other European nations, which also developed their own styles, notably in the Netherlands, Germany, and Poland. In the Netherlands especially, the term landscape (*landschap* in Dutch) has deep cultural significance, because much of the land in the nation has literally been "made," reclaimed from the sea (Fig. 18-11).

The Germans borrowed from the English approach but contributed a more scientific understanding of nature, laying the groundwork for contemporary concepts of ecology and sustainability. The Poles combined formal and informal spaces, in conscious melding of nature and culture, at places such as the grounds at Wilanów Palace and Lazienki Park (Figs. 18-12, 18-13).

Figure 18-13   Detail of the Wilanow Palace Garden, Warsaw, Poland (M. Cieszewscy).

Figure 18-11   Dutch polder.

The Industrial Transition and the Rise of the Landscape Profession

While members of the English landscape school were looking back to what was envisioned as a more picturesque era, or were turning to the Orient for a more natural vision of the land, Europe was changing from an agrarian culture to an industrial one. The Industrial Revolution began in England and quickly spread to Europe and North America. Its impact on people was profound, as deep as that of the earlier transition to agriculturally based nation-states from hunting and gathering nomadic tribes.

The new products of the Industrial Revolution made life easier and increased the amount of leisure time for many people. It also increased urbanization, poverty, pollution, and urban squalor, depicted so vividly in Charles Dickens' acidic portraits of England during the mid-nineteenth century. In response to these patterns of industrialization and rapid urbanization, the English parks movement was begun. In the 1830s and 1840s, several parks were built in London: St. James' Park, Green Park, Hyde Park, Kensington Gardens, and Regent's Park. Although these parks remained the property of the Crown, they were open to the public and continue to be enjoyed by Londoners and visitors today.

The Transformation of the Landscape in the United States

The Industrial Revolution moved quickly to the United States, where the agrarian democratic ideals of Thomas Jefferson had been influential in the establishment of the new nation. Jefferson believed a strong democracy would be based on a nation of small farmers who owned their land. The forces of industrialism challenged this ideal. Partially in reaction to the industrial transition, the Transcendental movement grew in popularity in the United States. Transcendentalism is a philosophy that asserts the primacy of the spiritual and intuitive over the material and empirical. The New England leaders of the movement, Ralph Waldo Emerson and Henry David Thoreau, stressed the presence of the divine within people as a source of truth and a guide to action. This philosophy was based on the writings of the German philosopher Immanuel Kant and was influenced by the Society of Friends, or Quakers.

Transcendentalism and the English landscape school influenced several designers in the United States. In 1841, the young horticulturist and landscape gardener Andrew Jackson Downing (1815–1852) published his popular A *Treatise on the Theory and Practice of Land-*

scape Gardening Adapted to North America. Downing designed country estates along the Hudson River, north of New York City. Like previous estates, these were owned by the wealthy, but this wealth was broader-based than that of Europe, a new affluence created by the Industrial Revolution. The Hudson River Valley was transformed from wilderness to farmland, then to suburbs, and finally to a connected piece in the puzzle of urbanization—a cycle that would recur many times throughout the industrializing world.

Olmsted and His Collaborators

Landscape architecture in the United States came into being after several decades of gestation in the English style. Downing was an adherent of the English school of landscape gardening. Frederick Law Olmsted (1822–1903), Sr. (Fig. 18-14) had been influenced profoundly by the more informal or organic English style, especially at Birkenhead Park, which he visited during an 1850 trip to the British Isles. Birkenhead is a suburb of Liverpool, and its park was designed specifically for the public by Joseph Paxton (1803–1865) in 1844. Previous parks in England and elsewhere in Europe were the estate gardens of the aristocracy donated to a city or loaned to the public.

Figure 18-14   Frederick Law Olmsted, Sr. (c. 1860; courtesy National Park Service, Frederick Law Olmsted National Historical Site).

A second direct influence from the British Isles on Olmsted's work was his partnership with the English architect Calvert Vaux (1824–1895). In spite of the strong English influence, Olmsted was an original. He altered the English name of the field from "landscape gardening" to "landscape architecture" and established a new discipline that transcended the creation of gardens for the very rich and powerful.

Olmsted's incredible start in landscape architecture was the design and construction supervision with Vaux of Central Park in New York City, beginning in 1857. Through Central Park, Olmsted sought to bring the benefits of open space to the urban masses. The urban park would provide a healthy antidote to the crowding and pollution brought on by the Industrial Revolution. Central Park was an immediate success (Fig. 18-15). This led Olmsted to establish a landscape architecture practice, initially with Vaux and later with his sons. The practice was responsible for urban parks in Brooklyn, Boston, Chicago, Montreal, and eventually throughout North America.

The discipline that Olmsted founded was defined by the scope of his own work as well as that of his son (Frederick Law Olmsted, Jr. 1870–1957) and nephew-adopted son (John C. Law Olmsted, 1852–1920). In addition to urban parks, Olmsted designed Riverside, Illinois—a prototypical suburban new community—and contributed to the preservation of Yosemite National Park and Niagara Falls, setting the stage for national and international parks. He also participated in the planning of the World's Columbian Exposition of 1893, which created the inspiration for the City Beautiful Movement. Toward the end of his prolific career, Olmsted, Sr., also designed the Biltmore estate for the very wealthy George

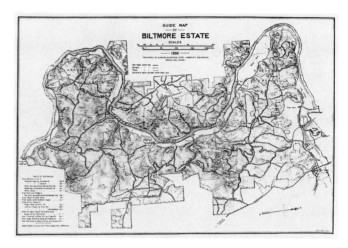

Figure 18-16 George Vanderbilt's North Carolina Biltmore estate, designed by Olmsted, Olmsted and Eliot in 1896 (courtesy National Park Service, Frederick Law Olmsted National Historical Site).

W. Vanderbilt (Fig. 18-16). Biltmore was also an experimental forest and farm where the French-trained forester and conservationist Gifford Pinchot (1865–1946) first applied his "multiple use, sustained yield" concept, a precursor to contemporary sustainability.

While the Olmsteds broadened the scope of landscape architecture, the style they employed was strongly English-influenced. The "pastoral aesthetic," as well as the associated Whig political philosophy, resonated within the United States. This aesthetic was appropriate for large portions (but not all) of the North American continent. When Olmsted worked in California on the design of the Stanford University campus, he adopted a style that was more Spanish than English and more suitable for the climate and history of the state (Fig. 18-17). He also designed many other university campuses.

"GREENSWARD," THE ORIGINAL PLAN FOR CENTRAL PARK, 1858 (above)
MAP OF THE PARK AS IT APPEARED ca. 1870   right
Although there were numerous modifications of details, Olmsted and Vaux's basic conception was carried out for the lower park (below 85th Street); extension of the upper park to 110th Street permitted them to develop that area, as they had the lower park, in accordance with the natural topography. Sunken transverse roads were included right from the beginning as a unique part of the Olmsted-Vaux plan. In defense of the numerous grade divisions Olmsted remarked that "to the visitor, carried by occasional defiles from one field of landscape to another, . . . the extent of the park is practically much greater than it would otherwise be"
[Olmsted Office Portfolio]

Figure 18-15 "Greensward," the original 1858 Plan for Central Park by Frederick Law Olmsted and Calvert Vaux (courtesy National Park Service, Frederick Law Olmsted National Historical Site).

Figure 18-17 Stanford University Campus Plan (courtesy National Park Service, Frederick Law Olmsted National Historical Site).

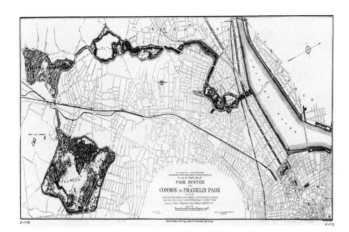

Figure 18-18   Boston Park System, Boston, Massachusetts. Plan of a portion of the "emerald necklace" from Boston Common to Franklin Park. Olmsted, Olmsted and Eliot, landscape architects, January 1894 (courtesy of the National Park Service, Frederick Law Olmsted National Historic Site.)

Olmsted was also involved in other aspects of higher education. He was a strong supporter of the land grant colleges established by Justin Morrill (1810–1898) in 1862 to offer education in the agricultural and mechanical arts and sciences. Morrill, Olmsted, and others believed that the interests of agriculture and industry had been ignored by the established universities in the United States, which had more elitist goals. Many of these land grant schools began requiring landscape gardening courses in the late nineteenth century, and one (Iowa State) offered Olmsted its presidency.

Landscape architecture impacted the elite schools too. Perhaps Olmsted's brightest young collaborator was Charles Eliot, son of the president of Harvard University. The younger Eliot organized probably the first comprehensive, multidisciplinary ecological inventories of Mount Desert Island in Maine during the 1880s. With the Olmsted firm, Eliot developed a plan for the Boston metropolitan region in 1893. He proposed an "emerald necklace" for the region that linked park and open space systems while making environmental improvements for flood control and water quality (Fig. 18-18). Eliot died of spinal meningitis prematurely at 38 in 1897. In his memory, his father established the landscape architecture program at Harvard that would lead the discipline throughout much of the twentieth century.

The Modern Movement in Landscape Architecture

In the early twentieth century, landscape architecture established itself as a profession in North America,

northern Europe, and Japan. Professional associations were founded, including the American Society of Landscape Architects (1899), and leading universities and the growing land grant schools initiated departments or programs. However, much of the idealism of the Olmsteds dwindled as the progressive branch of the field embraced the new profession of city planning. The leading landscape architecture historian, Norman Newton, noted that "single-track eclecticism" took over, especially at Harvard, as practitioners flocked to build estates and exclusive neighborhoods for the wealthy.

However, it was at Harvard that a countermovement against this eclectic garden design dominance began. In the late 1930s, students rebelled against the Harvard curriculum. Their quest for a more modern, more creative approach to landscape design coincided with the arrival of Walter Gropius (1883–1969) at Harvard in 1937. Gropius helped institutionalize the Bauhaus philosophy of design within this leading academic institution.[3]

Meanwhile, in California, Thomas Church (1902–1978) had developed a practice focusing on gardens for the middle and upper middle classes. Celebrated in *Sunset* magazine, the Church garden provided an ideal for the suburban lifestyle (Fig. 18-19).

Between the rebellious Harvard students and Church, a modern movement in landscape architecture developed. This modernism is characterized by its democratic spirit, making the benefits of landscape design available to a wide spectrum of people, as well as by its spare Cubist- and Surrealist-inspired forms. A good example is Garrett Eckbo's Depression-era multifamily housing in California built for the Farm Security Administration. These schemes are functional spatial arrangements designed to provide shelter and a delightful

Figure 18-19   Donnell Garden in California by Thomas Church, 1948 (M. Treib).

Figure 18-20 Hideo Sasaki, circa 1950s (courtesy of Sasaki Associates, Inc.).

environment for working people in challenging economic situations. Eckbo was one of many landscape architects who contributed to the economic and social recovery of the nation through various public works projects ranging from the greenbelt new towns to the national parks and forests.

Modernists found inspiration in the works of the Brazilian Roberto Burle Marx (1909–1994) and the Mexican Luis Barragán (1902–1988). Modernism in landscape architecture arguably coalesced in the work of Hideo Sasaki (1919–2000) and Lawrence Halprin (b. 1916). As both student and teacher moving between the University of Illinois and Harvard, Sasaki defined landscape architecture during the 1950s. Through his San Francisco–based practice, Halprin's work reflected a free spirit that was in harmony with the 1960s. The work of both men returned in scope and scale to that established in the previous century by the Olmsteds—urban parks, new communities, campuses, and, increasingly, corporate headquarters (Fig. 18-20).

The Ecological Transition

During the 1960s, the way people viewed their relationship to the Earth changed fundamentally. Since World War II, the specter of nuclear destruction had clouded the future. In their quest to prevail in the arms race, the Soviet Union and the United States raced to the moon. Something unexpected happened. Images of the Earth

from space were transmitted to living room televisions and breakfast newspapers. On July 20, 1969, Neil Armstrong stepped on the moon and altered our view of Earth. From that barren orb, it became clear that the Earth is alive. Boundaries are human impositions. The world we inhabit is both fragile and beautiful.

Even before these images were broadcast, voices for protecting the Earth had been raised. Ado Leopold (1886–1948) urged people to view land as community, and Rachel Carson (1907–1964) demonstrated the dangers of poisoning our nest. To this chorus, Ian McHarg (1920–2001) chimed in with a demand that we "design with nature." His book with the same title provided a new theory for landscape architecture and altered other fields as well, notably planning, architecture, and the environmental sciences.

From his University of Pennsylvania base, McHarg's new approach married a traditional landscape architecture technique with contemporary concepts. Map overlays had been used by landscape architects since the time of the Olmsteds and Eliot. But McHarg suggested that such information should be collected in a systematic chronological order to reveal ecological interactions, relationships, and patterns (see the discussion of the layer-cake model in Chapter 26). Natural phenomena, such as climate and geology, influence processes like water flow and soil development, which in turn affect the location of plants and animals. McHarg suggested that by conducting such an ecological inventory of a place, opportunities and constraints on various possible land uses can be identified. The values of people living in the place can then be used to determine how these opportunities and constraints indicate a range of suitability for potential land use. This approach influenced how environmental impact assessments are undertaken and

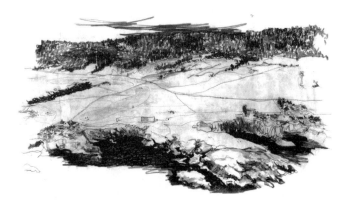

Figure 18-21 Lawrence Halprin's "Ecoscore" for Sea Ranch, California (The Architectural Archives, the University of Pennsylvania).

provides the underlying theory for geographic information systems (GIS). GIS is used for displaying, analyzing, and storing spatially related data in map overlays.

McHarg recognized that in order for human communities to take full advantage of ecological knowledge, a fundamental value shift was necessary, especially in Western nations. He argued that the Judeo-Christian philosophy of "multiplying and subduing the earth" has deleterious consequences for the environment. McHarg found hope in Native American and Asian religious beliefs, which stressed harmony with nature rather than dominance.

Future Prospects: Following Nature's Lead

The ecological revolution promulgated by McHarg at the University of Pennsylvania went beyond influencing techniques and technology. It advocated a fundamental shift in the way we design and plan. Ecology is the study of how all living creatures, including people, interact with each other as well as with their physical and biological environments. Such understanding is essential for sustainable development and regenerative design. **Ecological design** involves understanding the regional context in which humans live, recognition of natural limits and capacities, and an ability to build at an appropriate scale.

Landscape architects such as Andropogon in Philadelphia, Jones & Jones in Seattle, and Design Workshop in Colorado have continued to refine and advance McHarg's concepts of ecological design and planning (Figs. 18-22 to

Figure 18-23 Crosby Arboretum, Picayune, Mississippi, Ecological Plan by Andropogon Associates, pavilion design by architect Faye Jones (Photo by Ed Blake, courtesy of Andropogon Associates).

18-25). Iconoclastic practitioners such as A. E. Bye (1919–2001) in Connecticut, Jones & Jones and Rich Haag in Seattle, and Laurie Olin in Philadelphia have adopted a less empirical, more intuitive, yet still ecological approach to their work (Figs. 18-26, 18-27).

Figure 18-22 Andropogon Associates in a field of wild flowers, 1975 (Photo by A. Kobernick, courtesy of Andropogon Associates).

Figure 18-24 Jones & Jones Partnership, Seattle (photograph courtesy of Jones & Jones).

Figure 18-25 Grant Jones reviewing the design of one of the world's first landscape immersion exhibits, created by Jones & Jones for Seattle's Woodland Zoological Park (photograph courtesy of Jones & Jones).

Landscape architects are unique among artists and architects in that their media for creation are mostly living entities. They work with natural processes and materials, which is a complex undertaking. As the Roman architect Vitruvius observed in his second book on architecture, "all things are generated as the Nature of Things has determined, not for the pleasure of [people], but disparate as though by chance."

The need to understand the nature of places is basic to the art and science of landscape architecture. Ecology provides the language for reading landscapes and for gaining a sense of place. Such understanding leads to an appreciation of critical regionalism. Understanding the cultures of places is fundamental to such regionalism.

Figure 18-26 Gas Works—a historic industrial area now reanimated into one of Seattle's most popular parks (designed by Rich Haag).

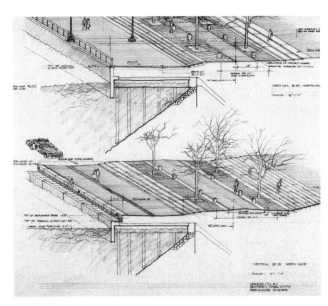

Figure 18-27 Alternative cross sections for New York City's Battery Park City esplanade and master plan by Hanna/Olin and Alexander Cooper Associates, 1980 (Olin Partnership).

Landscape architecture in the United States appears to be adaptable to many places internationally. Such internationalism is neither an international "style" nor a form of cultural imperialism; rather, it is a flexible approach, sensitive to cultural pluralism.

Landscape design was first recognized in the formal Moorish gardens of Spain and in the hillside Renaissance villas of Italy, as well as in the more informal contemplative places of China, Korea, and Japan. All the early examples represent cultural adaptations to climate and topography. The Italian style was expanded to grotesque proportions in the French Baroque and was then muted to the practical scale of the Dutch polders. The picturesque English landscape school leaped the formal garden wall and introduced landscape aesthetics to the city, the suburb, and the wilderness. Landscape architecture is now crossing continental divides and finding the importance of designing with nature throughout the world at every level of integration.

Acknowledgments

This chapter has been adapted from Frederick Steiner's essay "Landscape Architecture," which appeared in the *Encyclopedia of the Social and Behavioral Sciences*.[4] I appreciate the help with typing this manuscript provided by Mack White, as well as the illustrations by Pamela Peters. Illustrations were provided by Tom Bartuska,

Carol Franklin of Andropogon Associates, Pamela Morris of Jones & Jones, Marc Treib, Jusuck Koh, Sujeong Park, Ewa Kaliszuk, Mariusz Cieszewscy, Laurie Olin, Michele Clark of the Olmsted National Historic Site, and Emily Cooperman and Laura Stroffolino of the University of Pennsylvania Architectural Archives.

References

Alofsin, A. *The Struggle for Modernism: Architecture, Landscape Architecture, and City Planning at Harvard.* W. W. Norton, 2002.

Birnbaum C. (ed.). "Preserving Modern Landscape Architecture." Papers from the Wave Hill–National Park Service Conference. Spacemaker Press, 1999.

McHarg, I. *Design with Nature.* Natural History Press, 1969 (2nd ed. Wiley, 1992).

McHarg, I., and F. Steiner (eds.). *To Heal the Earth.* Island Press, 1998.

Newton, N. *Design On the Land: The Development of Landscape Architecture.* Belknap Press of Harvard University, 1971.

Olin, L. *Across the Open Field: Essays Drawn from English Landscape.* University of Pennsylvania Press, 2000.

Rybczynski, W. *A Clearing in the Distance: Frederick Law Olmsted and America in the Nineteenth Century.* Scribner, 1999.

Steenbegen, C., and W. Reh. *Architecture and Landscape: The Design Experiment of Great European Gardens and Landscapes.* Prestel, 1996.

Walker, P., and M. Simo. *Invisible Gardens: The Search for Modernism in the American Landscape.* MIT Press, 1994.

Watkin, D. *The English Vision: The Picturesque in Architecture, Landscape and Garden Design.* Harper and Row, 1982.

Endnotes

1. D. Watkin, *The English Vision: The Picturesque in Architecture, Landscape and Garden Design* (Harper and Row, 1982).

2. See Note 1.

3. A. Alofsin, *The Struggle for Modernism: Architecture, Landscape Architecture, and City Planning at Harvard* (W. W. Norton, 2002).

4. A. Weddle, *Techniques of Landscape Architecture.* (American Elsevier, 1967).

CHAPTER 19

Landscape Architecture Today: Purpose, Process, and Palette

Kenneth R. Brooks

Careful planning and design of the landscape provides a more useful and pleasant context for human activities. It improves the natural and built environments and enhances human safety, health, and enjoyment of that environment. Land planning and design is an intentional, conscientious process, carried out by landscape architects and other environmental designers/planners, to apply and integrate a wide range of science, art, and technology to improve the built environment.

The Purpose and Goals of Landscape Architecture

The purpose of landscape architecture is to provide the knowledge, inspiration, and experience necessary to bring people's interests and aspirations for the use of land together with the opportunities and limitations of the natural and built environments. When it is done well, this process creates a modified built environment in which people can live, work, and play in a manner that creates the greatest amount of enjoyment, safety, and value with the least amount of damage or pollution (Fig. 19-1). Planners and designers try to increase the

benefit/cost ratio of human-environmental relationships. The level of **health** and **fitness** between environment and human activities is increased when landscape architects, along with other designers and planners, are able to create more utility, enjoyment, and/or safety in the use of land and decrease the cost of development and environmental damage. As suggested in the definition of landscape architecture, landscape planners and designers do a variety of planning and design activities in their effort to improve the use of land and the management of environmental resources.

> Landscape Architecture encompasses the analysis, planning, design, management and stewardship of the natural and built environment.[1] It is a profession that deals with the science and art of modifying land areas by organizing natural, cultivated or constructed elements . . . requiring special knowledge, skill and experience relating to natural systems, physical processes and human relationships.[2]

By law, licensed landscape architects are required to make sure that their designs protect the health, safety, and welfare of the public.

Human activities in landscapes (such as housing and neighborhood developments, commercial and shopping

229

Figure 19-1 The San Antonio, Texas, Riverwalk is a designed landscape that provides a stimulating and aesthetically pleasing setting for a variety of outdoor activities (walking, shopping, eating at outdoor cafes, socializing, and entertainment) and forms an important part of the city's image. It also helps preserve historic properties and assists with stormwater management (W. Winslow).

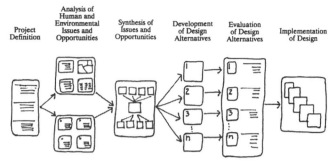

Figure 19-2 Diagram of important phases of a systematic/integrative design process.

areas, and recreation) are usually referred to as "land uses." Landscape architects apply their talents in designing these land use activities at a very wide range of scales, from a sitting area at a bus stop to huge resort developments or whole new cities or regional plans. Landscape architects are especially involved with design that addresses **sustainability**, security, and quality-of-living issues.

The Land Design Process

Landscape architects use many methods to plan and design projects. Their efforts are usually referred to as "the design process." The word "the" suggests only a single method or process, while in reality, there are many variations and approaches to the processes of landscape planning and design. The **design process** is usually broken up into several tasks that consider various issues of the project at hand. In spite of the variation in methods for landscape design, most share several similar characteristics. They are organized to be thorough, systematic, and ecologically sensitive to human and environmental issues, characteristics they also share with the other design disciplines. Figure 19-2 illustrates a general approach in the decision-making process for landscape planning and design projects.

Thoroughness in the design process is demonstrated when careful consideration is given to all of the possible environmental, cultural, functional, economic, and aesthetic factors that might influence the success of a project or its impact on the environment. Such a systematic and careful evaluation of a full range of parts and wholes as potential factors is often referred to as a **comprehensive** (or holistic) **ecological approach** to planning and design.

Systematic/Integrative Approaches to the Design Process

The systematic characteristics of landscape planning and design can be seen in the ways that professional consultants evaluate various human and environmental factors for a landscape design or planning project by breaking down broad areas of consideration into component parts. Hierarchy theory is often a useful tool in organizing these factors. An example of the orderly way in which landscape architects consider the whole and its parts is the use of ecological models. An ecological model of a project is created and then broken down into parts— processes and elements. **Ecological processes** are further broken down into subparts such as nutrient cycles and energy cycles, while ecological elements are subdivided into such subparts as geology, physiography, soils, hydrology, vegetation, and animals. Landscape architects often use checklists to make sure that they have systematically considered all of the major components, all of the human activities and interests, along with environmental options and constraints related to the project at hand. Environmental designers **analyze** these broad human-environmental issues, their subcomponents and the relationships, then **synthesize** them to arrive at the best alternatives for the design or plan. This holistic **analysis-synthesis** process is common to all design and planning fields.

Considering Human Needs and Values in Land Design

The planning process ideally focuses on human uses of and aspirations for the land. This part of the design process seeks to answer questions about client(s), user(s), and the ways in which they will use the land. The following are typical questions and issues considered as part of the human aspects of land design:

- Who will be using this land?
- What are their needs and desires?
- How will they use the land (are there primary and secondary uses)?
- Do users have identifiable cultural characteristics that should be accommodated in the design?
- What are the characteristics of the spaces that will be planned to meet the needs of users (such as number, size, function, nature of activities, and safety)?
- What is the relationship of the various land uses or activities within the project?
- Are there related technologies, utility, or support uses that will enhance the project?
- How can the special aesthetic qualities of the project be celebrated?
- How will the project's land use activities be affected by off-site influences and in turn affect off-site areas?
- Are there any potential environmental impacts anticipated from the project?

This kind of detailed, systematic analysis of users' and clients' needs and desires is often referred to by environmental designers as "project programming." In this part of the process, the designer considers all of the possible factors about the projected use of land and the probable users and develops recommendations for the best way to organize and accommodate users' interests and human needs.

Environmental Considerations in Design

Landscape architects and other design and planning professionals who are trained ecologically are advocates of environmental quality. As part of the land design process, they evaluate the landscape to determine its suitability and sustainability for proposed land use(s) and to assess their potential damage to ecosystems—either on or off the site. Landscape architects often take a lead in reducing environmental hazards and in making site design sustainable.[3]

On relatively small projects, most landscape architects conduct a "site analysis," a study of the environmental conditions of the site and their suitability for the project. For larger projects, landscape architects may conduct an extensive and intensive study of environmental conditions, and the suitability and potential impacts of the proposed project on local ecosystems. Large studies may be divided into several components: environmental conditions; a suitability analysis that evaluates the capabilities of the site to accommodate the various land uses that are or may be part of the project, or an **Environmental Impact Statement** (EIS) that evaluates the potential of a project to cause degradation or pollution of local ecosystems, as well as to propose means to mediate these environmental impacts. Some of the concerns and questions addressed in this type of analysis include the following:

- What is the ecological structure of this land, and what kinds of ecological processes naturally occur within it? A more detailed discussion of the analysis of the ecological process, that is, McHarg's layer-cake method, occurs in Chapter 26.
- What are the natural conditions of the land and its features (such as geology, slope, topography, soils, vegetation, animals, and climate), and how might these conditions limit the development of the proposed design project? Are there any endangered species, wildlife habitats, or corridors on site?
- What special environmental conditions of the land would be especially suitable for the proposed project? What is the carrying capacity of the ecosystem, that is, what intensities of human use can it absorb without a major disruption to the system?
- How would development of the proposed project impact the land's present ecosystem?
- How would development of this project impact other ecosystems on adjoining land?
- Would the development of this project create irreversible changes in the landscape or significant loss of nonrenewable resources?

Design Synthesis: A Search for Fitness

Landscape architects and ecologically oriented designers use holistic and comprehensive evaluations of the land, the users, and the probable project to prepare a variety of schematic alternative solutions that explore a range of ways in which the project program and the land could be brought together to accommodate the needs and interests of future users and the land's ecological systems. Designer(s) and client(s) must both evaluate the suitabil-

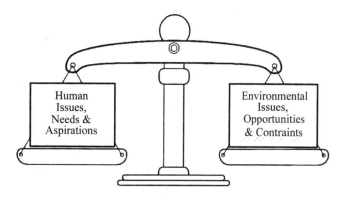

Figure 19-3   The goal of landscape planning and design is to integrate human interests and land conditions in balance and to create healthy and fit human-environmental land uses.

ity and potential impacts of alternatives and then select a design option that will lead to the best fit of user interests and environmental conditions. The strategy is to adapt the program (human aspects) and the site environment to each other in a manner that provides the greatest user utility, enjoyment, and safety with the greatest amount of environmental quality and sustainability—a goal of seeking balance (Fig. 19-3).

The Design Palette— The Materials/Elements/Spaces of Landscape Design

In the planning and design of built landscapes, the beauty and utility of a site may come as much or more from selection of materials as from the way they are arranged. Just as fine artists may use clay or ink to create their works, landscape architects have a large palette of materials available for use in the design of landscapes.

Other chapters in this book show the built environment to be made up of a large number of component levels (products, interiors, landscapes, structures, cities, regions, and the Earth) that come together to form human-environmental settings. The dynamic relationships between context and content have been used as a means of integrating these various levels. A similar application of this context/content method can be used to describe the design of built landscapes. Landscapes are usually perceived as areas where a variety of activities may occur or where one or more structures may be built. To understand the way a landscape is designed, one must take the whole and analyze it as a set of component parts.

A **landscape** can be viewed as made up of a number of individual spaces, much as a building is defined by its

various rooms and interior spaces. Individual **spaces** are components that come together within the context of a total built landscape, while each space can be seen at the same time as the context for its parts. In exterior spaces or landscapes, the elements that provide structure and organization—"walls, floors, and ceilings"—are created with hills, masses of plants, walls, paving, lawns, and other installations. Interior spaces are not only formed and defined, but are furnished and decorated with equipment to meet the functional and aesthetic intent of the designer. Exterior spaces can also be furnished and decorated to enhance interest and beauty. Landscape furnishings (called "street furniture") may include benches, trash containers, signs, lighting, and other equipment. Decorative components are **elements** that do not materially affect the use or structure of a space, but that add interest and enhance its character. These elements can be created in a wide variety of ways, such as with special patterns in the paving, decorative ironwork, or colorful plantings. Structural, furnishing, and decorative elements can be further analyzed by examining the **materials** from which they are formed.

As indicated in Figure 19-5, materials are put together to make up elements; elements are combined to form spaces, and spaces are organized to make the total built landscape. The concept of a **material-element-spaces-landscape hierarchy** diagrammed in Figure 19-5 uses the term "element," implying objects that are put together to create design spaces. We could also use the term "product" as a synonym in many of these discussions, and that term would be consistent with the discussion of product design elsewhere in this book. Benches, light bollards, and

Figure 19-4   A variety of materials (concrete, plants, water, and stone) are used to create elements (paving, seating, fountains, bollards, and plantings). The elements are combined to make spaces within a plaza (R. Forsyth).

(a)

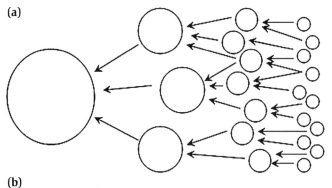

(b)

Landscapes	Spaces	Elements	Materials
A Designed Landscape	Spaces That Make Up the Landscape	Elements That Make Up the Spaces	Materials That Make Up the Elements
City	entry	signs, lighting	carved wood,
	parking	paving, signs, plantings	concrete, plants, wood, metals
Park	ball fields	structures, fences, furniture, plantings	concrete, wood, plants
	picnic area	benches, plantings, trash receptacles	wood, concrete, plants
	tot lot	play equipment, benches,	wood, steel, sand, plants,
	etc.	plants, etc.	etc.

Figure 19-5 (a and b) Diagram and examples of materials, elements, and spaces forming a landscape.

similar items can be interchangeably termed "designed products" or "elements." Some designers might use the term elements when referring to products that are built in place (such as paved surfaces, earth berms, or plantings).

Materials of Built Landscapes

To be able to design with the large variety of available materials, one must know and understand the inherent characteristics and properties of those materials, and how they relate and fit together. The materials of the landscape architect's palette are both natural and built.

They include such things as earth (soil), rocks, plants, wood, masonry, water, concrete, asphalt, and metals. Building materials have a variety of properties that determine their utility, beauty, and character in the landscape.

To understand the design potential of various materials, it is useful to explore the characteristics of building materials as shown in Table 19-1. Landscape architects must consider a large variety of visual (aesthetic), physical, and functional properties when selecting materials for built landscapes. The character and setting created within a landscape will strongly reflect the properties of the materials that make up that landscape. The fitness, quality, and character of landscapes are significantly influenced by the characteristics of the materials used in the design.

Designing a landscape with a large proportion of processed, modular, hard, or massive materials will give the resulting space a feeling of strong human control, commonly referred to as a **hardscape**. By contrast, if the designer creates a space or landscape dominated by natural, irregular, and/or soft materials, it will feel like a more natural landscape, commonly called a **softscape**.

Many people think of the landscape as made up primarily of **plant materials**, without considering the many other materials discussed in this chapter. Plants are not the only material, but they are a very important and useful material for landscape development. Trees, shrubs, and flowers not only contribute oxygen to the atmosphere (a basic human need) but also add beauty and make functional contributions to the fitness of landscapes. Designers often think of the uses and values of plant materials in five general ways: (1) architectural uses; (2) engineering uses, including maintenance and water use; (3) for climate modification; (4) aesthetic uses; and (5) other uses of landscape plant materials.[4]

Architectural use of plant materials means arranging plants for the purpose of creating spaces in a landscape. The engineering category includes the use of plants to solve technical environmental engineering problems in a landscape. The climate modification category includes the use of plants to change climatic conditions within a landscape. Aesthetic uses of plants are intended to appeal to the visual, olfactory, and intellectual senses. The fifth category, other uses, refers to additional uses that do not fit easily into one of the other categories.

Elements of Built Landscapes

In applying the context/content model of integrating levels in the built environment, the materials described in Table 19-1 can be combined to form various defining elements used in design of landscapes. For a further discus-

Table 19-1 Outline of Characteristics of Landscape Materials

CHARACTERISTICS	EXAMPLES

1. Physical Characteristics
  a. Origin
   • Natural
   • Processed
  b. Form (shape)
   • Modular or regular
   • Plastic or irregular
  c. Firmness (rigidity)
   • Hard
   • Soft
	
	• Plants, driftwood, rough timbers, native stone, flowing water, ponds, or lakes
	• Brick, tile, dimensioned lumber, cut stone, processed metals, water in fountains
	
	• Brick, dimensioned lumber, sheared hedges
	• Untrimmed plants, poured concrete, undulating landforms
	
	• Paving, fencing, architectural structures
	• Planting, flowing or languid water, fabric (banners, flags)

2. Visual Characteristics
  a. Color
   • Warm vs. cool colors
   • Bright vs. subdued colors
  b. Texture
   • Coarse vs fine textures
  c. Size
   • Large vs. small size
  d. Mass
   • Heavy vs. light mass
	
	• Red, yellow, and orange colors vs. blue, green, and lavender colors
	• Bright floral displays and painted surfaces vs. weathered or earth-toned surfaces
	
	• Large-leaved oaks vs. honey locusts with very small leaflets
	
	• Big oak tree vs. small dogwood tree
	
	• Solid block of granite for a bench vs. light wood for a bench

3. Functional Characteristics
  a. Utility
  b. Economic
  c. Dynamic vs. static
	• Material for a specific use, such as concrete used for paving
	• High-cost granite pavers vs. lower-cost asphalt paving
	• Static materials like stone vs. changing materials like plants

sion of design elements, see Chapter 7. A rich variety of elements can be used to create the "walls," "floors," "ceilings," and "furniture" of landscape spaces:

• Landforms
• Walls and fences
• Plantings
• Furniture
• Paving
• Lighting
• Terraces/decks
• Other structures

The floor, or ground plane, provides the base for human activities. Ground planes can be made from natural and processed materials such as earth, sod, or paving. Ceilings, often created by architectural coverings, by tree canopies or trellises, form the cover and protection for landscape spaces. Walls, made from plants, landforms, or architectural materials, create the vertical elements that mark the edges of spaces. They enclose and define spaces and subspaces.

Landforms are created by earth (soil and rock). They may be flat, rolling, or steep. Land provides the base for structures and for human activities. Flat and gently sloping areas usually provide the "base plane" for spaces in a landscape and serve the same function as a floor in a building. Steeper areas usually are perceived as boundaries for a space or as a transition between spaces.

Plantings are a very visible part of the landscape. In natural landscapes, plants form communities that interact with each other and with the environment. In the built environment, plants may be arranged singly, in groups, or in natural associations. Plants can serve a variety of uses in built landscapes, some of which are described in the last section of this chapter.

Paving is a very useful product in built landscapes. Paving materials are regularly used in places where there will be intense human activity, such as pedestrian or vehicular circulation. Paving may be designed as linear elements (like walks or roads) to accommodate traffic or as cover for larger areas (such as malls, plazas, and terraces). Its materials not only provide the structural support necessary for intense activity, but can also be used

Figure 19-6 A pastoral setting is created with generous use of plant materials. An irregular stone path adds to the casual nature of the space. Even the deliberate use of light and shadow adds to the mystery and interest of the space (R. Forsyth).

to define spaces and subspaces within a landscape. Paving can also direct people through a landscape or provide places where they can gather. Detailed changes in paving can provide direction and orientation, as well as additional visual interest.

Figure 19-8 Color in the paving pattern organizes the spaces in this plaza. Firmness and durability create a surface that can support intensive pedestrian activity. Plant materials help define subspaces within the plaza (R. Forsyth).

Terraces/decks are very similar to paving in that they provide a base plane for activity. They are often somewhat different from the harder paving materials in that they are usually suspended above the surface and are usually made of wood or other softer material. Although they may be placed in the middle of a public space, they are more likely designed as auxiliary space adjoining a building.

Walls and fences have a very powerful effect on landscapes because of their vertical position and processed nature. Vertical elements are quite visible because they contrast with the dominant horizontal nature of most landscapes and with the base plane. Just as walls in a building are clear definers of interior space, vertical elements in a landscape signal the end of one

Figure 19-7 Hard materials are used to create paving and sitting walls. Earth berms and plant materials soften and help subdivide the plaza (R. Forsyth).

Figure 19-9 Elements making up this space include balustrades, fountains, benches, paving, hedges, tree rows, and lighting (T. Bartuska).

space and the start of another. Walls can be transparent, such as a series of pillars or trees, or they can be solid and opaque. The exterior wall of a building can also serve as a wall for the exterior space adjacent to it. Besides serving as edges of spaces and as screens, some walls, with landfill behind them, provide a transition in topography.

Furniture, known as "street furniture" to landscape architects, serves several functions in a built landscape. Just as it may enhance the utility of interior spaces, furniture can be selected and arranged to meet the needs of people using a landscape. Benches, chairs, tables, trash receptacles, water fountains, signs, lights, and other furnishings are intended to provide for such needs as sitting, trash disposal, wayfinding, and similar functions to improve the comfort, utility, and attractiveness of a site for users. Furniture can be used to separate two spaces or to subdivide areas within one space. It can add interest and help determine the character of a space through the expression of materials used, their style, and their placement in a landscape.

Examples of Plant Material Used in Designed Landscapes

Architectural Uses of Plants

- Defining spaces with walls, floors, and ceilings created by plants
- Controlling views and framing vistas
- Creating screening for privacy or to eliminate an undesirable view
- Marking the location of an entry or a pathway
- Creating groupings to create linkages or connections between other elements

Environmental Engineering Uses of Plants

- Reducing glare and screening unwanted light
- Controlling and/or directing traffic
- Reducing soil erosion and protecting the soil surface
- Intercepting rainfall, slowing runoff, and directing drainage
- Reducing wind flow
- Absorbing and reducing noise
- Absorbing and reducing air pollution

Climatological Modification Uses of Plants

- Temperature modification by the cooling action of plants
- Modification of relative humidity through evapotranspiration

- Retaining daytime heat and preventing nighttime loss within the tree canopy
- Channeling air movement for ventilation
- Trapping static air around buildings with plants for insulation

Aesthetic Uses of Plants

- Creating visual interest through color, form, texture, and movement of plants
- Adding attractive and pleasant fragrances
- Creating special interest or attention with highly visible plantings
- Influencing the mood of the landscape through color and texture

Other Uses of Plants

- Wildlife habitat
- Food value (for humans and wildlife)
- Educational values
- Recreational values
- Historical and social values
- Economic good such as building materials, fuels

Space Components of Landscapes

The next level of context/component integration in built landscapes is the combination of elements—landforms, plantings, paving, decks, walls, fences, furniture, and others—to form space. Space is the primary product of the landscape architect. It is the ultimate component of the media of landscape design, because it is in space that

Figure 19-10 Trees serve as columns in a wall to define the principal vertical division of space. Other plantings provide spatial separation and enclosure. The tree canopy provides shading from summer sun, and the turf contributes to cooling and humidification (R. Forsyth).

Figure 19-11   A slope next to a tennis court becomes a sitting space in Luther Burbank Park in Seattle, Washington. It is designed with hard materials as a series of sitting walls and steps. Tree plantings help to provide vertical elements to separate sitting spaces from the tennis court.

buildings are built and human activities occur. Space is not the void that is left after all of the materials have been installed. It is the positive commodity created by design. Materials and elements are designed to define space.

Spaces are usually classified according to their uses. People think about landscape spaces in terms of their intended uses, and they usually define these spaces by those uses before they think of the qualities that make any one space different from other spaces. It is the way spaces are used that gives them their value. Uses may be active (such as circulation or recreation) or passive (such as sitting or viewing).

Common spaces found in the built environment (although not all necessarily in the same landscape) include entries, playing fields, playgrounds, malls, courtyards, plazas, sitting areas, patios, circulation systems, gardens, and open space. This is not intended to be an exhaustive list of possible landscape spaces, but rather to suggest some common ones.

The nature of landscape spaces in the built environment can be explored by looking at their inherent properties in much the same manner used to compare the properties of landscape materials. Spatial definition is one of the properties of a built landscape space: Where are the boundaries of a space? How strong and definite are they? Is the space easy to perceive as a space or is it rather informally delineated? The form or shape of a space makes a big difference in the character and the use of that space. Spaces with specific edges give better definition to the activities for which they were designed. The more formal or geometric the shape, the greater the affinity with a more rigidly controlled environment; the more informal, picturesque, and organic, the greater the affinity with nature.

The firmness of a space, like the firmness of building materials, is a measure of how hard or how soft the materials are that define its character. Hardscape spaces are suited for more intense activity, while softer materials enhance feelings of relaxation and casual activity. Some activities require a solid base plane, while others are better suited to a softer, more relaxed environment.

Landscape architects plan spaces to serve a variety of uses, but once the project has been built, the characteristics of landscape spaces influence the kinds of activities or uses that occur there. Each activity (such as walking, driving, sitting, playing softball, getting a drink, collecting trash, or delivering the mail) has its own needs in terms of size, form, and characteristics. Some spaces require such specialized design that other activities cannot be well accommodated. Other areas can be designed to accommodate a variety of activities. Landscape activi-

Figure 19-12   The Capitol Mall in Madison, Wisconsin, is a streetscape project that provides a major urban link between the University of Wisconsin campus and the state capitol grounds. Vehicular and pedestrian circulation, sitting, gathering, and display spaces make up the mall.

ties can be classified as active (such as playgrounds or entrance areas for major public buildings) or passive (such as gardens, sitting areas, or patios). Designers carefully analyze various user activities, and organize or zone spaces to separate incompatible activities and to integrate complementary uses. Integration of similar activities may be accomplished by arranging complementary spaces next to or near each other while separating or buffering incompatible activity spaces. A major part of the design process in such cases involves analyzing the relationship of one activity space with each of the others in a landscape design.

The character and organization of a space—the way it feels, the way it influences our senses—is a large part of the art and science of landscape architectural design. Designers are interested in creating spaces that not only work well (functionally and ecologically), but also stimulate human users physically, psychologically, and emotionally. Such properties are the special defining characteristics that one should consider when designing and integrating materials into elements, elements into spaces, and spaces into total landscapes.

Conclusion

A wide variety of ways can be found to evaluate the design of landscapes in the built environment. The holistic landscape can be subdivided into spaces, the spaces into elements, and the elements into materials. It should be clear that the organizational structure of a landscape, its use and function, and its character, beauty, and per-

Figure 19-14 The Cannery in San Francisco, California, is an example of a hardscape where the landscape architect has used materials, design elements, and landscape spaces to provide a stimulating environment for shopping and socializing.

sonality, result from careful consideration and combination of materials, elements, and spaces. The process in which landscape architects use materials to create elements that define spaces is systematic and comprehensive. A comprehensive ecological process and design palette can harmoniously bring together human needs and aspirations with natural land opportunities to improve the interrelationships between environments and human life.

In the coming years, population will continue to rise, natural resources will be strained by consumption, and people's quality of life will continue to be challenged by human/social/cultural, environmental, and technology issues. Landscape architects and other designers of the

Figure 19-13 Constitution Plaza in Hartford, Connecticut, is made up of refined circulation and sitting spaces and subdivided with mounds and plantings in raised planters (R. Forsyth).

Figure 19-15 The Japanese Garden in Golden Gate Park in San Francisco, California, is a softscape with a rich variety of materials, elements, and spaces that enhance urban life and provide a dramatic contrast to the bustling character of the dense city around it.

built environment must be able to use their skills and knowledge to create livable communities with quality spaces that have a good fit with the natural world and are functional, aesthetic, and sustainable.

Additional information about landscape architects and the issues they are concerned about can be found on the Internet at the Web site of the American Society of Landscape Architects.[5] A Google™ search of the Web for "landscape architecture" will generate over 75 million other Web site hits.

References

ASLA. American Society of Landscape Architects, 2006: www.asla.org.

Booth, N. *Basic Elements of Landscape Architectural Design*. Elsevier, 1990.

Furgeson, B. *Introduction to Stormwater*. Wiley, 1998.

Kirkwood, N. *The Art of Landscape Detail*. Wiley, 1998.

LAG. Landscape Architectural Guide, 2006: www.gardenvisit.com/landscape/LIH/history/definitions.

Laurie, M. *An Introduction to Landscape Architecture*. Elsevier, 1986.

Lyle, J. *Design for Human Ecosystems: Landscape, Land Use, Natural Resources*. Van Nostrand, 1985.

Pierceall, G. *Sitescapes: Outdoor Rooms for Outdoor Living*. Prentice Hall, 1990.

Potteiger, M., and J. Purinton. *Landscape Narratives: Design Practices for Telling Stories*. Wiley, 1998.

Robinette, G. D. (compiler). "Plants, People and Environmental Quality." U.S. National Park Service in collaboration with the American Society of Landscape Architects Foundation, 1972.

Thompson, J., and K. Sorvig. *Sustainable Landscape Construction: A Guide to Green Building Outdoors*. Island Press, 2000.

Endnotes

1. ASLA (American Society of Landscape Architects), 2006: www.asla.org.
2. LAG (Landscape Architectural Guide), 2006: www.gardenvisit.com/landscape/LIH/history/definitions.
3. B. Furgeson, *Introduction to Stormwater* (Wiley, 1998) and J. Thompson and K. Sorvig, *Sustainable Landscape Construction: A Guide to Green Building Outdoors* (Island Press, 2000).
4. G. D. Robinette (compiler), "Plants, People and Environmental Quality" (U.S. National Park Service in collaboration with the American Society of Landscape Architects Foundation, 1972).
5. See Note 1.

CHAPTER 20

Comparative Campus Design and Planning

Phillip S. Waite

A community campus, whether a college, corporate, or civic campus, is a distinctive form in the built environment. Campus planning combines multiple environmental design and planning disciplines in such a way that the whole is greater than the sum of its parts. Although a campus deals with many of the same issues that affect cities, it often has many of the positive attributes of an urban environment without many of the negative aspects. This chapter examines various types of campuses and campus planning concepts, looking for lessons that can be applied by designers to improve the built environment of our cities.

Introduction to Campus Planning

Campus planning is a unique endeavor, combining many design and planning disciplines. A campus is a unique community with an integration or synergy between the whole and the parts. Various types of campus planning and design, and their lessons, can be translated into the design and planning of other community and urban settings.

The word "campus" comes from the Italian word *campo,* which means country or field.[1] In North America, the original use of the word referred to the grounds of a school or university. This stems from the fact that the first colleges and universities were simply a building or group of buildings around a central grassy field. Over time, the term came to include not just the grounds, but also the buildings and all the interconnected voids and interstitial spaces of the landscape between the buildings.[2] Current usage of the term has further expanded beyond the combination of the grounds and buildings of a school, college, or university. It now includes a variety of settings such as corporate campuses, business "parks," office complexes, medical complexes, civic centers, recreational and entertainment parks, and even Olympic sports villages.[3]

There are two critical and related concepts that are vital to our understanding of campus design and planning. The first is that campus represents more than just buildings and more than just the grounds or landscape. It represents a whole that is greater than the sum of its parts. Like most community environments, a campus consists of special fabric woven from the strands of landscape, buildings, and the activities that occur therein. This stands in contrast to the way we usually conceptualize and experience our environments. We tend to segregate inside environments from outside environments as well as corresponding experiences. When we think of a residence, we think of the house or the yard, but we rarely conceive of them as one integrated whole. The Italian word *villa,* like campus, carries this distinctive

Figure 20-1 A quadrangle at Stanford University, California.

connotation, referring to the place as a whole—not to either house or grounds alone but to the total complex seen and experienced as a single unit.[4]

The second and perhaps more important concept in understanding campus planning is that a campus is also an **ideal community**.[5] When first founded, many institutions of higher education were viewed as the means of promoting utopian and democratic social visions. The campus was more than a collection of buildings; it included an entire community of those who voluntarily joined together in pursuit of knowledge and social change. Thomas Jefferson, in designing the University of Virginia, described his goal as the creation of an "academical village"—an ideal democratic community of scholars.[6] Some have argued that well-designed campuses, as ideal communities, serve as both "role model and antidote for society."[7] This is because a campus is a microcosm of a city. Campus planning is, in essence, a subset of urban planning. Campuses, as microcosms of our cities, feature the same elements and the same issues as cities. Like urban planning, campus planning integrates many diverse disciplines: interiors and interior design, architecture, landscape architecture, transportation planning, engineering, infrastructure and utility planning, politics, economics, sociology, ecology, and psychology, just to name a few. Generally speaking, campuses accomplish this integration of disciplines more

effectively than do our cities. It is important to realize that lessons learned anywhere in the built environment can have application elsewhere in design and planning. Lessons learned in planning campuses can be translated into the larger discipline of urban planning and design. But before we look at some of the lessons that they have to teach about the built environment, let's compare and contrast college, corporate, and civic campuses with a typical urban environment. Such an analysis will highlight the unique characteristics and qualities of each environment.

Comparing Campus Communities

The following discussion of the various types of campus environments is, of necessity, one of generalities. Exceptions and examples that contradict each statement readily abound. But for the most part, these considerations hold true. The following discussion compares and contrasts campuses in light of several analytical categories: human and social issues, environmental issues, technical issues, and design issues.

College Campuses

Education is the purpose of a college campus. Its mission and focus is on learning. Obviously, the average age of those populating a college campus varies, depending on whether it is a community college, a rural residential college, an urban college, or a university. Regardless of the average age of persons at an institution, the largest demographic cohort is usually a relatively homogeneous group of mainly students between 18 and 24 years old. Factors affecting the planning and design of campuses include politics and the long tradition of shared governance in higher education. Commerce and business play little role in planning and design. Most institutions are "owned" by a single entity such as a government, a religious organization, or a private entity. The students, faculty, and staff use the grounds of a campus for circulation, socialization, recreation, and both formal and informal learning. Many campuses, especially residential campuses, operate 24 hours a day. Though many students, faculty, and staff may arrive on campus by walking, bike, mass transit, or vehicle, once there, most move around campus on foot. The architectural style on most campuses is fairly uniform, reflecting a unity of scale, design, materials, fenestration, roofs, and detailing. Architecture on campuses tends to be oriented and designed to a human scale and for human needs. All

Figure 20-2   Landscape and buildings at the University of California, Berkeley.

these aspects suggest lessons for the built environment, especially cities.

Corporate Campuses

The mission and purpose of a corporate campus is to increase the enterprise's profitability. The focus of much of campus planning in this case is efficiency, but with a heavy emphasis on corporate image and reputation. The population using a corporate campus is the employees. Their demographics, while broader than those of the population of a college campus, are still somewhat homogeneous, with most employees falling within the 25 to 55 age range. In the corporate setting, organizational politics and the employees have little input into the design result. Rather, design decisions are authorized by corporate governance (e.g., the owner, chief executive officer, or corporate boards) and based on business goals. Corporate ownership plays a major role as well in influencing planning and design decisions. The landscape in a corporate campus is used primarily for circulation between facilities. Some corporate campuses include site amenities such as water features and recreational amenities like jogging trails. But unlike a college campus, where activities occur throughout the day and night seven days per week, most of the activities on a corporate campus occur within a narrower day time frame (e.g., 8 A.M. to 5 P.M., Monday to Friday). The mode of transportation on a corporate campus is primarily pedestrian, although employees may arrive at the site by private vehicle or mass transit. Most corporate campuses have a comprehensive plan that guides the design of the buildings and grounds.[8] This means that

there is often a high level of uniformity in the architecture and in the landscape across the campus. If manufacturing is occurring on a corporate campus, some buildings may be more focused on the needs of machines rather than people.[9]

Civic Centers

In a civic center, the mission is to support civic life. The types of buildings and elements in a civic center include city halls, libraries, museums, law enforcement, administrative/office functions, legislative buildings, performing arts, and monuments or memorials. The focus is on image, often monumentality, and the ongoing life and activities of the community. Civic center users are heterogeneous demographically, consisting of a healthy mix of ages, ethnicities, races, abilities, and gender. The campus landscape is used for circulation, socialization, regular activities, and special events. In most instances, a civic center operates 10 to 12 hours a day, including weekends, with special events extending the hours of operation. Factors affecting planning and design include politics and governance, but usually not commerce. And of course, the civic campus is owned by a single, albeit public, entity. Modes of transportation on a civic campus include walking and bicycle, but also mass transit and automobiles. The design styles are generally uniform but can be mixed. The design of civic centers is usually focused on ceremonial and monumental forms, out of scale with the individual but appropriate when viewed and experienced as the embodiment of a community's aspirations and ideals.

Figure 20-3   The Jefferson Memorial on the capital "campus" of Washington, DC.

Figure 20-4   San Francisco's City Hall campus.

Urban Campus Environments

In contrast to all of these is the urban environment, which typically includes residential, educational, recreational, and entertainment uses. A major difference is that commercial development usually drives the form of urban environments. The demographics of a typical urban environment are, like that of a civic center, heterogeneous, embracing the full range of ages, races, abili-

Figure 20-5   Mixed and uneven architectural character in Boston, Massachusetts.

ties, and socioeconomic status. The open landscape of urban environments, unless planned as recreational space (a park) or specifically designed as a public open space (plazas, courtyards, etc.), is the interstitial space left between buildings and dominated by streets and alleys. Thus, most open space in urban areas is used for circulation. While pedestrians, bicyclists, and public mass transit should be emphasized in transportation planning, it is unfortunate when the private automobile dominates most transportation in cities. The variety of designs in urban areas is uneven, mixed, and eclectic, spanning as it does broad stylistic eras. In urban areas, the focus of architecture is mixed as well, some being focused on people, others on corporate images or machines. Perhaps the most telling aspect of quality in urban areas is the orientation and priority given to the pedestrian compared to the automobile. The best communities emphasize pedestrians, while the worst design for automobiles. Factors influencing planning and design include, to a minor degree, politics and governance. The major influences on planning and design, however, are commerce and ownership. The influence of commerce on the visual environment cannot be overstated. Advertising and signage alone dominate many visual environments. Lastly, in urban areas capital is owned by multiple entities, some public and some private. This factor alone explains why the typical urban environment stands in such sharp contrast to campus-type environments.

Table 20-1 summarizes the previous discussion comparing and contrasting the different types of campuses.

Lessons in Campus Design and Planning

Now that we have, however briefly, defined the distinctive qualities and characteristics of each type of campus community and how they contrast with one another and with a typical urban environment, what are the lessons that a good college campus can teach us about the design of other campuses? Further, what knowledge and human, environmental, and technical understanding can be translated into the design and planning of other community and urban environments?

It should be noted that most campuses in the United States began with a comprehensive plan to guide physical development. Many campuses adhered to their plans as they developed over time. Some campuses built their historic core according to a comprehensive plan and have since sprawled incrementally beyond their compact and

Table 20-1 Comparative Campus Planning

ISSUES:	COLLEGE CAMPUS	CORPORATE CAMPUS	CIVIC CENTER	TYPICAL URBAN ENVIRONMENT
Human/Social Issues • Focus/mission • Demographics • Control and ownership	• Education and learning • 18–26 students • Single entity: the institution itself	• Profit and image • 25 to 55 employees • Single entity: the corporation	• Civic life and image • 0–100 citizens • Single, but a public entity	• Business and profit • 0–100 citizens • Multiple entities, both public and private
Environmental Issues • Site/landscape uses	• Circulation, socialization, and learning	• Circulation	• Circulation, socialization, and events	• Circulation, socialization, and business
Technical Issues • Modes of transportation • Hours of operation	• Pedestrian, bike, and vehicle • 24 hours/day	• Pedestrian • 12 hours/day	• Vehicle, transit, pedestrian, and bike • 12 hours/day	• Vehicle, transit, pedestrian, and bike • 24 hours/day
Design/Planning Issues • Design styles • Design/planning focus	• Usually uniform • Focus on humans	• Usually uniform • Focus on production	• Often uniform, at times uneven • Focus mixed: monumental or ceremonial	• Uneven and mixed • Focus mixed: tendency to orient to the automobile

identifiable core. Others simply took their plan as a starting point but grew in an ad hoc, unstructured way. More buildings were built on campuses in the United States between 1950 and 1975 than in the prior 200 years.[10] It was during this postwar explosion of construction that many campuses lost much of the coherence and architectural consistency that had marked their previous existence.[11] Nevertheless, many campuses are trying to retain the characteristics that have marked them as special places, and they remain worthy examples for our study.

The following discussion examines four patterns or principles of planning and design evident on noteworthy campuses. No doubt there are other lessons to be learned as well, especially as they pertain to pedestrianization, transportation, automobiles, the integration of residential and mixed land uses, and the importance of adaptable utility infrastructures. But these four stand out as vital to the overall experience of a campus as a unique and distinct type of environment. The lessons are:

• The importance of the landscape and positive exterior space
• Architectural continuity and coherence
• Edges, entrances, and centers
• Pedestrian orientation

The Importance of the Landscape and Positive Exterior Space

On the classic campus, the landscape is accorded as much respect as the buildings, and buildings are subordinate to the spaces in which they participate.[12] This results from the knowledge that a campus is more than just buildings and their rooms. It is also the rational organization of outdoor spaces and all they include. The campus landscape is the matrix or fabric that holds the buildings together.[13] The experience of a campus includes all of the exterior spaces around buildings, both those that are planned and designed and those that are simply leftover, unplanned spaces. The landscape of a campus—its quadrangles, planted areas and lawns, plazas, courtyards, and recreational fields—is critical to the everyday experience of place. Several authors have noted the importance of the landscape in the experience of place, and these observations hold true for campus landscapes as well.[14] The best campuses exhibit this holistic understanding of the importance of the landscape and express it through simplicity of design. The classic campus landscape in the United States is primarily just mowed lawns and large trees. This simplicity of design enhances longevity and ease of maintenance—

Figure 20-6   The trees and lawn of Harvard University at Cambridge, Massachusetts.

Figure 20-7   A landscaped courtyard at the University of Texas, Austin.

the perennial budgetary challenge of campuses. There are, of course, ecological factors that must be taken into consideration, and this park-like model of grass and trees is not universally appropriate. But the notion of simplicity of design is universally appropriate. It's been said that the art of campus design is primarily one of shaping spaces, not decorating them. Well-designed campuses are composed of both site materials and plant materials that will endure for many generations.[15] Positive exterior space can be defined as an outdoor space with a distinct and definite shape. The greater the sense of enclosure, the greater the sense of **positive space**.[16]

The edges of the space can be defined by buildings or landscape elements or both. Without a sense of enclosure, space seems to bleed out at the perimeter. The best campuses have a hierarchy of outdoor spaces from small to large. There are five different spatial types in outdoor spaces on a campus.[17] The smallest is a patio, followed by, in increasing order of size, a courtyard, quadrangle, lawn, commons or green, and fields. The predominant characteristic of those spaces is that they have a significant level of enclosure—they have positive space. These campus spaces are thought of as outdoor rooms in which buildings and landscape borders are the walls, lawns and walkways the floor, and trees and sky the ceiling.[18]

The lessons to be learned for cityscapes are (1) the primacy of buildings and the landscape in shaping space; (2) the necessity of positive exterior space of varying scales; and (3) that simplicity of design can often be more enduring and effective than overdesigning.

Architectural Continuity and Coherence

One of the hallmarks of a campus as a unique type of built environment is the visual coherence and harmony of its architecture. While there may be stylistic differences, there is usually a consistency in the scale of architecture, the type and use of materials, fenestration, roof design, and detailing. Thus, regardless of building type or building style, there remains a continuity of design language and expression. Further, this harmonious quality has been maintained through time.

One of its [a campus's] most important qualities is a peculiar state of equilibrium between change and continuity. As a community, it is like a city, complex and inevitably subject to growth and change, and it therefore cannot be viewed as a static architectural monument. But it is not exactly like a city; it requires a special kind of physical coherence and continuity.[19]

Figure 20-8 An older building at the University of Colorado, Boulder.

That required **coherence and continuity** are best articulated in the architecture of the campus. The lesson for urban settings is that much could be gained by more harmony and coherence in design qualities within the community, or at the least the avoidance of jarring and discordant contrasts.

Edges, Entrances, and Centers

Three patterns of design that include edges, entrances, and centers, are all linked. A good campus exhibits all three to varying degrees. All three are critical to the definition of a campus as a distinct and special place. Clear edges delineate the boundary of the place and define the need for access (i.e., a recognizable entrance). Recognizable entrances define and celebrate access to the place. An identifiable center acts as a device for orienting movement and creating a sense of gravitational integrity to hold the community together as a special and distinct place. Campuses that have been most effective in establishing themselves as distinct physical entities within their surrounding contexts have done so by having clear edges. Sometimes that edge is an actual physical barrier, such as the gated wall that surrounds parts of Harvard University. Other campus communities, especially those built in rural areas, demark their boundaries with defined areas of development (a green belt) and/or landscape maintenance. In urban settings, edges may be defined by distinctions in style or scale. However, the clarity of a boundary is essential to defining a campus, neighborhood, or city.[20] The campus cannot maintain its

Figure 20-9 A newer building at the University of Colorado, Boulder, using many of the same forms and materials as older buildings on that campus.

own definable character if its edge is ill-defined. That said, it is also important to have some edges that are ambiguous. Campuses often grow incrementally, and the edge where they expand into the neighboring context is often a rich, lively, and dynamic area supporting a wide array of land uses and functions that sustain both on-campus and off-campus activities. Developing clear

Figure 20-10 A portion of the wall and gated entrance to Harvard University at Cambridge, Massachusetts.

Figure 20-11 The east "gateway" to the University of Idaho.

edges and growth boundaries for cityscapes would at least slow, if not inhibit, unmitigated urban sprawl.

The pattern of recognizable entrances goes hand in hand with having clear edges. At some point, the edges of campuses must be penetrated to provide access. Rather than simply acknowledging that access must occur somewhere, the best campuses (and neighborhoods, communities, and cities) celebrate those penetrations by creating gateways and recognizable entrances. Recognizable entrances notify newcomers that they have indeed arrived and are welcomed at their destination. Creating a sense of arrival also provides visual and psychological cues that help differentiate between on-campus and off-campus behaviors. The recognizable entry clarifies that one has now entered a special place, a place different from the surrounding context. "A gateway can have many forms: a literal gate, a bridge, a passage

Figure 20-12 The "center" of the University of Virginia campus.

between narrowly separated buildings, an avenue of trees, a gateway through a building. All of these have the same function: they mark the point where a path crosses a boundary and help maintain the boundary."[21] Most of our urban communities would benefit from clear edges and recognizable entrances beyond the prosaic highway sign that informs arrival by designating the exit number for an off-ramp.

Most campuses have an identifiable center. Campuses without an identifiable center lack a sense of place— "there is no there there."[22] In contrast, "most of the finest campuses have a definable center—such as the famous lawn at the University of Virginia—a place where, if someone says to meet him or her 'at the center of [the] campus,' no further explanation is necessary."[23] Often this central space, whether quad, lawn, courtyard, or plaza, is acknowledged with an architectural landmark as well. These places are the crossroads of the campus. Sometimes a campus has multiple centers: an emotional and ceremonial center, a historical center, and a social center. In the best campuses, these are all combined into one space and that space creates enough "gravitational force to hold the entire institution together."[24] A similar sentiment has been expressed regarding city centers: a well-defined center and a compact core can give coherence to a whole built environment.[25]

Pedestrian Orientation

The most memorable campuses, like communities, should have a pedestrian orientation. A pedestrian orientation is created in three ways. The first two deal with scale, and the third deals with amenities. The first scale is a horizontal scale. On most campuses, academic buildings are grouped within a walking distance circumscribed by a circle with a diameter between 300 and 450 meters (1,000 and 1,500 feet or one-fourth of a mile). This is the distance that most people feel comfortable walking between classes or from a transit stop or parking lot to a class. When campuses grow past this size, they tend to be grouped like buildings in "quads" or precincts so that students with a given major can stay within walking distance of the majority of their classes. Recently, transit-oriented developments and new urbanist town planning have identified the same approximate distances for a pedestrian scale and orientation.

The second scale in a pedestrian orientation is a vertical scale. A vertical scale is perhaps more important than a horizontal scale. Traditional campus environments have limited the height of architecture to between four and six stories. One campus planner and architect has

Figure 20-13 The clock tower "center" at the University of British Columbia, Vancouver, Canada.

stated, "the style of the campus building is important; but style is not so important as the village-like atmosphere of all buildings and their contained spaces. . . . **Scale, not style, is the essential element in good cam-**

Figure 20-15 Pedestrian-scaled patio outside the student union building at the University of Texas, Austin.

pus design."[26] A four-story limit is the ideal height for maintaining a pedestrian scale.[27]

The last element of a pedestrian orientation is the presence of site amenities that support the pedestrian experience. Examples include plenty of benches, drinking fountains, public phones, sculpture and art, shaded walks, and informal gathering places. The lesson to be learned for cityscapes is that regardless of the stated intent of a campus, neighborhood, or city to be pedestrian-oriented, the absence of these amenities results in an environment that is less than friendly to the pedestrian. Pedestrians will especially use environments that have a

Figure 20-14 A major pedestrian walkway at the University of California, San Diego.

Figure 20-16 This built-in seat at a building edge is an example of what once was, but is no longer, a pedestrian amenity at the Berklee College of Music, Boston, Massachusetts.

pedestrian scale and spaces with the physical amenities that support a vibrant pedestrian experience.

Conclusion: Mirror or Lantern?

A metaphor sometimes used to explore literature and other design disciplines is that of a mirror or lantern. Some view the purpose of design as holding up a mirror to society, reflecting the best and worst of contemporary culture. As a mirror, design cannot show potentials but can only expose **what is**. Others argue that the purpose of design is to function like a lantern that lights the way in the darkness. Rather than merely reflecting what is, like a mirror, the lantern shows **what can be** and what potentials might be realized. As a subset of urban planning, campus planning and design that functions as a mirror misses the mark. It reflects in microcosm the larger macro issues and problems but doesn't provide answers. We ought rather to conceive of planning and design as a lantern that leads the way, providing not a reflection of society, but rather a guide and model for what is possible in the design of successful communities and urban places.

> To visualize the potential unity, order, and richness of the . . . environment, which is now so tragically marred by disunity, disorder and poverty, one must go to our more handsome colleges and universities. For it is on the campus, as virtually nowhere else in the country, that architectural permanence, rational organization of diverse activities, generous provision of open space, liberal respect for the arts and sciences, and—in some ways most significant of all—freedom from the automobile and from advertising, can be seen acting together to provide an organic milieu for civilized life . . . the campus, at its finest, embodies principles of design which may be fruitfully employed throughout our civilization. . . . [28]

Although some might quibble with the above description of a campus as a locale for "civilized life," the point is, nevertheless, well taken. A campus, when viewed and designed as a whole, coherent, and ideal community, does have the potential to inform design efforts elsewhere in the built environment.

References

Alexander, C., et al. *A Pattern Language*. Oxford University Press, 1977.

Carr, S., et al. *Public Space*. Cambridge University Press, 1992.

Chapman, M. P. "Social Change and American Campus Design," *Planning for Higher Education*, March 1994.

Dober, R. *Campus Architecture: Building in the Groves of Academe*. McGraw-Hill, 1996.

Kaplan, R., and S. Kaplan. *The Experience of Nature: A Psychological Perspective*. Cambridge University Press, 1989.

Lang, J. *Creating Architectural Theory: The Role of the Behavioral Sciences in Environmental Design*. Van Nostrand Reinhold, 1987.

Lang, J. *Urban Design: The American Experience*. Van Nostrand Reinhold, 1994.

Newton, N. *Design on the Land: The Development of Landscape Architecture*. Harvard University Press, 1971.

Polyzoides, S. "On Campus-Making in America." In *Campus and Community*. Rockport Publishers, 1997.

Rush, S., and S. Johnson. "The Decaying American Campus: A Ticking Timebomb." American Association of Physical Plant Administrators, 1988.

Sensbach, W. "Restoring the Values of Campus Architecture," *Planning for Higher Education*, January 1991.

Temko, A. *No Way to Build a Ball Park and Other Irreverent Essays on Architecture*. Chronicle Books, 1993.

Turner, P. *Campus: An American Planning Tradition*. MIT Press, 1984.

Van Yahres, M., and S. Knight, "The Neglected Campus Landscape," *Planning for Higher Education*, April 1995.

Van Yahres, M., "Van Yahres and Associates, Landscape Architects." Promotional materials, 1996.

Whyte, W. *City: Rediscovering the Center*. Doubleday, 1987.

Zwart, F. "The Campus as Model Habitat," *Planning for Higher Education*, February 1994.

Endnotes

1. P. Turner, *Campus: An American Planning Tradition* (MIT Press, 1984).

2. S. Polyzoides, "On Campus-Making in America," in *Campus and Community* (Rockport Publishers, 1997).

3. J. Lang, *Creating Architectural Theory: The Role of the Behavioral Sciences in Environmental Design* (Van Nostrand Reinhold, 1987).

4. N. Newton, *Design on the Land: The Development of Landscape Architecture* (Harvard University Press, 1971).

5. See Notes 1 and 2.

6. See Note 1.

7. F. Zwart, "The Campus as a Model Habitat." *Planning for Higher Education*, February 1994: 35.

8. J. Lang, *Urban Design: The American Experience* (Van Nostrand Reinhold, 1994).

9. See Note 8.

10. S. Rush and S. Johnson, "The Decaying American Campus: A Ticking Timebomb" (American Association of Physical Plant Administrators, 1988).

11. M. P. Chapman, "Social Change and American Campus Design," *Planning for Higher Education*, March 1994, and

R. Dober, *Campus Architecture: Building in the Groves of Academe* (McGraw-Hill, 1996).

12. W. Sensbach, "Restoring the Values of Campus Architecture," *Planning for Higher Education*, January 1991.

13. M. Van Yahres, Van Yahres and Associates Landscape Architects, Promotional materials (1996).

14. R. Kaplan and S. Kaplan, *The Experience of Nature: A Psychological Perspective* (Cambridge University Press, 1989), and S. Carr, et al., *Public Space* (Cambridge University Press, 1992).

15. See Note 13.

16. C. Alexander et al., *A Pattern Language* (Oxford University Press, 1977).

17. See Note 2.

18. See Note 12.

19. Turner, *Campus: An American Planning Tradition*: 304.

20. See Note 16.

21. Alexander et al., *A Pattern Language*: 277.

22. This is Gertrude Stein's famous comment about Oakland, California, and is applicable not just to some campuses, but to much of the urban environment.

23. M. Van Yahres, M. Knight, and S. Knight, "The Neglected Campus Landscape," *Planning for Higher Education*, April 1995: 22.

24. See Note 13.

25. W. Whyte, *City: Rediscovering the Center* (Doubleday, 1988): 338.

26. Sensbach, "Restoring the Values of Campus Architecture": 11.

27. See Note 16.

28. A. Temko, *No Way to Build a Ball Park and Other Irreverent Essays on Architecture* (Chronicle Books, 1993): 137.

CITIES
Urban Design and Planning

Introduction

What is a city? One answer might be that it is the ultimate artifact. Another might be that it is the most complex and celebrated expression of human creativity, culture, and civility at best or a manifestation of human neglect at worst. Still another is that current urban patterns of sprawling developments represent human folly.

Cities are the fifth component of this study and are difficult to delineate. Their human/social, environmental, and technological aspects combine and form perhaps the most complex component of the built environment.

A city is a place created or built for people to live, work, visit, and play. Aristotle did not call the city a place built with houses; he said that it is a company.[1] Shakespeare much later agreed; Hamlet says, "what is the city but the people?" And that is the point: the more people there are, and the more sophisticated their needs and values, the more they modify their environment into a human creation, an increasingly rich, complex, and varied creation—the city.

Cities are further illustrated by a four-part definition. The defining four characteristics also clarify the city's content-component-context interrelationships:

- **Cities** (which combine products, interiors, structures, and landscapes in various ways) are humanly made or arranged;
- to fulfill human purpose, to satisfy human needs, wants, and values; and
- to mediate the overall environment;
- while affecting their context (regions and the Earth).

The city is a human creation, an assemblage of parts and interrelationships. It has content and a context, as recognized by the continuum that also has organized this book:

Products—Interiors—Structures—Landscapes—
Cities—Regions—Earth

Cities have various quantitative and qualitative dimensions. Many countries classify them by size, others by quality. People consider a city a higher form of civilization, and for a city to even exist, to function, requires a high level of organization. This image of a city as a higher form is widely reflected even in official nomenclature. In Britain, "city" is used as a qualitative term that identifies only important centers of culture and civilization. British cities can be small or large, but they must have an important qualitative aspect of society (a cathedral, an outstanding university, etc.). In Canada, a city is generally defined as a municipality of the largest size. For example, in Ontario, a village is traditionally an urban place of 2,000 people or less. A town is 2,000 to 15,000. A town, on reaching the magic number of 15,000, can become a city, at which time it is separated from the jurisdiction of county government. In the United States, Iowa provides a similar example, in that cities of the first class are those of 15,000 or more and cities of the second class are those ranging from 2,000 to 15,000. Ohio originally divided its municipal corporations into cities (urban places with over 5,000 inhabitants), villages (200 to 5,000), and hamlets (incorporated places with fewer than 200 people). Other terms are used to define even smaller community subdivisions such as "neighborhoods," "communities," "subdivisions or clusters of houses."

Some find it useful to describe a city as a forcefield in which transactions take place as exchanges of energy and resources, similar to various organic systems. The field concept, used in a number of places in this book, is useful in defining an important aspect of cities, that of human-environmental-technological interactions, exchanges, and circulation. It is useful to understand the city as a dynamic interaction field that allows a necessary humanistic shift in focus, emphasizing the relationships among people as an important feature of community at all levels.

All this means that the best cities are inclusive rather than exclusive and segregated; they are integrated rather than disintegrated and fragmented. And they are part of, rather than apart from, their context and the region within which they are located. In other words, they should be the epitome of health, fitness, and creativity: healthy, pleasant places to live; fit within their environmental context; an expression of human culture and creativity. Unfortunately, cities are too often void of these human-environmental qualities. This should not discourage citizens and designers from striving to realize the promise that is inherent in the purpose or idea of a city.

The city is an expression of our culture and "virtually all of civilization and indispensable in this role."[2] Lewis

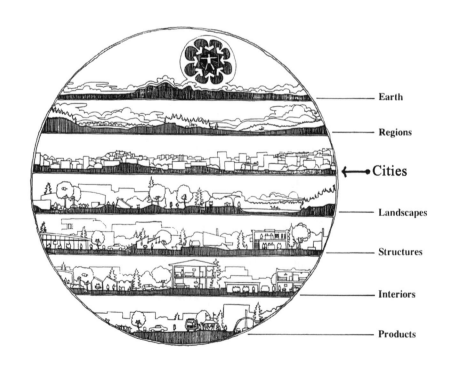

Earth

Regions

Cities

Landscapes

Structures

Interiors

Products

Mumford has suggested that the city is "at once a microcosm and a microscope, containing and magnifying the best and worst of humanity." The best, he says, derives from the level attained, "the scale of the city [being] one of its chief sources of enjoyment and edification." The best cities enrich the lives of those who understand and/or participate in their creation. Great cities are a dynamic expression of culture and civilization, an important symbol and contribution to future generations. Great cities demonstrate important connections between the **city, civility, citizenship,** and **civilization**. The worst cities are plagued by so many problems that it is hard to know how to help them, causing too many of us not to care about the quality of our cities or get involved in maintaining or revitalizing them.

The chapters in this section examine the city, its problems, and its potential. They emphasize the best, discuss ways to reanimate the rest, and remind the reader of the importance of these inherited resources of civilization:

The History of Urbanization
by Robert J. Patton

This chapter analyzes the way cities have developed through time and space, examining the city as the largest, most dynamic manifestation of any living organism's interaction with its environment. The chapter analyzes the evolution of urbanization as it relates to the changing needs, wants, and values of society and defines the characteristics that are common to all settlements, from the first villages to the urban developments of today. It illustrates the common characteristics (constants) that have evolved over the long history of urban development and emphasizes that they are still present in the cities of today.

The Inherited City as a Resource
by Robert M. Baron

This chapter examines the city as a critically important cultural and material resource. In the recent past, the particular role of inherited urban resources in the cultural and social life of contemporary society has not been fully understood or appreciated. Processes for urban transformation that manifest in changes of urban components and urban form (morphology) are discussed. Changes are discussed that are gradual and evolutionary, achieved through adaptation and reuse, and others that

are cataclysmic as the result of urban renewal. The chapter also discusses strategies for historic preservation, including preservation, rehabilitation, restoration, and reconstruction, and their capacity to sustain components of the city as well as their collective inherited form.

Cities Today: The Imprint of Human Needs in Urban Patterns and Form
by Tom J. Bartuska

Cities of today reflect the best and worst aspects of contemporary society. This chapter examines the human aspects of cities today—how human needs are manifested in the ways land is used and the ways connections are made through urban infrastructures. Both land use and infrastructure define the patterns and form of cities. Great cities convey a collective story of some of civilization's greatest achievements. The stories they tell are expressed in supportive human-environmental collaboration and effective design and planning strategies.

Urban Design and Planning
by Michael S. Owen

Few people understand how cities are actually planned and designed. The final chapter in this section surveys the various legal and procedural developments that define urban planning and design in the United States. Most cities, U.S. cities in particular, appear to be highly complex, complicated, and chaotic. It is true that they are complex, but most cities exhibit an underlying order or rationale. This rationale is brought into being by the processes of urban planning and design. This chapter describes some basic concepts related to these processes and the professionals who carry out the work.

References

Each chapter concludes with a list of relevant references.

American Planning Association (APA): www.planning.org
Association of Collegiate Schools of Planning (ACSP): www. acsp.org
Smart Growth Institute (SGI): www.smarthgrowth.org
Urban Design Group (UDG): www.udg.org.uk
Urban Design Research Institution (UDRI): www.udri.org
Urban Land Institute (ULI): www.uli.org

Resources

Elyot, Sir Thomas. *The Image of Goueraunce.* Compiled by the Actes and Sentences Notable, of the Most Noble Emperour Alexander Seuerus. Bertheletter, 1540.

Fabun, D. *Dimensions of Change.* Glencoe Press, 1971.

Mumford, L. *Technics and Civilization.* Harcourt, Brace, 1934.

Shakespeare, W. *The Works of William Shakespeare.* "Hamlet." Macmillan, 1923.

Valery, P. *An Anthology.* Princeton University Press, 1977.

Wordsworth, W. *The Complete Poetical Works of William Wordsworth.* Houghton Muffin, 1904.

Endnotes

1. Sir Thomas Elyot, *The Image of Goueraunce,* Compiled by the Actes and Sentences Notable, of the Most Noble Emperour Alexander Seuerus (Bertheletter, 1540).

2. P. Valery, *An Anthology* (Princeton University Press, 1977).

CHAPTER 21

The History of Urbanization

Robert J. Patton

The city is the largest, most dynamic manifestation of any living organism's interaction with its environment. It is challenging to analyze the total complexity of forces that created the city. This chapter discusses the evolution of urbanization as it relates to the changing needs, wants, and values of society throughout history and defines characteristics common to all settlements considered to be urban.

Two sets of aspects help us to understand urban characteristics and qualities historically. The first set of aspects is **variables**, dynamic human, environmental, and technical variables: size and growth; cultural, political and social character; natural context; and the resultant built environment. It is difficult to understand urban evolution only in terms of variables. Variables change radically from culture to culture, so they alone are insufficient to describe the evolution of urbanization.

The second set of aspects is **constants** common to all cities: permanence, density, institutionalism, segregation, dominance—and, later, decentralization and subcentralization. These constants were energized during the process of urban evolution and are revealed in the cities of today. It is through these constants that the evolution of the city can best be understood.

The Village

The constants of permanence and density have their roots in preurban or village society dating back more than 10,000 years. During this period (known as "prehistory"), people were nomadic, existing at the simplest level of material technology, often limited to what could be carried by individuals. The precise time in history when preurban people altered their nomadic, wandering lifestyle is not clear, but the probable cause is domestication of plants and animals, which led to horticulture and agriculture, to herding, cultivating, and harvesting, which allowed stabilization of the food supply and development of village settlements.

Permanence

With the advent of domestication, the first villages appeared as permanent settlements. **Permanence** provided two qualities of life important to ultimate development of the urban unit. It gave people an opportunity to identify with a **sense of place** within the larger environment, a refuge to which they could return no matter where they roamed. It also provided a sense of community, creating new kinds of relationships not previously experienced between people. A strong sense of place is an expression of the composite built form of an urbanized area and is still today a memorable quality of successful cities.

Density

The pattern of early villages reveals another characteristic: an image of various built elements clustered in close

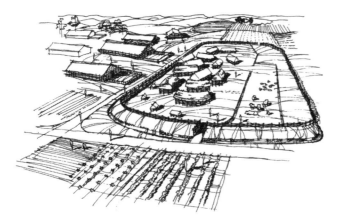

Figure 21-1 Permanence established through the domestication of animals and the development of agriculture, as illustrated in an early village settlement.

spatial proximity. This clustering or compactness results in greater **density** of people. Such clustering provided mutual protection, efficient sharing of the workload, and the opportunity for increased social interaction. The concepts of permanence and density are common to all cities throughout history, including those of today.

If two of the constants of urbanization, permanence and density, were formed in preurban society, what then differentiates village settlement from urbanization? The difference resulted from a change caused by a revolution in village society occurring somewhere between 10,000 and 5,000 years ago. This change is referred to by historians as the **urban transformation**.

Village society was based on a tribal or communal hierarchy oriented toward cooperative action to fulfill the needs of the group.[1] The organizing methods of an urban society are quite different. They are based on dominance hierarchies, a division by power, a structure in which the

Figure 21-2 Density expressed in the compactness of village settlements. Istalif, Afghanistan (T. Bartuska).

needs of one part of the group are often achieved at the expense of others.

In the late preurban village society, one segment of the population appears to have risen to a position of dominance over others. Villages were increasingly producing surpluses beyond sustenance needs, making them ripe for urban transformation. A dominance power structure created an opportunity to make the village even more productive, thereby raising the level of existence for some to that of affluence. As a result, the village was transformed into what is defined as an urban unit, characterized by mobilization of the workforce, division of labor, and separation of classes.

The Preindustrial City

As a result of the urban transformation, a new set of constants emerged, creating an urban unit referred to as the "preindustrial city." The preindustrial city spanned the period from approximately 3000 B.C.E. to 1760 C.E. in Western civilization and included the ancient cities of Mesopotamia and Egypt, the classical cities of Greece and Rome, the medieval guild cities, and the metropolises of the Renaissance.

The urban constants that emerged in preindustrial cities were **institutionalism**, **segregation**, and **dominance**. These constants were not prominent in village settlement, but all of them evolved in the preindustrial city and are basic to urban settlements today.

Institutionalism

Archaeologists have determined that the city of Ur in Mesopotamia contained a population of 5,000 by 3000 B.C.E. Records show that the population of Rome had grown to 1 million by the first century B.C.E. During this growth process, religious, political, and economic activity intensified, creating three dominant power structures having a simultaneous impact on this vast new urban society. To ensure their individual strength and identity, each group intensified its organization and structure, institutionalizing its social, economic, and religious purposes. The resulting institutionalism transformed these power groups into the major organs of the urban body.

Segregation and Dominance

Once institutions were structured, a dynamic ordering process took place in the preindustrial city known as **segregation**. It was partly ecologically based and partly

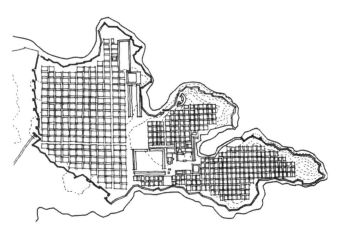

Figure 21-3 Segregation of public and private urban activities, Greek colonial town of Miletus, fifth century B.C.

Figure 21-5 Spatial dominance of a public square, Siena, Italy (T. Bartuska).

socially based. Ecologically, it resulted from a tendency for people and institutions with similar characteristics and interests to cluster together. By doing so, they attained a stronger sense of identity, as well as separation from those that seemed incompatible.

Segregation was also planned. The military, the laboring class, the merchant class, and others were forced to live in segregated residential districts. Governmental, cultural, and religious buildings, palaces, or guildhalls were often built centrally, depending on which were the dominant institutions.

Segregation affected the physical appearance of preindustrial cities. Patterns were generated that expressed sharp lines of demarcation. The lines established territorial limits to preserve institutional identity. Some boundaries were natural, based on topography, rivers, lakes, or vegetation. Others were constructed, the most common being the street system.

Some institutions and their pattern of segregation dominated because of physical size and/or position. This was often planned purposely to exert, by virtue of visual presence (be it religious or autocratic), a prominent influence on the inhabitants.

Interestingly, **dominance** had a positive influence on the pattern of preindustrial cities. In some cases, it punctuated the otherwise monotonous character of the city. In others, the center of the city was dominant, providing a feature of orientation and a social place of assembly. The scale of spaces and buildings provided a background for exciting civic life, a stronger sense of place. Centralized dominance is not unfamiliar to us today. It exists as the manifestation of economic institutionalism in the central business districts of almost every major city.

The Industrial City

Toward the end of the eighteenth century, a second social change occurred that was even more extensive in terms of its impact on preindustrial cities than that of the urban transformation made on village life 5,000 years before. The **Industrial Revolution** significantly altered the course of urban development. The industrial city was created, imposing new human-environmental and technological complications that have left their mark on the development of all major cities throughout the world.

Invention of the steam-powered assembly line and related advances in technology and manufacturing in the eighteenth century caused the Industrial Revolution. The factory was built around the assembly line, establishing a new and powerful economic institution. It created a great

Figure 21-4 Dominance by physical size of a medieval cathedral over the city, Chartres, France (T. Bartuska).

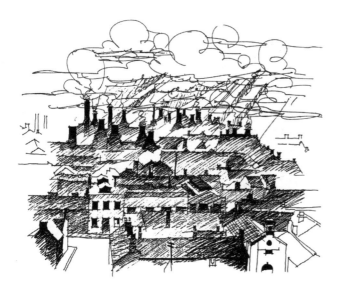

Figure 21-6 Image of the eighteenth-century industrial city.

demand for products and for people to produce those products.

Factories grew in two places. One was in rural areas near the sources of raw materials. These factories became a catalyst for the rapid and disorderly development of new factory towns. Factories were also imposed on large, existing preindustrial centers, taking advantage of population concentrations to provide a labor force and centralized locations for markets and trade. The advent

of the factory system caused one of the greatest immigrations in human history. Rural, agrarian people flooded into the cities, hoping to increase their prosperity.

At this point, trouble began for the city as an environment for human habitation. The politics of the new industrialists perpetuated a belief that if economic enterprise were allowed to flourish, free of any governmental control, the system would be self-organizing. This type of unregulated, speculative growth is commonly referred to as "laissez-faire development." The new society believed that an ordered urban environment would also result.

It did not work. No period in the evolution of urbanization is more impoverished than that of the late eighteenth and nineteenth centuries. Every aspect of urban life became subordinate to the factory. No plan determined its location. It usually claimed the most amenable sites on flat land near water. Mass substandard housing was located near the noxious factory to create close proximity between home and work for the labor force. Many cities today are still trying to correct these unfortunate, deregulated laissez-faire developments.

Decentralization

The coming of the factory changed the dynamics of the city; one result was a deteriorating environment for living. The upper classes began to move out of the city. They settled in rural locations just far enough away to avoid the crowdedness and blight, yet close enough to easily access the city for working, entertainment, and material commodities. Some of the earliest forms of public transportation (streetcars and commuter trains)—before the advent of the automobile—facilitated such changes.

This outward movement of a segment of the population gained momentum to the point where it began to affect the demography of the urban population pattern. This dynamic movement, referred to by urbanologists as "decentralization," was a major factor affecting the transition of the industrial city into the postindustrial city, the metropolis that we know today.

The Postindustrial City

Extensive **transit-oriented developments** (TODs) by commuter railroads further accommodated the continued decentralization of settlements. Originating at the center of the city and projecting outward, the railroad connected a series of planned suburban residential vil-

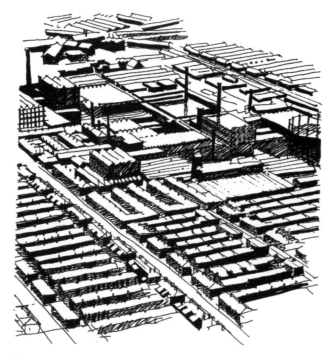

Figure 21-7 Crowded industrial housing developed adjacent to factories caused the outward movement of decentralization.

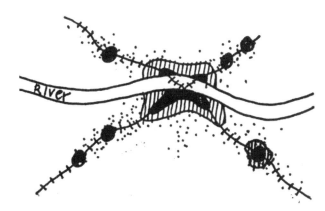

Figure 21-8 Radial patterns of urban development: a central city and surrounding decentralized villages served primarily by rail transit.

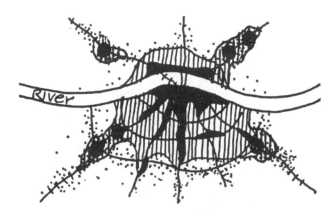

Figure 21-9 Spider web pattern of urban development, illustrating subcentralized growth between villages and the city primarily served by the automobile.

lages. Although built on a speculative basis, these villages had certain amenable environmental qualities and an identifiable sense of place. They were spaced evenly along the rail routes and surrounded by greenbelts of agricultural land or forest. These communities were planned for populations of 5,000 to 10,000, to be walkable, and dependent on local community services. They were successful planned examples of effectively clustered urban development and remain today as promising strategies for the future. Clustered development (TODs) could be supported by inexpensive railroad fares, and this efficiency allowed a broader segment of the population to move out of the city. This increased decentralization created a demand for more residential land, and speculators began buying, platting, and building between the clustered suburban villages.

Subcentralization

With the increase in decentralized development, the automobile arrived on the scene. The car was individually owned, convenient, and small enough to negotiate the urban and suburban street patterns, which was the norm for many rapidly expanding cities. Automobile use was actually very costly, because it caused the demise of public mass transportation and perpetuated the creation of the low-density, detached, single-family suburban living unit.[2] The expanding villages merged and soon ceased to be places with any special identity.

As decentralization continued, major urban commercial establishments began to build in the outer areas to take advantage of the suburban economic market. These new commercial centers set up origin-destination routes that ran across the original radial transportation pattern of railroads and roads leading to and from the city. Cross-

roads were built, and subsequent residential construction along these routes filled in the remaining open spaces. The original concept of TODs and the commuter railroad came into conflict with this new sprawling suburban density. The railroad had to make too many stops to serve the large population and lost its efficiency as a mass transportation system.

In this way, a continuous settlement was created, surrounding cities and extending across the countryside without any clear point of termination. Auto-driven decentralization is referred to as **subcentralization**, from which the familiar term **suburb** is derived.

The suburb is an environment particularly characteristic of the postindustrial metropolis and continues today. Other characteristics are the dominant economic center, massive industrial and transportation complexes, and the intricate vehicular freeway system tying it all together. Subcentralization and its market-driven speculative development, commonly referred to as **suburban**

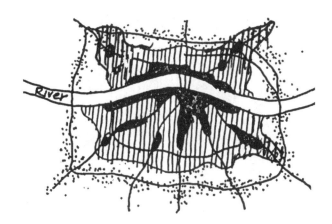

Figure 21-10 Extensive subcentralized development and auto-driven suburban sprawl.

Figure 21-13 Extensive auto-driven suburban sprawl and strip development, Phoenix, Arizona (T. Bartuska).

Figure 21-11 Deteriorated areas surrounding the city caused by subcentralization near the North Side of Chicago, Illinois (T. Bartuska).

sprawl and **strip development**, continue in most U.S. cities today and are creating new **edge cities** that follow the freeways and surround the original city in a donut pattern. The speed of sprawl makes "the new" seductive, leaving behind other kinds of TOADs—temporary, obsolete, abandoned or derelict sites.[3] Sprawl perpetuates

more auto-driven lifestyles and significant challenges for society today. The long-term human, environmental, and technical costs of sprawl are significant and are exceeding society's ability to pay (through taxes) for their construction and maintenance. The costs of low-density sprawl include the loss of regional resources, the loss of a sense of community, more traffic congestion and accidents, ineffective use and maintenance of infrastructure (roads, utility networks, public safety/services, parks and schools, etc.), crime, obesity, and global warming. The costs affect not only the city but also all levels of the built environment and extend far into the regions around the Earth.

In the recent past, a saturation of untenable complexities has rendered most U.S. central cities nearly unlivable. Cities will always be places people love or hate, but their presence as part of civilization will have an impact

Figure 21-12 Continued subcentralization, auto-driven suburban sprawl, and the creation of edge cities (lower half of the diagram).

Figure 21-14 Dominance and density of a contemporary city core and the delightful qualities of a livable city—the reanimation of an industrial site into an enjoyable urban environment, Gas Works Park, Seattle, Washington (T. Bartuska).

on the human condition far into the indefinable future. Major steps are being taken to unravel and limit the negatives. Programs and policies, such as the **growth management acts** (GMAs) are being developed to control sprawl and save regional resources while promoting inner-city renewal and pedestrianization; open space planning; new TODs, mixed-use developments, and new multimodal transport systems are slowly bringing new livability and sustainability back to the city. Many of these challenges to revitalize and humanize our inherited urban and now suburban patterns are further explored in following chapters.[4]

References

Barnett, J. *The Fractured Metroplis: Improving the New City, Restoring the Old City and Reshaping the Region.* HarperCollins, 1995.

Calthorpe, P., et al. *The Regional City: Planning for the End of Sprawl.* Island Press, 2001.

Duany, A. *Suburban Nation: The Rise of Sprawl and the Decline of the American Dream.* North Point Press, 2000.

Eisler, R. *The Chalice and the Blade.* HarperCollins, 1987.

Gallagher, W. *The Power of Place.* Poseidon Press, 1993.

Gallion, A. *The Urban Pattern.* Van Nostrand, 1986.

Garreau, J. *Edge City, Life on the New Frontier.* Random House, 1991.

Hawkes, J. *Pre-History and the Beginnings of Civilization.* Harper and Row, 1963.

Hayden, D. *A Field Guide to Sprawl.* W. W. Norton, 2004.

Jacobs, J. *The Death and Life of Great American Cities.* Vintage, 1992.

Jenks, M., and N. Dempsey. *Future Forms and Design for Sustainable Cities.* Architectural Press, 2005.

Kunstler, J. *The Geography of Nowhere.* Simon and Schuster, 1993.

Mumford, L. *The City in History.* Harcourt, Brace and World, 1961.

Shoup, D. *The High Cost of Free Parking.* American Planning Association, 2006.

Spreiregen, P. *The Architecture of Towns and Cities.* McGraw-Hill, 1965.

Endnotes

1. R. Eisler, *The Chalice and the Blade* (HarperCollins, 1987).

2. D. Shoup, *The High Cost of Free Parking* (American Planning Association, 2006).

3. D. Hayden, *A Field Guide to Sprawl* (W. W. Norton, 2004).

4. M. Jenks and N. Dempsey, *Future Forms and Design for Sustainable Cities* (Architectural Press, 2005).

CHAPTER 22

The Inherited City
as a Resource

Robert M. Baron

The built form of the inherited city must be considered a great cultural resource for the future development of society. What is an inherited city? The inherited cities, including their assembled components of the built environment, which have evolved over time, are great artifacts that reveal a sense of place and cultural identity. The urban artifact is constructed through a process of adaptation and incremental growth in which each addition or modification contributes to an evolving inherited city. The evolution of an urban settlement into a place arises out of a human need to provide an existential foothold. At times, modern design and planning have been impatient with the existing urban conditions and utopian in their vision of the future city, which has led to the erosion of a sense of place.

The purpose of a town or city is to make a place for people to dwell—to fulfill individual and collective needs and values. Thoughtful additions to the built environment make legible the meaning of the inherited built environment. The past urban form is not seen as an impediment but as an opportunity for integration of past forms and present life. Towns and cities, like historic buildings, have often demonstrated an enormous capacity for transformation. Historic preservation has made people more aware of the importance of their existing urban inheritance in achieving a sense of place in the future city.

The particular role played by the built environment in the cultural and social life of contemporary society has not, however, been fully understood or appreciated. Geographical and sociological research has not always acknowledged the role of the built form of the city in influencing social and cultural life. Adaptive reuse of historic environments suggests a different perception of the value of the historic city. Historic preservation is becoming more assimilated into contemporary design and planning. These issues are also examined in Chapter 14.

In the United States, past interest in historic preservation was based on economic, cultural, and political imperatives. A nostalgic desire for the cultural integrity of the premodern world has emerged with ecological consciousness, an ethic of sustainability, and criticism of modernism.

Many successful developments, such as Ghiradelli Square in San Francisco, have resulted from this intersection of values.

Historic preservation is the general term that focuses attention on the importance of the historic artifact of the city as an inherited resource on which to build, rather than as a liability to be overcome in future development. These issues depend on understanding certain terms and premises. Inherited components of the city need to be evaluated in terms of historic, cultural, and environmental value so that appropriate responses can be adopted. Some aspects will be significant because of an historical event associated with the site. Others have value because of the quality of the design. In the United States, four approaches to historic preservation have evolved to address historic aspects of the city: preservation, restoration, rehabilitation/adaptive reuse, and reconstruction. **Preservation**, the least invasive approach, generally focuses on the ongoing maintenance and repair of the historic fabric rather than extensive replacement or new construction. **Restoration** concerns "the measures necessary to sustain the existing form, integrity and materials of a historical property and . . . involves accurately depicting the form, materials, features, and character of a property as it appeared at a particular period of time. Restoration retains as much of the historic fabric as possible. Inconsistent features may need to be removed and missing features faithfully reconstructed in accordance with the restoration period."[1]

Rehabilitation concerns the adaptation of "a property for continuing or new compatible use through repair, alteration, and additions, while preserving those portions or features that convey historical, cultural, or architectural values."[2] Rehabilitation involves determining a new compatible use and transforming the historic building through addition, erasure, and insertion. This response to the historic building always involves determining the appropriate relationship between the inherited and the new. The terms "adaptive reuse" or "reanimation" are also used to express similar attempt at renewing a component of the city. Finally, the process of **reconstruction** seeks to "accurately depict by means of new construction the form, materials, features, and character of a historical property that no longer exists, as it appeared at a particular period of time, in its historic location."[3]

The rehabilitation of the San Francisco Cannery into a shopping center with reconstruction and the restoration of colonial Williamsburg, Virginia, will provide clarification of these terms.

Originally built in 1907, the San Francisco Cannery Warehouse was adapted as a contemporary shopping center during the 1960s. At Williamsburg, the historic town plan and buildings were reconstructed according to what the archaeologists thought was the town's eighteenth-century form. Even the Williamsburg docents are dressed in period clothing. The subsequent built layers of Williamsburg that had accumulated in the nineteenth and early twentieth centuries were demolished so that the site could be reconstructed as a colonial town. Consequently, Williamsburg became frozen in time; only the

eighteenth-century layers became visible. By contrast, the Cannery reveals in its rehabilitation the conjunction of two layers: a contemporary mixed-use shopping center and a nineteenth-century warehouse. New fenestration, signage, mechanical (HVAC) systems, lighting, and furnishings are juxtaposed with the inherited thick masonry walls and trussed roof structure of the warehouse. Both historic preservation strategies can be deployed in the same project to produce a balanced design that preserves the inheritance as an important sense of place in the memory of the city and provides a place that continues to be useful.

Urban morphology is the study of the built form of the city and changes to its parts both individually and collectively over time. It involves describing and analyzing the physical form and changes. Urban form can be analyzed by classifying the typology of its parts and understanding the structure that organizes each component into larger contexts. Parts can include the plan of the city as a whole and its monuments, streets, sidewalks, buildings, parks, neighborhood, districts, and so

Figure 22-1 Rehabilitation of a nineteenth-century warehouse into an urban shopping and office center, the Cannery, San Francisco, California (T. Bartuska).

Figure 22-2   Restoration of a historic town, the Governor's Mansion, Williamsburg, Virginia.

on. Each of these parts could be further broken down into smaller parts—"the whole physical mass of marble, bricks and mortar, steel and concrete . . . metal conduits and rails—the total artifact."[4] Particularly interesting are the ways that the urban artifact is formed and adapted through time as it is adjusted to its inhabitants' changing social, cultural, and economic conditions. In many historic cities, for instance, one can clearly see this evolutionary process at work through cycles of growth and adaptation. Few cities have been developed from a clean slate.

More importantly is a need to appreciate the growth and change of a city's forms and patterns. **Urban morphogenesis** is the study of this process of growth and change of urban morphology—the evolutionary changes in the form and patterns of cities.[5]

The built environment is a collectively constructed total environment that manifests itself at different scales—in regions, farms, towns and cities, neighborhoods, landscapes, streets, squares, parks, avenues,

buildings, interiors, and products. These parts are considered artifacts of cultures and can be studied as such. Cities need to be understood as both built environments and symbols of the intention of the members of a society to live, work, and play together in communities. Acts of design and planning intervention operate collectively to bring intelligibility to the built environment.

A Break in Urban Continuity: Modern Urbanism

Most **urban renewal** projects constructed in European and U.S. cities between 1930 and 1980 have been destructive to the traditional city. Most Modernist attitudes have led to morphological fragmentation and to demolition of historical cities. The net effect of this all too prevalent tendency has been to create conditions that prevented the preservation, reuse, or adaptation of existing parts and provoked a rupture in social/cultural and morphological continuity. These Modernist attitudes are still prevalent in society today, and the reasons for their disruptive impact are numerous and complex. However, most observers agree that Modernism failed because it was not based on the premise that a city is a continuous production made by periodic adaptations and that continuity, in morphological, social, and cultural terms, is an essential condition to be nurtured and conserved.

Modern or avant-garde movements active at the beginning of the twentieth century reacted against the traditional city and its culture, losing sight of the need for continuity. Designers and theorists were reacting to what they thought was a society, culture, and city in need of revolutionary change. The most revolutionary of the avant-garde were the Italian Futurists, whose rhetoric was anti–traditional city and who considered the existing city as obsolete.

Most designers followed the "progressive" urban theories of Robert Owen, Charles Fourier, Soria Mata, Tony Garnier, and Ebenezer Howard, who proposed to replace the traditional city with a new Modernist form. Their planning concepts were presented as utopian settings in which open space, landscaping, and fresh air became symbols of social progress. As a result, many early Modernist designs were unrelated to the patterns of existing cities. Le Corbusier, a prominent leader in the modern movement, created powerful images of a new type of urbanism. Most postwar urban renewal was, in fact, based on ideas present in Le Corbusier's Voisin Plan of 1922, a design project funded by the Voisin Automobile

Figure 22-3 Le Corbusier's Voisin Plan for Rebuilding Paris, 1925 (© 2006 Artists Rights Society [ARS], New York/ADAGP, Paris/FLC).

Company. It proposed an almost total rebuilding of the historic center of Paris. In order to realize his idealized vision of an entirely new society, Le Corbusier proposed that the urban fabric of Paris be razed and rebuilt as a new pattern of street grid overlaid with radiating auto connectors, high-rise slabs, and housing blocks set in vast parks. The traditional street space for people to shop, to greet, and to socialize was to disappear. The new urban morphology was to be strictly zoned to separate urban functions like housing from workplaces. Not designed for the conventions of Parisians, Le Corbusier's design proclaimed a new way to live. The zoning indicated in the plan would have resulted in dissolving networks of interaction between related functions. As Jane Jacobs observed, this kind of zoning leads to disintegration of lively social vitality and diversity and breaks down social contact among individuals.[6]

Postwar Urbanism: Urban Renewal

In the United States, Le Corbusier's Voisin Plan was implemented in housing developments like the Alfred E. Smith Project of 1948, the Stuyvesant Middle-Income Project of 1947, and the Polo Grounds Middle-Income Project as late as 1964–1967. These developments, inserted into New York City, became emblems of the U.S. interpretation of the Voisin Plan. To many designers/planners of the 1950s and 1960s, these designs connoted social progress and enlightened urban policy that seemed consistent with national social goals. Many up-to-date young architects, landscape architects, and planners began thinking about the built environment in these visionary terms, ignoring existing physical and social contexts. The influential architectural historians Sigfried Giedion and Nikolaus Pevsner claimed that Modern architecture expresses the "spirit of the age."[7] Under this

Modernist theory, the historical city and its various historical styles seemed outdated and required continual rebuilding to capture the spirit of the time (zeitgeist). This kind of history implied that each new age required its own form; old forms corresponded to past times and were not relevant today. For instance, the medieval city belonged to the Middle Ages and the neoclassical city to the eighteenth century alone. What then is to be the form of the modern city? The continuous historical city was perceived as irrelevant to contemporary life. Here is the basis of an ideology of historicism and discontinuity and a rejection of the past in the present. Three case studies illustrate the problems of answering the question of form for the modern city.

Cataclysmic Urban Renewal: Lincoln Center Redevelopment Area

Complete destruction of a whole inner-city neighborhood is recorded in the history of New York's Lincoln Center Project, directed by Robert Moses, a master implementer of modern urbanism. In this project, the existing buildings in the area were totally destroyed. Its poor residents were relocated. So, the existing neighborhood was physically and socially razed. After the area was cleared, housing towers and an expensive Performing Arts Complex (Lincoln Center) were built in its place. Robert Stern, an influential architectural critic, calls these developments "cataclysmic urban renewal."[8] A kind of "frontal lobotomy" was performed on the urban body. The logic for this strategy was to revitalize a sagging inner-city economy, but for whom? Certainly not for its original residents. Neither the morphology nor the social life of the neighborhood was seen by its developers as an important resource to be studied and rehabilitated.

Antiurban Myths: The Oak Street Connector Project

In his criticism of the Oak Street Connector Project in New Haven, Connecticut, Vincent Scully identified four persistent anticity myths given expression in the project: "the city is bad; tear it down; get on the road; and be a pioneer."[9] These myths, long present in U.S. social and cultural history, have joined with modern urbanism to produce a rather potent monster. In New Haven, a "slum" was cleared (the city is bad; tear it down) to provide space for a freeway connector (get on the road), which was built to bring suburbanites (be a pioneer) into the city center to work and shop but not to live there. Scully observed that the decay of public transportation during the 1950s resulted in an urgent need for the city to encourage the construction of yet more automobile connectors, which eventually destroyed the existing historic neighborhood and block pattern of New Haven, isolating areas and the people who lived there. This "new development syndrome" and its side effects worked like a self-fulfilling prophecy. In the end, the old neighborhood was totally replaced by vast open spaces, new commercial buildings, and luxury apartment slabs. Regrettably, this is a recurring pattern of development that can be traced across the country during the post–World War II period.

Urban Transformation

Modernist scholars of the city have not paid enough attention to **urban transformation**—how urban form slowly evolves. There exist important **ecological relationships** between the urban form and the way people and society organize the city over time. Urban transformation is a slowly evolving process. Although political and social institutions may change, these changes do not transform cities. After 1945, Eastern Europe underwent major political-economic changes, which did not affect the historic core of many cities. Sofia, Budapest, and Prague have persisted in their prewar form, and these inherited resources are treasured today. Urban morphology seems to act independently of institutional processes and can be adaptable to changing functions. Why does urban morphology behave in a quasi-autonomous way? James Vance gave three reasons:[10]

• Since biological and psychological qualities of humans persist, built forms relate to human scale; for example, the height of doors does not change very much.
• Properties of the physical world, like geographic characteristics, are relatively unchanging. Due to its materiality, urban morphology changes less than human institutions.
• Physical change is evolutionary. Old buildings are slowly being transformed or replaced by new ones following precedent in materials and in form. This perpetuates the existing form of the city.

As defined earlier, urban morphogenesis is concerned with the processes that establish and transform urban form over time, the constantly changing form-function relationships found in any historic city. Urban form has some autonomy. Building types like ancient Roman basilicas and amphitheaters have undergone dramatic changes of function and yet remain in continuous use. For exam-

ple, the Roman basilica evolved from a covered market to a court of law and finally to a church. The form of the basilica remains fundamentally the same, even though its functions and meanings have changed.

Vance also suggested that urban transformation occurs in stages, each stage synchronized with its patterns of social use. As social activities and values change, the physical environment will have to be reanimated or adapted. An adaptive process, therefore, is at work mediating between stages. The process works in two ways: (1) adaptation of existing morphology from one stage to another and (2) adaptation from one form-function relationship to another. In both cases, the physical form is an inherited resource to be appreciated and preserved through an incremental urban transformation process.

Adaptation from One Stage to Another

The urban morphology of Bath, England, is indicative because it reveals six morphological stages, each integrated into the others: (1) Roman settlement, (2) abbey town, (3) medieval market town, (4) society town of the eighteenth century, (5) home of the British Admiralty during World War II, and finally, (6) the Bath of today.[11] Each stage has left its permanent mark. Because of rapid population growth, its Palladian eighteenth-century form, however, is still the most dominant.

Rome provides another example of the layering of old and new forms through eight stages of growth: (1) Etruscan Rome, (2) an early republican city, (3) an imperial Rome, (4) a medieval Rome of successive sackings and

Figure 22-4   Plan of Rome, 1873.

political neglect, (5) a papal Rome reflecting the planning of Sixtus V at the end of the sixteenth century, (6) a Rome of King Victor Emmanual II during the unification of Italy in the mid-nineteenth century, (7) a Rome of Mussolini, and finally, (8) a modern Rome with auto connectors, auto businesses, and suburban tower developments. Today, Bath and Rome (and many other cities) are intriguing urban collages or palimpsests of all these previous periods. The sense of historic continuity in these places is remarkable. This kind of continuity in the two cities' urban transformation was not arrived at by a Modernist policy of "urban renewal." Ancient streets and civic buildings have been continuously reanimated. All previous stages of morphogenesis have been touchstones for further development.

Adaptation from One Form-Function Relationship to Another

One of the most amazing morphological adaptations of an ancient site occurred in Split, Yugoslavia. Originally, it was a palace complex built for a retired Roman emperor, Diocletian. During the Early Middle Ages, it was converted into an entire town. In Europe, examples of this kind of reanimation abound.

Figures 22-6 and 22-7 Transformation of a historic railroad station into an urban mixed-use center, St. Louis, Missouri (T. Bartuska).

Figure 22-5 Aerial view of a Roman amphitheater adapted into a piazza in Lucca, Italy.

The arena of the Roman amphitheater at Lucca was changed into a piazza, and the ancient amphitheater at Arles, France, was converted into a fortified town. The same adaptive reuse strategies are at work in the United States, with the transformation of a chocolate factory and old warehouses into popular retail centers in San Francisco. There are also many examples of railroad stations converted into city halls or community centers, warehouses turned into loft apartments, and preservation in historic districts. Other examples are discussed in Chapter 14.

Both urban forms and functions can be successfully adapted and changed to enhance the urban transformation process. In his study of Savannah, Georgia, Stanford Anderson observes that past historical studies have focused on the origin of environments and not on the ways that such environments adapt to change. He notes that the urban pattern can be studied to identify the permanent adaptable parts and to understand the complex interactions between environmental form and its social (functional) context. Anderson asserts that every built environment can support multiple uses and interpretations. Positive urban transformation undergoes a pattern of changes through the interplay of physical conditions and social behaviors. Anderson shows that the city plan of Savannah has been adapted to support a series of different patterns of habitations. He concludes his investigation with the observation that all urban environments can be understood through analysis of two systems: (1) social spaces (functions) and (2) environmental resources (forms). All of the above examples challenge the "form follows function" doctrine. Function also follows form.[12]

Modernists claim that the use of a building determines its particular shape. If this is true, then what happens to the form when the original functions change? Does this lead to a nonfunctional state? Most urban forms of any age—like individual buildings, topography, and street patterns—are being used for very different purposes than those originally intended. The Modernist/functionalist renewal policy has led to massive destruction of established urban environments.

Equally mistaken is the reverse notion that function follows form, that is, that urban form shapes human behaviors. This suggests that if the original function were changed, then the past form would no longer be relevant in the future. Recent research has shown that designed environments, like rooms or plazas, can accommodate numerous types of uses and visual meanings. Therefore, as Anderson suggests, every physical form can be adapted to support multiple uses and meanings. He rejects determinism and embraces a concept of transformation, which better explains the adaptive relationships between people and their environments. Many aspects of historic cities, sites, and buildings are special because they can be creatively adapted to new uses; they possess transfunctional qualities.

Designing/Planning with Inherited Built Resources: Strategies for Reuse and Recycling

As cities mature, new uses and projects are inevitably inserted into an existing urban context of irreplaceable quality (like historic buildings or districts with valuable physical characteristics). These new developments need to be carefully adjusted to inherited urban resources. If

not, designers/planners/developers do not take advantage of existing potentials and invariably insist on development plans that require total replacement of urban settings. If the built environment has a transfunctional or ecological relationship with social/cultural life and evolves through adaptive use, a process of **negotiation** occurs. This is quite different from the functionalist approach. A process of negotiation enables designers and users to appreciate ways to respond to the limits and opportunities of both the form and function of the urban environment—ways to negotiate the idea that form suggest uses and that uses suggest form. Throughout history, urban environments have been reanimated in three general ways: (1) as **quarries** for building materials, (2) as **foundations and founding plans** for new developments, and (3) as **supports and frameworks** for new space/form insertions.

Quarries

Using existing built resources as quarries for new construction is a useful form of recycling, one that has occurred throughout history. For example, many Roman constructions were made from the parts of dismantled older buildings. The Roman Forum and Coliseum were used as quarries for new constructions during the Middle Ages. The composition of inherited parts combined in a contemporary building creates a "temporal collage." This temporal ensemble can be seen in many of the eighteenth-century etchings of Piranesi, who was fascinated by ancient ruins. His etchings provide an image of a kind of urban recycling operation that was common in the premodernist city and illustrates the potential for future urban transformation.

Figure 22-8   Basilica, Pompeii (120 B.C.), used as a resource quarry for building material throughout the ages.

Figure 22-9 A Piranesi engraving of the Theater of Marcellus, a theater transformed into an apartment building in Rome.

Figure 22-11 Plans of the Santa Croce district of Florence showing the circular amphitheater converted to housing (P. Fontana, 1603).

Foundations and Founding Plans

As discussed earlier, the urban plan, like the foundation, is a permanent feature. The founding plan offers a fixed context for the evolving spatial structure of social territories and boundaries. These relationships between people and things become defined and associated with law and custom and are nearly impossible to eliminate. For example, the Stadium of Domitian became the foundation for the buildings surrounding Piazza Navona in Rome. Piazza Navona was originally a Roman racetrack, but now its enclosed form has become a wonderful urban plaza. This is an archetypal example of how an existing form can be

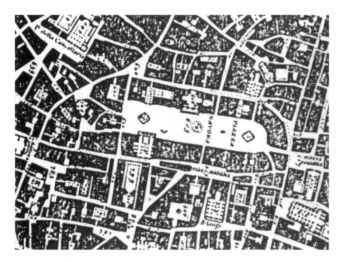

Figure 22-10 A section of 1748 Nolli plan of Rome; the Piazza Navona is at the center.

used as a foundation and founding plan for new uses and urban development. Another example can be found in the Santa Croce district of Florence, Italy. Absorbed in the residential textures is the foundation of an ancient amphitheater. The existence of the ancient building is hardly noticeable.

In Turin, Italy, and London, England, founding plans laid by colonial Romans and recycled through development in the medieval societies still persist in the dynamic cores of their morphological development. The Spaniards employed the existing plan of Cuzco, Peru, as the Inca left it when building their colonial town (the second stage in its morphogenesis). The Spanish builders subdivided and provided a context for development of new buildings and urban spaces.[13] The founding plan provided possibilities for changed uses.

Supports and Frameworks

The urban fabric of a city must be both well defined and adaptable so that it can both accommodate the variety of existing forms and future interventions that will occur. The Rue de Rivoli in Paris is such a morphological support: within it you find a rich population of shops, restaurants, cafes, and even hotels. Many urban buildings carry an amazing variety of social functions over time. The Coliseum in Rome, which became the site of two proposed reanimation operations, has a fantastic transfunctional character: a proposed transformation into a wool

Figure 22-12 Central Square, Cuzco, Peru, as developed by the Incas before their conquest and later transformed by the Spaniards in the 16th century C.E.

factory with workers' apartments and a later proposal to adapt it and create a forum for a centralized church.[14]

Streets and squares, as morphological parts, have provided support for public functions like strolling, dining, waiting, entertaining, sitting, selling, shopping,

Figure 22-13 Central Square, Cuzco, Peru, today (T. Bartuska).

Figure 22-14 City center development connects new buildings on the left with a reanimated historic school on the right with a glass-enclosed street. Vancouver, British Columbia, Canada (T. Bartuska).

horse racing, political rallies, parking, and public processions. Amsterdam's old lot pattern, with its brick walls perpendicular to the street, provides a structure for insertions. The lot space is six meters, the distance needed to span the space with a wooden beam spanning one masonry wall to another. This kind of supporting system has given the city a remarkable consistency since the Middle Ages.

A foundation is a horizontal connecting element, while its support components are vertical links for inser-

Figure 22-15 Arles, a town built within a second-century C.E. Roman amphitheater (J. Noble de la Lauziere).

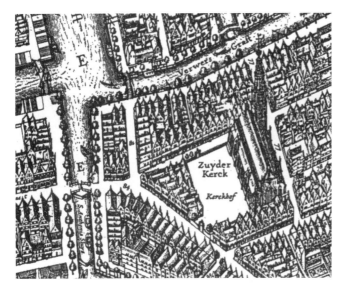

Figure 22-16 A segment of a 1625 map of Amsterdam, Holland.

tions or additions to established urban patterns. Charles Moore's extensions to the Citizens Federal Savings and Loan Association Building in San Francisco provide a contemporary example. The existing bank building furnishes support, linking Moore's addition to the street and block pattern. As noted before, the Yugoslavian town of Split is a dramatic demonstration of the use of an inherited urban framework. As a support for its inhabitants, the ruined palace of Diocletian was dramatically reused to establish social space marking private and public spaces. The wealthy, for example, made homes in the larger palatial apartments, while the poor found accommodations in the basement chambers. The ruined unroofed basilica became a public square. The palace provided the framework for new social uses.

Figure 22-17 Amsterdam today, showing how the 6-meter (20-foot) module is now used (T. Bartuska).

The true significance of any inherited urban form, then, is its value as a cultural resource, with great capacity for being reused as social functions change. This understanding of the adaptability of all the built environment's components of the city leads to the conservation of resources and societies' identity and sense of place.

References

Anderson, S. "The Plan of Savannah and Changes of Occupancy During Its Early Years: City Plan as Resource," *The Harvard Architecture Review*, Spring 1981.

Corboz, A. "Old Buildings and Modern Functions," *Lotus International*, 1976 Dec. V.13, pp. 68–79.

Fitch, J. *Historic Preservation: Curatorial Management of the Built Environment*. University Press of Virginia, 1992.

Giedon, S. *Space, Time and Architecture*, 13th printing. Harvard University Press, 1997.

Habraken, N. "The Leaves and the Flowers." In *VIA: Culture and Social Vision*, 1980.

Jacobs, J. *The Death and Life of Great American Cities*. Vintage Books, 1961.

Perez deArce, R. "Urban Transformation: The Architecture of Additions," *Architectural Design,* January, 1978.

Pevsner, N. *History of Building Types*, 5th printing. Princeton University Press, 1997.

Rossi, A. *The Architecture of the City*. MIT Press, 1982.

Scully, V. *American Architecture and Urbanism*. Praeger, 1969.

Secretary of the Interior. "Archeology and Historic Preservation Standards and Guidelines." 2006: www.cr.nps.gov/local-law/arch_studs_0.htm.

Stern, R. *New Directions in American Architecture*. Braziller, 1969.

Summerson, J. "Urban Forms." In *The Historian and the City*. MIT Press, 1963.

Vance, J. *The Continuing City: Urban Morphology in Western Civilization*. Johns Hopkins University Press, 1990.

Venturi, R., et al. *Learning from Las Vegas*. MIT Press, 1972.

Endnotes

1. Secretary of the Interior, Archeology and Historic Preservation Standards and Guidelines. 2006: www.cr.nps.gov/local-law/arch_stnds_0.htm, and J. Fitch, *Historic Preservation: Curatorial Management of the Built Environment* (University Press of Virginia, 1992).
2. See Note 1.
3. See Note 1.
4. J. Summerson, "Urban Forms," in *The Historian and the City* (MIT Press, 1963).
5. J. Vance, *The Continuing City: Urban Morphology in Western Civilization* (Johns Hopkins University Press, 1990).
6. J. Jacobs, *The Death and Life of Great American Cities* (Vintage Books, 1961).

7. S. Giedon, *Space, Time and Architecture*, 13th printing (Harvard University Press, 1997), and N. Pevsner, *History of Building Types*, 5th printing (Princeton University Press, 1997).

8. R. Stern, *New Directions in American Architecture* (Braziller, 1969).

9. V. Scully, *American Architecture and Urbanism* (Praeger, 1969).

10. See Note 5.

11. See Note 5.

12. S. Anderson, "The Plan of Savannah and Changes of Occupancy During Its Early Years: City Plan as Resource," *The Harvard Architecture Review*, Spring 1981.

13. R. Perez de Arce, "Urban Transformation: The Architecture of Additions," *Architectural Design,* January 1978.

14. A. Rossi, *The Architecture of the City* (MIT Press, 1982).

CHAPTER 23

Cities Today: The Imprint of Human Needs in Urban Patterns and Form

Tom J. Bartuska

Cities of today reflect a collective vision of society. They convey an inclusive story of some of civilization's greatest achievements and some of its worst. The stories they tell are expressed in human-environmental patterns, evolution, and change.

Great cities are civil places and an important expression of civilization. Most livable cities are the dynamic and civil hub of the economic, cultural, and social activities of their regions, sometimes of their countries, and even of the world. Many cities are delightful places to live, work, and play—places worthy of our attention and care.

Unfortunately, some cities have been neglected. Many significant problems of decaying cities are related. First, blight causes serious human/social, economic, and environmental problems, which manifest in disincentives to improve the city. Urban blight influences a second major and related problem: the decision by many people to escape difficult urban conditions by moving outside of the city. The process of outward migration from the city is known as **suburbanization**. People commute to the city for work but choose to live and shop outside of the urban core, no longer providing revenues that are needed to maintain necessary community amenities and infrastructure. The consequences of suburbanization can be even more serious than those of urban blight and more difficult to correct. In the worst cases, workplaces have also moved to suburban areas, further depriving the city of its necessary human and monetary resources. The high economic, social, and environmental costs of suburbanization (auto-dependent suburban sprawl) are tremendous. Regardless of the measure, sprawl is costly in energy (excessive auto use and large homes); in loss of prime agricultural land; and in monetary expenditures (higher taxes to provide necessary but defused community services and infrastructure). Unfortunately, few people connect the high cost of living, and even high crime rates, with the dual problems of urban decay and suburban sprawl. Urban problems are like tooth decay; they can be prevented by daily maintenance or by more invasive corrective surgery (which is expensive and painful).

An abundance of good news does exist. Many cities are healthy and exciting places to live, work, and play in.

277

Figure 23-1 The animated built environment of the city of Reading, England.

The great cities of the world are as vivid in our memories as they are in the following popular lyrics:

• I left my heart in San Francisco . . .
• Chicago, it's a wonderful town . . .
• Wonderful, wonderful Copenhagen . . .
• I love Paris . . .
• Things will be great when you go downtown, everything's waiting for you . . .

Great cities are more sustainable—by effective clustering, they conserve vital human/social, economic, and environmental resources. They are even lovable; they have many wonderful qualities, services, and facilities, such as great parks and fountains, museums, hospitals, governmental services, fine restaurants and pubs, jobs, markets, theaters and concert halls, sports, zoos and aquariums, art galleries, police and fire safety services, festivals, and parades. Great cities are the dynamic center of some of the best aspects of human achievements. They are societal life support systems and fulfill human needs, and celebrate and express the collective qualities of a civil life.

It is easy to dismiss cities or to focus on their negative aspects. But most cities are resilient places; they can be revitalized with care and concern. Everyone—citizens and the design/planning professionals—plays an important role in helping to reverse the trends of urban decline and to offset the effects of auto-driven suburban sprawl. We must all help to revitalize urban neighborhoods and to breathe new life and excitement into cities as places to celebrate, not denigrate, human and community life, and create enjoyable places to live, work, shop, socialize, and express our collective vision of culture.

Human/Social Needs and the City

Infrastructure and **land use** are important yet almost invisible or abstract elements that help determine the nature of a city. Equally important are the more visible elements of urban form, including buildings, blocks, streets, landscapes, and spaces between buildings. Individually and collectively, these elements help shape the form, visible character, quality, and spatial dimensions of the city. Land use patterns, commonly called "zones," define the various functions of a city (residential, commercial, governmental, and industrial zones of activity). **Infrastructure** (societal support systems developed to fulfill human needs and values) ties land uses together. Infrastructure is externally expressed in the circulation patterns (walkways, bike lanes, public transit, and auto systems) that allow people and goods to move and interconnect. Infrastructure also includes other important but less visible systems, such as energy (electric, gas, oil, etc.), utilities (water and sanitation, telephone and cable systems), and services (police, fire, health services, and street maintenance). Infrastructure is complex and costly. These relatively invisible support systems are critical to the city and are very similar to the support technologies discussed in earlier chapters. It is a tremendous accomplishment for society to organize, build, and operate these life support systems. Readers are encouraged to explore their dependencies on the life support infrastructures of a community. Trace and compare yours with the example in Table 23-1.

Creating positive environments in cities is important to everyone—environmental design professionals, political leaders, and most of all, the general public. It has also become imperative to analyze, repair, and correct the negative aspects and to reinvest time and resources in reanimating the inherited city—a significant human and cultural resource.

Human-Environmental Patterns: The Doorknob and Its Urban Context

Human needs and values create a definite imprint upon the city and are defined in land use and infrastructure. The imprint of each and every individual is part of the excitement and complexity of the city. These patterns, like fingerprints, begin with the individual and radiate outward into the city. They are expressed as patterns of **human-environmental relationships** (HE/HER) and

Table 23-1 Human/Social Needs and Urban Institutions and Infrastructure

EXAMPLES OF HUMAN NEEDS AND ACTIVITIES	URBAN INSTITUTIONS AND INFRASTRUCTURE
The music from the clock radio comes on at 6:45 Tuesday morning. Although cold outside, the warm bedroom is a welcome transition to what will be a busy day. To erase the darkness, Chris flicks on the lights on the way to the bathroom and shower. Refreshed, clean and dressed, Chris goes to the kitchen alcove for breakfast. Coffee, cereal and milk are hastily retrieved from the refrigerator. The 7:20 news comes on as the newspaper headlines are quickly reviewed before cleaning up and leaving for work. The evening rainstorm has freshened the air. Workers are busily cleaning the storm drains of debris to ease the water ponding before the rush hour traffic intensifies. The pace of activities quickens as the sidewalks and streets fill with people hustling to work. The pedestrians seem irritated to have to wait for the cars and to have them, as if in a different world, spray water onto the curb. The lights are not working and a police officer is actively directing traffic. Fortunately, Chris is able to catch the 7:45 transit and is whisked off to the city center. It is a more relaxing time to finish reading the paper and reflect upon the challenges of the day. At the city center, Chris leisurely walks to work through the beautiful landscaped walkways. A few people pause to view the urban park where city workers are busy setting up for the noon concert. The weather, as predicted, looks promising. On time at work, Chris reviews the computer screen for important messages, responds to two by phone and transfers others via e-mail. The office seems warm and Chris feels a bit sleepy. By 10:00, interoffice, regular, and express mail is sorted and reviewed. At 11:45, Chris anxiously awaits a luncheon date with a close friend. The once introverted city dramatically changes as its people discharge onto its outdoor spaces. Chris and Jean meet at the museum and decide to go to the concert instead of the waterfall park for a chat and lunch. The restaurants and outdoor cafes are busy, so they pick up a sandwich from a street vendor. An ambulance speeds by and muffles their conversation. The concert is wonderful; the people, music and the waterside park landscape animate the city's finest qualities. The city clock tower strikes 1 P.M., Chris hastily says farewell and returns to the office refreshed and motivated to continue . . .	• Radio/electrical energy • Time: who invented time to organize our lives? • Heat and ventilation/energy • Lighting/electrical energy • Water/sanitation systems • Clothes and food: commercial institutions • Appliances/electrical energy • Communication networks: newspapers, radio, and telecommunications • Street maintenance • Recycling services • Storm drain systems • Walking and bikeways • Streets systems • Traffic control, public services • Auto/road systems/energy • Public safety officers • Public transit systems/energy • Time/schedules • Pedestrian priority circulation networks • City maintenance staff • Weather services and satellite systems • Urban parks and their programs • Computer networks/energy • Heat, ventilation, and lighting systems/energy • Communication systems (phone and mail: interoffice, local, national, and international addresses) • Time, scheduling • Diversity of employment • Urban parks and open space • Social/cultural institutions • Cultural institutions (art museums and galleries, churches, entertainment) • Restaurants and food distribution systems • Urban parks and services • Public service (police, fire, health and safety, government) • Time, scheduling • Diversity of employment

Source: Royston (1985).

can be traced, starting with the individual and his or her doorknob and radiating outward into the neighborhood, the city, and its region.

HE/HER patterns are like a stone thrown into a still pond. At impact, the object becomes the center of concentric waves radiating outward. The patterns of two or more stones create intersecting rippling patterns. In a similar way, urban patterns radiate outward in waves from each person's door, intersecting other patterns from other households throughout the city.[1] The patterns in water are beautiful, as they should be in the city.

The **doorknob** is a small individual object, a product of human creation, an object embedded in the complexities of the smallest home (a house or apartment) and the grandest city. The doorknob is functional and symbolic; opening the door to the outside provides insights into the rich complexities and qualities of a community, including neighboring structures, landscapes, and urban patterns. Inside the door is, of course, the personal or private domain—the products, the interiors, and the enclosing structure. The doorknob is conveniently and proudly placed on the door at the threshold between inside and outside, with access in both directions. It controls access to the private realm of the dwelling unit. The door is designed to be part of an inviting entryway or porch. The entry relates to a front garden, a lawn, a sidewalk, and a street. Society has established ways of defining the intersecting relationships of private territories. Fences, landscaping, gates, and terraces are commonly used elements to define property lines—elements that give clarity to the built environment.

Like the design of a good doorway, semiprivate aspects are essential to understand and express in the design of the community/urban environments. When effectively expressed, they can be considered signs of a responsive, healthy environment—one that shows personal definition, involvement, and pride. When these factors are not expressed, apathy can become a problem, human-environmental patterns deteriorate, and crime and vandalism can increase.

Semiprivate territories created by the **doorknob-door-porch-garden** relate to nearby houses, walkways, and streets. Such neighboring elements are commonly referred to as "semipublic patterns" or "activities"—"semi" because they are subdivisions of more public

Figures 23-3 and 23-4 Defining human-environmental territories in sprawling suburban (Chicago) and clustered urban housing (Vancouver, Canada).

Figure 23-2 Diagrams of human-environmental imprints/patterns: doorknob to dwelling, like stone-caused ripples in a pond.

places. Residential walkways and streets connect clusters of neighbors together to form a neighborhood.

The **neighborhood** is a fundamental building block, a basic planning unit in the design of cities. Good neighborhoods create important connections between the individual and society and, when well defined, foster a sense of community and civic pride. In their most effective form, they provide some of the basic needs of society—a small grocery shop, meeting places, a neighborhood park and playground, and especially an elementary school to which young children can walk safely to school and chat and play on the way home. "Neighborhoods [are] instruments of civilization . . . preserve and strengthen [them] as the basic . . . cell in the urban organism."[2]

Once again, the doorknob has a basic function; it opens the door to neighbors, to neighborhoods, to the neighboring environment. Neighborliness binds individuals and families and establishes the positive qualities of an urban community. A neighborhood connects the people behind each door to the basic social, cultural, and recreational networks of a friendly social unit and the city. In cities throughout the world, old and new neighborhoods

Figure 23-5 Subdivision patterns of walkways and streets. Village Houses, Davis, California (courtesy of Sandra Satterlee).

are being created and/or revitalized with sensitive clustered housing and accessible neighborhood facilities.

A more complex pattern develops when neighborhood units combine to form a larger urban **district**. Some

Figures 23-8 and 23-9 Old and new clustered housing in an urban neighborhood. San Francisco, California (top), and Portland, Oregon.

cultures define this scale of urban development as a **village** or **town**. Planning for such units should include accessible schools and recreational, commercial, medical, governmental, and cultural facilities to serve a larger population.

Districts or villages combine to form the **city**. The larger the city, the more districts and neighborhoods it will have, as well as places with a diversity of social/cultural, commercial, and recreational opportunities. The focus of the traditional city is the city center. Besides the basic functions of government and workplace, the most livable cities have a healthy heart—a **city center** that provides restaurants, concerts, festivals, art galleries and museums, parks and river walkways, open markets, city government, and entertainment to celebrate life and make being in the city fun. Labeling city centers "central business districts" (CBDs) is limiting and one-dimensional. Cities need business to provide goods, services, and jobs, but also life-enhancing places to live and play. Accepting that a city center can be replaced by shopping malls is even worse. New shopping malls built on the edges of

Figures 23-6 and 23-7 Subdivision patterns of walkways and streets—when originally developed and now. Village Houses, Davis, California.

cities drain city centers of their vitality, increase transportation problems and costs, and foster suburban sprawl. With subcentralization (see Chapter 21), city centers decline. Vacant stores, lonely streets, and lack of nighttime activities are symptoms of this erosion of vitality. But city centers are resilient; like neighborhoods and their nurturing amenities, centers can be revitalized through positive leadership, proactive government, and concerned citizens who understand and support the importance of civility and the city.

Fortunately, in many city centers, these difficult challenges are being met: they are being revitalized and enjoyed by increasing numbers of people who want to live and be part of the dynamics of a great city. Amenities like walkable streets, waterfronts, and parks with views of mountains and forests give city centers an exciting contrast between urban/built environments and the natural environment.

Figure 23-12   Enjoying the special qualities of the city. Seattle, Washington.

Figures 23-10 and 23-11   Dynamic qualities of the city center or strip commercial development. Boston, Massachusetts (top) and almost anywhere in the United States.

Cities also impact the surrounding **region** in multiple ways. Cities combine into even larger urban units, commonly referred to as **metropolitan regions**. Too many cities, as they grow, sprawl over their boundaries onto rural areas, obliterating farm and forest lands, absorbing or annexing smaller outlying communities as they expand. The regional requirements of people in urban places for food, water, energy, and other essentials are huge. Fulfilling these requirements is a very complex task and underlines the extent to which cities depend upon regional, national, and even international resources, as well as manufacturing and distribution systems. Table 23-2 itemizes the daily requirements of food and energy for New York City. Imagine supplying a city with 108,000,000 eggs each day—almost 40 billion a

Table 23-2 Daily Resource Needs for the City of New York

Energy and Water Supplies	
• Electricity	2,600,000 kilowatt hours
• Oil and gasoline	5,500,000 gallons*
• Water	1,000,000,000 gallons
• Sewage	1,000,000,000 gallons
Food Supplies	
• Vegetables	5,200,000 lbs.
• Meat	2,700,00 lbs.
• Poultry	1,300,000 lbs.
• Eggs	108,000,000 eggs

*if used in cars, 110,000,000 pounds of CO_2 will be released into the air.
Source: Royston (1985).

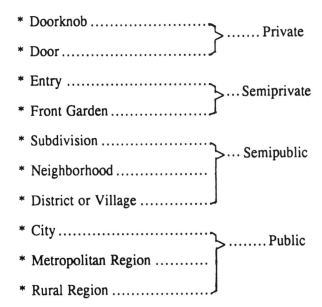

* Doorknob ....⟩ .... Private
* Door ....⟩

* Entry ....⟩ ...Semiprivate
* Front Garden ....⟩

* Subdivision ....⟩ ... Semipublic
* Neighborhood ....
* District or Village ....⟩

* City ....⟩ .... Public
* Metropolitan Region ....
* Rural Region ....⟩

Figure 23-13   Urban patterns: private-to-public territorial continuum.

year. Accomplishing such a task may seem incredibly complex, but it is far more efficient than having each individual trying to fulfill his or her needs separately from the urban/regional unit. For eggs alone, that would require at least two or three chickens behind every door in the city.

The complexities of cities can be better understood by looking at them as a series of patterns radiating outward—from the private domain of the individual to the most public aspects of a city and its regional context. These interlocking sets of urban patterns are difficult to observe when walking or traveling through a city. They are more apparent from the air. The problem is analogous to studying the human body. True health and beauty are not just skin deep. External observation can be appreciated, but the health of a person requires X-ray and laboratory studies of the structure (skeleton) and biological systems. An X-ray vision of urban patterns is required to more fully understand and effectively design urban places and spaces. The patterns define a continuum: private-to-public territorial zones of space and facilities.

History has proven that cities are more effective and efficient if the relationships among their parts are well defined and integrated. This not only requires knowledge of the significant defining patterns of cities, but also people who care and get involved to ensure that such relationships are created and maintained. As emphasized throughout the chapters in this book, "Integration may well be the key word in good design. Not only does it

mean the correct combining of parts into a whole; but it implies [that] by association, integrity, soundness and honesty . . . environmental design, now and in the future, is and will be a matter of expert teamwork supported by public appreciation [awareness] and participation."[3]

A Community Test

Putting people first is a simple test for evaluating successful neighborhoods and cities. The basic test question is, can families, especially children, **walk** to school, a park, and a shop to buy a loaf of bread? In most successful urban places, planners and designers have been able to enhance the public realm with human qualities and amenities such as easy access to work, diversity of shopping, child care and schools, public transit, and affordable housing. These basic amenities enable all city dwellers—including and perhaps especially those who have low incomes—to lead a quality life. The success of Portland, Oregon, as a city and as a place to live derives from a simpler set of priorities: put pedestrians first, then design for public transit, and, lastly, accommodate the car. Simple priorities can have far-reaching implications.

One wonderful example: the planners in Portland banned dwellings with jutting, full-fronted garages creating a "garagescape," not a people-friendly **streetscape**. These are also what Portland calls "snout houses" because they failed the "trick-or-treat test"—children couldn't find the front door on Halloween night.[4]

Creating successful pedestrian zones in cities requires a set of diverse activities (commonly called **"mixed use"**), moderate clustering or density of those activities, and a sense of twenty-four-hour life (requires housing near or above shopping areas). Sprawling low-density developments lack efficient density and are too diffuse to be successful pedestrian zones. In these neighborhoods the auto comes first, requiring an extensive and expensive auto-oriented infrastructure to support its wasteful inefficiencies. Auto-oriented cities often become places people want to leave, creating more sprawl. Clustered pedestrian-oriented cities are those that people enjoy, write songs about, and want to inhabit. Too many people believe the advertisements that suggest they can only be happy with the latest sport utility vehicle and need to live in a huge house out in the suburbs. Such choices are very expensive to individuals and society in terms of social-economic-environmental costs (SEE variables). They isolate young and old from the wonderful enriching qualities of a healthy neighborhood and an animated city.

Clustered developments also minimize the length of expensive infrastructure and maximize land use efficiencies by increasing the density. In general, clustered urban forms are most efficient; sprawling forms are least efficient and most costly.

A walking environment creates an optimum density of housing. Walking requires short distances (0.5 to 1 kilometer or one-fourth to one-half of a mile) and pleasant pathways to schools, parks, and shops. Neighborhood facilities require a certain population to support them. The population dictates the number of housing units. Walking distance determines the radius of the area in which most of the housing and community amenities need to be built. Walking communities need a housing mix effectively designed for a moderate density (generally calculated at 10 to 15 dwelling units per acre [D/A]). Most neighborhoods of single, detached housing (generally two to five D/A) are too spread out to encourage walking or the efficient use of public transit. Traditional neighborhoods built before World War II, where houses are sited on smaller lots and close to downtown districts, are a notable exception and provide good examples of walkable communities. The fact remains—to work, neighborhood units require convenient facilities within walking distance and a range of housing choices.

Leading the Way to a Better Future: London

Planning with these patterns of human-environment relationships in mind makes a lot of sense for all cities, new and old. This method of defining HE/HER patterns was extensively used in the planning of London during and after World War II. The 1946 Greater London County (GLC) Plan and the resulting strategies are internationally renowned. At that time, London and New York City were the two largest cities in the world. London, like all industrial cities, was experiencing tremendous growth. Urban/suburban growth was spreading outward, eating up the surrounding countryside and prime agricultural resources at an alarming rate. The infrastructure (transportation network and public services) was being extended to serve these sprawling developments at a very high public monetary cost and inefficiency. Uncontrolled sprawling development was overtaxing the existing systems (auto, public transit, water and sewage, air pollution, energy, police and fire protection, etc.). This condition continues in many other sprawling cities

today. These sprawling use patterns and extensive infrastructure were like a cancer—uncontrolled, unhealthy growth of the urban organism, destroying itself and its regional amenities and resources.

Through extensive study and bold national legislation, London made the following critical decisions about urban **growth management** (GM) and clustered urban patterns.

A. Establish Growth Management Policies to Control Sprawl

Before the GLC growth management policies and plan, London was circled by miles of the same kind of low-density sprawl that surrounds most cities. In this case, however, all the growth occurred before World War II. In order to stop uncontrolled growth, a **green belt** or "girdle" was placed around London and other cities to contain sprawl, preserve the surrounding rural resources and countryside, and stop inefficient expansion of the urban infrastructure. Now with the green belt, sprawl is contained and the beautiful countryside, and rural landscapes of agricultural farms and villages are retained. The contrast is remarkable.

Green belts are like a land bank and provide an effective strategy to contain growth within a defined area. These GM strategies are being used throughout the world to control sprawl and preserve regional resources. Successful examples of this important land banking strategy in the United States include Boulder, Colorado; Davis, California; and Portland, Oregon.

B. Cluster Development in New Towns and Revitalize Old Towns

To allow normal urban growth to continue, the GLC Plan proposed, and the British government implemented, **town and country** growth policies. New towns were established and built some 30 miles from London, beyond the green belt. Thirteen new towns were built around London with an approximate population of 30,000 to 80,000 each. About 40 new towns were built throughout Britain around other major cities that implemented similar GM strategies. There is even one called Washington, named after George Washington's ancestral home. In addition to new towns, and where appropriate, clustered expansion was planned for existing towns outside of London as well as in London's internal villages. These new towns and revitalized old towns are connected to London by fast rail.

Figure 23-14   Green belt placed around London to contain its subcentralized growth and the development of new towns and expanded existing towns to accommodate clustered growth. Greater London Plan, 1946.

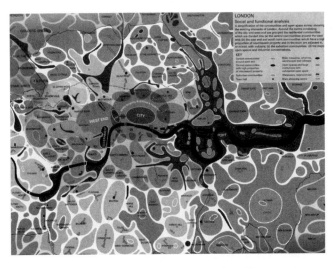

Figure 23-15   The excellent Greater London Plan creating a city of clustered urban neighborhoods and villages interconnected by public transit and defined by greenways, parks, and open space.

Today, the new towns are complete—and successful. London's complex system, though not problem-free, is considered an excellent model for effective design/planning strategies for the management of urban and regional developments.

C. Reanimate Urban Neighborhoods and Villages

In order to improve inner London, villages were defined as important planning units. The villages were the focus of further internal development/redevelopment, and many were surrounded by parks and open space. Today, London is known as a unique city, a city of villages.[5] These communities may not be completely recognizable to an untrained eye, but local people strongly identify with their clustered urban villages and neighborhood units. This clustered development is interconnected by public transit (the famous London tube, the first interurban rail transit system in the world).

Throughout the world, many cities are actively refocusing and developing clustered neighborhood and village patterns. Seattle's Vision 2020 program discovered, through an extensive public participatory process, that the public (a resounding 90%) prefers clustered urban growth interconnected by transit and surrounded by open space. Unfortunately, the visionary 2020 plan for clustered growth is being stymied by regressive tax initiatives that support auto dominance and sprawl while limiting funding for public transit.[6]

The ABCs of Urban Design and Planning

Cities are a symbol of the civilized world. A proactive attitude is critical for them to thrive and prosper as centers of human activity. Cities, like all components of the built environment, need enlightened citizen participation and effective leadership and governance, guided by expert teamwork from all the design, planning, and scientific disciplines. Effective urban design strategies can strengthen the capacity of cities to achieve their civil potential as the heart of human activities and culture—to become animated places that people cherish and maintain. Effective strategies for enhancing the human-environmental relationships of cities today are presented next.

A. Human Strategies

A1. Proactive Citizen Participation. Put people first. It is fun to become aware of and involved in human-environmental issues. Citizen participation is an important quality of a democratic society. Sharing ideas, viewpoints, and perspectives is critical—with friends, civic organizations, local news media, governmental representatives, and administrative officials. Cities like Chattanooga, Tennessee, lead the nation in advancing the power of citizen participation to bring together and revitalize a struggling city.[7] This proactive vision process has engaged the public, civic leaders, and the design/planning community (educators, students, and professionals). In the process, a very successful Downtown Planning and Design Center was cre-

Figures 23-16 and 23-17   Poster and Downtown Planning and Design Center in Chattanooga, Tennessee. The Center was designed as an urban meeting place with a small park and Meeting/Market building (center), an outdoor stage (bottom right), and restaurants (lower floor right), with the Downtown Planning and Design Center on the second floor.

ated to help implement many of the citizens' ideas.[8] Chapter 4 more fully addresses the importance of citizen participation and discusses additional ways people can get involved in generating ideas and action programs.

A2. Effective Leadership and Government. Democracies welcome citizen awareness and participation (or at least they should). City committees, design and planning commissions, and city councils generally welcome public input. The primary purpose of these governmental organizations is to represent the populace, so it is useful to understand the governmental planning process (this is explored in the next chapter).

A3. Collaborative Environmental Design and Planning. The design and planning of urban settlements is a complex task. Professionals are trained and licensed to guide and shape development of the built environment. Because of the exciting multidimensional aspects of most urban issues, a holistic perspective and collaborative efforts of design/planning disciplines and the general public are critically important.

B. Environmental Strategies

Be sensitive to healthy human-land use patterns—from the doorknob to the dynamics of the urban environment.

B1. Strengthen Neighborhoods. Friendly, integrated neighborhoods are a key element in making healthy linkages between the individual and the community. Citizens need to encourage and support neighborhood activities and critical amenities: accessible schools, parks, and recreational activities, walking and bike paths, convenient shopping, garage and craft sales, and so on. People should encourage city officials to develop neighborhood associations or planning groups to clarify and strengthen quality assets and solve problems. Neighborhood action plans can be part of the comprehensive planning process. Avoid, at all cost, the closure of neighborhood support facilities (especially schools). Avoid plans for traffic routes that cut through cohesive neighborhoods. Mixed housing densities can offer a range of more affordable dwelling alternatives. Increasing the mix and density of housing can provide a rich diversity of people and support more accessible neighborhood facilities at reduced cost.

B2. Revitalize City Centers. The traditional focus of a city is its center, its heart that needs to beat with the rhythms of the city. City centers should be the "living/family room" of the community and a special place, the focus of a civil society and a manifestation of all human

Figures 23-18 and 23-19 Interdisciplinary team of designers and planners participating in a public workshop. Citizen participation (making comments on proposals, verbally above and graphically on drawings below). Seattle, Washington.

support institutions and services. Many city centers are being revitalized by adapting old buildings—important and irreplaceable parts of a city's heritage—for exciting new uses and by building new structures to fit in with the cityscape. Landscaping, water amenities, and street furniture are widely used strategies to enhance urban spaces. More and more city centers are filling with people instead of cars. Restaurants and cafes, farmers' markets, arts and craft shows, outdoor concerts and parades, landscaping, even flower boxes and banners are enriching the diversity and enjoyment of city centers. Single-function business districts, strip developments, and

Figure 23-20 Urban neighborhood and fine clustered housing. Bainbridge Island, Washington.

Figure 23-21 Dynamic human-environmental qualities of some cities today. Munich, Germany.

sprawling shopping centers should be avoided because they siphon resources and activities from the city center.

B3. Protect Regional Resources and Avoid Auto-Driven Suburban Sprawl. This dual problem requires effective and coordinated urban and regional GM policies and procedures. Such programs are not anti-growth, but pro-meaningful growth while conserving finite regional (and global) resources. Careful planning can achieve both objectives. Refocusing city centers and developing cohesive neighborhoods can help prevent suburban sprawl and minimize costly infrastructure services.

C. Interrelationship Strategies (Infrastructure: Circulation, Utilities, and Services)

Through interrelationship strategies, more efficient, less costly infrastructure systems can be developed to improve services and reduce personal and societal costs.

C1. Put People First and Balance All Transportation Systems. Citizens and officials should demand design in the public realm that puts people first. A multimodal balance of all circulation systems should be encouraged, which includes placing the highest priority on encouraging and supporting pedestrian activity and biking, putting public transit second, then car and van pools, and giving the lowest priority to the inefficient single-occupancy automobile. Because of society's love affair with the private automobile, most U.S. cities are hopelessly out of balance; autos consume huge amounts of space for roads and parking infrastructure; create noise, gridlock, congestion, air pollution, and high energy use; and cause some 50% of global warming in the United States (see Chapter 28 for a discussion of U.S. cities that are adopting the Kyoto Protocol on reducing global warming).

Studies have shown that up to two-thirds of the land use in most auto-oriented cities and one-third in suburban areas is given over to auto circulation, parking, and related services; that does not leave much space for people, services, buildings, landscaping, and open areas. These huge personal and societal costs are hidden in everything we buy and do. Cars are costly to own and operate and consume about half of the nation's petroleum resources; they emit a significant portion of greenhouse gases. Government subsidies for parking approximate the size of the U.S. Medicare Program budget.[9] Multimodal transportation systems can minimize costly inefficiencies and pollution while providing more options for children and the elderly who cannot drive a car. Reduced auto dependency can make cities healthier and more enjoyable places to live, work and play. Table 23-3 summarizes the relative efficiencies of various circulation systems in terms of energy per passenger mile and land use. The automobile is by far the most inefficient. The bi-cycle, an amazing example of appropriate technology, is approximately 40 times more efficient than the automobile in terms of energy, 3 times more land efficient, and 120 times more efficient when land and energy are factored together.

C2. Minimize Infrastructure Costs—Cluster, Don't Sprawl.

Clustered community development with a mixture of moderate densities can create cohesive neighborhoods and achieve efficient infrastructure patterns without compromising residential qualities. An efficient infrastructure can enhance the cost effectiveness of public services and minimize utility and property taxes. Low-density sprawl is the most costly and wasteful form of urban growth.

Figure 23-22 Putting people first, transit second. Portland, Oregon's, pedestrian and transit streetscape.

The human-environmental relationships and strategies described in this chapter are complex and highly interrelated. Cities were not built in a day. They cannot be remade in a day. Time and positive human effort can help strengthen urban communities as places that express and celebrate human civility and cultures. Apathy can foster urban decay and create higher monetary and human and environmental costs, both locally and globally. The suggested collaborative design/planning strategies can help those who want to creatively guide cities to become more healthy, sustainable, environmentally fit places to live, work, and play.

References

Brebbia, C., et al. *The Sustainable City: Urban Regeneration and Sustainability.* WIT, 2002.

Chattanooga Adventures, 2006: www.co-intelligence.org/S-Chattanooga.html.

Chattanooga's Design and Planning Center, 2006: www.rivercitycompany.com/about/design.asp.

DeBell, G. *The Environmental Handbook.* Ballantine Books, 1970.

Duany, A., et al. *Suburban Nation: The Rise of Sprawl and the Decline of the American Dream.* North Point Press, 2000.

Greenbie, B. *Space: Dimensions of Human Landscape.* Yale University Press, 1981.

Hayden, D. *A Field Guide to Sprawl.* W. W. Norton, 2004.

Jacobs, J. *The Death and Life of Great American Cities.* Vintage Books, 1961.

Jenks, M., and N. Dempsey. *Future Forms and Design for Sustainable Cities.* Architectural Press, 2005.

May, G. *The Future of the City: Issues for the 21st Century.* Futures, 1990.

Rasmusen, S. *London: The Unique City.* MIT Press, 1983.

Table 23-3 Relative Efficiencies of Various Urban Circulation Systems: Energy in Passengers per Mile, Land Use in Passengers per Lane Width (DeBell, 1970), and Relative Efficiencies of Both Factored Together

CIRCULATION TYPES	ENERGY	LAND	ENERGY × LAND
Bike	40	3	120
Walking	28	2	56
Public Transit Bus	4	17	68
Public Transit Rail	3	12	36
Automobile	1	1	1

Riding, A. "London: Next City of the Sky?" *New York Times,* June 30, 2004.

Royston, R. *Cities 2000.* Paulton Books, 1985.

Rudlin, D., and N. Falk. *Building the 21st Century Home: The Sustainable Urban Neighborhood.* Architecture Press, 2000.

Shoup, D. *The High Cost of Free Parking.* American Planning Association, 2006.

Von Eckardt, W. *Back to the Drawing Board: Planning Livable Cities.* New Republic Books, 1978.

Endnotes

1. B. Greenbie, *Space: Dimensions of Human Landscape* (Yale University Press, 1981).

2. W. Von Eckardt, *Back to the Drawing Board: Planning Livable Cities* (New Republic Books, 1978): p. 203.

3. R. F. Reekie, *Design in the Built Environment* (Edward Arnold, 1972): pp. v and 5.

4. D. Hayden, *A Field Guide to Sprawl* (W. W. Norton, 2004).

5. S. Rasmusen, *London: The Unique City* (MIT Press, 1983).

6. M. Jenks and N. Dempsey, *Future Forms and Design for Sustainable Cities* (Architectural Press, 2005).

7. Chattanooga Adventures, 2006: www.co-intelligence.org/ S-chattanooga.html.

8. Chattanooga's Design and Planning Center, 2006: www. rivercitycompany.com/about/design.asp.

9. D. Shoup, *The High Cost of Free Parking* (American Planning Association, 2006).

CHAPTER 24

Urban Design and Planning

Michael S. Owen

Few people realize that cities are actually planned and designed. Most cities may appear to be highly complex, complicated, and chaotic. It is true that they are complex, but most cities do exhibit an underlying order or rationale. This order is brought into being by the deliberate processes of urban planning and design. This chapter describes some basic concepts related to these processes and the professionals who carry out the work.

The Authority to Plan

Do private property owners have the right to do whatever they choose with their land? The answer is "not entirely"; the drafters of the U.S. Constitution believed in a balance between private rights and public welfare. Drawing from English law, two primary authorities were granted to the federal government under the Constitution: the authority of eminent domain and police powers. These authorities were intended to provide the federal government with the legal means for regulating the use of private property on behalf of the general welfare of the community.

Under the authority of **eminent domain**, the federal government has the power to own property and to expropriate property from private landowners. The Fifth Amendment to the Constitution (part of the Bill of Rights), however, stipulates that private citizens have the right to be compensated for the compulsory taking of their prop-

erty when the federal government appropriates it for public use. In other words, the federal government is required to pay private citizens the fair market price for their property.

Among other powers governing the health, safety, and welfare of U.S. citizens, **police powers** were established in the Constitution to allow the federal government to regulate the use of privately owned property. Similar powers were given to state governments in 1928 under the Standard State Planning Enabling Act. In turn, each state legislature has given police powers to local, city, and county authorities through enabling legislation. Cities and counties, then, also have the power to expropriate and regulate private property under the authority of the Constitution. Most property-related issues, therefore, are argued on constitutional grounds, often to the level of the U.S. Supreme Court.

General Welfare of the Community

Most people intuitively understand what is meant by the general welfare of the community. If tax dollars are traced to government responsibilities and related functions, the wide array of infrastructures, facilities, and services that the government provides is revealed. At the local level, they include:

- **Safety**: fire protection and emergency services
- **Security**: police protection

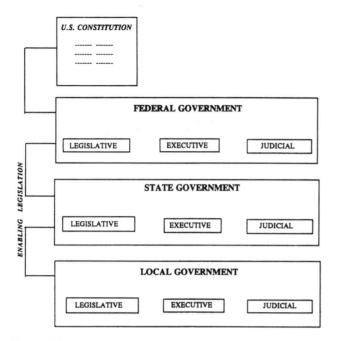

Figure 24-1   Graph showing the transfer of authority by the U.S. Constitution to the three levels of government.

- **Health**: adequate provision of air, water, sanitation, light, emergency, and hospital services
- **Transportation**: walkways, bikeways, mass transit, streets, highways, and traffic regulations
- **Education and recreation**: schools, parks, playgrounds, and civic and cultural amenities

Along with this obvious list is a function that most people would not immediately consider: the preservation and stabilization of community and personal property values. This is an inherent part of the government's responsibility for protecting the general welfare of the community. The mechanisms for carrying out this responsibility are called **comprehensive planning** and **zoning**.

Administrative Planning Structure

By definition, urban planning and zoning in the United States are carried out by local governments: cities and counties. Note, in Figure 24-1, that the organization of government in the United States has a similar structure at each level: a legislative branch, which writes and enacts laws; an executive branch, which administers the laws; and a judicial branch, which interprets the laws. At the city level of government, the legislative body is called the "city council" and the executive is called the "mayor." Local courts typically have jurisdiction over small (dam-

age) claims and traffic violations and do not play a role in planning or zoning. When the courts do get involved with planning and zoning, it is typically at the state and federal levels.

City Council

Members of city councils are elected officials whose role is to govern on behalf of the general welfare of the community within their geographic boundaries—the city limits.

In this capacity, councils write and enact laws called **ordinances** and **codes**. City councils are the final authorities for regulation of land use within these jurisdictions. All planning, zoning questions, and disputes for a particular city are decided by the council. A similar organization exists at the county level. At the state level, the governor and legislature function in a similar way.

Since planning and zoning are only a small part of the total responsibilities of any city council, most cities create an advisory body (to the council) called a **planning commission**, which is composed of local citizens appointed by the mayor. As an advisor to the council, the planning commission makes recommendations pertaining to the adoption of plans and ordinances and to arbitration of zoning disputes. For planning and zoning issues, the city (or county) council has the final authority. Councils may approve, revise, or reject any or all of a planning commission's recommendations.

In larger cities, a subcommittee of the planning commission, called the **board of adjustment**, is also maintained to review and arbitrate specific requests for zone changes, conditional uses, and variances. These functions may also be carried out by an individual hearing examiner.

The actions of all persons involved in zoning arbitration are strictly governed by regulations in the local zoning ordinance. Final interpretation of the regulations is made by the city council.

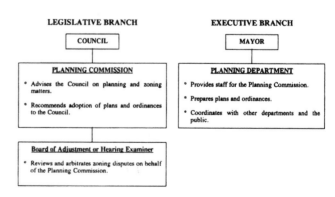

Figure 24-2   Graph showing how local governments are organized to carry out planning and zoning.

If property owners want to dispute a finding of the city council, they must bring a suit in a court of law. Typically, suits focus on one of two issues: first, "due process" or "fairness"—whether the council acted in compliance with its own ordinance; second, "constitutionality"—whether the zoning ordinance itself is in compliance with the U.S. Constitution. In either case, the city must demonstrate that the decision it made against the property owner was not arbitrary or capricious.

Public Participation

In all of the instances mentioned above, decisions by a city council, a planning commission, a board of adjustment, or a hearing examiner are made only after the public has had an opportunity to comment on the issue in a **public hearing**. Public hearings are part of the process of government in a democratic society. Such meetings are typically advertised in local "newspapers of record" and often posted, with letters sent to all property owners within 200 to 300 feet of the location of a proposed action.

The intent of the public hearing is to encourage public participation in order to air all views; it is part of the fact finding necessary to evaluate a proposal. The final decision affecting a land use is not necessarily based, however, on public sentiment. It is based (presumably) on careful deliberation of all facts and fair judgment in accordance with the interpretation of accepted planning principles. Sometimes this process requires city councils to make unpopular decisions, but hopefully it serves the general welfare of the community over the long term.

Planning Department

As mentioned, the city council is part of the legislative branch, and the mayor is the head of the executive branch of local government. As elected positions, they can change with the political cycles inherent in a democratic form of government.

To govern a city, the mayor relies on an organization of administrative departments. The department responsible for planning and zoning in city government is the **planning department**, which is composed of persons trained in urban planning, urban design, and/or other related fields. The planning staff, sometimes with the help of outside professional planning consultants, prepares the planning ordinances of the city. Although the city council has the final authority for planning and zoning, the planning department has the technical expertise and professional knowledge of the field.

In addition to preparing plans and ordinances, the planning department has the responsibility of issuing development approvals based on developers' compliance with the zoning ordinances. If planners determine that a development proposal is not in compliance with the zoning ordinances, it will be turned down and/or referred to the board of adjustment for review.

Ultimately, it is the responsibility of the planning department to bring professional knowledge to bear on the preparation and administration of city plans and ordinances. At times, the recommendations of the planning department run counter to the political objectives of the elected officials. The conflicting goals of environmental conservation and protection versus economic growth and development often represent the type of disputes that can arise.

Such tension is an inherent result of the democratic process and the system of checks and balances. Essentially, and ultimately, all land use and development decisions are economic and political in nature. They bear on the fundamental constitutional rights of individuals to "life, liberty, and the pursuit of happiness" while protecting the general welfare of the community. This balance is what citizens charge both elected officials (mayors and councils) and professional staff (planners and administrators) to negotiate on their behalf. Citizens—"the public"—are the third essential ingredient to ensure that the process works. To protect the public interest, citizens should insist upon an open process and should be involved enough to gain, and then maintain, the necessary knowledge and understanding of how the system works.

The Comprehensive Plan

A **comprehensive plan** is not a law; it is a policy document that, through (ideally) rigorous research, analysis, and public input, identifies the goals, objectives, and methods of providing for the orderly growth and development of a municipality. Comprehensive planning is an ongoing activity performed by the planning department. From time to time, depending on the rate of change a city is experiencing, a comprehensive plan will be updated and printed to represent the culmination of analysis and recommendations for a certain period until it is again updated in a subsequent plan (generally every 5–10 years). The comprehensive plan for a small town may consist of a single volume, while plans for large cities can run to dozens of volumes and thousands of pages. All governmental decisions regarding land use must be in compliance with the comprehensive plan; otherwise, such decisions can be challenged as arbitrary and capricious.

Analysis Elements

As noted, the intent of the comprehensive plan is to provide policies and general guidelines for the development of a city. As such, it must address the goals and objectives of every aspect of urban life, including:

- Population growth and distribution
- Environmental quality
- Energy consumption/conservation
- Transportation
- Housing, commerce, industry/manufacturing
- Health, education, and welfare
- Public safety and security
- Public recreation and culture

Note how these compare to the elements that make up the general welfare of the community. This is because the comprehensive plan is intended to guide government decision making as it relates to both public and private development.

In recent years, planners have attempted to incorporate into the comprehensive planning process an element of urban design or aesthetics. These are often called "urban design framework plans" and provide design guidelines for visual consideration of specific parts of the city. Often, design commissions or design review boards are appointed to review developers' compliance with the design guidelines. Urban design is discussed later in this chapter.

After the goals and objectives for future development of the city are compared with an inventory of existing conditions, a set of recommendations will be stipulated in the comprehensive plan. This plan of action will indicate what programs and policies must be developed to achieve the goals and objectives. Typically, this will result in plans for each subelement, as discussed in the following paragraphs.

The **land-use plan** is of primary concern to urban planning and design because it specifies general categories of the division of land in the city and the policies, guidelines, and standards that will govern their development. It also identifies potential land for annexation if the city determines the necessity to grow. As part of the comprehensive plan, an analysis of the new land-use plan is performed to bring the zoning ordinance into compliance with the new land-use designations.

The **circulation plan** includes a list of changes and improvements to the system of city streets and highways.

It is typically written in conjunction with such items as changes in land use, extending city boundaries through annexation, schedules of repairs, or replacement of existing roads.

The **capital improvements plan** includes a list of projects (and associated costs) to extend or repair the physical infrastructure of the city. As such, it may include new public amenities such as new buildings for schools; fire and police protection; parks; libraries; courthouses; sidewalks, bikeways, transit and streets; and utilities.

Implementing Ordinances

The primary "tools" used to regulate the physical development of a city are building codes, environmental impact assessments, subdivision ordinances, and zoning codes. Of these, zoning codes are the most fundamental to implementing the comprehensive plan and therefore receive the most detailed coverage here.

Building codes regulate the safety of individual structures. They are concerned with the structural capability of buildings to stand up under the various conditions they might be subjected to: occupant loads, seismic (earthquake) loads, wind and snow loads, impact loads, and the loads imposed by their own weight. Codes are also concerned with fire safety, both in terms of the fire resistance of construction materials and the protection of life and property—for example, adequacy of exits and sprinkler systems. They are also concerned with plumbing, electrical power, and sanitation. Building codes actually reference a variety of specialized regulations published nationally, including the International Building Code or the Uniform Building Code. Most municipalities adopt the national codes and supplement them with local regulations to formulate their own proprietary building ordinances.

Environmental impact assessment requirements were enacted nationally in the United States early in the 1970s to ensure that all developments, both public and private, are evaluated prior to implementation for their adverse impacts on the natural and human environments. All developments larger than a two-family attached dwelling (duplex) must have an environmental checklist identifying potential impacts. A threshold determination of "significance" or "nonsignificance" is then made by a government authority. If the development is considered to have significant impacts, an environmental impact statement must be prepared that identifies all adverse impacts and the measures to be taken by the developer to mitigate them. City-related environmental assessment is typically governed by the

State Environmental Policy Act (SEPA). Overall federal coordination is regulated by the National Environmental Policy Act (NEPA). Compliance with SEPA is required when state funding is involved in a project, and NEPA compliance is required when federal funding is involved.

Subdivision ordinances regulate the requirements for the subdivision of land for the purpose of sale. The end result of a subdivision proposal is a plat map, which designates the legal boundaries of private property, street rights of way, and public easements. The initial layout of street and property sizes, geometries, and relationships can significantly impact the density and quality of development of an area.

Zoning codes are the specific laws that regulate land use in accordance with the comprehensive plan. In general, zoning refers to the division of land into districts, a description of how the land within each district may be used, and a list of standards for the land's development. A zoning code consists of a map showing the designated zoning districts and a description of the regulations governing each district.

The primary districts of most cities include residential, commercial, and industrial areas. The standard notation for designating a district includes a letter (e.g., "R" = Residential, "C" = Commercial, etc.) and a number designating the allowable intensity of use (e.g., "R-1" allows single-family detached homes, "R-2" allows single-family detached homes and duplexes, "R-3" allows multifamily attached dwellings such as townhouses, "R-6" allows multistory apartments, etc.). Typically, designations with lower numbers are more restricted in their use.

Each zone designation indicates the types of uses that are permitted. Certain other uses may be permitted if they comply with conditions specified in the ordinance. Uses not stipulated in these categories are banned outright unless a developer can demonstrate that the proposed use can be made compatible with other uses in the designated zone. In this way, zoning is unique because it provides individual citizens the right to change the law if the change can be demonstrated to benefit the general welfare of the community.

Within the zoning ordinance, each district is governed by a set of development standards (discussed in the next section). Since zoning standards are written to meet general assumptions about land subdivisions and adjacent uses, unique circumstances often arise (such as odd-shaped lots). If property owners can demonstrate that due to unique circumstances they will suffer a hardship by complying with zoning standards, then they may petition for a variance. **Variances** are routine administra-

Figure 24-3 A typical zoning map showing districts of a city and their zone designations (courtesy of the city of Pullman, Washington).

tive modifications built into the standard procedures of most zoning ordinances and do not require a change to the comprehensive plan.

Under certain circumstances, city councils have the authority to allow a nonconforming use to occur if the new use meets special conditions. For example, school districts with surplus school buildings as a result of demographic shifts have petitioned city councils and planning commissions to allow the buildings to be used for noneducational functions (e.g., a community center) until the facility is needed again as a school. Hence, a change of use is allowed under the condition that it revert back to a school if circumstances change at some point in the future. **Conditional use permits** may be granted by city councils without a corresponding change to the comprehensive plan.

Citizens may also petition city councils to change the zone designation of a district. This is a long process that requires a corresponding change to the comprehensive plan. It may result in a down zone (a change to a more restrictive use category) or an up zone (to a less restrictive use category). Again, as long as the petitioners can demonstrate that the change will benefit the general welfare of the community, and that it is consistent with the goals and objectives of the comprehensive plan, the change may be enacted.

For each designated zone, in addition to permitted uses, specific development standards apply to each property. Keeping in mind that the intent of zoning is to regulate property use for the benefit of the community, it is necessary for the ordinance to set limits of building size, site access, and other elements that impact the environmental qualities of the zone. Accordingly, most zoning ordinances set a variety of standards.

For example, there is a direct relationship between building height and intensity of land use, quality of views, amount of public access to fresh air and light, and solar insolation/shading. Ordinances set building heights by establishing maximum limits. Sometimes heights are set by establishment of overall building envelopes, which also sets the volumetric shape or bulk of the building.

A related limitation is that of **lot coverage**, or the relationship between the building and open space on a site. Lot coverage can be regulated in several ways, the most common being setbacks from property lines and floor area ratios. Typically, residential zones limit built areas on lots by establishing setback standards for front, side, and back property lines.

Downtown, city center sites are generally regulated by the **floor area ratio** (FAR). Downtown sites normally do not require setbacks of buildings from the property line at ground level. To ensure greater flexibility in building design, however, the building's height and bulk are governed by a ratio of building floor area to lot area. For example, a FAR of 2.0 allows a two-story building to cover the entire lot (100%) or a four-story building to cover 50% of the lot. The four-story building would allow 50% of the lot to be used as open space and would be a taller, slimmer building.

In many districts, developers are required to provide a designated number of on-site parking spaces to avoid overloading city streets with cars—one parking space for every 300 square feet of building in office structures, for example, or one and a half spaces for every unit of multifamily residential development. More forward-thinking cities, such as Portland, Oregon, have tried to encourage transit use and reduce congestion by enacting codes to limit the amount of parking developers can provide for new construction within the downtown area.

The zoning ordinance covers many other aspects of site use and development. Auxiliary structures, such as signage, fences, garages, and sheds, are regulated, as well as such uses as home occupations. Often, the latter is recommended for residential areas as part of a city's overall energy strategy. Persons working at home do not drive their cars, thereby saving on gasoline, reducing traffic, and lowering transit demands.

A final set of standards being incorporated into many zoning codes are those governing aesthetics—landscaping, building styles, colors, and shapes. Such standards are called **design guidelines** and are tied to designated districts. They form the basis for the multidisciplinary field called "urban design."

Urban Design

Most urban planning is concerned with the preparation of two-dimensional plans or maps and related ordinances. Urban design considers the city in three-dimensional terms, with emphasis on the visual spatial quality of the overall built environment. Urban designers must find ingenious ways to integrate their ideas into the city because they do not always have control over individual building and landscape designs. They are able to influence the shaping of cities by using the standard city planning tools like zoning coupled with design guidelines. In this way, they are able to design cities without designing individual buildings.[1]

Conventional zoning codes are based on a strict separation of land uses (residential, commercial, industrial) and rigid regulations. In the 1970s and 1980s, cities added more flexibility to the codes by allowing **overlay zones** aimed at retaining or enhancing the character of certain districts. The Pike Place Market in Seattle, Wash-

Figure 24-4   Seattle's Pike Place Market was restored after its designation as a historical district.

Figure 24-5 An example of Santa Barbara's Mission Style architecture.

ington, for example, was designated an historical district and, through public and private investment, was renovated and restored to its original character. In addition to restoring streets, sidewalks, and buildings to their original character, the city used **inclusive zoning** to require that all renovated and new housing in the district include a proportion of handicapped and single-room occupancy units, and that rents for these units be subsidized. This resulted in retaining the handicapped and the retired elderly population in the area, thus encouraging a range of socioeconomic classes, which many felt contributed to the original charm of the market. **Mixed-use zoning** (commercial at street level with housing and/or offices above) is also used to bring more activities and diversity to neighborhood village centers and urban districts.

Other cities have designated large areas as **architecturally unified zones**. Two cities that require all new buildings to be designed in accordance with a particular

character are Santa Barbara, California (Spanish Mission style), and Santa Fe, New Mexico (Pueblo style). As a consequence, these cities have been particularly successful in attracting upscale commercial and tourist activities.

Another innovative technique of urban designers is the use of incentive zoning to involve private developers in the creation of public amenities. Essentially, city planning authorities permit private developers to exceed floor area limitations established in the zoning ordinance if the developers also agree to construct certain public amenities at their own expense. Public amenities might include parks, lobbies, and atriums; connections to public transit; squares and plazas; second-level walkways and bridges (skywalks). The incentive for the developer is that although there is a higher front-end construction expenditure, this cost will be recovered and profits will be made on the long-term rental of additional space. Also, public amenities often result in the ability to charge higher rents.

An excellent example of incentive zoning is the Calgary, Alberta, "Plus-Fifteen" skywalk system in Canada. It is the most extensive system of second (third and fourth)-level pedestrian walkways in the world. It incorporates stair connections for every bridge. Bridges are wider than usual—4–7 meters (12–20 feet) in Calgary versus the standard 2.5–4 meters (8–12 feet) used in most cities. The system connects over 50 atrium buildings downtown, many of which include usable indoor and outdoor open space at the ground and second levels. The elevated walks and indoor atriums are part of the city's response to the climate (see Chapter 5) and allow city dwellers to enjoy the urban environment during the very cold winters.[2] All of these features resulted from incentive zoning using the principles stated above.

Whereas overlay zoning is effective in maintaining the existing character of an area, **planned unit develop-**

Figure 24-6 Downtown Sante Fe; the city has adopted the traditional Pueblo Style for its buildings.

Figure 24-7 A pedestrian bridge and street in Calgary, Alberta, Canada (T. Bartuska).

Figure 24-8 One of the over 50 atrium buildings in Calgary, Alberta, Canada. Often these spaces are filled with artistic hangings to celebrate seasonal holidays.

ments (PUDs) provide opportunities for creating vibrant new communities. PUDs differ from the typical planning approach by allowing the developer to meet performance criteria rather than adhering to specific prescriptive regulations. PUDs combine concepts for subdivision design and zoning within the same development. The city provides the developer with a set of performance standards for a piece of property; then the developer subdivides, zones, and designs it with a variety of densities, building types, landscaping, and amenities. This provides developers, urban designers, landscape architects, and architects greater latitude in creating innovative schemes, which often achieve higher qualities of social integration, energy conservation, and environmental protection. The widespread acceptance and popularity of the PUD concept by both city planners and developers laid the groundwork for a new alternative to conventional zoning—the New Urbanism.

The New Urbanism

Since the 1990s, a radical shift has taken place in the structuring of zoning codes. Most critics agree that (conventional) zoning as applied in U.S. cities has encouraged separation of zones, urban sprawl, and auto-dependent development. A new town planning movement called the **New Urbanism** advocates restructuring zoning codes to promote compact, mixed-use, pedestrian-oriented communities using **traditional neighborhood design** ideas. Whereas conventional zoning separates homes, schools, workplaces, and shopping, New Urbanism mixes building types, sizes, and prices. Townhouses and one-story shops with apartments above share neighborhoods with single-family homes, which may have a rental apartment over the garage.

Conventional zoning creates sprawling suburbs where people are forced to make dozens of car trips per day. The New Urbanism approach tries to ensure that basic goods and services are available within a five-minute walk, facilitated by sidewalks, narrow streets, and proximity of commercial and residential areas.

Most suburban residential subdivisions consist of cul-de-sacs and "garagescapes." The New Urbanism places garages and trash bins out of sight in alleys. Communities are more compact and interactive; houses are close to each other and close to the street. The design intent is for residents to gather on front porches, in nearby parks, and in open plazas. Neighbors share driveways, walkways, and alleys.

The New Urbanist vision can be applied to all scales of the built environment—regional, rural, urban, and

Figure 24-9 The New Urbanist planned unit development of Seaside, Florida. Note the pedestrian path, low fence, and variety of "front porches" based on traditional neighborhood design (Jan Gehl).

Figures 24-10 and 24-11   Downtown Portland, Oregon, linked to the surrounding communities with light rail public transit and abounding in pedestrian amenities (T. Bartuska).

their surrounding communities."[3] Examples are the Seattle Housing Authority–sponsored rehabilitation of the low-income family communities of New Holly/Holly Park, Rainier Vista, and High Point.

Portland, Oregon, has combined many of the features of the New Urbanism to revitalize its downtown and surrounding neighborhoods and to address the interdependent transportation issues of surrounding suburbs. The key to Portland's planning success in the past three decades has been its commitment to giving priority to pedestrian amenities and public transit and reducing dependence on the automobile. This has been achieved by committing to revitalization of the downtown core and working with the State of Oregon's progressive **Growth Management Act** (GMA) to establish an **urban growth boundary** for Portland's metropolitan area. The GMA was implemented by creating a new political entity called Metro, composed of elected officials and planning

suburban—and to large-scale new developments as well as inner-city infill developments. New projects on raw land are called **greenfield** developments. Two of the most well known are the town of Seaside, Florida (Fig. 24-9), and the town of Celebration (developed by the Disney Corporation) in Orlando, Florida. There are also innumerable inner-city New Urbanist–inspired projects called **brownfield** developments (e.g., on vacant lots and former industrial sites). These projects advocate mixed-use and mixed-income housing and, like their greenfield counterparts utilize traditional neighborhood design concepts.

For example, the **U.S. Department of Housing and Urban Development** (HUD) has incorporated New Urbanist design principles into its vast program of restructuring the nation's low-income housing projects by "changing the physical shape of public housing by demolishing the worst developments—high-rises and barracks-style apartments—and replacing them with garden-style apartments or townhouses that become part of

Figures 24-12 and 24-13   Pedestrian-friendly streets, Santa Barbara, California, and Portland, Oregon (T. Bartuska).

professionals, to direct and coordinate land use and transportation policies for the area.

In addition to conventional zoning procedures, Metro has adopted New Urbanism guidelines to support **transit-oriented development** (TOD). These guidelines require that the region be linked by transit (light rail trains and buses) between population centers in the outlying areas and downtown Portland. Metro requires that transit lines and stops be in place before new development can occur so that transportation can precede and help to direct growth. Such planning, called Smart Growth, must be carried out at the regional planning scale (Figs. 24-10 and 24-11).

The objective of **Smart Growth** is to accommodate population increase in an area in ways that are land and resource efficient and sustainable, with a corresponding reduction in the use of the automobile for commuting. When the latter is achieved, pollution, traffic jams, and sprawl are in turn reduced. Urbanized regions are composed of a **hierarchy of central places** ranging in scale from villages to cities. Smart Growth's hierarchy of central places clusters urban growth in compact, well-defined communities framed by a network of open space and connected by public transit (TODs). In turn, public transit, and strategies such as ride sharing, support the central place concept by moving people instead of automobiles, especially during peak traffic periods. Smart Growth emphasizes higher densities in existing residential areas to make public transit feasible and the clustering of new, high-density residential communities around convenient transit stations. These are effective strategies, tested and implemented some sixty years ago in London's GLC town and country plan (see Chapter 23).

Conclusion

Urban design and planning are ongoing processes that have major impacts on all of our lives. Although it is important, few people really understand the intentions and processes involved and how they are carried out. Few classes on the subject are offered in schools; civics classes, for example, focus on political, not physical, structure. Typically, people become aware of comprehensive planning and zoning only when they want to subdivide, buy, or develop a property and when they must obtain city or county permission. Often these encounters are confrontational because the average citizen is not aware of the complex laws that govern land use and development.

Once citizens understand the principles and processes involved in planning and zoning, they can use this knowledge to achieve their personal goals as well as contribute to the general welfare of the community. The U.S. Constitution and corresponding local ordinances are structured to ensure a balance between private interests and public good. For development-related issues, this is achieved through comprehensive planning, environmental review, and public participation. After nearly a century of planning and zoning test cases, the legal precedents and procedures for controlling the shape of U.S. neighborhoods, towns, cities, and regions are in place. It is now up to an informed partnership between government leaders and an active, concerned citizenry to provide the vision, energy, and guidance necessary to realize the potential of urban environments.

References

Bohl, C. "New Urbanism and the City: Potential Applications and Implications for Distressed Inner-City Neighborhoods." *Housing Policy Debate*, 11: 4761. Fannie Mae Foundation, 2000.

Calthorpe, P., and W. Fulton. *The Regional City: Planning for the End of Sprawl*. Island Press, 2001.

Duany, A., E. Plater-Zyberk, and J. Speck. *Suburban Nation: The Rise of Sprawl and the Decline of the American Dream*. North Point Press, 2000.

Duany, A., E. Plater-Zyberk, and J. Speck. *Smart Growth Manual*. McGraw-Hill, 2003.

Gallion, A., and S. Eisner. *The Urban Pattern*, 6th ed. Wiley, 1993.

Gindroz, R. *Urban Design Handbook: Techniques and Working Methods*. Urban Design Associates, 2003.

Katz, P. *The New Urbanism*. McGraw-Hill, 1994.

Kelly, E., and B. Becker. *Community Planning: An Introduction to the Comprehensive Plan*. Milldale Press, 2000.

Rudlin, D., and N. Falk. *Building the 21st Century Home: The Sustainable Urban Neighbourhood*. Architectural Press, 2000.

The Winter Cities Association. 2006: www.wintercities.com.

Endnotes

1. R. Gindroz, *Urban Design Handbook: Techniques and Working Methods* (Urban Design Associates, 2003).
2. The Winter Cities Association, 2006: www.wintercities.com.
3. C. Bohl, "New Urbanism and the City: Potential Applications and Implications for Distressed Inner-City Neighborhoods." *Housing Policy Debate*, Vol. 11, Issue 4 (Fannie Mae Foundation, 2000): p. 761.

REGIONS

Regional Planning and Management

Introduction

The region, the sixth component of the built environment, is of interest for a number of reasons. The concept of a region as an artifact is an invention of the human mind and, though useful in real terms, should be recognized as such. Regions are defined, their boundaries established by social/political and/or economic systems. Regions may also be defined by natural conditions such as geology, ecology, or climate. Society is becoming increasingly concerned about manipulation of various environments at the regional scale; humans have spilled over the boundaries of their cities, states, and even nations, causing numerous impacts at the regional or multiple-regional level. In the attempt to solve larger problems of pollution, transportation, or the loss of valuable farmland to suburban sprawl, representative governments have enacted regional planning procedures and comprehensive plans. In addition, some of the most impressive and significant artifacts of the built environment have been created as links between regions, more clearly emphasizing the nature of regions while interconnecting them: regional canal networks; national highways and interstate systems; watershed management projects; pipe and power networks; and regional and international airports, among others.

Region is not easily differentiated from other middle-level expressions of the built environment such as landscapes or cities. It is possible, for example, to speak of an urban landscape or an urban region. People in eastern Washington and northwestern Idaho interchangeably use the terms "Palouse landscape" and "Palouse region" when describing the area's rolling hills.

Perhaps the easiest way to clarify this issue is to describe regions more specifically in terms of a level of the built environment with specific focus on a set of design/planning disciplines—regional planning and management. Again, there is overlap, but the concept of levels of integration has been used in this book to help deal with overlap, to conceptualize an interrelated, integrated continuum. So, the distinctions made are for the sake of organizational clarity. Both content and context should always be kept in mind; regions, like all other components, are holons made up of parts and are part of something larger.

Therefore, for the purposes of this book, regions indicate categories as well as relationships. Landscapes are local entities, either rural or urban, more encompassing than a single structure but less comprehensive than a region. A city can be within a region, is usually clearly defined by the edges or boundaries of urbanization, is usually made up of numerous landscapes, and is part of a region. A region is normally thought to represent the next level of part-whole relationships, including many landscapes, several cities, and their surrounding environs. This content-component-context relationship can once again be shown below and symbolized in the text logo:

> Products—Interiors—Structures—Landscapes—
> Cities—**Regions**—Earth

The purpose of regions can be further clarified by the following four-part definition:

- **Regions** contain products, interiors, structures, landscapes, and cities and are, in part, humanly made, arranged, or maintained;
- to mediate the overall environment (to manage farm and resource production, to provide a coordinating subunit of the globe); and
- to help fulfill human purposes and the need for organization;
- while affecting their context, the Earth.

The chapters in this section explore the various ways regions can be defined how their many human/social, environmental, and technical factors can be more clearly understood, managed, and planned.

Defining and Planning the Regional Context
by Barbara M. Parmenter

This chapter examines the significance of regional perspectives for planning, design, and management professionals and how they use regional concepts in their work. While for many planning professionals it is not necessary to explicitly define what they mean by "region," people working in the public sector need to implement plans across a region and must set a bound-

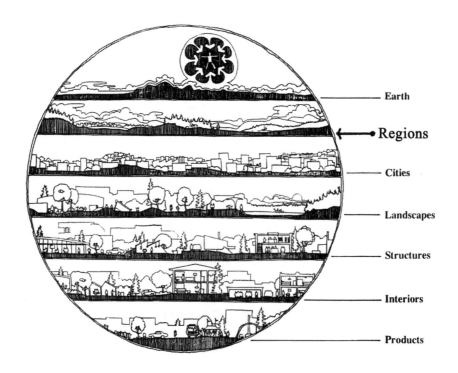

ary for their efforts. Examples of regional boundaries are presented and explored. Finally, the chapter looks at current regional practices and technologies like geographic information systems (GIS) that offer greater opportunities to integrate environmental, social, and economic factors into regional planning and design.

Regional Planning: Historic and Contemporary Developments
by Frederick R. Steiner

This chapter explores how regional planning has gained prominence during two periods of the twentieth century and has new relevance today. Grounded in intellectual movements of the early twentieth century, regional planning played an important role during the New Deal of the 1930s. A resurgence of regionalism during the 1960s led to many important planning initiatives. The twenty-first century is the first urban century. As urbanization and population increase, regional planning will be essential to create and manage a sustainable built environment.

Connections: Products to Regional Planning and Policies
by William W. Budd

This chapter links the levels of the built environment, from products to regions. It examines important connections between people's values and attitudes and their perception of environments at the regional level. It establishes these connections by tracing the waste materials generated by the manufacture and use of products and how they affect design/planning and management processes and policies for all components of the built environment.

References

Each chapter concludes with a list of recommended references.

American Planning Association (APA): www.planning.org
Association of Collegiate Schools of Planning (ACSP): www.acsp.org
Environmental Protection Agency (EPA): www.epa.gov
National Association of Regional Councils (NARC):www.narc.org
Smart Growth Institute (SGI): www.smartgrowth.org
Urban Land Institute (ULI): www.uli.org

CHAPTER 25

Defining and Planning the Regional Context

Barbara M. Parmenter

This chapter examines the significance of regional perspectives for planning and design of the built environment. While for many design and planning professionals it is not necessary to explicitly define what they mean by "region," people working in the public sector to implement plans across a region must usually set a boundary for their efforts. Examples of the different types of regional boundaries are presented and explored. Finally, the chapter looks at current regional practices and technologies like geographic information systems (GIS) that offer greater opportunities to integrate environmental, social, economic, and technological factors in regional planning and design.

Why should society be concerned with a regional perspective when most design, planning, and construction projects involve much smaller scales of products, interiors, buildings, landscapes, sites, developments, neighborhoods, and cities? The simple answer is that many phenomena that impact the projects originate in the wider region. In turn, development of the built environment in a particular town or city exerts wider influences on the surrounding region. These impacts and influences include environmental factors like air, water, energy, and habitat modifications; economic conditions and markets; and social, demographic, and cultural characteristics. Every new road, building, public space,

school, and subdivision will be affected by at least some of these factors, and will in turn help modify to some degree the regional context for future development.

If we think of **sustainable design and planning** as integrating concerns for the environment, the economy, and social equity, then a regional approach is critical. From an environmental perspective, the region's climate, ecological systems, geology, topography, and soils present certain conditions, opportunities, and limits for the development of a sustainable built environment. Buildings, parks, transportation networks, and land uses can be designed productively to take into account these biophysical factors in a way that is energy and resource efficient and helps maintain resources like clean air and water, open space, and healthy communities of plants and animals. From an economic and social equity perspective, a regional approach can help resolve imbalances between cities, suburbs, and rural areas in terms of housing, jobs, educational opportunities, and tax burdens while helping to attract stable, long-term economic investments. From a quality perspective, designing and planning the various components of the built environment that relate to the region's history, its evolving cultural resources and values, and its landscape qualities can create a distinctive sense of place for residents and substantially add to the overall quality of life. This sense of **regionalism** has

Figure 25-1 House in Austin, Texas, combining U.S. southern and Hispanic aesthetic qualities characteristic of the region.

emerged as an important issue in a number of chapters (see Chapters 5, 14, 15, 18, 23, 26, 28, 29, and 32).

Defining Regions

Given that a regional approach is important for designers of the built environment, how is "the region" defined, bounded, and determined? Unlike the other levels of the built environment discussed in this book, regions are often not clearly defined. In the hierarchy used here, landscapes and cities are smaller units of analysis, while the Earth encompasses the entire context. All of these can be fairly well conceived if not precisely defined territorially. But regions are different and seem at times to be arbitrary. We hear frequently of the western United States as a region, but we also speak of the Southwest, southern California, and greater Los Angeles as regions. The European Union is a regional political body, but the south of France, the Scottish Highlands, and the Rhine Valley are also distinctive regions within this larger structure.

The disparities between these regional definitions can be traced to issues of purpose and scale. The concept of a region is subjective in that we define the boundaries of a region differently for different purposes. Thus, "the West" (in the context of the United States) makes some limited historical and cultural sense because it was the context for very rapid U.S. expansion and settlement in the nineteenth and early twentieth centuries, exposing the entire area, despite its great diversity, to important common experiences (e.g., the building of transcontinental railroads, the displacement of native peoples, rapid town development, and a common land survey system). Yet, such a large, diverse region is not practical for planning or administrative purposes, so the West is

further divided into regions defined by more specific criteria. For example, the Northwest or Southwest shares many common elements in terms of its cultures, history, climate, vernacular styles, landscapes, and water resources and still stand out today as a distinctive cultural region. Thinking of a region is useful largely because of its cultural and landscape qualities, which provide a rich palette for design and planning. In addition, common water issues can be usefully approached at the regional level. For most other planning purposes, however, it is still too large and diverse to constitute a practical regional boundary.

Within the Southwest, southern California is a smaller region with distinct cultural and economic developments. Its economy grew rapidly over the twentieth century by utilizing oil and agricultural resources, manipulating water and energy supplies, and creating for itself a leading role in the defense and entertainment industries. Thinking about it as a region makes sense in several ways, including purposes of industrial and business site location, decision making, marketing, and economic development. But it also shares a common human-environmental context that benefits from a regional approach, and people across the region need good intercity transportation alternatives to take advantage of work and recreation opportunities. Finally, distinctive southern California qualities have been promulgated both within the region and nationally (and in some instances globally).

Planners and designers look to the even finer regional scale of the greater Los Angeles area not so much for its shared cultural and historical traits, but for purposes of developing and managing its transportation and resource infrastructure, its financial and property markets, and its role as a global economic and cultural hub. At this scale, we finally arrive at a region that is at least theoretically appropriate for urban planning and administration in the sense that local political leaders and citizen stakeholders can work out plans and legislation to coordinate important regional infrastructure and facilities like transportation, water and wastewater, and open space, as well as manage regional air and water quality. An emerging planning field, **bioregional planning**, considers all cities, towns, and landscapes that share the same ecosystem.

Defining a region, then, depends in part on purposes in mind and/or applications. The examples indicate that regions are sometimes defined by environmental and cultural dimensions and sometimes by political, economic, and transportation functions. Nevertheless, the regional concept should not be considered completely arbitrary. Landscape ecologist Richard Forman offers a useful starting point that incorporates multiple dimensions. He states that a region is "a broad geographical area with a common macroclimate and sphere of human activity and interest."[1] Climate, geology, and topography provide the basic framework. These, in turn, influence soils and vegetation. Together these elements impose broad limits on human and animal life. But within those limits (and we can argue about just how limiting they are), human settlement, resource use, economic exchanges, and technological development mold the geographical context over time and impart distinctive characteristics beyond the physical setting. These characteristics include such things as ways of making a living, land-use patterns, types of local governance, vernacular styles, modes and patterns of transportation, language dialects and accents, and culinary styles. Forman gives the example of New England as a relatively clearly defined region; it has a generally cool climate, a town meeting government tradition, an integrated regional transportation network, and "cultural nuances including architecture, religion, and language." In Forman's perspective, regions are rich in diversity in terms of ecosystems, landscapes, and human communities. Thus, in the New England example can be found a distinctive assembly of cities, suburbs, dairy farms, old mill towns, salt marshes, and several types of forest ecosystems.[2]

What, then, can designers and planners take from this definition? How can they make it useful in their work? The answer may differ according to the profession. For an architect or interior designer, a region's cultural and climate characteristics may be important. Vernacular building styles and craft traditions can stimulate design ideas. Efforts to build energy-efficient structures require a regard for climate, seasonal patterns, and energy resources. Landscape architects might likewise relate their work to regional cultural and historical qualities, but they must keep an even keener eye on biophysical characteristics like climate, soils, vegetation, and water availability. Design professionals are all enmeshed in regional economic conditions, land markets, development practices, and building and land-use regulations. Within this context, designers and their clients working at the site level can/should integrate regional qualities into their work. Their choices and the ways in which they combine elements can, in the best practice, create wonderful places that both relate to the local region and are refreshingly innovative and forward-looking.

Public sector planners perhaps face the largest challenge in determining a regional context, for not only do they incorporate regional qualities into their work, but also they frequently act as advocates for regional implementation of plans through governmental initiatives,

Figure 25-2 Frederick Law Olmsted's home and office in Brookline, Massachusetts, showing New England regional elements.

regulations, and guidelines. These have significant consequences on all residents and businesses within a community, affecting property rights, pocketbooks, commute times, and quality of life. If we think of regional planning as the process of ordering development of the built environment on a scale larger than an individual city or town, the implication is that a regulatory, financial, and political framework overlaps and may extend beyond the authority of individual local governments. Citizens and political leaders alike are often loath to give up their power even as they recognize the need for regional strategies. The definition of a region for planning purposes can thus be difficult and contentious. Because laws in the United States typically give individual cities significant land planning authority, coordinated implementation of truly regional plans is still rare but is an increasingly important phenomenon.

Regional Types in Practice

In practice, there are two main bases for "regionalization," or the process of determining a region for planning purposes (as distinct from incorporating regional elements into design practice). Some planning organizations, especially those concerned with resource management and environmental planning, attempt to determine their region of work using biophysical characteristics. Most planning organizations rely on political/jurisdictional boundaries to determine the appropriate regional boundaries for their work.

Ecological or Biophysical Regions

Watersheds are one of the most widely used biophysical regionalization schemes. Watersheds can be defined at various scales, from a river basin to a tiny stream. The U.S. Geological Survey (USGS) defined a structure of hydrologic units for the United States in an attempt to standardize river basin and watershed mapping and management. Hydrologic units are categorized into four hierarchical levels. In the first level, the United States is divided into twenty-one major geographical regions corresponding to the drainage area of a major river or a set of rivers. At the second level, major regions are divided into 222 subregions. The third level of 352 accounting units is nested within the subregions. Finally, a fourth level is derived, called "cataloging units," numbering 2,150 altogether in the United States.[3] Watersheds as planning units have a physiographical logic in that they encompass a hydrological and topographical structure that can be mapped and modeled.

River basins have been advocated as planning units since John Wesley Powell surveyed the Colorado River in the nineteenth century. Regional planning advocates hoped that the Tennessee Valley Authority (TVA), under way in the late 1930s, would prove the benefits of a regional approach. Today river basin authorities like the TVA are primarily concerned with power generation and water distribution. However, since both energy and water are critical for development, these authorities have a significant influence on the way their regions grow.

The use of smaller, more local watersheds as planning and management units gained in popularity over the last two decades of the twentieth century. The U.S. Environmental Protection Agency (EPA) and the U.S. Fish and Wildlife Service (FWS) both advocate a watershed approach to resource management and in particular water quality protection.[4] Many states have some sort of legislation requiring or encouraging watershed management. As control of individual point source pollution improved, water resource managers recognized a need to examine nonpoint sources of water quality degradation and the larger range of activities that affect water quality in an area. The latter include urban and agricultural runoff, groundwater contamination, and physical alteration of streams and other water bodies. Because upstream and uphill conditions have a major impact on water quality and quantity, the watershed concept makes sense for managing many water resource issues.

Yet, as a regional concept for planning and resource management, the watershed approach can be problematic. First, watersheds do not coincide with administrative boundaries. Second, while watershed boundaries may be adequate for monitoring and managing water quality and quantity, they are not nearly as good for managing or planning other human activities or even for understanding basic ecosystem characteristics and functions. There are many environmental factors, including human activities, vegetation, geology, and soils that do not correspond to topographic watershed boundaries. Third, in arid and semiarid regions, groundwater flow and aquifers may be quite different from the surface flows delineated in watersheds and may be of major importance to water quantity and quality management. And in large areas of the country, watersheds may be difficult to define—for example, in flatlands and areas of karst (underground stream) topography.[5]

Some scientists have argued that the delineation of ecoregions is a useful complement to watersheds for environmental resource management. The concept of an "ecoregion" (also know as a "bioregion") has evolved over the past two decades, and although there is not yet complete agreement on the details, in general, **ecoregions** are defined as areas in which the combination and arrangement of ecosystem components is distinctively different than that of adjacent areas. An ecoregion shows certain recurring local ecosystems in a more or less predictable pattern. This pattern enables managers to extrapolate working management practices from one area of an ecoregion to another area in the same ecoregion.[6]

National and state agencies in the United States, including the EPA, have made substantial efforts in ecoregion mapping. As with hydrologic units, there is a hierarchical structure, with four levels so far described.

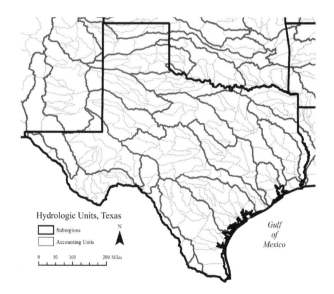

Figure 25-3 Watershed regions of Texas.

Figure 25-4 Ecoregions in the 48 contiguous states of the United States (with the political regions of the states).

For a local or regional focus, Levels III and IV are the most significant.

For example, in the northwestern United States, Level III ecoregions include the coast range, the Puget Sound lowlands, the Willamette Valley, and the Cascades. At Level IV, the Willamette Valley is broken down into the Portland/Vancouver Basin, the Willamette River and Tributaries Gallery Forest, Prairie Terraces, and Valley Foothills.[7] The ecoregion concept is somewhat controversial among scientists because it is defined by both quantitative and qualitative factors and in the end represents a subjective regionalization structure. But proponents of the concept argue that this constitutes a strength. Because it is based on distinctive and recurring patterns of local ecosystems, the ecoregion concept requires human perception to sort out these patterns and their relative differences from other areas. The process of delineating ecoregions at Levels III and IV involves bringing together a group of expert resource managers from local, state, and national agencies and the utilization of many different maps and data sources. The experts' knowledge, based on experience, is as important as other, more quantitative sources of information. The result, ideally, is a regionalization scheme that has substantial scientific validity for research and is practical for cross-disciplinary efforts to investigate, monitor, and manage a broad array of environmental resources.

The delineation of ecoregions for local and regional resource management is relatively new, and therefore the performance of this concept cannot yet be evaluated. It is pertinent to note that several national government agencies (e.g., the EPA and the USGS) utilize both the watershed and the ecoregion concept. While this use may be complementary, it also indicates that the scientific community remains uncertain about how best to determine regional boundaries.

Political Regions

Most organizations involved in regional planning determine regions based on political jurisdictional boundaries. These regions seem in some ways the antithesis of watersheds in that they often lack a clear relationship to physical terrain. A look at the varied ways that metropolitan regions are defined offers numerous examples of this approach. Often they consist of a set of counties grouped together, as in the Metropolitan Statistical Areas defined by the U.S. Census Bureau. The county boundaries themselves are frequently arbitrary in that they correspond to survey lines laid down during the period of early settle-

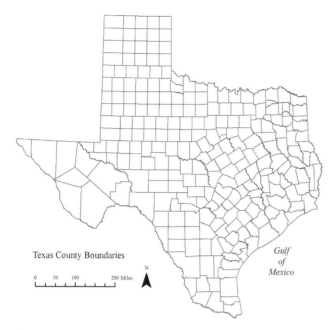

Figure 25-5 Political regions of Texas.

ment or statehood. Their modern grouping into regional planning initiatives is generally based on the notion of a metropolitan economy within which people travel to and from work and goods are exchanged. Thus, the latest Regional Plan of New York, a voluntary effort aimed at offering guidelines for local political leaders, encom-

passes the "Tri-State Metropolitan Region" of 31 counties, 1,600 cities, and nearly 13,000 square miles spread across parts of New York, New Jersey, and Connecticut.[8]

On the other side of the United States, the State of Oregon requires coordinated regional planning by local governments. In Oregon, Portland's Metro was established as an elected regional governing body that covers three counties. Metro is responsible for regional coordination and planning.[9]

In many U.S. urban areas, some planning takes place at the regional level but without the comprehensiveness implied by regional plans such as those of New York or Portland. To get federal funding for roads and highways, an urban area must have a **metropolitan planning organization** (MPO) that devises regional transportation plans meeting federal regulations. The MPO's service area typically extends well beyond the boundaries of any one city to cover the region's main transportation network. Which areas are included can be a contentious political issue. In addition, many states have **regional councils of governments** (COGs) that also typically consist of a group of counties. COGs are voluntary associations, usually without regulatory authority. They may undertake regional planning, or they may simply provide a venue for cross-jurisdictional discussion and focus on providing services, training, and information related to economic development. Often there are other non-

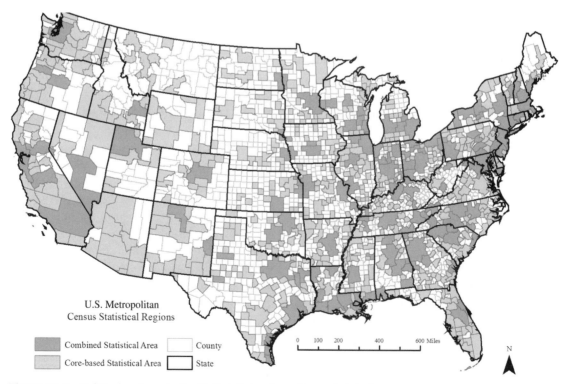

Figure 25-6 Political regions in the United States (counties and states).

governmental groups lobbying for regional strategies as well. These range from regional business associations to environmental and community development organizations. It is not unusual for an urban area to have an MPO doing regional transportation planning, be part of a COG doing regional economic and community development, be included in a regional watershed or river basin utility, and have one or more nongovernmental organizations advocating regional planning or development strategies. Austin, Texas, is an example of this, and every one of the above organizations defines the region differently.

In may be interesting to note the different geometric characteristics of the political/cultural regions across the United States and magnified in the State of Texas. Those in the East were created earlier and are more organic, relating to the biophysical characteristics of the land. Those in the Midwest were subdivided later and illustrate the application of the township and range system, a 1-mile grid system created by Thomas Jefferson's Land Survey Ordinance of 1785 (see Chapter 3). Those in the West are a combination of the formal Jeffersonian grid and the organic and more informal patterns created from the land's dramatic biophysical characteristics. Some regions in the Southwest are also influenced by Spanish terriorities (established before the U.S.-Mexican war of 1846–1848). Those various historic cultural imprints are dramatically displayed in the political regions of Texas.

The Return to Place-Based Regional Planning

After World War II, regional planning focused mostly on economic development and the infrastructure to support economic growth. Planners working with this functional concept of region were primarily concerned with allocation and organization of activities across space. The space itself could be defined primarily by networks and nodes, that is, for transportation and exchange of labor, goods, and services. Other than that, this regional space was largely featureless and unrelated to the actual terrain on which it was laid. This concept of region, at whatever scale chosen to define it, could be modeled on a computer, often without the need of a map.

But this was not always the case. A real geographical context, a territorial extent filled with landmarks and places as well as roads, rivers, and power lines, had been central to earlier advocates of regional planning. In the 1890s, the Scottish biologist and town planner Patrick Geddes, inspired by French geographers, set up a "Civic Observatory and Laboratory," known as the Outlook Tower, in Edinburgh. Geddes argued that a thorough understanding of the physical, cultural, and historical evolution of a city and its regional hinterland was critical for good planning. To this end, Geddes argued, residents and schoolchildren should be engaged in civic surveys that document a wide assortment of regional characteristics, including geology, climate, soils, vegetation, the historical evolution of communities, and the ways that people make their living.

Geddes' work influenced a generation of British and U.S. planners and urbanists, including Lewis Mumford, who forcefully argued for regional approaches to planning from the 1920s to the 1970s. For Mumford, regional planning clearly implied a territorial view of human settlements and required understanding regions as loci of natural, social, and cultural processes. This place-based concept of regionalism lost ground in the 1950s and 1960s as planners concentrated on what they felt were more economically rational and efficient models of urban and regional development, defining the optimum spatial location of service nodes and an efficient transportation network for the unhindered flow of goods and people.

Although it can be argued that the planning practices of the mid-twentieth century achieved success in terms of housing and employing a growing middle class, they failed to arrest the continuing environmental degradation leading to disastrous results for central cities. The rise of the environmental movement, on the one hand, and community-based, often grassroots, development organizations, on the other, helped rekindle place-based planning. Environmental planners and designers were especially important for reestablishing a regional framework, while community development planners often worked at the neighborhood level. Nonetheless, regional planning today is increasingly concerned with issues of social equity and economic development, along with environmental conservation and enhancement.

For designers and planners of the built environment, the place-based concept of regionalism is critical. They are, by profession and inclination, focused more on the creation and maintenance of human-scale places and contexts for living than on the flow of labor, goods, and services that constitute a more functional view of regions. It is clear, however, that the two concepts are and must be closely related. To be sustainable, regions must have healthy ecosystems and land patterns integrated within a functioning and well-designed framework of communities and open space, transportation and communications networks, and utilities that support economic development.

Interrelationships and Multiple Scales: Implications for Planning and Design

From this discussion, several lessons can be drawn. First, regional definitions are closely related to purpose and will always be subjective to some degree. A watershed or ecoregion or metropolitan area will work for some needs and not for others. Second, the use of regions requires a sophisticated understanding of interlinkages between elements and scales. That regional boundaries are difficult to draw was recognized long ago by Lewis Mumford. Writing in the 1930s in support of regional planning, Mumford observed:

> As soon as human communities are considered, the region becomes even more plainly a system of interrelationships that overflow and become shadowy at the margins. . . . This means that all boundaries in black and white are, to one degree or another, arbitrary. Reality implies a certain looseness and vagueness, a certain failure of definition. To define human areas, one must seek, not the periphery alone but the center.[10]

Like later environmental scientists, Mumford saw the need to explore multiple relationships as a complex system rather than trying to draw simple boundaries. Understanding these interrelationships continues to be a challenge, but there is at least growing acceptance of the need to think about the interactions between economics, social equity, and environmental quality.

Third, regions should be examined at multiple scales, with increasing levels of detail as we move down in scale from cities to landscapes to neighborhoods. Thus, individual neighborhoods should be seen as part of the larger city, which is embedded in a larger region. Architect Peter Calthorpe and planner William Fulton argue that "designing the region is designing the neighborhood" and that to do either one without the other will increase the problems we already face.[11]

> First and foremost, the region and its elements—the city, suburbs, and their natural environment—should be conceived as a unit, just as the neighborhood and its elements—housing, shops, open space, civic institutions, and businesses—should be designed as a unit. . . . Just as a neighborhood needs to be developed as a whole system, the region must be treated as a human ecosystem, not a mechanical assembly.[12]

The neighborhood and the region share important qualities, with implications for design. "Both need pro-tected natural systems, vibrant centers, human-scale circulation systems, a common civic realm, and integrated diversity," observe Calthorpe and Fulton. Rather than thinking of drawing boundaries, society needs to be creating these building blocks at multiple scales. Specifying land uses and the intensity of use in a zoning map is less important than structuring centers and districts, creating corridors, and interweaving a network of open spaces that sustain working ecosystem functions. This approach is currently being taken in a number of urban regions, including Chicago, the Salt Lake City area, and Central Texas, by Calthorpe and planner John Fregonese.[13]

Visualizing Regional Interrelationships and Multiple Scales

Advocates of a geographical concept of regionalism have long argued for the need to visualize our knowledge of people and the environment as a means for exploring interrelationships, scales, and patterns. Geddes' Outlook Tower was one attempt to do this. Mumford and his colleagues in the Regional Planning Association of America also made intensive use of maps and other visualization methods to understand and sort out regional patterns and relationships. In the 1960s, Ian McHarg and others began experimenting with map overlay techniques to explore the fit between design, nature, and cultural values. By overlaying "single-purpose" maps at the same scale, questions about suitability and the appropriateness of design interventions could be analyzed and explored. In McHarg's framework, the combination of spatial map layers should also express a time dimension. Geological and climatic information represent the oldest data; topography, soils, and hydrology follow. Vegetation and animal life, and finally human systems, derive from and in turn modify the older foundations.[14] McHarg's ecological method of designing with nature is further examined in the next chapter.

Today, geographic information systems (GIS), databases, and three-dimensional visualization techniques make possible spatial data collection, analyses, and graphic displays that these early thinkers could only dream of. Single-purpose environmental maps like those depicting soils, geology, vegetation, topography, and hydrology can be shown in combination with human-related dimensions like demographics, infrastructure, land regulation, and health information. In theory, and increasingly in practice, many of these layers can be examined at multiple scales. Overlay analyses are used to prioritize land for conservation based on aggregate threat and vulnerability factors. They are also used to explore suitability for proposed land uses, given multiple criteria to estimate land supply for development and for many other purposes.

The strengths of GIS technologies lie in their ability to manage large data sets, integrate spatial data from a number of disparate data sources, visualize relationships and patterns between elements, and move relatively easily between scales. As we have seen, these strengths are all necessities for regional planning, and GIS has become an indispensable tool for regional planning efforts. For example, Portland, Oregon's, regional government authority, Metro, has created a state-of-the-art GIS to support regional growth management policies mandated by state legislation.[15] Data layers produced and maintained in this effort are available to the public. Researchers, citizens, and nongovernmental organizations can utilize the database for their individual purposes.

The wide use of spatial database technology in planning today is a far cry from the abstract functional models used by planners in the 1950s and 1960s. But what implications do they have for the way we conceive regions? First of all, they make it possible to produce high-quality maps and other visualizations of geographical areas at a variety of scales. This can be done quickly in response to new issues, citizen queries, and political debates. The opportunity for planners, politicians, and citizens to see and examine a geographical region and its many components on a dynamic map allows the discussion of what we mean by our region to be fleshed out and argued in a collaborative setting. While these technologies do not provide answers and are far from perfect sources of information, they allow a focused discussion of values and purposes and the ability to understand more fully the complex interrelationships that Lewis Mumford and other regionalists have long urged us to explore.

Conclusion

Regional boundaries are not so much arbitrary as they are pragmatic. There is a clearer consensus today than at any time in the past that the region, however defined, must be integrated into society's ecological, economic, and social processes—the triad variables of sustainable development. The problems inherent in a city-by-city or neighborhood-by-neighborhood planning approach are clear—there are too many wasted regional opportunities and resources when communities compete against each other. This lack of integration and lack of linkages between individual plans cause significant imbalances

between housing and jobs, transportation inefficiencies and gridlock, a worsening environment, and the proliferation of built forms that have no regional distinctiveness, resulting in what one popular author has called "the geography of nowhere."[16] Planners and designers are calling for the integration of spatial, environmental, and social-economic components to productively bring society and the professions together again. The challenge of regional planning and design remains daunting, but new understanding and vastly better visualization and mapping tools allow exploration of regions more comprehensively than ever before.

References

Calthorpe, P., and W. Fulton. *The Regional City.* Island Press, 2001.

Envision Utah. 2003: www.envisionutah.org.

Forman, R. T. T. *Land Mosaics: The Ecology of Landscapes and Regions.* Cambridge University Press, 1995.

Kunstler, J. H. *The Geography of Nowhere: The Rise and Decline of America's Man-made Landscape.* Simon and Schuster, 1993.

McHarg, I. *Design with Nature.* Doubleday Natural History Press, 1969.

Metro. 2002: www.metro-region.org.

Mumford, L. *The Culture of Cities.* Harcourt Brace, 1938.

Omernik, J. M., and R. G. Bailey. "Distinguishing between Watersheds and Ecoregions." *Journal of the American Water Resources Association,* May 1997.

U.S. Environmental Protection Agency. "Ecoregions of the United States." 2002: www.epa.gov/bioindicators/html/usecoregions.html.

U.S. Environmental Protection Agency. "Watersheds." 2003: www.epa.gov/owow/watershed.

U.S. Fish and Wildlife Service. "An Ecosystem Approach to Fish and Wildlife Conservation." Conceptual Document. U.S. Fish and Wildlife Service, 1995.

U.S. Geological Survey. "Hydrologic Unit Maps: What Are Hydrologic Units?" Water Resources. 2003: water.usgs.gov/GIS/huc.html.

Yaro, R., and T. Hiss. *A Region at Risk: The Third Regional Plan for the New York-New Jersey-Connecticut Metropolitan Area.* Island Press, 1996.

Endnotes

1. R. T. T. Forman, *Land Mosaics: The Ecology of Landscapes and Regions* (New York: Cambridge University Press, 1995): 13.
2. Forman, *Land Mosaics:* 23.
3. U.S. Geological Survey, "Hydrologic Unit Maps: What Are Hydrologic Units?" *Water Resources,* 2003: water.usgs.gov/GIS/huc.html.

4. U.S. Environmental Protection Agency, *Ecoregions of the United States*, 2002: www.epa.gov/bioindicators/html/usecoregions.html, and U.S. Fish and Wildlife Service, *An Ecosystem Approach to Fish and Wildlife Conservation*, Conceptual Document (Washington, DC: U.S. Fish and Wildlife Service, 1995).

5. J. M. Omernik and R. G. Bailey, "Distinguishing between Watersheds and Ecoregions," *Journal of the American Water Resources Association*, May 1997.

6. See Note 5.

7. U.S. Environmental Protection Agency, *Ecoregions of the United States*, 2002: www.epa.gov/bioindicators/html/usecoregions.html.

8. R. Yaro and T. Hiss, *A Region at Risk: The Third Regional Plan for the New York-New Jersey-Connecticut Metropolitan Area* (Island Press, 1996).

9. Metro, *Metro*, 2002: www.metro-region.org.

10. L. Mumford, *The Culture of Cities* (Harcourt Brace, 1938): 315.

11. P. Calthorpe and W. Fulton, *The Regional City* (Washington, DC: Island Press, 2001).

12. Calthorpe and Fulton, *The Regional City*: 49.

13. Envision Utah, *Envision Utah*, 2003: www.envisionutah.org.

14. I. McHarg, *Design with Nature* (Doubleday Natural History Press, 1969).

15. See Note 9.

16. J. H. Kunstler, *The Geography of Nowhere: The Rise and Decline of America's Man-made Landscape* (New York: Simon and Schuster, 1993).

CHAPTER 26

Regional Planning: Historic and Contemporary Developments

Frederick R. Steiner

Regional planning gained prominence during two periods of the twentieth century and has renewed relevance in this century. Grounded in intellectual movements of the early twentieth century, regional planning played an important role during the New Deal of the 1930s. A resurgence of regionalism during the 1960s led to many planning initiatives today. Because of global population growth and migration to cities, the twenty-first century is fast becoming the first urban century, and regional planning will be essential to create a sustainable built environment.

In some areas of the world, the natural environment and the culture of the region are closely linked to its government. Many parts of Europe come to mind—France, Italy, Germany, England, and the Low Countries. In France, for example, one can experience the unique qualities of a particular village, which distinguish it from other villages, by drinking local wine and savoring cuisine in a restaurant or garden that reflects the character of that specific place.

Prior to the sixteenth century, when Europeans began invading South, Central, and North America in large numbers, the native people lived in a variety of cultural regions. The U.S. ethnographer and explorer John Wesley Powell recognized this and, as a result, proposed a plan for the southwestern United States based on its ecology.

Powell's 1879 report to Congress about the Southwest "stressed the need for new land and water use policies, an adapted land-settlement pattern, and an adapted institutional organization and way of living that was intimately suited to the conditions of the arid and semi-arid lands."[1]

These concepts, and those presented in the previous chapter, have long been used by planners, often in an eclectic manner. The origins of regional planning in the United States are relatively easy to trace. Frederick Law Olmsted, Sr., and his protégé, Charles Eliot, developed metropolitan park plans for the Boston region in the late 1800s. The concept of **regionalism** flourished as a form of cultural philosophy in the 1920s and 1930s. This activity was encouraged by a small group of intellectuals organized in 1923, the Regional Planning Association of America (RPAA), which included leading designers and intellectuals like Catherine Bauer, Benton MacKaye, Lewis Mumford, Clarence Stein, Henry Wright, and others.

During the 1940s, Benton MacKaye linked regional planning explicitly to ecology. He defined regional planning as "a comprehensive ordering or visualization of the possible or potential movement, activity or flow (from sources onward) of water, commodities or population, within a defined area or sphere, for the purpose of laying therein the physical basis for the 'good life' or optimum human living."[2]

Figure 26-1   The Palouse region of eastern Washington and northwestern Idaho. The wheat in this region has been carefully bred to increase productivity. Because of the steep slopes, special farm machinery has been designed to manage the landscape (T. Bartuska).

According to MacKaye, a comprehensive ordering referred to "a visualization of nature's permanent comprehensive 'ordering' as distinguished from the interim makeshift orderings of people." MacKaye found the purpose of the "good life" or optimum human living incorporated in what the U.S. Congress has called the "general welfare" and what Thomas Jefferson called the "pursuit of happiness." MacKaye concluded that "regional planning is ecology."[3]

Social Vision and the Harnessing of Human and Natural Resources

Regionalism has influenced planning in the United States and elsewhere at various times in different ways. The ideas about regionalism developed by Mumford, Mac-Kaye, and others were embraced on a broad scale during Franklin D. Roosevelt's New Deal. The regional planning programs of the New Deal were enacted in response to the human suffering of the Great Depression. These efforts marked the first of two major periods in which regional planning especially flourished in the twentieth century. Examples of such programs include the Tennessee Valley Authority, the Columbia Basin Irrigation Project, and Greenbelt new towns. Other nations embarked on similar projects that involved the harnessing of human and natural resources for social purposes. Throughout Europe, road building, electricity and telephone extension, and water and sewer construction received considerable attention. The Zuiderzee reclama-

tion works provide a notable example of ambitious, large-scale planning in the Netherlands. Dutch planners and engineers transformed an inland sea (the Zuiderzee) and flood-prone coastlines into new lands with productive farmlands and planned new communities.

Tennessee Valley Regional Planning

The Tennessee Valley Authority (TVA) stands as one of the more successful examples of regional planning in the United States or internationally. The TVA stresses cooperation among various levels of government and the provision of multiple benefits for citizens. The jurisdiction of the TVA is generally limited to the drainage basin of the Tennessee River, but some of its activities extend beyond this area. As a result, the TVA provides a model for Eugene Odum's ideal of the use of **watersheds** (river basins) as the optimum unit of planning. The Tennessee River drainage basin, an area of almost 41,000 square miles (106,149 square kilometers [km]), covers parts of seven states: Alabama, Georgia, Kentucky, Mississippi, North Carolina, Tennessee, and Virginia.

The U.S. Congress established the TVA in 1933 as part of the New Deal to lift the nation out of the Great Depression. President Roosevelt asked Congress to create "a corporation clothed with the power of government but possessed of flexibility and initiative of a private enterprise." Under this innovative legislation, a broad plan was proposed for the Tennessee River drainage basin. Congress established the semi-independent authority to pro-

Figure 26-2   Norris Dam was started in 1933 and completed in 1936. It was the first dam built by the TVA. Located in Clinch River in east Tennessee, it is 265 feet high and 1,860 feet long. Its reservoir has a storage capacity of 2.5 million acre-feet of water, of which 1,922,000 is useful, controlled storage. The power installation consists of two 50,400-KW units (courtesy of the Tennessee Valley Authority).

mote the economic and social well-being of the people of the entire region. Before the TVA, the rich timber and petroleum resources of the region had been ruthlessly exploited, leaving a derelict landscape and an economically depressed population. The people of the Tennessee Valley ranked among the poorest in the United States at the height of the Great Depression.

The TVA legislation recognized the potential of water as a basic resource that could be used to revitalize the region (Fig. 26-2). Congress granted the TVA three broad basic powers: the control of flooding, the development of navigation, and the production of hydroelectric power. As a result, the TVA was conceived as having multiple purposes. A multiple-use plan was developed that extended beyond the three basic purposes to include reforestation, soil conservation, outdoor recreation, new community building, the retirement of marginal farmland, and the manufacture of fertilizer.

Columbia Basin Regional Planning

A second regional effort, also a product of New Deal legislation, was the Columbia Basin Irrigation Project, located in east-central Washington State. Like the TVA, the project involved the harnessing of water resources for social purposes through comprehensive planning. The general authorization for the project came from the National Industrial Recovery Act of 1933, with specific project authorization from the Rivers and Harbors Act of 1937 and the Columbia Basin Act of 1943. The project, like the TVA, incorporated several purposes: irrigation, power generation, navigation, regulation of stream flow, flood control, and recreation.

Before the project, the Columbia Basin was a sparsely populated desert region. Although lands close to streams were successfully settled, attempts to homestead the region from the late nineteenth century on had been thwarted by lack of water and lack of the appropriate irrigation technology. Irrigation became feasible with the construction of the Grand Coulee Dam (another New Deal project). From the 1930s on, much effort was devoted to planning the Columbia Basin Project, covering some 1.1 million acres (445,500 hectares [ha]).

The planning activities encompassed extensive resource inventories of the Columbia Basin, land classification, suitability analysis, the establishment of optimum farm sizes, and economic and transportation studies. The U.S. Bureau of Reclamation coordinated the planning efforts under the leadership of Secretary of the Interior Harold Ickes, a strong supporter of the project. The combined venture of federal, state, regional, and local agencies was called the Columbia Basin Joint Investigations.

The Columbia Basin Joint Investigations, begun in 1939 and completed in 1942, published a variety of reports involving three hundred people, representing 40 federal, state, local, and private agencies that studied 28 separate problems in 16 divisions. These coordinated endeavors generated a general, comprehensive plan for development and settlement, which provided the basis for the Columbia Basin Act of 1943. After the completion of the Grand Coulee Dam in 1941, the Columbia Basin received its first water in 1948, and development continued into the 1980s.

In the early 1990s, further irrigation development ended as a result of environmental concerns. Since then, more emphasis has been placed on other purposes, such as fish and wildlife, recreation, and power generation. Still, farmers continue to irrigate some 671,000 acres (271,755 ha) of land. Water for these lands is supplied by 300 miles (483 km) of main canals, about 2,000 miles (3,218 km) of laterals, and 3,500 miles (5,632 km) of drains and waterways.

Greenbelt New Towns

The Greenbelt new towns provide a third example of regional planning during the New Deal era. Intellectual impetus came from those involved in the newly formed RPAA, in this case the architect Clarence Stein and Henry Wright, an architect who became a landscape architect. They were influenced by the British garden cities of Ebenezer Howard, idealized in the United States by planners in the RPAA. They advanced a straightforward idea: a regional approach could alleviate urban squalor. The establishment of new communities, buffered by gardens or green space, formed a key element in this approach and continues to influence planning strategies today (see Chapter 23).

The New Deal economist Rexford Guy Tugwell provided leadership for the Greenbelt new towns. As undersecretary of the U.S. Department of Agriculture, he proposed the Resettlement Administration, established to develop a comprehensive approach to alleviate the socioeconomic problems of rural regions. In less than two years, from 1935 to 1936, Tugwell's agency planned and constructed three new communities and started a fourth.

The three new communities built were Greenbelt, Maryland; Greenhills, Ohio; and Greendale, Wisconsin. The fourth, Greenbrook, New Jersey, was planned but never constructed. Tugwell's ideas for these new

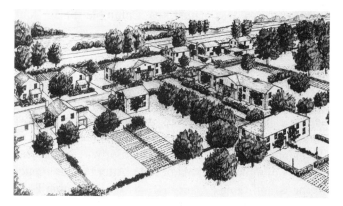

Figure 26-3   Apple Court drawing, Greendale, Wisconsin, 1936 (Alanen and Eden, 1987).

Figure 26-4   Detached houses and pedestrian pathway, Greendale, Wisconsin, 1939 (J. Vachon from Alanen and Eden 1987).

Figure 26-5   Happy and healthy children, Greendale, Wisconsin, 1939 (J. Vachon from Alanen and Eden 1987).

communities dovetailed with those of the RPAA in his unbiased acceptance of the automobile as an element to be affirmatively considered in the planning process. For example, Mumford and MacKaye believed cars were essential for the fourth migration: a "backflow" of people into rural regions that were largely bypassed by earlier North American migrations.[4] The design of the new communities consisted of low-rise single- and multifamily housing units, with a pedestrian-oriented traditional design, clustered commercial and public facilities, a surrounding greenbelt, and a road network linking the communities to their metropolitan region (Figs. 26-3 to 26-5). Each town had its own interdisciplinary design team consisting of architects, planners, and civil engineers. John Nolen, a leading early-twentieth-century town planner, advocated that each team be led by a landscape architect to ensure "the proper placing of the plan upon the ground. . . . "[5] These communities remain quite popular with their residents today, and are still exemplars of new town planning in the United States and throughout the world.

Zuiderzee Regional Planning

The New Deal planning programs in the United States had, and continue to have, an international influence. The Zuiderzee reclamation works actually began earlier than the projects of the New Deal. Even so, its planning was influenced by the TVA and Greenbelt new towns. Like the U.S. undertakings, this Dutch example involved a comprehensive regional approach to harness natural resources in order to solve social problems.

The Zuiderzee reclamation works is a long-term, large-scale planning effort. It shaped the Dutch landscape through human intervention in natural processes, and is maintained as an eloquent equilibrium between people and their environment. The Zuiderzee (Southern Sea) was an extension of the North Sea into the heart of the Netherlands (Fig. 26-6). As early as 1667, the Dutch speculated on damming the Zuiderzee and reclaiming it but lacked the appropriate technology. However, in the late nineteenth century, the engineer Cornelis Lely developed serious plans for reclamation.

In 1918, the Dutch parliament passed the Zuiderzee Act. That legislation established goals for flood protection, water control, the formation of a freshwater reservoir, transportation, and the creation of farmland. Engineers realized these goals by damming the Zuiderzee and creating a large lake—the Ijsselmeer. New land, called "polders," displaced this lake under the direction of a government agency—the Ijsselmeerpolders

Figure 26-6 Polder landscape in the Ijsselmeerpolders, the Netherlands.

Figure 26-7 John Friedmann, professor emeritus of the University of California–Los Angeles, 2001, and Honorary Professor of Community & Regional Planning, University of British Columbia (L. Sandercock).

Development Authority. New farmlands were created, and new villages and cities were built. Dutch planner-architect Coen van der Wal[6] calls this Herculean effort "planning the ordinary," but an extraordinary national commitment was required to create the seemingly normal places for people to live and to work.

Economic Equity and Ecology Parity

After noteworthy beginnings in the early twentieth century, regional planning languished, and for years it was considered an oddity in many academic circles. It rebounded in the 1960s—a rebirth that came in the form of fraternal twins. For the sake of simplicity, the writings of John Friedmann (1964 and 1973) epitomize one twin, while those of Ian McHarg (1969, 1996, 1998 with Steiner) illustrate the other (Figs. 26-7 and 26-8).

Friedmann defined regional planning as "concerned with the ordering of human activities in supra-urban space—that is, in any area which is larger than a single city."[7] McHarg no doubt would have accepted this definition, for he described metropolitan regions in a similar way: "A city occupies an area of land and operates a form of government. The metropolitan area also occupies an area of land but constitutes the sum of many levels of government."[8]

From here on, however, each offers widely different perspectives. According to Friedmann, "regional planning theory has evolved out of special theories in economics (location) and geography (central places); [while] city planning theory is based on human ecology,

Figure 26-8 Ian L. McHarg with colleagues Bob Hanna and Nick Muhlenberg, University of Pennsylvania, c. 1975 (by The Architectural Archives, University of Pennsylvania, photo B. Young.)

land economics and the aesthetics of urban form."[9] This view of regional planning, based on economics and social science, may be contrasted to McHarg's natural science approach. McHarg stated repeatedly that "the world, the city and [people] as responsive to physical and biological processes—in a word to ecology—are entirely absent from the operative body of planning knowledge. If the planner is part social scientist, part physical planner, [he or she] is in no part natural scientist or ecologist."[10]

John Friedmann studied in the Program of Education and Research in Planning at the University of Chicago and then taught for many years at the University of California–Los Angeles before retiring to Australia. The Chicago school had pioneered the social sciences since the early twentieth century. For a brief spell, this school provided the leadership in changing the planning profession in the United States by introducing techniques of sociology and economics. As a result, many planners abandoned the environmental design and came to think of themselves as applied social scientists.

McHarg revolutionized planning in a different direction. He and his University of Pennsylvania colleagues initiated new ways to apply the biophysical sciences to the planning process. As discussed in other chapters, his book *Design with Nature* was and still is one of the most influential works on planning, which clarified the importance and means to achieve a more **ecological approach** to design and planning. McHarg suggested that environ-

mental information be organized in what he called a **layer-cake model** (Fig. 26-9). According to this model, information is organized with older components, like geology, on lower layers than elements prone to shorter time horizons, like wildlife. This model helps form the theoretical basis for computer mapping programs called "geographic information systems (GIS)."

In addition to teaching at the University of Pennsylvania, McHarg was a founding partner in a multidisciplinary firm called Wallace McHarg Roberts and Todd (now Wallace Roberts and Todd). With this firm, McHarg developed an ecological plan for a new town, the Woodlands, near Houston, Texas, in the early 1970s. McHarg and his colleagues used the natural drainage of the site to structure the plan. As a result, the Woodlands has not experienced the devastating flood damage that plagues other communities in the region. The Woodlands also maintained much natural vegetation and, as its name indicates, is a series of neighborhoods in woodlands.

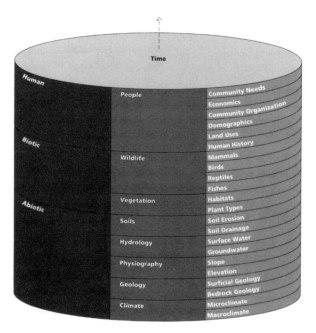

Figure 26-9 McHarg's layer-cake model (F. Steiner's *The Living Landscape*, 2nd ed.).

Figures 26-10 and 26-11 Woodlands, Texas, a new town designed/planned "with nature" by Ian McHarg and colleagues.

The sociologist Carl F. Kraenzel proposed an approach to regional planning somewhere between those of Friedmann and McHarg. According to Kraenzel:

> Regionalism and regional planning recognize that geographic and natural environment forces still set the broad limits within which culture can function. Culture, in cooperating with nature rather than fighting it, can also, within limits, use natural and geographic forces to its own ends. Regionalism and regional planning assist in defining the natural and physical limits within which culture can operate and aid in pointing the way for a dynamic coordination between culture and natural forces.[11]

Late-Twentieth-Century Regional Planning

The ideas about social and economic fairness and ecological relationships discussed in academic circles during the 1960s influenced legislation for new regional planning programs. These programs reflected social, economic, and environmental concerns, which later emerged as the key triad relationships in sustainable development. A few examples of such programs include the Appalachian Regional Commission, New York's Adirondack Park Agency, the Tahoe Regional Planning Agency, and the New Jersey Pinelands Commission. Today societal interest in smarter growth management, environmental quality, livability, and sustainability is prompting renewed interest in regional planning. The Regional Planning Association can trace its efforts from the early twentieth century through the environmental decades to sustainability. The following regional planning programs further illustrate these important societal developments toward a more sustainable future.

Appalachian Region

John F. Kennedy had been deeply moved by the poverty he encountered in the West Virginia mountains during his presidential campaign. As a result, he formed a presidential panel and directed it to draft "a comprehensive program for the economic development of the Appalachian Region." President Lyndon B. Johnson used the commission's report as the basis of what became the Appalachian Regional Development Act of 1965. Its provisions included establishment of the Appalachian Regional Commission.

The Appalachian Regional Commission covers some 200,000 square miles (517,800 sq km)—all of West Virginia and parts of 12 other states with a population of about 22 million. The Commission is comprised of representatives from the federal and state governments. The president appoints a co-chairman, with another elected by the governors of the participating states. The Appalachian Regional Commission affects local government too through its multicounty development districts represented by city and county officials.

The Appalachian Regional Commission concentrates on economic development and thus illustrates the Friedmann orientation to regionalism. The Commission's activities encompass highway building and community development. Programs have included a regional development highway system, vocational education projects, health projects, child development, community infrastructure development (roads, solid waste disposal, housing, and water and sewer systems), and environmental and natural resource projects. The Appalachian Regional Commission continues to undertake projects that address the five goals of its strategic plan: developing a knowledgeable and skilled population; strengthening the region's physical infrastructure; building local and regional leadership capacity; creating a dynamic economic base; and fostering health.

Adirondack Park

New York's Adirondack Park Agency is an example of a multicounty regional planning effort within one state. The agency focuses on natural resource management and economic development. The Adirondack Park encompasses some 6 million acres (2,430,000 ha) and was created by the New York legislature in 1892, having been set aside as a forest preserve in 1885. The park includes 107 towns and villages in 12 counties and consists of a patchwork of private and state lands. The Adirondack Park Agency was established in 1971 after growing land-use conflicts in the region and discussion about converting the area to a national park. The legislature directed the agency to accomplish two tasks: write a comprehensive plan for the state-owned lands and propose legislation for land use on private lands within the park. The public owns approximately 2.5 million acres (1 million ha) of the park, with the rest in private ownership.

The plan for state lands was immediately adopted with little controversy, but the plan for private lands resulted in considerable debate and court action. The private lands plan provides for control by the Adirondack Park Agency over projects with strong regional impact.

Projects with less regional impact are subject to local government review but must be approved by the Adirondack Park Agency. Currently, the Adirondack Park Land Use and Development Plan regulates land-use and development activities on the 3.5 million acres (1,417,500 ha) of privately owned land.

Lake Tahoe Region

As in the Adirondack region and other parts of the United States, many city, county, and state governments and federal agencies overlap jurisdictionally—often with conflicting policies and programs. During the 1960s, the Lake Tahoe Basin grew at a rapid rate. The region's natural beauty and recreational opportunities attracted many visitors and new residents. In 1969, the legislatures of Nevada and California created the bi-state Tahoe Regional Planning Agency. This agency attracted heated controversy and debate between environmental groups and development interests throughout the 1970s.

To help resolve these conflicts, the U.S. Congress passed, and President Jimmy Carter signed into law, the Tahoe Regional Planning Compact in 1980. This compact gave federal recognition to the regional agency and empowered it to establish environmental threshold carrying capacities, an approach that illustrates a more McHargian orientation to regional planning. Congress defined the threshold **carrying capacity** as "an environmental standard necessary to maintain a significant scenic, recreational, educational, scientific or natural value of the region or to maintain public health and safety within the region." Congress further directed that these thresholds be incorporated into the basin's regional plan and its ordinances for implementation.

The agency adopted this plan in 1987, and it continues to evolve. The implementing ordinances of the plan regulate, among other things, land use, density, growth rates, land coverage, excavation, and scenic impacts. The Tahoe Regional Planning Agency's regulations attempt to bring the region into conformance with threshold standards for water and air quality, soil conservation, wildlife habitat, vegetation, noise, recreation, and scenic resources.

Pinelands

The 1-million-acre (405,000-ha) New Jersey Pinelands, a United Nations–designated Biosphere Reserve, is situated in the midst of the most densely populated region of the United States (Fig. 26-12). The plan for the area

Figure 26-12 Cranberry harvesting in the New Jersey Pinelands (photograph by Francis Rapa, courtesy of the New Jersey Pinelands Commission).

(known locally as the Pine Barrens) derives from designation by the U.S. Congress in 1978. Pinelands was the country's first national reserve. To implement this regional program, the Pinelands Planning Commission was established to coordinate the planning activities of local, state, and national governments.

The Comprehensive Management Plan developed by this Commission broadcasts a number of strategies for the region and also reflects a McHarg-influenced approach. The components of this plan include a natural resource assessment; an assessment of scenic, aesthetic, cultural, open space, and outdoor recreational resources; a land-use capability map; a comprehensive statement of land-use and management policies; a financial analysis; a program to ensure local government and public participation in the planning process; and a program to put the plan into effect. The plan was the culmination of intensive research and planning efforts.

The Pinelands Comprehensive Management Plan evolved at the same time as the Lake Tahoe plan. Although the regions differ, their plans and implementing regulations possess similarities. The Pinelands plan attempts to balance preservation and development. It sets aside some areas for protection and targets others for growth. Land use and development are regulated through environmental standards for wetlands, vegetation, wildlife, water resources, air quality, scenic resources, fire, and history. In addition to its regulatory and economic development programs, the Pinelands Commission maintains ongoing educational efforts concerning the ecology and cultures of the region.

Regional planning undertakings for the Appalachians, Adirondack Park, Lake Tahoe, and the Pinelands reflect the social and environmental awareness of their time and demonstrate important directives for the future. The Pinelands plan, in particular, influenced greenway planning throughout the United States.

Greenways, Sustainable Development, and the Future

Greenways exhibit more similarities to European national parks than to their U.S. cousins. Instead of blanket public ownership, both public and private entities own lands within greenlines. Regional cooperation must occur among government agencies, environmental organizations, businesses, and individual citizens for greenways to be successful.

A greenway, or greenline park, is a large scenic landscape protected by law and regulation from degradation by unplanned development to the extent that it retains its significant attributes. Often, a greenway is a region that remains in productive use by land-oriented industries like fishing, farming, ranching, or forestry. The protections for such a region are cooperatively arranged and managed by citizens and agencies on the local, state, and federal levels, usually through a joint commission. Examples of such commissions include the New Jersey Pinelands Commission and the Columbia River Gorge Commission in Oregon and Washington. Greenway planning, or greenlining, is the process of establishing and maintaining such a region. Both citizens and government are involved in analyzing the region's ecology, deciding on priorities for conservation and development, establishing legal protections, and following through by managing the region according to an agreed-upon plan.

Greenway planning began in 1970, when a 25-year-old North Carolina State University landscape architecture graduate student named Bill Flournoy developed a greenway plan for his hometown of Raleigh. Greenways from Raleigh, North Carolina, to Yakima, Washington, have proven to be a popular form of regional planning (Figs. 26-13, 26-14). Large scenic landscapes and regional water systems have been protected. Regional recreational opportunities have been created. As the quality of life has improved, so have regional economies, as businesses have chosen to stay or have been attracted to areas with open space amenities.

In its third regional plan for the New York–New

Figures 26-13 and 26-14 The Yakima greenway in Washington combines openspace protection and recreational use (courtesy of R. Dix, Yakima Greenway Foundation).

Jersey–Connecticut metropolitan area, the Regional Plan Association (RPA) built on the greenway movement as well as on its own heritage and experience. An emphasis on sustainability was incorporated as well. By the early 1990s, the Brundtland Commission's call for sustainable development began to influence society and its policymakers, designers, and planners around the world. This impact became evident in the Regional Plan Association's third regional plan, published in 1996.[12]

The RPA incorporated in 1929 and produced its first plan that year. The RPA should not be confused with the Regional Planning Association of America (RPAA). In fact, Lewis Mumford of the latter group criticized the

1929 plan for not being strong enough in its efforts "to restrain development and deconcentrate the urban core."[13] Thomas Adams, the planning director of the RPA and the principal author of its first plan, opted for strategies to accommodate growth instead. The Adams-Mumford dichotomy echoed four decades later with the reemergence of regionalism under the banners of Friedmann and McHarg (who, after all, was a protégé of Mumford's).

The RPA completed its second metropolitan-wide plan in 1968. This plan attempted to address the issues of suburban sprawl, urban decline, and transportation. It "helped to protect hundreds of thousands of acres of open space and guided the rebuilding of regional commuter rail systems."[14]

Building on the three foundations of sustainability—social equity, environment, and economy—the most recent plan seeks to optimize the intersections of these (too often viewed as competing) interests. The ultimate goal is to improve the quality of life in the region. The third RPA plan presents bold visions, including, among other things, the creation of eleven regional open space reserves linked by a greenway network and eleven downtown centers supported by transit-oriented development.

To implement this vision, interdisciplinary teams of designers and planners from the RPA work in a open, participatory way with diverse civic and business groups as well as government agencies. The New York regional planners also cooperate with their counterparts in other large metropolitan regions, including Milan, Shanghai, and Tokyo, to refine and advance their vision. For example, sites in Milan and New York were selected so that planners from both metropolitan regions could explore the theme of "transforming the places of production."[15] Both the New York and Milan regions are bustling industrial and manufacturing centers facing decline and renewal, especially emergence of the new information-based economy. In both regions, planners conducted on-location workshops for one site in the metropolitan core, for a regional center, and for a site reflecting landscape and historic preservation values. These cross-cultural, binational exchanges sought to strengthen and transfer expertise in regional planning research and expertise.[16]

Considerable interest exists, at present and for the foreseeable future, in the planning of metropolitan regions. The world's population is increasing and is expected to grow from its current 6 billion to around 9 billion by 2030. Increasingly, people are living in city regions. In fact, we live in the first urban century because more than half of the world's population lives in city regions. As a result, the design and planning of the future

of all (metropolitan and rural) regions will be an important challenge.

Acknowledgments

I appreciate the help with illustrations received from Pamela Peters, Arnold Alanen, Lynette Marie Neitzel, Russ Dix, Keith Witt, Lilly Chin, John Friedmann, and Bob Yaro. Mack White provided the word-processed manuscript, and his contribution is appreciated.

References

Alanen, A., and J. Eden. *Main Street Ready-Made, The New Deal Community of Glendale, Wisconsin*. State Historical Society of Wisconsin, 1987.

Fossa, G., R. Lane, D. Palazzo, and R. Pirani (eds.). *Transforming the Places of Production* (*Trasformare i luoghi della Produzione*). Edizioni Olivares, 2002.

Friedman, J. "Regional Planning as a Field of Study." In W. Alonso (ed.), *Regional Development and Planning*. MIT Press, 1964.

Friedmann, J. *Retracking America*. Anchor Press/Doubleday, 1973.

Kraenzel, C. "Principles of Regional Planning: As Applied to the Northwest," *Social Forces*, December 1947.

Kraenzel, C. *The Great Plains in Transition*. University of Oklahoma Press, 1955.

MacKaye, B. *The New Exploration*. Harcourt, Brace, 1928.

MacKaye, B. "Regional Planning and Ecology," *Ecological Monographs*, Vol. 10, No. 3 (July 1940).

McHarg, I. *Design with Nature*. Doubleday Natural History Press, 1969.

McHarg, I. *A Quest for Life*. Wiley, 1996.

McHarg, I., and F. Steiner (eds.). *To Heal the Earth*. Island Press, 1998.

Van der Wal, C. *In Praise of Common Sense: Planning the Ordinary. A Physical Planning History of the New Towns in the Ijsselmeerpolders*. 010 Publishers, 1997.

Yaro, R., and T. Hiss. *A Region at Risk, The Third Regional Plan for the New York–New Jersey–Connecticut Metropolitan Area*. Island Press, 1996.

Young, G. "Human Ecology as an Interdisciplinary Domain." *Advances in Ecological Research*, 1974.

Endnotes

1. C. Kraenzel, "Principles of Regional Planning as Applied to the Northwest," *Social Forces*, December 1947: 376.
2. B. MacKaye, "Regional Planning and Ecology," *Ecological Monographs*, July 1940: 349–353.
3. MacKaye, "Regional Planning and Ecology,": 95–124.
4. B. MacKaye, *The New Exploration* (Harcourt, Brace, 1928).
5. A. Alanen and J. Eden, *Main Street Ready-Made, The New*

Deal Community of Glendale, Wisconsin (State Historical Society of Wisconsin, 1987): 8.

6. C. Van der Wal, *In Praise of Common Sense: Planning the Ordinary. A Physical Planning History of the New Towns in the Ijsselmeerpolders* (010 Publishers, 1997).

7. J. Friedmann, *Retracking America* (Anchor Press/Doubleday, 1973): 69.

8. I. McHarg, *Design with Nature* (Doubleday Natural History Press, 1969): 153.

9. J. Friedmann, "Regional Planning as a Field of Study," *Regional Development and Planning* (MIT Press, 1964): 63–64.

10. G. Young, "Human Ecology as an Interdisciplinary Domain," *Advances in Ecological Research*, 1974: 46.

11. C. Kraenzel, "Principles of Regional Planning": 376.

12. R. Yaro and T. Hiss, *A Region at Risk, The Third Regional Plan for the New York–New Jersey–Connecticut Metropolitan Area* (Island Press, 1996).

13. Yaro and Hiss, *A Region at Risk: 1.*

14. Yaro and Hiss, *A Region at Risk: 2.*

15. G. Fossa, R. Lane, D. Palazzo, and R. Pirani (eds.), *Transforming the Places of Production* (*Trasformare i luoghi della Produzione). (Edizioni Olivares, 2002).*

16. See Note 15.

CHAPTER 27

Connections: Products to Regional Planning and Policies

William W. Budd

How individuals perceive the environments around them, and the relationship of those perceptions to values and attitudes, are central to the design/planning process. The objects, institutions, and organization of the built environment that emerge from these processes develop an understanding or a vision of human-environmental- and technical relationships. Under general and ideal conditions, these relationships are seen as ones of balance and harmony, of health and fitness. It is not society that interacts with the environment, but rather the collective action of individuals interacting within a dynamic series of social, economic, and ecological dimensions.

> Recognizing the limitations of human nature . . . is a necessary prerequisite to designing a social system that will minimize the effects of those limitations . . . that too . . . is a means of modification of human behavior.[1]

Understanding the relationship between design/planning and the environments that result must encompass all levels of society, from individuals and groups to national and international policies and leaders. It is through individual team collaboration and creativity that design becomes tangible. But, in form and content, "designing with nature," to use the title of Ian McHarg's seminal work, entails and requires a much larger responsibility. It is everyone's responsibility and the designers' charge to understand and become sensitive to the collective interactions of humans, society, and nature. It is vital to envision design and the resulting built environment as interconnections within a series of integrated levels. To understand these connections, it is essential to know the magnitude and extent to which change at any level may affect other levels of integration.

The integrative process has come to be known as **synthesis**. It is a vision, an understanding, a sensitivity to all the components of the built and natural environments, which operates from the level of products to those of regions and global systems. This chapter is about this integrative vision. The questions examined are: To what degree can changes at one level of integration affect other levels? And, given these relationships, what are the implications and responsibilities for design and planning?

Assessing Actions Across Levels: The Importance of Culture

How do humans assess the effects of their actions on the environment? What are the "right" sets of "things" to measure? How are these measurements made? These are

Figure 27-1   The challenges of comprehending human-environmental relationships. Czechoslovakian exhibition wall at the World Expo, Montreal, Canada (T. Bartuska).

premise that a new technology can always be developed to treat any problem. As new technologies are created, new problems are also created, which require newer technologies. The cycle appears endless.

The critical questions that must be asked are: What are the challenges (opportunities and limitations) that such a connective vision places on society and on the design, planning, and management fields? How can citizens, planners, and designers respond to the challenges presented by a connective, integrated vision of human-environmental relationships?

difficult questions that continue to challenge decision makers and professionals because the nature of the problems that societies address is constantly changing. Where do we start?

All too often, people lose sight of the fact that in addressing a problem, whether perceived or realized, any action has human-environmental impacts. Humans alter environments to provide an improved quality of life, an improved sense of well-being, of purpose, of achievement. There is nothing inherently negative or positive about such efforts; indeed, they may well be viewed as noble. However, humans often forget, or ignore, that these interventions are occurring within a dynamic system, a system within which humans are but one dynamic component. It is, however, a system that exists by balance, interactions, change, and adjustment. In this sense, culture is inseparable from nature. Human societies exist at the interface between **cultural** processes and **natural** processes. Changes in culture do have effects on natural systems. Too often, human assessments are rooted in the space and time of social constructions but not of natural processes. Human actions on any scale will have ramifications on a variety of other scales.

In general, societies, and more specifically industrialized societies, have failed to recognize and to incorporate into their behavioral patterns and traditions an understanding of these connections. Even within the fields of planning and design, the very fields in which such revelations would seem most likely to occur, the incorporation of a holistic perspective has been slow to develop. At times, tradition and practice have served as obstructions to such a visionary change. People operate under the

From Products to Households: The Unseen/Unexpected Toxic Problem

Perhaps the most fundamental relationship in the built environment is the interactions of products consumed by humans and their personal everyday lives. In developed societies particularly, there is a perceived need for a diversity of products and goods. Unfortunately, the costs associated with a wide variety of consumer products are hidden, and all too often those costs are not assessed or in many instances are not well known. This problem is most severely felt in the major time delays (disconnects) for products that exhibit hazardous or toxic characteristics. For example, more than a quarter century after regulatory reform curbed the use of asbestos in buildings (1970s) and its use peaked, deaths from asbestosis are rising in the first decade of the twenty-first century and are expected to continue to rise for at least another ten years.

Despite what people think or feel, the risk of developing cancer from exposure to asbestos, from chemicals in drinking water, or from paint strippers and other solvents found in homes is greater than the risk from the same chemicals found in a hazardous waste site.

The link between individual actions and their effects on fresh air and water should be apparent to most individuals. Fresh air and water are fundamental human needs. Although the connections may indeed be "apparent" and of "vital importance," a cursory review of the ledger of human interactions with these resources suggests a different level of understanding. Water provides a vivid example. **U.S. Environmental Protection Agency** (EPA) figures show that nearly 2,000 publicly owned treatment works have recorded organic (e.g., solvent) contaminant levels in excess of those considered to be safe. This translates into an affected population of nearly

1 million. Nearly 67% of all rural drinking water supplies have a measurable level of contamination.

What is even more revealing about this particular problem and society's lack of understanding about the interconnections between products and, in this case, water quality is that use of groundwater (the major source being contaminated) has been increasing. As a consequence, individuals have been increasingly exposing themselves to many of the most toxic compounds known to humankind—many of which likely came from their own kitchen shelves. Readers are encouraged to review the warning labels (and Web sites) of all products used in the home and elsewhere, places where they may work and play.

Most people are not aware of it, but the chemicals used to clean and beautify their homes may be doing quite a bit more. Some of the same toxic materials found in hazardous waste sites are used in paints, paint thinners, cleaners, and other household goods. More importantly, the amount of material individuals are exposed to in the everyday use of these materials can be higher than if the home was next to an abandoned hazardous waste facility.

Major offenders are the pesticides used so freely in the United States. The most widely used garden pesticides are 2-4-D, benomyl, chorothalonil, and glyphosphate (read the labels of products on the store shelves to see how common these are). The most common toxic materials found in and around the home are the following:

- **Asbestos**: insulation, floor and ceiling tiles, paints, and joint compounds
- **Radon**: in rock and soil beneath houses
- **Combustion Gases**: from gas appliances, wood stoves, and furnaces
- **Household Chemicals**: in pesticides, paints, paint strippers, and cleaning fluids
- **Artificial Fragrances**: perfumes/colognes, soap and detergents, drier sheets, air fresheners, etc.
- **Water Pollutants**: lead in water pipes or pipe solder and chemicals that leach into water supplies

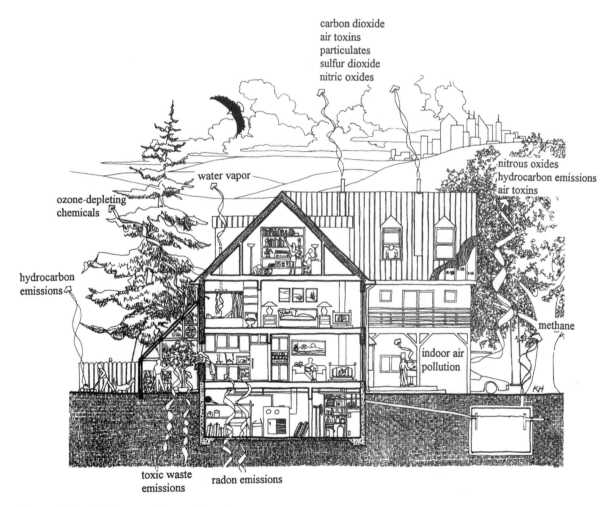

Figure 27-2 Toxic materials entering a house.

- **Formaldehyde**: in cabinets, bookcases, and other furniture constructed with particleboard or plywood, as well as drapes, upholstery, carpets, and wallpaper adhesives
- **Allergens**: molds, bacteria, dust, and pollen that collect in air-conditioning vents, humidifiers, and dehumidifiers

These chemicals are all linked to cancer and reproductive problems. An example of a serious offender is the compound chlordane, the most widely used termite-killing agent in the United States. It has been linked to cancer, to a host of neurological disorders, and to miscarriages. It was banned because of these effects, but the government graciously permitted exterminators to use up the supplies of this material stored in their warehouses.

In fact, approximately 70,000 different chemicals are in everyday use in the United States. Monsanto Corporation, a major chemical manufacturer, asks, "Where would we be without chemicals?" In quantitative terms, this statement seems justified. But look a little more closely at this claim: Of those 70,000 chemicals, the EPA indicates that thousands are potentially hazardous to human health and the environment. What is even more disturbing is that of these thousands of known toxics, good information concerning exposure, effects, and risks has been developed for only a handful. For the overwhelming majority of these compounds, using them means exposure to risks.

The Toxic Substance Control Act was passed in 1976 to provide some level of protection and evaluation for the public. But there too there has been bureaucratic obstinacy. Since 1976, the EPA has received health and environmental results on only 22 chemicals and has assessed the test results for only 13 of them. Although the agency has determined that some of these compounds are dangerous, it has taken no regulatory action because it believes the chemicals do not post "significant or unreasonable risk."[2]

But blame cannot be leveled just at agencies and governments in this regard. Think for a moment about the passion in the United States for a green, well-manicured lawn. The EPA estimates that the sale of lawn care pesticides exceeds $700 million annually. Further, about 67 million pounds of active ingredients from these sales are applied to lawns and parks nationwide each year. In addition, approximately 5,000 lawn care firms are doing $1.5 billion in annual business servicing about 12% of the remaining homes in the United States.[3] Central to all of these environmental concerns are individuals and personal choice. Even artificial fragrances in many perfumes, colognes, shampoos, laundry soaps, and drier sheets are made from petrol chemicals and can cause health problems. Unfortunately, the manufacturers of these products are not required to list the chemical used.

Many chemicals are being tested, and the contents of various products are being listed; also, when necessary, warning labels are placed on the containers. In addition, more detailed information is available in product data sheets from manufacturers.

Many chemicals interact with one another in what could be considered multiple-chemical soup. Individually, toxins up to certain threshold levels may be relatively safe, but no one knows the compound interactions with others. For example, a person gets up, uses a shampoo and showers (with questionable personal care products), uses some perfumes/colognes/hair spray, then applies a weed killer on a lawn and afterward does a load of laundry, uses drier sheets, and wears "freshly scented" clothes. Thereafter, he or she might go out and pass other lawns or breathe in the exhaust from vehicles or visit with others who might use the products. Or this person may spend the day working in a building that uses other cleaning products and may have poor air quality, interacting with people with other fragrances and with off-gassing materials. In any day, we all experience this **multiple-chemical environment**. The human body has limits and reacts with headaches, burning eyes, allergic reactions, nervous system disorders (at increasing rates in our children), and even birth defects and cancer. Many people find that the body is saying that it's had enough; they are experiencing a rather new illness—**multiple chemical sensitivity** (MCS). MCS is challenging the medical community and society to more fully understand and be more careful about the interaction of all the chemicals used and then concentrated in our indoor and outdoor environments. Unfortunately, the chemical industry is trying to shift the name and blame of the problem by calling it an "environmental sensitivity."[4]

From Products to Communities: Solid Waste

The relationship of culture and the effect of changes in human needs and values on design and planning is nowhere more explicit than in the evolution of cities. Cities represent and are expressions of human-environmental relationships. The demand for shelter and security is fundamental to the human species. Although more efficient than sprawl, many urban environments have a history of neglect and distress. The critical questions are, why did this happen and what was the role of design?

It is important to recognize that human-environmental relationships in cities are dynamic. For example, city officials and urban populations have not always viewed refuse, trash, and pollution as social evils. During the early years of the Industrial Revolution, pollution was a sign of progress. Pollution and waste produced the "smell of money." During this period, industrialization was the primary social objective, and buildings and cities were constructed to meet specific social and economic needs.

As discussed in the component on cities, the ideas of free market (laissez-faire) growth coupled with the rapid increase in wealth that characterized the Industrial Revolution, spawned a wide range of social and environmental concerns. By 1880, New York had changed from a walking "town" to an industrialized city. Along with large numbers of factories, mills, and tanneries, some of the largest slums in the world were created. Cities began to reek of a variety of odors. Ammonia gases, sulfur, offal rendering, bone boiling, animal wastes, manure heaps, and unwanted litter were found everywhere. The standard practice for dealing with these problems was to find an empty lot or the nearest river and dump the waste. Epidemics began to occur with alarming frequency. Typhoid fever, cholera, dysentery, and yellow fever were commonplace. Each of these diseases has its root in pollution. To get rid of the mass of wastes, cities began to use rivers and lakes, only to have these environments deteriorate and, in some instances, die. Ultimately, changes were made, but for several decades these actions were used and tolerated.

In an evaluation of planning or design, clear documentation is now available about the broader interconnections between the city and a wide range of other levels of integration. Individuals and products specific to regional watersheds are examples of levels adversely affected by the cities. They are aggregate representations of human preferences. The design and planning process in today's cities is being forced, or conditioned, by global factors.

Cities are concentrations of material wealth. As societies have become wealthier, there has been a tendency for many to consume more. For a wide range of reasons, most of which are obvious, increased disposable income leads to an increased desire for material goods. To meet this demand, a wide variety of products are created. As populations have grown, the demand for more and more goods has also increased. This demand for greater quantities and diversity in goods has had a tremendous impact on the design and planning disciplines. People in these fields are in great demand because they provide and define the forms of the objects being consumed: from increasingly large single-family homes to vacation condominiums sited on sand dunes, from glass bottles to flip-top cans, from the paper and plastic wrapping on packages to disposable coffee cups and lids. Society "reads" consumer demand and then responds.

In 1990, the average person in the United States generated 7.7 kilograms (17 pounds) of solid waste every day, and this amount nearly doubled by the year 2000. This means that an average family of four generates more than 3 tons of solid waste each year. Viewed collectively, this is enough solid waste to fill the Superdome in New Orleans twice every day for an entire year. As a result of high levels of waste production, U.S. citizens

- Import more goods
- Waste more energy
- Suffer increased inflation
- Endure more environmental degradation
- Expose more individuals to increased health risks

The financial and environmental costs associated with managing this problem are substantial.

These impacts cannot be viewed as attributable exclusively to designers or planners. These are problems that have at their heart a lack of understanding of connections and an unfortunate shared social belief that the planet is nothing more than an infinite resource base. This attitude fosters careless consumption patterns and demands for goods without any thought as to how these goods are produced and without any prior assessment of the long-term impacts on the environment and human life. This can be illustrated by vivid examples of packaging and chemical and electronic waste.

Examples of the Solid Waste Dilemma

Packaging

About 50% of all the paper, about 8% of all the steel, about 75% of all the glass, about 40% of all the aluminum, and about 30% of all the plastics produced in the United States are used to wrap and decorate consumer products. This means that $1 out of every $10 spent on product is for packaging, an item that will ultimately be thrown away (or, hopefully, reused/recycled).

This increased demand for stylish and fancy packaging is a relatively recent phenomenon. The trend was initiated around 1958, often referred to as "the packaging explosion year." If U.S. society was less interested in and designers did not respond to the demand for products that contain so much packaging waste, tremendous amounts of energy and money would be saved and far less solid waste would be generated. Excessive paper wrappers and plastic packaging for fast-food burgers, for example, has fallen by the wayside. This decision by the fast-food industry has had the net gain of reducing waste and the associated costs of dealing with waste. If packaging levels were held to those of 1958, 566 trillion BTUs of energy would have been saved every day—an equivalent of 267,000 barrels of oil every day![5]

Container packaging is another example of product effects at higher levels of integration in the built environment. Large numbers of people consume milk. In fact, 70 million families in the United States consume at least a half-gallon of milk every week. If those households bought that milk in half-gallon containers rather than two single-quart containers, the amount of paper discarded by our society would be reduced by approximately 42 million pounds per year. The amount of plastic discarded each year would be reduced by 6 million pounds. About 146 million dollars per year in packaging would be saved, along with about 1 trillion BTUs of energy. That is enough energy to heat and cool a community of 7,500 households for an entire year—just by reducing the number of milk cartons.

Another not at all trivial example: plastic shopping bags—the ubiquitous sacks used to carry groceries, books, or clothes; to wrap strawberries or chicken for the freezer; and, if used again (too rare an occurrence), to pick up doggie doo. Estimates vary between 500 billion and 1 trillion bags in use every year around the world—the low number dismaying, the high one overwhelming. These bags are made from nonrenewable petroleum, and scarce energy resources are used in their manufacture and distribution. Thrown-away bags (350,000 in one concerted pickup effort on the East Coast of the United States) become a litter problem (called "white pollution" blowing around the streets of China and the "national flower" in the countryside of South Africa). And the bags can do serious harm to wildlife: Planet Ark, an international environmental group, claims that, globally, the bags kill 100,000 whales, seals, turtles, and other marine animals each year. Some countries have banned the bags or slapped a use tax on them (e.g., Ireland's PlasTax) in efforts to reduce the damage. To date, the United States has not done much to address the problem, except for meager efforts by plastic manufacturers to head off regulations by showcasing recycling efforts.[6]

While solid waste illustrates a direct and visible connection of products to effects at higher levels, the translation of change into energy and resource savings is difficult for the average citizen to envision. Even the cost savings are often muted because when the data are disaggregated to the individual level, the perception of the problem changes. It simply does not seem to be a real concern.

Individual behavior must change to solve the solid waste problem, but this process can be difficult and slow. For attitudes and behavior to change, alternative products must be developed and their use encouraged. Simpler packaging and the use of recyclable materials can have a significant impact, as the illustrations above indicate. Moreover, with new products, planners can begin to develop policies that will encourage individuals and society to practice the three Rs—first, **reduce** the use of packaging; then **reuse**; and, finally, **recycle**. Society is responding to the last (recycling) but not as much to the first two priorities (reduce and reuse).

Chemical Waste

A far more insidious problem is the use of and demand for chemicals by society. Chemicals are a pervasive part of society; tremendous quantities of synthetic fabrics and petroleum products are consumed. The demand for new and different paint products, the desirability of buildings constructed with preserved wood products, and the desire to have that bright, clean shine on linoleum floors are a few examples of the use of chemicals in our society.

Prior to 1977, industry in the United States indicated that it was annually generating about 23 million metric tons (MmT) of hazardous waste. In 1977, following a study by the EPA, it was discovered that this figure was slightly off and that U.S. society was now generating about 35 MmT of hazardous waste. But the more alarming finding of the study was that only 10% of the waste was being disposed of in a manner consistent with what then were proposed regulations for managing hazardous wastes.

In fact, 50% of the waste was being placed in open lagoons, 30% was being disposed of in unsecured landfills, and 10% was being dumped directly into sewers. Further studies show that today the demand for chemical products has produced a monstrous environmental problem. It is estimated that people in the United States are now generating approximately 600–750 MmT of hazardous waste each year. What is more, this quantity is increasing at a rate of about 4% per year.

The true tragedy of this problem is that the principal mechanism to dispose of these materials has been the land. Here, as with the quantity of solid waste generated, the figures are staggering. In 1979, industry reported that 3,383 waste sites had been used from 1950 to 1976. But only six months later, the EPA revealed that the figure was more like 30,000–50,000 waste sites, 2,000 of which posed an immediate threat to human health. Today it is generally believed that there are 180,000–390,000 waste sites, 20,000 of which pose a serious threat to human health and/or the environment. What makes this problem so serious is that these materials include some of the most dangerous compounds on this planet—carcinogens, mutagens, and teratogens—and increasingly they are showing up in the water that people use most directly—by drinking it.

Humans too often fail to recognize context and relationships. But nature does, modifying, transporting, and inserting back into our lives materials placed and hidden in the bowels of the earth. From the seeds of convenience, consumer economics, and/or design, humans are now reaping cancer, mental retardation, pain, suffering, and death. The most fundamental activity in the built environment, the development of a product, is not immune to interaction with other levels of integration. Indeed, like the city, products cannot be viewed as end states. The definition and acceptability of products change with changes in human behavior.

As with solid waste, the roots of the chemical waste problem lie in human behavior. What is needed is not a better technology, but a better understanding of the connections between what people use and their collective impacts on the world around them. To minimize chemical waste generation requires investigation and promotion of waste reduction, reuse, and recycling, as well as source reduction and treatment programs. U.S. laws require these changes for major businesses, but they must also apply to households for the chemical waste problem to be resolved. Individuals must recognize their role in the chemical cycle. Without changes at the level of the individual, chemical waste will remain one of the most serious crises facing societies for decades to come.

Electronic Waste

Electronic waste, commonly referred to as "e-waste," is fast becoming a major challenge in this century. Millions of computer monitors, televisions, and cell phones are being discarded and replaced with newer, more advanced systems. In the United States alone, 60 million computers are already buried in landfills, with another 250 million to become obsolete by 2009 (that's 136,000 per day), along with some 100 million cell phones. Most

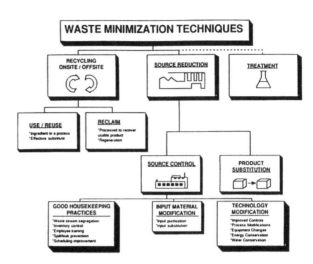

Figure 27-3 Opportunities for future change in hazardous waste management (GAO, 1988).

e-wastes contain toxic heavy metals (antimony, silver, chromium, zinc, tin, and copper). If they are buried in landfills, the metals can leach into soils and water. If burned, they will emit dangerous toxins that are harmful to health, especially that of children.

What should society do with this growing e-waste problem? Who should pay for protection from it—the user, the manufacturer, or society? Regardless of who pays, the cost will be carried over to the consumer through added costs, taxes, or impacts on human and environmental health. Can these products be designed to last longer or adapt to new technologies by inserting modules? Can these discarded electronic products be recycled and become a renewed resource? These are

Figure 27-4 E-waste—part of a department's used supply of computer equipment waiting to be reprocessed (Pamela Overholtzer).

what McDonough calls **technical nutrients**, which he believes must be the responsibility of the creators, that is, the manufacturers, and returned to them for recycling and reuse.[7] As discussed in Chapter 13, this cradle-to-cradle approach would encourage the responsible company to design products that would last longer and be made of materials can be reused or reprocessed. In some European countries, the cost of recovering and recycling these products into new resources is added to the purchase price. In the United States, many states are considering similar programs.

From Product to Region: Acid Deposition

Energy is central to all components of the built environment. At all levels of integration, energy is the critical factor in determining what is produced, what is planned, and what is constructed. Energy determines in a real way the form of the built environment. More energy is consumed in the United States than anywhere else on this planet. The principal sources of energy are fossil fuels—coal, oil, and natural gas. The United States consumes, for example, about 22% of the electrical power generated in the world. Coal is used to generate a significant portion of this electrical energy.

One of the by-products of using coal to generate electrical power is pollution. The original pollutant of concern associated with coal combustion was particulate matter. The particulate problem came abruptly to public awareness in 1952, when a climatic inversion settled in over the city of London, resulting in a buildup of pollution that killed 3,000 people. A similar incident, fortunately with many fewer deaths, affected Johnstown, Pennsylvania, in 1954. Communities near power facilities became concerned about these particulates; they were viewed as serious, but as a local problem.

To resolve this problem, industry designed a new technology. Tall stacks were erected to deposit the pollution high in the atmosphere. The rationale: the atmosphere is but another endless resource for human use—**dilution is the solution to pollution**! The impacts of this solution to the particulate problem were not manifested for nearly thirty years. Since 1968, however, a noticeable change has been occurring downwind from these stationary sources of pollution. "Downwind" here means thousands of miles, distances that transcend political boundaries and the institutions that humans establish to manage environmental issues. This has created a

new problem, continental in scale, of acid deposition (acid rain).

Like global warming (discussed in the next chapter), acid deposition is a secondary form of pollution. The problem, as the term suggest, is that by-products of fossil fuel combustion lead to large regional deposits of acids. The acids are not emitted directly, which is why the problem is referred to as "secondary pollution." The term "deposition" is used because the acidic inputs can be either wet (i.e., rain or snow) or dry (i.e., particulates). The specific acids of most concern are sulfuric and nitric, and the major precursors of these acids are sulfur dioxide and nitrogen oxides.

Acid deposition is a complex phenomenon. At all levels, natural and cultural, the problem requires dealing with transformations and transfers over large regions and over time. There is considerable uncertainty about what acid deposition does, how it occurs, and who or what is responsible.

Some general known and potential effects of acid deposition have been identified. These effects graphically illustrate the degree to which developments and actions at a low level of integration affect higher levels. More importantly, this particular example illustrates that controls are mostly lacking at higher levels.

Scientists know that in certain sensitive aquatic systems, changes in acidity can lead to wide changes in fauna and flora. Some sensitive lakes are acidifying in Canada, the northeastern United States, and Scandinavia. A second major possible/probable impact of acid deposition is on forest growth. Some forests in regions experiencing acid deposition for several decades are showing signs of decline. Many scientists believe that this change is a direct or indirect consequence of acid deposition. The mechanisms associated with such declines, however, are very complex, involving, at a minimum, nutrient flows, plant physiology, and plant-soil interactions, all of which are operating across regions and over decades, making it difficult to be certain. It is clear that increased rainfall acidity occurred during the same period of time that declines in growth were noted. This may be coincidental, but it may also be causal.

Finally, evidence exists to indicate that structures of the built environment are being affected, that increased damage to buildings and monuments has been caused by acid deposition. Misinterpretations and false analyses regarding nonliving effects have occurred. For example, damage to Cleopatra's Needle in New York City was originally thought to be associated with acid deposition. In 1978, the *New York Times* commented, "The city's atmosphere has done more damage than three and a half millennia in the desert, and in another dozen years the hieroglyphs will probably disappear." This proved to be false. The damage was actually from advanced salt decay and the increased humidity of New York City, coupled with some misguided attempts at preservation. Nevertheless, it is clear that acidic deposition does cause significant incremental damage to nonliving materials beyond that brought about by natural processes.

Dealing with issues such as acid deposition requires large, farsighted, transboundary institutions that have yet to be created. Costs, benefits, and reduced risk have dominated outcome evaluation, measures that have become institutionalized and, therefore, continue to influence design and planning. More concerted efforts on the part of individuals, professionals, and institutions are needed to integrate knowledge about natural processes with knowledge about social and economic processes.

Resolving the problems of acid deposition, like most problems involving human-environmental relationships, requires changing the level and degree of interactions and changing human behavior. There is a tendency for individuals to throw up their hands when asked what should be done about acid deposition. Opportunities for individual actions are complex and difficult, and are perceived to be even more so. Change, however, can come about through energy conservation programs and political action. Change can also come about by individuals voicing concerns to political representatives. Again, the primary determinant affecting change is individual action.

From Region to Planet: International Management of Toxins

The effects of human actions extend well beyond products to regions and to the planet, which is in many ways quickly becoming a global society. Within this context, the effects of regions, or more precisely nations and collections of nations (supranational regions), market traditions, culture, products, and certainly pollutants, through interactions with other nations on natural systems and the Earth as a whole integrated system must be better understood. The costs of such transactions are often not always fully measured or assessed. In this case, the damage is particularly profound.

The effect of this type of cultural influence can best be shown in economic development. At the conclusion of

World War II, there was a great interest in promoting economic development in the Third World. The societies involved in this effort are commonly referred to as "market societies." When reaching out to help developing nations, developed societies imposed their own model, their own perspective of the built environment. This influenced (in many cases established) the prevailing manner in which humans interact with nature. Developed societies have changed the nature and degree of human interactions with the natural environment, locally and on a global scale. The results have been dramatic.

In traditional societies, the use of natural resources developed from an immediate dependency on the natural environment. The very livelihood of individuals, families, and small groups in Third World societies depends upon immediate environmental feedback. The use of resources—and the development of a built environment within this context—mandated designing "with" nature and the maintenance of ecological stability. In contrast, developed societies, with the exception of a few professionals and interest groups, have been desensitized to the interrelationships between their well-being and the natural environment.

In developed societies, strong incentives exist to produce as much surplus as can be sold. This stockpiling behavior is perceived as necessary because it leads to increases in material wealth and power. In this type of system, there is little incentive to conserve. While conservation is not precluded from this framework, it is also not a driving force or primary criterion for evaluating changes in human surroundings—the natural and built environments.

On a substantive level, the effects of more developed regions on global processes can have profound meanings. An increasing number of toxic outputs have become ubiquitous. There is simply nowhere on this planet that a person can go without encountering some amount of these added chemicals. Examples include radionuclides, polychlorinated biphenyls (PCBs), and, more recently, a number of pesticides.

The pesticide issue is of particular interest. The impacts of pesticides are a growing global concern. The use of these substances is increasing in all areas of the planet, and with this use comes increased risks and consequences. The issue is more than simply applying and using a dangerous material; the pesticide case represents adoption of a particular view of human interactions with the environment. Again, it is a short-term production, surplus generation model that developed societies impose on nations that they intend to "help."

But look at the costs. While it is true that the gross national product of many developing nations has increased by about 3% each year, has an analogous change occurred in the quality of life of the people being aided? Between 400,000 and 2 million pesticide poisonings occur worldwide each year. Most of these are happening in less developed countries; approximately 10,000 to 40,000 of these incidents result in death. Compare this figure to the number of deaths that resulted from the chemical plant tragedy at Bhopal, India, an accident that resulted from a system failure in the built environment: a valve failed, management was poor, and response capabilities were absent. In this case, the resultant release of a toxic gas led to the deaths of over 2,500 individuals. Upon learning of this disaster, the world was outraged! At the same time, U.S. citizens, officials, and advertisers ignore the fact that promoting the use of pesticides creates the potential equivalent of 4 to 16 Bhopal-level accidents each year.

Pesticide use in agriculture could likely be cut in half and industrial waste cut by a third in the future. For societies to realize the benefits of such change, policies and funding priorities need to be changed to actively promote the use of new agricultural practices and sustainable methods of production. As Wendell Berry (1977) notes, "Food is a cultural product; it cannot be produced by technology alone. . . . A healthy culture is a communal order of memory, insight, value, work, conviviality, reverence, aspiration."[8] To effect change at the level of societies, individuals must change. This can include changing the products consumed to only those that are pesticide free, insisting on increased monitoring for such chemicals in food, and supporting policies that seek to promote sustainable methods.

Conspectus

> The ancient spiritual teachings of the Cheyenne Indians tell us that we meet ourselves in almost everything we confront. . . . When we meet an animal, feel a touch, or take a hike down the street, we see a reflection of ourselves and of humanity.[9]

Can the design and planning fields provide the guidance and foresight needed to improve or eliminate the myriad destructive elements in the built environment? What skills are required? What knowledge is needed?

Decisions about the distribution of scarce resources are critical in today's world. "We do not live in the timeless days of a dog or sparrow. As we become aware of what we as a society are doing, we bear responsibility for those allocations that will be made as well as for what has already been done in our names."[10]

In dealing with pollution and waste outputs, U.S. society can be characterized by the phrase "out of sight, out of mind." We have designed our buildings and communities so as to hide waste cans and dumps. We have used air, water, and land to dump wastes, and now we are seeing that there is a price.

There are alternatives. They require innovative minds, new designs, and new institutions. The design fields are on the cutting edge of this challenge. From the development of new product designs to community and regional planning, individuals in these fields provide both the tools and the procedures by which the future of humans and environments will be managed. Using this information effectively requires learning to foresee the impacts of products, to incorporate uncertainties and contingencies into plans, and, above all, to view problems and activities within a holistic context while adopting more ecologically safe and sustainable ways. Figure 27-5 shows the future potential of managing society's outputs of toxic materials. In the past they were viewed as waste, but in actuality they are chemical resources that need to be recycled and reused.[11] As McDonough and Braungart state, society needs to **eliminate the concept of waste**[12] and find ways to reintegrate and recycle the outputs back into the industrial process. The diagram shows (from left to right) how society has tried to control the dumping of waste by (1) pollution controls. Now industry needs to (2 and 3) reintegrate the output within the overall processes. This leads to (4), a rapidly expanding interdisciplinary field of **industrial ecology** that looks at outputs and inputs within a closed-loop system. And then this could lead to (5)—a sustainable society that reintegrates all of its outputs and eliminates the concept of waste.

What, then, can individuals do? There is no formula, no model for success that will provide greater understanding of the relationships examined in this chapter and this book. A number of key aspects, however, are important for any program seeking to strengthen training in this area. First, the challenge has too often been limited to establishing discipline-specific relationships and to emphasizing the strength and uniqueness of each—an effect called "siloing." To understand the interconnections between levels of integration, individuals must be able to transcend their discipline and acquire a comprehensive worldview. This is happening, as with the authors of this book and with many practitioners. Second, it is vital that scholars develop conceptual skills that have methodological rigor. **Conceptual power without analysis is impotent;**

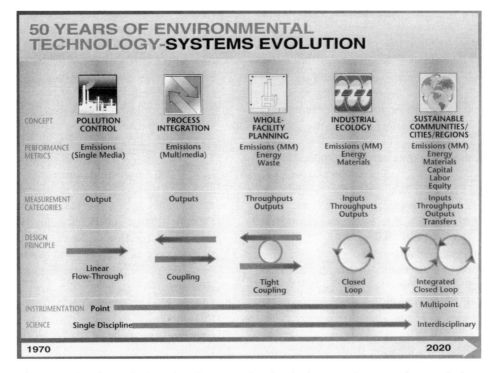

Figure 27-5   The evolution of environmental technologies—moving away from end-of-waste-pipe controls to an integrated systems approach that eliminates the concept of waste, which is required for a truly sustainable society (NETC, 1995).

analytical rigor without synthesis is lethal. Finally, all participants need to practice the **three Rs**—first, **reduce**; then **reuse**; and, finally, **recycle** and think in terms of complete ecological/sustainable systems.

Humans will continue to use natural resources to meet basic needs, as well as to achieve social goals and objectives. What they must learn is how to use those resources in a sustainable way. Planning and design, in their best interdisciplinary mode, can help meet these goals and transcend limited levels of interaction. The impact of all fields is tremendous because they affect activities that affect human behavior, and it is human behavior that is the core of all human-environmental and technical problems.

One final note: there is no assurance that humans will be able to avoid the types of problems discussed in these pages. What emerges, however, from an increased sensitivity to the importance of connections in human-environment-technical relationships is a new paradigm for interactive, interdisciplinary learning. It is a paradigm that does not seek to provide humans with prescriptions for change, but rather forces humans to recognize the impacts of their decisions across multiple levels.

Environmental problems exist because humans have not taken to heart a multilevel, holistic framework for learning. Most people remain ignorant of the array of

connections that immerse them in and bind them to the complex natural and built environments in which they live. Erasing that ignorance, in oneself especially but in others as well (friends, associates, clients, politicians, etc.), is a major challenge in the design, planning, and management of the built environment.

References

Berry, W. *The Unsettling of America: Culture and Agriculture.* Sierra Club Books, 1977.

Calbresi, G., and P. Babbitt. *Tragic Choices.* W. W. Norton, 1978.

Computer Take Back Campaign, 2006: www.computertake-back.com.

Freeze, R. *Environmental Pendulum: A Quest for the Truth about Toxic Chemicals, Human Health and Environmental Protection.* University of California Press, 2000.

General Accounting Office. "Toxic Substances: EPA's Chemical Testing Programs Has Not Resolved Safety Concerns," GAO/RCED-91-136, June 1991.

General Accounting Office. "Lawn Care Pesticides: EPA Needs to Assess State Notification Programs," GAO/RCED-91-208, September 1991.

Hazeldon Foundation. *Touchstones.* Harper and Row, 1986.

Heij, G., and J. Erisman. *Acid Rain Research: Do We Have Enough Answers?* Elsevier, 1995.

Konner, M. *The Tangled Wing.* Holt, Rinehart and Winston, 1982.

Liu, D., P. Bouis, and B. Liptak. *Hazardous Waste and Solid Waste*. CRC Press, 1999.

Lowy, J. "Plastic Left Holding the Bag as Environmental Plague." Scripps Howard News Service, 2004.

McCampbell, A. Multiple Chemical Sensitivities Task Force Report: "Multiple Chemical Sensitivities Under Siege." 2001: www.mindfully.org/Health/MCS-Under-Siege or Townsend [News] letter for Doctors and Patients, 210, January: www.tldp.com.

McDonough, W., and M. Braungart. *Cradle to Cradle: Remaking the Way We Make Things*. North Point Press, 2002.

National Science and Technology Council. *Bridge to a Sustainable Future*. Interagency Environmental Technologies, 1995.

Rainbow, P., and M. Crane (eds.). *Forecasting the Environmental Fate and Effects of Chemicals*. Wiley, 2001.

Royte, E. "e-gad!" *Smithsonian*, August 2005.

Selke, S. *Packaging and the Environment: Alternative Trends and Solutions*, rev. ed. CRC Press, 1994.

Tammemagi, H. *Waste Crisis: Landfills, Incinerators, and the Search for a Sustainable Future*. Oxford University Press, 1999.

Tchobanoglous, G. *Handbook of Solid Waste Management*. McGraw-Hill, 2002.

Endnotes

1. I.M. Konner. *The Tangled Wing* (Holt, Rinehart and Winston, 1982): p. 406.

2. General Accounting Office, "Toxic Substances: EPA's Chemical Testing Programs Has Not Resolved Safety Concerns" (GAO/RCED-91-136, June 1991).

3. General Accounting Office, "Lawn Care Pesticides: EPA Needs to Assess State Notification Programs" (GAO/RCED-91-208, September 1991).

4. A. McCampbell, Multiple Chemical Sensitivities Task Force Report: "Multiple Chemical Sensitivities Under Siege," 2001: www.mindfully.org/Health/MCS-Under-Siege or Townsend [News] letter for Doctors and Patients, No. 210, January 2001: www.tldp.com.

5. S. Selke, *Packaging and the Environment: Alternative Trends and Solutions,* rev. ed. (CRC Press, 1994).

6. J. Lowy, "Plastic Left Holding the Bag as Environmental Plague" (Scripps Howard News Service, 2004).

7. W. McDonough and M. Braungart, *Cradle to Cradle: Remaking the Way We Make Things* (North Point Press, 2002).

8. Konner, M. *The Tangled Wing* (Holt, Rinehart and Winston, 1982): 406.

9. Hazeldon Foundation, *Touchstones* (Harper and Row, 1986).

10. G. Calbresi and P. Babbitt, *Tragic Choices* (W. W. Norton, 1978): p. 199.

11. National Science and Technology Council, *Bridge to a Sustainable Future* (Interagency Environmental Technologies, 1995).

12. See Note 7.

EARTH

Global Policies, Planning, and Management

Introduction

Earth itself is the seventh level and final selected component of the built environment. It is the region that contains all other regions. It is, of course, possible to take such an organizational series further—to the solar system, then the galaxy and the universe. Although societies are sending space probes to these distant environments (and leaving their waste), the Earth is still the measure of the present limits of human domain. To a degree, the Earth itself is an artifact, manipulated, however inadvertently, by human actions.

The earth viewed as artifact is a challenging concept. And it is not an artifact in the same sense as those discussed in previous sections: it was not created by human hands. But it is an artifact in the sense that so many of its complex systems are now impacted and altered by humans to the farthest reaches of the globe.

This condition is illustrated most vividly by the fact that no place on or above the Earth, even the most remote places of the atmosphere and oceans, remains untouched by the effluents of industrial civilization. The by-products of creating a built environment can now be found in Antarctic ice (and in the penguins there), in the jet stream sweeping down from the Arctic, in the vast reaches of the stratospheric ozone layer, and in sediments at the bottom of the deepest oceanic trench. Even the by-products of running cars, manufacturing materials, and heating/cooling buildings are affecting the temperature of the planet. The more immediate realm of life, the biosphere, has been dramatically impacted, irreversibly, on a global scale. Humans have saved themselves from lethal infectious diseases by eradicating the tiny bacterial sources. Similarly, though less deliberately, humans have placed the largest mammals of the ocean, the whales, and many large land creatures—polar bears, tigers, and elephants—near the brink of extinction.

Earth's finite resources, the materials and energies required to construct and manage the built environment, are being consumed at an alarming rate. A sustainable conservation ethic in design and planning (recycling products, using renewable resources, conserving energy, etc.) must continue to help change wasteful, foolish attitudes and consumptive ways.

In essence, the chapters in this section make the point that all individuals—laypeople, politicians, and designers/planners alike—must try to expand their consciousness, to share and collaborate and become more aware of the interconnections that tie everything and everyone to other organisms, to all systems around the world. The point is repeated that the boundaries humans draw around each discipline, each nation or region, are intended to help organize our world, not limit our view of it.

Having accepted the basic organizational structure of this book and its levels of integration, we know that one level of the built environment builds upon the next and then the next. Humans will continue to use natural resources to achieve individual and social goals and objectives. What they must continue to learn is how to use those resources in a renewable and sustainable way. Planning and design, because they are interdisciplinary and involve overarching contexts, can help meet these

goals and help transcend limited levels of interaction. Their potential is tremendous because they affect activities that impact human behavior, and it is human behavior that is the core of all human-environmental activities, including both successes and failures.

The definition of the Earth and its manipulation as a level of the built environment can be clarified by the following:

- The **Earth** contains all aspects of the built environment (products, interiors, structures, landscapes, cities, and regions) and is consequently, in part, humanly changed, arranged, or maintained;
- to mediate the overall environment (to manage resource production, to provide a coordinating subunit of the globe);
- to help achieve human purpose (needs, wants, and values);
- while affecting itself; the final context is the Earth.

The final content-component-context relationship is once again symbolized in the text logo:

Products—Interiors—Structures—Landscapes—
Cities—Regions—**Earth**

One final note: there is no assurance that humans will be able to avoid the types of problems discussed in these

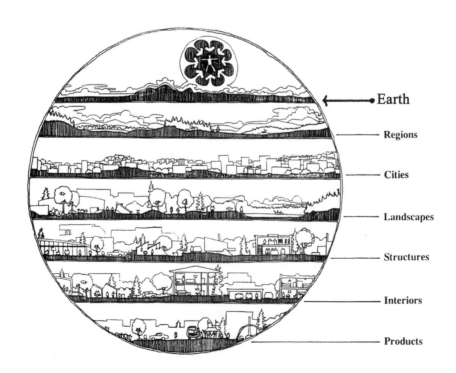

pages. Humans may not yet seem capable of planning or designing perfect systems. There is no certainty that problems will be averted. What emerges, however, from an increased sensitivity to the importance of connections in human-environment-technical relationships is a new paradigm for interactive, collaborative, interdisciplinary learning and behavior. It is a paradigm that does not seek to provide humans with prescriptions for change. Instead, it challenges humans to appreciate, understand, and attempt to make the positive contributions and avoid the negative impacts of their decisions across all seven levels.

Human-environmental problems exist because humans have not taken to heart a multilevel, holistic framework for learning and for living. To change, we must learn how to learn—and then put that knowledge into action. The following chapters in this section explore the various ways the Earth can be defined, how the Earth's many human/social, environmental, and technical factors can be more clearly understood, designed, planned, and managed.

Global Life-Support System and the Built Environment
by Eldon H. Franz

The global environment—including all life on the planet—constitutes a unique life-support system. The ecological stability and reliability of services provided to support human activities by this life-support system depend on all species and the natural environment. All human activities related to the built environment are continually involved in dynamically balancing interactions with the natural environment. These interactions are currently producing changes, including global warming, linked to land-use change, change in the composition of the atmosphere, and loss of biodiversity. Society and the built environment professionals now have a growing array of options for mitigating global change and creating a more sustainable world.

Taking Local-Global Action in the Built Environment
by Diane Armpriest

A consistent supply of information describes numerous human-caused environmental problems. The ramifications of these problems can be overwhelming, and it is essential to develop an attitude that allows us to maintain a sense of hope and to take positive, creative action. The purpose of this chapter is to provide a framework for taking action in response to global human-environmental concerns. The chapter begins with a brief introduction to critical environmental issues, followed by a summary of particular problems and examples of strategies for finding collaborative solutions. It concludes with ideas about how environmental designers and planners can take local action to improve both the built and natural environments.

References

Each chapter concludes with a list of relevant references.

Earth Charter: www.earthcharter.org
Ecological Footprint: www.myfootprint.org
Eco Trust–Conservation Economy (see the interactive pattern map): www.conservationeconomy.net
Environmental Protection Agency (EPA): www.epa.gov
Global Planning Education Association Network (GPEAN): www.gpean.org
Kyoto Protocol: en.wikipedia.org/wiki/Kyoto_Protocol
Living Planet Report: www.wwf.org.uk/filelibrary/pdf/living planet2002.pdf
Sierra Club: www.sierraclub.org
United Nations (UN): www.un.org
United Nations Division of Sustainable Development: www.un/esa/sustdev/
United Nations Millennium Development Goals: www.un/esa/millenniumgoals/
The World Conservation Union (IUCN): www.incn.org
The World Watch Institute: www.worldwatchinstitute.org

CHAPTER 28

Global Life-Support System and the Built Environment

Eldon H. Franz

The global environment, including all life on the planet, constitutes a unique life-support system. The ecological stability and reliability of services provided to support human activities by this life-support system depend on all species and the natural environment. All human activities related to the built environment are continually involved in dynamically balancing interactions with the natural environment. These interactions are currently producing changes, including global warming, linked to land-use change, change in the composition of the atmosphere, and loss of biodiversity. Society and the built environment professionals now have a growing array of options for mitigating global change and creating a more sustainable world.

In the early years of the twenty-first century, we are more mindful than ever that the global environment, the Earth as a whole, is the ultimate context for all of our personal and professional activities. As the implications of this fact for our lives, for our children's lives, and for those of future generations become more familiar to us, the nations of the world are increasingly turning to international and global regimes to ensure our common future.

The maxim "think globally, act locally" has served us well as both a necessary and, throughout most of human history, a sufficient guide to action. Credit for the phrase is attributed to both David Brower, founder of "Friends of the Earth," and Rene Dubos, advisor to the UN conference on the Human Environment. Local action will always be a necessary complement to global thinking, and for many reasons will always have primacy among our responsibilities. It is now becoming clear, however, that local actions can no longer stand alone because they no longer provide a sufficient basis for action to ensure our future and the future of the planet. Local action alone cannot address the global challenges that lie ahead.

Think globally, act globally is now also informing human actions in a world community. The twin maxims reflect the need to take action directly at both the local and global levels for the sake of our future and the future of the Earth as a whole. The need to understand the social, environmental, and economic dimensions of global changes—such as warming climate and loss of biodiversity—and the need for international cooperation in designing global environmental regimes to implement solutions to the challenges of global environmental change—have never in history been more apparent than now.

Global thinking motivates us to learn as much as we can about the world and to access and use the knowledge that science and technology provide about the way the global ecological systems of the Earth work in order to make the world a better place. As always, this knowledge enables us to take action locally with awareness of the presence and significance of global impacts.

Figure 28-1 The Earth as viewed from space reminds us of the need to think globally.

Now, however, the aggregate and cumulative effects of local activities can be detected at the scale of the globe as a whole. Changes in the dynamics of the global environment involving patterns of land use, the distribution of water and wetlands, the composition of the atmosphere, and the complex patterns of biodiversity and climate all have significant implications for all human activities. Many of these dynamic Earth system processes directly influence the workings of society and the environmental design/planning and management professionals everywhere.

This chapter examines the nature of the Earth as the context for the work of all designers and planners of the built environment of the Earth. Connections are explored between global processes and the themes that have been presented throughout this book. The professional decisions that will determine the structural and functional attributes of the built environment from this point on are connected to the future of the global environment.

The Life-Support System

Knowledge of environmental conditions on the surface of the moon, Mars, Venus, and other planets in the solar system, vastly augmented by the space explorations of the last half-century, confirms the uniqueness of the Earth. The Earth is a living system. So far, it is the only one that humans know.

That there is only one Earth seems trite to say, but it takes on added significance when we realize that anything humans do to induce global change represents a global experiment without any possible control. It also leads naturally to the question of how the unique conditions for life on the Earth are maintained.

In some measure, the total amount of life must hold the key to Earth's uniqueness and the stability of conditions for supporting life. One measure of the total amount of life is the number of species. Recent estimates suggest that the total number of species is between 10 and 100 million. Of that number, only 1.5 million species or so have been identified by science and have been given scientific names. *Homo sapiens* is one of the named species, an increasingly dominant one among the 10 to 100 million others.

We now know that favorable physical and biological conditions for life on Earth are maintained by a system of feedbacks. The natural environment of the Earth is organized to provide a life-support system that operates at the scale of the Earth as a whole. The reliability of the life-support system is entirely due to other species. For the vast majority of the Earth's 4.6 billion years, in fact, the global impact of *Homo sapiens* as a single species has been small. Before there was a built environment there was a natural environment. The built environment was virtually nonexistent and of little consequence until very recently.

How recently these changes have occurred can be illustrated by scaling the last 2 million years of human history to a lifetime of 70 years. On that time scale, it was not until eight months after their 69th birthday that humans began to settle into villages.[1] It was not until then that the built environment as we now define it really began to grow. And only since the last half of the day before their 70th birthday have the global impacts of the built environment been widely and routinely recognized and reported in the daily news.

The long-term memory and experience of the human species thus constitute a very brief experiment for a planet where the natural environment has dominated the built environment and maintained conditions capable of supporting people and their machines, a **life-support system** primarily mediated and maintained by other species. Now we are challenged to imagine a future very different from that of the past. Now the dynamic balance continually being set by interactions between the built and natural environments is dominated by human activity. The balance between the life-supporting processes maintained by other species and the impacts of the built environment on those processes is rapidly changing.

Biodiversity, the Carbon Cycle, and Global Change

To appreciate the nature of global change, it is necessary to understand how the life-support system works. The total amount of life, now generally called **biodiversity**, is its most remarkable emergent property.

> Biologists are inclined to agree that it is, in one sense, everything. Biodiversity is defined as all hereditarily based variation at all levels of organization, from genes within a single local population or species, to the species composing all or part of a local community, and finally to the communities themselves that compose the living parts of the multifarious ecosystems of the world.[2]

In one sense, biodiversity is everything and is certainly a subject for global thinking. Although scientific knowledge of biodiversity is still growing rapidly, perhaps the most significant insight into how this "everything" works was published by Jean-Baptiste Dumas in 1844. Dumas wrote that plants and animals were nothing but condensed air. According to his understanding at the time, what plants absorb from the air, animals release back to it. The primary material basis of life is thus based on elements that cycle in and out of the atmosphere.

Organisms are approximately 50% water. Water, of course, is continuously cycled through the atmosphere, condensing in clouds and falling back to Earth. Most of the remaining half consists of approximately equal amounts of carbon, present in the atmosphere as carbon dioxide (CO_2), and oxygen, present in the atmosphere as molecular oxygen. The rest is made up of much smaller amounts of nitrogen, sulfur, phosphorus, calcium, potassium, iron, and so on, totaling altogether less than 5% or 6% of the atmosphere.

Carbon is the basic building block of life. The dry weight of organisms, what is left after water is removed, is nearly 50% carbon and consists mostly of other elements attached to a string of carbon atoms. As such, carbon, and the biogeochemistry of carbon, are fundamental to the structure and function of everything that lives. At one level of integration, then, biodiversity and the carbon cycle are functionally the same.

Dumas' profound insight is the essence of global thinking. The life-support system works through a series of transfers from the atmosphere to plants to animals and back to the atmosphere through the force of solar energy and cycles of chemical transfers. It should be noted, of course, that this is only the barest basis and not the whole explanation. For this process to work, optimal amounts of the other essential elements, protection from toxic elements, and a host of other suitable ecological conditions are required.

The insight of Dumas further suggests a profound separation of Earth's biodiversity into two primary functional groups, autotrophs (plants) and heterotrophs (animals). Dumas links them to the two primary biochemical processes that make up the **carbon cycle**: **photosynthesis** and **respiration**.

If you think about these two processes in terms of millions of species, each making its various withdrawals and deposits of carbon dioxide and oxygen out of and into the atmosphere, the dynamic balance of all outputs and inputs will always be revealed by the total amount of those gases that are being stored in the atmosphere at any time. If you think about this in terms of the idea of dynamic balance, a time plot of the atmospheric concentration of a gas would never change if the outputs exactly equal or compensate for the inputs.

Such time plots of the carbon dioxide concentration have been compiled on a monthly basis since 1958 at the Mauna Loa Observatory in Hawaii (Fig. 28-3). More recent data are shown in Figure 28-4. The pattern has been and continues to remain consistent. What the graphs show is not the expected constant CO_2 concentration that would result from a balanced compensation of

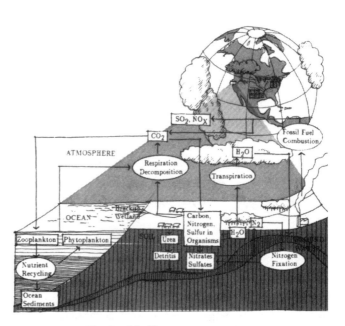

Figure 28-2 The Earth's life-support systems.

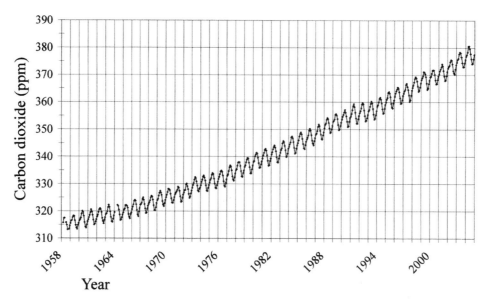

Figure 28-3 Increase in CO_2: monthly/yearly average concentrations in the atmosphere (parts per million), Mauna Loa, Hawaii, 1958–1993 (Keeling, 2005).

inputs and outputs. Instead, the graphs vividly illustrate that the concentration has been increasing over time and that it fluctuates on a fairly regular intra-annual basis.

The first value for every year is the concentration estimated for the 15th of January and so on for every month. Counting the months ahead from there each year verifies that the maximum is reached in April or May every year and the minimum four or five months later, in September of each year. There are fewer months on the downside than the upside, so the pattern does not correspond exactly to half a year up and half a year down.

Since it is the balance of inputs and outputs of carbon dioxide that is being recorded here, any fluctuation must be the result of an imbalance between photosynthesis and respiration that shifts once each year. The key to this

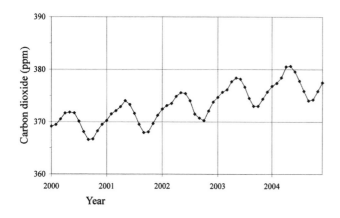

Figure 28-4 Cycle of CO_2: monthly/yearly average concentrations in the atmosphere (parts per million), Mauna Loa, Hawaii, 1997–2005 (Keeling, 2005).

shift is easy to recognize when the months involved are considered. From September to April or May, the concentration is increasing. That means that the inputs of carbon dioxide to the atmosphere are greater during that time period than the outputs. Thus, respiration of the Earth's systems must be greater than photosynthesis. During the period from April or May to September, the reverse is true: photosynthesis must be greater than respiration.

What is clear from these yearly cycles recorded at Mauna Loa is influenced by the seasons in the Northern Hemisphere. The processes of photosynthesis and respiration are arrayed across the globe, but most of the photosynthetic activity is confined to the spring and summer months, when the active green plants absorb CO_2 and in the process release oxygen. While people may think in the abstract of the four seasons as being of equal duration, in global ecological terms they are not. In the Northern Hemisphere, the **green wave** of spring passes from south to north over a period of months, and the summer in the far north is only a few weeks' duration. Photosynthesis, when globally averaged in this way, exceeds respiration for only four or five months a year. As summer ends, the **brown wave** of autumn passes from north to south, and by September, much of the photosynthetic capacity of the Northern Hemisphere is shutting down for the winter. The intra-annual fluctuation of the carbon dioxide concentration of the atmosphere at Mauna Loa, then, results from the dynamic relationship between inputs and outputs mediated by the changing balance of photosynthesis and respiration in the Northern Hemisphere.

From one cycle to the next, the concentration is gradually increasing. Each summer sees a higher minimum and each winter a higher maximum. Longer records indicate that the carbon dioxide concentration was about 270 ppmv just before the beginning of the Industrial Revolution. In the past three years, the concentration has passed 370 parts per 5 million (ppmv), a dramatic increase of 100 parts per 5 million (ppmv), or 27%.

The rise is due principally to the combustion of fossil fuels, but a portion of it is also due to deforestation, drainage of wetlands, and loss of carbon stored in the soil, all related to human activity. While the intra-annual fluctuation is most directly linked to the nature of the Earth's biodiversity and natural environment, the recent increase is attributable to activities of the built environment. Human activities are beginning to dominate the activities of other species and are altering the dynamic system balancing the global carbon cycle.

The Greenhouse Effect and Global Warming

Human domination of the carbon cycle has implications for global temperature and climate because of the effects of carbon dioxide on the radiation balance of the Earth. Carbon dioxide, water, and certain other gases in the atmosphere that absorb long-wave, infrared radiation are known as "greenhouse gases." Their effect on the global radiation balance, global temperature, and climate is known as the "greenhouse effect."

Global temperature has always been sensitive to changes in the concentration of carbon dioxide. As the concentration of carbon dioxide in the atmosphere increases, the extra absorption of long-wave radiation increases the global temperature and global warming. Concentrations of other greenhouse gases are now also increasing. Some of these, such as ozone, methane, and nitrous oxide, have sources in the natural environment but, like carbon dioxide, are increasing because of human activities in constructing and maintaining the global built environment. Some, like ozone and nitrous oxide, are linked to the combustion of fossil fuels. Others, such as the chlorofluoromethanes, industrial compounds used as refrigerants, solvents, and propellants for aerosol cans, have no known natural sources and are entirely products of the built environment. The current level of global warming resulting from these increases is approximately half due to carbon dioxide and half to the other greenhouse gases. At projected rates of increase of

the concentrations of greenhouse gases in the atmosphere, a warming of several degrees is expected by the middle of this century.

Human Appropriation of Net Primary Production

It is clear from the global carbon cycle and the greenhouse effect that human activities are producing global change. Just how great an impact these activities now have, and how it might change in the near future, can be estimated also from our relationship to the **net primary production** (NPP) of the globe. NPP is the total amount of food available to all organisms that do not produce their own food by means of photosynthesis. That includes humans and essentially all other species except green plants and a few microorganisms; it includes all animals and fungi and the vast majority of microorganisms.

Human appropriation of net primary production (HANPP) includes direct consumption of NPP for food, as well as the effects of all human activities on NPP. When the global population stood at 5 billion in 1986, HANPP was estimated to be 40%. At current rates of population increase and constant fertility, world population is expected to exceed 10 billion by 2040 according to the most recent United Nations estimates.[3] That represents a doubling in 54 years, or an average annual rate of exponential growth of 1.3% per year. Such an increase in the size of the human population will result in a rebalancing of the relationship between global NPP and HANPP.

Increasing the human share of global NPP is certain to cut the amount available to support other species and accelerate the rate of extinction. The capacity of the natural environment and other species to support human population, machines, and the built environment has been a condition we have taken for granted in the past, but it is, at best, uncertain for the future.

People are now significant agents of global change and the most dominant species on the planet. The impacts of the built environment have global effects. For much of human history, adaptation to the environment involved primarily local choices with local effects. Management of local ecosystems sometimes degraded local ecosystems, leading even to extinction of species, but there were few, if any, truly global effects. As the scale, magnitude, and duration, as well as the kinds of human impacts on the environment, have changed, so too has the potential for global effects. The future course of human interactions with environments will be defined and limited not only in relation to local processes, but also by global change.

Global Change and the Built Environment

Global changes in the carbon cycle, the greenhouse effect, HANPP, and the threat to biodiversity all contribute to a growing recognition of the need for creative solutions to mitigate global environmental problems through interdisciplinary collaboration, especially among scientists and design/planning professionals.

Global change involves a complex set of ever-present interactions between the natural environment and the built environment (diagrammed in Fig. 28-5). A change in any single factor triggers feedback responses in other factors, and the dynamic balance of the entire system changes. Because of the large expenditure of energy and materials involved, these interactions are also tightly linked to travel decisions. Land use and transportation planning are central to the mitigation of global change processes.

The Importance of Transportation

The transportation sector of the U.S. economy accounts for approximately one-third of all CO_2 emissions and is the most rapidly growing source. Fuel use for transportation accounts for seven of every ten barrels of oil consumed. This increasing level of consumption is caused by auto-oriented lifestyles, sprawling settlement patterns, and large, inefficient vehicles. The U.S. transportation system alone emits more CO_2 than the entire economies of every other country except China. Public roads and roadsides occupy about 1% of the land area of the United States, covering a total area about the size of the State of Indiana. Auto-oriented services, roads, and parking consume one-third of suburban land and two-thirds of urban land. The ecological effects of roads, including impacts on biodiversity, soil, and water quality, extend well beyond roads, however, to a zone comprising 20% of the total land area.[4] Each person in the United States makes the equivalent of one trip around the world in personal vehicles, totaling 4.8 trillion miles for all vehicle miles traveled.

Protecting Environmentally Sensitive Areas

State and local governments have designated and mapped many different types of habitats and resource lands for special treatment in land-use planning. Sensitive area protection is extended to vital components reflecting values that communities wish to protect. The most commonly used techniques of sensitive area protection involve wetlands, riparian zones, and greenbelts.

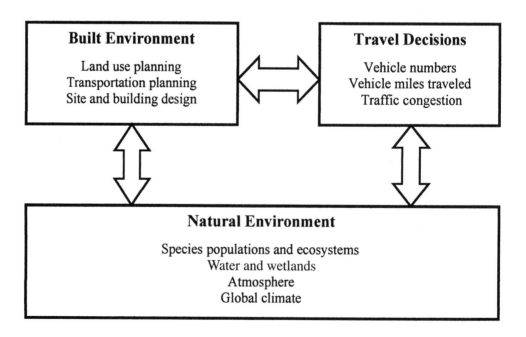

Figure 28-5 Interactions within the built and natural environments.

Figure 28-6 Auto-driven sprawl. Although the sign says "one way," it is not the only way or the best way to plan our communities (P. Overholtzer).

Wetlands are of particular concern because of their relationship to water quality: pollutant loads in streams increase as the proportion of wetlands in a watershed decreases.

Despite current understanding of the ecological values and benefits of wetlands, wetland loss is a worldwide problem. The extent of this problem is well illustrated by data from the United States. Recent estimates suggest that wetlands accounted for a total of about 105.5 million acres in 1997, or 5.6% of the land area of the contiguous United States, an area approximately the combined size of Kentucky, Illinois, Indiana, and Ohio. This 1997 acreage represents a loss of 53% of the 221 million wetland acres that existed in the early 1600s. Six states have lost over 85% of their wetlands and 22 others over 50%. On the high end of the scale, California has lost 91% and Ohio, 90%. On the low end, Alaska has lost only 1%, New Hampshire, 9%, and Hawaii, 12%.

Recognizing the tremendous ecological and economic costs of such losses, the Emergency Wetlands Resources Act sets a goal of "No Net Loss." To monitor progress toward that goal, the U.S. Fish and Wildlife Service conducts status and trend studies of the nation's wetlands and periodically reports the results to Congress. In the latest report, the agency estimates that annual wetland losses have been reduced from 290,000 acres per year in the 1970s and early 1980s to approximately 58,000 acres per year in 1997. From 1986 to 1997, a total of 664,000 acres were lost, 51% from expansion of the built environment (30% from urban development and 21% from rural development). Wetland drainage for agriculture (26%) and forestry (23%) accounted for the rest.

The patterns of wetland losses worldwide are consistent with the range of variation in wetland losses from state to state in the United States. Such variation is to be expected because the extent of wetland loss is a product of several factors that weigh in to different degrees at different locations around the globe. Those most directly linked to the built environment include:

- Pressures for modifying wetlands for urban and rural development, agriculture, or forestry
- Changes in hydrological systems due to construction of dams or diversions, and increases in runoff from impermeable surfaces and other changes in land cover such as the clearing of forests
- Changes in water quality caused by increasing pollutant loads

It is clear from this list of factors that a range of wetland losses—from nearly zero in some areas (e.g., remote mountainous regions) to nearly 100% in others (densely populated urban, suburban, and agricultural regions)—would be expected. It is also clear from the nature of these causes that local action is insufficient to deal with the problem of wetland loss. All of these factors are also strongly linked to land use and market pressures generated at regional and global scales.

Since wetlands drained and converted to other uses generally promise higher market returns, wetland losses can always be justified on economic grounds unless nonmarket ecological values are somehow factored in. Since ecological values have not been well represented historically, it is not surprising that wetland elimination has been popular and that the rate of wetland loss has been so high, especially in more populated regions.

Now that the essential ecological values of wetlands are more widely understood and recognized, attitudes about wetland loss and their value have started to change. Interdisciplinary collaboration on the management of runoff and pollution problems associated with development of the built environment has led to ecological and engineering criteria for integrating wetlands and wetland functions into designs across all levels of the built environment. This area of science and technology is only a few decades old, but progress has been rapid. One of the most significant advances has been the development of design criteria to account for the important functions provided by wetlands. This need to focus on function has become especially clear since studies of constructed wetlands have repeatedly indicated that the establishment of wetland plants does not necessarily indicate that an area is providing the same level of services that natural wetlands do. The take-home lesson is that existing natural wetlands and watersheds need to be integrated into the landscape mosaics of the built envi-

Figures 28-7 and 28-8   A city designed with networks of wetlands and water systems. Woodlands, Texas, by Ian McHarg et al. (T. Bartuska).

ronment to preserve their supportive services before they are lost.

Sustainable Development of the Built Environment

The way people view their place on Earth has been changed forever by recognition of the fact that the globe functions as an ecological whole. Virtually every aspect of human activities in the built environment is linked in some way to the globe as a whole. Trace the linkages of any artifacts of the built environment; can any be identified that are not? For that reason, the global context has become basic to any understanding of the built environment. The built environment at any level can be sustained only if the integrity of the Earth's living system is maintained.

Humanity is now beginning to recognize the significance of designing with nature. Indeed, if sustainable

development had been achieved by any civilization in the past, history would have been drastically rewritten. Historians have repeatedly observed that rapid environmental degradation has been a significant factor in the decline of civilizations.

How did civilized [societies] despoil this favorable environment? [They] did it mainly by depleting or destroying the natural resources. [They] cut down or burned most of the usable timber from forested hillsides and valleys . . . overgrazed and denuded the grasslands that feed [their] livestock . . . killed most of the wildlife and much of the fish and other water life . . . permitted erosion to rob farmland of its productive topsoil and clog the streams and fill reservoirs, irrigation canals, and harbors with silt. In many cases, [they] used and wasted most of the easily mined metals or other needed minerals. Then [their] civilization declined amidst the despoliation of [their] own creation. From ten to thirty different civilizations have followed this road to ruin (the number depending on who classifies the civilizations).[5]

The goal of sustainable development is "a development strategy that manages all assets, natural and human resources, as well as financial and physical assets for increasing long-term health and well-being. Sustainable development, as a goal, rejects policies and practices that support current living standards by depleting the productive base, including natural resources, and that leave future generations with poorer prospects and greater risks than our own."[6]

The **World Conservation Strategy**[7] is a blueprint for sustainable development through the conservation of living systems. Three requirements are presented as necessary for achieving the conservation of living systems. The last two require achievement of the first.

- The maintenance of essential ecological processes and life-support systems primarily requires careful planning and allocation of uses and high-quality management of those uses.
- The preservation of genetic diversity primarily requires the timely collection of genetic material and its protection in banks, plantations, and so on in the case of on-site preservation.
- The sustainable utilization of ecosystems and species requires knowledge of the productive capacities of those resources and measures to ensure that utilization does not exceed those capacities.

For effective implementation of sustainable development, individuals and societies must be able to link their understanding of the global system to built environment activities. That means they must be able to qualify and characterize their ability to inhibit or promote local and regional development in relation to elements of global environmental change. Implementation must also include institutional and organizational changes toward more effective local, national, and international (i.e., global) research, policymaking, and management.[8]

One of the main obstacles to implementation is a "lack of environmental planning and of rationale use allocation."[9] Since rational planning is the first requirement for achieving the objectives of living systems conservation, this obstacle must be overcome. The World Conservation Strategy identifies ecosystem evaluation and environmental assessment as the best means of implementing environmental planning.

Policies for Environmental Assessment

In the United States, a number of steps toward rational environmental planning have been taken as (several were noted by other authors in this book). Perhaps the most profound of these was the passage of the **National Environmental Policy Act** (NEPA).[10] NEPA expresses an appreciation for the Earth's life-sustaining systems, which goes beyond strictly linear thinking:

> The U.S. Congress, recognizing the profound impact of [human] activity on the interrelations of all components of the natural environment, particularly the profound influences of population growth, high density urbanization, industrial expansion, resource exploitation and new and expanding technological advances and recognizing further the critical importance of restoring and maintaining environmental quality to overall [human] welfare and development . . . declares that it is the continuing policy of the Federal Government, in cooperation with state and local governments and other concerned public and private organizations, to use all practicable means and measure, including financial and technical assistance, in a manner calculated to foster and promote the general welfare, to create and maintain conditions under which [humans] and nature can exist in productive harmony, and fulfill the social, economic and other requirements of present and future generations.[11]

NEPA also requires that an environmental impact statement be written to "accompany every recommenda-

tion or report on proposals for legislation and other major Federal actions significantly affecting the quality of the human environment." In the United States, most states also adopt State Environmental Policy Acts (SEPAs) and require environmental assessment of major local and regional projects through an environmental impact statement process.

Environmental assessment has been a consistent theme throughout this book. Consistent application of a holistic "fitness test," examined across the entire range of scales—from creating the smallest product to comprehension of processes at a whole-Earth level—is necessary if humans are to live in quality built environments. That grasp of connections, from pencil to planet, will go a long way toward achieving the goal of sustainable development.

The Kyoto Protocol

Global action to control the emissions of greenhouse gases is linked to an international agreement known as the Kyoto Protocol, which went into effect on February 16, 2005. By that time it had been ratified by 141 nations, but not the United States. Recognizing the importance of U.S. action on climate change, Seattle Mayor Greg Nickels announced his intention on that day to meet or beat the Protocol's targets and challenged other mayors to do

Figure 28-9 Mayor Greg Nickels, celebrating the public release of Seattle's Green Ribbon Commission Report to an enthusiastic standing-room-only audience. The delegates on the left side of the podium were local, state, and national political leaders including former Vice President Al Gore (a global leader on global warming). On the right side of the podium are Green Ribbon Commission members including Dennis Hayes (creator of the first Earth Day and Director of the Bullit Foundation of Seattle) (T. Bartuska).

the same. On June 13, 2005, the U.S. Conference of Mayors unanimously adopted the Mayor's Climate Protection Agreement (2006). As of January 10, 2007, the mayors of 358 cities representing a combined U.S. population of 55 million had accepted his challenge.[12]

Seattle's Green Ribbon Commission on Climate Protection presented their recommendations for action on March 24, 2006. The Kyoto target seeks to reduce greenhouse gas emissions by 7% from the 1990 levels by 2012. For the City of Seattle, that means a reduction of 680,000 tons per year. Seattle's plan would exceed those levels if fully implemented. Since transportation—cars, trucks, buses, planes, trains, and ships—represents the single largest source of greenhouse gas emissions in the region,

the action plan calls for significant changes in transportation as well as energy efficiency improvements in all areas of the built environment. In general, the Green Ribbon strategies include:

- Reduce dependence on cars and cut greenhouse gas emissions by 170,000 tons. Actions to achieve this goal include increasing public transportation, expanding the bicycling and pedestrian infrastructure, and planning to create green urban neighborhoods.
- Increase fuel efficiency and use of biofuels and cut greenhouse gas emissions by 200,000 tons. Actions to achieve this goal include significantly reducing emissions from diesel trucks, trains, and ships.

Table 28-1 Mitigation Strategies for the Built Environment

VARIABLES	THE NATURAL ENVIRONMENT	PLANNING GUIDELINES FOR REBALANCING THE NATURAL AND BUILT ENVIRONMENTS	THE BUILT ENVIRONMENT
1. Energy Source	Powered by the sun and photosynthesis	Expand the use of renewable energy	Powered by fossil fuel
2. Power Requirements	Low	Adhere to green building standards and specify the most efficient available technologies for HVAC, lighting, and appliances	High
3. Land Use	Desert/grassland/savannah/forest complex	Use available urban infill and redevelopment sites such as brownfields, and increase the quantity and quality of open space overall	Urban/industrial complex
4. Cost of Maintenance per Unit Area	Free	Replace high-maintenance water, nutrient, and pesticide-demanding turf with natural vegetation	High
5. Bioregenerative Capacity	High	Use living machines and other constructed wastewater systems. Also, an additional benefit of guidelines for variables 3 and 4	Low
6. Global Share of Biodiversity	High	Increase with guidelines for variables 3, 4, 5, 8	Low
7. Effect on Carbon Dioxide and Other GHG Emissions	Sink	Emphasize mass transit, walking, and biking	Source
8. Effect on Pollutants of Air and Water	Sink	Increase capacity with restored wetlands and native vegetation	Source

- Achieve more efficient and cleaner energy for homes and businesses and cut greenhouse gas emissions by 316,000 tons. Actions to achieve this goal include increasing urban density and ensuring that all new construction is energy efficient.[13]

Combined with the efforts of other cities nationwide, these actions will not only meet the Kyoto targets, but also promise to improve human and ecosystem health. The connection to human health is especially significant because the combustion of fossil fuels that produces greenhouse gases also produces harmful air pollutants. Research shows that when these harmful pollutants decline, a city benefits, with a directly proportional drop in death rates from pollution-caused illness. Actions taken to meet the targets set by the Kyoto Protocol thus have multiple benefits. Such actions provide the means to rebalance the effects of the built environment with the natural environment in mitigating the negative effects of global change.

Rebalancing and Mitigation Strategies

Guidelines for achieving the goals of mitigating the effects of the built environment on global environmental change and rebalancing with the natural environment are summarized in Table 28-1. Additional local-global action strategies for all seven selected components of the built environment will be explored in the next chapter. Since these guidelines are now widely represented among the goals established for planners—from local community to regional to global scales—the effects of global thinking are having a major influence on local to global action.

Recent analysis indicates that designs based on the best available science and technologies, such as those listed in Table 28-1 and discussed in Chapter 29 can increase the energy and material productivity for housing and ground transportation by a factor of four. Effective use strategies based on conservation and use of renewable rather than nonrenewable resources can quadruple the efficiency per unit of resources. These results could reduce global consumption by 50%. The net economic gain of the efficiency would be significant, doubling the value of each resource unit extracted. Such gains in productivity are also consistent with the goal of stabilizing the dynamic balance of the life-sustaining systems of the natural environment.

The benefits of global thinking include tangible bene-

fits for the sustainability of local to global environments, both natural and built.

References

Carter, V. G., and T. Dale. *Topsoil and Civilization.* University of Oklahoma Press, 1955.

Clark, W. C., and R. E. Munn (eds.). *Sustainable Development of the Biosphere.* Cambridge University Press, 1986.

Foreman, R. "Estimate of the Area Affected Ecologically by the Road System in the United States." *Conservation Biology,* January 2000.

Frumkin, H. "Beyond Toxicity: Human Health and the Natural Environment." *American Journal of Preventive Medicine,* April 2001.

IUCN. The World Conservation Union. 2006: www.iucn.org.

Keeling, C., and T. Whorf. "Atmospheric CO_2 Records from Sites in the SIO Air Sampling Network." *Trends: A Compendium of Data on Global Change.* Carbon Dioxide Information Analysis Center, Oak Ridge National Laboratory, U.S. Department of Energy, 2005.

LEED. Leadership in Energy and Environmental Design. 2002: www.usgbc.gov.

Mayor's Climate Protection Agreement. 2006: www.seattle.gov/mayor/climate.

Reaka-Kudla, M., D. Wilson, and E. Wilson. *Biodiversity II: Understanding and Protecting Our Biological Resources.* Joseph Henry Press, 1997.

Repetto, R. C. *World Enough and Time: Successful Strategies for Resource Management.* World Resources Institute Book, Yale University Press, 1986.

U.S. Congress. The National Environmental Policy Act of 1969 (Public Law 91-190), 1969.

U.S. Environmental Protection Agency. *Our Built and Natural Environments: A Technical Review of the Interactions between Land Use, Transportation, and Environmental Quality.* USEPA #231-R-01-002, 2001: www.smartgrowth.org/ library/built.

U.S. Environmental Protection Agency. *Inventory of U.S. Greenhouse Gas Emissions and Sinks 1990-2000.* USEPA #236-R-02-003, 2002: www.epa.gov/climatechange/emissions/usinventoryreport.

von Weizsacker, E., and A. Lovins. *Factor Four: Doubling Wealth: Halving Resource Use.* Earthscan Publications, 1997.

Endnotes

1. H. Frumkin, "Beyond Toxicity: Human Health and the Natural Environment," *American Journal of Preventive Medicine,* April 2001.
2. M. Reaka-Kudla, D. Wilson, and E. Wilson. *Biodiversity II: Understanding and Protecting Our Biological Resources* (Joseph Henry Press, 1997): 1.
3. United Nations Web site: http://esa. un.org/unpp.

4. R. Foreman, "Estimate of the Area Affected Ecologically by the Road System in the United States," *Conservation Biology* (January 2000): 31–35.

5. V. G. Carter and T. Dale, *Topsoil and Civilization* (University of Oklahoma Press, 1955): 8.

6. R. C. Repetto, *World Enough and Time: Successful Strategies for Resource Management*, World Resources Institute Book (Yale University Press, 1986): 15.

7. IUCN (The World Conservation Union), 2006: www.iucn.org.

8. W. C. Clark and R. E. Munn (eds.), *Sustainable Development of the Biosphere* (Cambridge University Press, 1986).

9. See Note 7.

10. U.S. Congress, *The National Environmental Policy Act of 1969* (Public Law 91-190, 1969).

11. See Note 10.

12. U.S. Mayors Climate Protection Agreement: www.seattle.gov/mayor/climate.

13. Seattle Climate Action Plan, Green Ribbon Commission: www.seattle.gov/mayor/report.

CHAPTER 29

Taking Local-Global Action in the Built Environment

Diane Armpriest

A consistent supply of information is available describing global human-environmental problems. The ramifications of these problems can be overwhelming, so it is essential to develop an attitude that allows people to maintain a sense of hope and enables positive action. For a creative person, problems can be considered opportunities. This chapter provides a holistic framework for taking action in response to global human-environmental concerns. The chapter begins with a brief introduction to critical environmental issues, followed by a summary of particular problems and examples of strategies for finding creative solutions. It concludes with ideas about how everyone, including ordinary citizens, civic leaders, business owners, design and planning professionals, and others can take action to improve local and global sustainability and the built environment.

The first step in this process is to realize that while one individual will probably be unable to change things at a global scale, it is quite likely that the same person can work at the local scale to develop effective strategies and political solutions that create significant change. These changes, when made by many, can improve conditions at a global level. In 1972 Rene Dubos, advisor to the UN Conference on The Human Environment, put this simply and elegantly when he stated, "think globally, act locally." In this process, it also becomes obvious that all of these issues are intricately interwoven and that action is required at all scales, and by individuals, business, and government, as well as by design professionals. As described by Eldon Franz in the previous chapter, the need to **think globally and act globally** is now also informing human actions in the world community.

Understanding Human-Environmental Issues

Industrial societies have created new processes and products that have substantially improved material standards of living worldwide. These developments were made possible by the intensive and extensive consumption of both renewable and finite, nonrenewable natural resources. Improvements in the name of progress have incurred environmental costs. Unfortunately, the ways of thinking that led to improved standards of living have not given equal consideration to mitigating the resulting environmental degradation. The U.S. Council on Environmental Quality and Department of State reported in the *Global 2000 Report to the President of the United States* (1980) that every aspect of the Earth's ecosystems and resource base is affected by the worldwide growth in population, redistribution of income, and depletion or degradation of resources. Many other global human-environmental studies have presented similar findings about the pervasive global impacts of human activities. Awareness of these problems has been raised by disasters such as the catastrophic accidents at the Chernobyl nuclear plant in the Soviet Union, the spill caused by the wreck of the *Exxon Valdez* oil tanker in the Gulf of Alaska, the ongoing conflicts in the Persian Gulf, and dramatic changes in weather patterns that are causing the polar ice cap to melt and producing more intense hurricane seasons.

As a result of the transformation from an industrial economy to a global information-based economy, a vast amount of high-quality research is now readily available. Organizations such as Worldwatch Institute[1] and the United Nations Division on Sustainable Development[2] have done an excellent job of studying and publicizing these issues. Dissemination has been greatly improved through the World Wide Web.

The first Earth Summit was held in Rio de Janiero, Brazil, in 1992. At this meeting, a global agenda was outlined and supported by over 100 nations. At the 2002 Earth Summit in Johannesburg, South Africa, it was clear that not all nations (including the United States) were committed to implementing the global agenda and that many of the problems would continue to grow worse. At the same time, there is a heightened global awareness about the root causes of the problems and a growing commitment to sustainable development.[3] Although the U.S. government failed to embrace the challenges established by the worldwide summit and to sign the Kyoto Protocol, an international treaty concerning the prevention of climate change, local governments are accepting responsibility. As discussed in Chapter 28, mayors of U.S. cities led by Seattle Mayor Greg Nickels have signed a formal agreement to help mitigate global climate change by agreeing to reduce greenhouse gas emissions. Their actions demonstrate that "local communities even more than nations can be pioneers of environmental reform."[4]

Experts agree a number of interrelated challenges are among the most important to address. They are listed relative to their critical importance to human survival—people can live for only 2–3 minutes without air, 2–3 days without water, and 2–3 weeks without food.

- **Air**: The emerging environmental stresses that affect the chemical and physical nature of the atmosphere and global warming
- **Water**: The decline in quality of the Earth's ocean and freshwater resources

Figure 29-1 Children and families enjoying their allotment gardens and community market on the historic Koppel Farm, Pullman, Washington (T. Bartuska).

- **Land, Food, and Fiber**: The permanent loss or degradation of land, agricultural, and forestry resources
- **Energy**: The impacts of nuclear energy and the loss of nonrenewable energy sources
- **Biodiversity**: The accelerating loss of plant and animal genetic resources

Finding Solutions

Environmental designers/planners are educated and trained to take on many of the challenges of a global agenda and are particularly well positioned to influence change at all levels. In this chapter, these human-environmental problems that result from current standard practices are outlined and examples of new ways to conceptualize the problems and develop solutions are presented.

Air Resources

A great deal of discussion has surrounded problems related to atmospheric pollution and degradation. A number of factors need to be considered. As discussed in Chapter 28, the greenhouse effect, which contributes to global warming, occurs because automobile and industrial gases (such as carbon dioxide, nitrous oxides, methane, and ozone) thicken the blanket of atmosphere surrounding the Earth, trapping heat and raising the average temperature of the Earth. The greenhouse effect is altering ecosystems, melting ice caps, and raising the level of the oceans. Atmospheric pollution, which renders air unsafe to breathe (for humans as well as other animals and plants), is caused by many of the same gases that produce the greenhouse effect. Atmospheric reactions with auto emissions create blankets of smog and cause major health problems for people and plants, eventually affecting health, crop yields, and fish populations.

Dependency on the automobile is perhaps the biggest contributor to these problems. Changing auto-oriented cultures and sprawling development patterns in industrialized nations, especially the United States, is required to solve them. This will entail not only a change in attitude about the car, but also the development of walkable/livable communities and accessible mass transit alternatives. In the meantime, a number of states are adopting emission control standards and testing procedures that are beginning to address some of the problems. It is also necessary to improve fuel efficiency and to explore alternative fuel sources, ideally derived from renewable resources. People experimenting with fossil fuel conservation in the United States have converted cars to run on used cooking oil, relying on fast food restaurants to supply this normally discarded resource (fuel). In recent years, hybrid gas-electric cars, that get two to three times more miles per gallon than standard vehicles, have been successfully brought to the mass market by Toyota and Honda. In addition, the technology required to develop hydrogen power from water is under development.

Design that is responsive to local climatic conditions minimizes heating and cooling loads and is another essential starting point. By improving the performance of buildings through energy-efficient siting, spatial organization, exterior enclosures, and lighting (for instance), energy requirements for building operation can be greatly reduced without compromising comfort.

Many materials used in products and building interiors are known to release toxic substances. Ongoing research is trying to determine the characteristics of these materials, and new, less hazardous materials are now becoming more available. It is the responsibility of the designer to be informed about these issues and to specify systems and products that require less energy to produce and do not contribute to indoor and atmospheric pollution. In addition, the development and utilization of solar, wind, and other renewable sources of energy must be a priority.

Increased use of plants in landscape and urban design, as well as engineering for highways and hillside stability, will increase opportunities for purification and reoxygenation of the atmosphere. Retaining wetlands and forests is critical to improving air and water quality and minimizing/reversing the greenhouse effect and global warming. Planners can work to develop local and regional zoning and building ordinances that encourage

Figure 29-2   Industrial relics provide the centerpiece for Gasworks Park, viewed from between mounds created from existing site debris (T. Bartuska).

energy conservation. They can also work to regulate the consumption and production of energy at larger scales.

Soils are also degraded as a result of both atmospheric pollution and the disposal of toxic substances on or below the surface of the Earth. Gasworks Park in Seattle, Washington (Fig. 29-2), was built on the site of an old gas plant where tons of toxic materials had leached into the soil. The site was sculpted with waste and debris and planted with highly tolerant and restorative grasses, and the industrial structures were retained to provide a striking reminder of the past. Soils were treated through natural means to restore natural balance to the site, and some of the equipment was turned into playgrounds. This park, designed by Richard Haag, has become a model for many other cities faced with the task of reclaiming abandoned industrial and Superfund sites.

Water Resources

Water, by tradition (and necessity), is the sustainer of life, yet humans now face serious problems related to the supply of and demand for water. Urban areas have developed in landscapes that are not capable of supplying the water and other natural resource needs of residents. In urban and suburban developments located in desert areas such as Phoenix, Arizona, and Los Angeles, California, these shortages are exacerbated by the public taste for water-intensive landscapes, such as green lawns, and water-consumptive lifestyles—frequent showers, use of dishwashers, swimming pools, and so on. All of these water use habits produce much larger-scale environmental, political, and economic consequences.

The quality of this precious resource is also declining. The Environmental Protection Agency identified more than 100 organic and inorganic toxic pollutants in U.S. waterways via urban runoff, industrial discharge, fallout, leaching from landfills, disposal sites, and chemical spills.[5]

One key to changing consumer attitudes toward water conservation is to recognize that society has always considered water to be a free commodity, and the prices paid for household and municipal uses of water are greatly discounted. It takes a vast amount of energy to develop dams, transportation facilities, and treatment systems and to pump water to provide clean water for individual and industrial use. If citizens were required to pay more realistic prices for water, there would be a greater economic incentive for conservation. If conservation becomes the norm, then fewer resources will be spent on the production of clean water.

By the time it reaches the ocean, the Colorado River has been nearly drained by uses such as agriculture, urban development, and the production of hydroelectric power. This creates serious conflicts among the inhabitants of all the states through which it flows and with Mexico. Planners have been active in developing policy related to the "rights of ownership" of water, an effort that requires new ways of conceptualizing the problem, and the development of a cross-boundary (bioregional) policy based on sustainability. Similar issues occur with underground water resources (aquifers), which are being mined at a rate that exceeds their natural recharge.

There has been a great increase in the development of water conservation devices and systems in new and remodeled buildings. The concept of the **xeriscape** is based on the use of native drought-tolerant plants in landscape design. This approach provides an effective alternative to enable the development of gardens, yards, and parks that require less water to sustain plants, yet still provide users with the amenities they desire. Other water conservation strategies include use of rainwater and graywater (water previously used but not contaminated with toxins) for residential yards, public parks, rights-of-way, and even decorative fountains.

Water quality can be addressed in a number of ways. Reducing pollutants at the source is perhaps the most effective strategy and has met with success in many communities. In the United States, manufacturers and municipalities alike are required by law in many areas to treat liquid effluents before discharging them into waterways. Such regulations have already produced major improvements in the quality of water in many rivers throughout the industrialized world. When toxins enter water systems through indirect means (nonpoint sources), they are much more difficult to control or regulate. Urban runoff resulting from heavy rains is a major contributor to water system pollution. Intensive development in floodplains, which increases the percentage of land covered by impermeable surfaces, and the clear-cutting of forestlands contribute to rapid urban runoff. Pavement not only prevents rainwater from penetrating the soil, it also intensifies the volume and speed of runoff during periods of heavy rainfall. New methods for managing stormwater are being developed, including systems such as **living machines**, artificial or **constructed wetlands**, and **bioswales** that detain and purify water on site and slowly release clean water into the larger system. Earthworks Park in Kent, Washington, is an internationally recognized work of environmental design and at the same time serves as a stormwater detention system, preventing flooding of businesses downstream. In Arcata, California, for example, treated effluent from the wastewater treatment system is discharged as a water feature in community parks and coastal wetlands, enhancing and restoring ecosystems while meeting community needs. In Moscow, Idaho, the Palouse-Clearwater Environmental Institute developed the concept of a braided stream to slow the pace of water runoff and retain excess water that would normally rush and cause downstream flooding. Slowing the flow of water also releases sediment, cleans the water, and allows more water to recharge underground sources. The site's stream ecosystem will provide an educational opportunity for a future school to be built on adjacent land (Fig. 29-4).

Figure 29-3 The lowest of seven ponds connected by waterfalls at Bishop's Lodge outside Santa Fe, New Mexico, serves as part of the sewage treatment system for this small resort. Plants help clean the water, which is subsequently used to irrigate adjacent pastures. The owners of the resort use their unique system in their advertising.

Figure 29-4 Once a straight channel, this braided stream and its more natural meandering course allow spring runoff to slow down, recharge groundwater, and reestablish a wetlands ecosystem. The changes were developed as a community program by the Palouse-Clearwater Environmental Institute of Moscow, Idaho (T. Bartuska).

Coastal ecosystems that have been destroyed by water pollution and siltation from clear-cutting and land development result in degraded habitats for wildlife and fish. Environmental planners are skilled in assessing the value of these sensitive lands and are learning to work with developers to come up with creative solutions.

Land, Food, and Fiber Resources

"Agricultural systems are [human-made] communities of plants and animals, interacting with soils and climate."[6] These systems (which include forest resources) are at risk for two major reasons:

- The systems are typically out of balance in an ecological sense.
- The land resources upon which they are based are being lost to urban development, soil erosion, and nutrient depletion.

Agricultural productivity has greatly increased in recent years as a result of changes in agricultural technology: the development of pest-resistant and highly productive strains of plants and oil-based fertilizers, herbicides, and pesticides. To be economically efficient, these practices require large areas of land and are intensive consumers of energy.

The consequences of this system of agriculture are that soil life is being destroyed; lakes, rivers, and groundwater are being polluted by the use of chemicals; the lives of agricultural workers are being endangered by the use of pesticides and herbicides; soil quality is being reduced by erosion and compaction from cultivation

practices; and diversity in agricultural ecosystems is being lost. Intensive farming on marginal lands also leads to desertification.

Agricultural (and forest) resources are gradually being lost to urban development and wasteful suburban sprawl. The loss of this land, along with changes in agricultural and forestry practices, often means that the products we consume can no longer be produced locally or even within the region. This increases the distance food must be transported to reach the market. It also serves to distance people from the resources that sustain them.

Reinvented agricultural practices, which in some ways are a return to methods developed centuries ago, are gaining momentum. This involves taking a long-term view of land and soil resources and seeking to establish a self-sustaining system of food production. Adopted practices involve crop rotation, the use of organically derived fertilizers and natural systems of pest and disease control, minimal tillage, and the production of a diversity of crops and animals. In addition, many concerned farmers seek out local or regional markets, reducing transportation costs (and saving additional resources).

Many cities are also encouraging urban farming through the development of neighborhood and allotment gardens established on vacant land within the city. These gardens not only provide the garden farmer with fresh fruits and vegetables, they also provide productive green spaces on land that once lay dormant.

Although forest resources are technically renewable, logging and other methods of clearing, such as burning, often leave soil resources eroded or completely stripped of nutrients and incapable of growing trees. This may also result in a reduction of water recharge and retention potential, the loss of wildlife habitat, and the extinction of plant and animal species that thrive in forest ecosystems. Other significant losses from extensive logging include a net increase in CO_2 from burning, a decrease in the absorption capacity of CO_2, and a decrease in the amount of oxygen being produced by photosynthesis.

A sound timber management policy is an obvious key. Forests must be managed and maintained for sustainability and long-range goals. An issue in the public eye is the preservation of the few remaining old-growth stands of redwood trees in northern California and southern Oregon. These are very old, slow-growing trees, highly valued for timber, and irreplaceable members of the forest ecosystems. In an effort to preserve the ecosystems and raise public awareness of the issues, protestors occupy the canopies of trees many feet above the forest floor so that loggers will not cut the trees. Actions such as these are controversial and yet sometimes lead to improvements in forest management planning.

Another response to the loss of forest resources is to reduce the consumption of wood products and their derivatives. Designers have made great strides in the development of manufactured wood products for structural and construction applications. Columns and beams made from small strands of wood that would otherwise have been wasted are in widespread use. Often these products are unseen, but they are also used as expressive elements for exterior and interior applications (Fig. 29-5).

In developing nations, where wood is the primary source of fuel, experimentation with solar and fuel-efficient ovens, pumps, and other devices is under way. On a larger scale, leading institutions such as the World Bank and regulatory bodies such as the International Monetary Fund are beginning to place strict environmental controls on projects they fund or support in developing areas.

Designing sites where land use is determined by the inherent capabilities and suitabilities of the land is an approach eloquently defined by the landscape architect/ecologist Ian McHarg in *Design with Nature* (see the Introduction and Chapters 5, 18, 19, 25, and 26). Using

Figure 29-5 The new Recreation Center on the University of Idaho campus uses manufactured wood products to form the roof trusses that emphasize the entry to the building. Designers used a wide variety of resource-efficient materials throughout the structure. Students were also deeply involved in setting the design agenda for their building, and its central location encourages pedestrian accessibility and minimizes the use of automobiles.

this system, relatively flat, fertile land would be used for agricultural purposes, ecologically sensitive areas (such as wetlands) would be protected (see Fig. 29-7), and less productive land would be used for more intensive urban development.

At the Woodlands New Town near Houston, Texas, McHarg and his associates demonstrated these principles in the design of an ecologically based new town plan. Site development and design were based on a careful analysis and evaluation of water flow and wetlands, as well as existing forest and plant resources, resulting in judicious cutting, improved erosion controls, and maximum revegetation of all sites. Buildings were clustered together rather than being dispersed. The area of impermeable surfaces was reduced, and semipermeable paving was used wherever possible to preserve and restore conditions to support healthy development of plant and animal ecosystems while achieving better flood control. This alternative approach also saved millions of dollars in development costs, and the town is thriving.

Principles used in the Woodlands are now being more widely applied by individuals developing and maintaining their yards and streetscapes. Planting strategies can effectively moderate climates; reduce heating and cooling loads in buildings; cool and shade roadways, sidewalks, and parking lots; control and enhance winter winds and summer breezes; filter particulates from the air; block or filter noise or create attractive sounds; provide habitat for birds and other wildlife; and increase the supply of oxygen.

Energy Resources

Today, most energy resources used in industrialized nations are derived from burning nonrenewable fuels such as oil, coal, and natural gas. These sources are in limited supply, and the environmental impacts resulting from their extraction, transportation, combustion, and transmission have been devastating. In addition, the economic and human-environmental costs of these fuels are significant.

Hydroelectric power, touted as being "clean," also leads to the alteration and destruction of ecosystems. In the United States, a movement has developed to breach some of the dams to help improve salmon habitat and migration.

Nuclear energy was once seen as the panacea to solve problems created by the approaching depletion of nonrenewable energy resources. Some experts now believe that while there may be great potential in nuclear power, the possibility for widespread and immediate loss of other human and environmental resources as a result of a nuclear accident is greater. Cautious development of this technology, as well as strictly enforced site planning, design, and operations standards for such facilities, are essential. In particular, the problem of dealing effectively with the extremely toxic waste by-products of nuclear energy production is a major challenge.

Again, the reduction of overall consumption of energy and nonrenewable resources is essential. Conservation measures introduced in the United States in the 1970s demonstrated the effectiveness of conservation as a strategy to deal with depletion of nonrenewable energy. The early focus was on strategies such as home insulation and increased efficiency of lighting, heating, and cooling systems. Great strides have been made in energy conservation but demand continues to outpace supplies, creating a strong need for more innovation. Environmental designers are well positioned to take leadership roles in energy conservation. Industrial and product designers can eliminate the concept of "disposability" from their vocabulary, develop products and processes that require minimum inputs of energy, and/or utilize energy produced by renewable sources. Architects, interior designers, landscape architects, and engineers can specify materials that are the least energy consumptive to produce or least damaging to the environment. For example, materials such as aluminum and concrete are extremely energy and resource consumptive to produce and should be used only when less resource-intensive products will not work.

Renewable energy resources, using systems such as passive and active solar energy, wind generation, and methane and alcohol fuels derived from agricultural production, are important alternatives. These resources can and are being developed for individual projects and for mass production.

The high winds that blow over the land throughout the world are now being harnessed as a renewable energy source by wind generators that cover the landscape while cattle graze below. Wind generators at sea, like the sailing ships of the past, are also becoming commonplace in northern Europe. Large-scale solar collection systems are under development in many locations throughout the world. These renewable resources can also be developed as an integral part of the building design process. Although significant progress has been made in the use of renewable energy sources in lieu of nonrenewable sources, there is still much left to do. A number of examples of creative and holistic thinking can be cited. Michael Reynolds, an architect practicing in New Mexico, has developed an earth-sheltered, passive solar housing type based on the use of old tires crammed with earth as foundations, discarded aluminum cans as

Figure 29-6   Wind turbines generating renewable energy in southern California (T. Bartuska).

building infill walls, and discarded bottles for greenhouse planter walls[7] (Fig. 29-6).

In another example, a dairy farmer in Pennsylvania has devised a two-tiered barn that allows him to house and milk the cows, collect their wastes and urine, and convert them to methane. This method of energy produc-

Figure 29-7   Students at the University of Cincinnati built an experimental passive solar greenhouse using all recycled materials, inspired by the work of Mike Reynolds. The materials included tires rammed with earth, bottles, and aluminum cans.

tion is being developed for small-scale applications in many areas.

Considerable research is under way to improve the performance of various building enclosure systems while allowing people to control individual workspaces. Transparent and translucent insulating wall systems, solar shingles, and light-sensitive devices are among the many new products coming to market.

Through effective climate and solar design and the use of wind and photovoltaic panels, many projects now can be energy self-sufficient. These projects produce their own energy needs, and some even sell excess power back to the energy grid for others to use.

Biodiversity

As emphasized in Chapter 28, species diversity is critical to keeping ecosystems balanced and functioning. Maintaining gene pools is also important to continue development of strains of plants for agriculture that are resistant to pests and disease. The Nature Conservancy estimates that as many as three species are being lost per day, in most cases because of loss or degradation of habitat and ecosystems. Extinction also results from hunting animals for trophies, for fur, for ivory, or for other fashionable commodities. Loss of habitat frequently results from development related to resource extraction (strip mining, logging, farming, etc.) or urbanization. The preservation and restoration efforts described in the section on "Land, Food, and Fiber Resources" apply here.

In urban and suburban conditions, a number of possible actions can be taken. At the level of the backyard or park, plantings are being designed to attract species of wildlife that will help control pests and support the development of a diverse ecosystem. The creation of diverse habitats is intricately interwoven and requires action at all levels. Consolidating and linking larger collections of urban open space and developing this land as wildlife habitat will achieve even greater benefits.

Wetlands provide habitat that supports particularly diverse collections of living things, and special efforts are being taken to preserve these areas. Legislation has been passed and regulations developed to ensure that appropriate sites are either preserved or replaced when large-scale developments are built.

It is also important to stop the killing of endangered species for the collection and production of trophies, souvenirs, health and beauty aids, or clothing. The most obvious action is to not purchase these items. Organized boycotts have actually resulted in department stores closing their fur salons, stopping the killing of dolphins,

Figure 29-8 Student volunteers working with the Palouse-Clearwater Environmental Institute and Earth Works are planting thousands of trees, and helping to restore the Paradise Creek wetlands and watershed (T. Bartuska).

and causing major tuna companies to change their fishing practices.

Taking Action

It is clear that many opportunities exist for thoughtful, well-prepared individuals to develop environmentally sound lifestyles and to contribute substantially to the solution of many problems presented throughout this book and summarized in this chapter. Table 29-1 outlines issues and identifies a few of the many possible actions that may be taken by individuals and groups of committed people.

Developing a personal lifestyle and professional practices based on the values of human-environmental responsibility may not be an easy undertaking but is becoming more feasible than it was just twenty years ago. The architect and educator William McDonough continues to provide leadership demonstrating the viability of design solutions at all levels of the built environment. "His designs range in scale from molecules to regions—from environmental optimization of product chemical compositions, to community plans that restore native habitat and hydrology while spurring economic development."[8]

It is important to become well informed and educated. Many mistakes are made by well-intentioned but ill-informed members of the general public and environmental designers. Establishing a network of informed and committed colleagues working together for the exchange of information and ideas can be a key to success. This can happen locally, nationally, and internationally, utilizing

Table 29-1 Human-Environmental Resources versus Design/Planning Strategies

RESOURCES	PRODUCTS/INTERIORS	STRUCTURES/LANDSCAPE	CITY/REGION/EARTH
Air	• Energy conservation • Develop pollution control devices • Nontoxic materials/methods in the home/workplace • Walk, bike, and use public transit	• Renewable energy and passive technologies • Energy-efficient buildings and landscapes • Reduce use of fossil fuel • Increase tree planting • Energy efficient	• Reduce suburban sprawl • Walk, bike, and use public transit • Minimize auto use • Design cities to maximize air circulation • Pollution control ordinances and incentives • Plant trees, retain wetlands
Water	• Water conservation devices for building and landscape • Low water planting design • Develop nontoxic materials	• Graywater recycling • On-site stormwater management • Eliminate toxic chemicals • Xeriscape and use native plants • Retain wetlands	• Wetland preservation • Recycle sewage and water treatment systems (living machines)
Land, Food, and Fiber	• Organic farming/gardening techniques • Tools and methods to eliminate erosion and increase productivity • Minimize materials in products • Eliminate need for packaging • Develop new building materials • Reduce, reuse, recycle	• Site design for erosion control • Reduce suburban sprawl • Reuse, restore existing buildings and landscapes • Utilize wood products that are easily regenerated • Eliminate rare/endangered hardwoods	• Design/plan with nature • Avoid development on agricultural land • Reduce suburban sprawl • Cluster developments • Develop urban forestry programs • Guidelines/zoning for forest management
Energy	• Passive and active solar technologies • Wind power • Develop materials with low embodied energy	• Energy-efficient site planning and landscape design • Design with climate • Superinsulated buildings • Daylighting • Use renewable systems: solar and photovoltaics	• Reduce/reuse/recycling programs • Use energy conservation incentives • Reduce suburban sprawl • Increase public transit, reduce use of autos
Biodiversity	• Avoid use of products from endangered species (fur, ivory, feathers, etc.)	• Planting design for diversity and ecosystem restoration • Wetland preservation	• Increase diversity for wildlife habitat • Strengthen/enforce legislation to preserve rare and endangered species

meetings, professional and scientific publications and journals, and the Internet to make connections. Most cities have excellent agencies that foster sustainable development.[9] Regionally, members of the Northwest EcoBuilding Guild[10] work together to develop and promote sustainable design solutions and construction practices.

Another strategy for implementation of change involves the "infiltration" of professional organizations by people committed to improving the environment or by like-minded designers making use of institutional power and resources. In leadership positions, such thinkers and doers can institute change from the top down. More extreme approaches are employed by organizations such as Earth First and Greenpeace, which use direct confrontation by nonviolent means to force change. The California tree-sitters have been effective in changing forest practices in northern California.

As this book repeatedly emphasizes, solutions are initiated at all levels of society: by individuals, professionals, community and national organizations, and global institutions in response to any number of human-environmental issues. Actions may involve developing new products or manufacturing processes or community or regional plans, getting them approved for use, and/or promoting and gaining public acceptance for the implementation of economically-socially-environmentally feasible solutions (see Table 29-1). In many cases, the choice to live in an area where there are problems also provides opportunities to become engaged in the development and implementation of innovative solutions.

While problems may sometimes seem insurmountable, it is also important to recognize that the present is one of the most exciting times in which to live. Engagement in design, planning, and management of all aspects of the natural and built environments is important today and will continue to be even more so in the future. There are opportunities for radical innovation and environmental change that have never before existed, and more than ever, citizens and designers are well equipped to make a difference. It seems that now, as never before, an international groundswell of interest in these issues is taking place and the time seems right for meaningful, sustainable action.

References and Resources

Christian Science Monitor. 2005: www.csmonitor.com/2005/0606.

Dubos, R. *Celebrations of Life.* McGraw-Hill, 1981.

Earthworks Group. *50 Simple Things You Can Do to Save the Planet.* Earthworks Press, 1989.

Forman, R., and M. Godron. *Landscape Ecology.* Wiley, 1986.

Hough, M. *Cities and Natural Process.* Routledge Press, 1985.

McDonough, W. McDonough and Partners. 2006: www.mcdonough.com.

Northwest EcoBuilding Guild. 2003: www.ecobuilding.org.

Palouse-Clearwater Environmental Institute: www.pcei.org.

Portland. Office of Sustainable Development. 2006: www.sustainableportland.org.

Reynolds, M. Earthship Biotecture. 2003: www.earthship.org.

Seattle Department of Sustainable Development. 2006: www.ci.seattle.wa.us/dpd/sustainability.

Spirn, A. *The Granite Garden.* Basic Books, 1985.

United Nations Division for Sustainable Development. 2003: www.un.org/esa/sustdev/index.html.

Council on Environmental Quality and Department of State. *Global 2000 Report to the President of the United States.* Pergamon Press, 1980.

Worldwatch Institute. 2002: www.worldwatch.org

Endnotes

1. Worldwatch Institute, 2002: www.worldwatch.org.
2. *United Nations Division for Sustainable Development,* 2003: www.un.org/esa/sustdev/index.html.
3. See footnote 1.
4. *Christian Science Monitor,* 2005: www.csmonitor.com/2005/0606.
5. A. Spirn, *The Granite Garden* (Basic Books, 1985).
6. M. Hough, *Cities and Natural Process* (Routledge Press, 1985).
7. M. Reynolds, 2003: www.earthship.org.
8. W. McDonough, McDonough and Partners, 2006: www.mcdonough.com.
9. Portland, Office of Sustainable Development, 2006 (www.portlandonline.com/osd) and Seattle, Seattle Department of Sustainable Development, 2006 (www.ci.seattle.wa.us/dpd/sustainability).
10. Northwest EcoBuilding Guild, 2006: www.ecobuilding.org.

PART IV

Challenges: Designing and Planning a Quality Sustainable Environment for All

The final section in the exploration of the built environment poses some critical questions in our continued search for understanding and effective solutions. How can humans collaborate to create quality environments for all, locally and globally? Can we continue to develop a comprehensive and integrated understanding of these immense and compelling social, environmental, and technical challenges? Can we harness the powers of effective design/planning and technology to their fullest potential as instruments for creating sustainable, quality built environments?

As discussed in previous chapters, creative paradigms exist for quality design responses within each layer of the built environment. Designs of products, interiors, structures, landscapes, cities, and regions can foster integrated, **symbiotic relationships**—designing with the nature of human-environmental-technological systems. A symbiotic paradigm evolves from a significant attitudinal shift to ways humans should collaborate with one another and interface with the ecological systems upon which all of life depends. The ultimate challenge is for local and global communities to cultivate a sustainable culture of expectations for all levels of the built environment and for such noble solutions to represent the rule rather than the exception. As Ian McHarg states in the Preface of this book: "The built environment must reflect the intelligence of humans, not their ignorance—a belated conclusion, not widely understood, it awaits application and realization."

What is needed is a plan or charter to direct our actions locally and globally. Many positive collaborative strategies are evolving, such as the *Global 2000 Report* (Chapter 29) and the UN Earth Charter:

> "The Earth Charter is a declaration of fundamental principles for building a just, sustainable, and peaceful global society in the 21st century. It seeks to inspire in all peoples a new sense of global interdependence and shared responsibility for the well-being of the human family and the larger living world. It is an expression of hope and a call to help create a global partnership at a critical juncture in history. . . . We stand at a critical moment in Earth's history, a time when humanity must choose its future."[1]

This concluding section addresses the challenge of designing and planning for quality and sustainable environments that support human activities in the developed and developing worlds. The chapters address urbanization and shelter in developing countries and creating livable, sustainable communities within the urban, suburban, and rural contexts in intensive-resource-use countries such as the United States. The section concludes with a conspectus that takes one last look back at the seven levels of the pervasive built environment and asks what the next steps might be.

One's Overall Impact on the Earth

A few more questions: Overall, how are humans doing in their efforts to maintain an appropriate balance with the Earth? What dynamic factors, when considered holistically, suggest guidelines for the future? What is the overall impact each human has on the Earth? Collectively, human activities vary, depending on numerous societal/cultural dynamics. As discussed, high-style and speculative societies tend to consume far more than vernacular and participatory ones. For example, many vernacular societies (unfortunately called "developing" countries) consume 10–25 times less than developed countries (sometimes called "over-developed"). This means that one person in a developed society has the same impact as 10–25 people in a vernacular society. As discussed throughout this book, many principles and creative strategies can be learned from vernacular societies about designing/planning with natural systems.

Many scientists and global planners are finding effective ways to holistically model and assess global systems. One simple yet very useful modeling method is the ecological footprint.[2] The **ecological footprint** method uses land as its basic comparative measure—how much land does it take to accommodate one's lifestyle, including material consumption, food production, forest resources, and energy? The reader is encouraged to calculate his or her footprint at www.myfootprint.org. This method allows people to easily calculate their overall impact on the

Earth,[3] summarize it and compare it with the overall demands of various societies/nations, and compare these needs with the maximum carrying capacity of the Earth.[4] The various footprints provide critical comparisons between vernacular and consumptive societies. The findings demonstrate that developed countries require 10–15 times more land than developing countries to support the needs of their citizens. Probably more revealing is that collectively, the current human needs and impacts of the world exceed the overall carrying capacity of the Earth by 30%.[5]

In the most basic sense, the ecological footprint of the typical human demonstrates the overall impact of each individual on the Earth. Barry Commoner, a renowned ecologist, states that the Earth is primarily affected by three basic human-environmental factors: population, affluence, and technology; he reiterates the need for a holistic perspective on how these factors are intertwined with global systems. It is also necessary to understand the multiple effects of these human-environmental-technical factors to realize the important challenges humans face on this Earth. These three factors are described as **human** population (P), affluent societies' induced consumption (C) of Earth's **environmental** resources, and the efficiencies (E) of **technology** and design. Taken together (PCE), they have a multiplying effect. The ecological footprint concludes that the current multiplying effect of $P \times C \times E = 1.3$ Earths, indicating that our current aggregate lifestyle is unsustainable. If the population of the Earth doubles in the next 50 years as predicted, along with overall consumption, and the efficiency of technology and design stays about the same, the overall multiplying effect would be $2 \times 2 \times 1 \times 1.3 = 5.2$ Earths. The result would be over five times as much resource consumption and related impacts on our shared human-environmental systems. Four more Earths are hard to find! But if the efficiency of technology and design were increased by five (cutting consumption by one-fifth), the overall effect of PCE would equal $2 \times 2 \times 1/5 \times 1.3 = 1.3$ Earths, or maintain the status quo and pose a formidable challenge to designers. If population increase is a given, per capita consumption must be reduced and the efficiency of technology and design must be increased to ensure a sustainable or, better, regenerative future for our progeny and our planet.

Being a 10

Projecting the above PCE calculations into the future, the global population is predicted to stabilize at two to three times the present number; consumption of resources, if shared in an equitable way to improve living standards throughout the world, will then increase by a factor of 3–4. This multiplying effect creates a need for efficiency improvements to reach 9–12 (1/9 − 1/12). For simplicity, **10 (or 1/10)** is an ideal design/planning goal (PCE = 2-3×3-$4 \times 1/10 = 1$ Earth).

Can we increase the efficiency of our design and planning in order to reach or exceed 10 (or, conversely, reduce consumption by 1/10th)? Can we challenge ourselves to be a 10 in efficiency *and* performance? This goal must be met to achieve a more equitable and harmonious future. Designing/planning symbiotic relationships with nature's renewable resources (or recycling used ones) can extend the usable life of systems and resources. Impressive efficiencies have been achieved in vernacular cultures and in nature. Studying and applying nature's symbiotic efficiencies is commonly referred to as "biomimicry."[6] Also, recycling products gives a second and a third life to these valuable resources and reduces the target efficiency by at least one-half, or the challenging 10 to 5.

Many products can be identified that have achieved efficiencies of 5 to 10—for example, the rapid evolution of computer technology. The first computers were huge, requiring room-sized equipment and tons of resources. Now computer notebooks are far more powerful, much smaller, and use a fraction of the energy (but the challenge still exists to recycle the e-wastes). Achieving a 10 can be as simple as using a disposable cup 10 times instead of just once and avoiding single-use, throwaway products. Hybrid vehicles achieve over 50 miles per gallon (mpg) and the Smart Car, popular in Europe, achieves 90 mpg while reusing and recycling many of its parts. Heavy, large vehicles use a disproportionate share of resources, with some getting less than 10 mpg. Walking is healthy and 28 times more efficient than driving a car, while riding a bike is 40 times more efficient (see Chapter 23). Traditional walking neighborhoods and planned cluster communities are substantially more efficient *and* effective in terms of human-environmental issues, energy consumption, and land use than low-density, auto-driven sprawl. Organic agriculture and sustainable forestry demonstrate very high efficiencies. As discussed earlier, quality and creativity are best determined by comparing and evaluating multiple sets of factors—hopefully, a combination of art and science, appearance and performance.

Shelter and community, housing and urbanization will be revisited in the next two chapters, and a final conspectus will be presented to review the many collaborative challenges facing humanity in creating a livable and sustainable society and world.

Urbanization and the Global Housing Crisis by Bashir A. Kazimee

Most people in the industrialized world take living in comfortable houses and apartments for granted. Yet, an increasing number of people around the world live in quite a different reality—they are literally homeless, living on the streets without shelter. They lack necessary life amenities. This chapter discusses the disparity in their quest for shelter, an especially critical issue in less developed countries, where significant numbers of rural people are moving to urban centers in search of work and a place to live. Providing adequate space and housing to this growing number of urban people is a critical challenge to society and to the design/planning professions. This dramatic need for shelter has profound implications for both human and environmental conditions throughout the world. Meeting the need, or not meeting it, will shape almost all aspects and scales of the built environment.

Livable/Sustainable Communities by Wendy R. McClure

Community and shelter are interdependent expressions of culture. Design and planning are powerful tools that can either support or undermine the quality of these aspects of the built environment and conditions for sustainability. Design decisions for each layer of the built environment, both individually and collectively, impact the capacity of a community and a region to achieve sustainability—socially, ecologically, and economically. This chapter provides an overview of the movement for sustainable development. Summary case studies involving key players from various design/planning professions are used to illustrate sustainable strategies for a range of contexts including urban, suburban, and rural environments.

Conspectus by Tom J. Bartuska

The final chapter challenges both author and readers to formulate some "conclusions-in-perspective" about this evasive and pervasive subject, the built environment. The built environment has been revealed, layer by layer, through concepts, components, and environmental design/planning professions that help give it substance and meaning. This chapter discusses the potential for a renewed spirit emphasizing the importance of ecological understanding of life and of the natural and built environments; a collaborative message for design and planning; and the critical need for proactive leadership, public awareness, and participation as we evolve toward a sustainable society throughout the world.

REFERENCES

Benyus, J. *Biomimicry: Innovation Inspired by Nature*. HarperCollins, 1997.
Commoner, B. *The Closing Circle*. Bantam, 1980.
Commoner, B. *Making Peace with the Planet*. New Press, 1992.
Earth Charter: www.earthcharter.org.
"Earth Day Footprint Quiz," 2006: www.myfootprint.org.

Ecological Footprint of Nations. *Rio5: Moving Sustainable Development from Agenda to Action*, 2004: www.ecocouncil.ac.cr/rio/focus/report/english/footprint.

Eco Trust-Conservation Economy (see interactive "pattern map": www.conservationeconomy.net.

Kribel, D. (ed.). *Barry Commoner's Contributions to the Environmental Movement: Science and Social Action.* Baywood, 2002.

Living Planet Report: www.wwf.org.uk/filelibrary/pdf/livingplanet2002.pdf.

McDonough, W., and M. Braungart. *Cradle to Cradle: Remaking the Way We Make Things.* North Point Press, 2002.

Wackernagel, M., and W. Rees. *Our Ecological Footprint: Reducing Human Impact on the Earth.* New Society Publishers, 1996.

ENDNOTES

1. UN Earth Charter: www.earthcharter.org.
2. M. Wackernagel and W. Rees, *Our Ecological Footprint: Reducing Human Impact on the Earth* (New Society Publishers, 1996).
3. Earth Day Footprint Quiz 2006: www.myfootprint.org.
4. Ecological Footprint of Nations, *Rio5: Moving Sustainable Development from Agenda to Action*, 2004: www.ecocouncil.ac.cr/rio/focus/report/english/footprint.
5. See Note 2.
6. J. Benyus, *Biomimicry: Innovation Inspired by Nature* (HarperCollins, 1997).

CHAPTER 30

Urbanization and the Global Housing Crisis

Bashir A. Kazimee

M ost people in the industrialized world take comfortable houses and apartments for granted. But the number of homeless people is increasing. Currently, there are 600,000 homeless in the United States, and on any given night at least 100,000 children are without homes.[1] They lack basic shelter and necessary life amenities.

The disparity in the quest for shelter is even more critical in less developed countries, where significant numbers of rural people are moving to urban centers in search of work and a place to live. Providing adequate space and housing for these growing migrant populations creates critical challenges for society and the design professions. This dramatic need for shelter has profound implications for both human and environmental conditions throughout the world. Meeting the need, or not meeting it, will shape almost all aspects and scales of the built environment, now and in the future.

Shelter and Urbanization

The availability and form of housing are influenced by many aspects of urban life—population characteristics, employment opportunities, and socioeconomic status. The housing crisis is linked closely to these overall forces of urbanization and the way these forces operate and influence each other. The primary force affecting the need for shelter is the dynamic increase in the population of cities, particularly in the less developed countries of Africa, Asia, and South and Central America.

Contemporary urban growth in and around the cities of the Third World is undergoing a dynamic revolution that has no precedent in the history of humankind. By 1985, the total urban population of the world had reached almost 2 billion.[2] More than half of this growth occurred in the metropolitan areas of less developed countries. Projections by the United Nations indicate that early in the twenty-first century, the urban population in Third World regions alone had increased to almost 2 billion. Cities and towns are experiencing a critical transformation from this remarkable growth in population. For example, Algiers grew from 450,000 inhabitants to over 2 million between 1950 and 1985 and is now one of Africa's larger cities. During the same period the population of Lagos grew almost 21 times, and those of Rangoon, Tehran, and Delhi increased fourfold. Kinshasa (Zaire) underwent a dramatic transformation, growing from 170,000 to 2.57 million—a 15-fold increase.[3]

There are many reasons for the massive growth in Third World cities. Besides the normal increase in population caused by improved life expectancy, increased birth

Figure 30-1 A view of the older squatter area on the east slope of Asmaye Mountain in Kabul, Afghanistan. The houses, in poor condition, are constructed of impermanent materials. The locality is at a saturated stage of development.

rates, and advances in health and nutrition, a significant share of this growth is due to rural-urban migration. Even more dramatic is the fact that this migration is often directed to principal and capital cities. Because most of the industries, commercial enterprises, and educational and national administrative centers are concentrated in the primary cities, they are experiencing the biggest impact from rural migrant populations. For example, Bangkok, the capital city of Thailand, with its extensive concentration of resources and urban amenities, has outgrown the second city, Chieng Mai, by more than 30 times.[4]

The causes of migration from rural areas to cities are multiple and complex. Aside from many personal and family motivations, scholars and other experts have identified three major factors—rural poverty, natural disasters, and political conflicts—as the root causes of rural-urban migration.

Rural Poverty

Push forces and pull forces are the primary causes of rural-urban migration. **Push forces** are the result of widespread rural poverty and the loss of both economic and social opportunities in rural areas that push people to urban centers. **Pull forces** are those that attract people to cities—employment, social and education opportunities, health and welfare services, and general city amenities and services. The synergy of pull and push forces has created a massive one-way movement of rural populations to urban centers. The result is distortion and imbalance in the economic and social orders in both the rural village and the city. Such forces impacted the developed nations in the nineteenth and twentieth centuries, when

the transformation to industrialization and urbanization was more complete than it is now in Third World regions. The changes were accommodated and accompanied by a better balance between economic development and prosperity in industrial and agricultural sectors. As discussed in Chapter 21, urban transformation in the developed world took place over a period of 200 years, while the cities of less developed countries are transforming in only 30 years.

The governments of less developed nations often place a high priority on expansion and development of the industrial sector of the economy. As a result of this policy, and of assigning a low priority to the agricultural sector, rural areas tend to lack modernization and development. Also, traditional methods of subsistence farming remain predominant in many Third World countries. Population growth in the agricultural sector exceeds the productive capacity of arable lands, contributing to a significant labor surplus and unemployment in rural areas. Outdated farming techniques, primitive irrigation systems, and the incidence of drought and pests all make farming less efficient and less able to support growing populations.

Natural Disasters

Natural disasters, although not limited to rural areas, are the second major cause of rural-urban migration. Natural disasters can also occur in urban areas, but amenities and support services in cities are equipped to provide basic assistance. Clearly defined strategies and precautionary measures to cope with such problems simply do not exist in rural areas. In these areas, both technical and economic means are limited. Upheaval from floods, cyclones, hurricanes, earthquakes, and tsunamis result in phenomenal loss of life and destruction of much of the physical environment. The effects of global warming may be equally devastating to all nations. These tragic events have frustrated already inadequate attempts by the governments of these nations to provide shelter for their citizens. In most cases, displaced people abandoned the countryside for the city. Effective land-use planning could protect settlement patterns from many natural disasters, but this has been difficult to implement.

Political Conflicts

Violent conflicts in the period of postcolonial and cold war politics, and ethnic or racial unrest, leave tragic footprints even in the sociohistorical structure of advanced societies. Both the conflicts and the consequences have

Figure 30-2 A view of the comparatively new squatter settlement on the south slopes of Asmaye Mountain in Kabul, Afghanistan. The dwellings are built from local materials, and many show advanced stages of development and a greater sense of community organization and permanence (T. Bartuska).

been far more dramatic and unfortunate in poorer countries. The Arab-Israeli conflicts of 1967 and 1973 in the Middle East brought drastic influxes of refugees to the cities. Approximately 250,000 refugees were added to the population of Amman in 1967, and almost 500,000 people moved to Cairo from the devastated settlements of the Suez Canal Zone following the 1973 war.[5] The Russian invasion of Afghanistan in 1978 imposed fourteen years of war on the general population, a war that disrupted and destroyed much of the socioeconomic fabric, as well as the land and resource base, on an unprecedented scale. The conflict killed 1.24 million people and forced almost 5 million refugees to migrate to the neighboring countries of Pakistan and Iran. These figures represent approximately a 40% displacement of the mostly rural postwar population. Consequently, the number of Afghan refugees in the border cities of Peshawar and Quetta in Pakistan is larger than that of native populations, and many of these desperate people are homeless. The U.S.-led invasions of Afghanistan in 2002 and Iraq in 2003 have created new disruptions.

Squatter Settlements

The shift of population from rural areas to urban centers creates a phenomenal impact on the general socioeconomic order of the rural and urban centers of the Third World. The capacity of urban areas to absorb and to cope economically and physically with an influx of migrants creates extreme stress and a tremendous challenge for society. The rate of population growth surpasses the

capacity to provide housing, community facilities, services, and other essentials of an urban community. Shortages of shelter have reached crisis proportions and adversely affect many aspects of life.

Many migrants arriving in the cities are not prepared or trained for urban life and employment. They are unaccustomed to new challenges in the urban labor market, a market that demands new skills. A majority strive to find employment and a place to live. Buying or renting a house or apartment is beyond the financial reach of most migrants. The inevitable result is that large segments of the migrant population in metropolitan areas attempt to help themselves by building their own shelters in slum areas and squatter settlements.

Squatters make illegal use of available public (and sometimes even private) land to build temporary shelters out of modest discarded materials. **Squatter settlements**, an almost overnight emergence of spontaneous growth, have become one of the most prominent shelter types in the urban landscape of developing countries.

Many squatter communities are doubling in population every 5 or 6 years, an annual increase of 15% to 20%. The normal growth rate of such cities is estimated at between 5% and 10% annually. Squatters constitute almost 33% of the population of Karachi, 40% of Caracas, 45% of Lima, 46% of Mexico City, and 50% of Ankara.[6] Of the more than 8 million people of Bombay (India), 54% live in slums and squatter settlements and an additional 2.5%, are pavement dwellers (living on the streets without shelter of any kind).

Squatter communities vary greatly in physical appearance and socioeconomic structure. Dwellings are constructed of any kind of salvageable rudimentary material available locally, ranging from cardboard cartons, petrol tin cases, straw, and matting to more consolidated structures and permanent materials such as brick, stone, wood, and earth. Generally, no standards for construction have been established, and the settlements lack even minimum conventional amenities. Municipal services such as water supply, sewage systems, street lighting or paved roads, and community facilities such as health, education, and police protection are virtually nonexistent in many squatter settlements.

The density of squatter areas is extremely high, so overcrowding and congestion are common. Poverty contributes to social disorganization, increased unemployment, crime, and delinquency. Rudimentary sanitation and unhygienic, squalid conditions (especially open sewage and drainage ditches) expose populations to constant dangers of epidemics of typhoid, malaria, and infectious diseases.

Government resources to provide assistance and community facilities for the poor are limited. Government officials tend to be passive and even indifferent to these complex challenges. Since housing the poor would require significant government subsidies, investment in this sector of the economy is least favored by many Third World countries. The widely accepted economic philosophy that investment in housing will tend to consume available resources rather than produce revenues makes the provision and improvement of public housing the lowest priority in national development policies. The magnitude and scale of the problem are such that interventions are beyond the means of most developing countries. Housing the homeless is not an easy task, even for an advanced and developed economy, and it is doubtful whether the majority of the less developed countries can ever satisfy the needs of their people.

Despite physical ills, poor housing, and squalor, the process of building squatter settlements does have some positive effects and does contribute to the socioeconomic life of the city. This participatory, self-help approach to problems is an effective and economical method for providing housing. Communities built this way are a source of labor and tend to stimulate small commercial and industrial enterprises in the urban area. The squatters generally try to be responsible citizens. They hope to overcome poverty and participate in the normal social and economic life of the city. Despite official views that shantytowns only deteriorate, many examples demonstrate that they are often improved gradually by their inhabitants. Citizens of squatter settlements attempt to provide a decent environment for their families and work very hard to improve their houses. "The root cause of squatting does not lie in the nature of the squatters themselves, but is a response to the lack of access to affordable housing or land. This is caused not only by insufficient production of houses, but also by the limited resources of society."[7]

One of the positive characteristics attributed to squatter settlements is a strong sense of community, a sense that reflects the inhabitants' rural values. Tribal and family ties, kinship, and extended family structures and village groupings encourage a continuity of custom and culture brought from rural village environments. In many cities of Africa, Southeast Asia, and the Middle East, squatter settlements follow the patterns of rural villages. Narrow streets and alleyways are designed primarily for pedestrian activity with no vehicular access. These alleys often function as meeting places for people and play areas for children. The continued use in squatter housing of both local materials and traditional con-

struction techniques is efficient and an obvious connection to the builders' sense of a regional vernacular tradition. Thus, "in third-world cities, we no longer see urbanization of the rural migrants, but rather a growing ruralization of the cities."[8] A study of Egyptian migrant adjustments to the city showed that more than one-third of the Cairo city population is comprised of migrants and that the majority are from rural areas of Egypt. Migrants who come to the city are equipped with rich customs of rural origin. They have a significant impact on shaping the culture of the city and contributing to it.

Squatter settlements are a recognizable force in the formation and growth of Third World cities. Reality suggests that this type of settlement is perhaps the only affordable method to provide shelter for the urban poor and will continue to be the way used by the majority of urban dwellers in Third World cities to achieve shelter.

Squatter Settlements of Rio de Janeiro, Brazil: A Case Study

There is a myth in Brazil that "God created the heavens and the earth in seven days, one of which was spent to make Rio de Janeiro." Surrounded by the beauties of a heaven-like natural setting, and the aura and attraction of a cosmopolitan center, Rio de Janeiro represents a true synthesis between humans and nature whose symbolism has become part of the Brazilian consciousness. Surrounded by vast stretches of Ipanema and other world-famous golden sand beaches and the magnificent seaside mountains of Sugarloaf and Corcovado, not to mention the charm of year-round amiable climate and sun, Rio attracts and inspires travelers from across the globe.

Despite its overriding urban attractions and its dazzling landscape, Rio is characterized by yet another reality. Much of the city's land is dominated by the harsh presence of slums and extremely poor neighborhoods. More than 1.4 million of Rio's approximately 6 million residents live in its 500 or more squatter or slum sites. Slums and squatter neighborhoods are increasing at a rate of 8% annually, occupy more than 10% of the urban territory, and have population densities three times those of the city as a whole. In the last few decades, their size has more than doubled and in some sites even tripled.

As in many cities in developing countries, the growth of squatter settlements in Rio was spurred by widespread poverty and economic depression in rural areas. These push factors, combined with the pull factors of employment and educational opportunities, continue to pro-

Figure 30-3 *Favelas* occupying a hill slope near the city center of Rio de Janeiro, Brazil.

mote the influx of migrants into the city. Migrants are extremely poor and unable to afford accommodation in speculative and hostile housing markets. The failure of government and city authorities to provide affordable housing for this low-income population forced Rio's migrants to erect dwellings illegally on public or private land through a self-help process.

Squatter settlements in Brazil are called *favelas*, and their inhabitants are referred to as *faveldos*. *Favelas* can be seen in all parts of the city of Rio; they are conspicuous on the hill slopes of the city (65%) and on low-lying areas near the bay on flat, swampy land (35%). The size of these communities varies from smaller settlements of about 500 people to much larger communities of more than 100,000. Before 1960, most of the *favelas* were established in the southern part of the city, but since then, the concentration has shifted to the northern and western regions.

Larger settlements are located close to commercial and industrial districts. The largest single agglomeration in Rio is located on prime real estate at the center of one of the wealthiest residential districts. The *favela* population of Rocinha is estimated to be about 200,000. Another large *favela*, known as Mare, houses an estimated 65,000 people.

Considerable variation exists in social and economic status, as well as in the physical conditions of housing in these communities. Generally speaking, the *favelas* exhibit a strong sense of community identity and organization. Their people are law-abiding and productive citizens with strong social ties to family and community. By comparison, the hillside squatter settlements are better off economically than areas near the water.

The layout of these sites is typically irregular, frequently taking the form of narrow, winding paths. Small houses are densely lined up at the edges of narrow walkways. In some areas, population density exceeds 300 persons per acre. (For comparison, the average density of most suburban developments in the United States is 10–20 per acre.) Dwelling units range from primitive one-room shanties to relatively well-built two-story houses. Many barely provide protection from the outside elements. Some *faveldos* make substantial improvements to their dwellings over time through a self-help process. It is not surprising to find houses lavishly plastered and painted, with fenced yards and porches and comfortably furnished rooms, often including a refrigerator and a television.

Since these settlements are constructed in a piecemeal, ongoing fashion without the sanction of law, their inhabitants have been denied basic services by Rio's municipality, resulting in limited and substandard urban services and infrastructure. Over time, a few settlements have been considered for improvements, either through government assistance and charity institutions or as a result of a self-help user participation process. Nevertheless, the quality of services in even the most urbanized *favelas* falls short in comparison to surrounding areas.

During the 1960s, the Housing State Agency of Rio de Janeiro (COHAB) was created in an effort to deal with the slum and housing problems of low-income populations in the city. The main initiative of this agency was removal of migrant settlements from the city center, based on the pretext that their sanitary problems had no solution and presented health problems for the city as a whole. An estimated 139,000 residents from 80 different *favelas* in Rio were forced to abandon their homes and move to publicly financed housing projects located on the outskirts of the city.

Figure 30-4 A view of the housing area with storefronts in an upgraded *favela* site in Rio de Janeiro, Brazil.

These public housing projects proved not to be equal to the task. They were expensive, badly constructed, and located farther away from the sources of employment and the city center. Some of these projects were soon abandoned by the poor who could not pay the monthly rents and who found their way back to dwellings in other illegal settlements. Some of those forced to leave squatter settlements in the central district of the city in the 1960s and 1970s were relocated to interior public housing projects. In recent years, new developments and new illegal subdivisions have proliferated in outlying areas.

Fortunately, a different approach is now being developed to help the people in squatter settlements and slums. Many societies are empowering the people and developing more realistic self-help or participatory responses to the housing problems of the poor. In contrast to reactionary policies of the past that resulted in the wholesale removal and evacuation of several sites and the failure of alternative solutions such as low-cost public housing programs, the main objectives of the new programs are to upgrade infrastructure, establish land ownership, and provide basic services. These rehabilitation programs are designed to empower the residents themselves to secure property titles, improve their houses, and access better infrastructure and services. This is the first step toward recognizing and integrating slum neighborhoods into the city. Under this program, the municipality of Rio changed its emphasis by setting goals to provide basic infrastructure, including a sewage system, garbage collection, and the provision of water and electricity. Implementation of infrastructure improvements has varied significantly, but many *favelas* now have some form of municipal water services, garbage collection service, and electricity.

Figure 30-6   A view of hillside *favela* housing in Rio de Janeiro, Brazil. Some of the houses are poorly constructed and built on stilts, a bad decision given the danger of landslides in rainy seasons.

Through municipal upgrading programs, an increasing number of settlements are being provided with a sewage network installed by the city. Sewage collection and treatment is still nonexistent for the remainder, creating an unhealthy situation in the rainy season, when sewage ditches commonly flood. During the rainy season in Rio, the precarious construction of the houses in *favelas* and the soil conditions around them at times result in landslides.

Faveldos have become increasingly active, organized, and aggressive participants in the political process. A proactive stance and increasing influence have significantly impacted their relationships to the governing authorities. Some of the squatter settlements in Rio take advantage of the political process, selling their votes during the elections to the highest bidder in exchange for favors to improve their neighborhoods. This process has been successful in attracting the attention of the authorities who control basic services. This mechanism has largely been responsible for the transformation of some of the settlements in the region.

Figure 30-5   A view of a newer public housing project built by the government close to a *favela* site in Rio de Janeiro, Brazil.

Figure 30-7 An affordable housing project built near the site of a *favela* on a hillside in Rio de Janeiro, Brazil.

Dealing with the problems of slum and low-income housing in Rio remains a very complex issue because of the huge size of the city's poor population. An estimated 1 million houses exist on slum sites in Brazil's major cities, and more than a quarter of this population lives in the city of Rio de Janeiro. In a developing economy such as Brazil's, this is a mammoth challenge, with limited financial and technical resources available. Investment in low-cost housing is considered risky since it consumes resources quickly rather than giving productive impetus to the economic cycle. Participatory programs to legalize land tenure in concert with strategies for income generation and social services are proving to be effective strategies in improving squatter settlements in Rio and throughout the world.

Conclusion

The task of ensuring that everyone is provided with adequate housing is challenging for both developed and developing societies. The scale of the problem is difficult to deal with, and the choices and solutions are few. Past practices and interventions by governments and international aid/lender organizations included successes and failures. Even though some nations are trying to improve rural village amenities and services, there is no evidence that the trend of mass migration from countryside to cities in developing countries will fade away, that the problems of squatters can be easily solved, or that appropriate alternatives can be found. Squatter and slum settlements will continue to shelter the majority of people in these cities. And that is not all bad; squatter settlements have several advantages in housing the urban poor. Squatters use tradi-

tional vernacular ways to build their shelters. They take advantage of self-help processes and participatory mechanisms that are economical and affordable. They build with local materials and do so incrementally to improve their houses and accommodate their growing families.

Squatter settlements throughout the world offer critical lessons to society and the design disciplines. The most important of these is that society must recognize the inevitable needs of people resulting from their mass migrations to cities and respond in the following ways:

- **Land Ownership**. Make land available for low rent or purchase by migrants who are settling in a given area. Award ownership and legalize land titles to squatters who are already settled and using a site.
- **Infrastructure and Services**. Provide an infrastructure and services (sewers, water supply, electricity, and schools) before or while settlements are being developed. This requires an incremental process of facility development as funds and resources become available. It is far more economical to provide service as settlement occurs rather than afterward.
- **Affordable Financing**. Provide small financing schemes over long periods of time to squatters for land purchase and improvements. Housing cooperatives and lending organizations secured by government guarantees can be effective in providing financial assistance for small self-help housing and business developments. Make loans to individuals for improvement of their dwellings rather than construct large public housing projects.
- **Participatory Methods**. The tradition of user participation in the planning and building process is just beginning to be appreciated and used in many societies. Offer encouragement to the self-help labor force and recognize the energies and resources that already exist in the skill and determination of people. Set up a self-help building advisory service to encourage safety and higher standards of construction.
- **Site and Service Projects**. Make provisions to allocate appropriate sites for low-income migrants to the city. Provide these sites with a minimum infrastructure of roads, water, sewer, and other necessary services that can be improved and expanded progressively.
- **Starter Shell**s. Provide a small room or shell with minimum space, sanitary facilities, and a small lot for the immediate needs of newly arrived migrant families. These shells can be expanded and improved in the future by self-help or participatory methods.
- **Rural Amenities and Services**. Since many of the migrants once had land and family housing in rural

areas, improving the desirability of rural villages by providing schools, health care, and employment would improve these communities and reduce the push and pull forces that encourage urban migration.

- **Participatory Governance**. Finally, recognize that the world housing crisis will not be solved until the people who need housing the most are invited to participate in its design and construction. Decisions concerning the future of these rural and urban communities should emerge from democratic discussions with community leaders and with the users. The necessity of community and user participation in self-help approaches is the key component for helping the poor get appropriate community services and housing.

Many of the above participatory responses are being effectively used in **Habitat for Humanity** programs that are implemented in communities across the United States and throughout the world.[9]

The greatest assets of a society are the hard work and energy of its people. The need to recognize them and use them to secure a dignified way of living is urgent. Recognizing their efforts as an asset and as part of the solution can enable them in innumerable positive ways.

References

Cohen, C., et al. "Urban Population Growth in the Case of the City of Rio de Janeiro." In *Cities for the 21st Century, Proceedings*. National University of Singapore and Singapore Institute of Planners, 1997: 63–72.

Drakakis-Smith, D. *Urbanization, Housing and the Development Process*. St. Martin's Press, 1980.

Evenson, N. *Two Brazilian Capitals: Architecture and Urbanism in Rio de Janeiro and Brasilia*. Yale University Press, 1973.

Gay, R. *Popular Organization and Democracy in Rio de Janeiro, A Tale of Two Favelas*. Temple University Press, 1994.

Ghosh, K. *Urban Development in the Third World*. Greenwood Press, 1984.

Habitat for Humanity International, 2006: www.habitat.org.

McAuslan, P. *Urban Land and Shelter for the Poor*. International Institute for Environment and Development, 1985.

Mountjoy, A. B. *The Third World: Problems and Perspectives*. St. Martin's Press, 1979.

Payne, G. *Urban Land Tenure and Property Rights in Developing Countries*. Intermediate Technological Development Group, 1997.

Pino, J. *Family and Favela: The Reproduction of Poverty in Rio de Janeiro*. Greenwood Publishing Group, 1997.

Ringheim, K. *At Risk of Homelessness: The Roles of Income and Rent*. Praeger, 1990.

Segre, R. "Rio de Janeiro Urban Symbols: Centrality, Power and Community." *Constructing New World*, ACSA Conference Proceedings, Rio de Janeiro, 1998.

UN. *Prospects of World Urbanization*. United Nations, Population Studies, No. 112: 1988, 1989.

Zwingle, E. "Where's Everybody Going?" *National Geographic*, November 2002: 70–99.

Endnotes

1. K. Ringheim, *At Risk of Homelessness: The Roles of Income and Rent* (Praeger, 1990).
2. UN, *Prospects of World Urbanization* (United Nations, Population Studies, No. 112: 1988, 1989).
3. See Note 2.
4. D. Drakakis-Smith, *Urbanization, Housing and the Development Process* (St. Martin's Press, 1980).
5. J. Abu-Lughod, "Migrant Adjustment to City Life, 1961." *American Journal of Sociology*, July 1973.
6. A. B. Mountjoy, *The Third World: Problems and Perspectives* (St. Martin's Press, 1979).
7. Drakakis-Smith, *Urbanization, Housing and the Development Process*.
8. Mountjoy, *The Third World*: 108.
9. Habitat for Humanity International, 2006: www.habitat.org.

CHAPTER 31

Livable/Sustainable Communities

Wendy R. McClure

Community and shelter are interdependent expressions of culture. The care used to plan and design a community and its most critical components such as shelter, public places, and civic places speaks to current and future generations about its cultural values. Take a close look at the community in which you live and ask some important questions: Does its built environment demonstrate good stewardship of land and wise use of resources? Do its citizens have adequate shelter and employment? Does its built environment celebrate the best of human potential and community? Can the less capable or elderly participate in community life? Will future generations have the resources to thrive in this place or will those resources be depleted? In essence, is your community sustainable?

Design and planning are powerful tools that can either support or undermine the quality of the built environment and conditions for sustainability in all communities. Design decisions for each layer of the built environment, both individually and collectively, impact the capacity of a community and region to sustain as a culture—socially, ecologically, and economically. This chapter provides a concluding overview of the movement for sustainable development. Summary case studies involving key players from various design professions are used to illustrate sustainable design ideas for a range of contexts including urban, suburban, and rural environments.

The potent message in Winston Churchill's insightful statement (first introduced in Chapter 1), "We shape our buildings and afterwards they shape us," has hopefully become more clear; quite simply, what we build as a society reflects who we are and what we value and helps to determine the quality of life for future generations. The built environment embodies a manifestation of human values, needs, and aspirations. Each generation adds a new layer to the human footprint. How will future generations view our current culture? Will they ask why our civilization abandoned its commitment to community building if they inherit a built environment that appears to have worshipped the car and consists largely of freeway infrastructure, strip shopping centers, big box stores, sprawling suburbs, abandoned city centers, and monotonous landscapes of garage-dominated cul de sac subdivisions? Why have so many communities, especially in the United States, lost the required skills and commitment that were intuitive to previous generations of community builders? According to author James Kunstler, the answer lies in the fact that we threw those responsibilities away in our efforts to become a "drive-in civilization." Unlike our ancestors with vernacular traditions who participated intuitively in building processes, we have "forgotten what it takes to make a good place."[1]

Will future generations ask why our civilization allowed its wealth of natural resources and diverse species to diminish? Why did designers consider resources to be so expendable that they encouraged a linear pattern of consumption—an open-cycle pattern of use or from "cradle to grave," as architect William Mc-Donough terms it? Could serious environmental problems have been averted through better design and planning?

Urban sprawl continues to expand its yoke around city cores and penetrate further into the rural landscape. Citizens of small towns and suburban communities impacted by growth are recognizing that regional differences are disappearing, that the dream of 1 acre in sprawling suburbs can no longer support a quality lifestyle of "country living," and that social, economic, and environmental costs can be hidden and high. Kunstler writes:

> There is a reason that human beings long for a sense of permanence . . . it touches the profoundest aspects of our existence: that life is short, fraught with uncertainty and sometimes tragic. We know not where we come from, still less where we're going, and to keep from going crazy while we are here, we want to feel that we truly belong to a specific part of the world.[2]

The impoverished state of our built environment presents compelling challenges to designers and their citizen partners. The time is ripe for new traditions that provide paradigms for long-term social, economic, cultural, and ecological health. Fortunately, numerous examples of better alternatives to standard development patterns provide opportunities for observation and study (Figs. 31-1 and 31-2).

Figure 31-1 Auto-oriented society. Typical highway strip where automobiles are given priority over pedestrians.

Figure 31-2 Sprawl. Residential sprawl onto former agricultural land outside of town is typical of development patterns nationwide.

Sustainability: What Is It?

As discussed throughout this collaborative work, sustainability is a critically important paradigm for solving many of society's design and planning challenges. "In its broadest scope, sustainability refers to the ability of a society to continue functioning into the indefinite future without being forced into decline through exhaustion or overloading of key resources on which that system depends."[3] At the 1993 annual convention of the American Institute of Architects, participants established a professional commitment to sustainability. Their approach echoed actions taken by the United Nations at a global summit on the environment and development held in Rio de Janeiro in 1992. At the Rio Summit, sustainability was defined as "that which insures the needs of the present are met without compromising the ability of future generations to meet their own needs."[4]

The concept of sustainability was recognized as a critical practice in fields such as forestry and agriculture well before the 1990s. Since the advent of managed forests, researchers for the U.S. Forest Service have attempted to determine sustainable yields in national forests so that harvesting of timber does not outpace the capacity to regenerate forests. In the case of responsible agriculture, crops and fields must be rotated to allow for soil regeneration if lands are to be used into the indefinite future.

Sustainability: How Can It Be Achieved?

The goal of achieving sustainability can be elusive because systems for measuring sustainable levels of consumption or yields face moving targets. For example, it is extremely difficult to determine sustainable levels of resource consumption when the world's population continues to increase by 250,000 people per day. Most of the 2% to 3% per year growth rate is occurring among nonindustrialized populations. Equally challenging are the consumption habits of affluent industrialized nations. In both the United States and Canada, for example, the average citizen uses 30 times more fossil fuel than a citizen of the nonindustrialized world. If everyone in the world lived by Western standards, consumption rates would quickly outpace known reserves of fossil fuels and many other nonrenewable resources. Ecological problems are further exacerbated in affluent societies by consumption patterns and wasteful practices, as discussed in previous chapters. Global energy consumption and waste production will escalate as Third World nations industrialize, creating a moving target for predicting future needs. Demand for life support systems and resources such as water and food will continuously increase as well. The global capacity to achieve an ecological balance will become even more elusive unless use patterns are changed from linear to regenerative.

Since the energy crisis of the 1970s, researchers and design professionals have largely focused on developing strategies to conserve energy and maximize the energy performance of the built environment. Ultimately, the pattern of resource consumption remains linear, however, leading to what McDonough labels "cradle to grave." As discussed earlier, McDonough promotes a new paradigm for renewable resource consumption that he calls "cradle to cradle." His design model is based on natural cycles in which food becomes waste, which in turn feeds a system that helps to generate food, creating a closed-cycle system. Consumption is sustainable when it becomes part of a closed cycle. Ultimately, design can become a potent tool to help achieve sustainability. If components of the built environment—products, structures, and landscapes—are designed to function within a closed- rather than an open-ended system, more sustainable levels of consumption can be attained.

Sustainable Community Development

The very nature of development implies that resources will be harvested or exploited to meet human needs and profit-making goals. **Sustainable development** requires paradigm shifts in how we as a society choose to live, our commitment to future generations, the value we place on

natural resources, and the philosophy of our economic systems. The inherent value of the planet Earth must be considered holistically; Earth's **natural capital** includes its crust, biosphere, ecosystems, and upper atmosphere and the life-sustaining services that the Earth and its ecosystems provide, such as air, water, climate stabilization, soil production, and maintenance of biodiversity. The Earth's systems perform irreplaceable tasks, such as removing pollutants and emissions. There is no humanly made substitute for natural capital. The ability to sustain natural capital is directly linked to social capital and economic capital. **Social capital** is defined by society's capacity to meet fundamental human needs such as food, shelter, and livable communities where the quality of life is measured by health, well-being, and happiness rather than by the level of material consumption. **Economic capital** in a sustainable society must ensure that fundamental needs are met, that wealth is distributed across as broad a spectrum as possible of current and future generations, and that economic systems are based on recognizing the value of, and sustaining, natural capital. Sustainable practices differ from those of conventional development because they integrate consideration of healthy natural, social, and economic systems and the well-being of future generations into decision-making processes.

The built environment is dynamic because it is constantly changing. It is shaped and reshaped by growth, development, and cultural values; development of new products and spaces, buildings and neighborhoods; design interventions within existing contexts; and planning decisions about city and regional land use and transportation. Design decisions impact patterns of resource utilization and generation of waste at various levels of resolution, including the individual, the community, and the city or region. Concepts for sustainability can be applied to design at each layer of the built environment. Individually and collectively, each design decision impacts the well-being of the planet Earth. Humankind is more capable of making choices at an individual or local scale than at a global scale. Each geographic region and culture will command a unique approach, hence the popular and profound expression "think globally, act locally." The downstream impacts of our local actions eventually contribute to global action in either a positive or negative way, so we cannot escape the fact that our actions are also global.

All of the design and planning professions are involved in making choices about the types of communities society will ultimately build. Each component of the built environment will either strengthen or weaken a community's capacity to live in harmony with natural systems. Designers of products, interiors, buildings, landscapes, or subdivisions can choose to promote more human-environmentally friendly concepts and practices as a fundamental part of their design processes. For example, product and interior designers can choose products made from natural materials to avoid indoor air pollution and design in support of healthy living and working environments. Architects and engineers can choose to use materials that are recycled or locally manufactured and design buildings to reduce dependency on mechanical systems. Landscape architects can select native plants that are well adapted to their region and require less water and chemicals. Urban and regional planners can encourage policies governing development that minimize dependency upon the automobile, provide affordable housing, strengthen neighborhoods, and preserve critical open space systems for agriculture, timber, recreation, and wildlife habitat and corridors.

In all cases, design and planning decisions about resource expenditures should incorporate long-term thinking and consider future as well as present needs. Sustainable design solutions optimize the full potential of art and science by using an integrated approach to creative problem solving. To be considered sustainable, creative designs, regardless of scale, utilize environmentally friendly technology to support functional needs and nurture the human spirit. Sustainable designs consider human, environmental, and technological factors holistically.

Different design strategies are required to address the unique challenges presented by each type of community context within a region, whether rural, suburban, or urban. Solutions to problems for individual contexts must be integrated to support a regional approach to problem solving. In his book *The Regional City*, architect Peter Calthorpe describes the interdependencies of each context in economic, social, and ecological terms. Strategies and approaches to sustainable development that have been successfully implemented in urban, suburban, and rural contexts can be illustrated by examples.

Key Concepts, Strategies, and Players

Urban Contexts

A variety of approaches to development, in combination, can enhance the livability of urban communities. Key concepts, players, and strategies will now be considered.

Revitalization. Revitalization of inner-city centers and neighborhoods is perhaps the ultimate recycling program. Historic urban fabrics embody investments of human and earth resources made by previous societies in the form of energy, materials, and culture. If buildings that are no longer serving their original purpose can be repaired and/or adapted for new purposes (adaptive use and rehabilitation), it is possible to create a closed-loop system for resource consumption. For example, historic materials contain **embodied energy**, resources that have already been expended to extract or manufacture original construction materials and transport them to construction sites. Reuse of buildings conserves embodied energy by sustaining materials that would otherwise be lost through demolition processes and disposed of in a landfill. New construction processes often perpetuate linear consumption patterns by requiring energy expenditures to extract resources for new materials, manufacture them, and transport them to construction sites.

Besides sustaining natural resources, revitalization also supports continuity of **cultural and human resources** by affording opportunities for future generations to experience firsthand contact with historic fabric. In addition to learning about historic environments and the aspirations of previous generations through literature and photographs, new generations can interact directly with residual historic fabric in their everyday lives. European cities feature layers of built fabric from ancient to modern times. City builders used inherited layers as foundations for the creation of new layers, resulting in a rich tapestry of built forms. The approach to city building in the United States has more typically been to erase previous layers or palimpsests and replace demolished structures with new construction. Since the 1950s, many U.S. cities have adopted a transient and resource-intensive attitude toward the built form through urban renewal programs in which entire neighborhoods are demolished and replaced with new development.

In many cases, rehabilitation supports a more economically sustainable approach to development than new construction. Less startup capital is generally required to initiate a project. Rehabilitation processes can be choreographed in phases. Existing historic districts in towns and urban neighborhoods are served by existing infrastructure including water and sewer systems, sidewalks, and streets, whereas infrastructure must be extended to support new development on **greenfields** (undeveloped sites) at the urban fringe. Economic justifications for developing outside of existing urban

Figure 31-3 Densification. Some cities, such as Vancouver, Canada, plan to grow vertically and to densify in order to preserve important city parks and prevent the city from sprawling into surrounding mountains.

Figure 31-5 Affordable housing. Portland, Oregon, constructed affordable housing in a neighborhood that is undergoing rapid gentrification. This construction project also represents the concept of densification, allowing more housing units per acre and demonstrating more efficient land use practices.

cores often include lower land costs. However, the actual costs of new development are frequently hidden and borne by taxpayers instead of developers because city and county governments must extend infrastructure, municipal services, and school districts to serve new developments. Rehabilitation of existing **brownfields** (existing urban sites that generally have infrastructure) is far more regenerative to a community than encroaching on new land.

Smart Growth. The national organization Smart Growth is dedicated to supporting sustainable development and combatting urban sprawl. Smart Growth promotes development strategies that include:

- **Densification** by increasing the number of housing units per city block, acre, or square mile (Fig. 31-3)
- **Rehabilitation** of existing structures to retain embodied energy (Fig. 31-4)
- **Brownfield** development by redeveloping sites that are served by existing urban infrastructure in existing neighborhoods (Figs. 31-5 and 31-6)
- New **infill construction** by developing empty lots or parking lots ("grayfield" sites) or redeveloping brownfield sites in existing neighborhoods (Fig. 31-7)
- **Mixed-use development** that includes housing and access to basic services within walkable distances (Fig. 31-8)
- Avoidance of sprawl and **greenfield** developments

Figure 31-4 Adaptive use. The ultimate recycling program. Embodied energy in this former warehouse in the historic Pearl District of Portland, Oregon, is captured with conversion of the structure to luxury condominiums to "warehouse" people.

Figure 31-6 Infill housing and densification. New housing in Portland, Oregon's, Park Blocks district affords easy pedestrian access to urban parks, downtown, and public transit.

Figure 31-7   New infill construction on a brownfield site. This mixed-use building, with housing in the upper stories over ground floor commercial space, replaced a single-story house. The development represents densification of a downtown area in the historic commercial district of Sandpoint, Idaho.

In combination, these strategies extend the capacity of existing communities and urban cores to accommodate growth, place priority on serving human needs rather than the automobile, and slow down or prevent the conversion of prime agricultural, forest, and open space. Another important goal of Smart Growth is to provide affordable housing choices to better accommodate an increasingly diverse population of elderly and single-parent households in addition to traditional family groups.

Figure 31-8   Mixed use. A more sustainable concept for a "big box" grocery store in Seattle's International district. This infill project features housing above and a pedestrian-scale outer layer of retail along the street.

Suburban Contexts

During the second half of the twentieth century, the center of population in the United States shifted from cities to suburban communities. Although this trend is reversing in many livable cities, the initial migration to suburban areas was supported by the construction of commuter rail lines in the early 1900s (for a more detailed discussion, see Chapter 21). Out-migration from urban centers and development of rural landscapes for housing intensified after World War II as the result of federal policies. Federal loan programs offered by the Federal Housing Administration and the Veteran's Administration favored construction of single-family homes in suburban locations. The 1956 Federal Highway Act subsidized construction of highways between suburbs and urban centers for commuters. Continued expansion of suburban development infringed upon agricultural lands and rural landscapes, resulting in a condition known as "urban sprawl."

Beginning in the late 1980s, several designers and planners developed seminal projects as alternatives to standard suburban developments. Their goals were to combat sprawl, encourage more sustainable land use, and strengthen regional character and identity. A discussion of key designers for the "new urbanism" and their strategies follows.

Traditional Neighborhood Development. Architects Andres Duany and Elizabeth Plater-Zyberk, partners of the firm DPZ, created plans for new communities based on development patterns of traditional towns. Their approach, known as "traditional neighborhood development" (TND), emulates the character and patterns of traditional neighborhoods that predated the automobile. New neighborhoods are served by multimodal transportation, including streets scaled to the pedestrian. The neighborhoods feature a mixture of uses and a diversity of housing choices. They include parks, civic centers, and commercial pedestrian establishments. In its design of Seaside, Florida, a vacation community along the northwestern coast of Florida, DPZ successfully incorporated elements of a traditional southern town. The community features small lots, houses with front porches, pedestrian-scaled streets, and community gathering spaces. Seaside's location on secondary land affords community access and joint ownership of sensitive dunes and beaches, ensuring access for all residents. The design received international recognition for its radical departure from surrounding coastal developments, which have destroyed the natural heritage of the region by constructing high-rise residential towers enveloped by asphalt parking lots and generic highway-oriented commercial strips directly on top of sand dunes.

DPZ's design of Kentlands, a new suburban development in Gaithersburg, Maryland, outside of Washington, DC, is also based on TND principles and provides a paradigm for year-round communities. Incorporation of public squares and alternative housing types into development plans provides a more richly textured community than the conventional suburb.[5]

Transit-Oriented Development.

Architect Peter Calthorpe planned transit-oriented developments (TODs) along transit lines in metropolitan areas of California. The developments are based, in part, on historic precedents for town and urban planning that preceded the automobile era. TODs provide an alternative to auto-dependent residential and strip commercial neighborhoods by including a mix of commercial and residential office uses and open space within walking distance of a transit stop.[6] TODs support multimodal transportation—walking, bicycles, and public transit in addition to automobiles. A reshaping of the form of suburban development is achieved by reducing dependency on automobiles, by providing alternatives such as pedestrian-oriented development and access to transit, and by rethinking design standards for streets and parking (Figs. 31-9, 31-10).

Most city zoning codes are land-use based, segregating residential neighborhoods from commercial districts. Streets are designed for automobiles, not people. New residential streets, even cul-de-sacs, are scaled to accommodate the 100-year party, since most zoning codes require that two off-street and two on-street parking

Figure 31-9 Mass transit. Light rail transit system stop in downtown Portland, Oregon.

Figure 31-10 New transit-oriented development (TOD). The town center of Orenco Station, a TOD outside of Portland, Oregon, features multistory buildings, with living and office units above and retail stores at street level (Fletcher Farr Ayotte Architects).

spaces be provided for each dwelling unit. Calthorpe scales streets based on traditional neighborhoods. They feature minimum curb-to-curb widths, with parallel on-street parking and a single travel lane to encourage traffic to slow down and to create a more pedestrian-friendly environment.

While acknowledging that the viability of commercial districts depends upon providing adequate parking, Calthorpe's designs encourage more efficient use of urban space. His design guidelines recommend changes to zoning standards to reflect use patterns and concepts for shared and on-street parking.[7]

Conservation Subdivisions.

During the 1990s, planner Randall Arendt developed a new paradigm for residential subdivisions on greenfield (undeveloped) sites in rural and suburban areas with the objectives of protecting sensitive ecological zones and conserving open space and wildlife corridors. The typical suburban residential development in rural locations is accomplished by subdividing large tracts of agricultural land into a system of large lots for single-family houses. By contrast, conservation subdivisions are based on the principles of clustering development, siting houses on small parcels of land, and pooling primary and secondary ecological zones as shared and/or protected open space.

Developers of conventional subdivisions typically subdivide to the limit allowable under local zoning codes (generally $1/2$-acre to 5-acre parcels in rural locations). Streets and other infrastructure must be designed to access each lot throughout the tract. Arendt's system seeks to simultaneously match or exceed the allowable

Figure 31-11 Conservation subdivision. A University of Idaho student team design demonstrates the application of Randall Arendt's concepts for open space subdivision planning on a 40-acre site in Moscow, Idaho.

Figure 31-12 Cluster development. As an alternative to conventional subdivisions, this cluster housing development in Port Townsend, Washington, features narrow streets and parking bumpouts instead of garages.

Figure 31-13 Shared open space. A path system affords access through common space in a clustered housing subdivision.

yield plan for conventional subdivision planning, provide usable open space, and reduce infrastructure costs by concentrating development (Figs. 31-11 to 31-13).

Rural Contexts

Citizens and civic leaders in rural towns throughout the United States must plan for potential as well as real socioeconomic changes, which may impact the future character and quality of their built environment. Some small towns are faced with declining populations and attrition of youth as the result of mechanization of agriculture. Towns with extraction-based economies, such as mining and mill towns, have traditionally experienced cycles of rapid growth and decline. In recent decades, they have been forced to plan for economic realignment with declining demands for, or exhaustion of, extractive resources. Towns proximal to recreational areas such as ski resorts or coastal and lake regions are known as "amenity towns." These communities must plan for explosive growth associated with second-home development and tourism. Towns located at the urban fringe are overwhelmed by suburban expansion and urban sprawl. Former ranch and agricultural lands are being subdivided according to patterns that consume land and resources and that require scarce community resources to extend infrastructure and services. Some communities have elected to revitalize existing downtown areas and to define urban growth boundaries within which new development must occur in order to prevent sprawl and preserve the important functions of agricultural, timber, and natural lands (Figs. 31-14 and 31-15).

Figure 31-14 Urban growth boundaries. This aerial view of Telluride, Colorado, demonstrates how the community has encouraged compact development and limited sprawl to protect surrounding open space systems.

Figure 31-15 Design guidelines. Citizens of Telluride, Colorado, enacted strict design guidelines to preserve the integrity of the historic buildings and the character, scale, and planning patterns of the former historic mining town.

Regardless of their economic circumstances, many citizens and civic leaders of small towns have a strong connection to place. Work with community groups on design and planning projects consistently reveals several commonly held values among small-town residents. In participatory design workshops, citizens typically rank "small-town atmosphere" and "quality of life" at the top of their list of community assets. When setting goals, they frequently articulate concerns about their economic future and view growth as a double-edged sword—important to economic well-being but potentially threatening to their unique regional identity and most cherished assets. Citizens hope to find balanced solutions and to direct the course of growth and development. By participating in the

Figure 31-16 Citizens and civic leaders in Star, Idaho, participate in a design workshop with University of Idaho students and faculty to envision a TOD for the center of town.

design process with citizens, business owners, and civic leaders as partners, design professionals can help their community partners envision appropriate solutions that are supported by the community (Fig. 31-16).

The **Main Streets** of small towns used to be the center of public life. In most places, historic downtown districts remain symbolic centers but the marketplace has moved to the malls, commercial strips, or large-footprint stores (commonly called "big box" developments). Several factors have contributed to the decline of downtowns, but foremost is a lack of collective responsibility for their well-being. The process of creating and maintaining meaningful public spaces is a shared responsibility requiring a culture of support from a diverse cross section of the community, including design professionals. According to James Kuntsler:

> The culture of good place-making, like the culture of farming or agriculture, is a body of knowledge and acquired skills. Indulging in a fetish of commercialized individualism, we did away with the public realm, and with nothing left but private life . . . we wonder what happened to the spirit of community.[8]

As a culture, we have abdicated our collective responsibility for the public places that nurture community spirit. Citizens no longer assume the role of caretaker because it is no longer intuitive to do so. To restore economic well-being and preserve historic continuity of downtown districts, it is necessary to first restore a culture of support. By engaging citizens and civic leaders in **participatory design** processes, progress can be made toward nurturing the custodial spirit required for successful community revitalization (see Chapters 4 and 23).

Through his work in rural northeastern communities and his book *Rural by Design*,[9] planner Randall Arendt creates more appropriate paradigms for commercial development than the strip patterns that characteristically align rural highways. As in his residential developments, Arendt advocates the conservation of open space and preservation of rural character by clustering commercial buildings and parking lots. To preserve the character of rural towns pressured by growth, Arendt designs new developments as integral additions to the town's existing plat. Unlike the standalone, discrete residential developments characteristic of the standard suburban model, Arendt's developments are designed as neighborhoods directly linked to existing street systems, appropriately scaled with smaller lots, and woven into existing neighborhood fabrics using common open space and path systems as connectors.

Research Models for Sustainability

University researchers develop theoretical paradigms for sustainable community development and regenerative design (cradle-to-cradle or closed-loop design) that advance our understanding of key strategies and concepts. Their studies can inform the design and planning work of design practitioners and planners. Architect William McDonough, for example, works in partnership with chemist Michael Braungart to research the chemical properties of products in order to determine their impact on the environment. McDonough's architectural firm, William McDonough and Partners, Architecture and Community Design, applies this information in the design of architectural projects. McDonough's award-winning design for Herman Miller, Greenhouse Factory Offices in Holland, Michigan, broke new ground in its use of environmentally friendly construction materials and attention to the health and well-being of factory and office workers. The company's investment in sustainable architecture has paid off in fewer sick days and higher productivity among employees.

An award-winning study of Pullman, Washington, by Washington State University faculty members Tom Bartuska, Bashir Kazimee, and Michael Owen, provides a model to evaluate a community's level of sustainability holistically and within each layer of the built environment, including the regional scale, city scale, neighborhood scale, and dwelling unit scale. Their case study demonstrates how to model and strengthen a community's overall performance using air, water, land, and energy as ecological variables.[10] Target goals are established for each variable so that consumption can be balanced by a capacity for renewal. Additionally, strategies to achieve a better balance among ecological variables are recommended for each scale of development. For example, by planting 4 million trees to convert carbon dioxide generated by development to oxygen, the Pullman community can achieve a sustainable air quality and balance out carbon dioxide emissions.[11]

Challenges and Expectations for Design and Planning of the Future

Within the context of a global and virtual society, it has become even more urgent for every person to feel connected to a real community and to develop a **sense of place**. As a society, we must nurture the places we inherit and build new places worth caring about. Those places, whether natural or humanly made, historic or new, support our daily experience, encourage positive human interaction, and communicate our aspirations as a culture to future generations. As individuals, members of a community, and part of a global society, we make choices about the types of communities we help to build. Our choices are either sustainable or not sustainable. As individuals, we make daily choices about whether to recycle an aluminum can or throw it in the trash; whether to walk to work, take public transit, carpool, or drive; whether or not to turn down the thermostat a few degrees and put on a sweater. As members of communities, we make choices about whether to invest our tax dollars in recycling centers or landfills; invest in alternative energy technologies or continue to expend nonrenewable resources; construct new highways or allocate more funding for public transit; promote conservation of resources or ignore the signs of overuse. Our individual and communal actions cause either a positive or negative reaction somewhere else on Earth. If we dispose of hazardous waste, it lands in someone else's backyard, because there is no "away." Remember, for a sustainable future, we must **act individually and think globally**.

The technical demands on society and on each design/planning profession will continue to expand. Correspondingly, accountability and liability for the impact of design decisions on the environment will increase. Designers of the future must be guided by a few clear principles:

- **Design/planning can be a potent tool** to help achieve sustainability.

Figure 31-17   Each citizen can make conscious, sustainable choices by taking local actions such as recycling to help reduce waste, pollution, and resource consumption.

Figure 31-18 The mayor of Moscow, Idaho, participating in a community landscaping project using native plants in front of the former high school that is being rehabilitated as a community center.

- **Our paradigms must be based on holistic thinking**—every design and planning decision must be considered as part of a greater whole.
- **Design/planning processes that are interdisciplinary, integrated, inclusive, and involve people** are more likely to achieve their full potential.

Preservation of healthy ecosystems is in the interest of human life—our welfare and survival. All who participate in the design of the built environment, whether as citizens or as designers of products, interiors, architecture, landscapes, or urban spaces, must face the limitations of resources and shift from the paradigm of linear consumption to regenerative systems. The Industrial Revolution enabled humans to view resources as unlimited and to disregard the need to design in concert with nature. In the interest of future generations, designers and society as a whole face several mandates. Individually and collectively, we must do the following:

- **Acknowledge the limits of resources** and use creative skills to extend capacity and help humanity find a balance between demand and the sustainability of natural resources.
- **Make decisions in the interest of natural systems**, not as something apart from humankind, but because everyone is an integral part of natural systems.
- **Change the focus of the design culture from signature design to sustainable design** by encouraging professional organizations to reward places that people use and cherish rather than because they are flashy or trendy.

Forward-thinking, creative professionals recognize design's power to improve the quality of the built environment and demonstrate its capacity through their work and their words. Architect Malcolm Wells challenges designers to use the wilderness as the goal post for their aspirations. Architect Bill McDonough provokes professional complacency with the comment "design that is less bad is not good design . . . it's just less bad." James Kunstler establishes a compelling need for citizens of the industrialized world to create "more meaningful places." Planner Randall Arendt challenges designers to stop participating in "moronic development." Society and designers/planners have a moral obligation to help build stronger communities spiritually, ecologically, culturally, and economically. As emphasized throughout this book, the built environment should reveal the aspirations and positive attributes of today's society to future generations so that they will want to become custodians of the places they have inherited from us.

Given all of the uncertainties about the future of the built environment and what each individual citizen and all designers and planners will contribute to it, there is one prevailing certainty: each and every object, space, or place that is designed, and every incremental design decision made, will either add to the quality of the built environment or diminish it in social, ecological, and technological terms. Designers of the present and future must continuously challenge themselves to create objects, buildings, and landscapes that help to shape more meaningful layers of the built environment. Collectively, each generation will leave a layer of built environment—either brilliant, creative, and workable or regrettable—that future generations will inherit.

References

Arendt, R. *Conservation Design for Subdivisions: A Practical Guide for Creating Open Space Networks*. Island Press, 1996.

Arendt, R., et al. *Rural by Design*. Island Press, 1994.

Calthorpe, P. *The Next American Metropolis: Ecology, Community, and the American Dream*. Princeton Architectural Press, 1993.

Calthorpe, P., and F. William. *The Regional City*. Island Press, 2001.

Duany, A., E. Plater-Zyberk, and J. Speck. *Suburban Nation: The Rise of Sprawl and the Decline of the American Dream*. North Point Press, 2000.

Ecotone. (view pattern map): www.conservationeconomy.net.

Kunstler, J. *The Geography of Nowhere: The Rise and Fall of America's Manmade Landscape*. Simon and Schuster, 1994.

McClure, W. *The Rural Town: Designing for Growth and Sustainability*. Center for Business Development and Research, 1997.

Porter, D. *The Practice of Sustainable Development.* Urban Land Institute, 2002.

Roseland, M. *Toward Sustainable Communities: Resources for Citizens and Their Governments* (rev. ed.). New Society Publishers, 2005.

Endnotes

1. J. Kunstler, *The Geography of Nowhere: The Rise and Fall of America's Manmade Landscape* (Simon and Schuster, 1994).
2. Kunstler, *The Geography of Nowhere:* 275.
3. AIA, 1993: www.aia.org.
4. United Nations, 1992. UN Earth Charter: www.earthcharter.org.
5. A. Duany, E. Plater-Zyberk, and J. Speck, *Suburban Nation: The Rise of Sprawl and the Decline of the American Dream* (North Point Press, 2000).
6. P. Calthorpe, *The Next American Metropolis: Ecology, Community, and the American Dream* (Princeton Architectural Press, 1993).
7. P. Calthorpe and F. William, *The Regional City* (Island Press, 2001).
8. Kunstler, *The Geography of Nowhere:* 273.
9. R. Arendt, et al., *Rural by Design* (Island Press, 1994).
10. T. Bartuska, B. Kazimee, and M. Owen. Washington State University, Architecture Department: www.wsu.arch.edu/sustain.
11. W. McClure, *The Rural Town: Designing for Growth and Sustainability* (Center for Business Development and Research, 1997).

CHAPTER 32

Conspectus

Tom J. Bartuska

The built environment has been revealed, layer by layer, through concepts, components, and design/planning professions, which all together help build understanding, substance and meaning, and the significant challenges society must address today and well into the future. The organization of this collaborative work is represented by the graphic logo of seven layers within a unified sphere, which symbolically provides a framework for analyzing the many components and then synthesizing them into a unified sphere of understanding and effective action. The uniqueness and definitions of the first six components—products-interiors-structures-landscapes-cities-regions—have been explored and integrated into the Earth, the final seventh component, fostering the need for **symbiotic relationships** with the Earth's natural systems. This collaborative investigation of each layer has revealed each component's historic precedents and contemporary issues and challenges. Each section individually, and as part of the collective work, has attempted to increase awareness, cultivate interest, and encourage participation in the design and planning of this humanly created world. Global thinker Buckminister Fuller stated, "the best way to predict the future is to design it."

Besides analyzing individual parts of the built environment, the authors have tried to synthesize or integrate the parts into meaningful wholes—carefully designing and planning symbiotic relationships with human-environmental-technical systems that shape the built and natural environments, locally and globally. Like pieces of a global puzzle, the pages, chapters, and sections of this book need to be integrated both one to another and to all the others. This spirit of **integration** should be extended to design and planning of all levels of the built environment.

Various ecological concepts were introduced and integrated throughout the book to foster such synthesis. **Levels of integration** is a conceptual tool that should help achieve this desirable goal. The integrative concept, as represented in the book's graphic logo—the seven levels within a unified sphere—awaits the reader's synthesis and creative integration. Fulfilling this premise requires both thought and action. The concept of **human-environmental relationships** (HE/HER) was another important unifying theme throughout the book. HE/HER activities reflect human interactions and are reflected in the initial definition and in its graphic representation.

Each letter of the alphabet used in this book is an artifact, and many are derived from common objects found in the built environment. For example, consider the letters BE (for "built environment"): the letter B originally represented a place to dwell, a shelter typified by a roof form and entrance; the letter E derives from the represen-

Figure 32-1 Deconstructing and reconstructing a global puzzle.

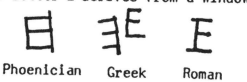

Figure 32-2 Original symbols of the letters B and E.

tation of a window (Fig. 32-2). Putting the two symbols together, the reader ends where the story began—sitting in a shelter, looking out of a window, observing the environment. The letters, as symbolized, represent our creative efforts, reminding us of ourselves, our homes, and our environments. The symbol fosters an inner view and an outer view, an introspection and outward-inspection . . . a conspectus.

Window and dwelling, inner and outer views suggests a dialectic, which was also implicitly intended as a theme in this book: analysis of the **content** of each

component, its **context**, and their ultimate synthesis and integration. A sense of achieved integration leads to the challenges of **health, fitness, creativity**, and questions of **livability and sustainability**, which were raised repeatedly throughout the book.

A concluding step is necessary. Each reader should look back and/or forward in time and space in an integrative way. Many of the chapters in this book did that, building on the **past** while addressing the problems and achievements of the **present** with those of the **future**. Whatever your perspective, we hope these integrative essays on the built environment have opened your eyes, compelling you to look more carefully through the window provided by this series of integrated frames of time, space, and human-environmental relationships:

Figure 32-3 The human lifeline connecting and influencing all the layers of the built environment.

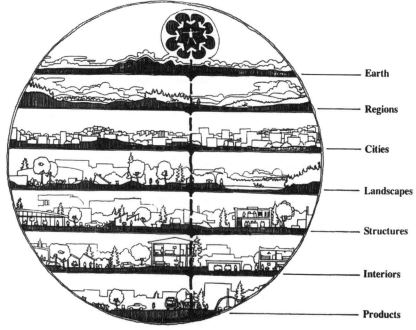

- Earth
- Regions
- Cities
- Landscapes
- Structures
- Interiors
- Products

products-interiors–structures-landscapes-cities-regions-Earth.

Readers, by adding one symbolic vertical line to the diagram—linking the person at the top to the bottom layer—may begin to fulfill this quest. The line represents the reader's **lifeline**. Each lifeline of experiences is like a tree, the branches and roots repeatedly penetrating into and through the layers of this delicate, interwoven fabric in both time and space.

Cultural Values, Dollars and Sense

One can gain insights from all the layers of the built environment. The symbols both small and large are everywhere and await the reader's discovery. We all carry these symbols with us wherever we go—in our minds and pockets. A reflective look at the coins we use reveals the same human-environmental-technical relationships. One side of most coins, the "head," has the figure of an important person within a circle. The other side generally shows his constructions, a building or image representative of a great accomplishment (and the circle that symbolizes unity and symbiotic relationships with the environment surrounds both sides). Thomas Jefferson, a founding father and third President of the United States, is featured on the 5-cent coin (and the 2-dollar bill). Besides being a national leader, he was a very creative inventor, designer, and planner. The profound words on the stone that marks his final resting place at the University of Virginia (the campus and buildings he designed) are "Author of the Declaration of Independence, of the Statute of Virginia for religious freedom, and Father of the University of Virginia." His legacy references what he created for future generations, not the important personal positions he held.

In England, Sir Christopher Wren, a renowned scientist and designer/planner, is featured on the old 50-pound note (bill). On one side of this paper bill is an image of the Queen of England; on the other side is an image of Wren and his great works—St. Paul's Cathedral and the intriguing medieval cityscape of London—a city he helped rebuild after the devastating fire of 1666. His final resting place simply states his legacy: "If you seek his memorial, look all around you."

Figures 32-4 and 32-5 Introspection of the symbolic meaning of money—U.S. coins and a UK note (bill).

Symbiotic Relationships: Trees, Tree of Life, and Tree of Knowledge

Trees provide another powerful symbol and symbiotic way to conclude this exploration of the pervasive nature and life-enriching qualities of the built environment. In many of the chapters, vernacular societies, designers, and planners have used natural analogies for inspiration. As Bruce Miller, a Skokomish Elder, professes: "The trees were our first teachers" (2006) and can offer lifelong inspiration. Malcolm Wells (1981), and later the Society of Building Science Educators (1999), use trees and the forest as inspiration to guide their work (see Chapter 15). They challenge us to do the same. A tree has many fascinating symbiotic qualities to honor and ponder: Can we use it as an ideal symbol for design and planning? Symbiotically, can we design a building or city as beautiful in **appearance** and significant in **performance** as a tree?

Trees are beautiful. Like people and the components of the built environment, they can exist in great variety and stand tall or grow up together, sharing space, time, and Earth's resources. They coexist in many combinations and enhance human and natural environments.

Figure 32-6 "Growing together" (photo-impressionism art © 2002 M&M Designs; courtesy of Milan & Marla Lackovic).

Figure 32-8 The use of plants and trees to cool and clean urban air, spaces, and buildings in Vancouver, British Columbia, Canada.

Deciduous trees are stunning with or without leaves and celebrate the special qualities of each season (four-season design).

Trees are generous; they share the fruits of their labor (beautiful blossoms, colorful leaves, fruits, nuts, etc.). Even their falling leaves create a rich blanket that pro-

vides organic matter to renew the Earth's systems. They provide free shelter for many species—animals, birds, insects, microorganisms, and some humans (especially those delightful tree houses created in one's youth).

Trees moderate climatic extremes, retain rainwater and soil, help prevent flooding, assist in recharging aquifers, cool by evaporative transpiration, and cleanse by absorbing toxins from the air and water. Many cities encourage the use of street trees and "green roofs" to cool the environment, save on air conditioning, and reduce water runoff. Environments, especially cities, without trees and living green surfaces, are not only less enjoyable but are also much hotter in the summer, colder in the winters, and generate more pollution. Collectively, these hostile conditions require a huge amount of energy to correct (and, of course, the more energy used, the more heat and toxic gases released into the atmosphere).

Humans (and all animals) are symbiotic partners with trees. Our combustion waste (carbon dioxide) is the plant's food and the tree's waste (oxygen) is our food. For our use and delight, plants also convert the toxic carbon into fiber—all our wood and paper products come from their growth processes. This fundamental partnership is an excellent example of the "**waste = food**" strategy.[1] As discussed in Chapters 28 and 29, the loss of forests and the continued burning of fossil fuels are one of the primary causes of **global warming.**

Trees are alive, and express critical symbiotic relationships and provide lessons for the built environment. Can one understand how these visible and invisible qualities and dynamic cycles affect the appearance and performance of design and planning the built

Figure 32-7 IslandWood's tree house classroom, Bainbridge Island, Washington.

Figure 32-9 Living machine (using plants to process and clean air and water). Islandwood: A School in the Woods, Bainbridge Island, Washington.

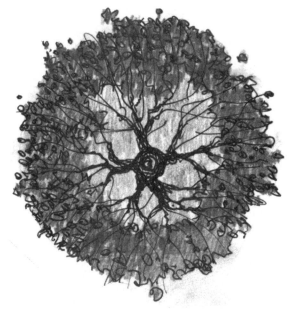

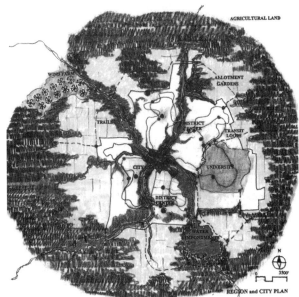

Figures 32-10 and 32-11 A plan of a tree (branches or roots) and a sustainable regenerative plan for Pullman, Washington. The central city branches out into neighborhoods, and the surrounding greenbelt moderates the climate while converting all the CO_2 produced into oxygen.[2]

environment? Can we design with natural systems as McHarg, Wells, and many of the vernacular societies did? Can we design and plan with all the dimensions of the built environment, including the normal three dimensions that express a design's visual **appearance**, as well as its **performance** over time and the invisible life-sustaining cycles and qualities of nature's systems? Can we design the components of the built environment to become as beautiful in appearance and performance as a tree?

Tree of Life

Besides their important life-giving qualities, trees also provide a wonderful way to measure and record time. Standing amid a virgin forest or a grove of the magnificent giants in a redwood forest is a humbling experience and challenges human-centered attitudes. By providing us with a longer view and record of time, this multigenerational perspective enables one to bridge the importance of history with the need to design/plan for a sustainable future. Many native cultures believed one should look seven generations into the future when making decisions about life, design, and the environment.

The growth rings of trees record time in cycles. Instead of measuring time in linear ways, trees record time in concentric growth rings. Each season, each year strengthens the tree, allowing it to grow strong and tall. Possibly this would be an effective way for us to think of time—each year and each new understanding is an important part of our growth and stature, our overall strength developing from healthy growth rings.

Tree of Knowledge

The book's investigation into the built environment can be compared metaphorically to the physical form of a tree. The roots of a tree have a symbiotic dependency on the Earth's resources and provide a strong foundation for the growth of complex, integrated living systems. Like a tree, people and all components of the built environment get their subsistence from the sun and the Earth's air,

Figure 32-12 The concentric growth rings of a mature tree (approximately 300 years old).

water, soil, and roots (Earth's finite resources). A healthy climate and an appropriate location enable humans and trees to prosper and aspire upward by branching out into the environment. Simi-larly, the body of information on the built environment, like a healthy tree, has solid roots and a trunk that support the development of the primary branches (possibly seven representing the selected seven components of the built environment). These branches grow and sprout smaller limbs (representing the chapters and numerous subtopics and ideas) and beautiful leaves that generate oxygen and fall, blanketing the earth (with quality design and planning ideas). All limbs interact, intersect, and share the space of other trees, branches, and limbs to symbolically and symbiotically represent the living, growing tree of knowledge of our built and natural worlds.

Like a tree, the built environment is a very delicate, responsive system. Hopefully, the authors of this collaborative work have cultivated a sensitivity and growing understanding of the built environment and a sense of the need for civility and professional responsibility—a personal and collaborative involvement in actively creating a quality and sustainable built environment for all, now and in the future.

We hope this collaborative inquiry into the built environment has fostered a deeper awareness of and interest in a topic close to us all, and is grounds for optimism about the power of design and planning to improve the natural and built environments, both locally and globally.

References

Berkebile, R. Keynote address at the Building Energy Conference, Boston, 2006: www.ArchitectureWeek.com/2006/0419/news_1-1.html.

McDonough, W. 2004: www.mcdonough.com.

McDonough, W., and M. Braungart. *The Next Industrial Revolution: The Birth of the Sustainable Economy.* Earthtone Productions, 2001.

McDonough, W., and M. Braungart. *Cradle to Cradle: Remaking the Way We Make Things.* North Point Press, 2002.

Miller, B. "Teaching of the Tree People," 2006: http://www.pselc.org/videos/treepeople/default.php.

Society of Building Science Educators (SBSE), 1999: www.sbse.org.

Wells, M. *Gentle Architecture.* McGraw-Hill, 1981.

Endnotes

1. W. McDonough and M. Braungart, *Cradle to Cradle: Remaking the Way We Make Things* (North Point Press, 2002).

2. T. Bartuska, B. Kazimee, and M. Owen, Sustainable Regenerative Proposal for Pullman, Washington. 1996. www.arch.wsu.edu/sustain.

Index

(Note: A boldface entry indicates that the entry is defined on that page.)